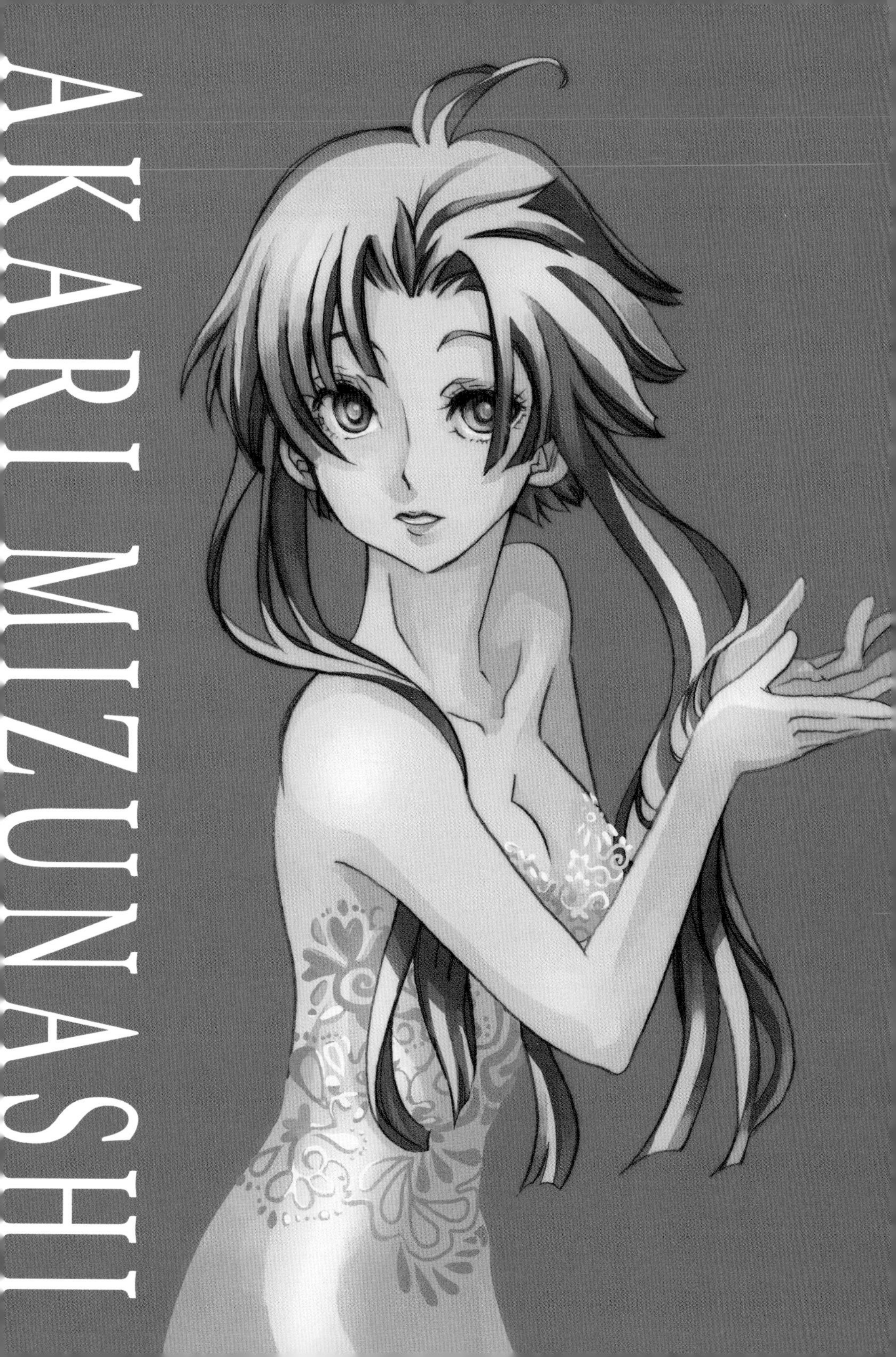
AKARI MIZUNASHI

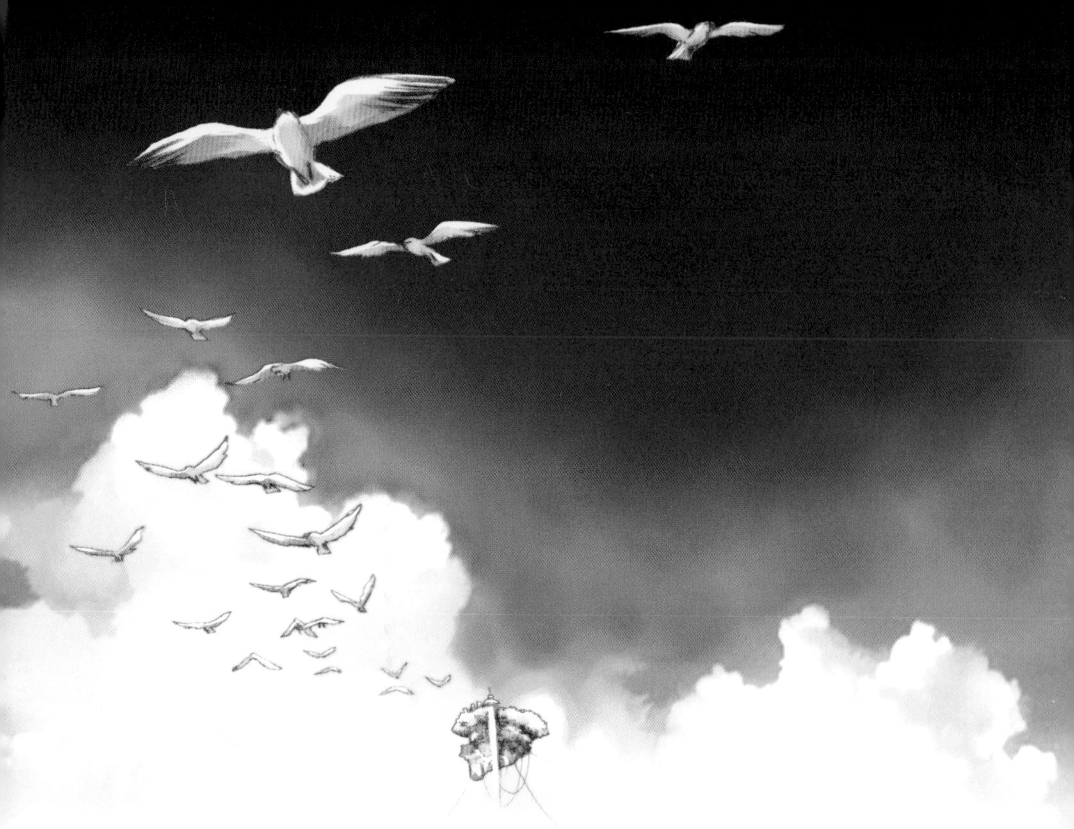

ARIA
The MASTERPIECE.1

contents

Navigation 01
The Water Planet

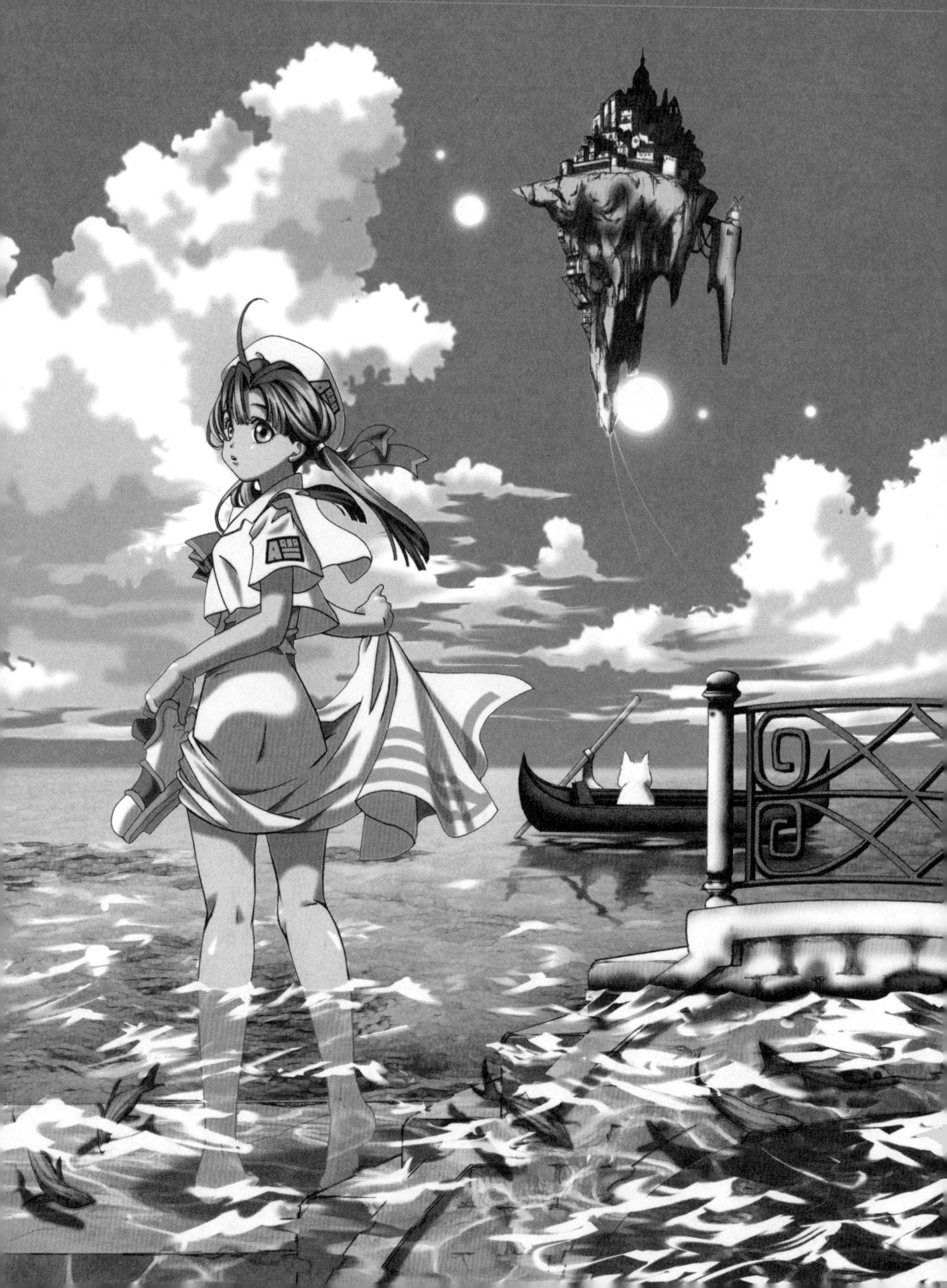

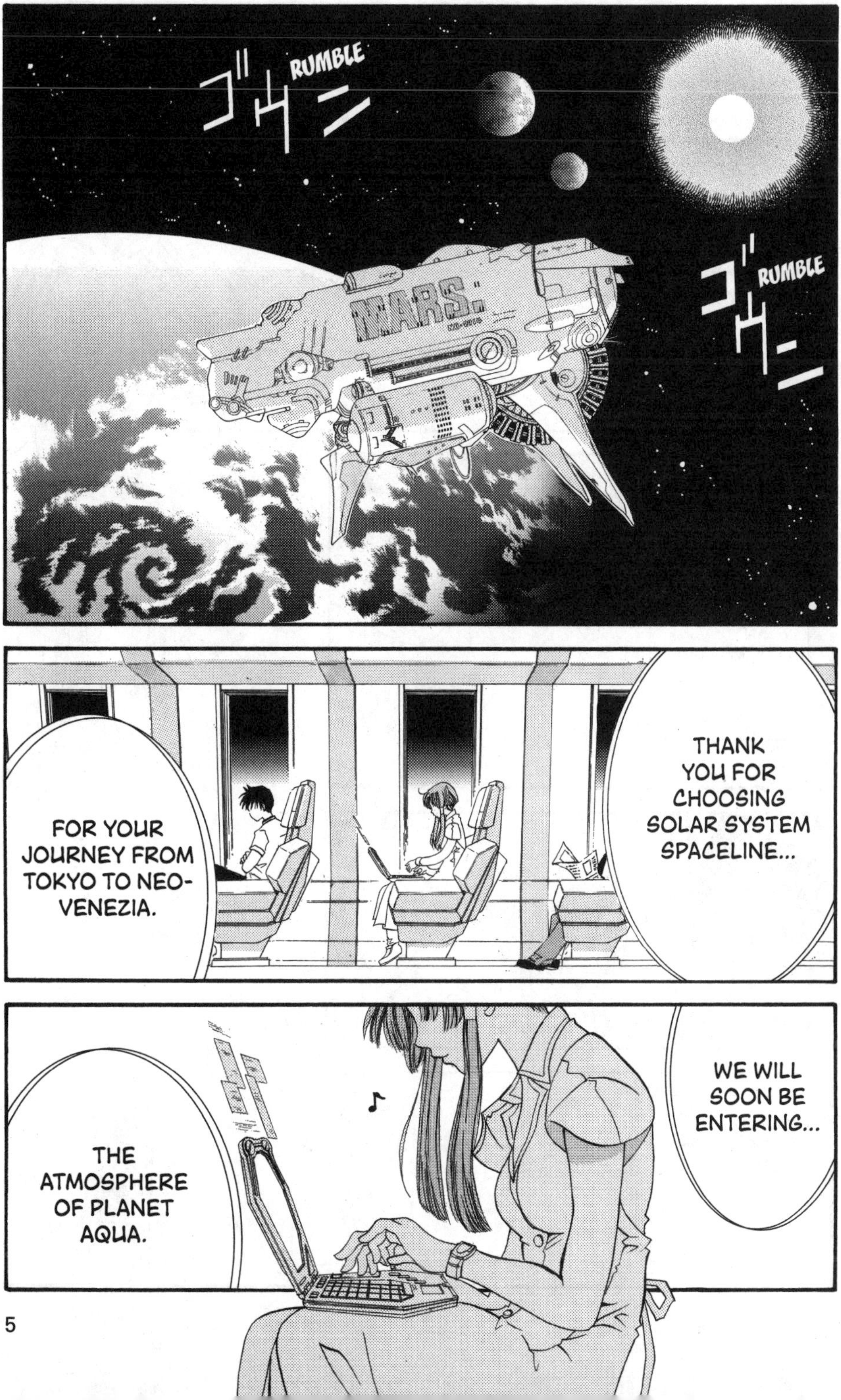
ゴウン RUMBLE
ゴウン RUMBLE
MARS.
THANK YOU FOR CHOOSING SOLAR SYSTEM SPACELINE...
FOR YOUR JOURNEY FROM TOKYO TO NEO-VENEZIA.
WE WILL SOON BE ENTERING...
THE ATMOSPHERE OF PLANET AQUA.

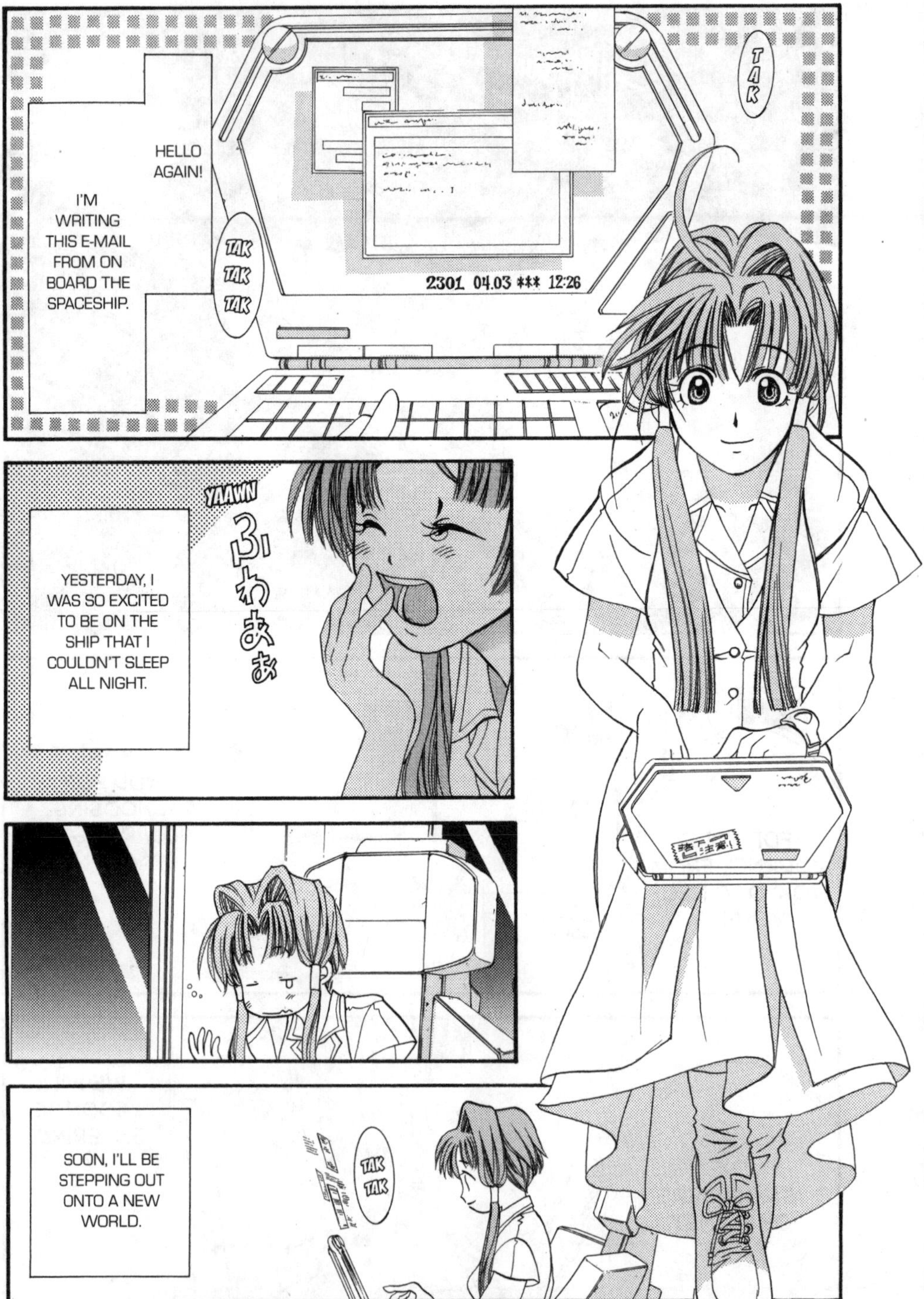
TAK
HELLO AGAIN!
TAK TAK TAK
I'M WRITING THIS E-MAIL FROM ON BOARD THE SPACESHIP.
2301 04.03 *** 12:26
YAAWN
ふわあぁ
YESTERDAY, I WAS SO EXCITED TO BE ON THE SHIP THAT I COULDN'T SLEEP ALL NIGHT.
TAK TAK
SOON, I'LL BE STEPPING OUT ONTO A NEW WORLD.

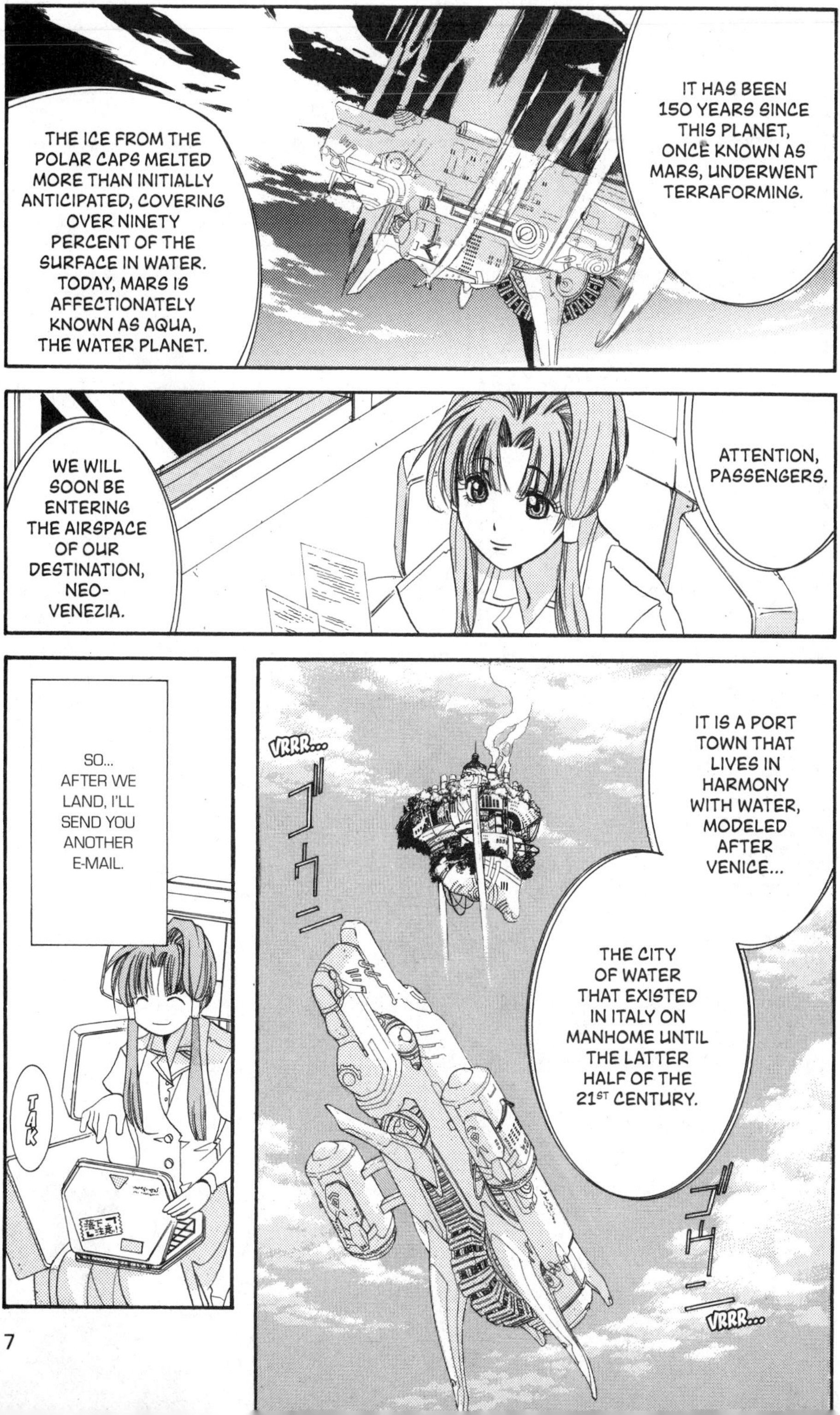
IT HAS BEEN 150 YEARS SINCE THIS PLANET, ONCE KNOWN AS MARS, UNDERWENT TERRAFORMING.
THE ICE FROM THE POLAR CAPS MELTED MORE THAN INITIALLY ANTICIPATED, COVERING OVER NINETY PERCENT OF THE SURFACE IN WATER. TODAY, MARS IS AFFECTIONATELY KNOWN AS AQUA, THE WATER PLANET.
ATTENTION, PASSENGERS.
WE WILL SOON BE ENTERING THE AIRSPACE OF OUR DESTINATION, NEO-VENEZIA.
IT IS A PORT TOWN THAT LIVES IN HARMONY WITH WATER, MODELED AFTER VENICE...
THE CITY OF WATER THAT EXISTED IN ITALY ON MANHOME UNTIL THE LATTER HALF OF THE 21ST CENTURY.
VRRR...
VRRR...
SO... AFTER WE LAND, I'LL SEND YOU ANOTHER E-MAIL.
TAK

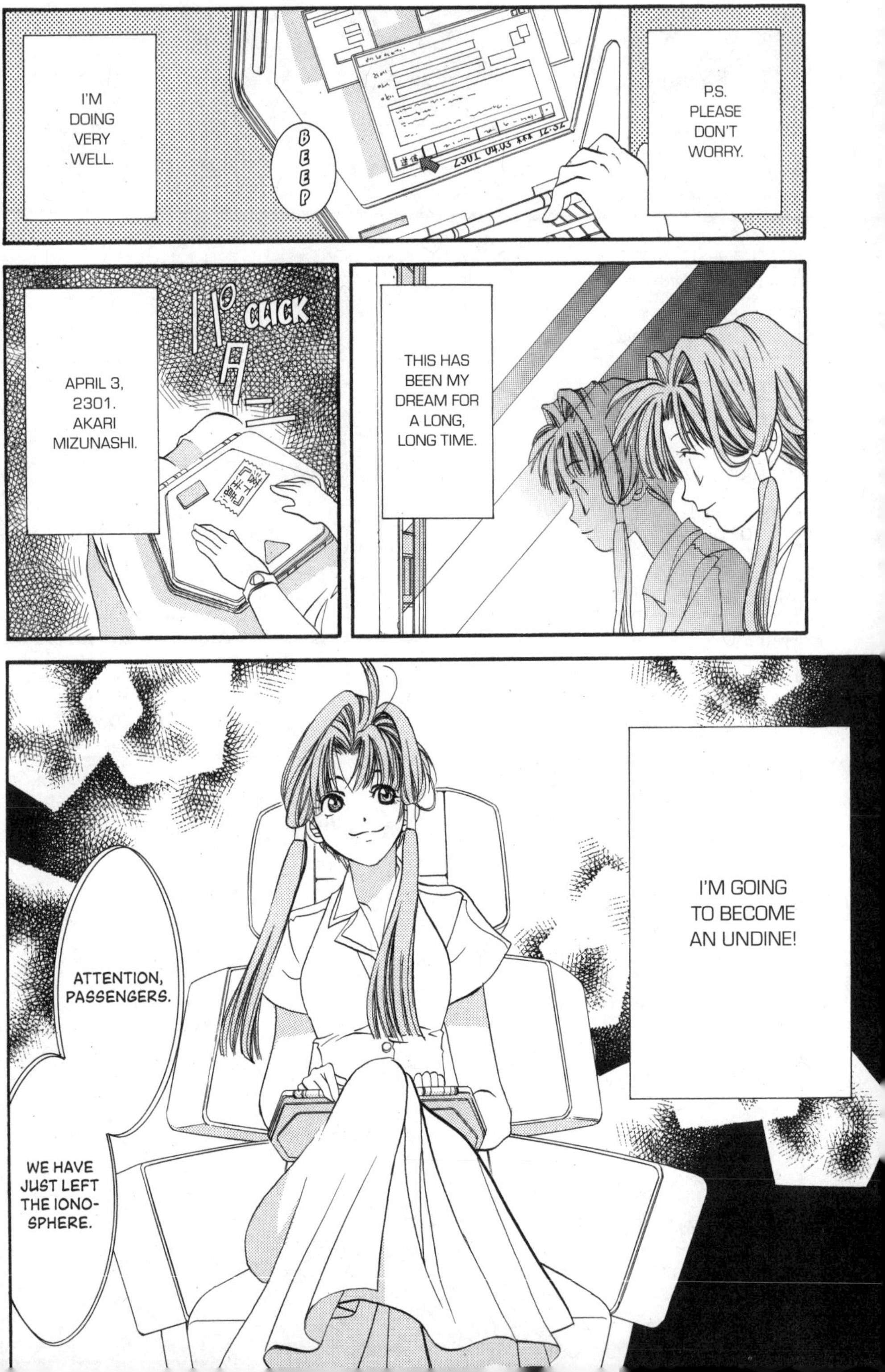
P.S. PLEASE DON'T WORRY.
BEEP
I'M DOING VERY WELL.
THIS HAS BEEN MY DREAM FOR A LONG, LONG TIME.
CLICK
APRIL 3, 2301. AKARI MIZUNASHI.
I'M GOING TO BECOME AN UNDINE!
ATTENTION, PASSENGERS.
WE HAVE JUST LEFT THE IONOSPHERE.

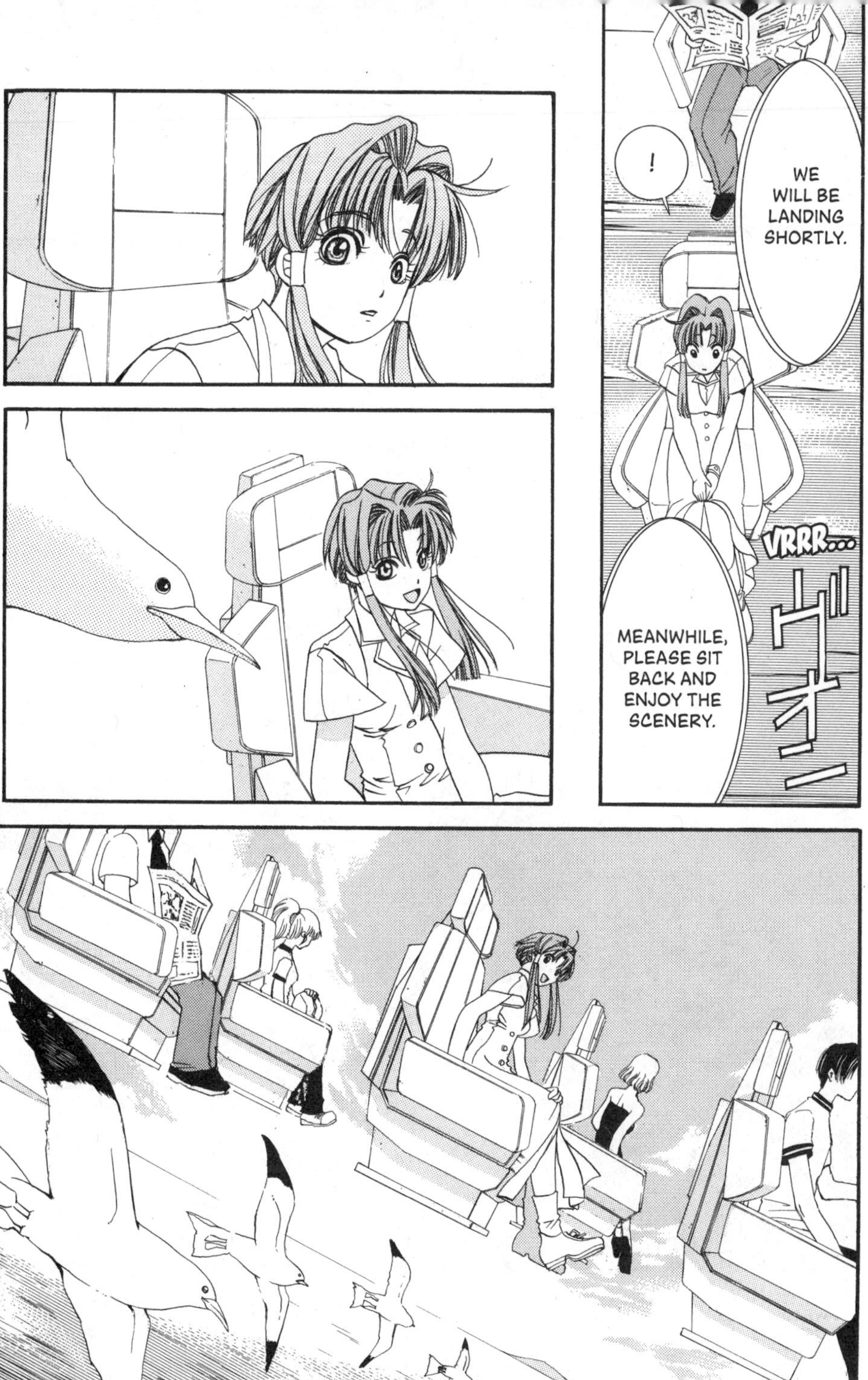
WE WILL BE LANDING SHORTLY.
!
VRRR...
MEANWHILE, PLEASE SIT BACK AND ENJOY THE SCENERY.

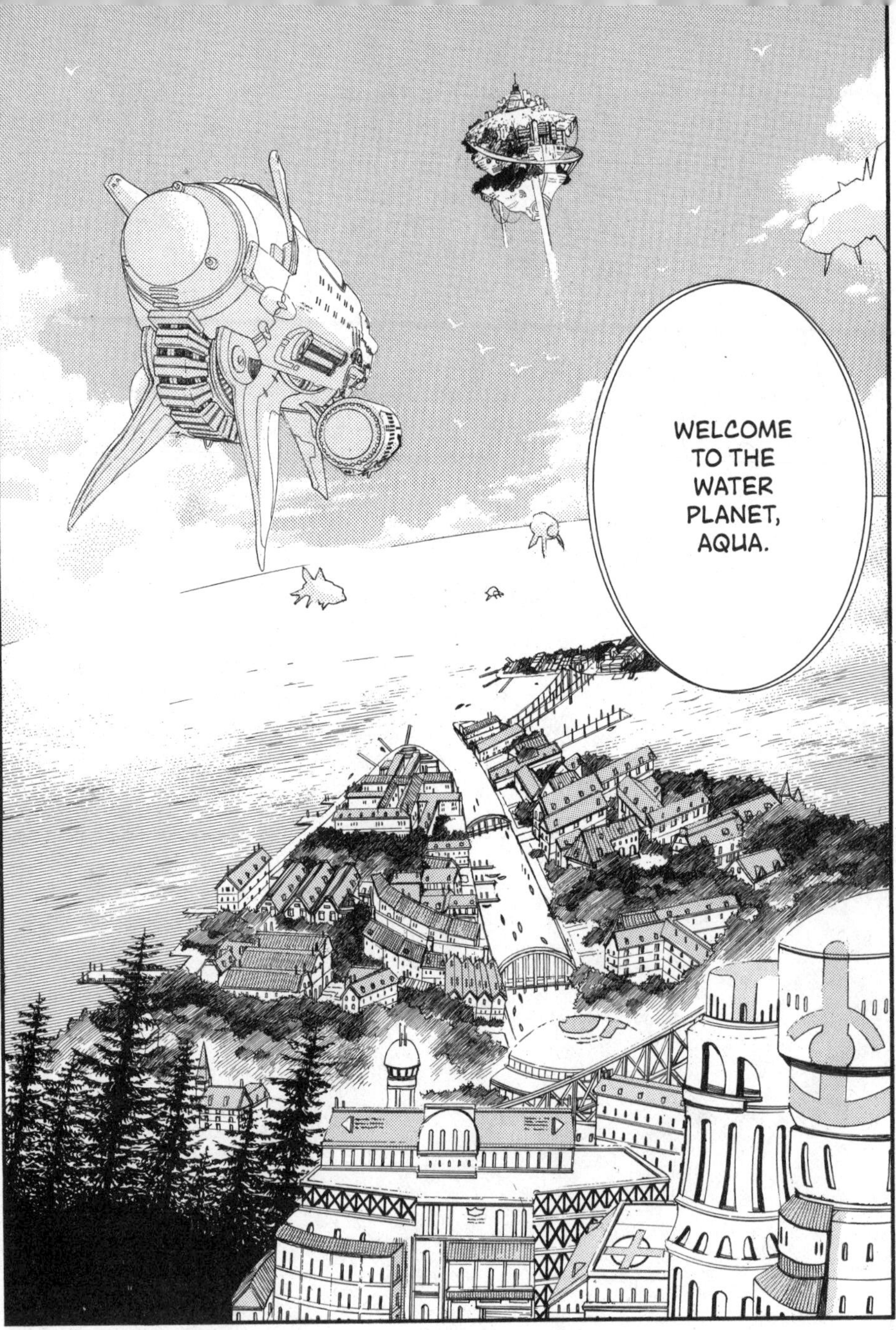
WELCOME TO THE WATER PLANET, AQUA.

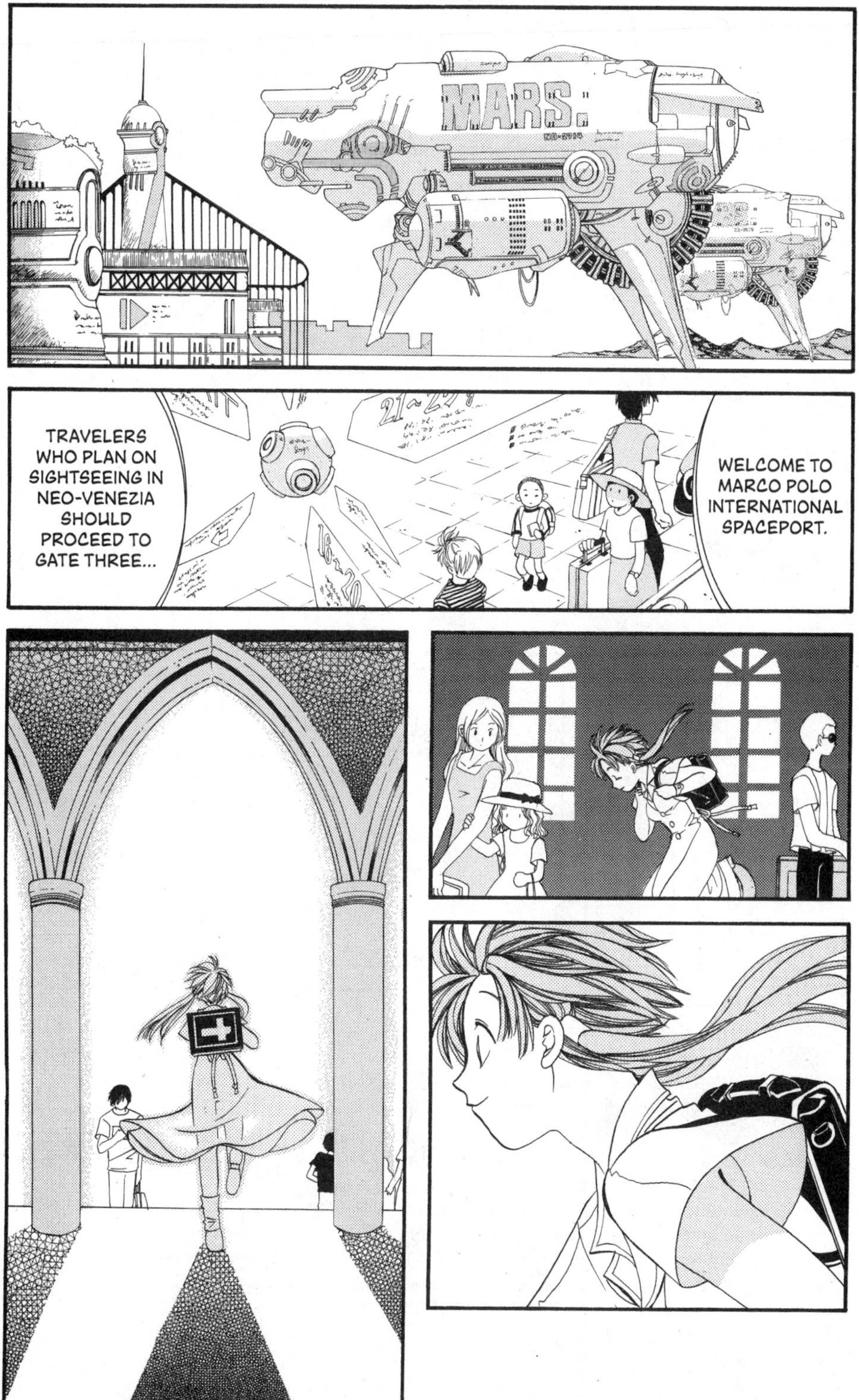
MARS.
WELCOME TO MARCO POLO INTERNATIONAL SPACEPORT.
TRAVELERS WHO PLAN ON SIGHTSEEING IN NEO-VENEZIA SHOULD PROCEED TO GATE THREE...

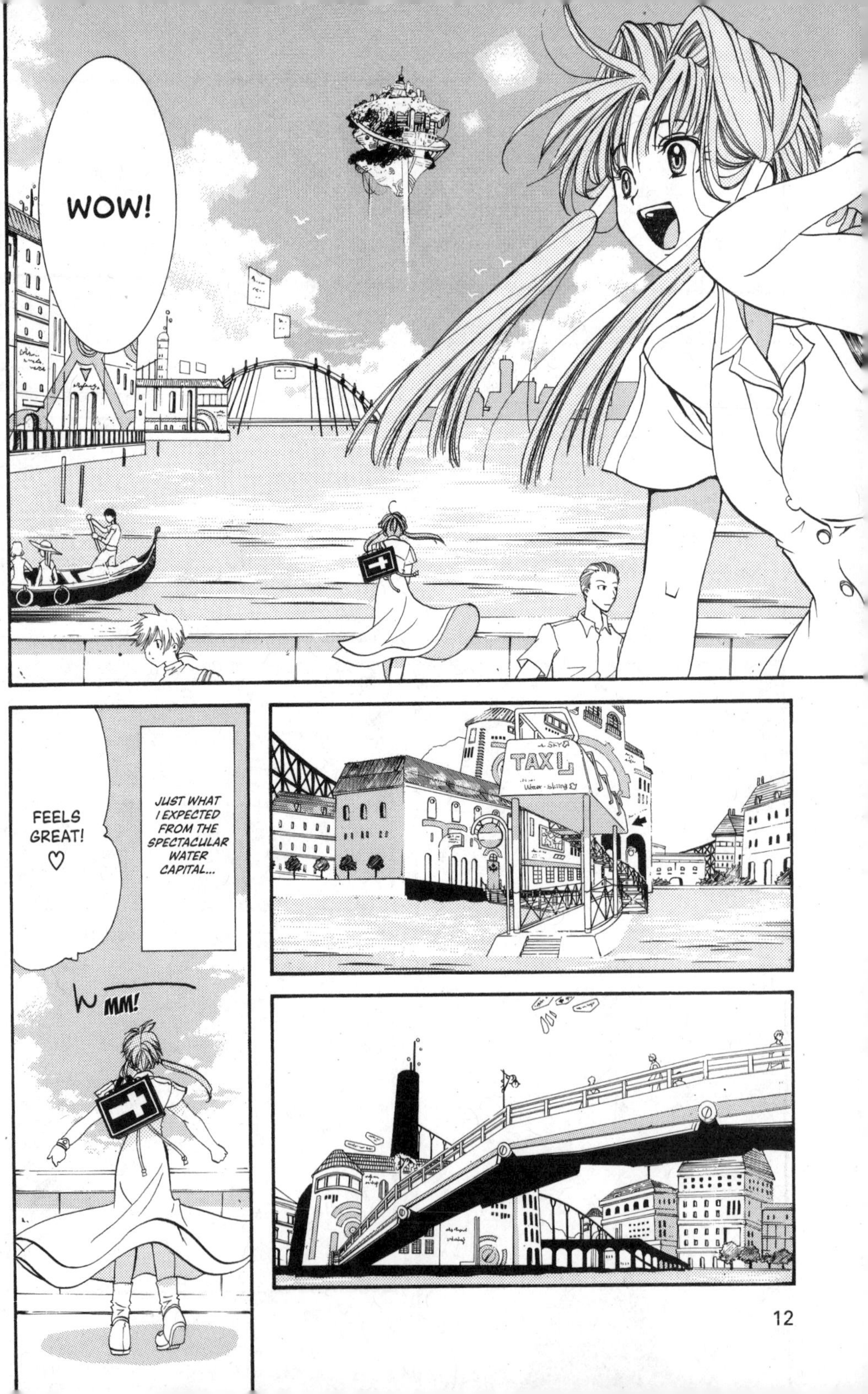
WOW!
TAXI
JUST WHAT I EXPECTED FROM THE SPECTACULAR WATER CAPITAL...
FEELS GREAT! ♡
MMM!

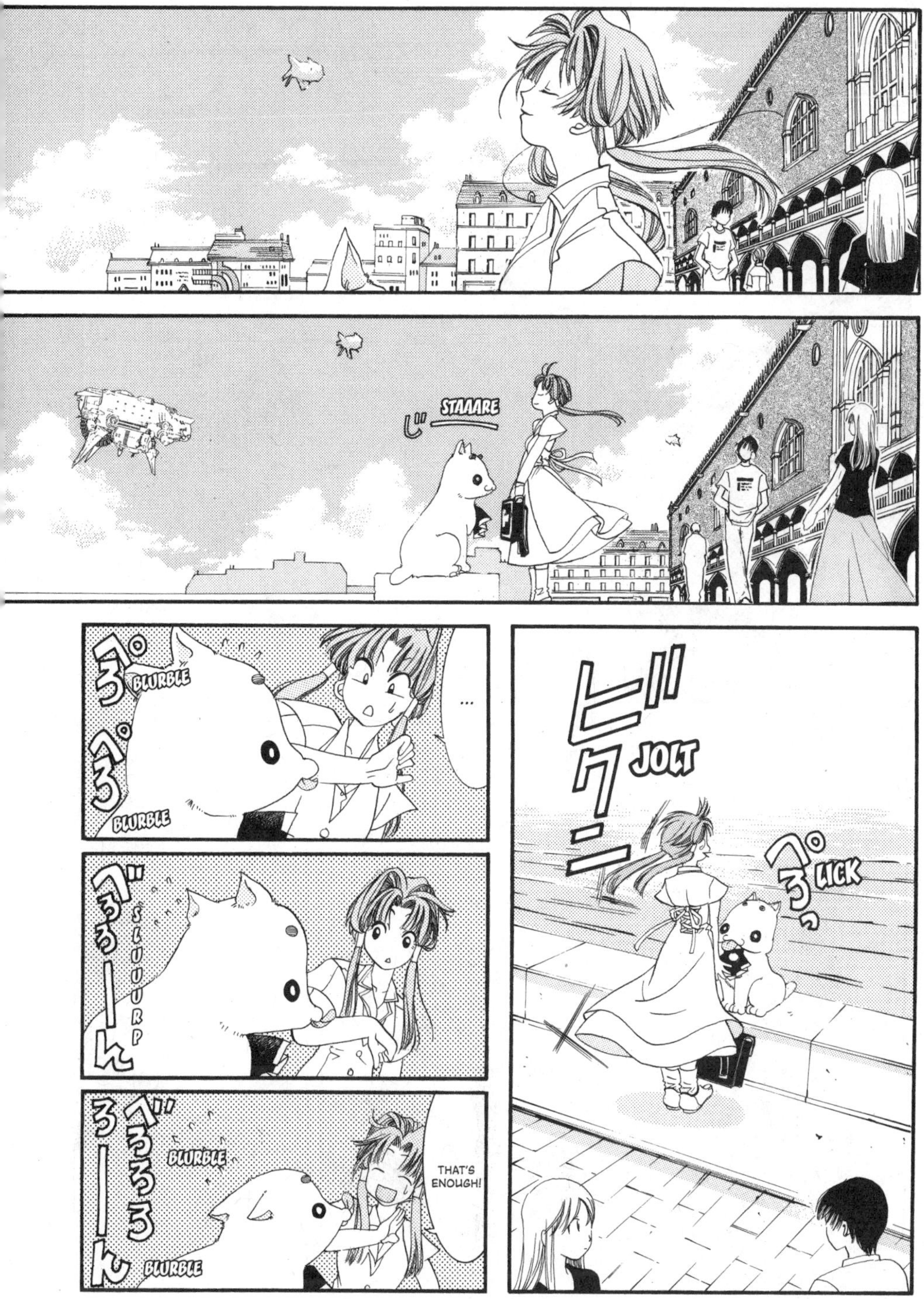

じー
STAAARE
ビクーン
JOLT
ぺろっ
LICK
...
ぺろぺろ
BLURBLE
BLURBLE
べろろーん
SLUUURP
THAT'S ENOUGH!
べろろろーん
BLURBLE
BLURBLE

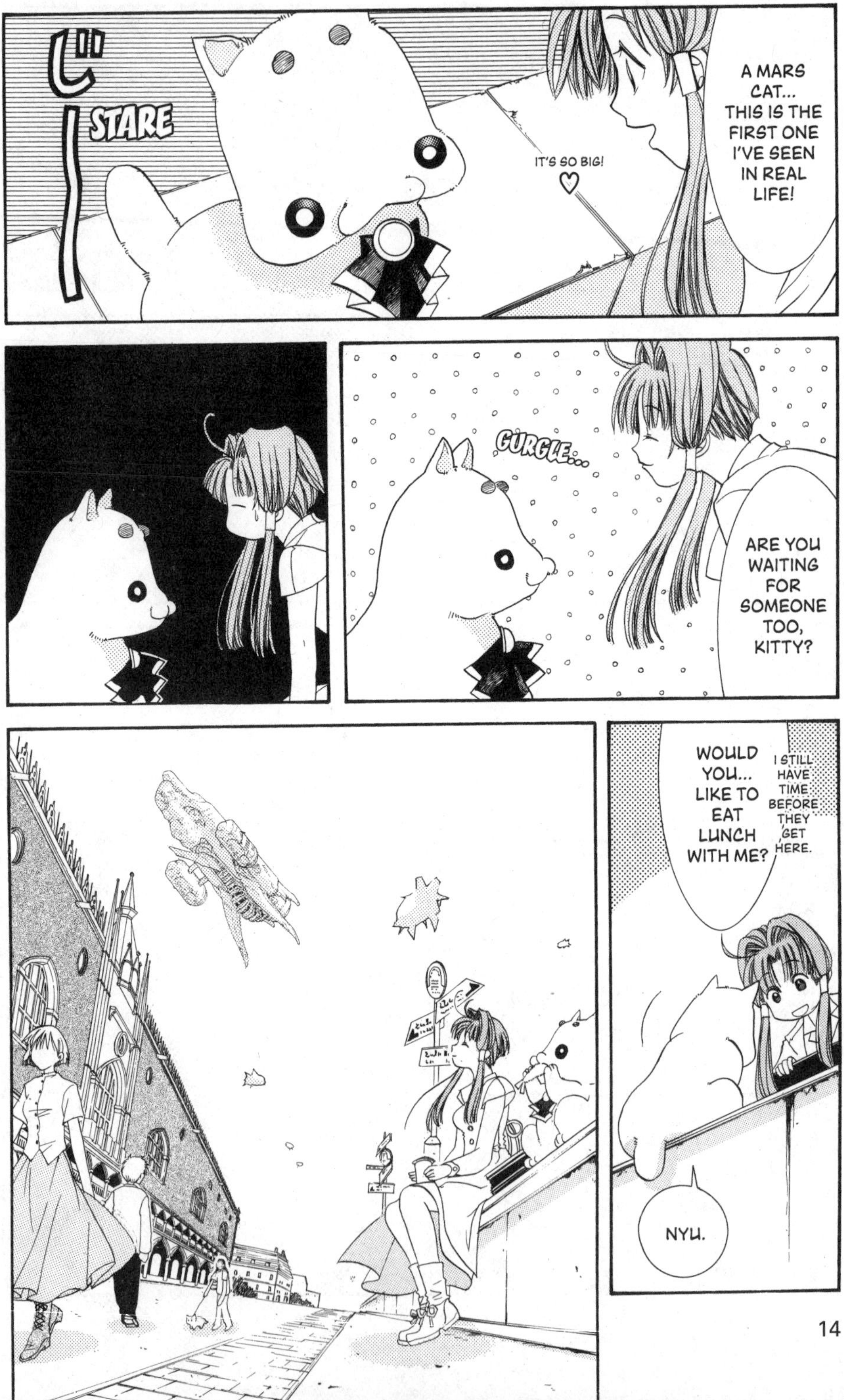
A MARS CAT... THIS IS THE FIRST ONE I'VE SEEN IN REAL LIFE!
IT'S SO BIG! ♡
じー
STARE
ARE YOU WAITING FOR SOMEONE TOO, KITTY?
GURGLE...
I STILL HAVE TIME BEFORE THEY GET HERE.
WOULD YOU... LIKE TO EAT LUNCH WITH ME?
NYU.

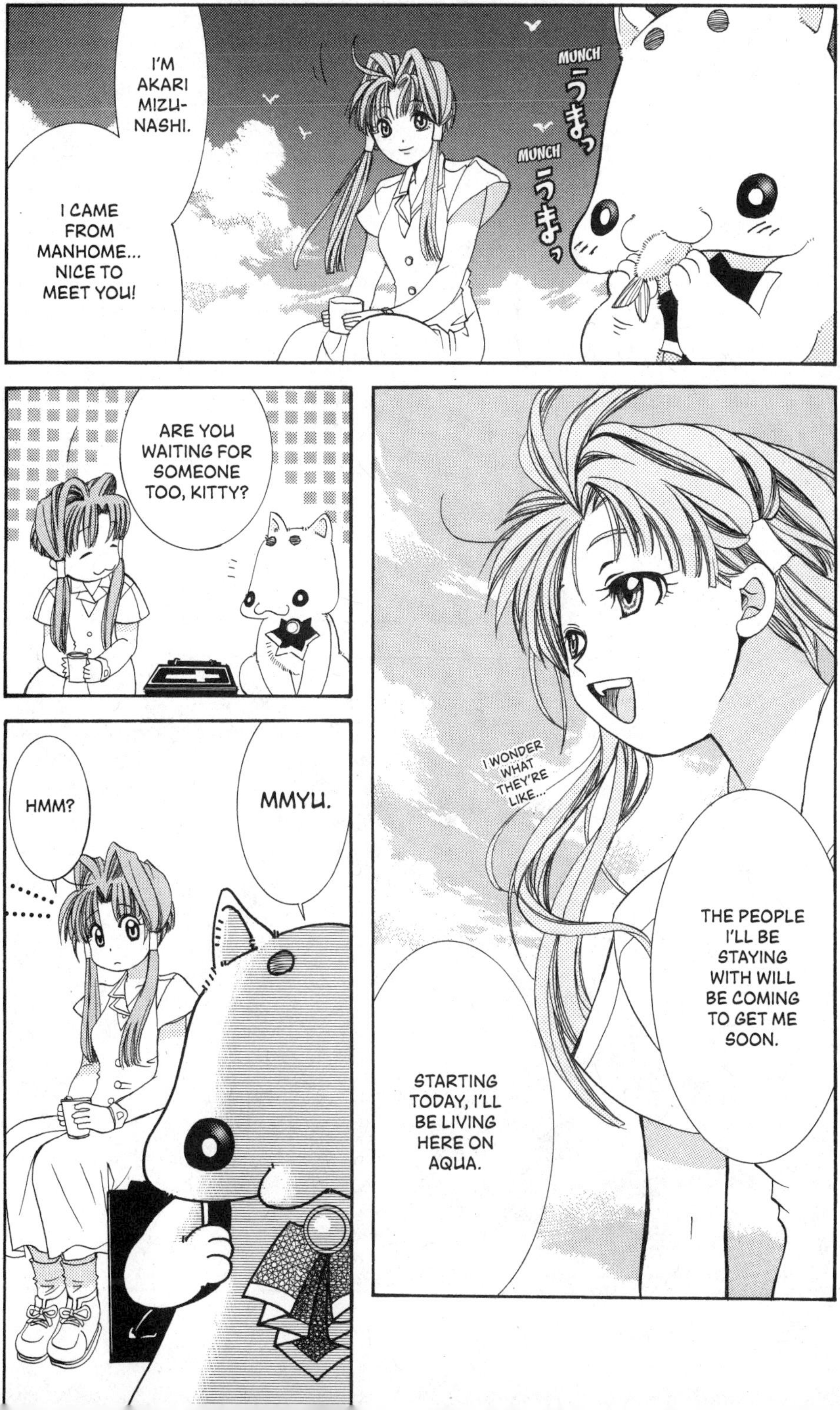
MUNCH
うまっ
MUNCH
うまっ
I'M AKARI MIZU-NASHI.
I CAME FROM MANHOME... NICE TO MEET YOU!
THE PEOPLE I'LL BE STAYING WITH WILL BE COMING TO GET ME SOON.
STARTING TODAY, I'LL BE LIVING HERE ON AQUA.
I WONDER WHAT THEY'RE LIKE...
ARE YOU WAITING FOR SOMEONE TOO, KITTY?
MMYU.
HMM?
......

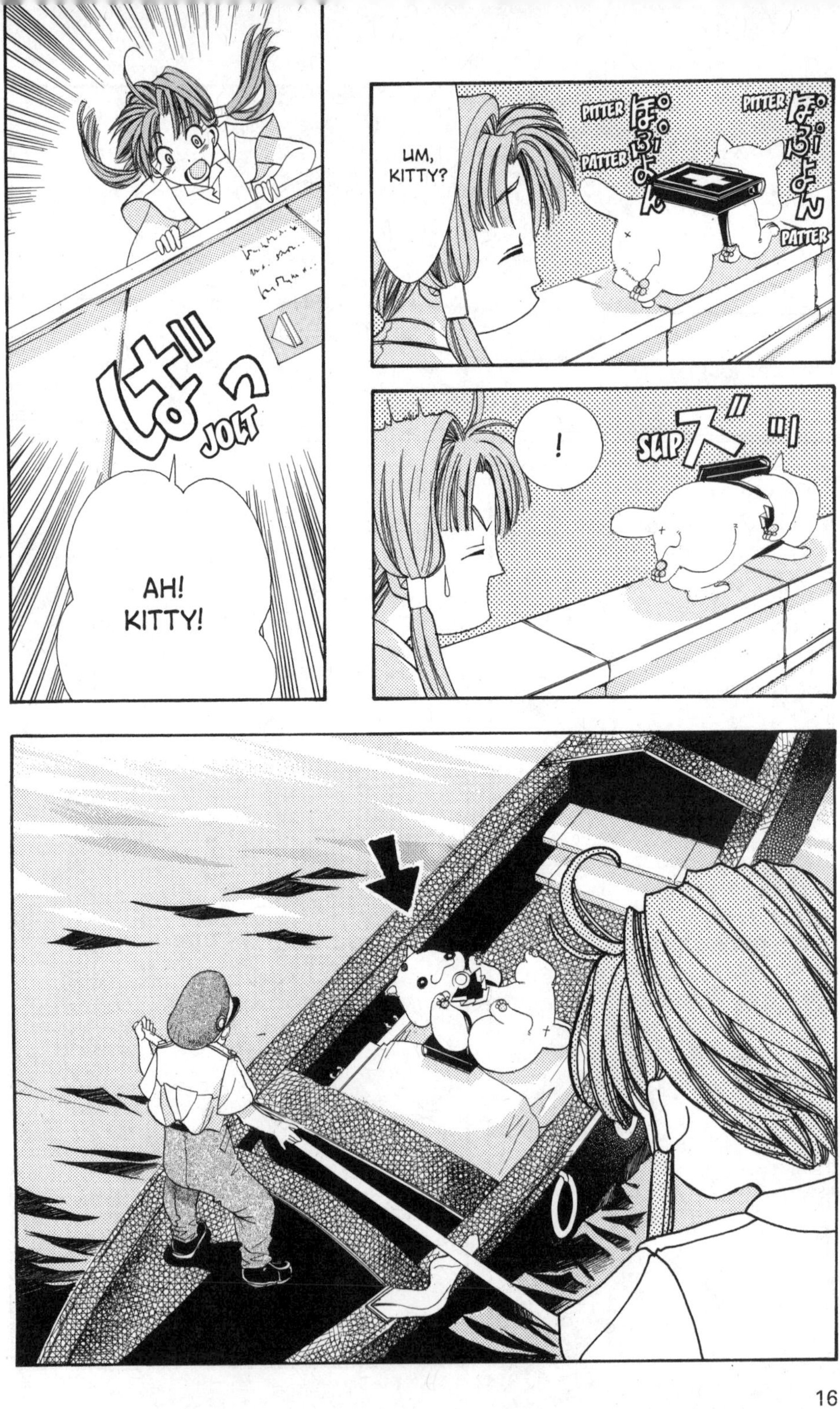

PITTER
ぽぷよん
PATTER
PITTER
PATTER
ぽぷよん
UM, KITTY?
SLIP
ズッ
!
ぱっ
JOLT
AH! KITTY!

SHWIP

UH... WAIT, HUH?

MY BAG!!

WHEW

ROW
ROW

...

SIR! EXCUSE ME?

SIR! PLEASE, WAIT!

17

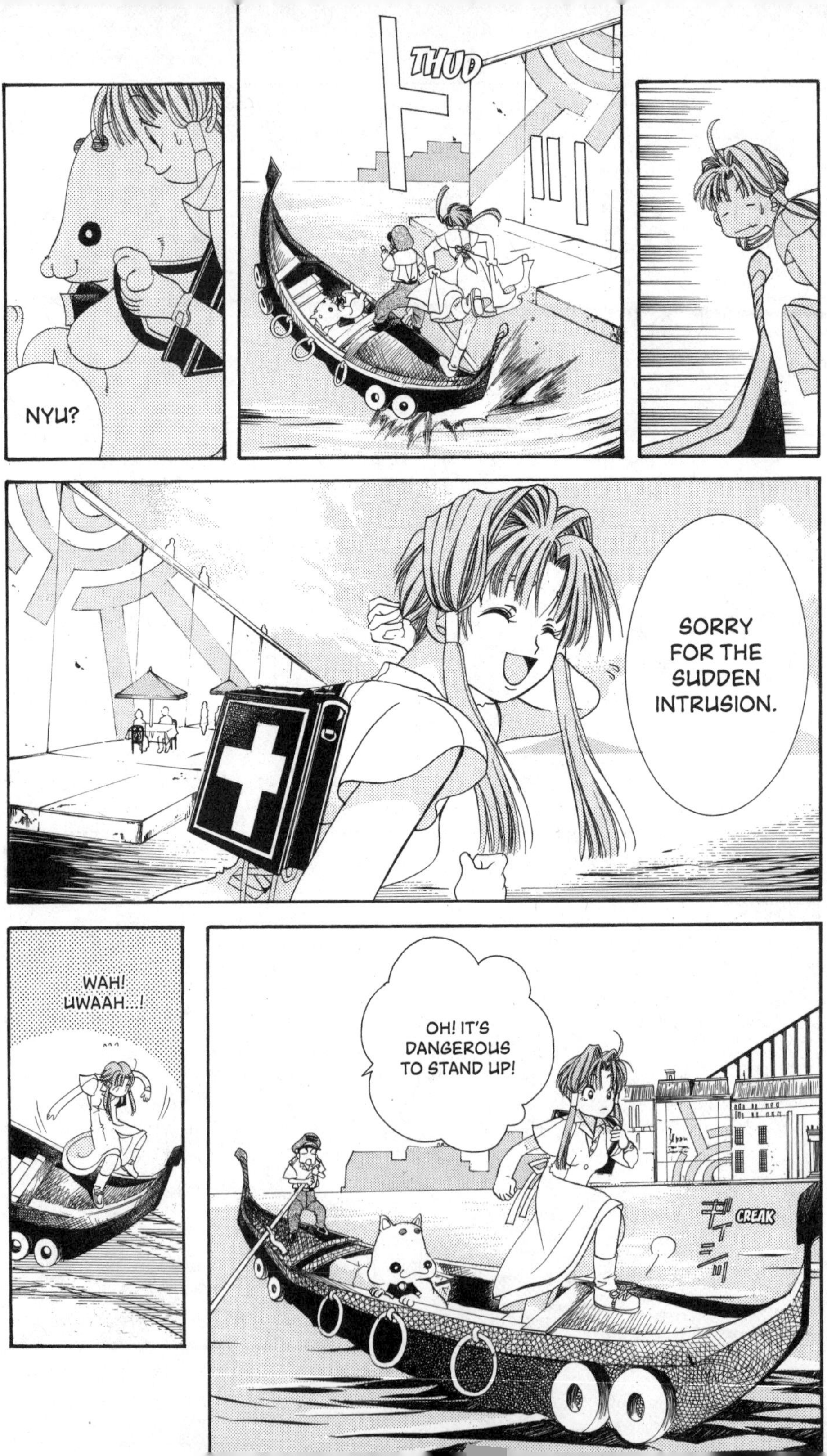
THUD
NYU?
SORRY FOR THE SUDDEN INTRUSION.
OH! IT'S DANGEROUS TO STAND UP!
CREAK
WAH! UWAAH...!

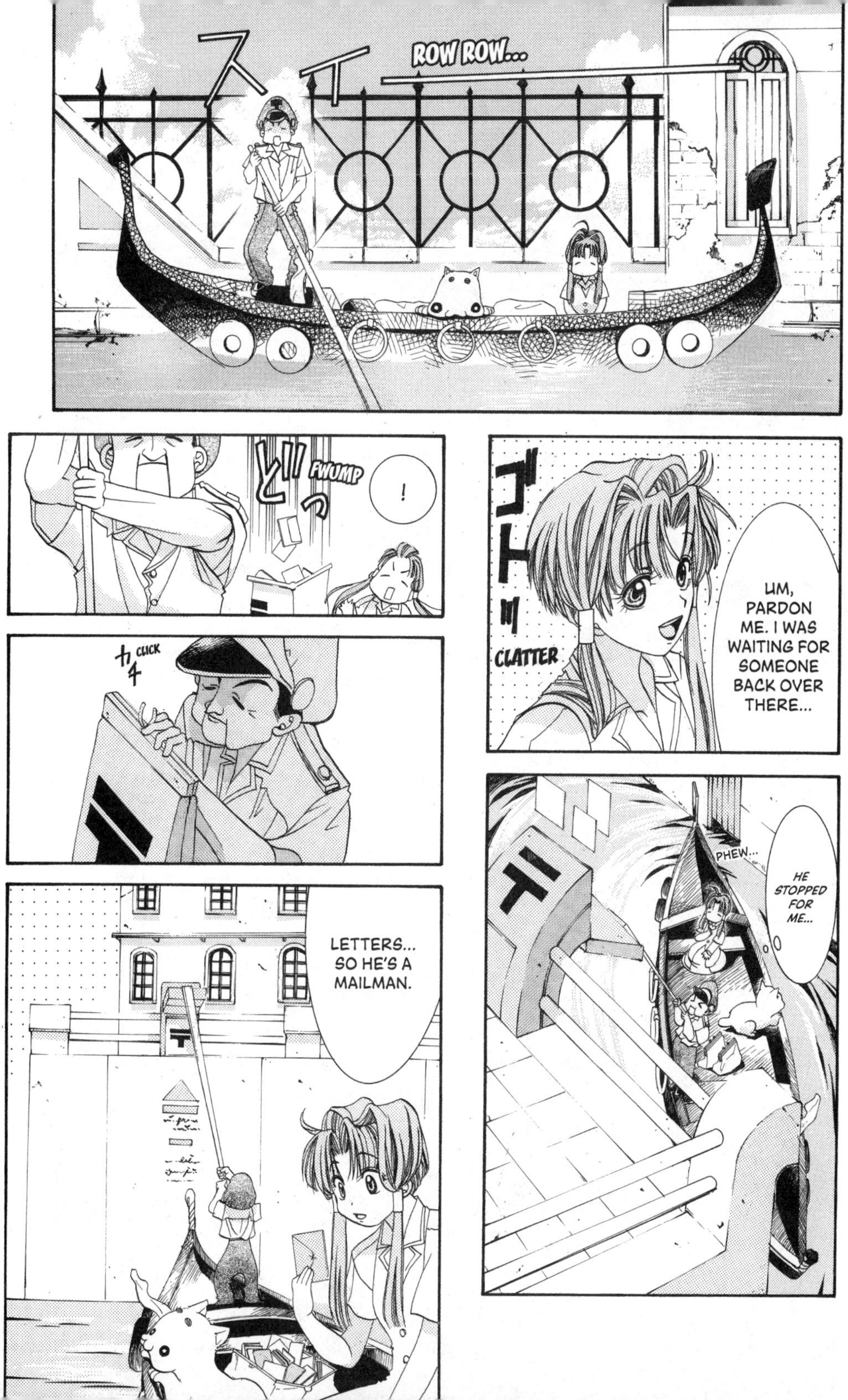

スイ
ROW ROW...
ゴトッ
CLATTER
UM, PARDON ME. I WAS WAITING FOR SOMEONE BACK OVER THERE...
どっ
FWUMP
!
カチ
CLICK
PHEW...
HE STOPPED FOR ME...
LETTERS... SO HE'S A MAILMAN.

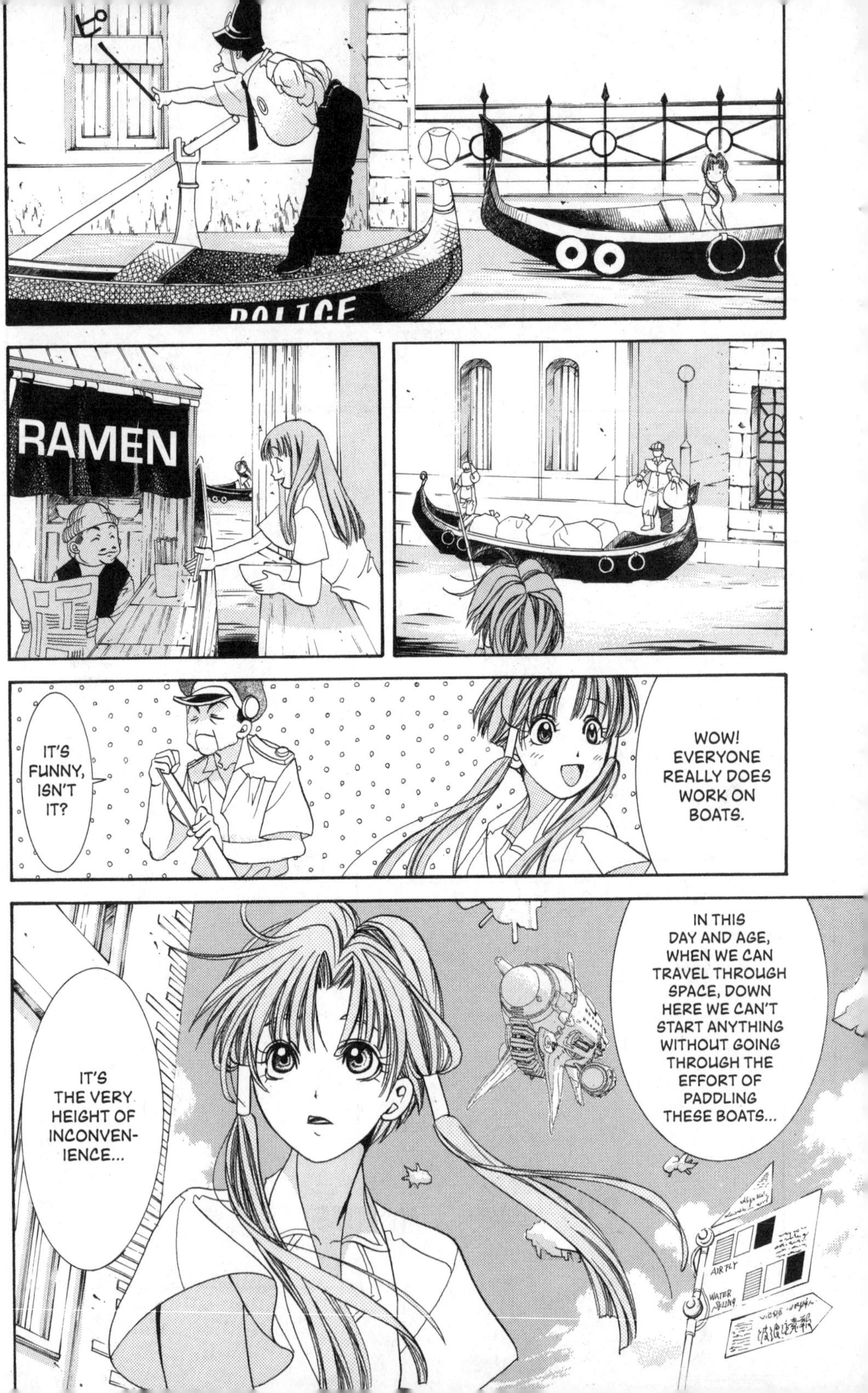
RAMEN
WOW! EVERYONE REALLY DOES WORK ON BOATS.
IT'S FUNNY, ISN'T IT?
IN THIS DAY AND AGE, WHEN WE CAN TRAVEL THROUGH SPACE, DOWN HERE WE CAN'T START ANYTHING WITHOUT GOING THROUGH THE EFFORT OF PADDLING THESE BOATS...
IT'S THE VERY HEIGHT OF INCONVENIENCE...
AIR FLY
WATER SKIING

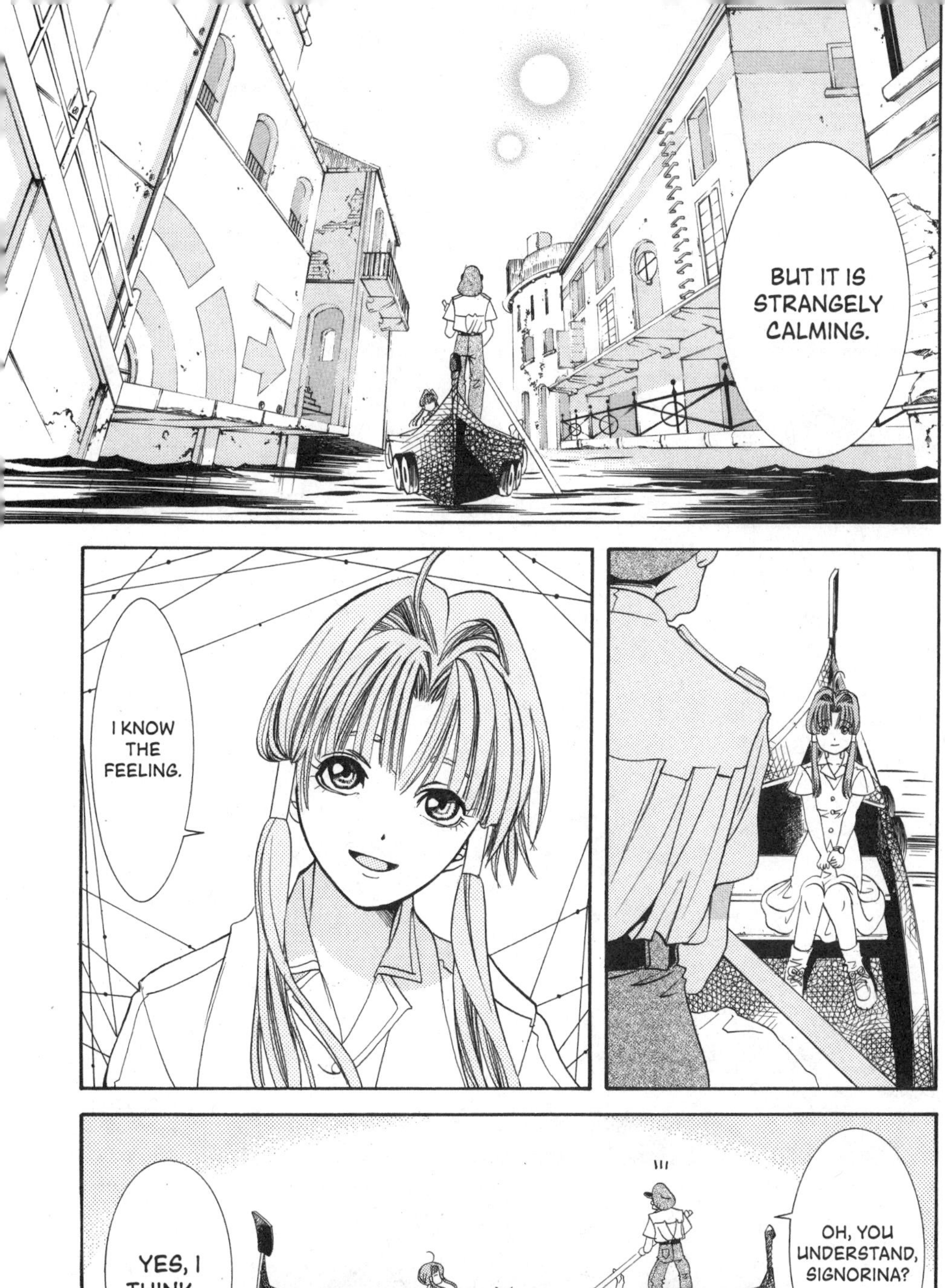
BUT IT IS STRANGELY CALMING.
I KNOW THE FEELING.
OH, YOU UNDERSTAND, SIGNORINA?
YES, I THINK...

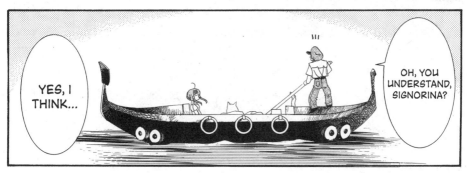

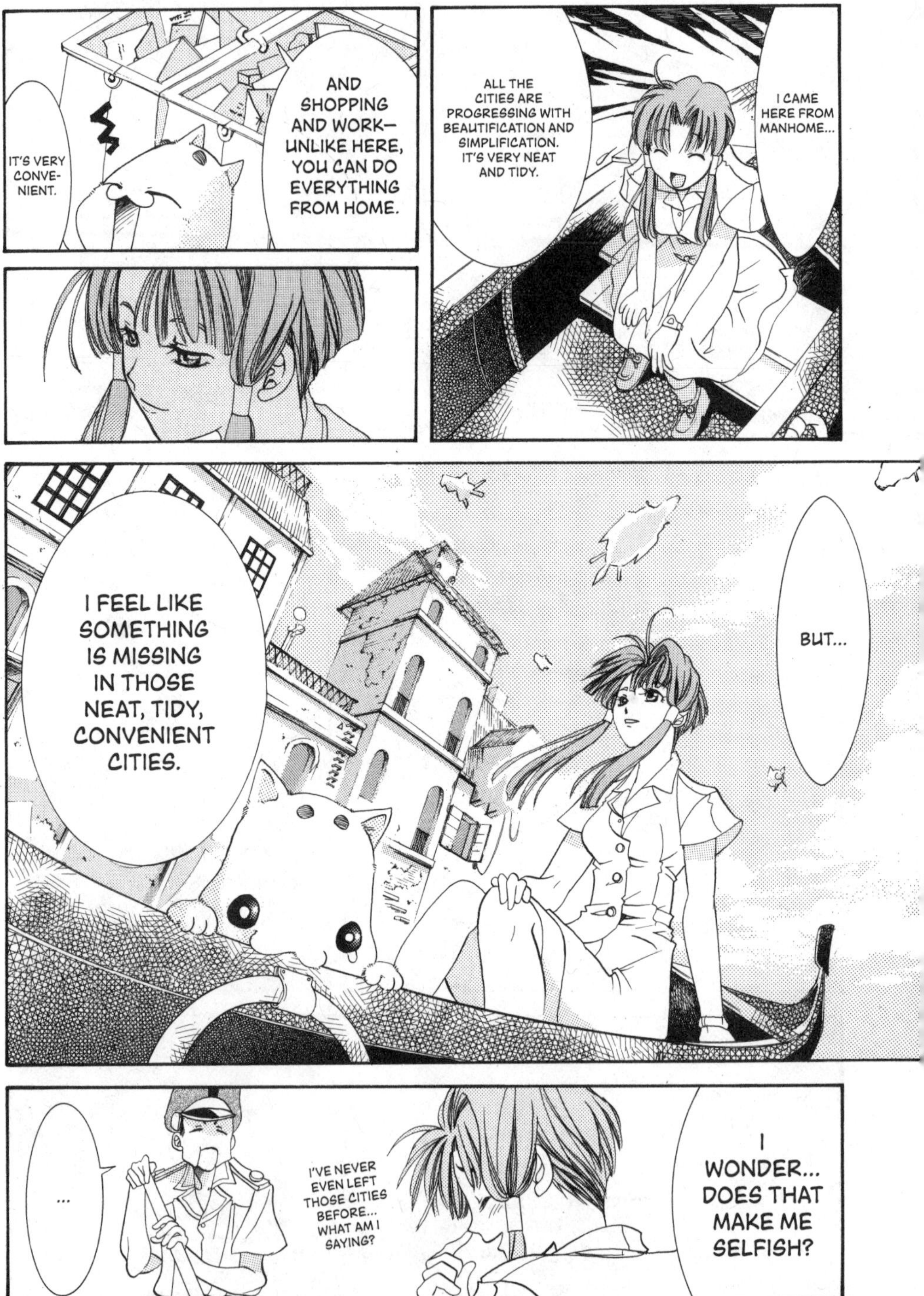
I CAME HERE FROM MANHOME...
ALL THE CITIES ARE PROGRESSING WITH BEAUTIFICATION AND SIMPLIFICATION. IT'S VERY NEAT AND TIDY.
AND SHOPPING AND WORK— UNLIKE HERE, YOU CAN DO EVERYTHING FROM HOME.
IT'S VERY CONVE-NIENT.
BUT...
I FEEL LIKE SOMETHING IS MISSING IN THOSE NEAT, TIDY, CONVENIENT CITIES.
I WONDER... DOES THAT MAKE ME SELFISH?
I'VE NEVER EVEN LEFT THOSE CITIES BEFORE... WHAT AM I SAYING?
...

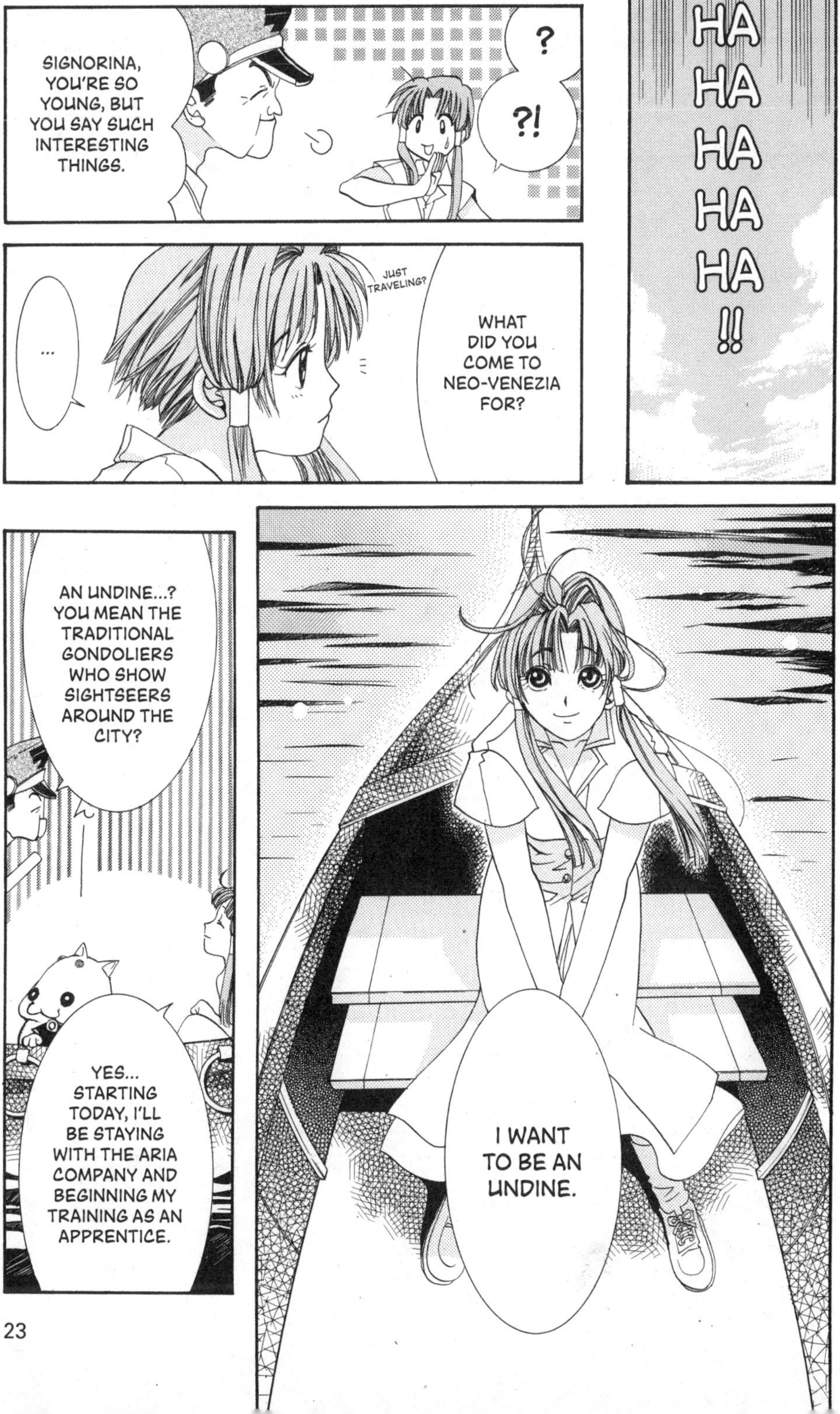
HA HA HA HA HA !!
?
?!
SIGNORINA, YOU'RE SO YOUNG, BUT YOU SAY SUCH INTERESTING THINGS.
JUST TRAVELING?
WHAT DID YOU COME TO NEO-VENEZIA FOR?
...
I WANT TO BE AN UNDINE.
AN UNDINE...? YOU MEAN THE TRADITIONAL GONDOLIERS WHO SHOW SIGHTSEERS AROUND THE CITY?
YES... STARTING TODAY, I'LL BE STAYING WITH THE ARIA COMPANY AND BEGINNING MY TRAINING AS AN APPRENTICE.

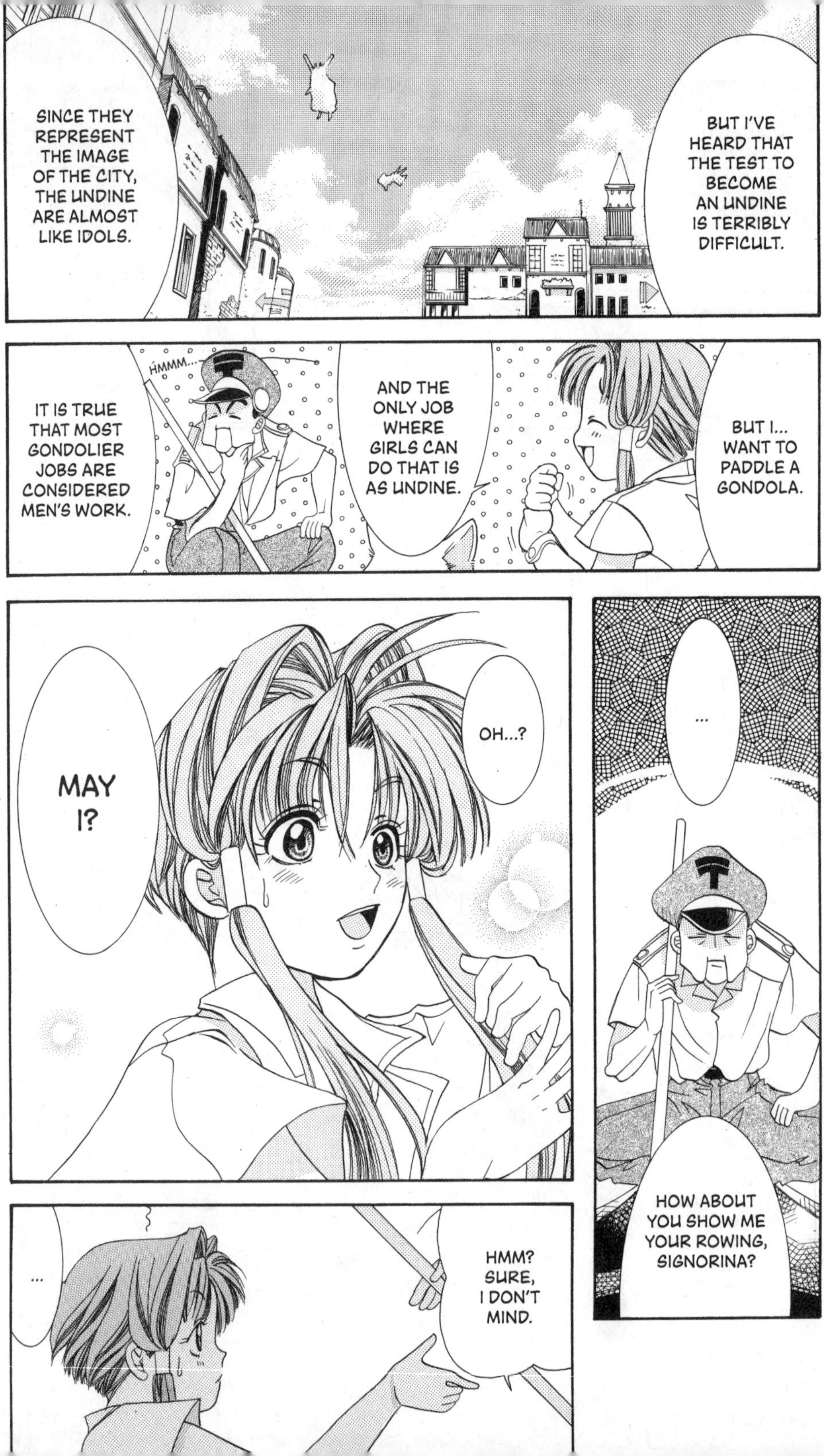
BUT I'VE HEARD THAT THE TEST TO BECOME AN UNDINE IS TERRIBLY DIFFICULT.
SINCE THEY REPRESENT THE IMAGE OF THE CITY, THE UNDINE ARE ALMOST LIKE IDOLS.
BUT I... WANT TO PADDLE A GONDOLA.
AND THE ONLY JOB WHERE GIRLS CAN DO THAT IS AS UNDINE.
HMMM...
IT IS TRUE THAT MOST GONDOLIER JOBS ARE CONSIDERED MEN'S WORK.
...
HOW ABOUT YOU SHOW ME YOUR ROWING, SIGNORINA?
OH...?
MAY I?
HMM? SURE, I DON'T MIND.
...

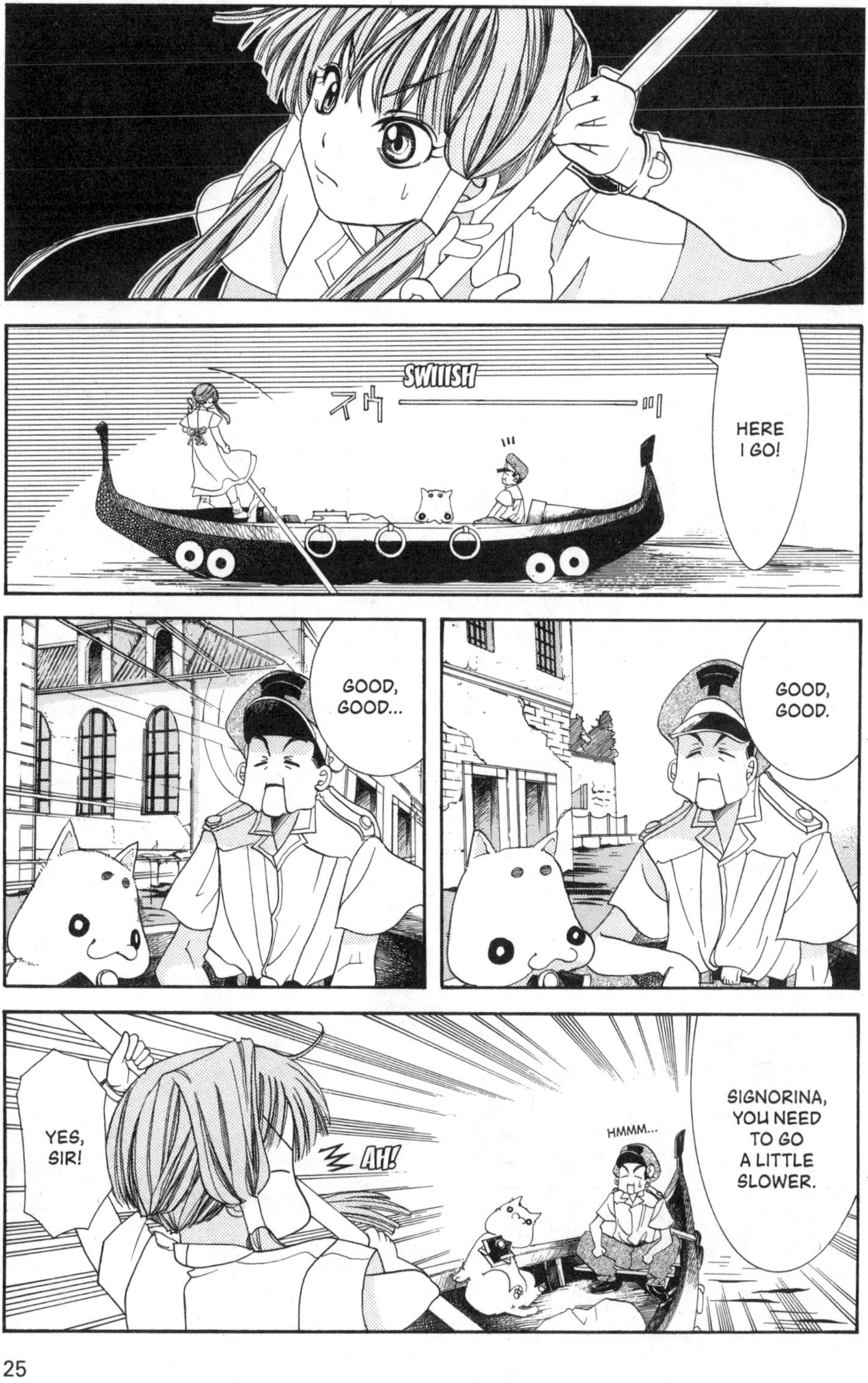
HERE I GO!
SWIIISH
GOOD, GOOD.
GOOD, GOOD...
SIGNORINA, YOU NEED TO GO A LITTLE SLOWER.
HMMM...
AH!
YES, SIR!

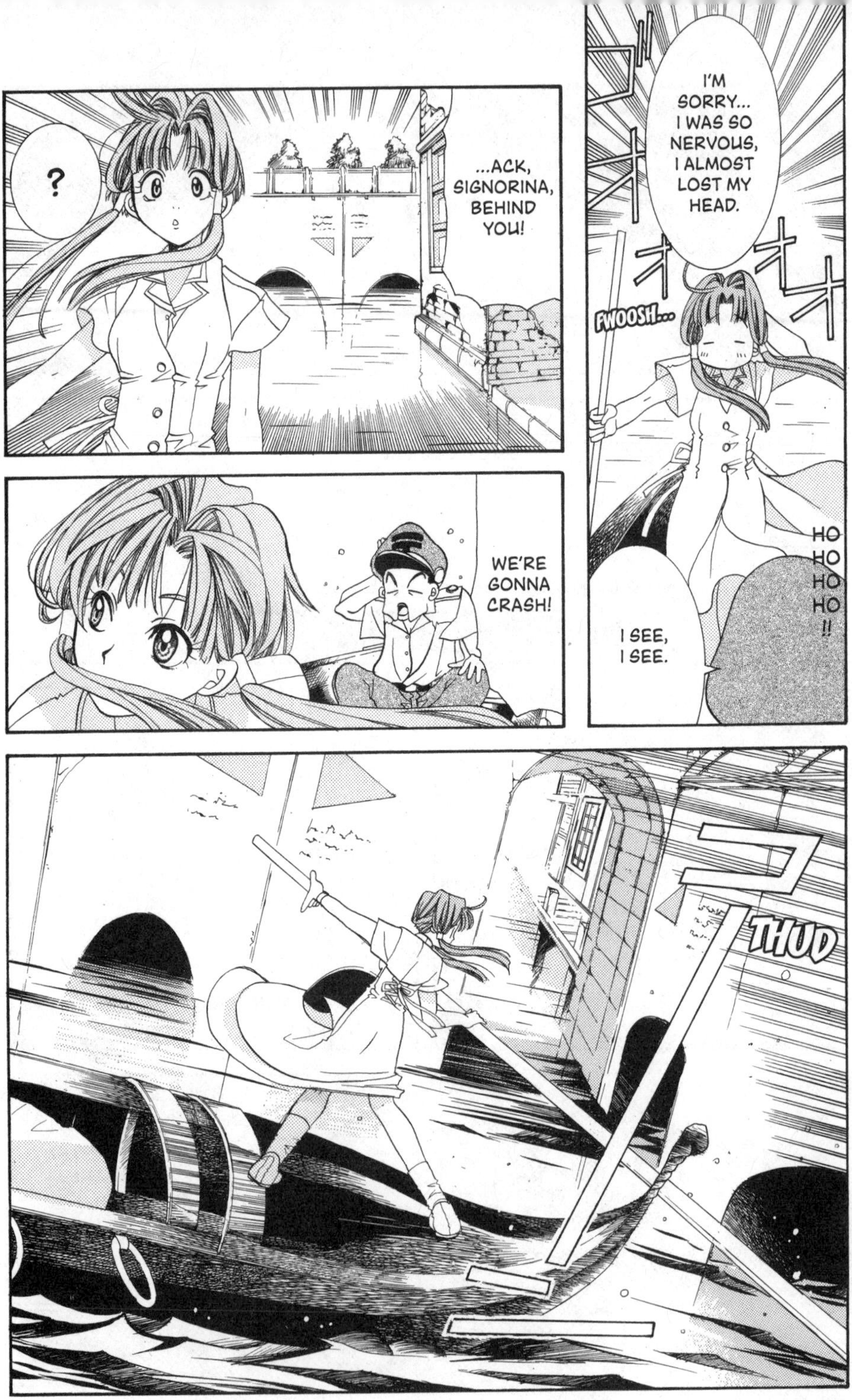
I'M SORRY... I WAS SO NERVOUS, I ALMOST LOST MY HEAD.
FWOOSH...
HO HO HO HO !!
I SEE, I SEE.
?
...ACK, SIGNORINA, BEHIND YOU!
WE'RE GONNA CRASH!
THUD

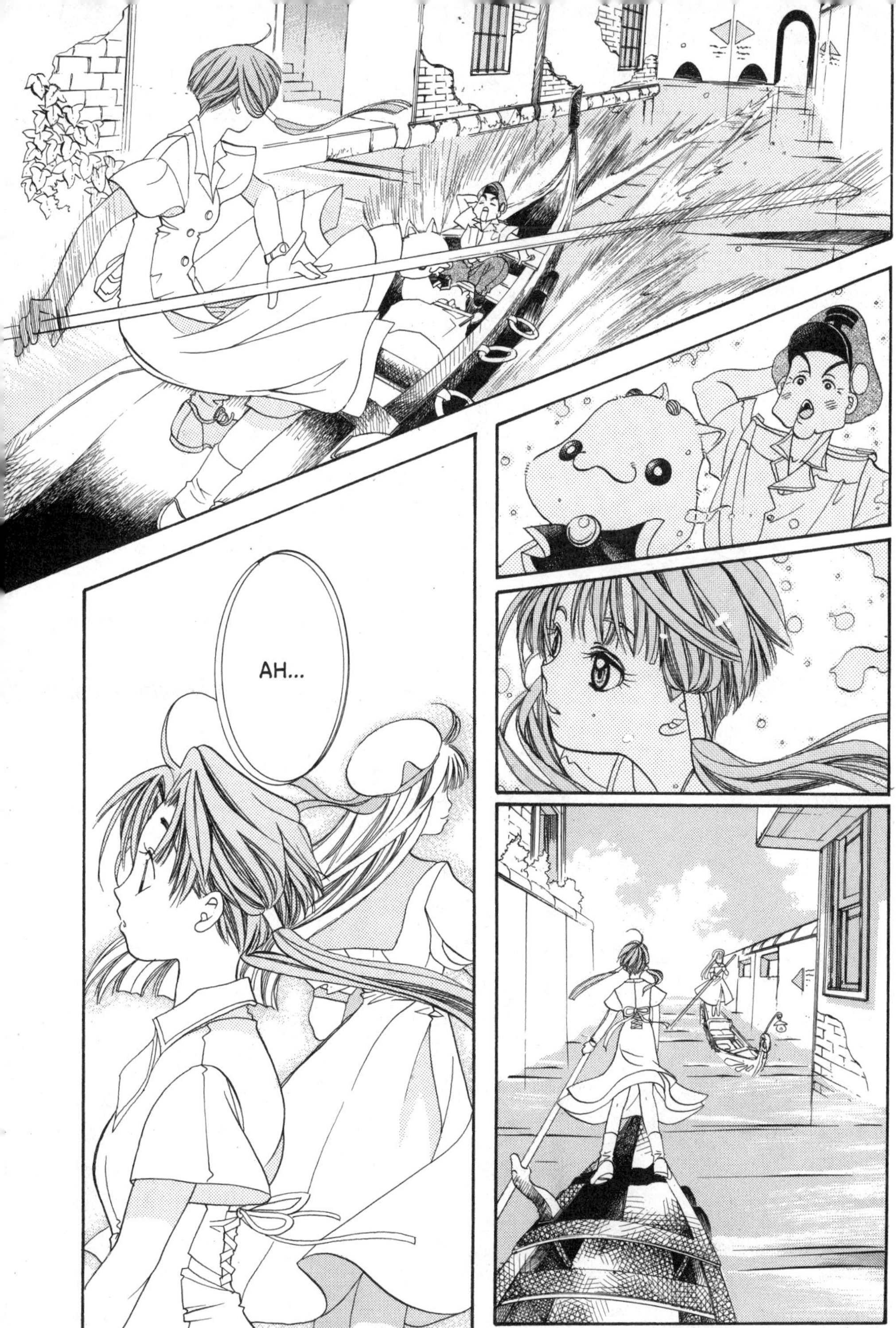
AH...

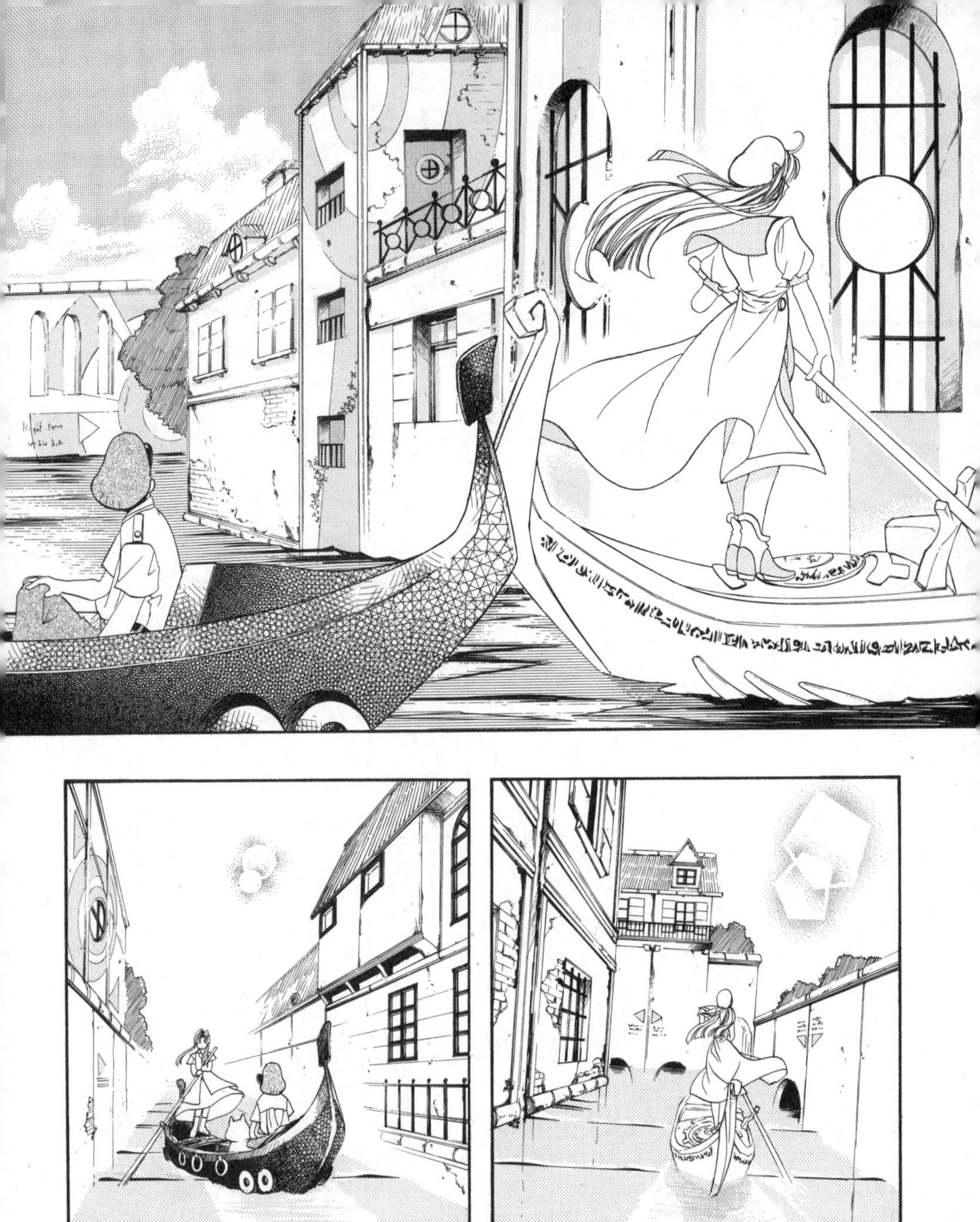

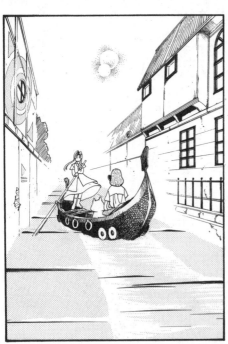

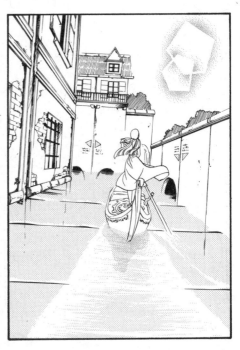

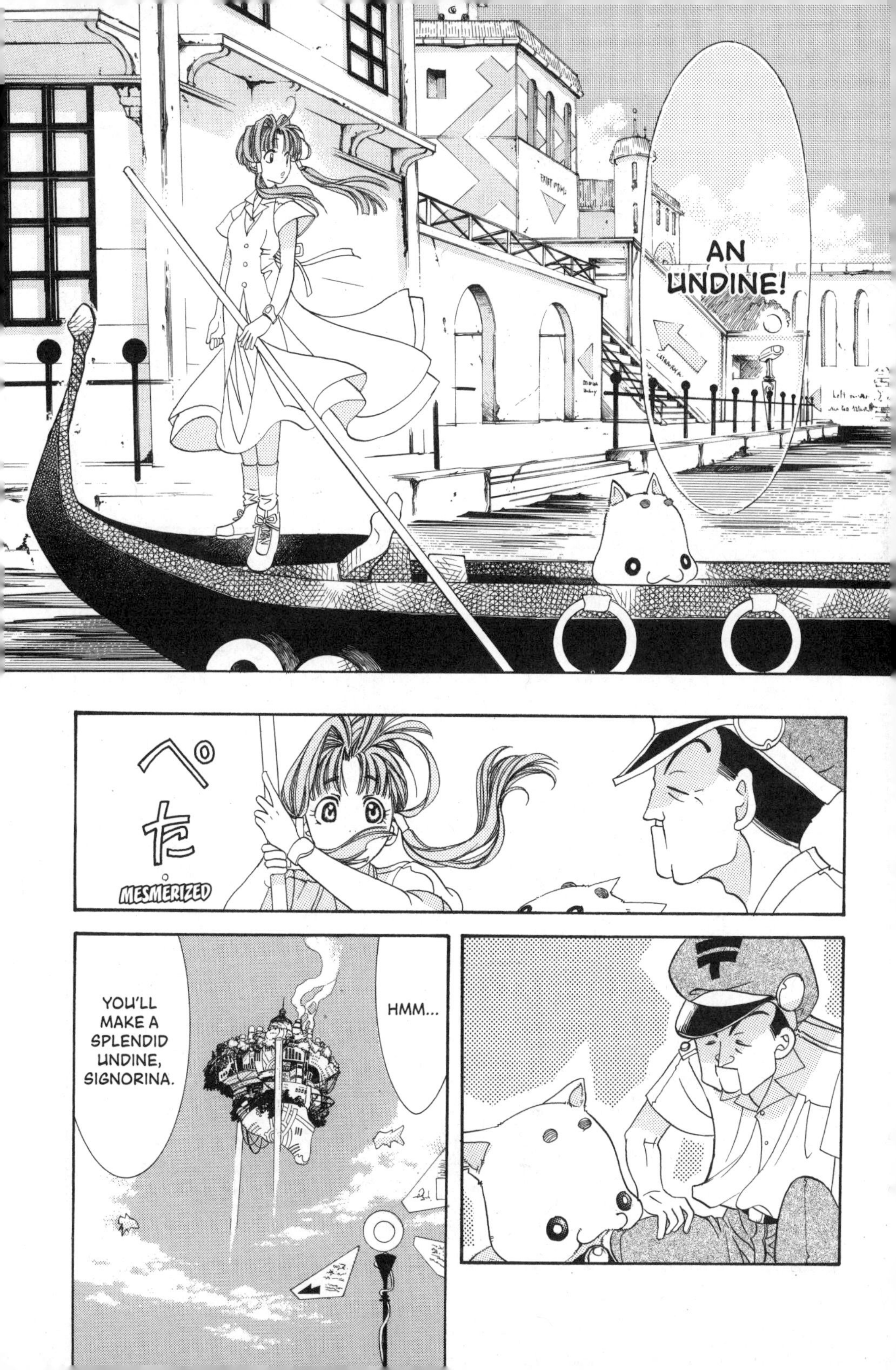
AN UNDINE!
ぺた
MESMERIZED
HMM...
YOU'LL MAKE A SPLENDID UNDINE, SIGNORINA.

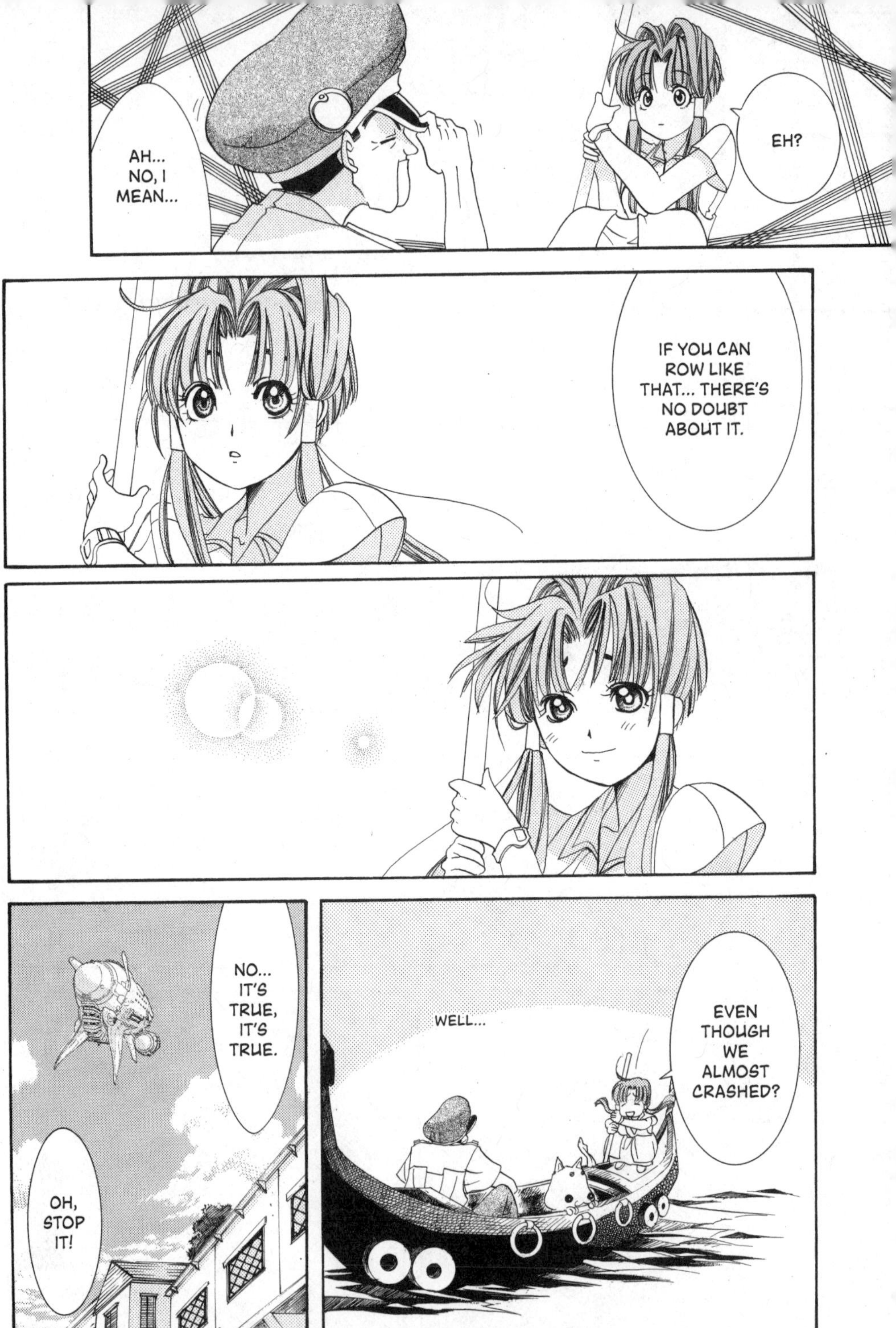
EH?
AH... NO, I MEAN...
IF YOU CAN ROW LIKE THAT... THERE'S NO DOUBT ABOUT IT.
EVEN THOUGH WE ALMOST CRASHED?
WELL...
NO... IT'S TRUE, IT'S TRUE.
OH, STOP IT!

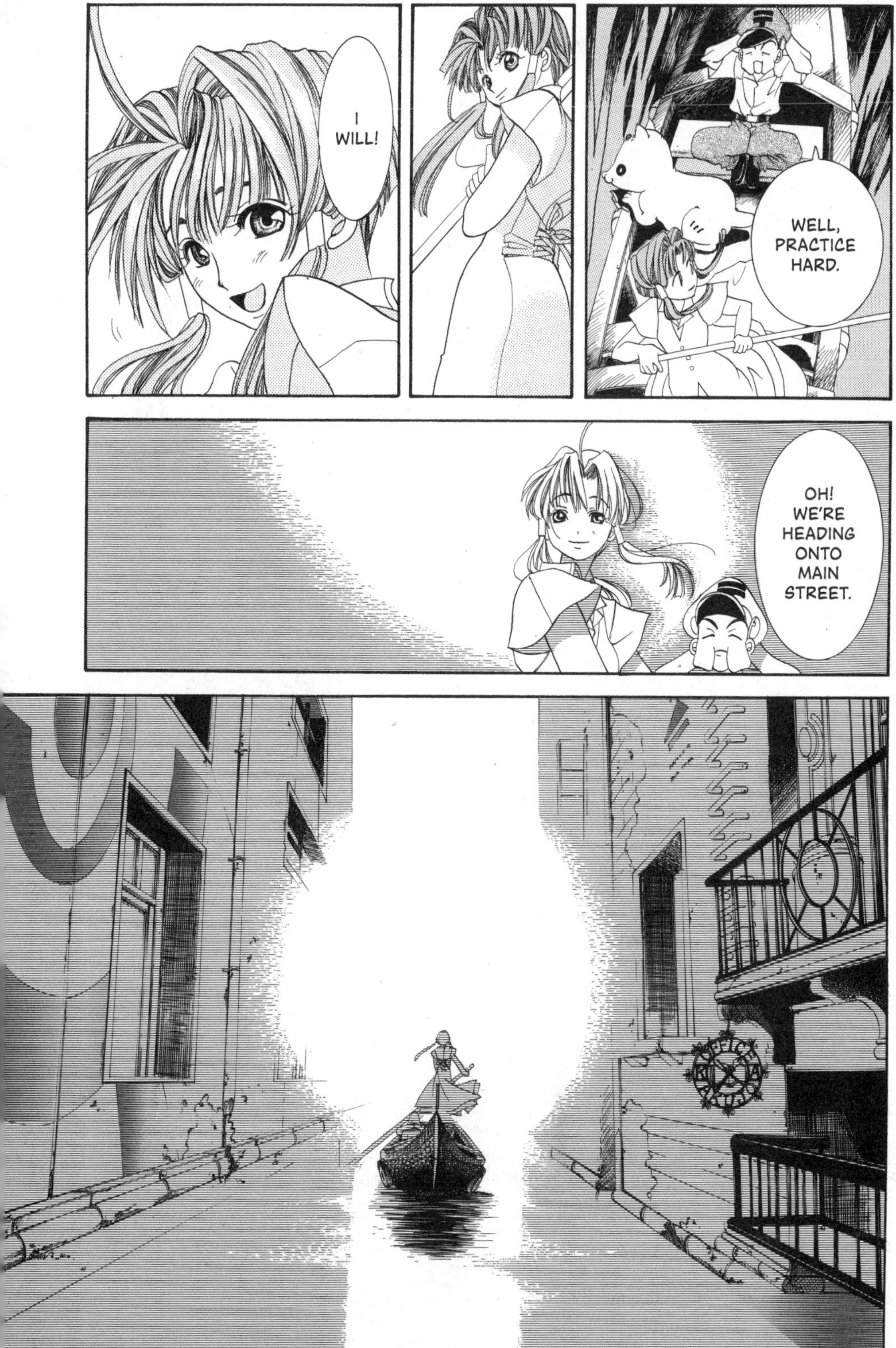
WELL, PRACTICE HARD.
I WILL!
OH! WE'RE HEADING ONTO MAIN STREET.

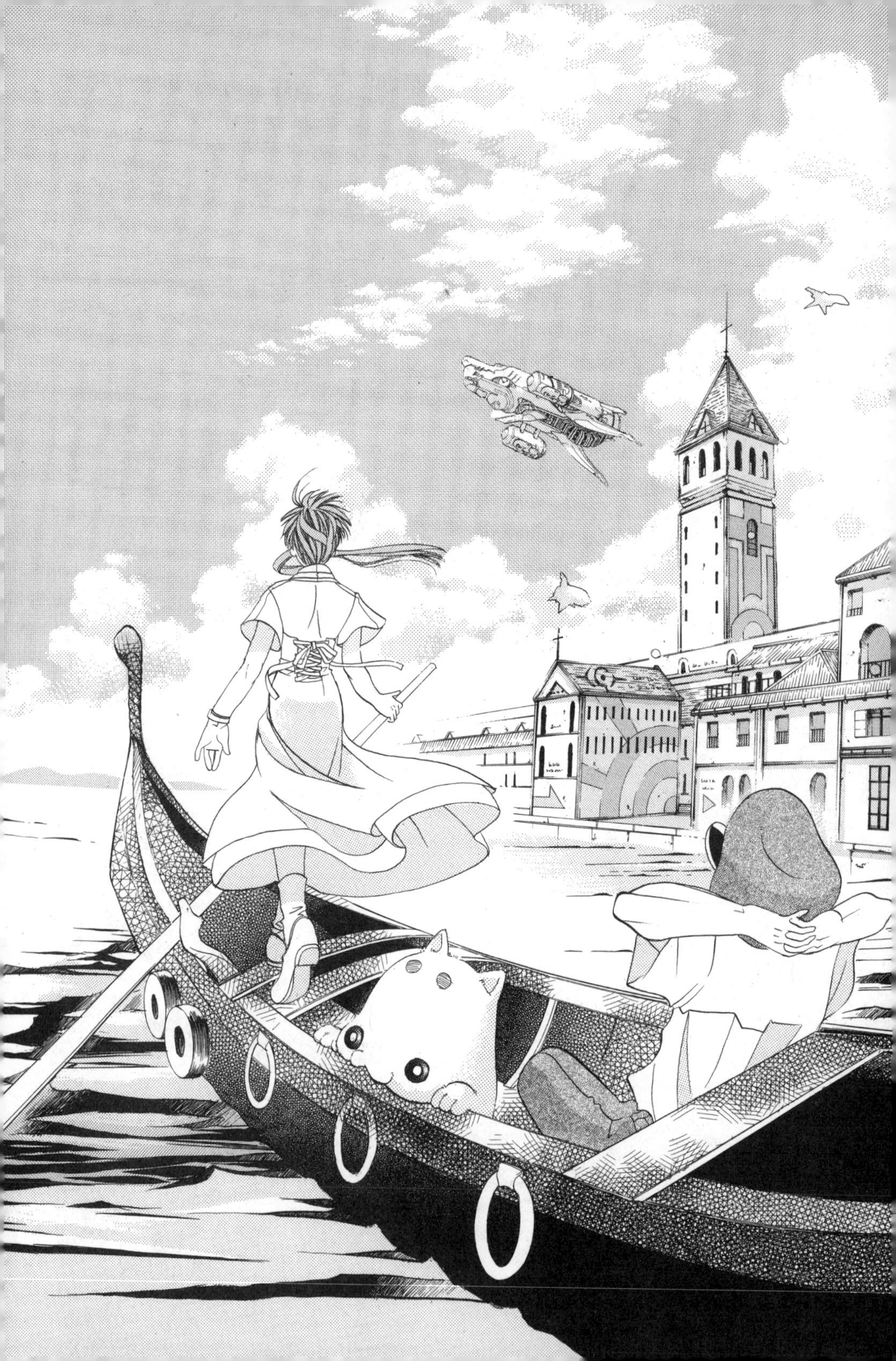

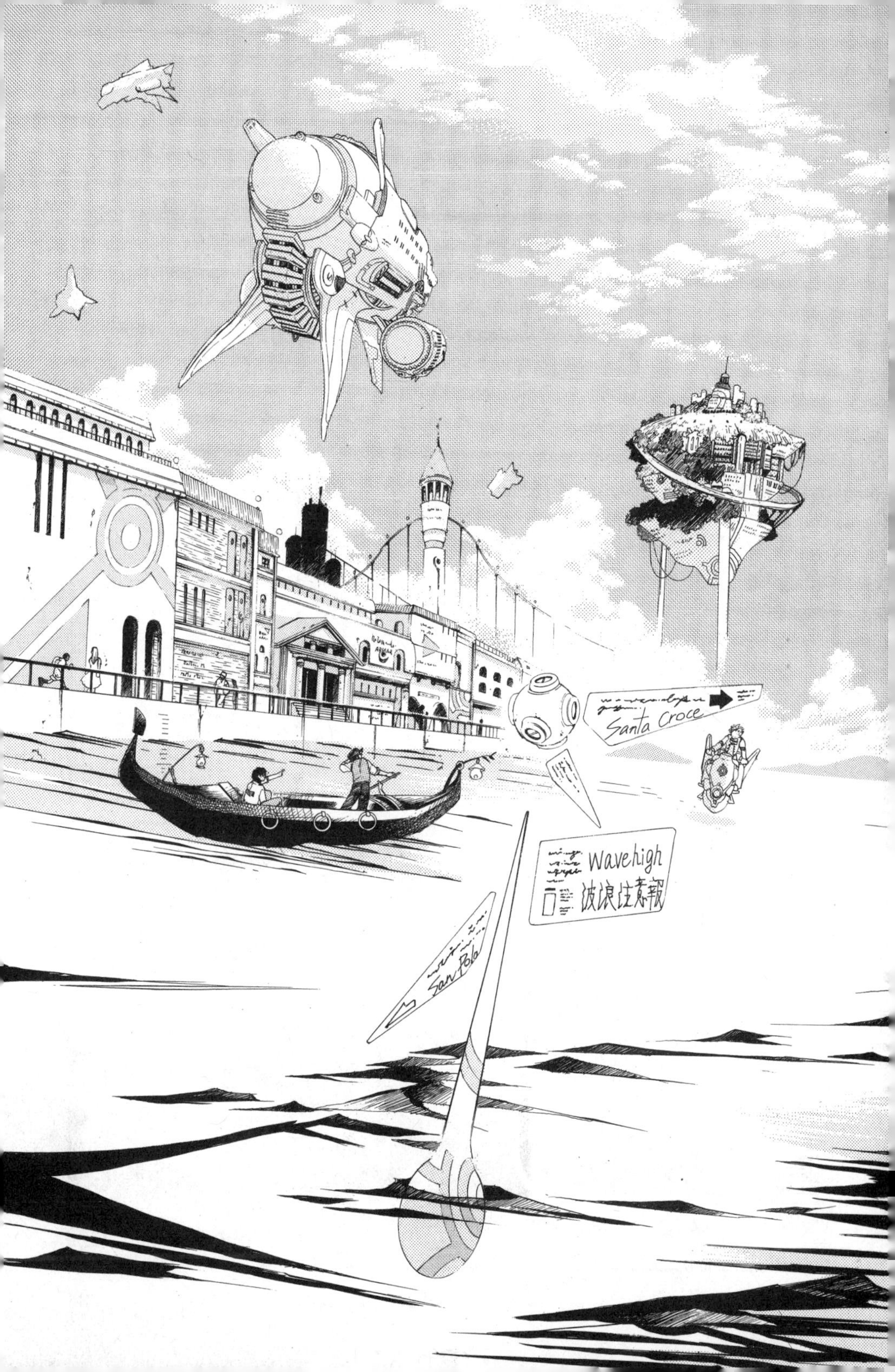
Santa Croce
Wavehigh
波浪注意報
San Pola

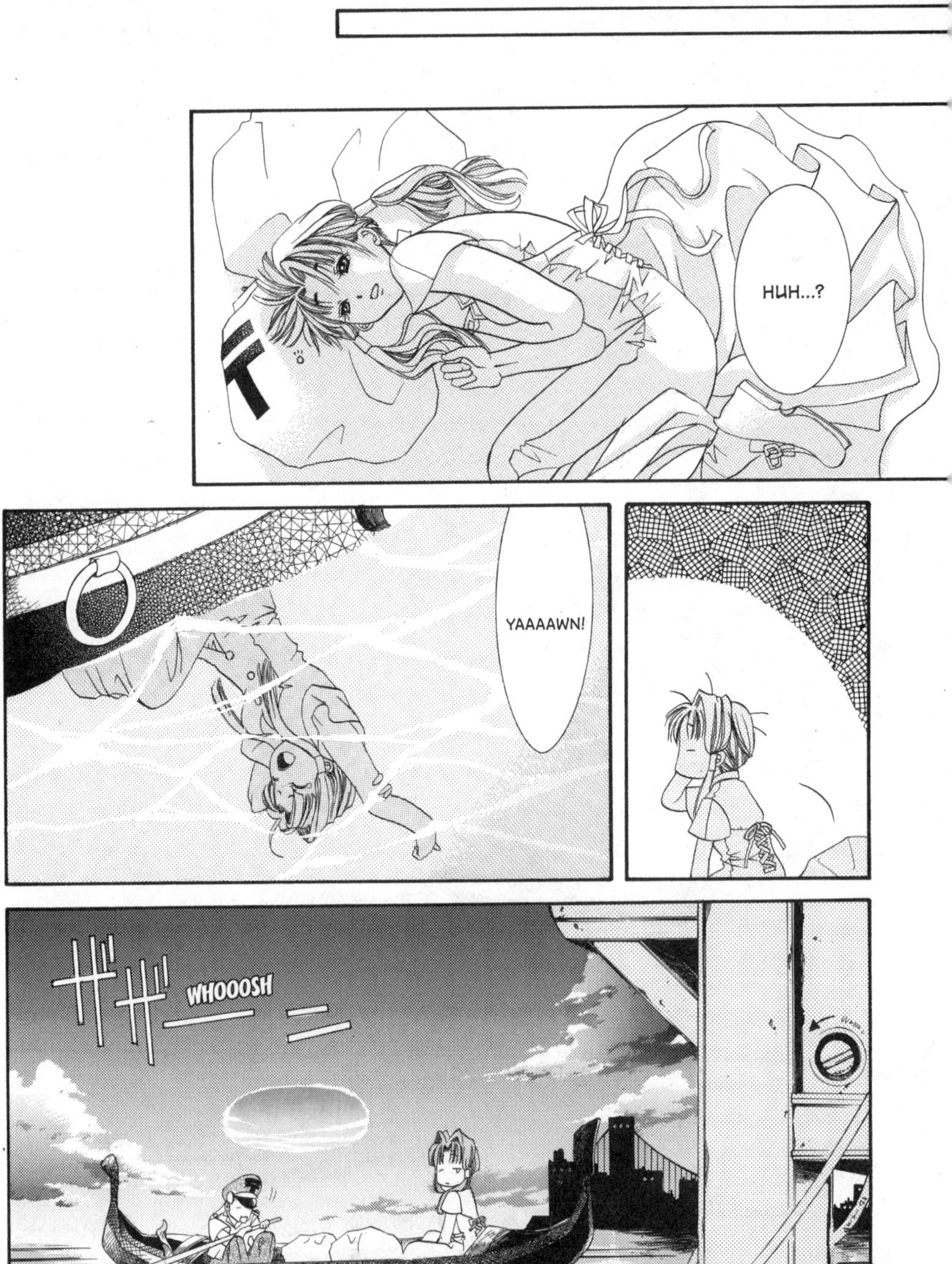
HUH...?
YAAAAWN!
ザザーー
WHOOOSH

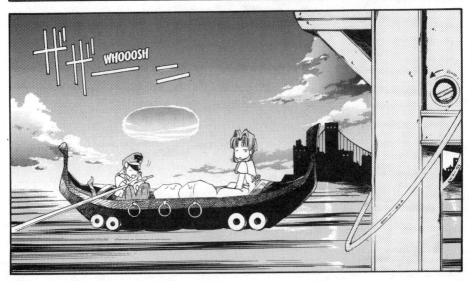

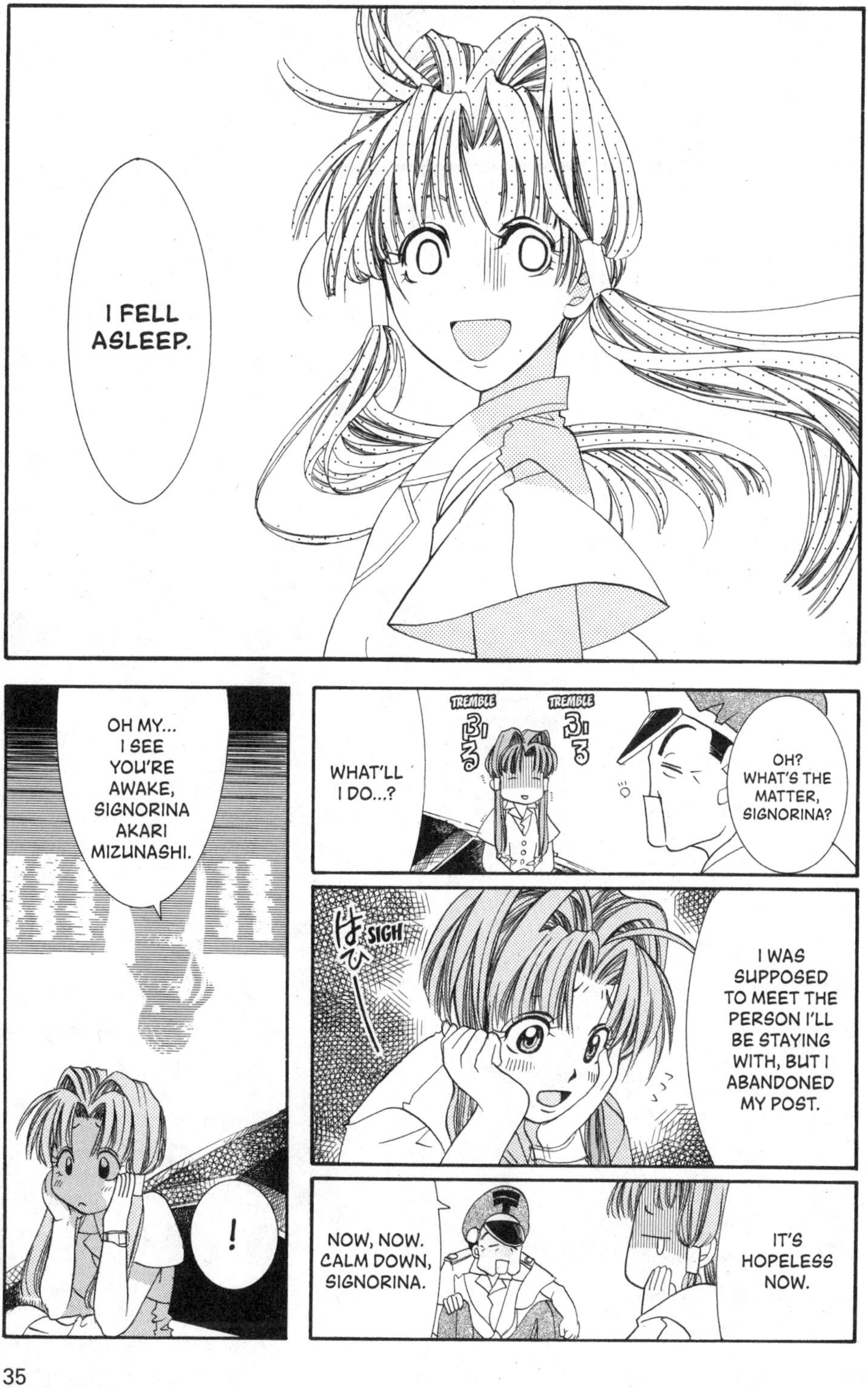
I FELL ASLEEP.
OH? WHAT'S THE MATTER, SIGNORINA?
TREMBLE
TREMBLE
WHAT'LL I DO...?
SIGH
I WAS SUPPOSED TO MEET THE PERSON I'LL BE STAYING WITH, BUT I ABANDONED MY POST.
IT'S HOPELESS NOW.
NOW, NOW. CALM DOWN, SIGNORINA.
OH MY... I SEE YOU'RE AWAKE, SIGNORINA AKARI MIZUNASHI.
!

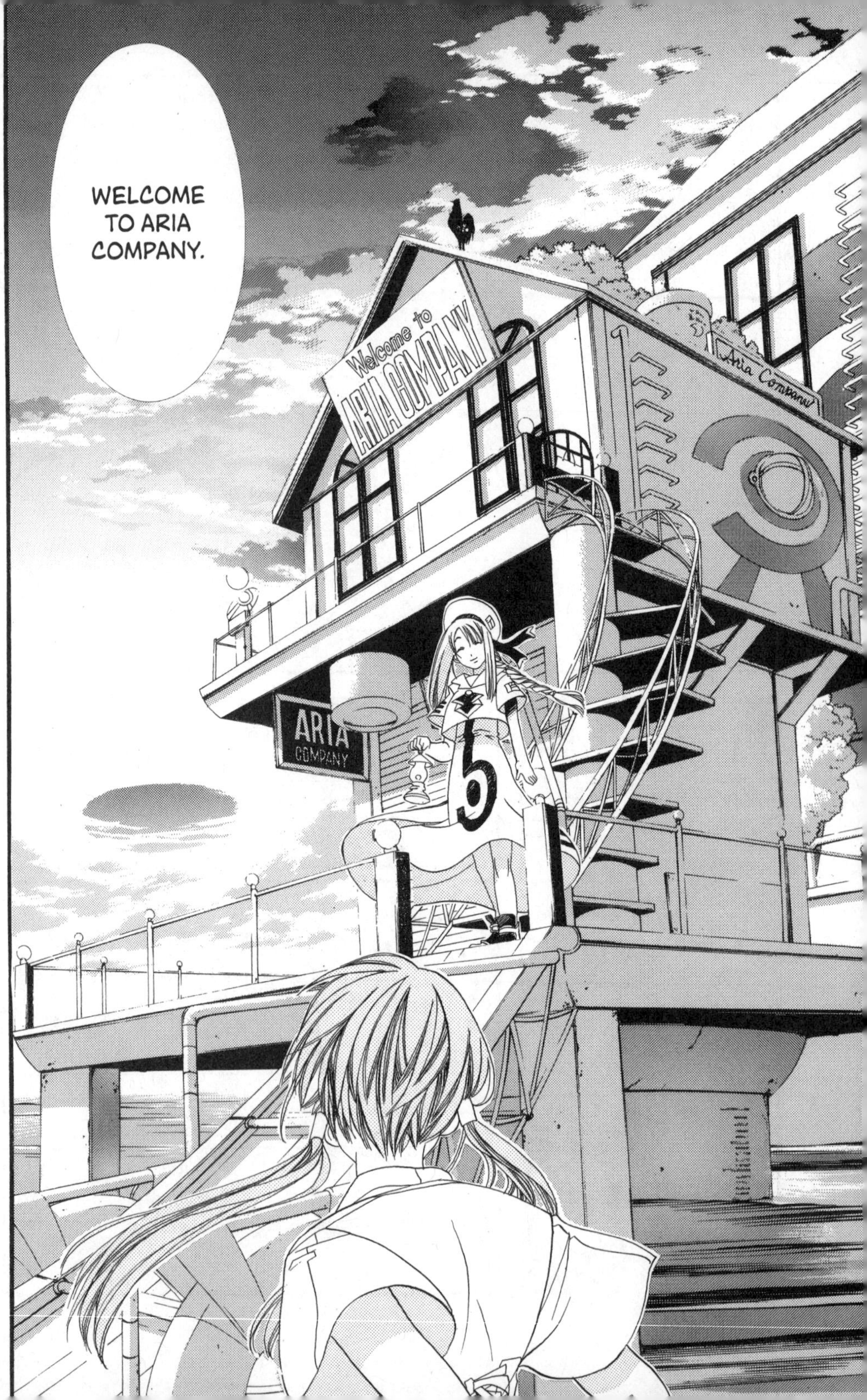
WELCOME TO ARIA COMPANY.
Welcome to ARIA COMPANY
Aria Company
ARIA COMPANY

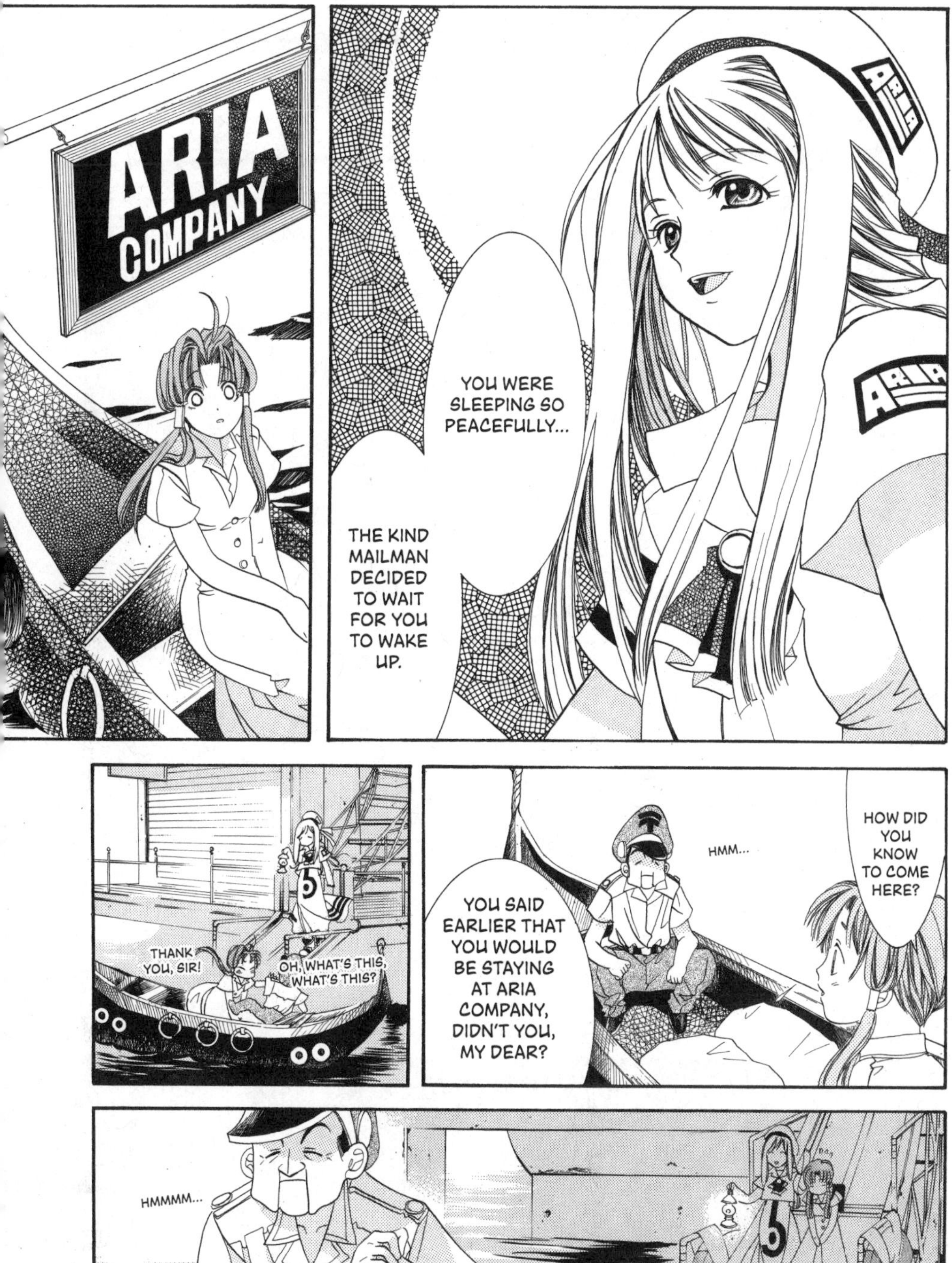
YOU WERE SLEEPING SO PEACEFULLY...
THE KIND MAILMAN DECIDED TO WAIT FOR YOU TO WAKE UP.
ARIA COMPANY
HOW DID YOU KNOW TO COME HERE?
HMM...
YOU SAID EARLIER THAT YOU WOULD BE STAYING AT ARIA COMPANY, DIDN'T YOU, MY DEAR?
OH, WHAT'S THIS, WHAT'S THIS?
THANK YOU, SIR!
HMMMM...

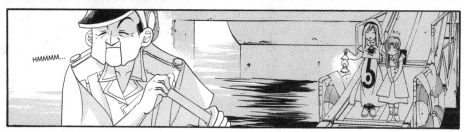

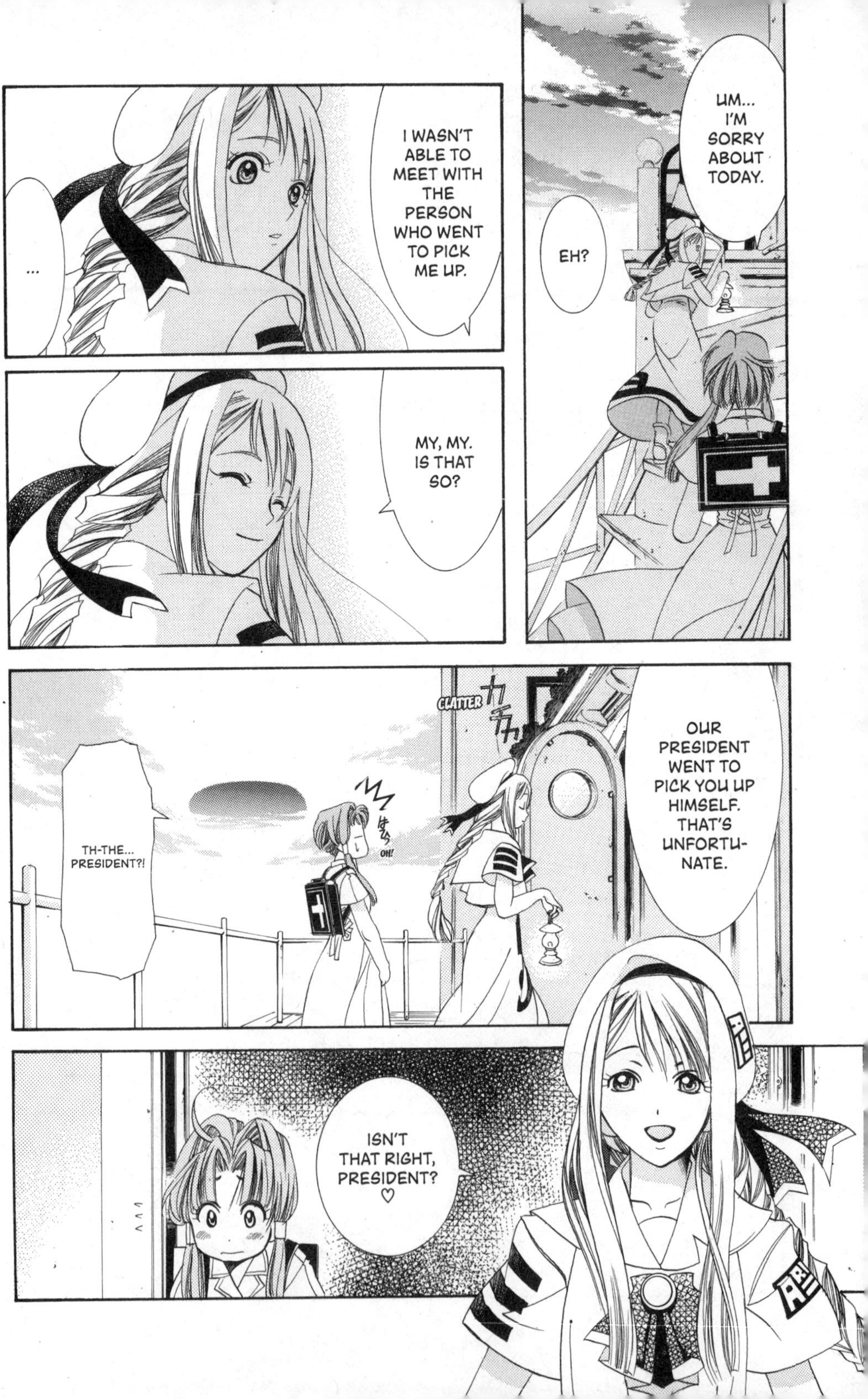
UM... I'M SORRY ABOUT TODAY.
EH?
I WASN'T ABLE TO MEET WITH THE PERSON WHO WENT TO PICK ME UP.
...
MY, MY. IS THAT SO?
CLATTER
OUR PRESIDENT WENT TO PICK YOU UP HIMSELF. THAT'S UNFORTU-NATE.
OH!
TH-THE... PRESIDENT?!
ISN'T THAT RIGHT, PRESIDENT? ♡

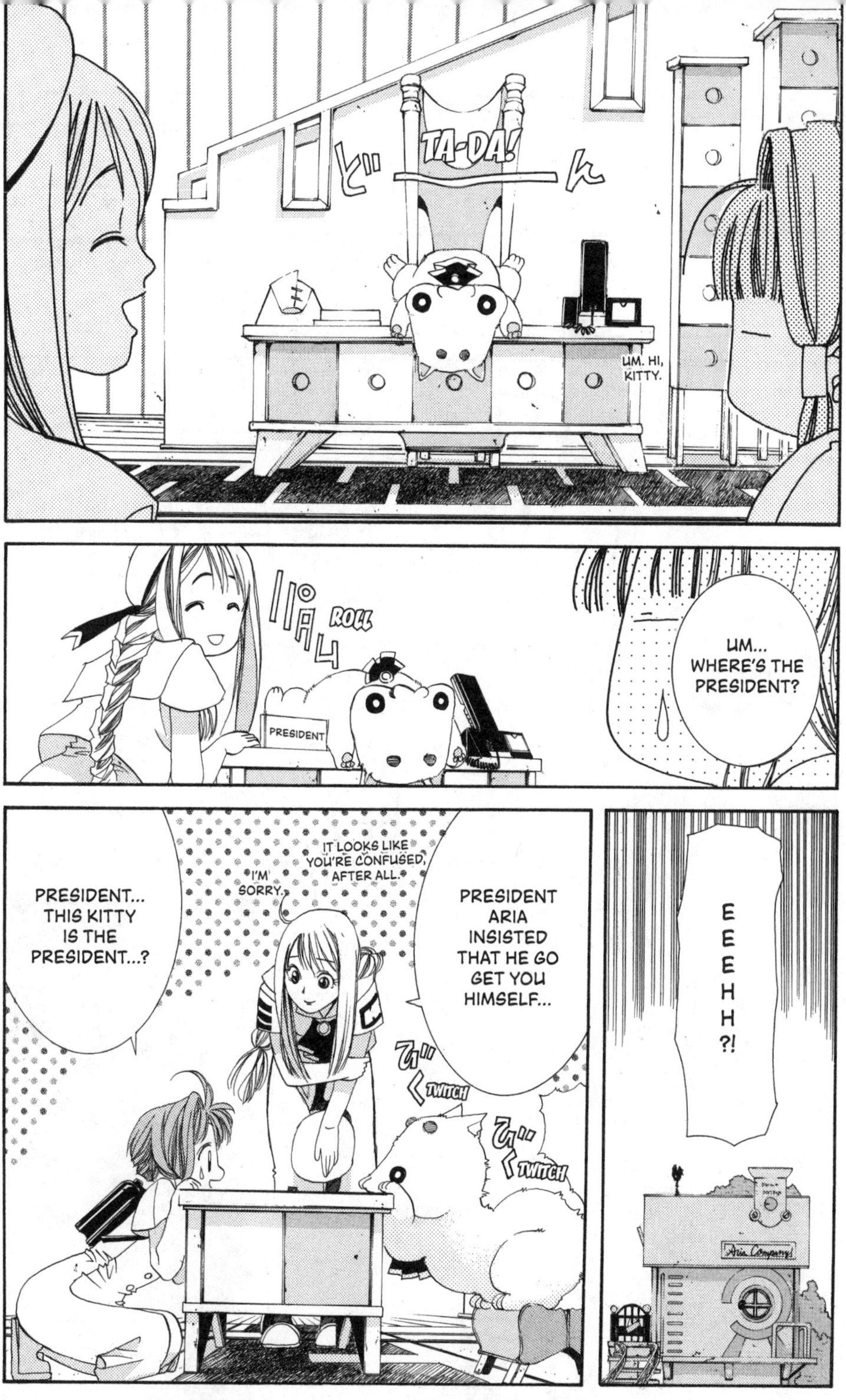
TA-DA!
UM. HI, KITTY.
UM... WHERE'S THE PRESIDENT?
ROLL
PRESIDENT
EEEEHH?!
Aria Company
PRESIDENT ARIA INSISTED THAT HE GO GET YOU HIMSELF...
IT LOOKS LIKE YOU'RE CONFUSED, AFTER ALL.
I'M SORRY.
PRESIDENT... THIS KITTY IS THE PRESIDENT...?
TWITCH
TWITCH

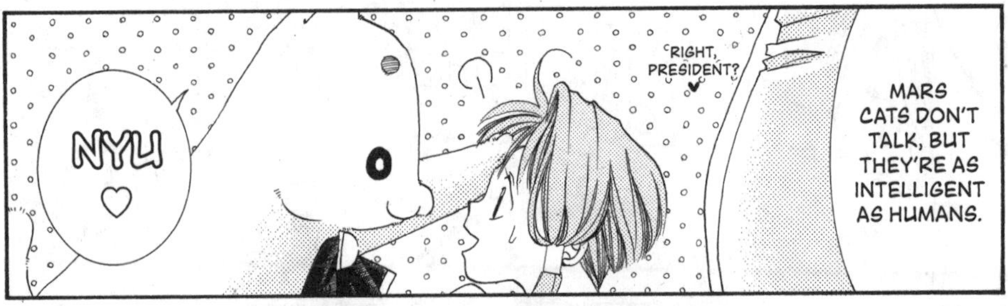
MARS CATS DON'T TALK, BUT THEY'RE AS INTELLIGENT AS HUMANS.
RIGHT, PRESIDENT? ♥
NYU ♡
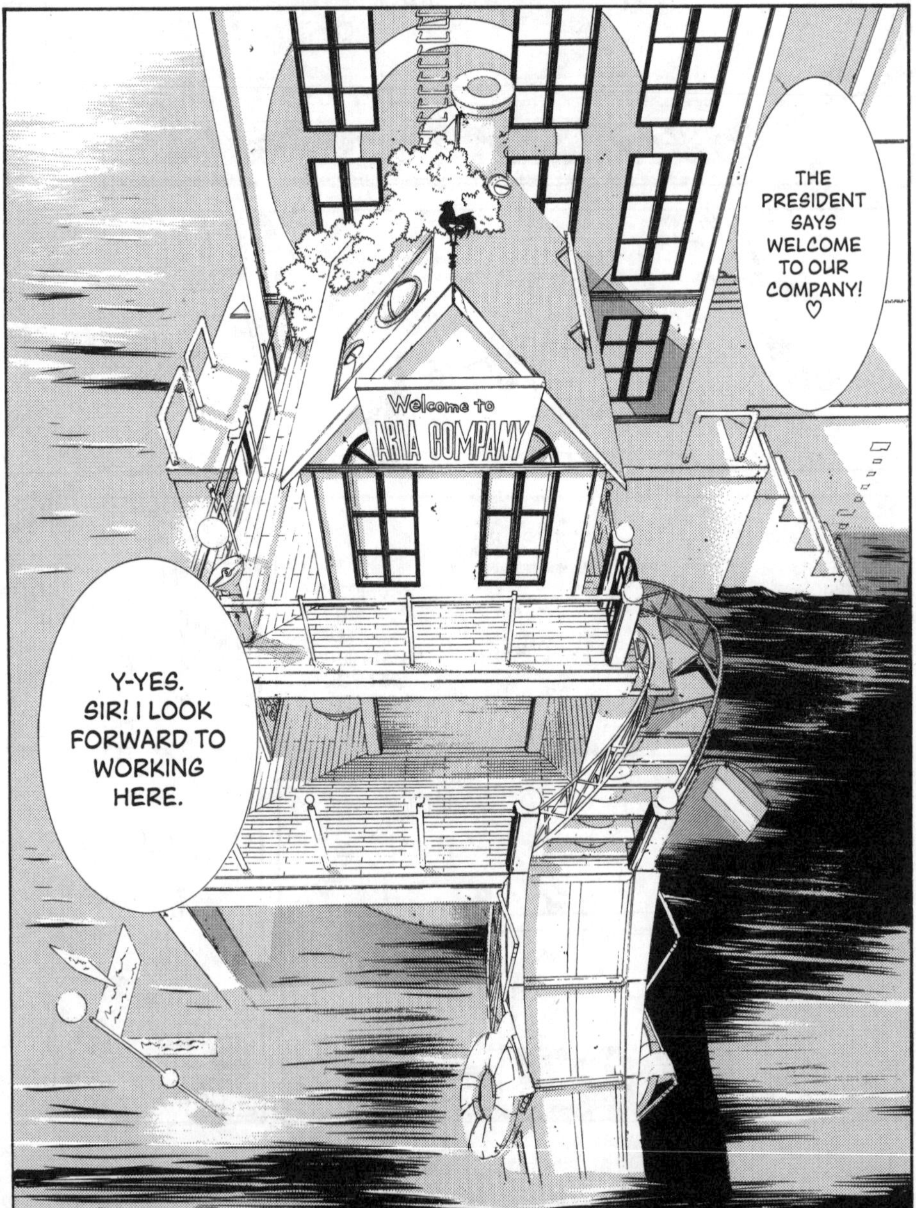
THE PRESIDENT SAYS WELCOME TO OUR COMPANY! ♡
Welcome to ARIA COMPANY
Y-YES. SIR! I LOOK FORWARD TO WORKING HERE.

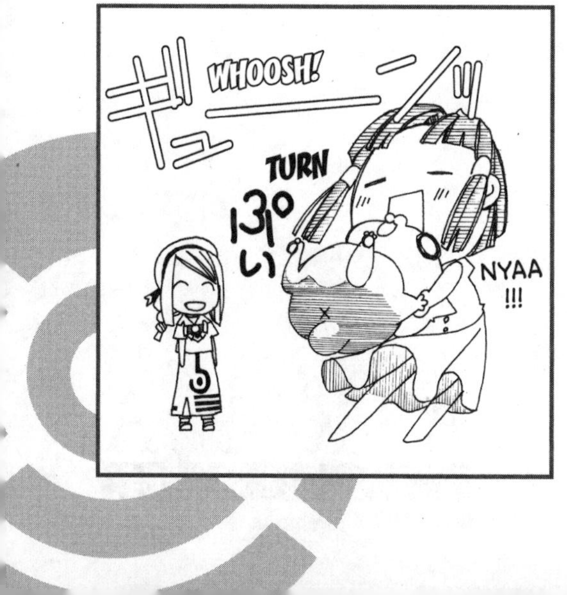
WHOOSH!
TURN
NYAA
!!!

ARIA

The MASTERPIECE

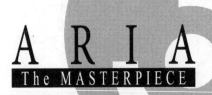

THIS IS MY FIRST MORNING ON AQUA.

HELLO AGAIN!

THE CURTAIN OPENS ON THE BEGINNING OF MY NEW LIFE.

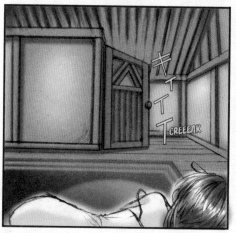

CREEEAK

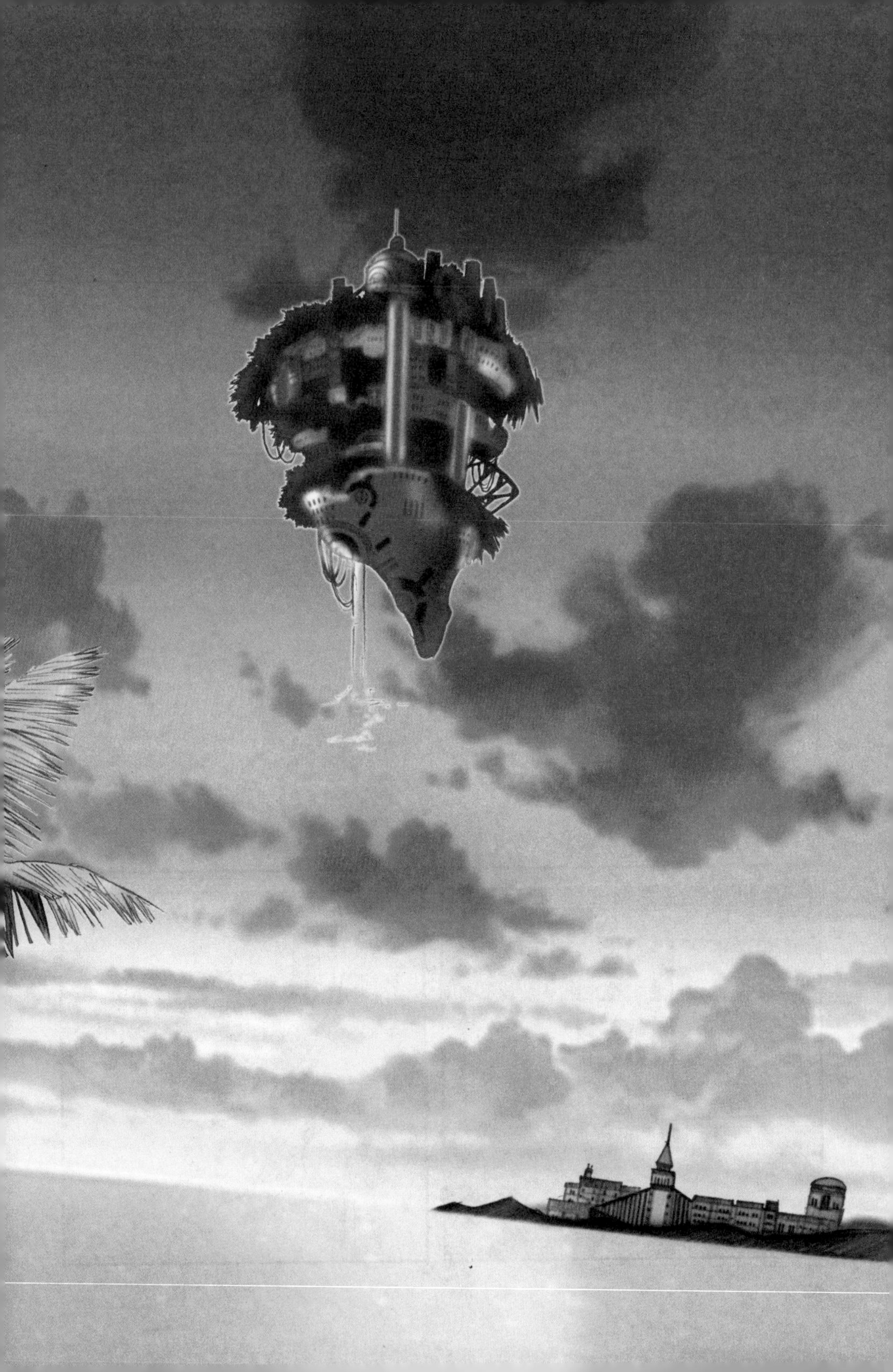

Navigation 02
The Guide on the Water

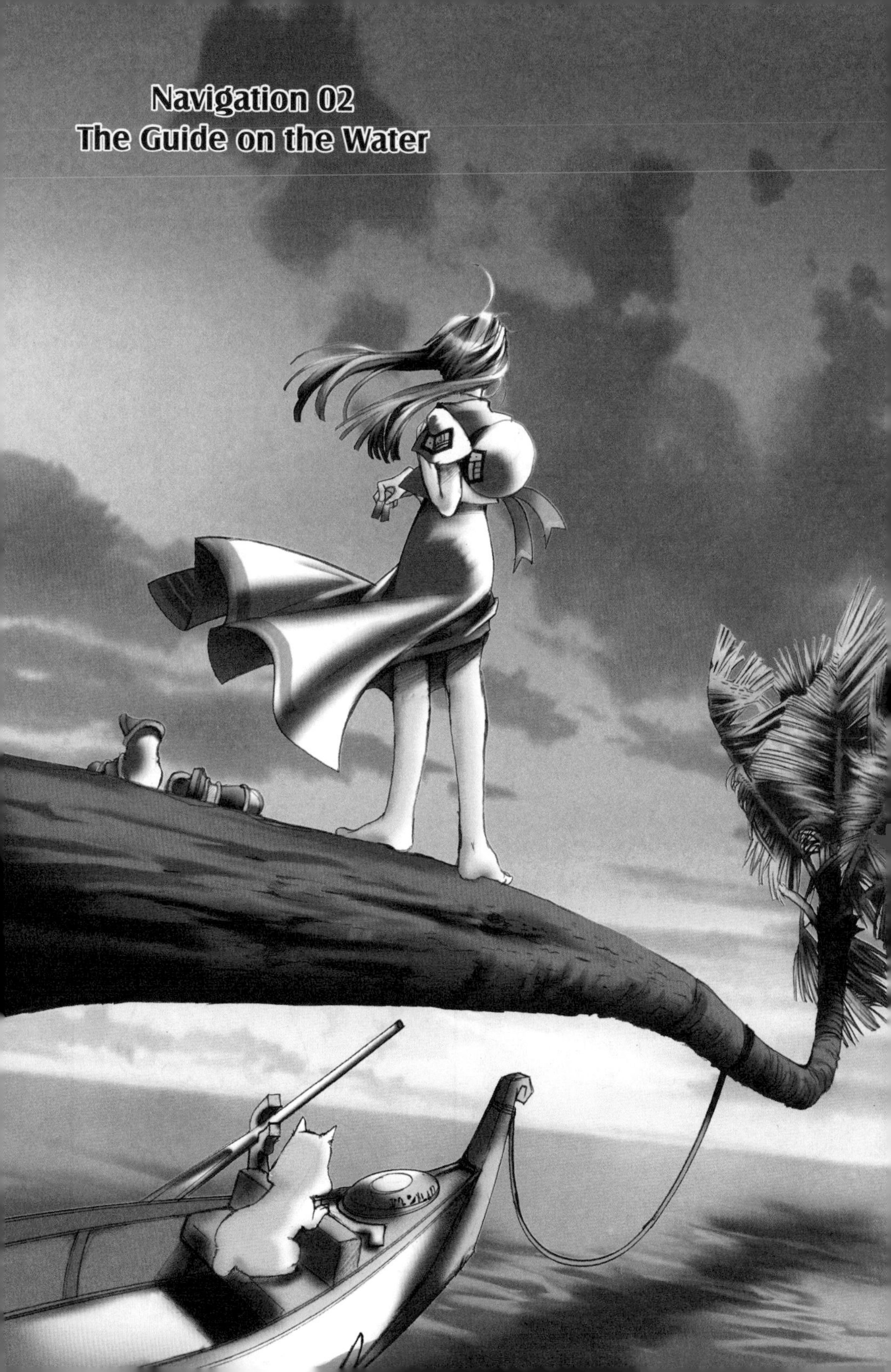

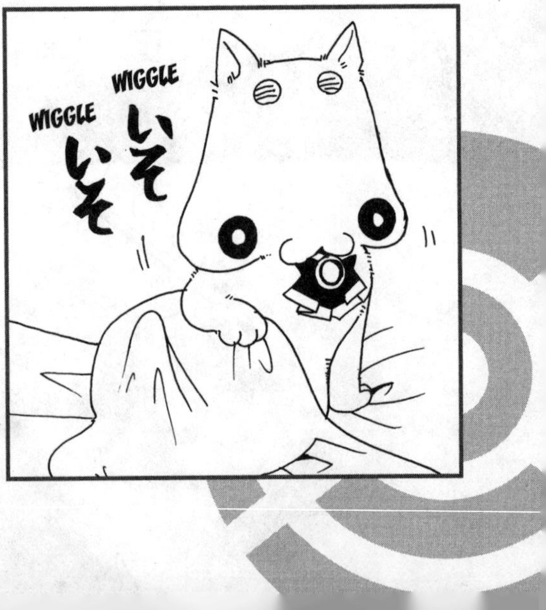
WIGGLE
いそ
WIGGLE
いそ

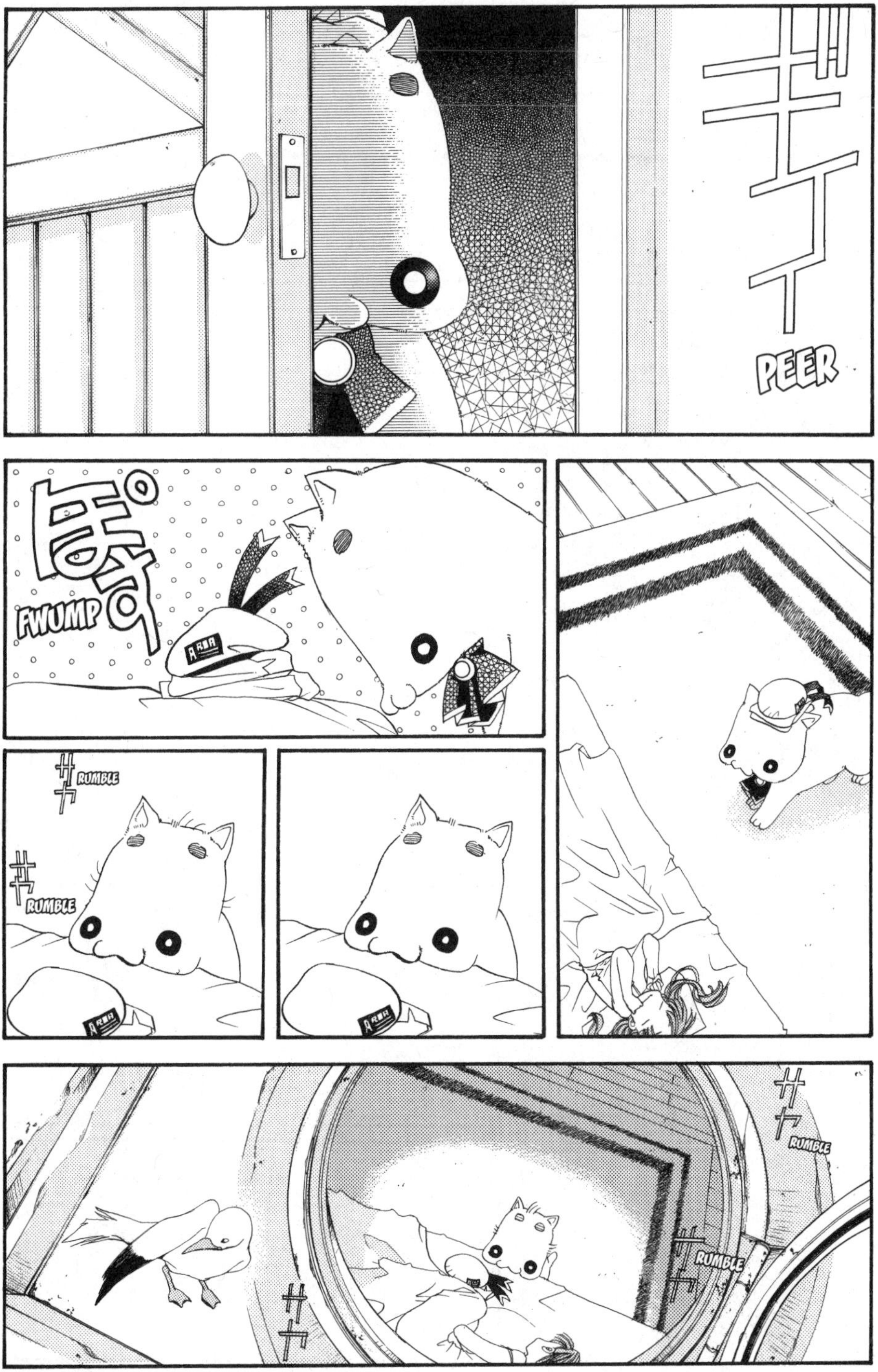

ギィィィ
PEER
ぽす
FWUMP
RUMBLE
RUMBLE
RUMBLE
RUMBLE

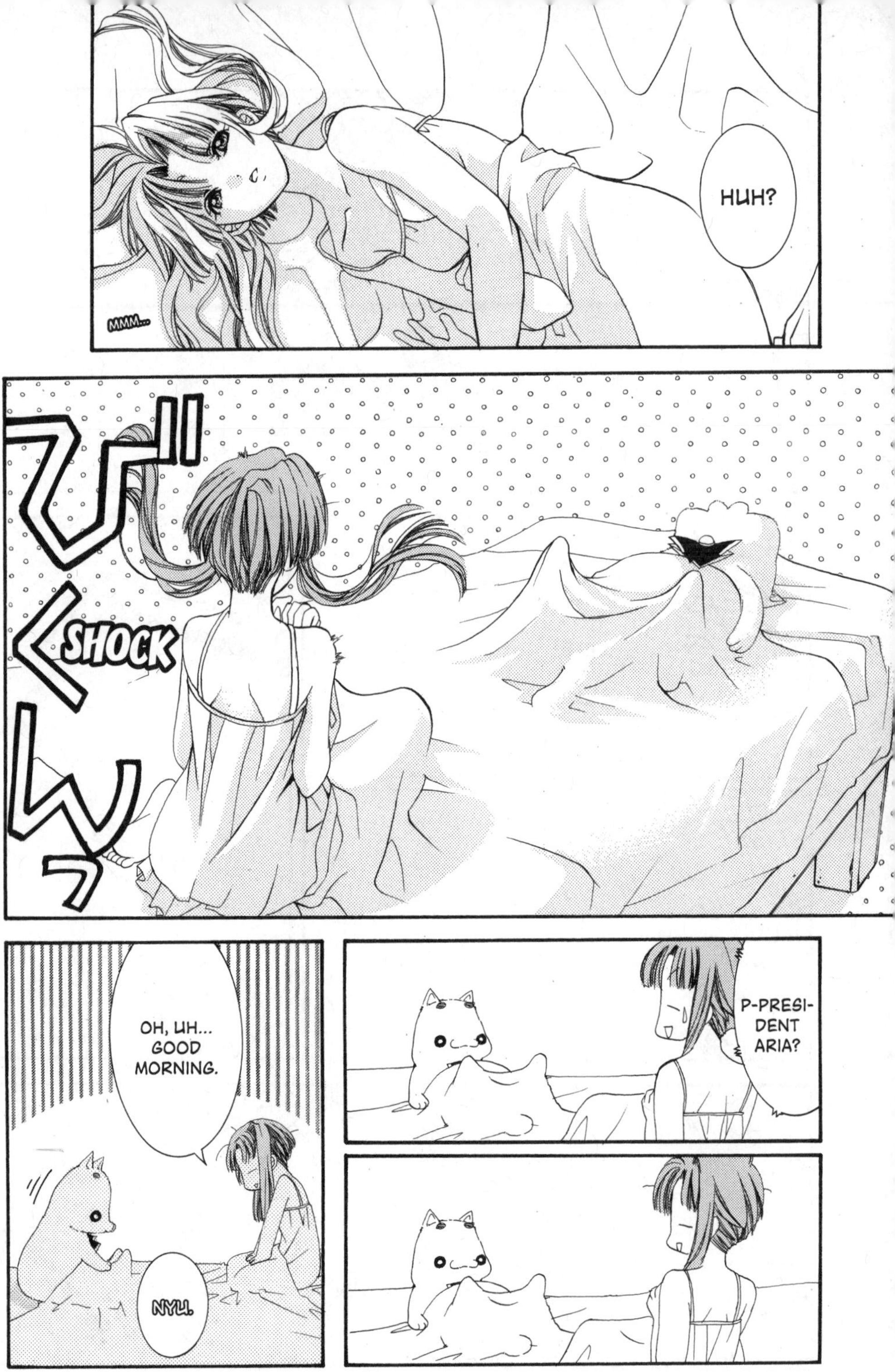
HUH?
MMM...
びくんっ
SHOCK
P-PRESIDENT ARIA?
OH, UH... GOOD MORNING.
NYU.

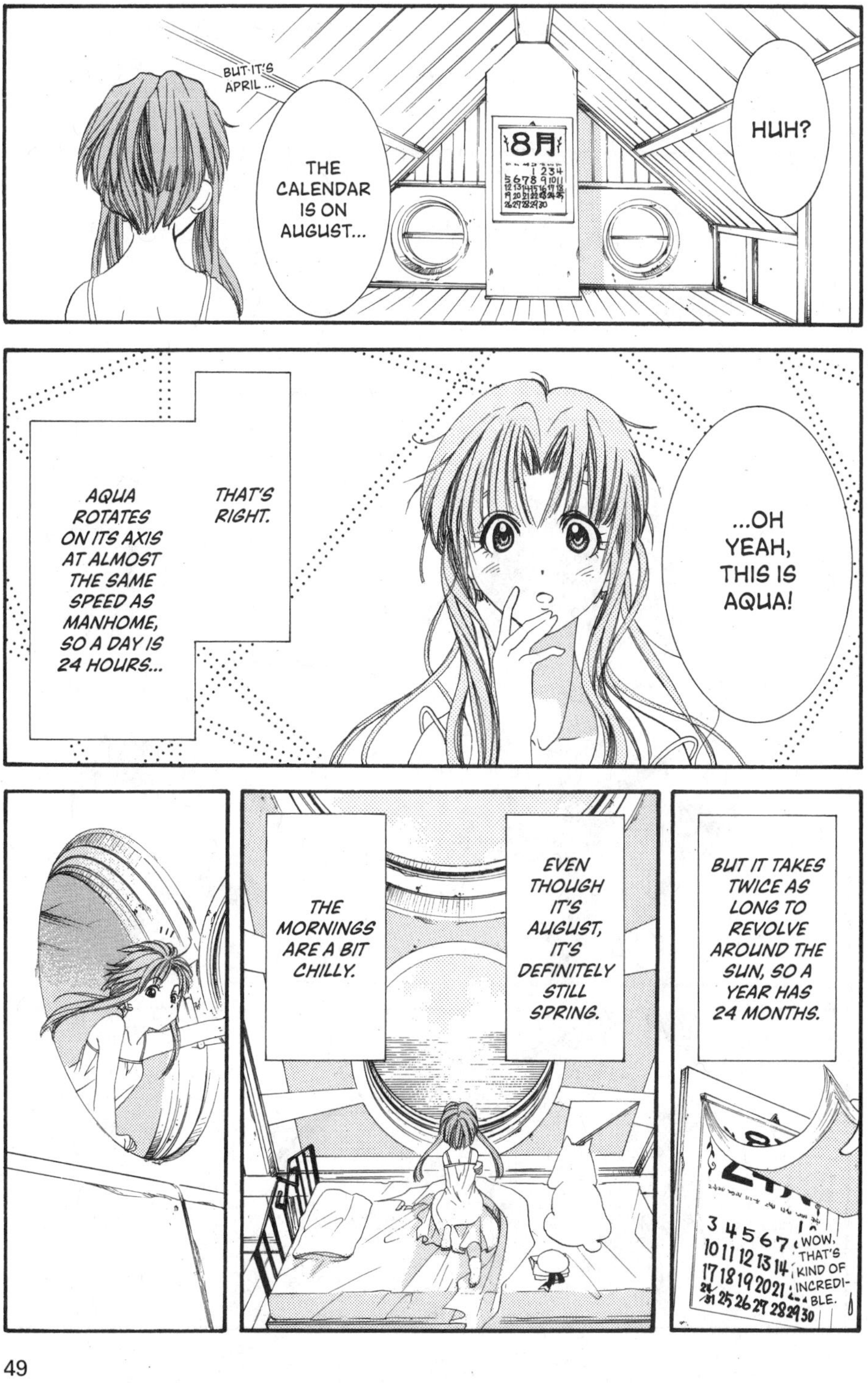
HUH?
THE CALENDAR IS ON AUGUST...
BUT IT'S APRIL ...
8月
...OH YEAH, THIS IS AQUA!
THAT'S RIGHT.
AQUA ROTATES ON ITS AXIS AT ALMOST THE SAME SPEED AS MANHOME, SO A DAY IS 24 HOURS...
BUT IT TAKES TWICE AS LONG TO REVOLVE AROUND THE SUN, SO A YEAR HAS 24 MONTHS.
WOW, THAT'S KIND OF INCREDI-BLE.
EVEN THOUGH IT'S AUGUST, IT'S DEFINITELY STILL SPRING.
THE MORNINGS ARE A BIT CHILLY.

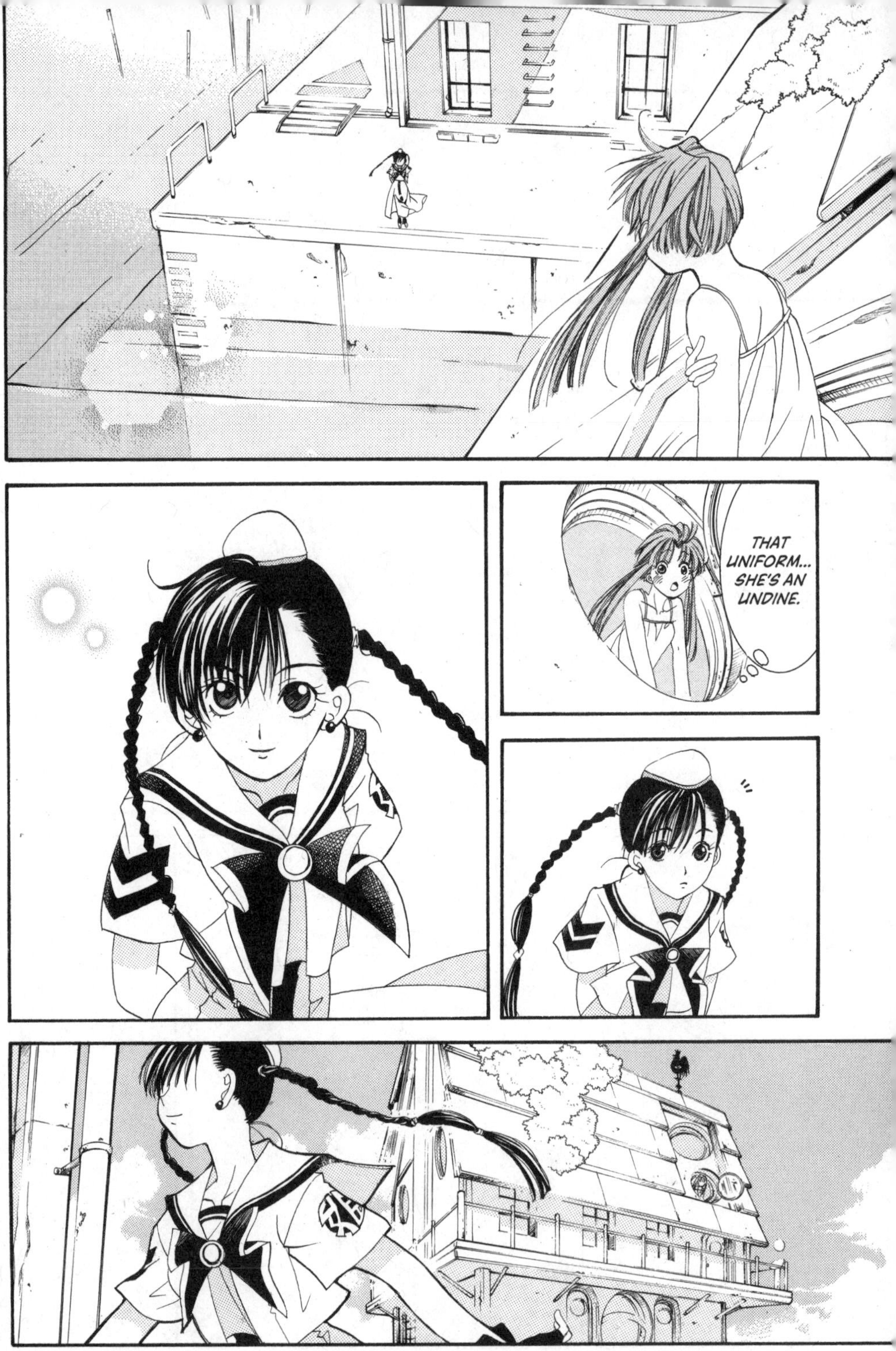
THAT UNIFORM... SHE'S AN UNDINE.

HUH?

STARE

PAT

PAT

BA-DUMP

THAT GIRL WAS ABOUT THE SAME AGE AS ME, WASN'T SHE?

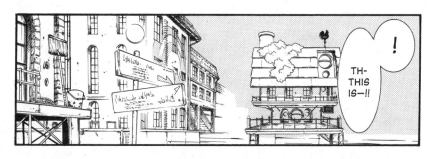

!

TH-THIS IS—!!

OH MY, GOOD MORNING, AKARI!

WHY ARE YOU HIDING?

GOOD MORNING, MISS ALICIA...

SIZZLE

SIZZLE

SIZZLE

SIZZLE

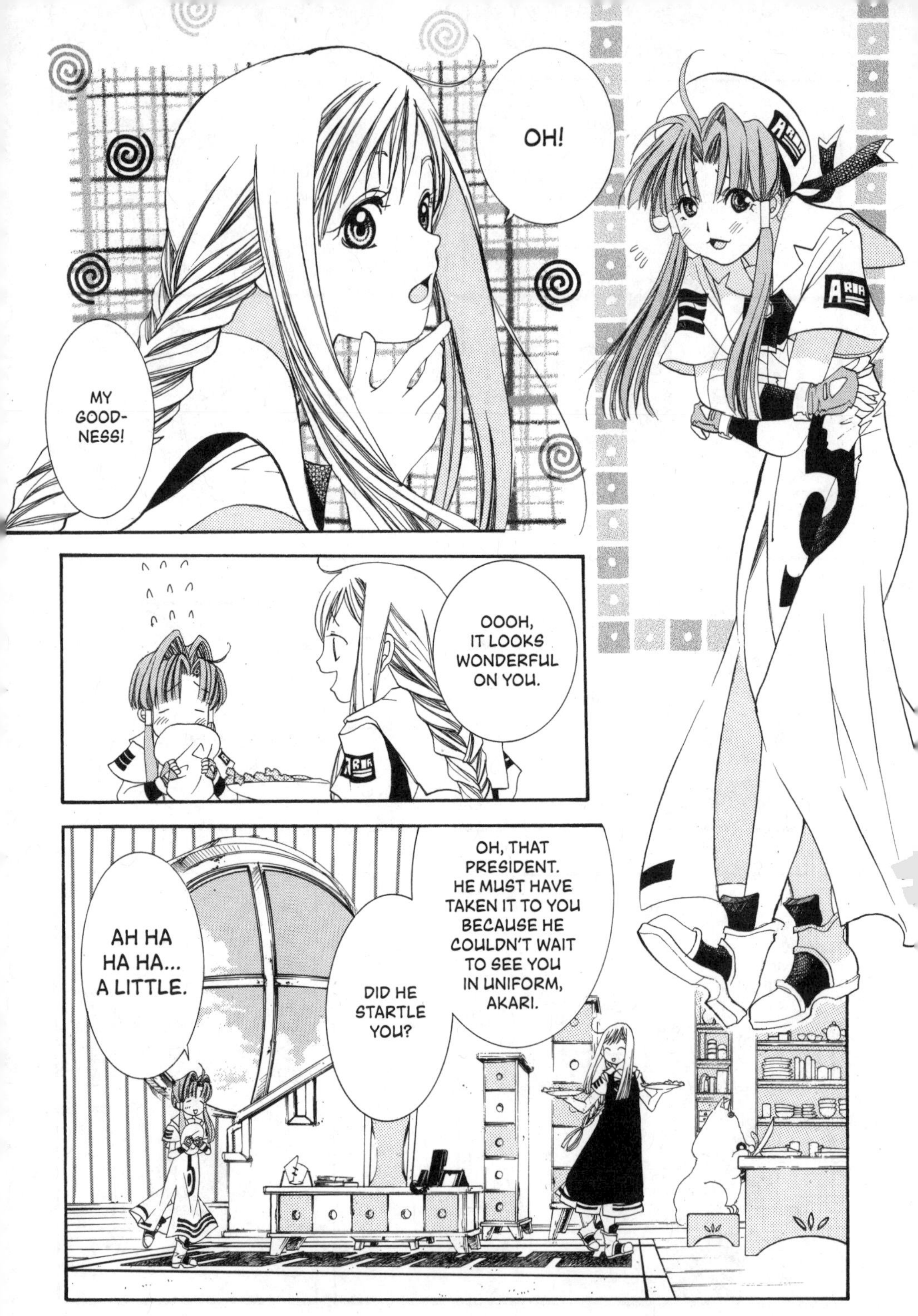
OH!
MY GOOD-NESS!
OOOH, IT LOOKS WONDERFUL ON YOU.
OH, THAT PRESIDENT. HE MUST HAVE TAKEN IT TO YOU BECAUSE HE COULDN'T WAIT TO SEE YOU IN UNIFORM, AKARI.
DID HE STARTLE YOU?
AH HA HA HA... A LITTLE.

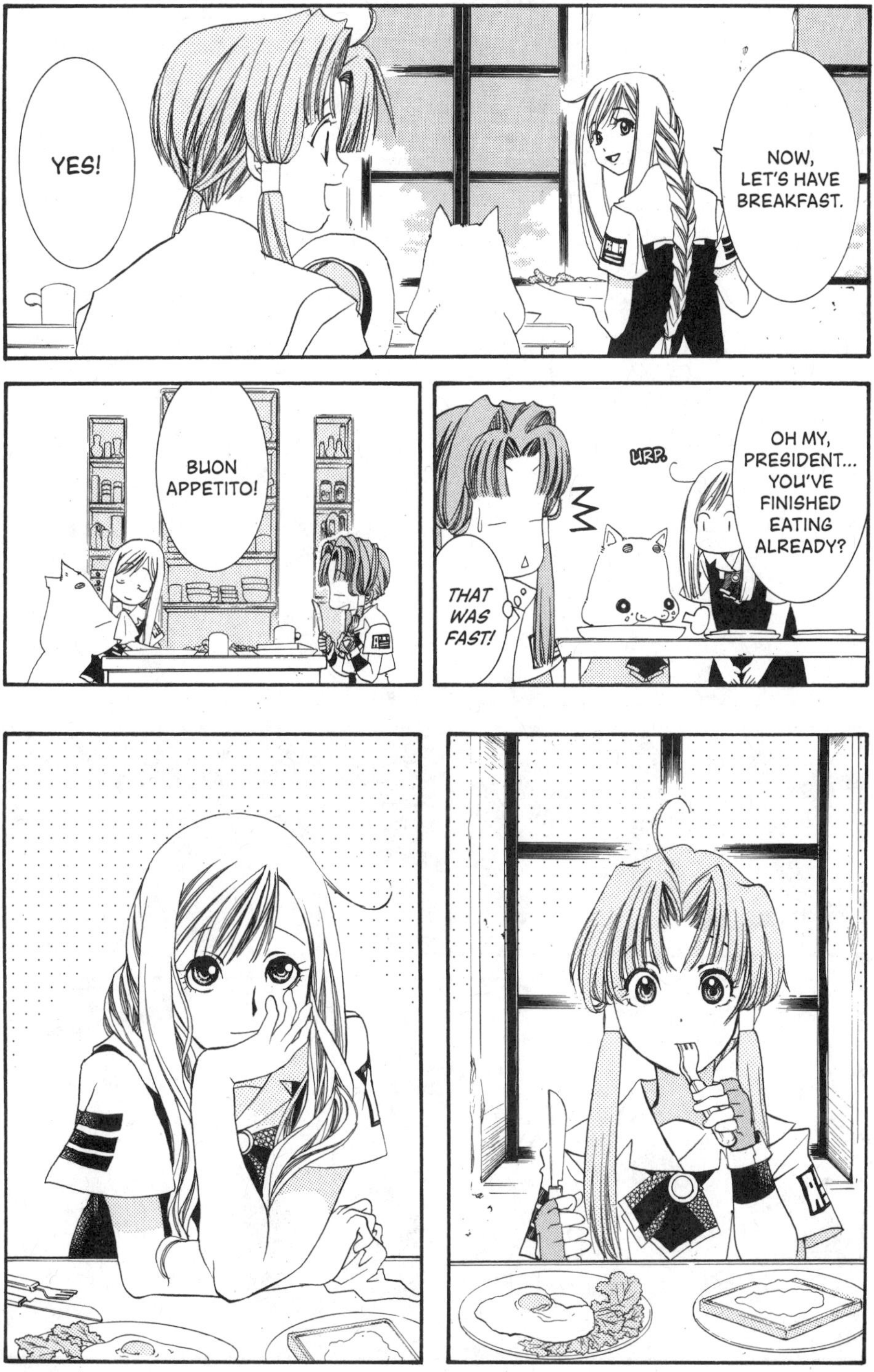
NOW, LET'S HAVE BREAKFAST.
YES!
OH MY, PRESIDENT... YOU'VE FINISHED EATING ALREADY?
URP.
THAT WAS FAST!
BUON APPETITO!

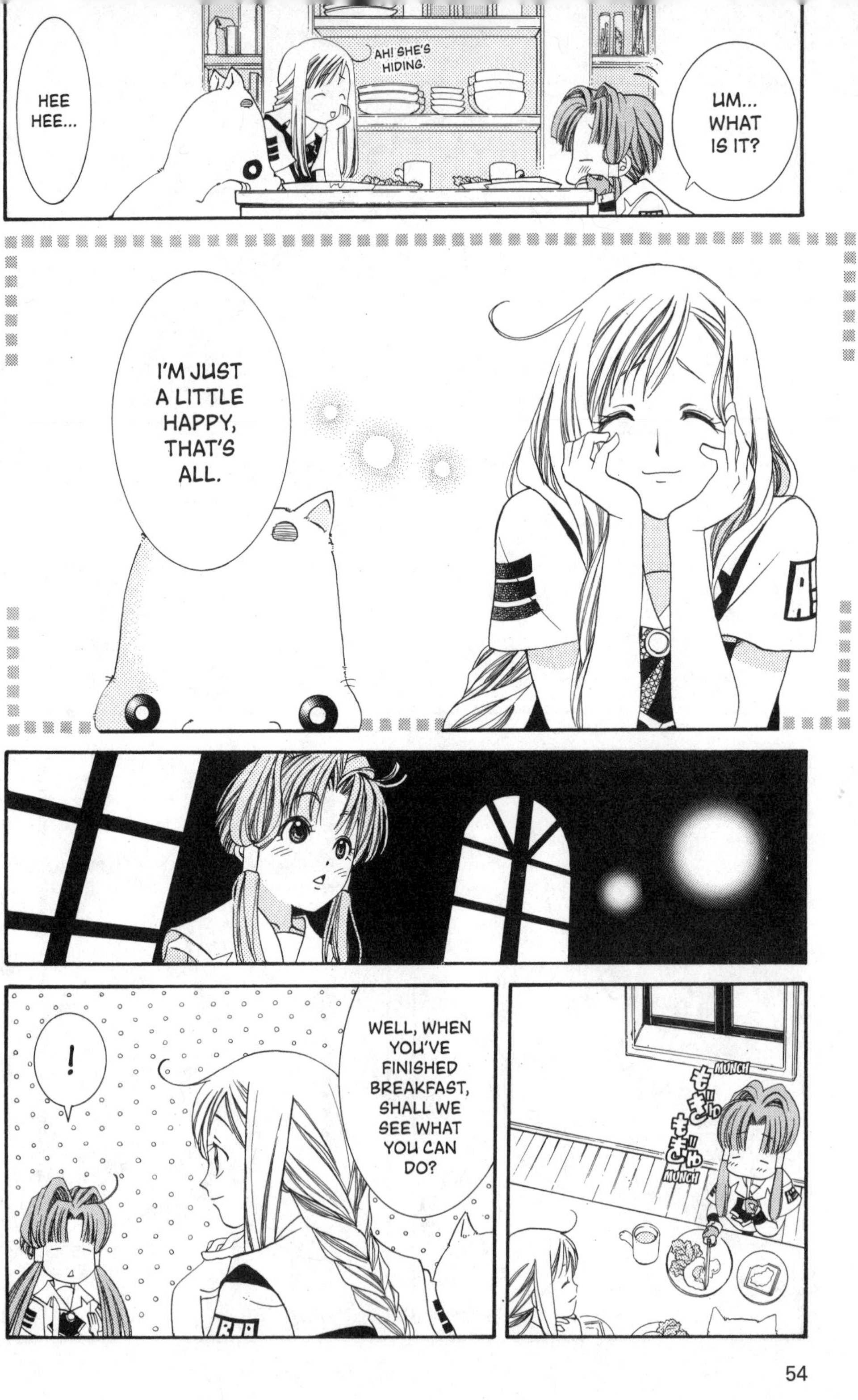
UM... WHAT IS IT?
AH! SHE'S HIDING.
HEE HEE...
I'M JUST A LITTLE HAPPY, THAT'S ALL.
MUNCH
MUNCH
WELL, WHEN YOU'VE FINISHED BREAKFAST, SHALL WE SEE WHAT YOU CAN DO?
!

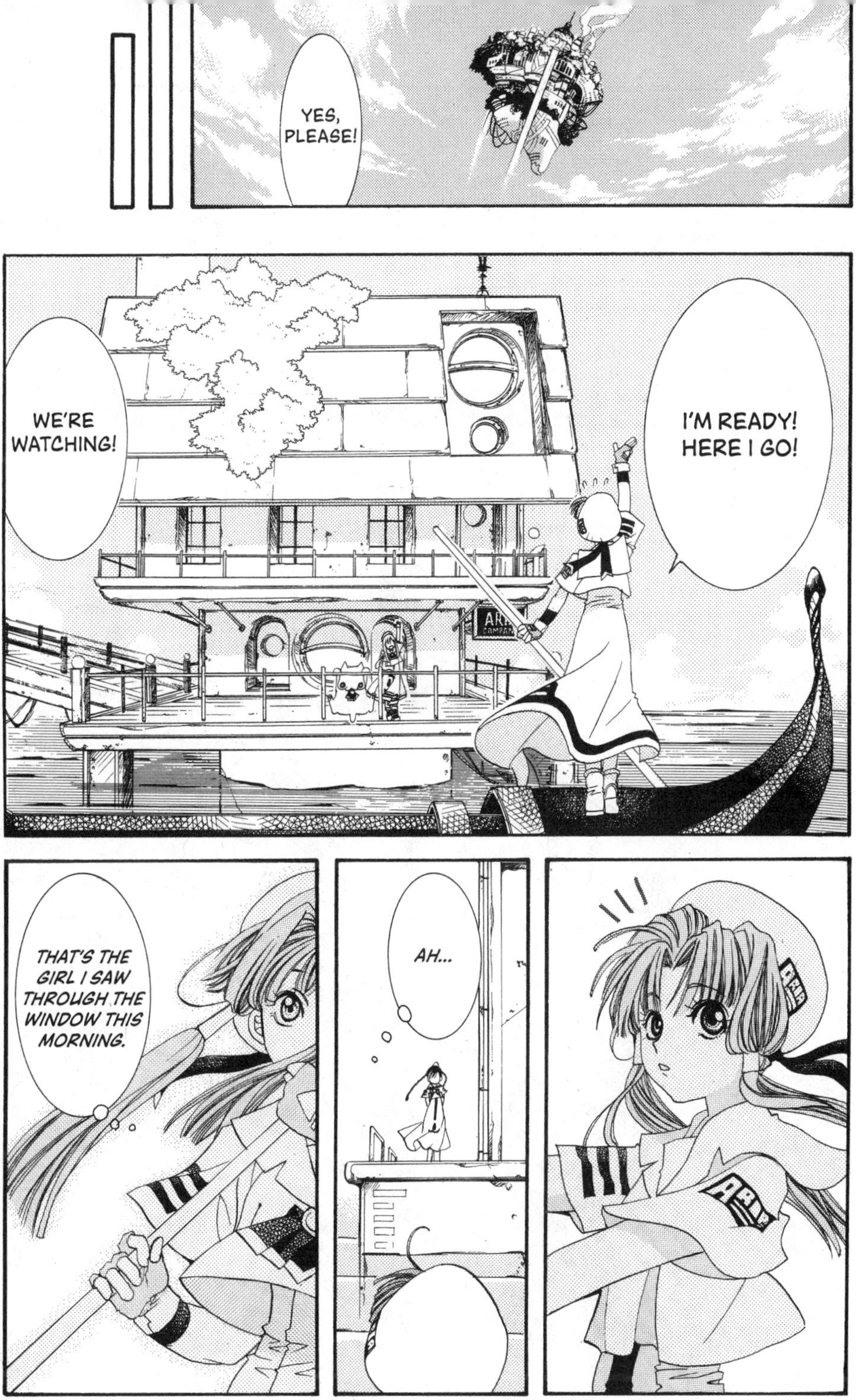
YES, PLEASE!
I'M READY! HERE I GO!
WE'RE WATCHING!
AH...
THAT'S THE GIRL I SAW THROUGH THE WINDOW THIS MORNING.

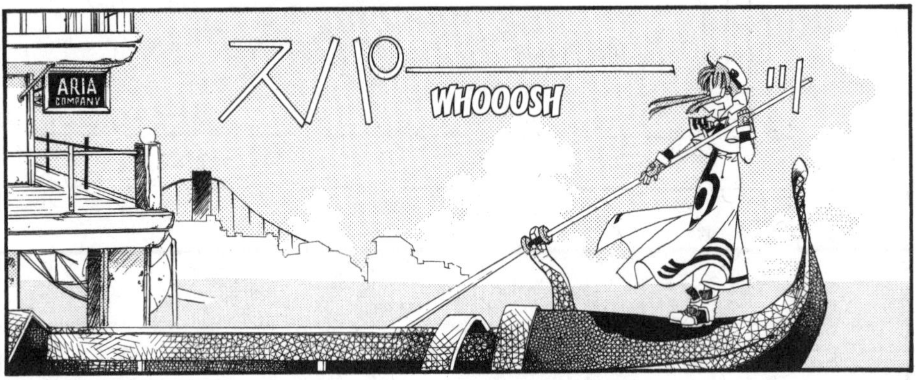
ARIA COMPANY
スパー
WHOOOSH
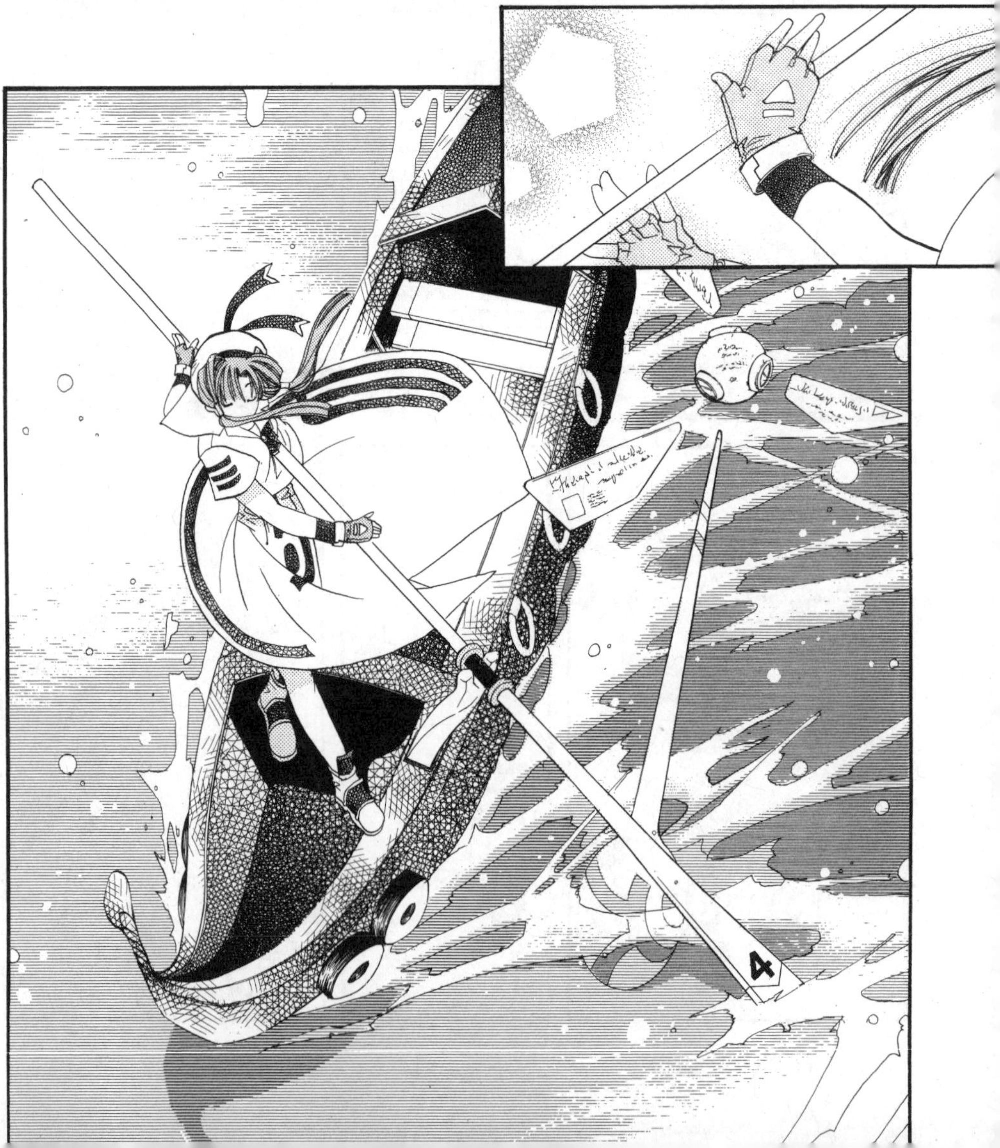

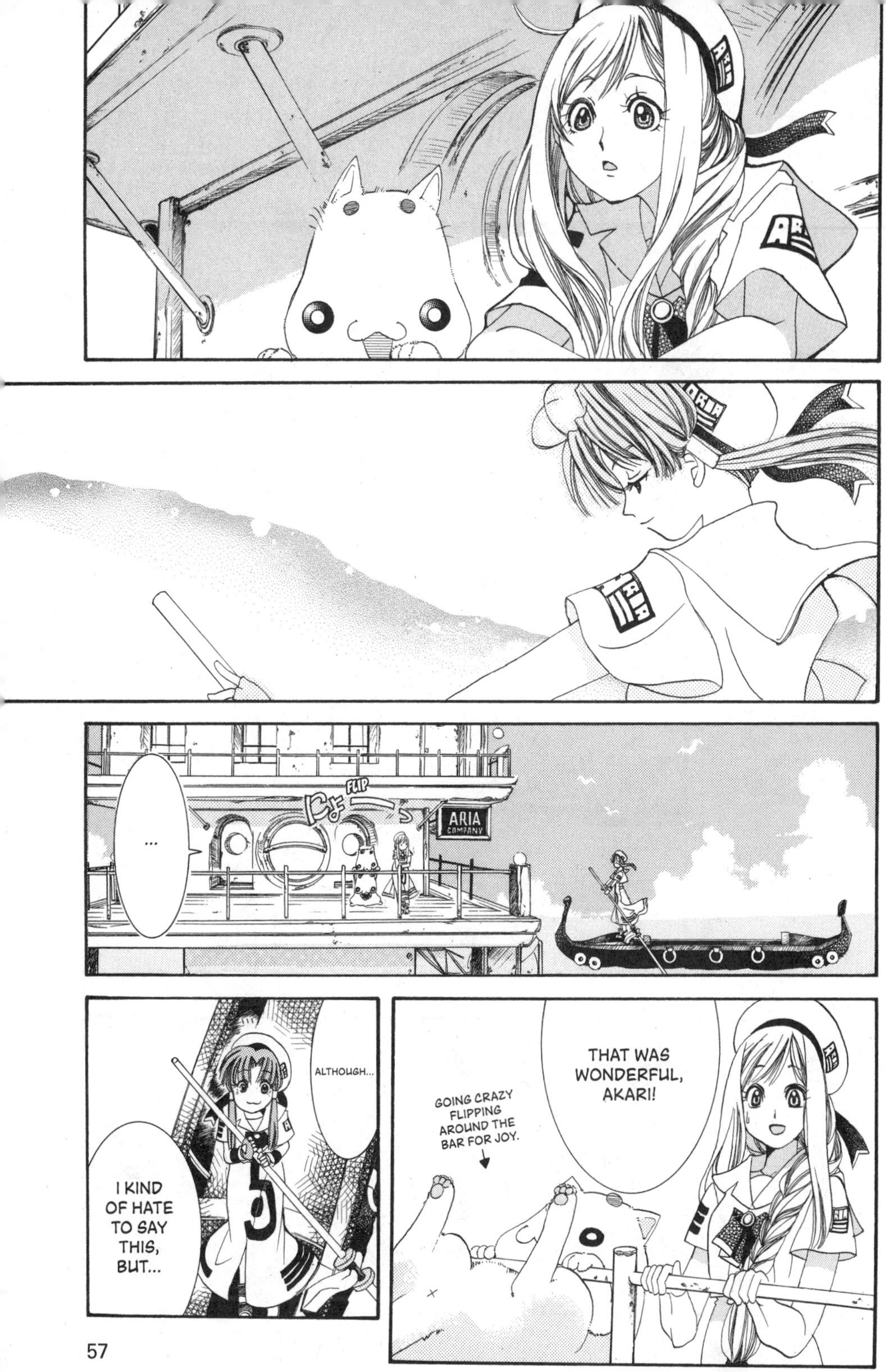
ARIA COMPANY
FLIP
...
THAT WAS WONDERFUL, AKARI!
GOING CRAZY FLIPPING AROUND THE BAR FOR JOY.
ALTHOUGH...
I KIND OF HATE TO SAY THIS, BUT...

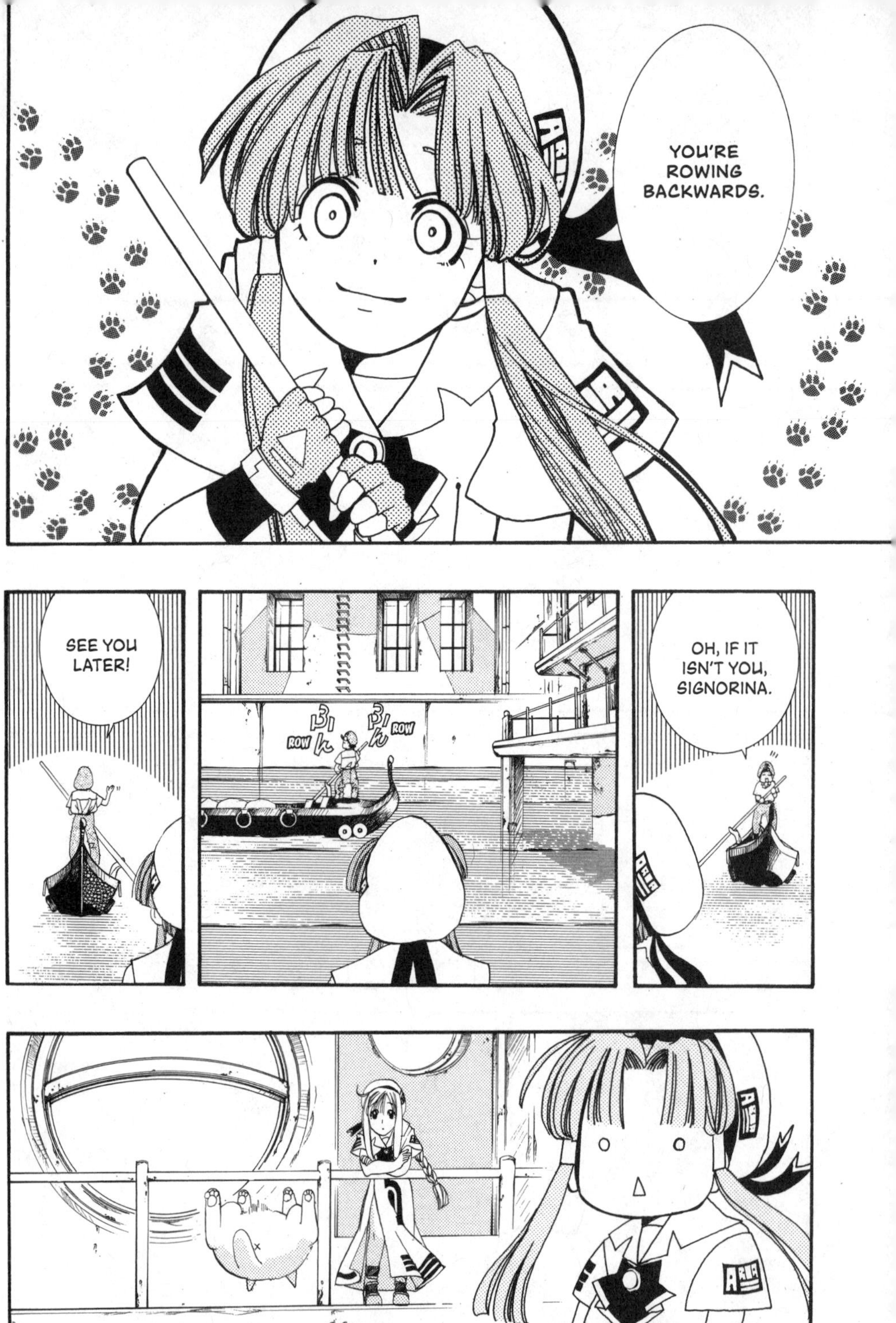
YOU'RE ROWING BACKWARDS.
OH, IF IT ISN'T YOU, SIGNORINA.
ROW
ROW
SEE YOU LATER!

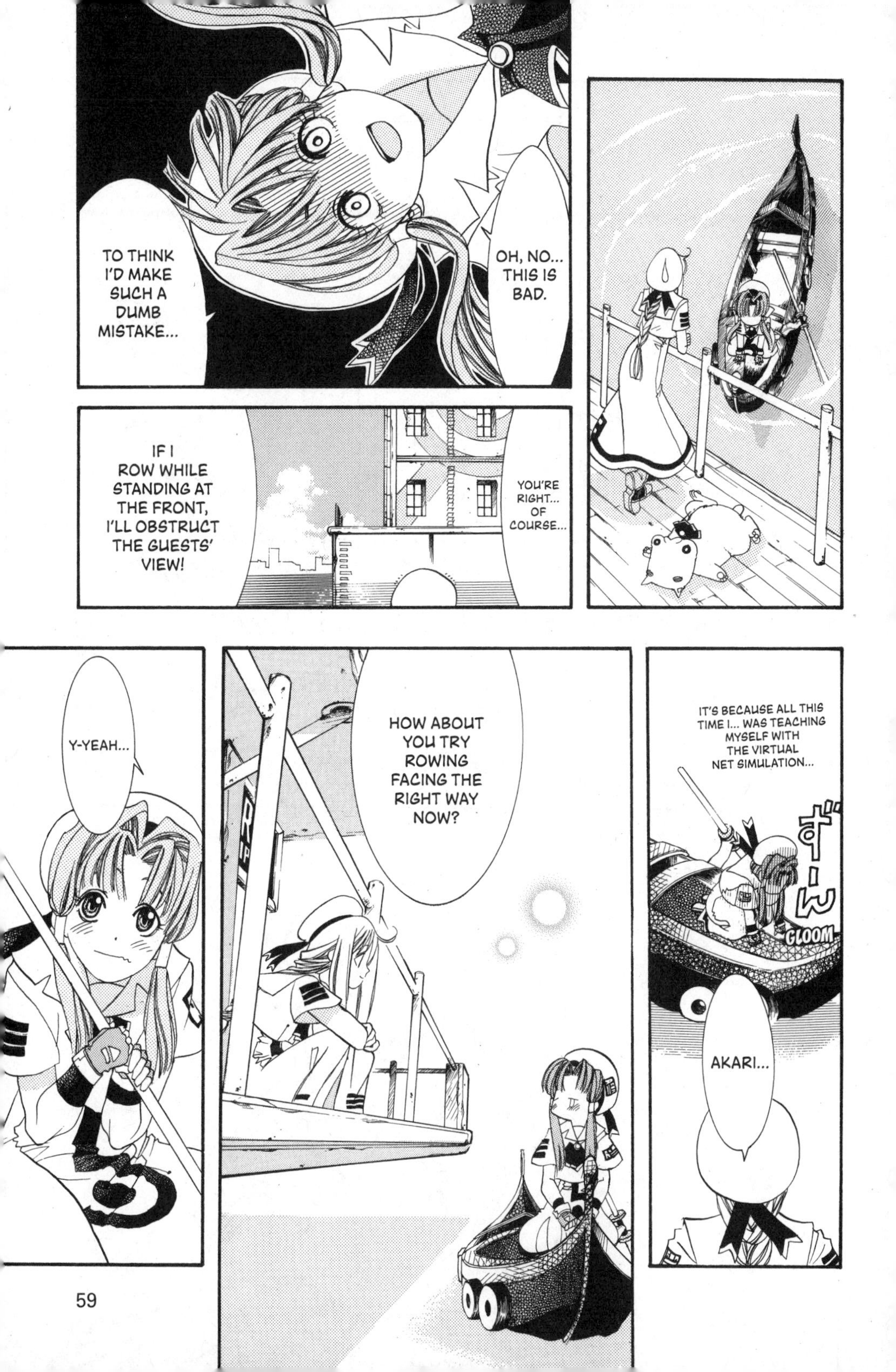
OH, NO... THIS IS BAD.
TO THINK I'D MAKE SUCH A DUMB MISTAKE...
YOU'RE RIGHT... OF COURSE...
IF I ROW WHILE STANDING AT THE FRONT, I'LL OBSTRUCT THE GUESTS' VIEW!
IT'S BECAUSE ALL THIS TIME I... WAS TEACHING MYSELF WITH THE VIRTUAL NET SIMULATION...
ずーん
GLOOM
AKARI...
HOW ABOUT YOU TRY ROWING FACING THE RIGHT WAY NOW?
Y-YEAH...

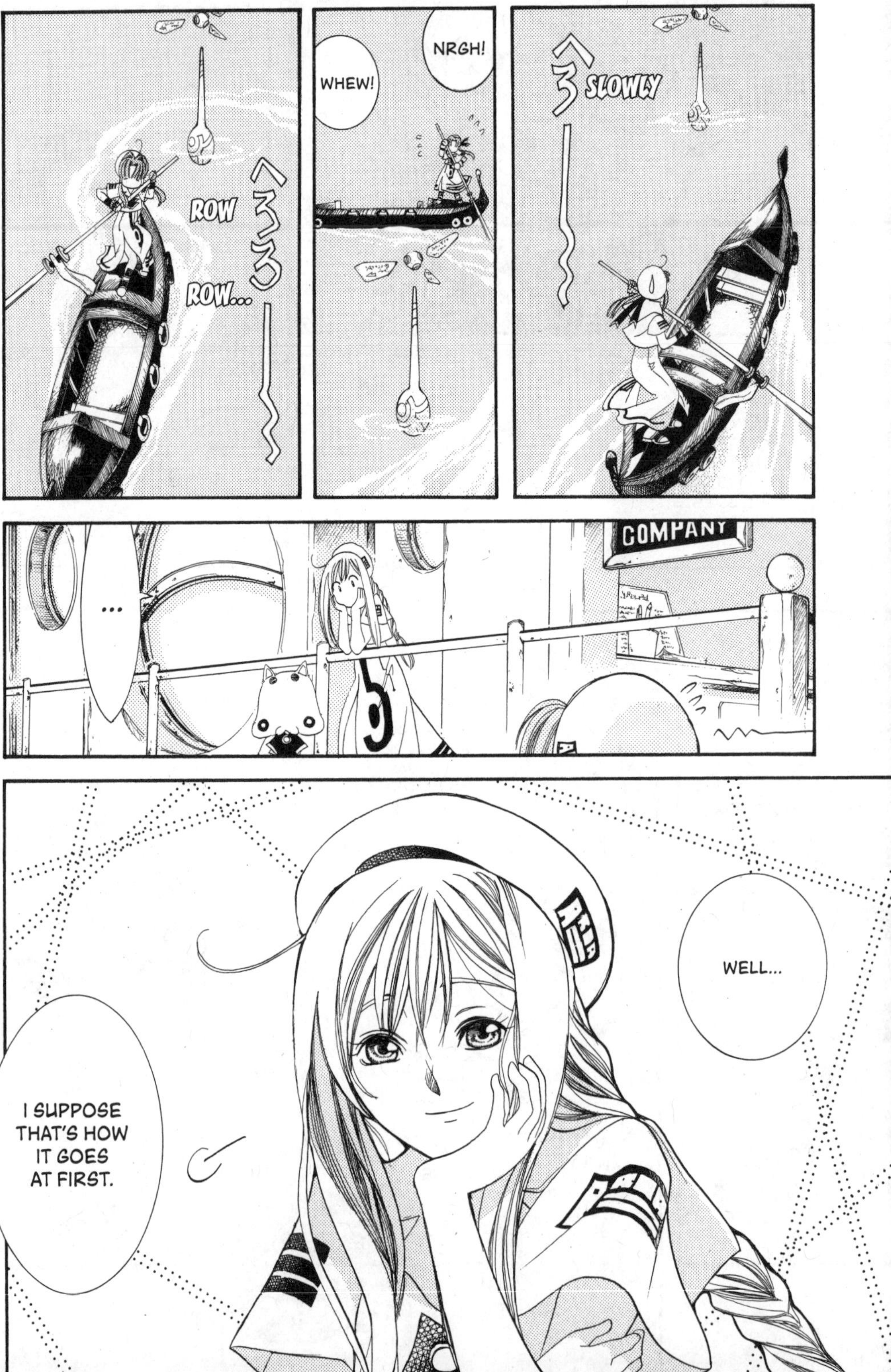
SLOWLY
NRGH!
WHEW!
ROW
ROW...
...
COMPANY
WELL...
I SUPPOSE THAT'S HOW IT GOES AT FIRST.

I'M SURE WE'LL ALL WORK HARD FROM NOW ON.

OH MY!

THANK YOU SO MUCH!!

FWUMP

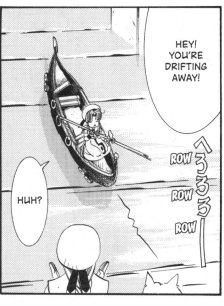

HEY! YOU'RE DRIFTING AWAY!

HUH?

ROW ROW ROW

E-EXCUSE ME!

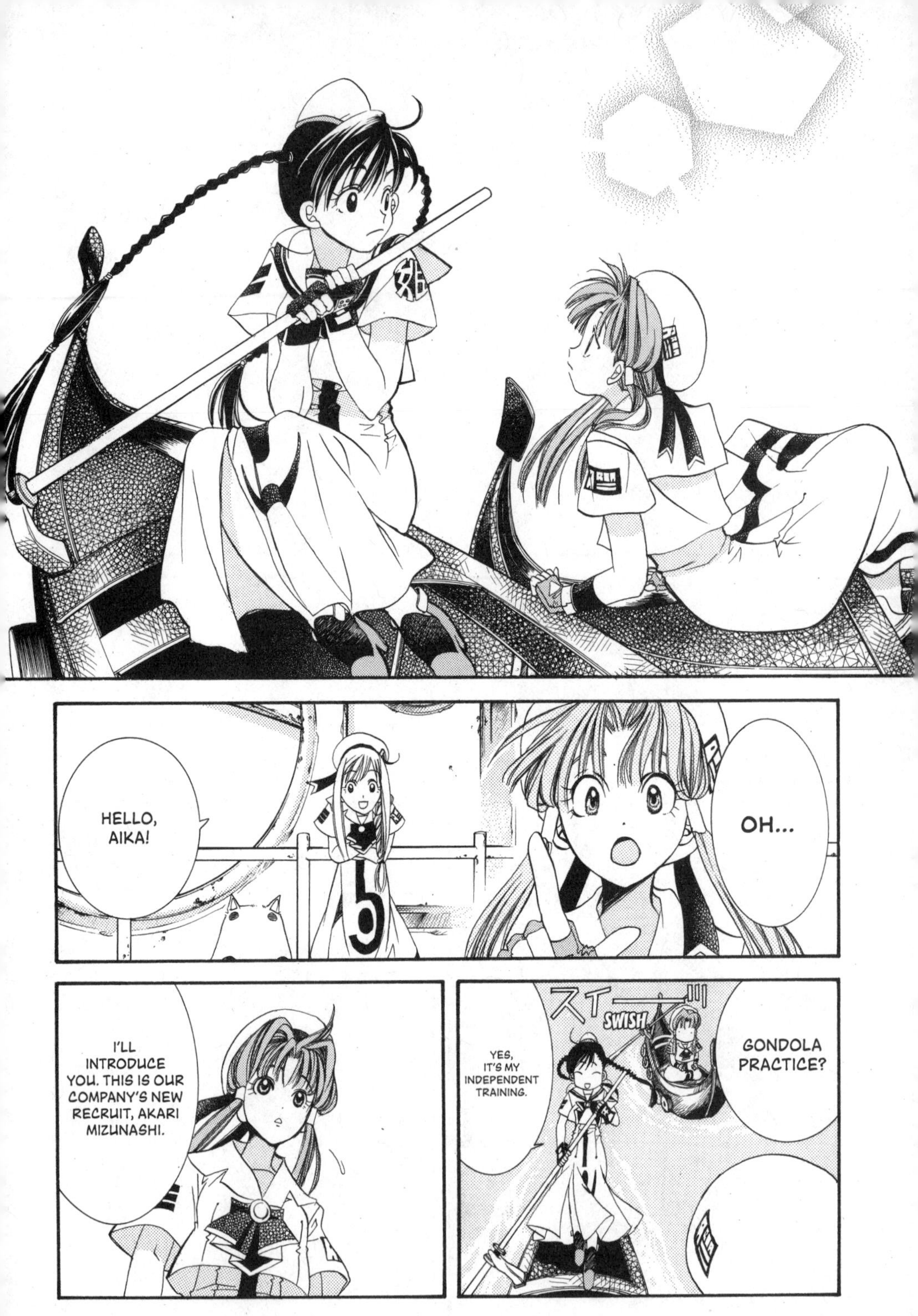
OH...
HELLO, AIKA!
GONDOLA PRACTICE?
スイー
SWISH
YES, IT'S MY INDEPENDENT TRAINING.
I'LL INTRODUCE YOU. THIS IS OUR COMPANY'S NEW RECRUIT, AKARI MIZUNASHI.

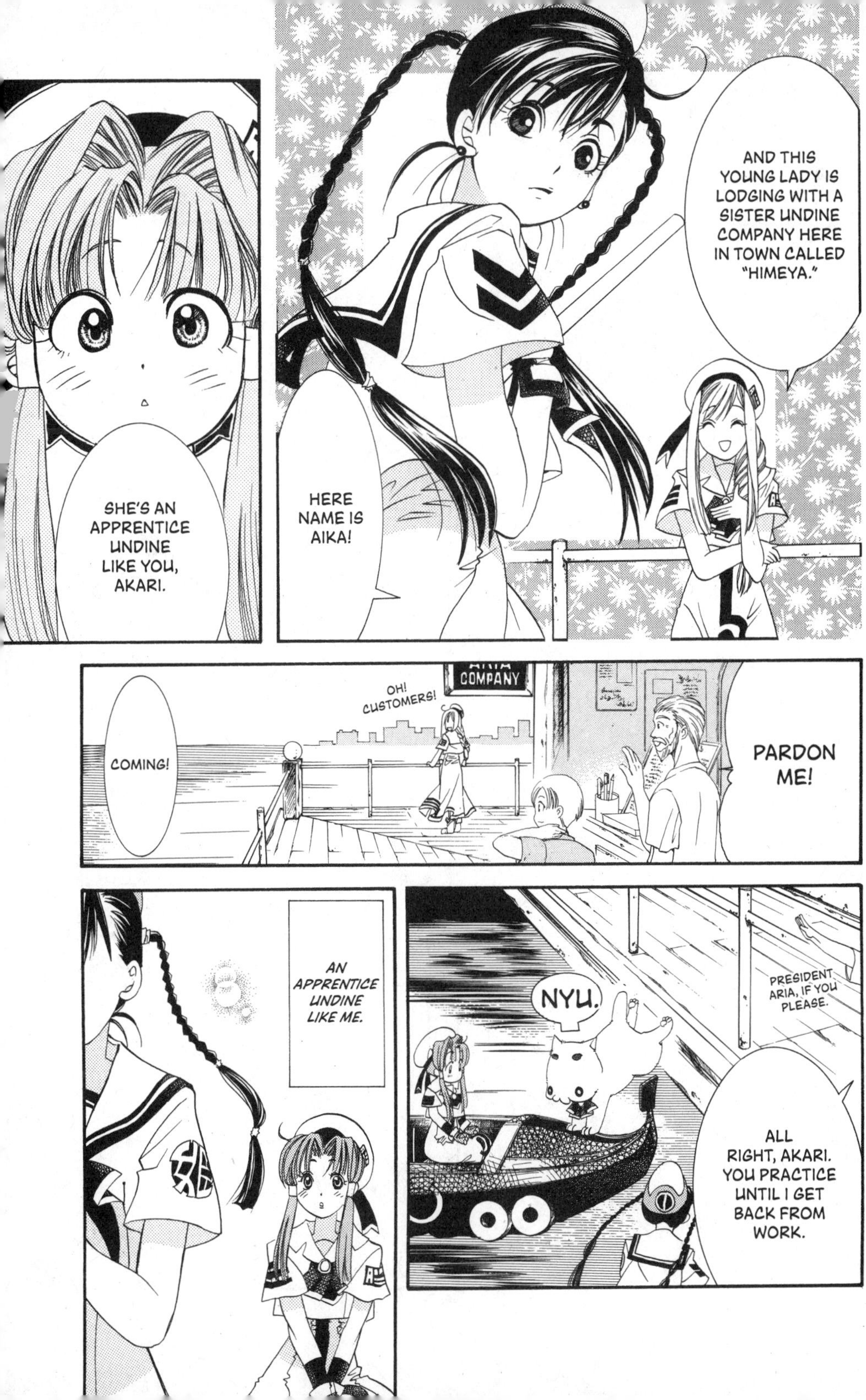
AND THIS YOUNG LADY IS LODGING WITH A SISTER UNDINE COMPANY HERE IN TOWN CALLED "HIMEYA."
HERE NAME IS AIKA!
SHE'S AN APPRENTICE UNDINE LIKE YOU, AKARI.
ARIA COMPANY
PARDON ME!
OH! CUSTOMERS!
COMING!
PRESIDENT ARIA, IF YOU PLEASE.
NYU.
ALL RIGHT, AKARI. YOU PRACTICE UNTIL I GET BACK FROM WORK.
AN APPRENTICE UNDINE LIKE ME.

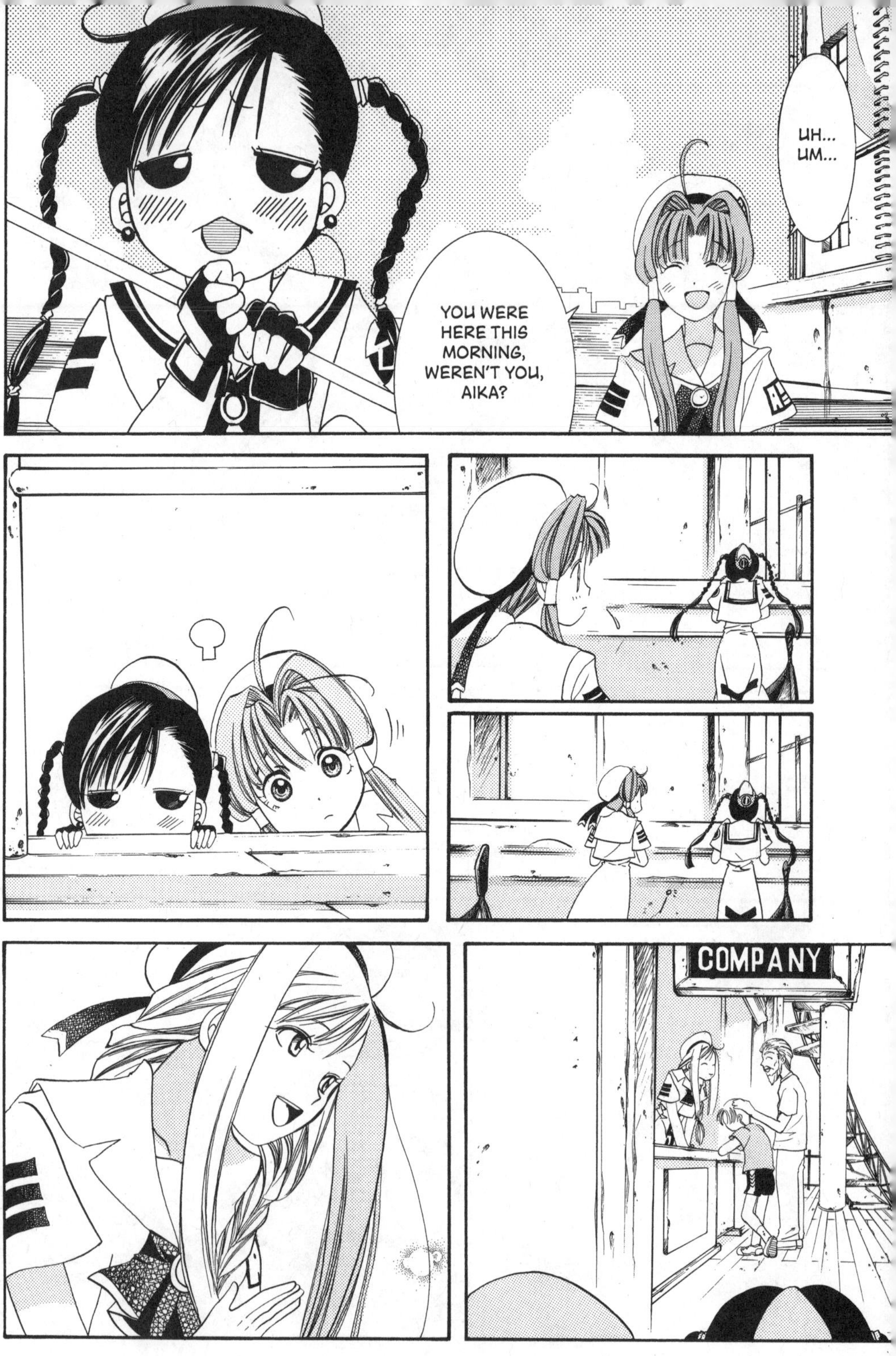
UH... UM...
YOU WERE HERE THIS MORNING, WEREN'T YOU, AIKA?
COMPANY

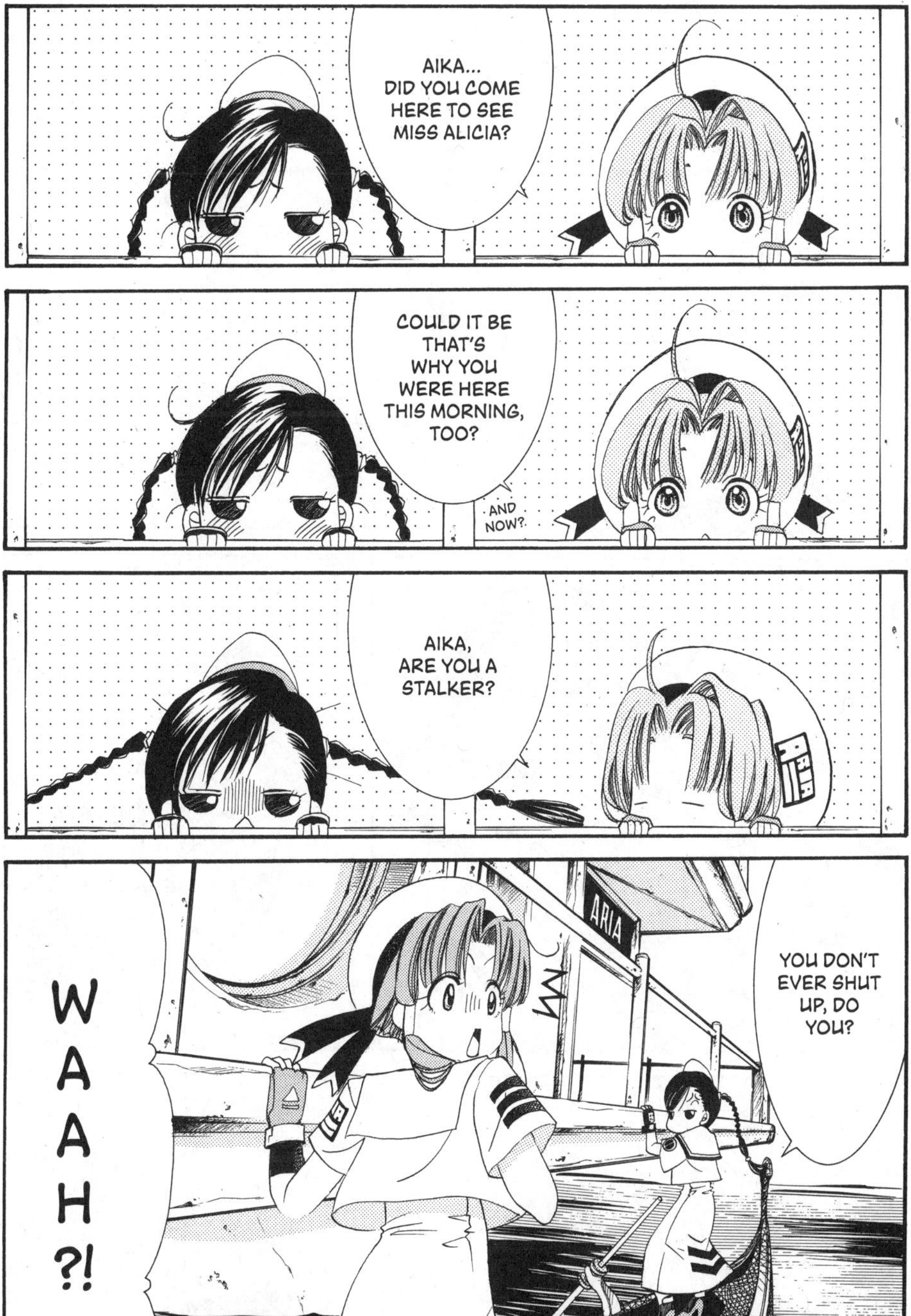
AIKA... DID YOU COME HERE TO SEE MISS ALICIA?
COULD IT BE THAT'S WHY YOU WERE HERE THIS MORNING, TOO?
AND NOW?.
AIKA, ARE YOU A STALKER?
YOU DON'T EVER SHUT UP, DO YOU?
WAAAH?!
ARIA

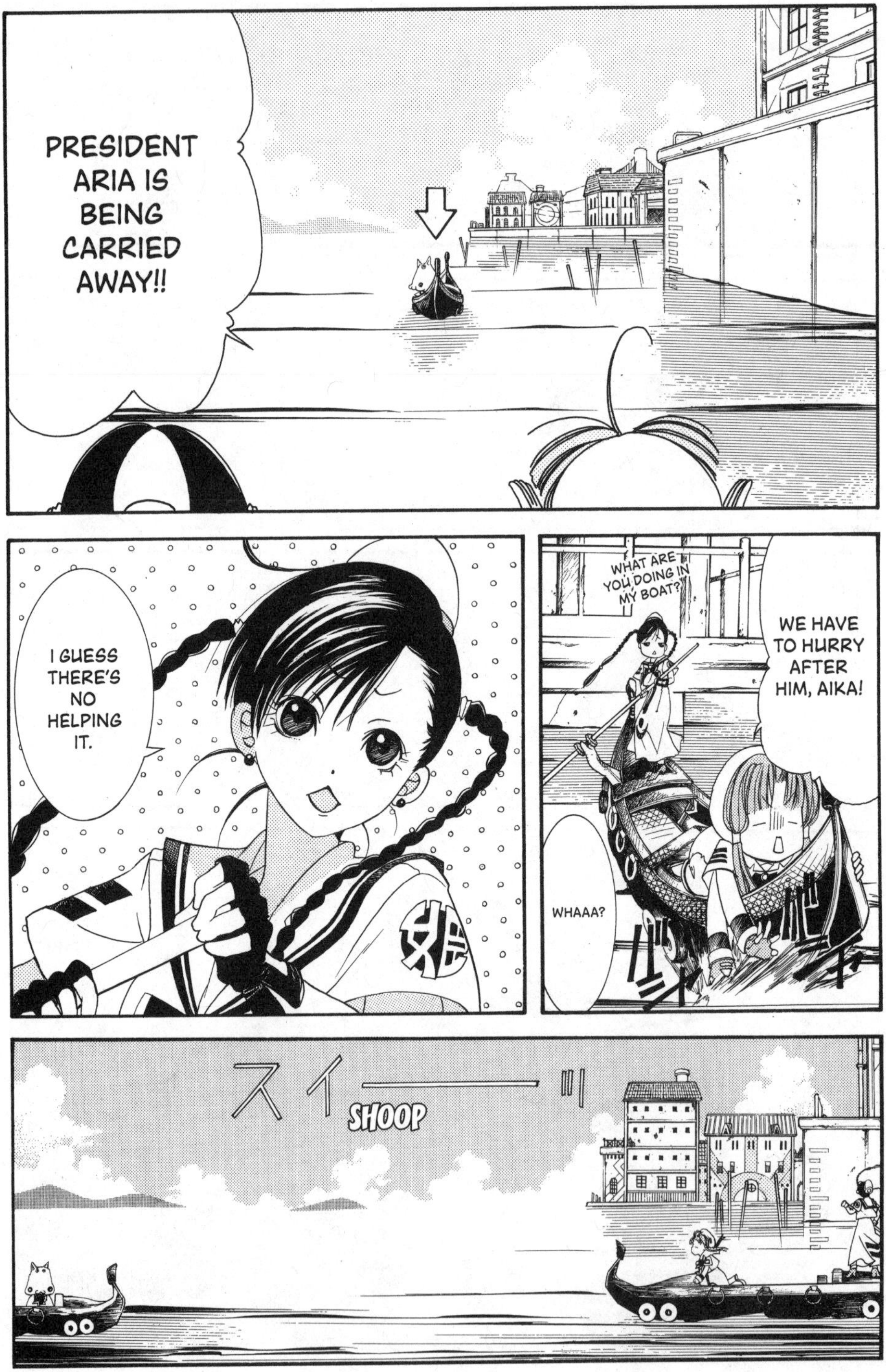
PRESIDENT ARIA IS BEING CARRIED AWAY!!
WE HAVE TO HURRY AFTER HIM, AIKA!
WHAT ARE YOU DOING IN MY BOAT?
WHAAA?
I GUESS THERE'S NO HELPING IT.
スイーーッ
SHOOP

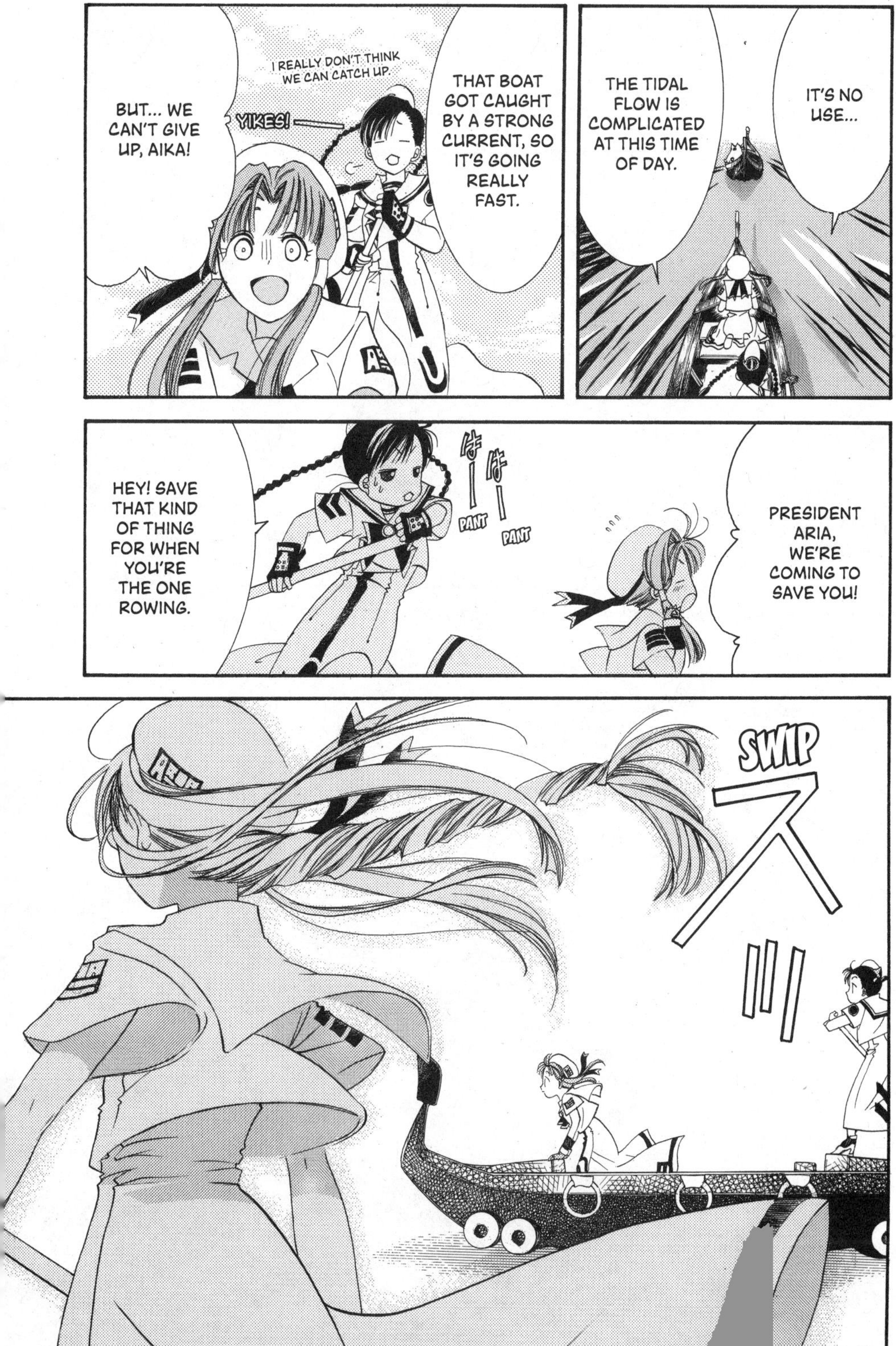
IT'S NO USE...
THE TIDAL FLOW IS COMPLICATED AT THIS TIME OF DAY.
THAT BOAT GOT CAUGHT BY A STRONG CURRENT, SO IT'S GOING REALLY FAST.
I REALLY DON'T THINK WE CAN CATCH UP.
YIKES!
BUT... WE CAN'T GIVE UP, AIKA!
PRESIDENT ARIA, WE'RE COMING TO SAVE YOU!
PANT
PANT
HEY! SAVE THAT KIND OF THING FOR WHEN YOU'RE THE ONE ROWING.
SWIP

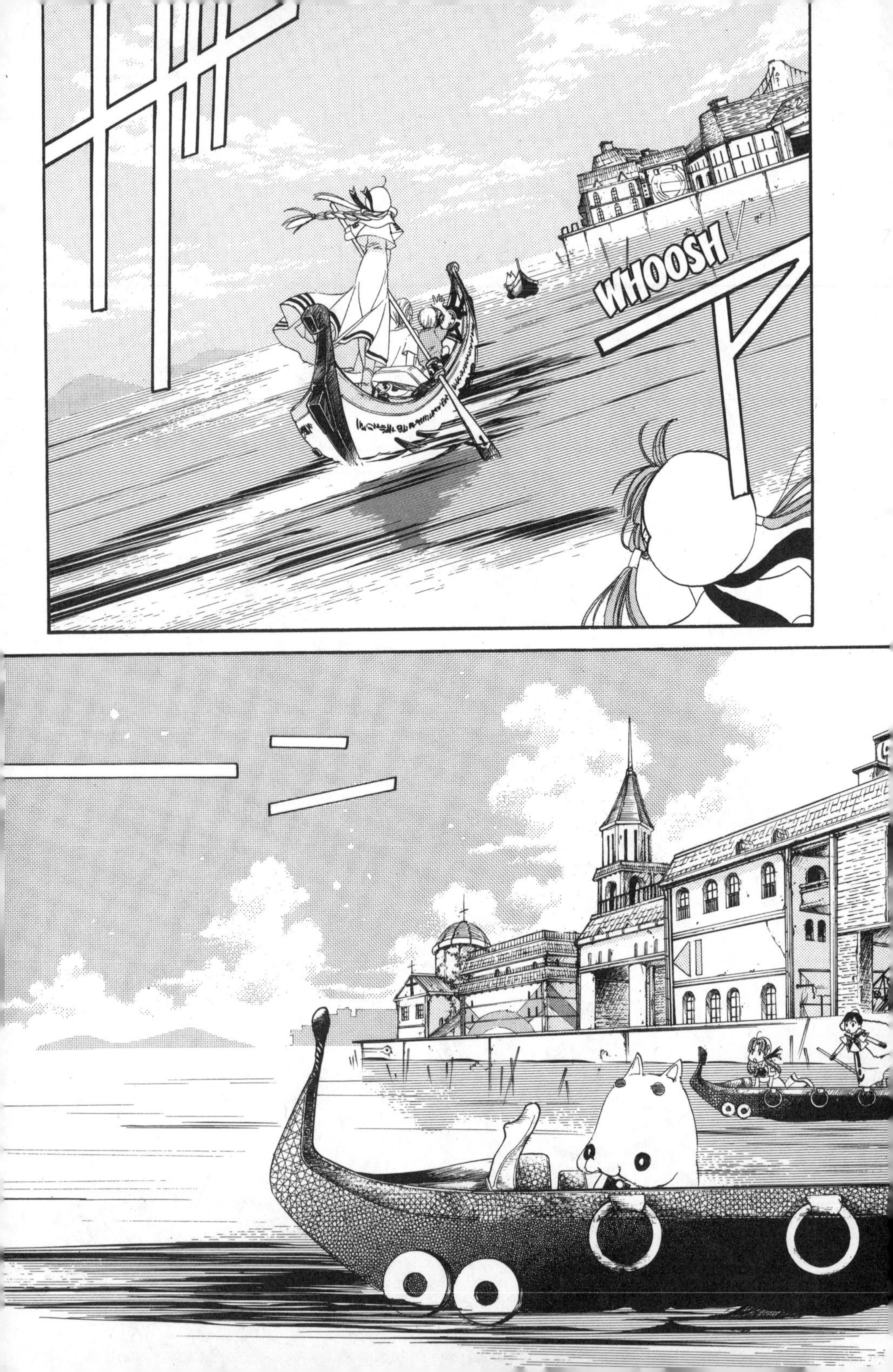
WHOOSH

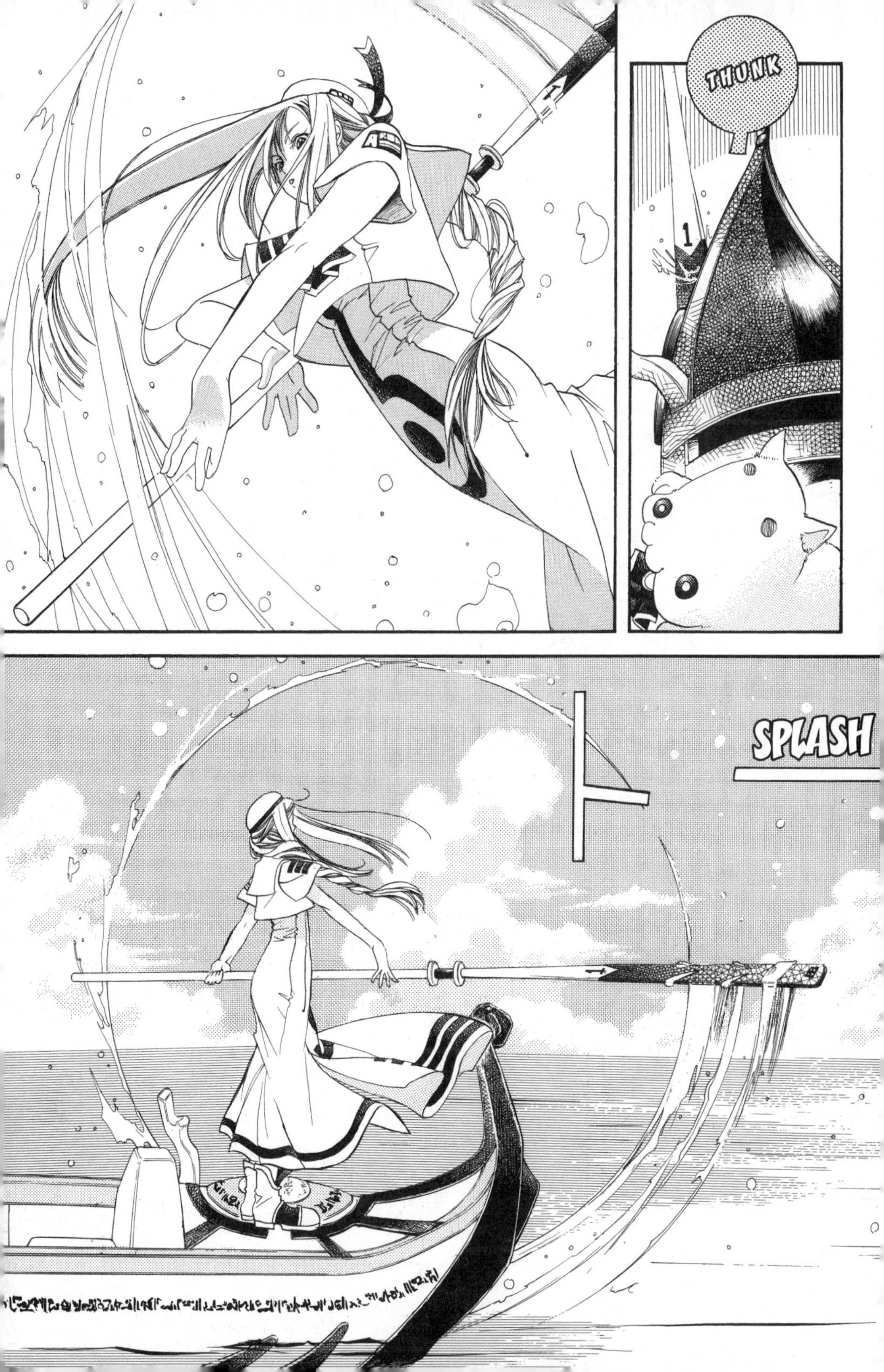
THUNK
SPLASH

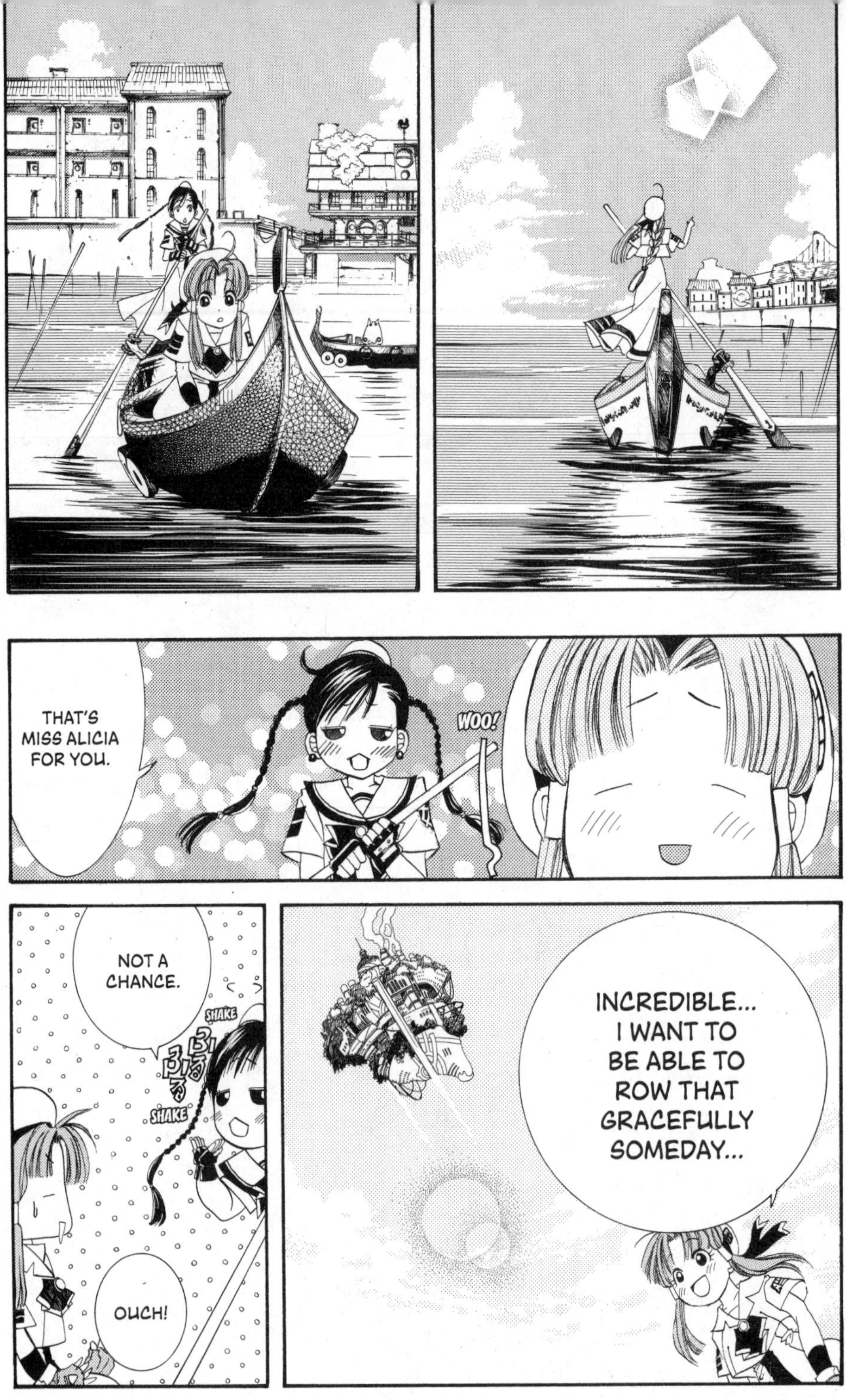
WOO!
THAT'S MISS ALICIA FOR YOU.
INCREDIBLE... I WANT TO BE ABLE TO ROW THAT GRACEFULLY SOMEDAY...
NOT A CHANCE.
SHAKE
ふるふる
SHAKE
OUCH!

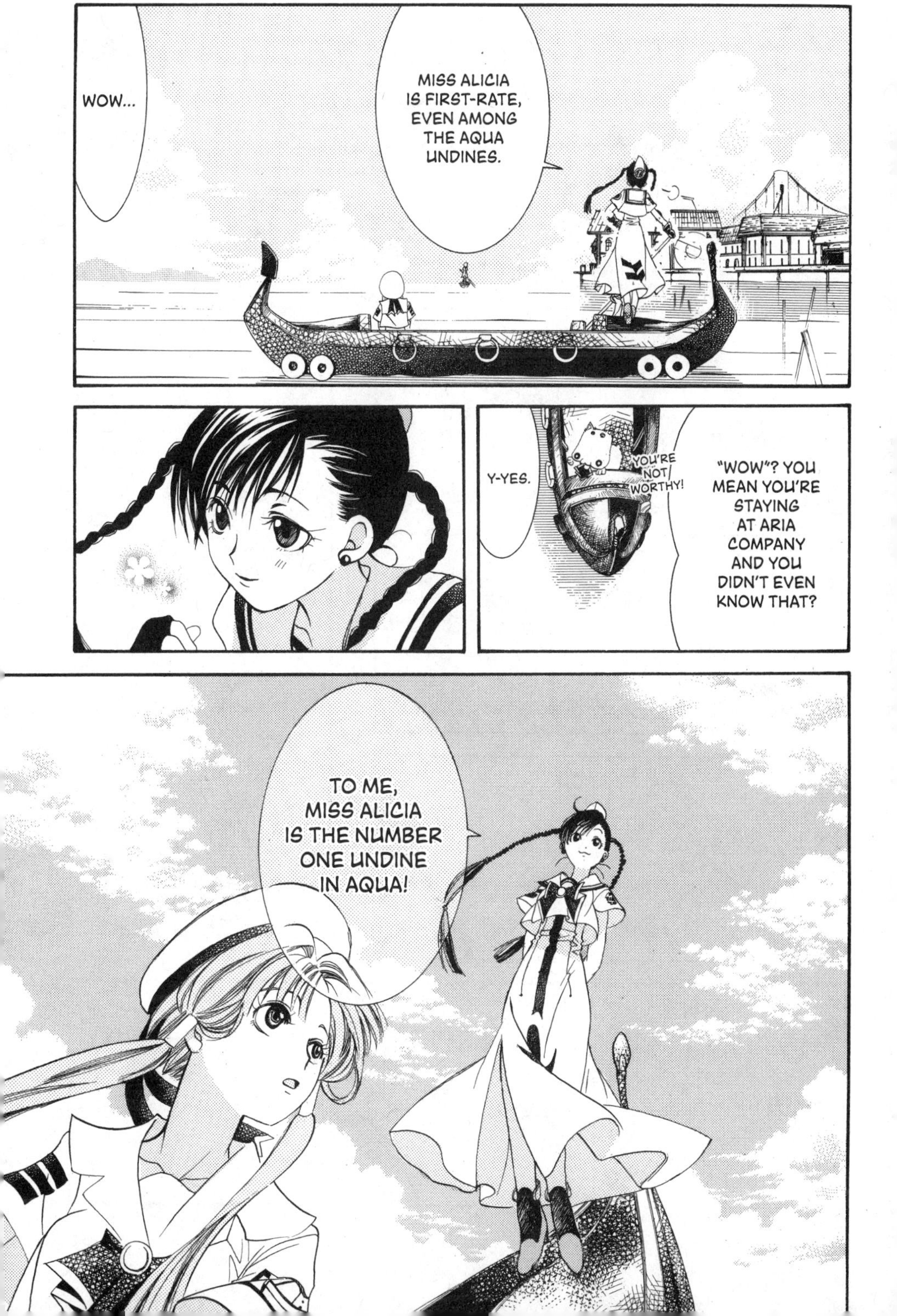
MISS ALICIA IS FIRST-RATE, EVEN AMONG THE AQUA UNDINES.
WOW...
"WOW"? YOU MEAN YOU'RE STAYING AT ARIA COMPANY AND YOU DIDN'T EVEN KNOW THAT?
YOU'RE NOT WORTHY!
Y-YES.
TO ME, MISS ALICIA IS THE NUMBER ONE UNDINE IN AQUA!

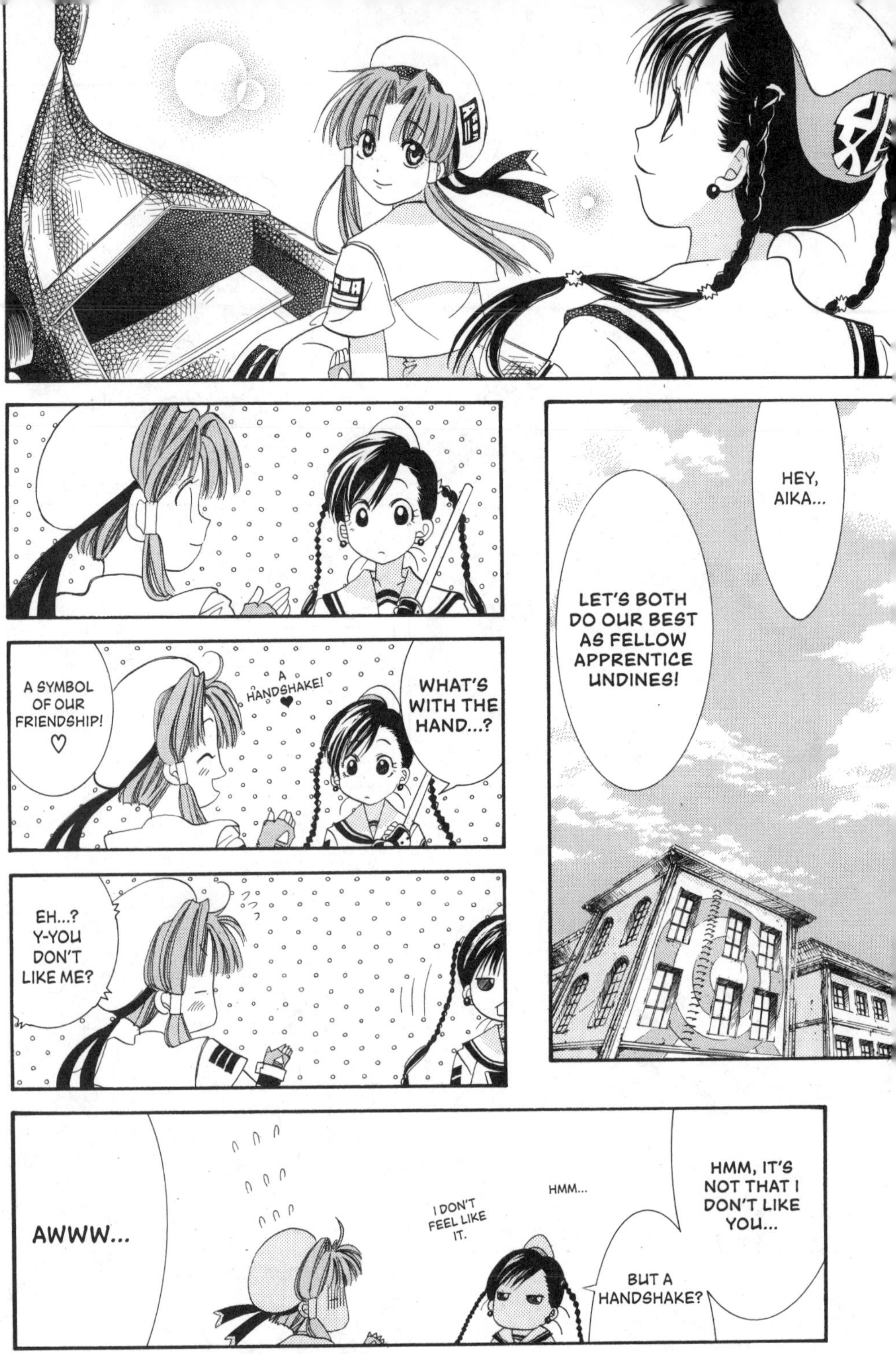
HEY, AIKA...
LET'S BOTH DO OUR BEST AS FELLOW APPRENTICE UNDINES!
WHAT'S WITH THE HAND...?
A HANDSHAKE! ♥
A SYMBOL OF OUR FRIENDSHIP! ♡
EH...? Y-YOU DON'T LIKE ME?
HMM, IT'S NOT THAT I DON'T LIKE YOU...
HMM...
BUT A HANDSHAKE?
I DON'T FEEL LIKE IT.
AWWW...

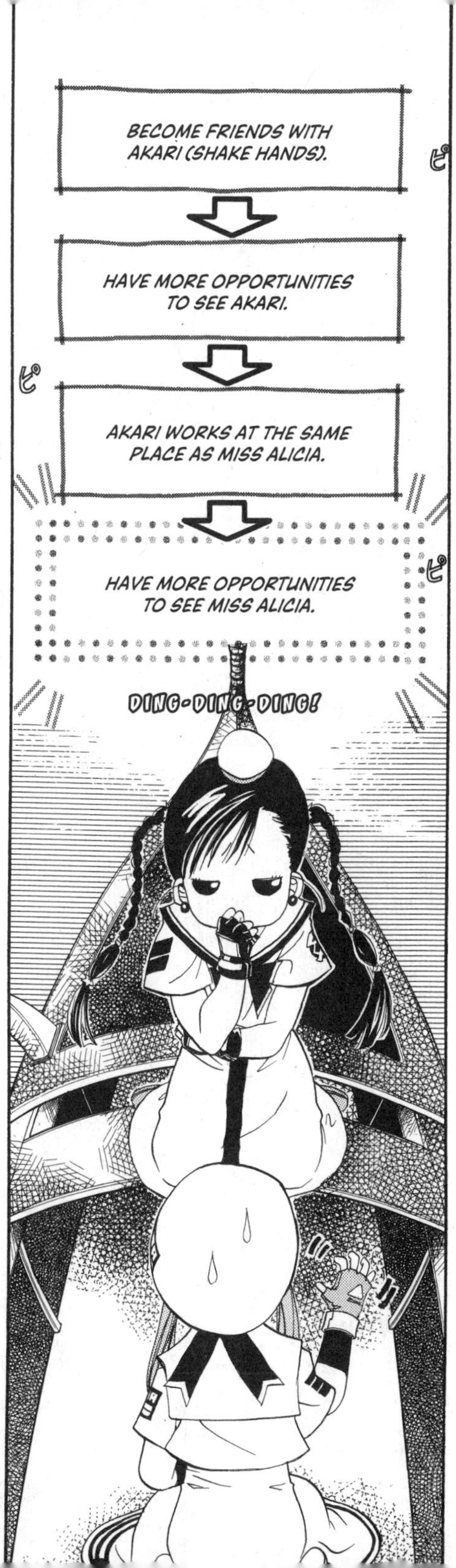
BECOME FRIENDS WITH AKARI (SHAKE HANDS).
ピ
HAVE MORE OPPORTUNITIES TO SEE AKARI.
ピ
AKARI WORKS AT THE SAME PLACE AS MISS ALICIA.
ピ
HAVE MORE OPPORTUNITIES TO SEE MISS ALICIA.
DING-DING-DING!

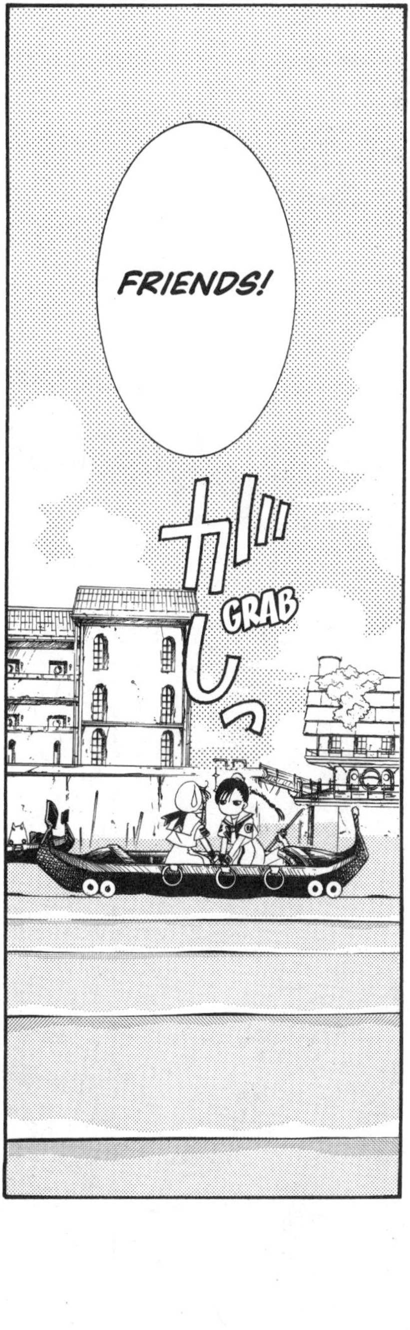
FRIENDS!
ガしっ
GRAB

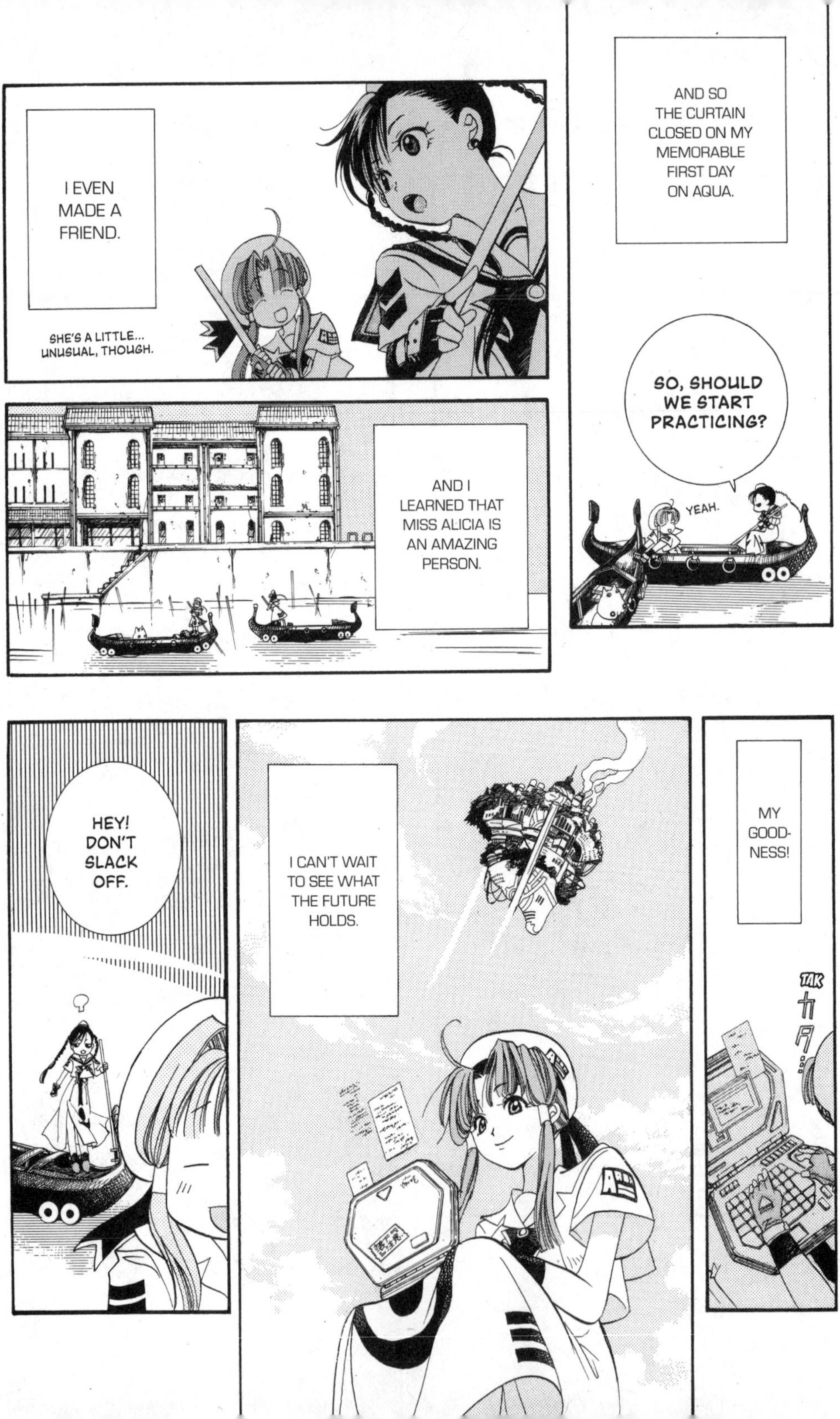
AND SO THE CURTAIN CLOSED ON MY MEMORABLE FIRST DAY ON AQUA.
SO, SHOULD WE START PRACTICING?
YEAH.
I EVEN MADE A FRIEND.
SHE'S A LITTLE... UNUSUAL, THOUGH.
AND I LEARNED THAT MISS ALICIA IS AN AMAZING PERSON.
MY GOODNESS!
TAK
カタ..
I CAN'T WAIT TO SEE WHAT THE FUTURE HOLDS.
HEY! DON'T SLACK OFF.

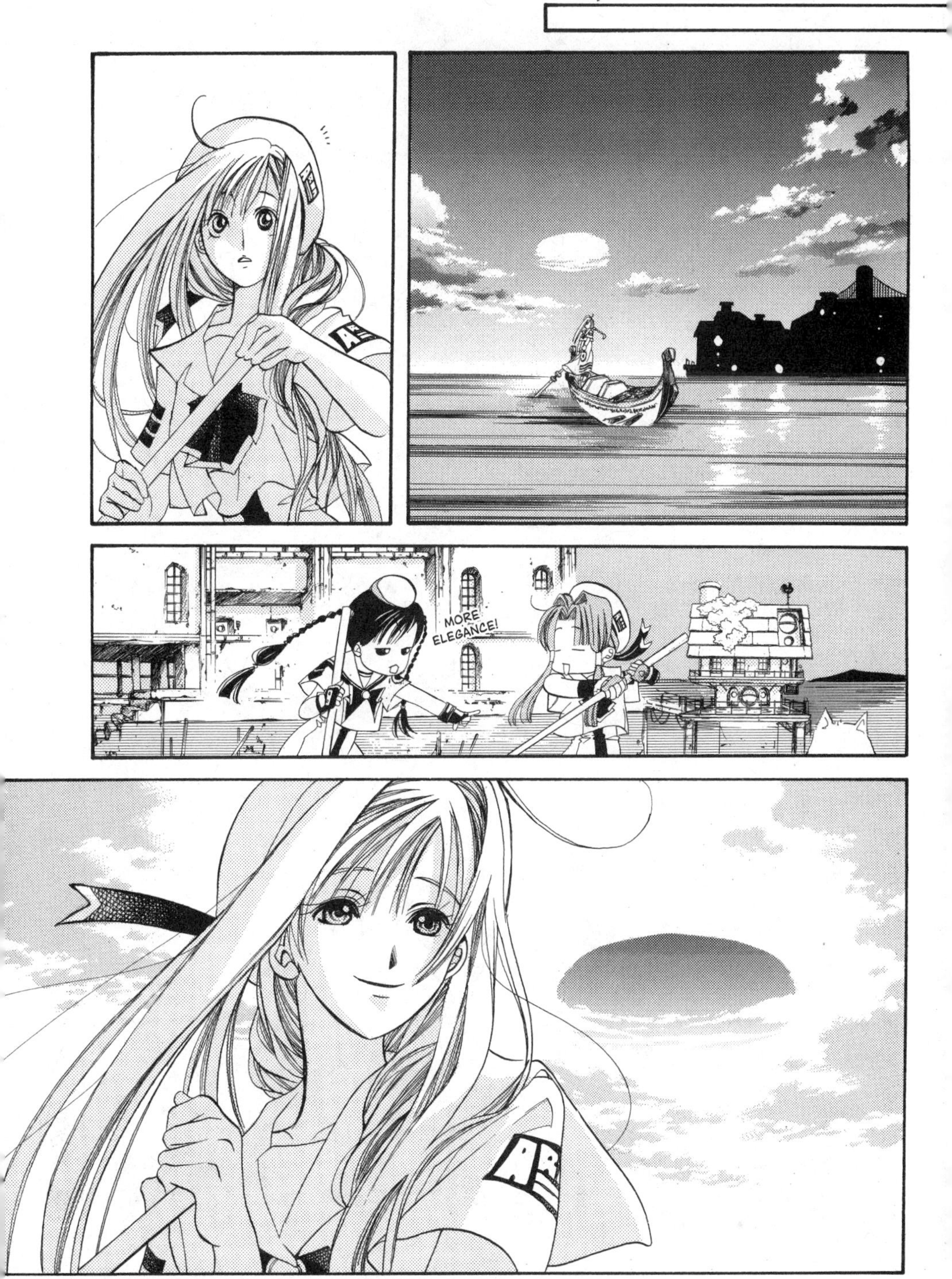
MORE ELEGANCE!

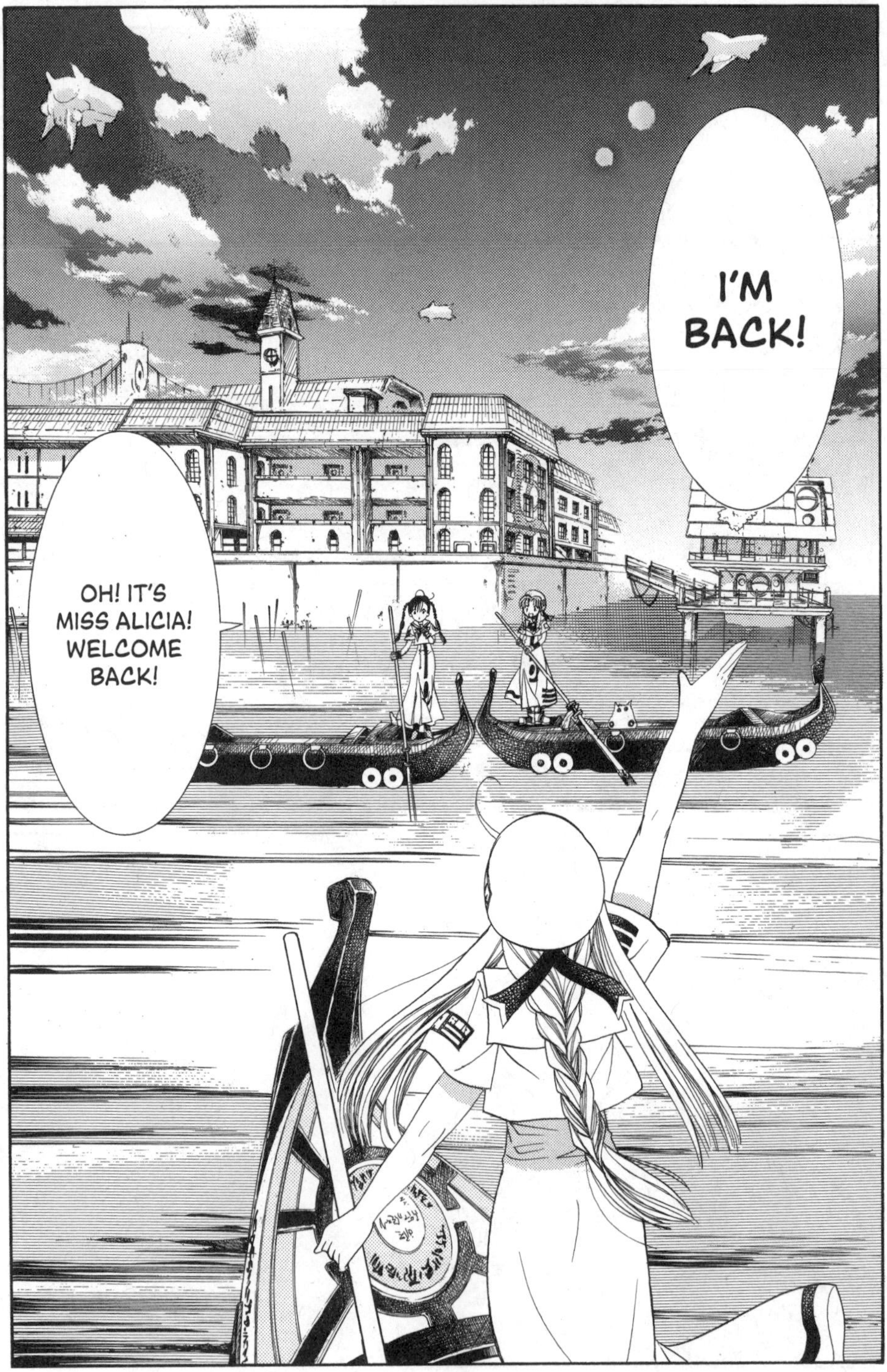
I'M BACK!
OH! IT'S MISS ALICIA! WELCOME BACK!

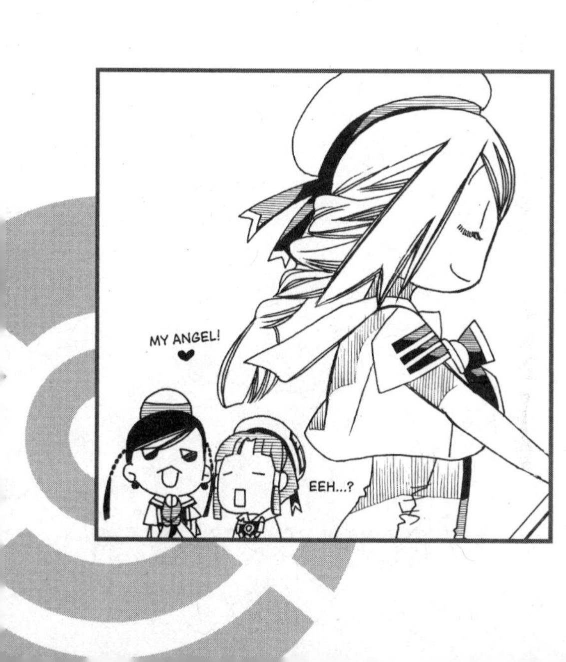
MY ANGEL!
EEH...?

ARIA
The MASTERPIECE

Navigation 03
The City Submerged

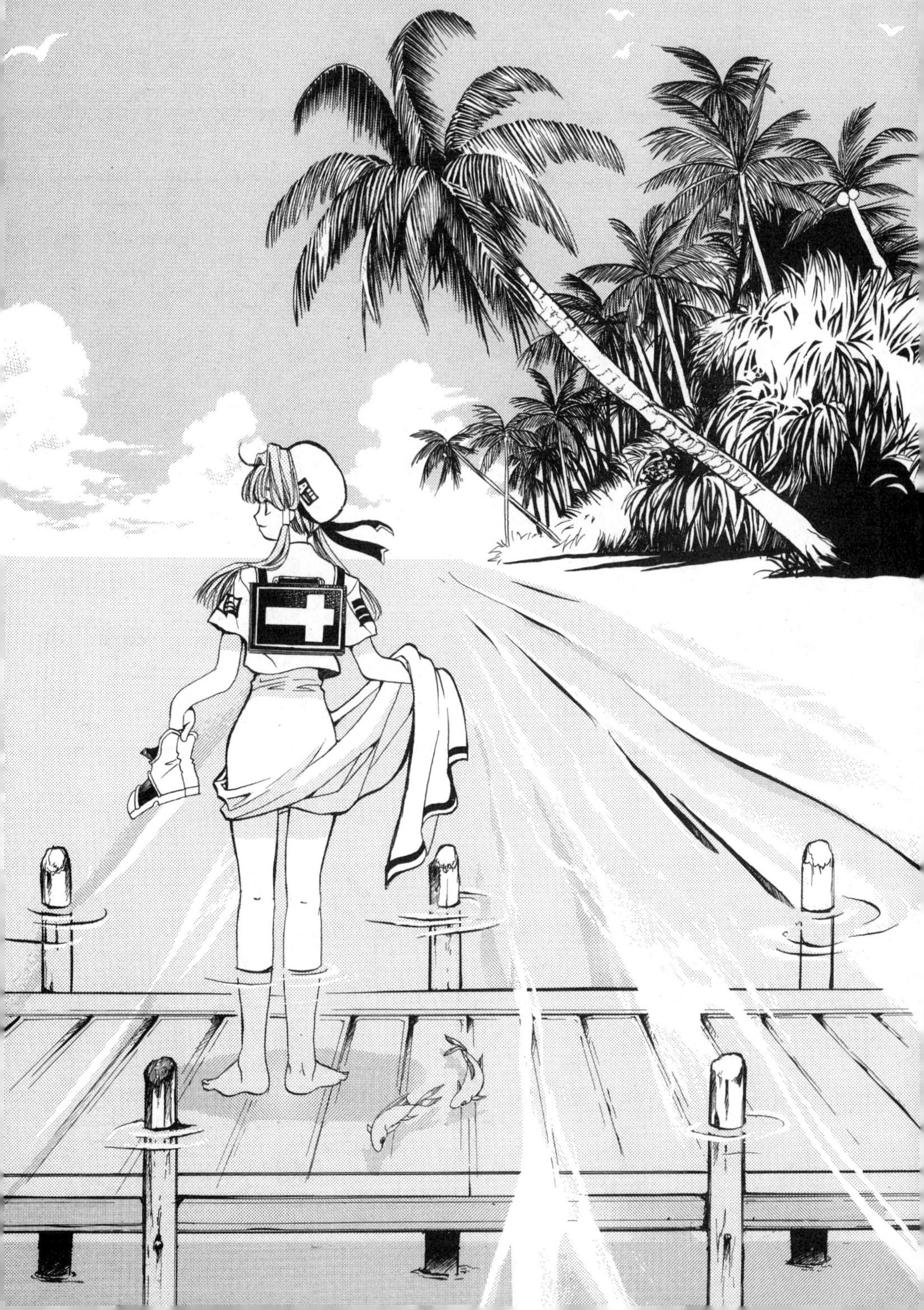

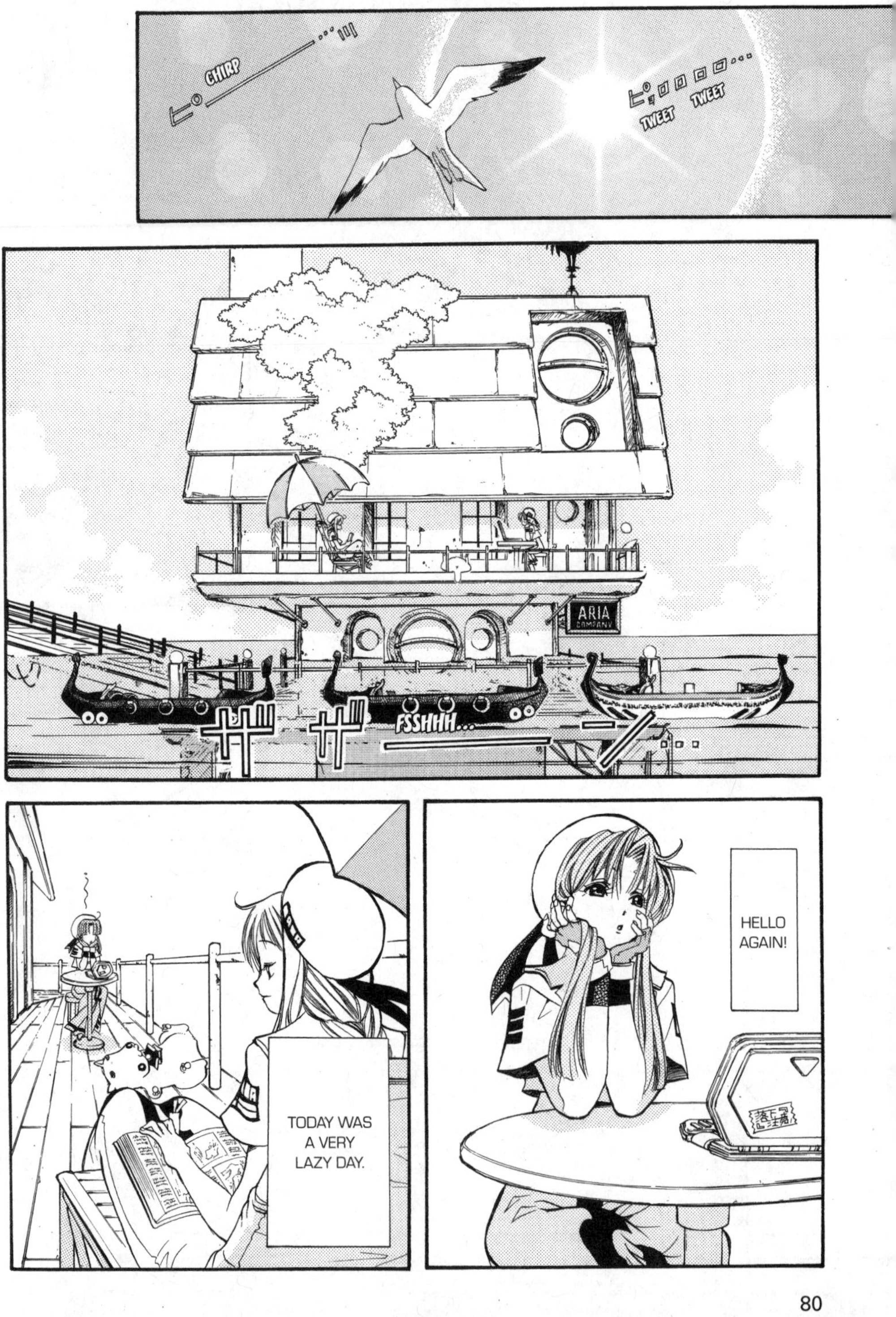
TWEET TWEET
CHIRP
ARIA COMPANY
FSSHHH...
HELLO AGAIN!
TODAY WAS A VERY LAZY DAY.

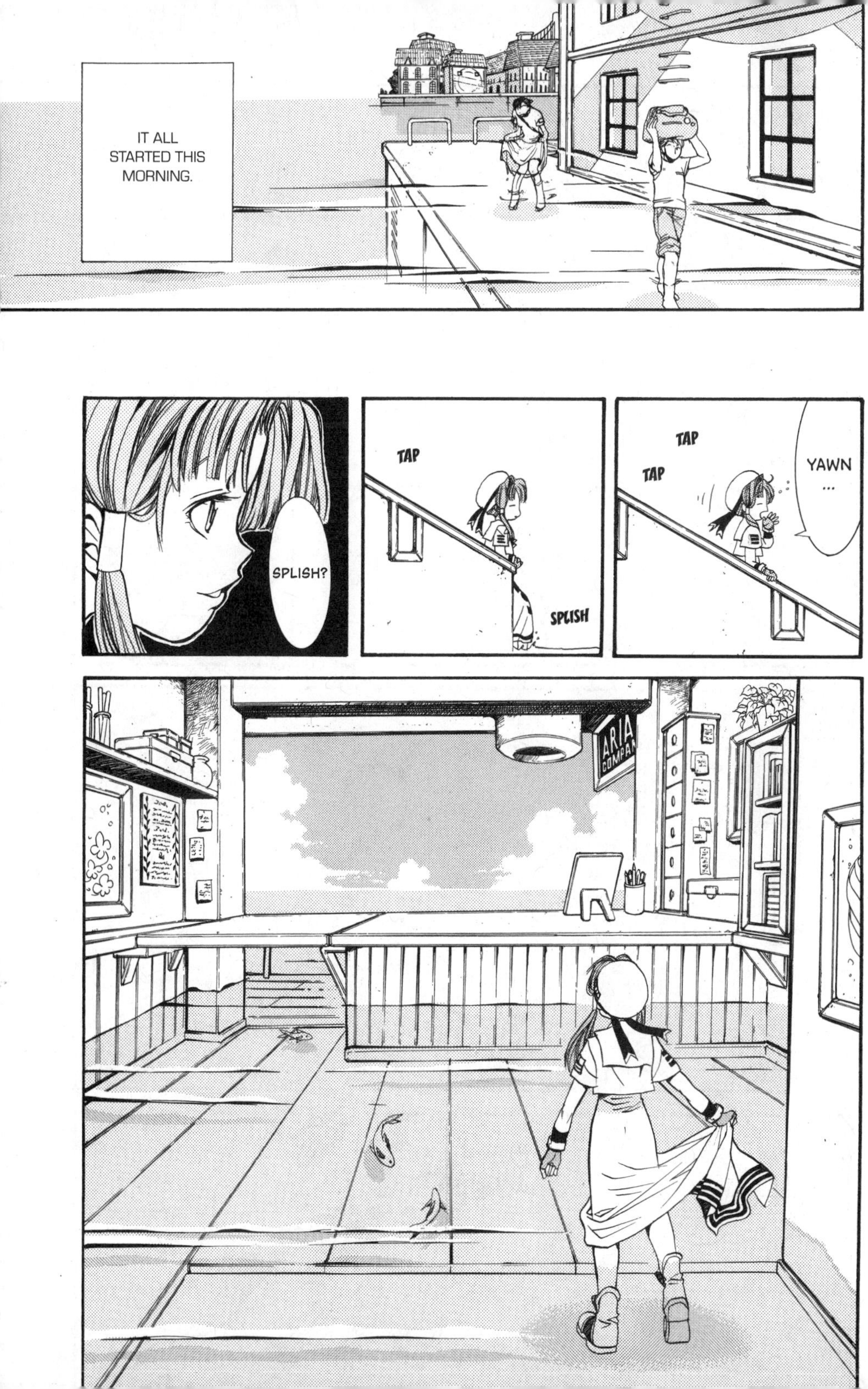
IT ALL STARTED THIS MORNING.
TAP
TAP
YAWN ...
TAP
SPLISH
SPLISH?

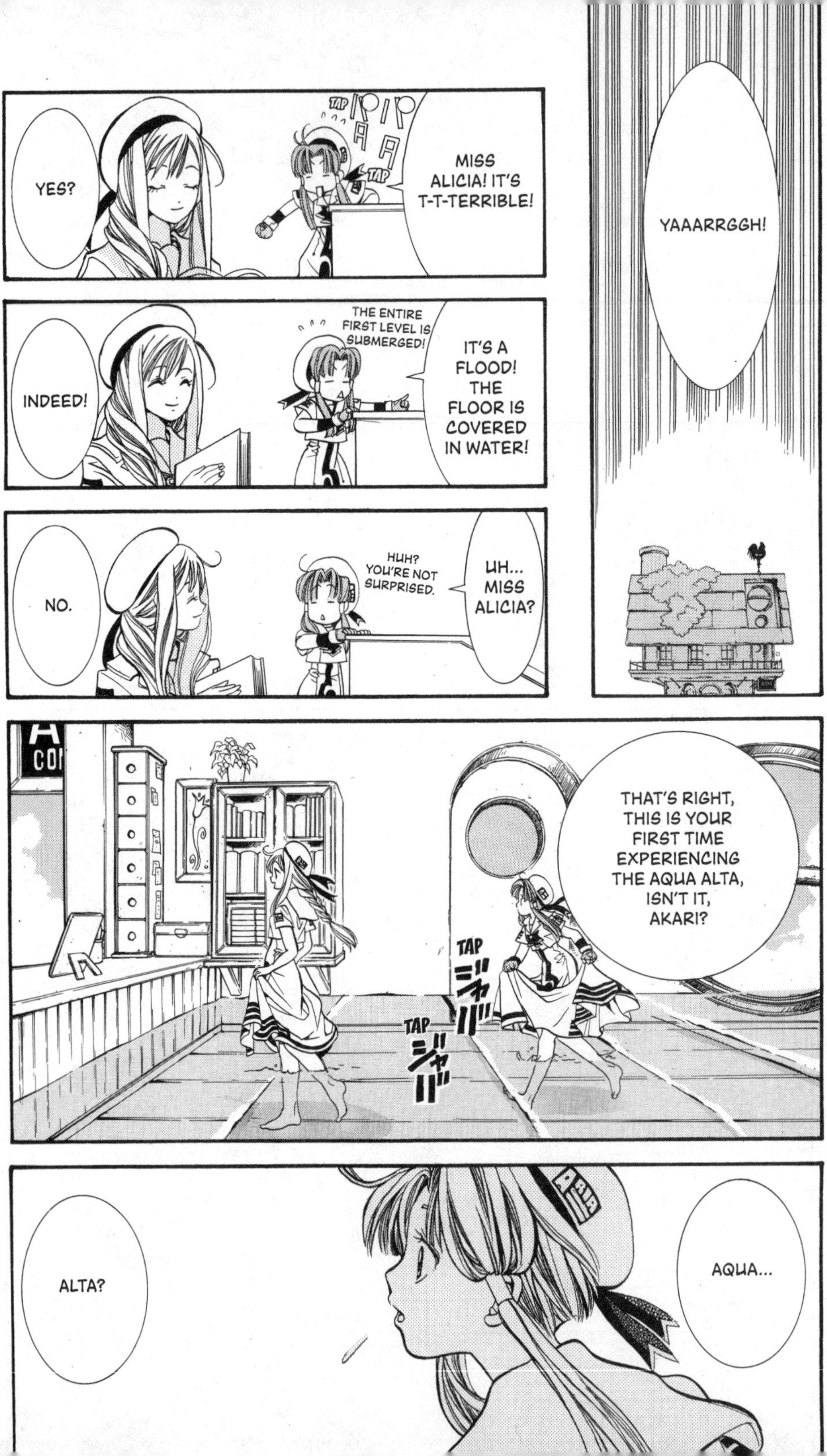
YAAARRGGH!
MISS ALICIA! IT'S T-T-TERRIBLE!
TAP
TAP
YES?
IT'S A FLOOD! THE FLOOR IS COVERED IN WATER!
THE ENTIRE FIRST LEVEL IS SUBMERGED!
INDEED!
UH... MISS ALICIA?
HUH? YOU'RE NOT SURPRISED.
NO.
THAT'S RIGHT, THIS IS YOUR FIRST TIME EXPERIENCING THE AQUA ALTA, ISN'T IT, AKARI?
TAP
TAP
AQUA...
ALTA?

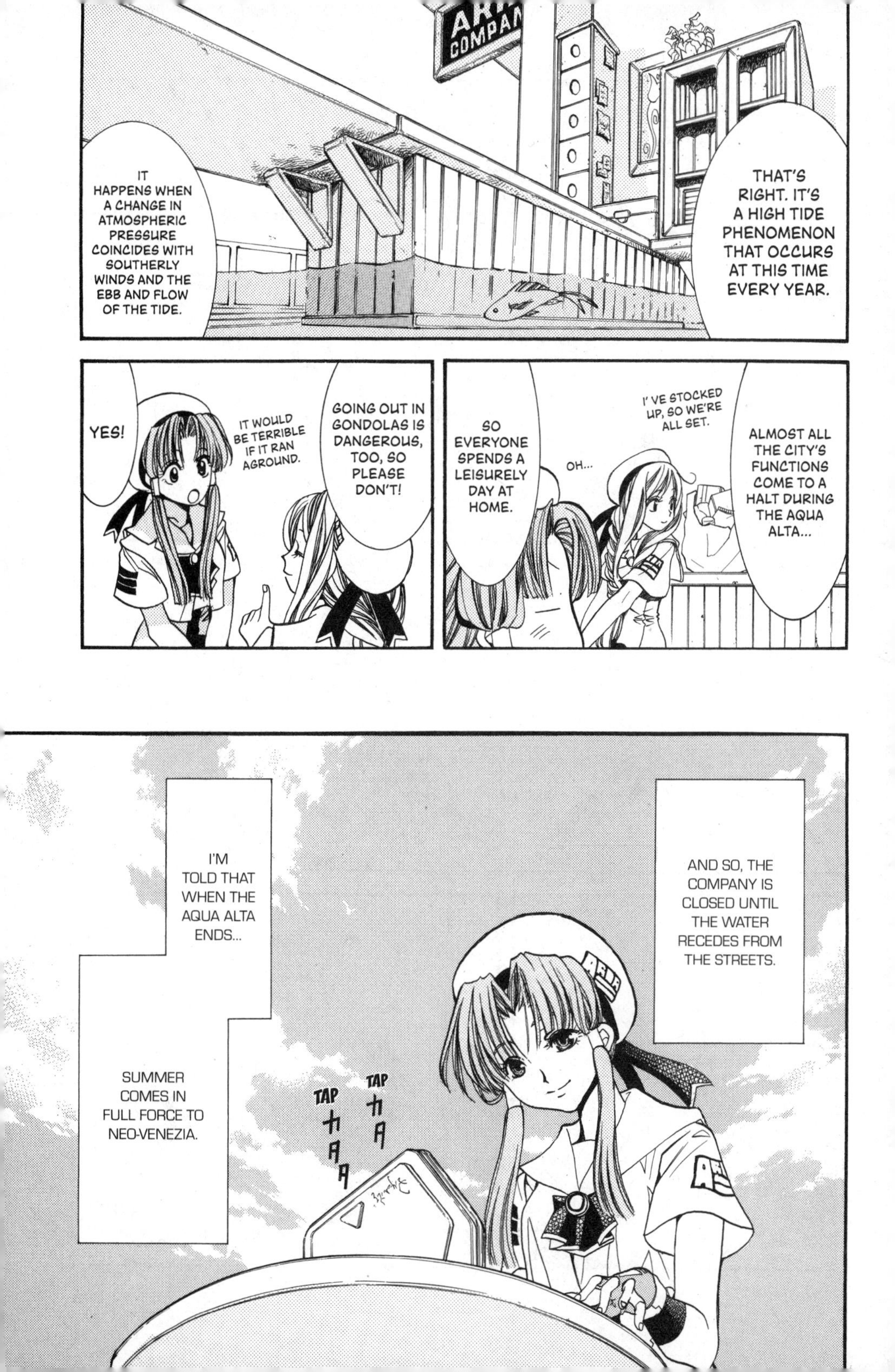
THAT'S RIGHT. IT'S A HIGH TIDE PHENOMENON THAT OCCURS AT THIS TIME EVERY YEAR.
IT HAPPENS WHEN A CHANGE IN ATMOSPHERIC PRESSURE COINCIDES WITH SOUTHERLY WINDS AND THE EBB AND FLOW OF THE TIDE.
ALMOST ALL THE CITY'S FUNCTIONS COME TO A HALT DURING THE AQUA ALTA...
I'VE STOCKED UP, SO WE'RE ALL SET.
OH...
SO EVERYONE SPENDS A LEISURELY DAY AT HOME.
GOING OUT IN GONDOLAS IS DANGEROUS, TOO, SO PLEASE DON'T!
IT WOULD BE TERRIBLE IF IT RAN AGROUND.
YES!
AND SO, THE COMPANY IS CLOSED UNTIL THE WATER RECEDES FROM THE STREETS.
I'M TOLD THAT WHEN THE AQUA ALTA ENDS...
TAP
TAP
SUMMER COMES IN FULL FORCE TO NEO-VENEZIA.

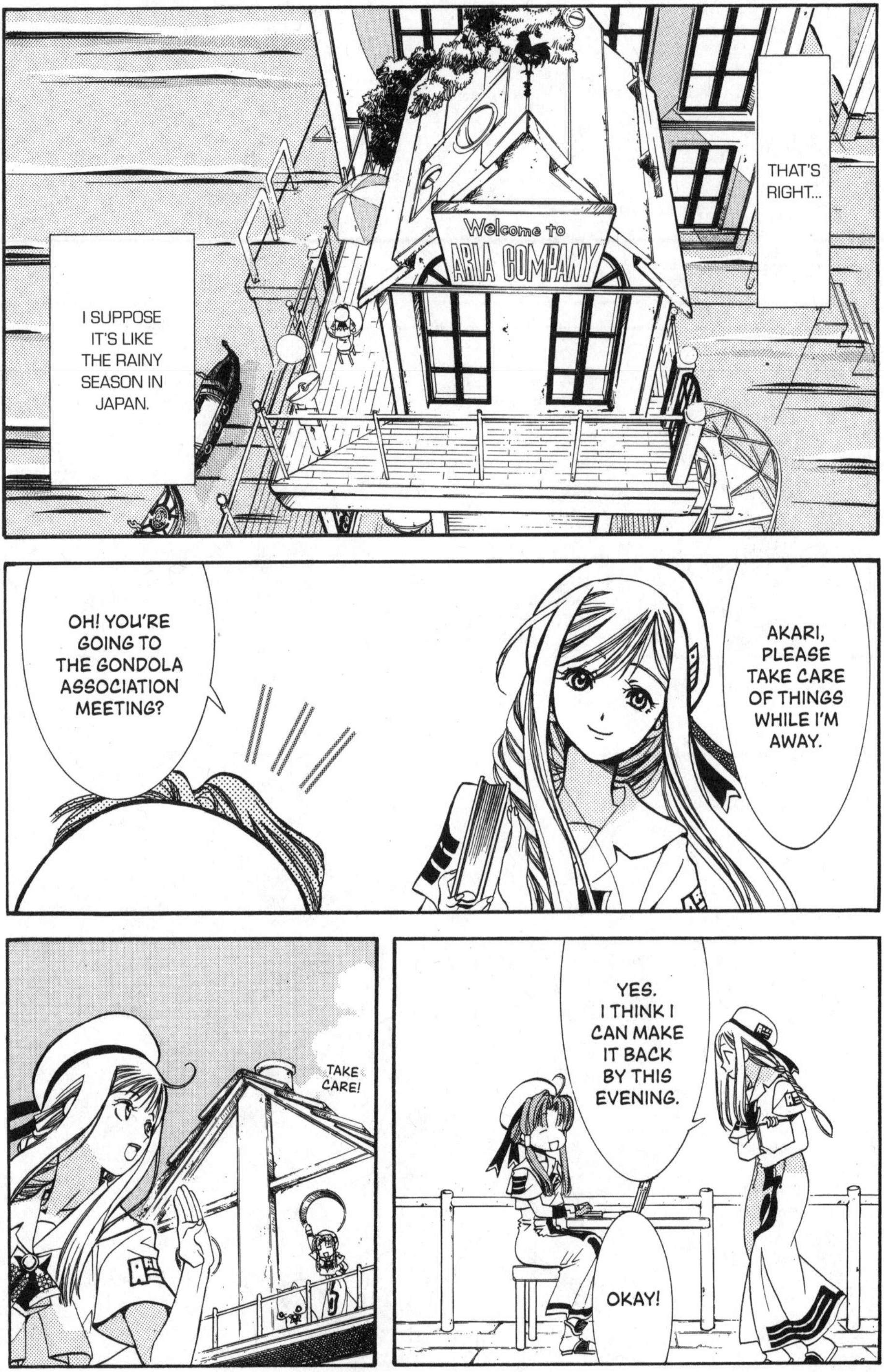
THAT'S RIGHT...
Welcome to ARIA COMPANY
I SUPPOSE IT'S LIKE THE RAINY SEASON IN JAPAN.
AKARI, PLEASE TAKE CARE OF THINGS WHILE I'M AWAY.
OH! YOU'RE GOING TO THE GONDOLA ASSOCIATION MEETING?
YES. I THINK I CAN MAKE IT BACK BY THIS EVENING.
OKAY!
TAKE CARE!

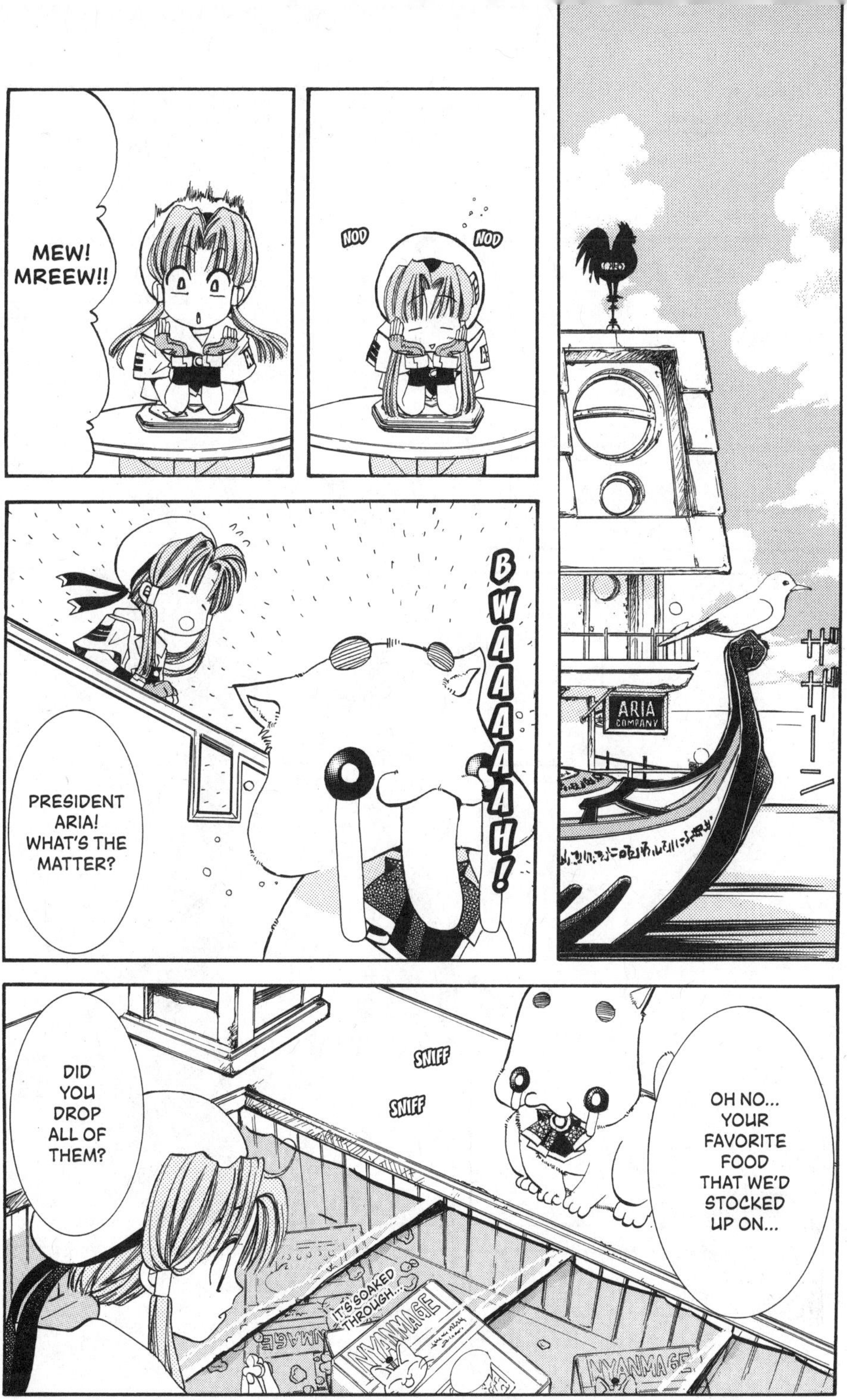
ARIA COMPANY
NOD
NOD
MEW! MREEW!!
BWAAAAAAAH!
PRESIDENT ARIA! WHAT'S THE MATTER?
OH NO... YOUR FAVORITE FOOD THAT WE'D STOCKED UP ON...
SNIFF
SNIFF
DID YOU DROP ALL OF THEM?
IT'S SOAKED THROUGH...
NYANMAGE
NYANMAGE

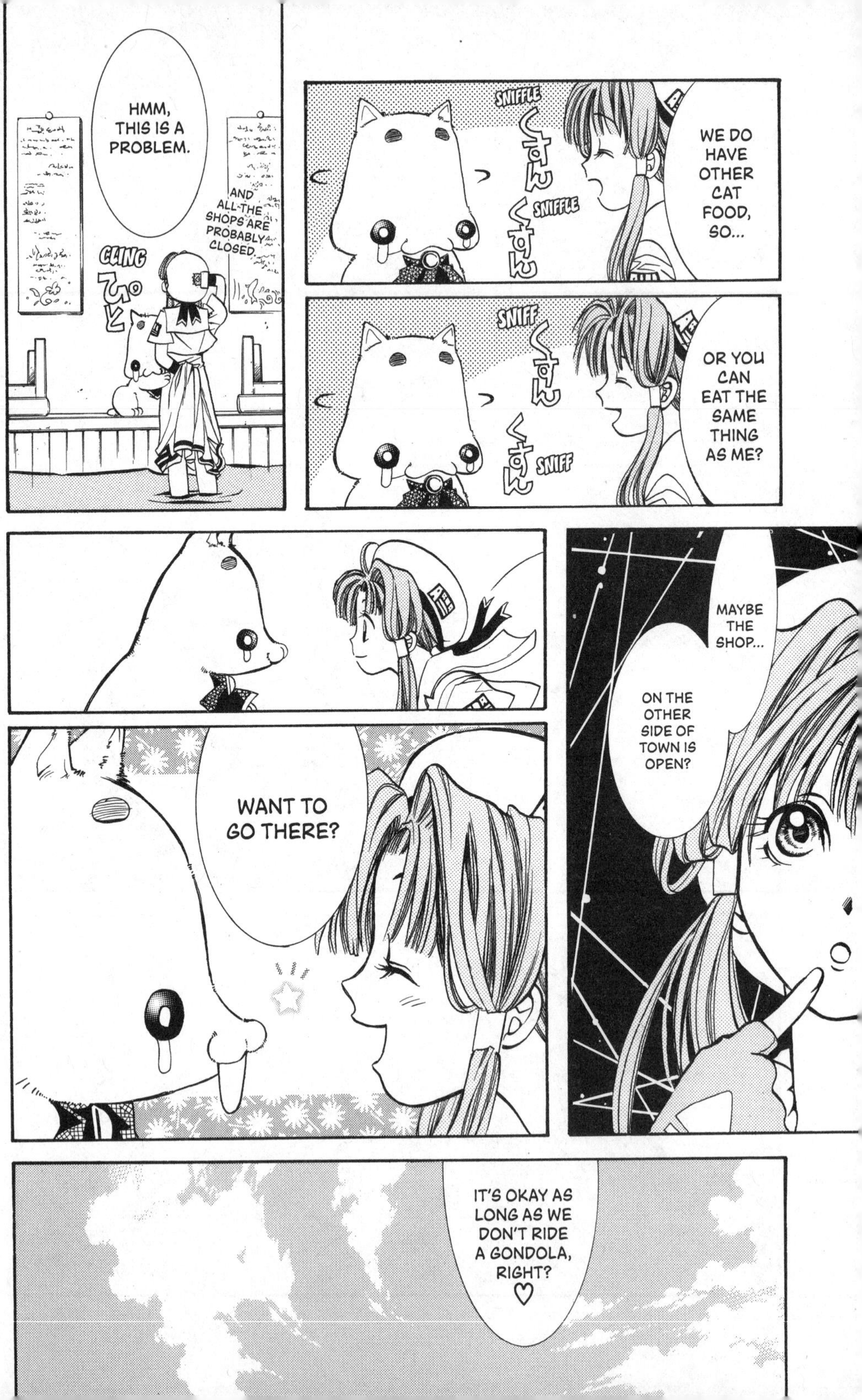

SNIFFLE
くすん
SNIFFLE
くすん
WE DO HAVE OTHER CAT FOOD, SO...
SNIFF
くすん
SNIFF
くすん
OR YOU CAN EAT THE SAME THING AS ME?
HMM, THIS IS A PROBLEM.
AND ALL THE SHOPS ARE PROBABLY CLOSED.
CLING
MAYBE THE SHOP...
ON THE OTHER SIDE OF TOWN IS OPEN?
WANT TO GO THERE?
IT'S OKAY AS LONG AS WE DON'T RIDE A GONDOLA, RIGHT? ♡

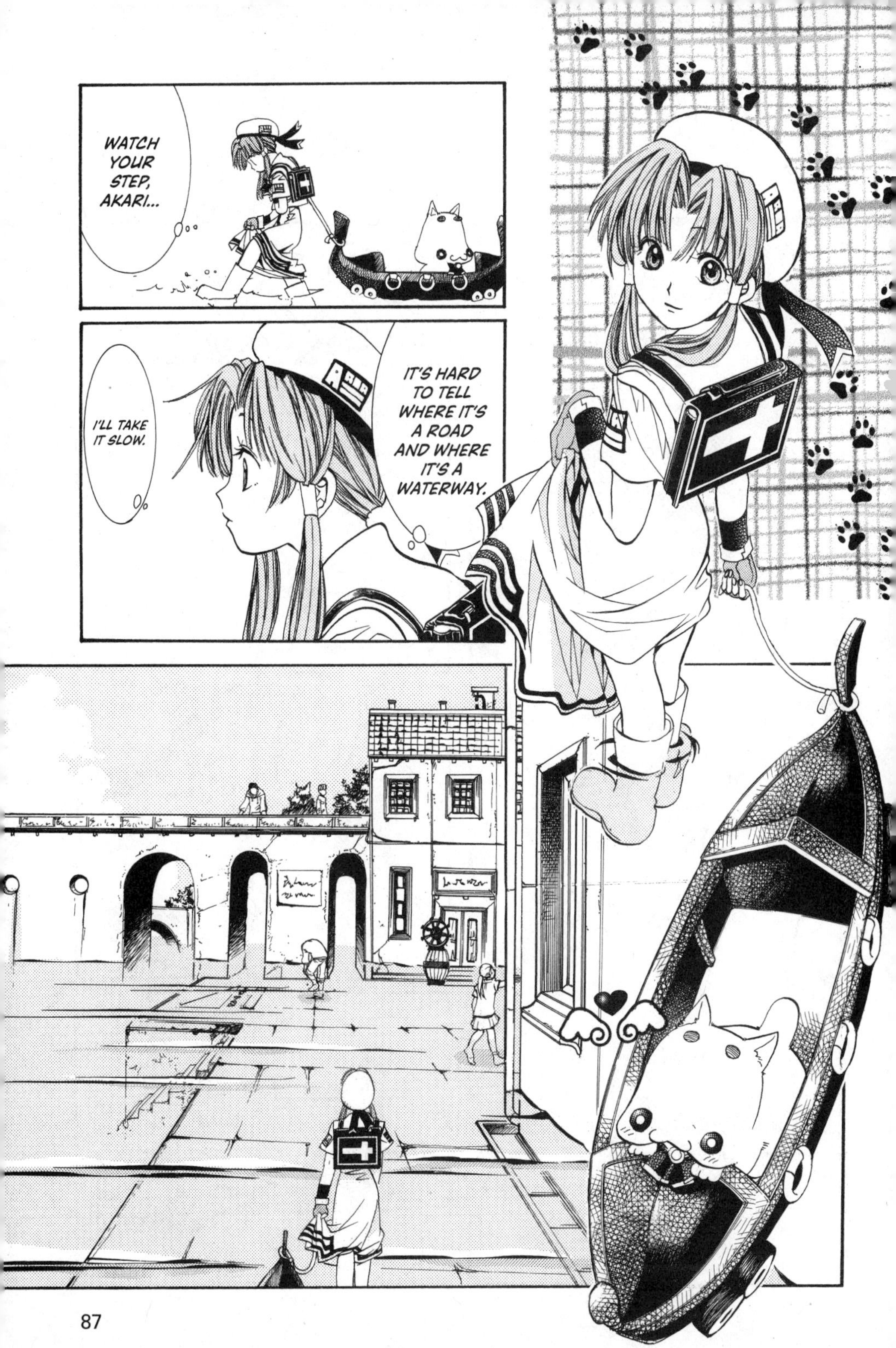
WATCH YOUR STEP, AKARI...
IT'S HARD TO TELL WHERE IT'S A ROAD AND WHERE IT'S A WATERWAY.
I'LL TAKE IT SLOW.

OOPS...

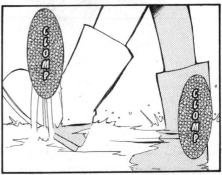

CLOMP

CLOMP

GLUB GLUB

GLUB GLUB

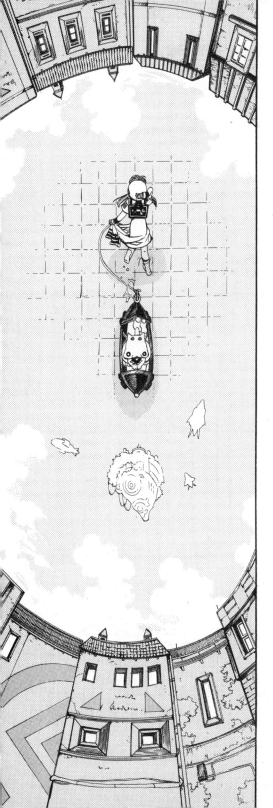

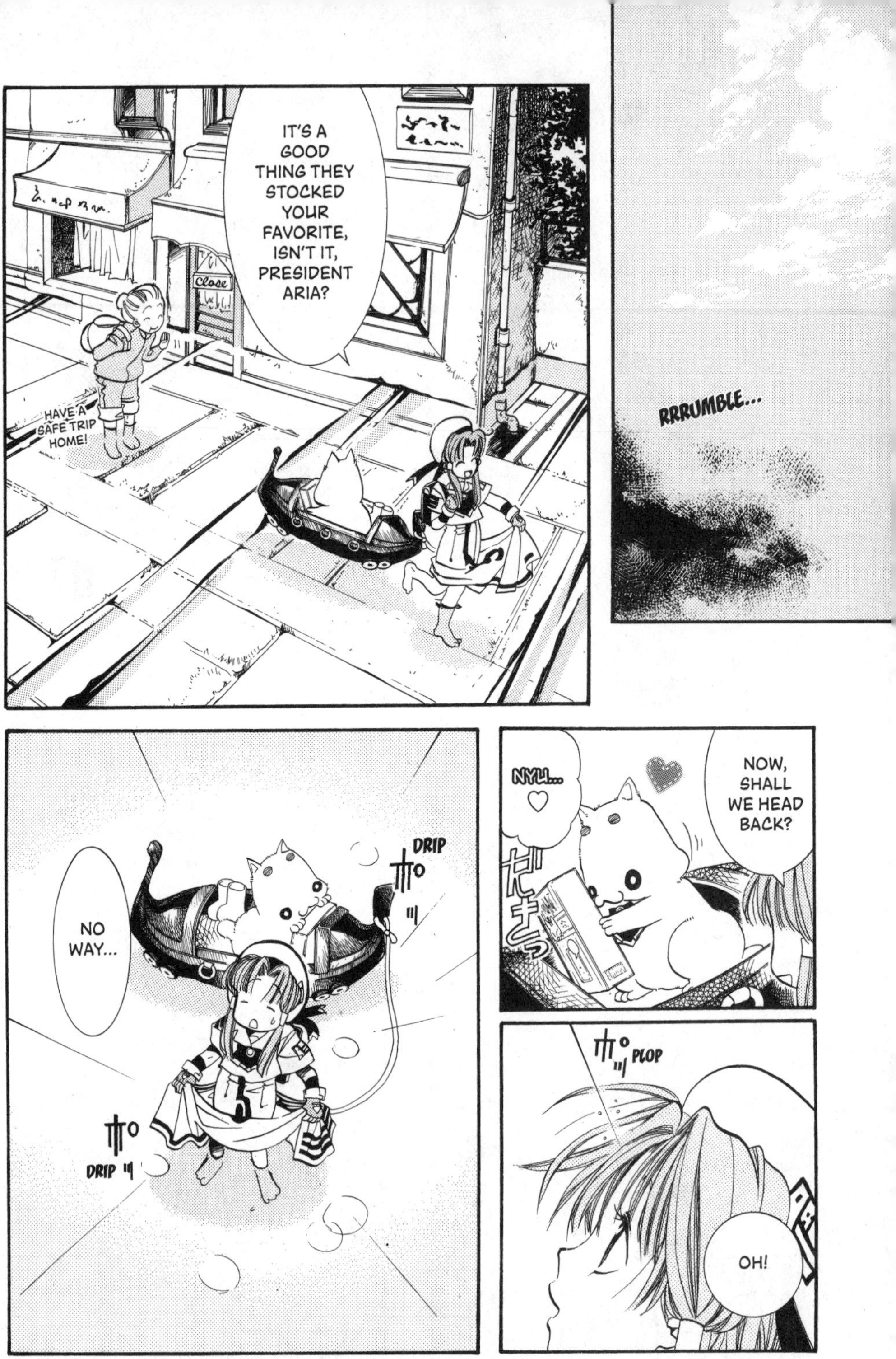
RRRUMBLE...
IT'S A GOOD THING THEY STOCKED YOUR FAVORITE, ISN'T IT, PRESIDENT ARIA?
HAVE A SAFE TRIP HOME!
NOW, SHALL WE HEAD BACK?
NYU... ♡
PLOP
OH!
DRIP
NO WAY...
DRIP

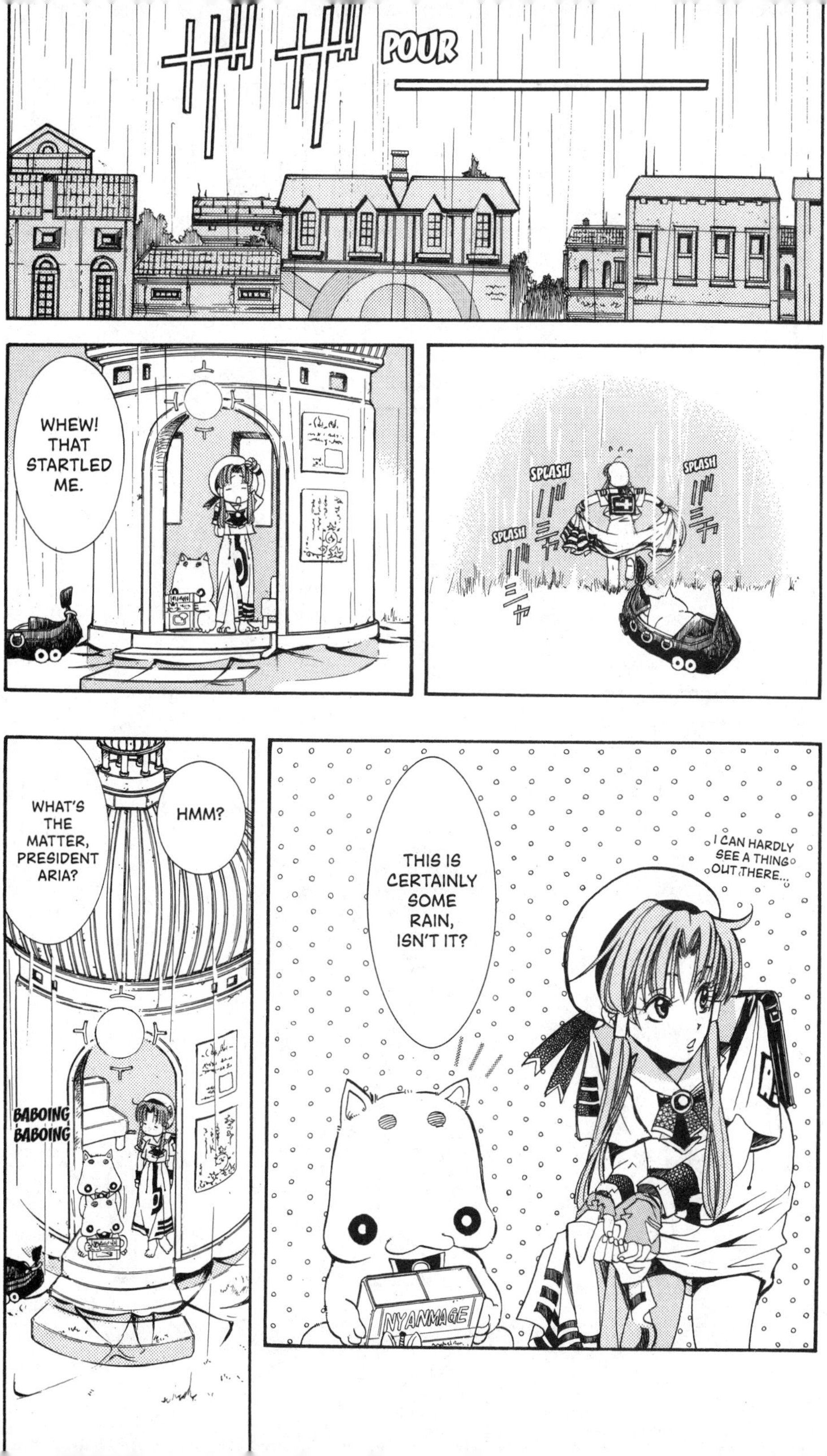
POUR
SPLASH
SPLASH
SPLASH
WHEW! THAT STARTLED ME.
I CAN HARDLY SEE A THING OUT THERE...
THIS IS CERTAINLY SOME RAIN, ISN'T IT?
NYANMAGE
HMM?
WHAT'S THE MATTER, PRESIDENT ARIA?
BABOING BABOING

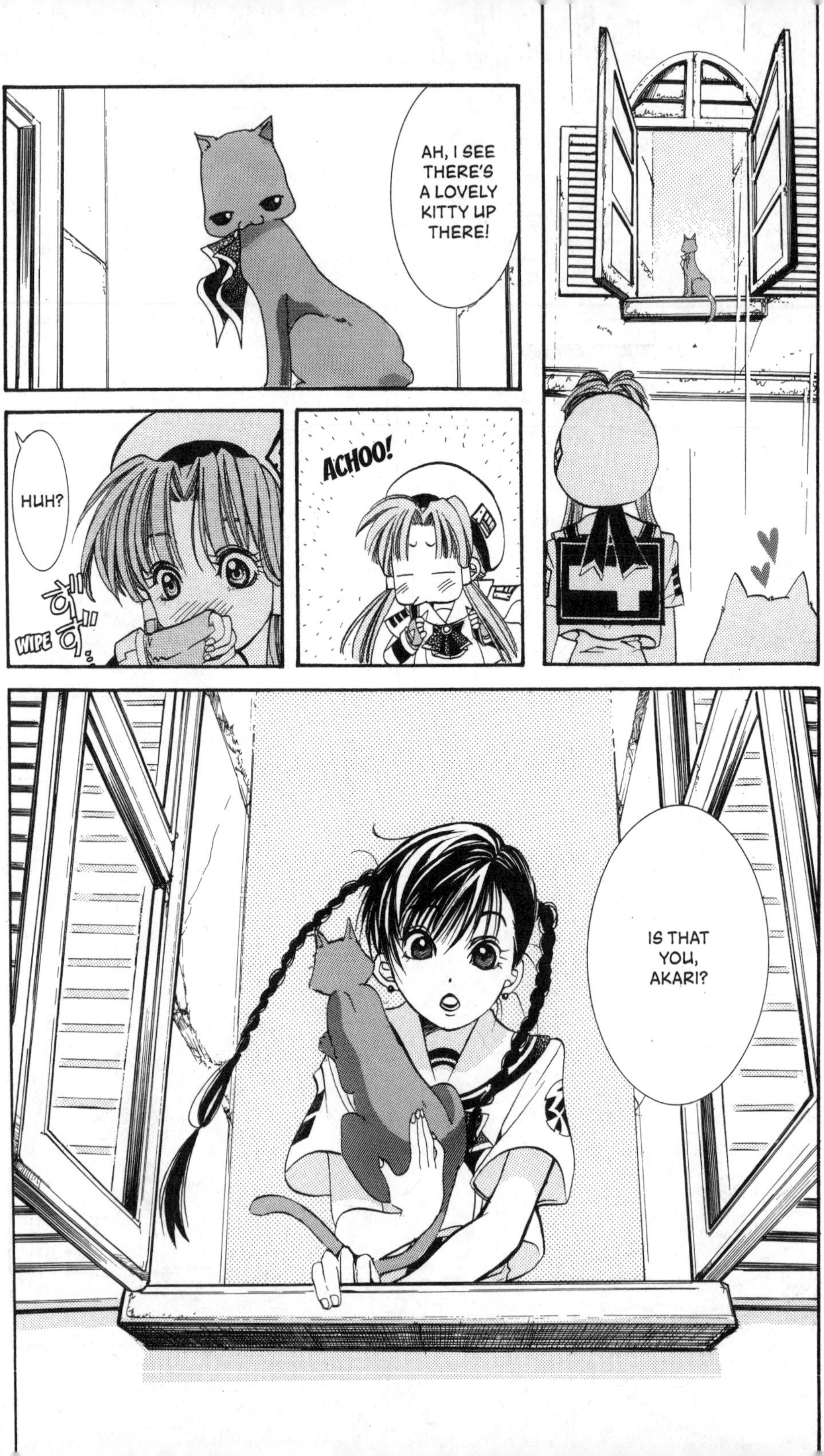
AH, I SEE THERE'S A LOVELY KITTY UP THERE!
ACHOO!
HUH?
WIPE
IS THAT YOU, AKARI?

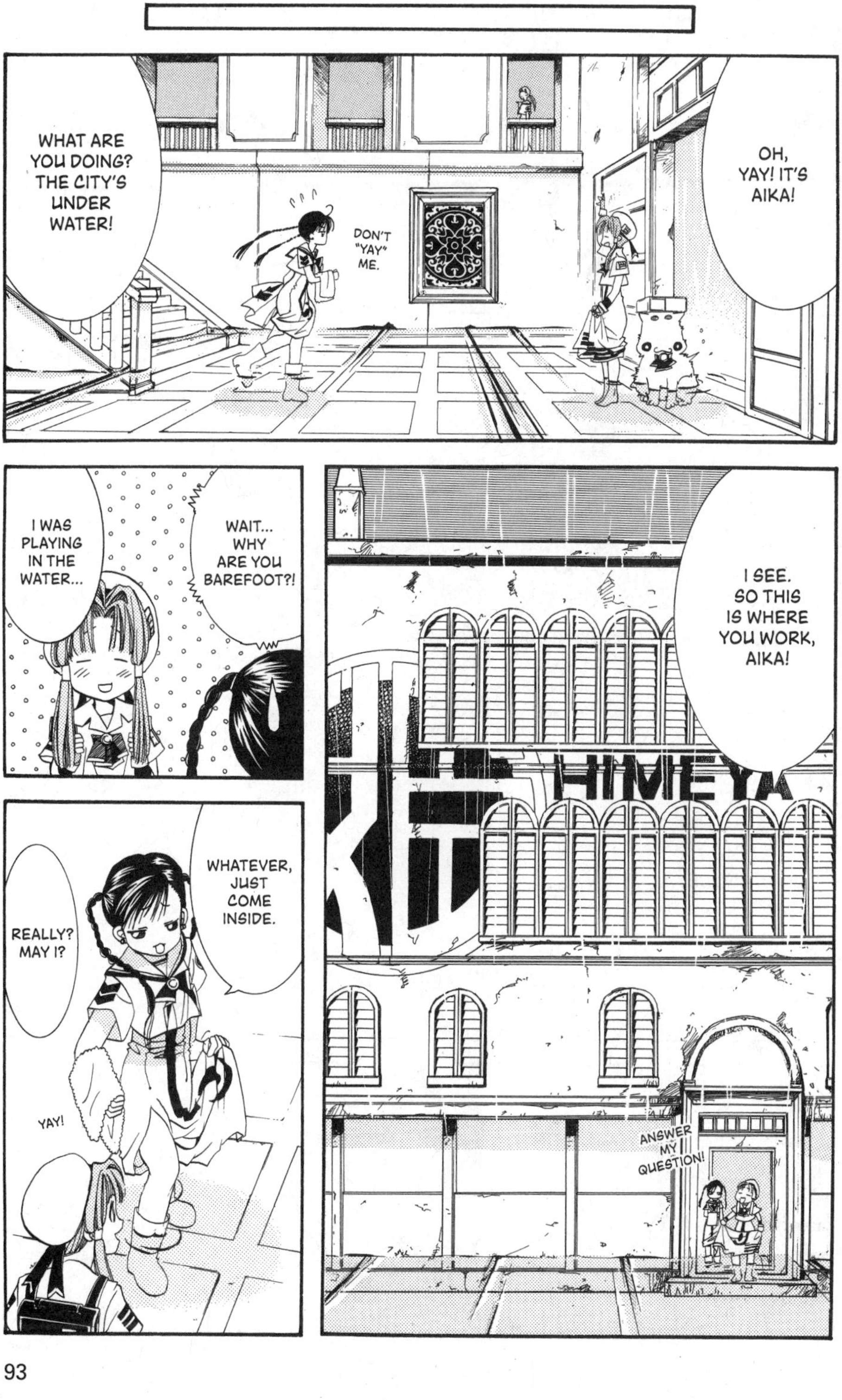

OH, YAY! IT'S AIKA!
DON'T "YAY" ME.
WHAT ARE YOU DOING? THE CITY'S UNDER WATER!
I SEE. SO THIS IS WHERE YOU WORK, AIKA!
HIMEYA
ANSWER MY QUESTION!
WAIT... WHY ARE YOU BAREFOOT?!
I WAS PLAYING IN THE WATER...
WHATEVER, JUST COME INSIDE.
REALLY? MAY I?
YAY!

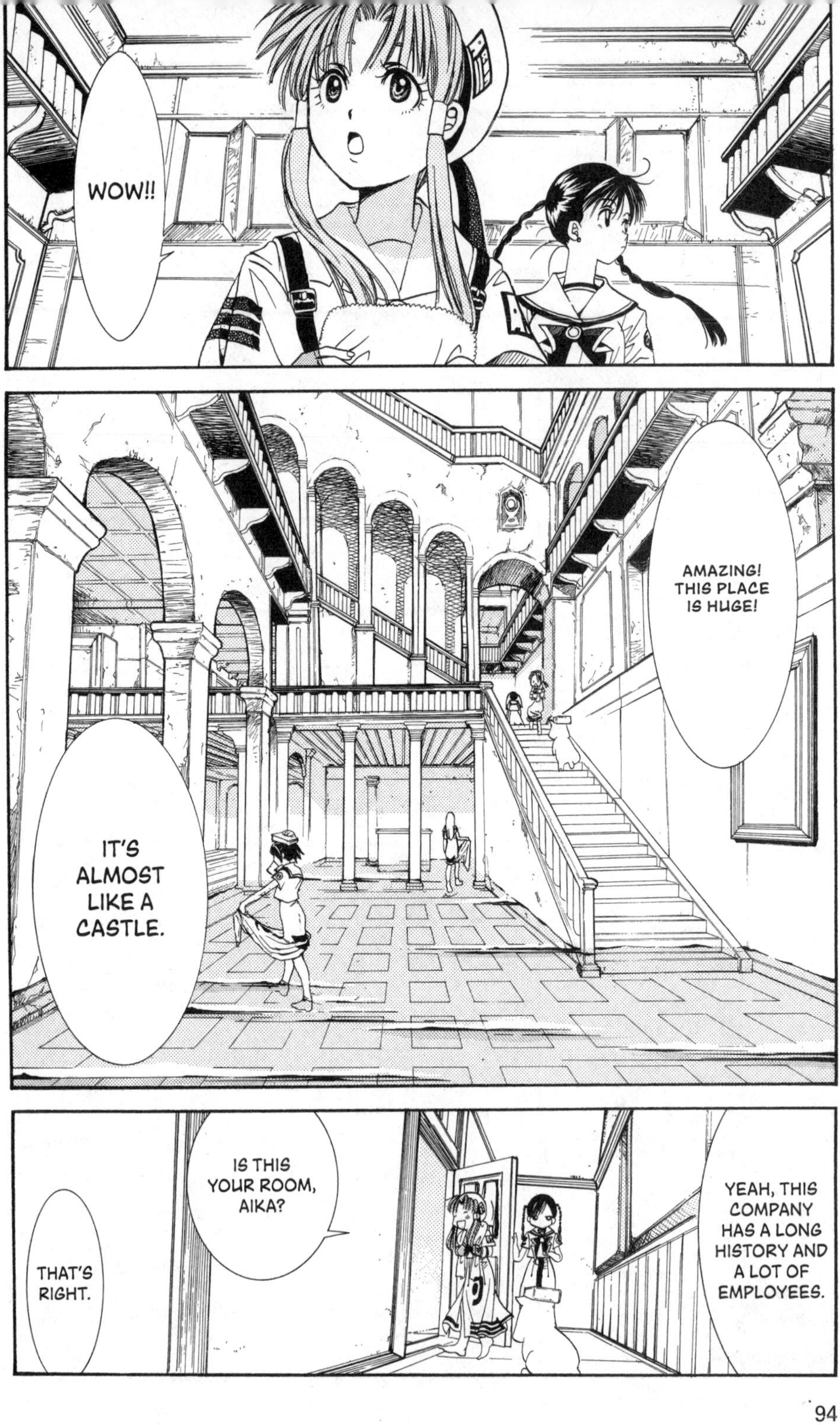
WOW!!
AMAZING! THIS PLACE IS HUGE!
IT'S ALMOST LIKE A CASTLE.
YEAH, THIS COMPANY HAS A LONG HISTORY AND A LOT OF EMPLOYEES.
IS THIS YOUR ROOM, AIKA?
THAT'S RIGHT.

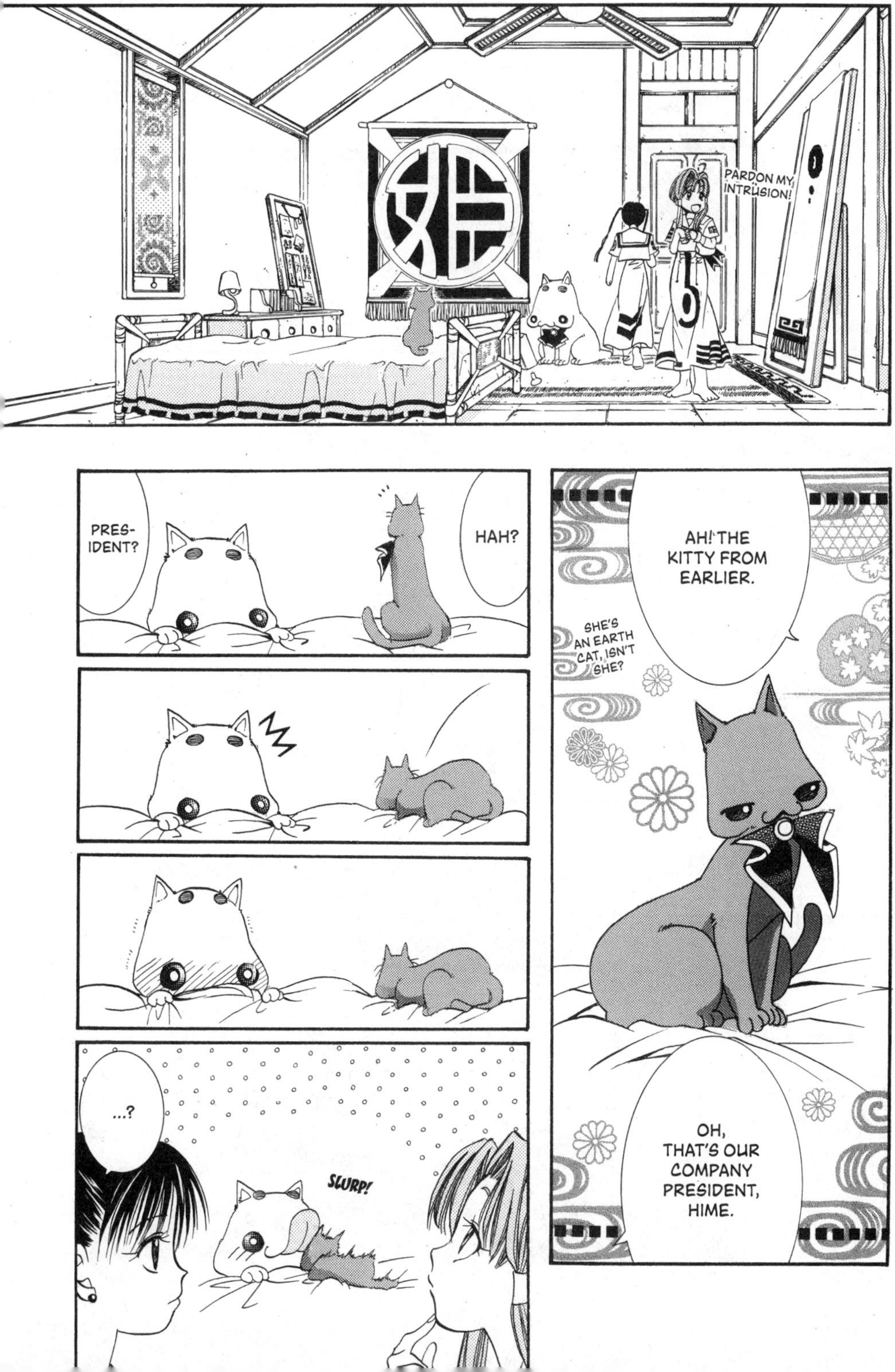
PARDON MY INTRUSION!
AH! THE KITTY FROM EARLIER.
SHE'S AN EARTH CAT, ISN'T SHE?
OH, THAT'S OUR COMPANY PRESIDENT, HIME.
HAH?
PRES-IDENT?
...?
SLURP!

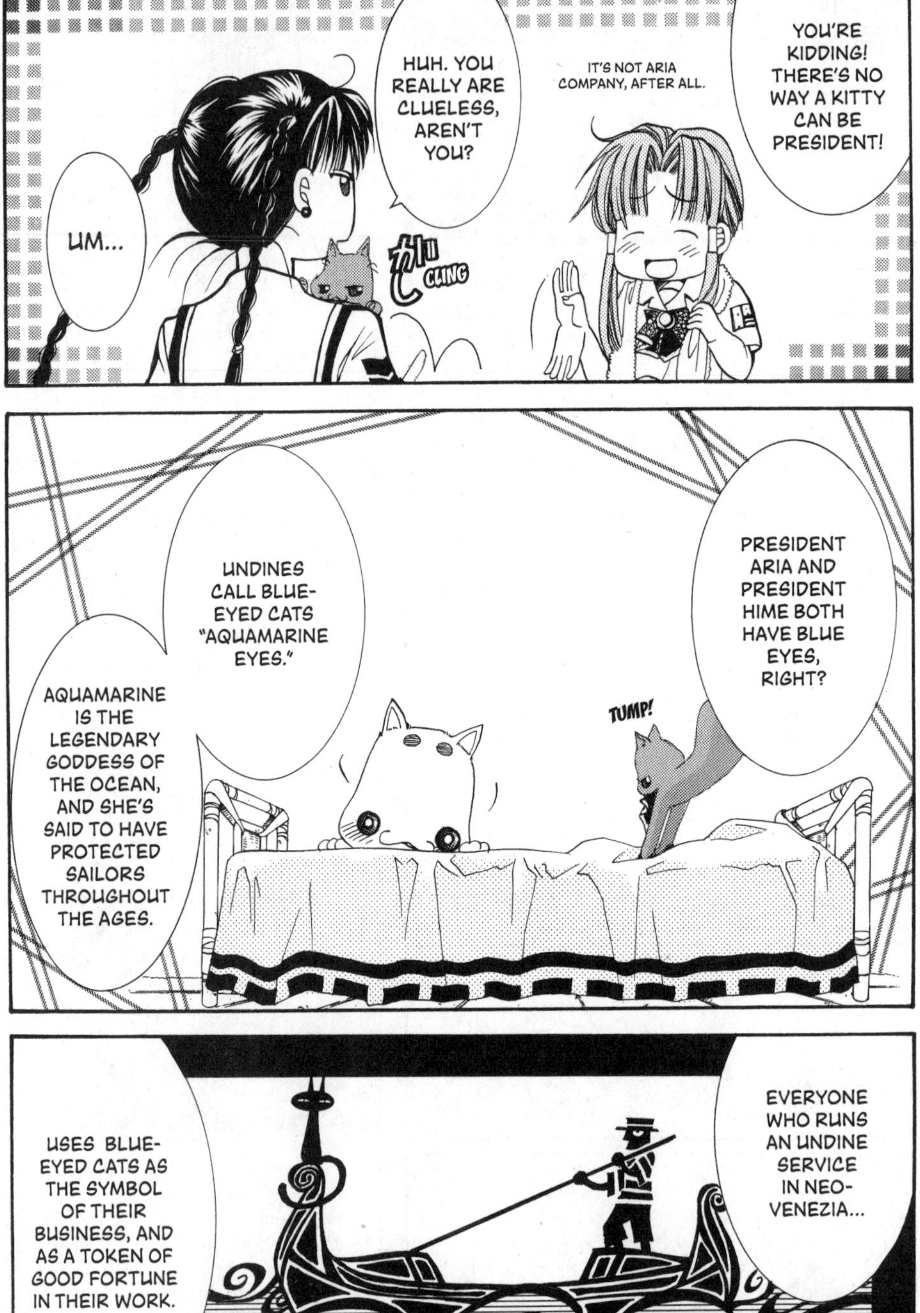
YOU'RE KIDDING! THERE'S NO WAY A KITTY CAN BE PRESIDENT!
IT'S NOT ARIA COMPANY, AFTER ALL.
HUH. YOU REALLY ARE CLUELESS, AREN'T YOU?
CLING
UM...
PRESIDENT ARIA AND PRESIDENT HIME BOTH HAVE BLUE EYES, RIGHT?
TUMP!
UNDINES CALL BLUE-EYED CATS "AQUAMARINE EYES."
AQUAMARINE IS THE LEGENDARY GODDESS OF THE OCEAN, AND SHE'S SAID TO HAVE PROTECTED SAILORS THROUGHOUT THE AGES.
EVERYONE WHO RUNS AN UNDINE SERVICE IN NEO-VENEZIA...
USES BLUE-EYED CATS AS THE SYMBOL OF THEIR BUSINESS, AND AS A TOKEN OF GOOD FORTUNE IN THEIR WORK.

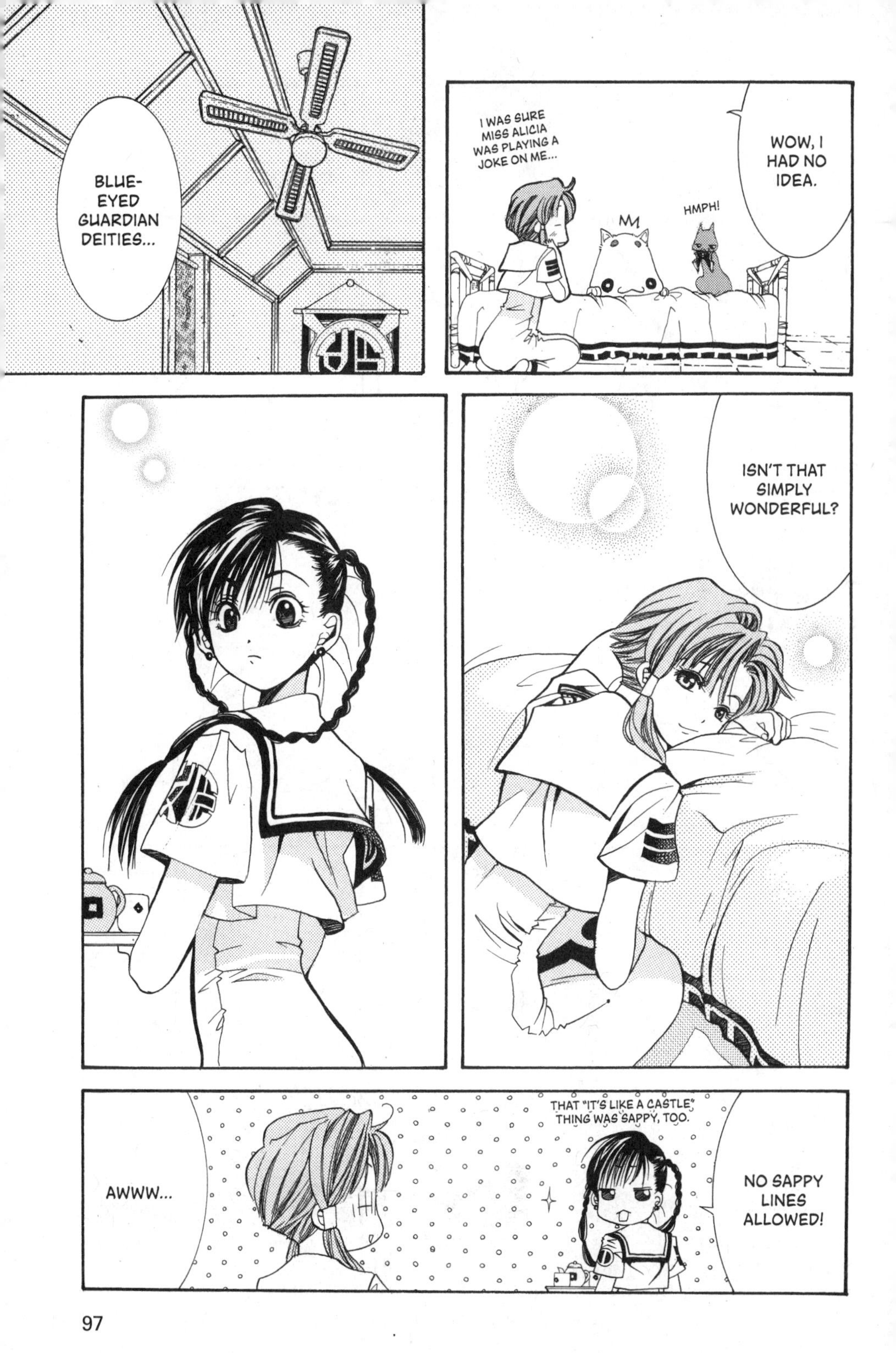
WOW, I HAD NO IDEA.
I WAS SURE MISS ALICIA WAS PLAYING A JOKE ON ME...
HMPH!
BLUE-EYED GUARDIAN DEITIES...
ISN'T THAT SIMPLY WONDERFUL?
NO SAPPY LINES ALLOWED!
THAT "IT'S LIKE A CASTLE" THING WAS SAPPY, TOO.
AWWW...

OKAY, I'LL HELP!

I WAS ABOUT TO MAKE DINNER. WANT TO EAT BEFORE YOU GO?

THANKS. THAT'D BE GREAT.

GURGLE

SORRY TO KEEP YOU WAITING!

HERE WE GO!

THOK

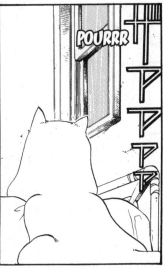

POURRR

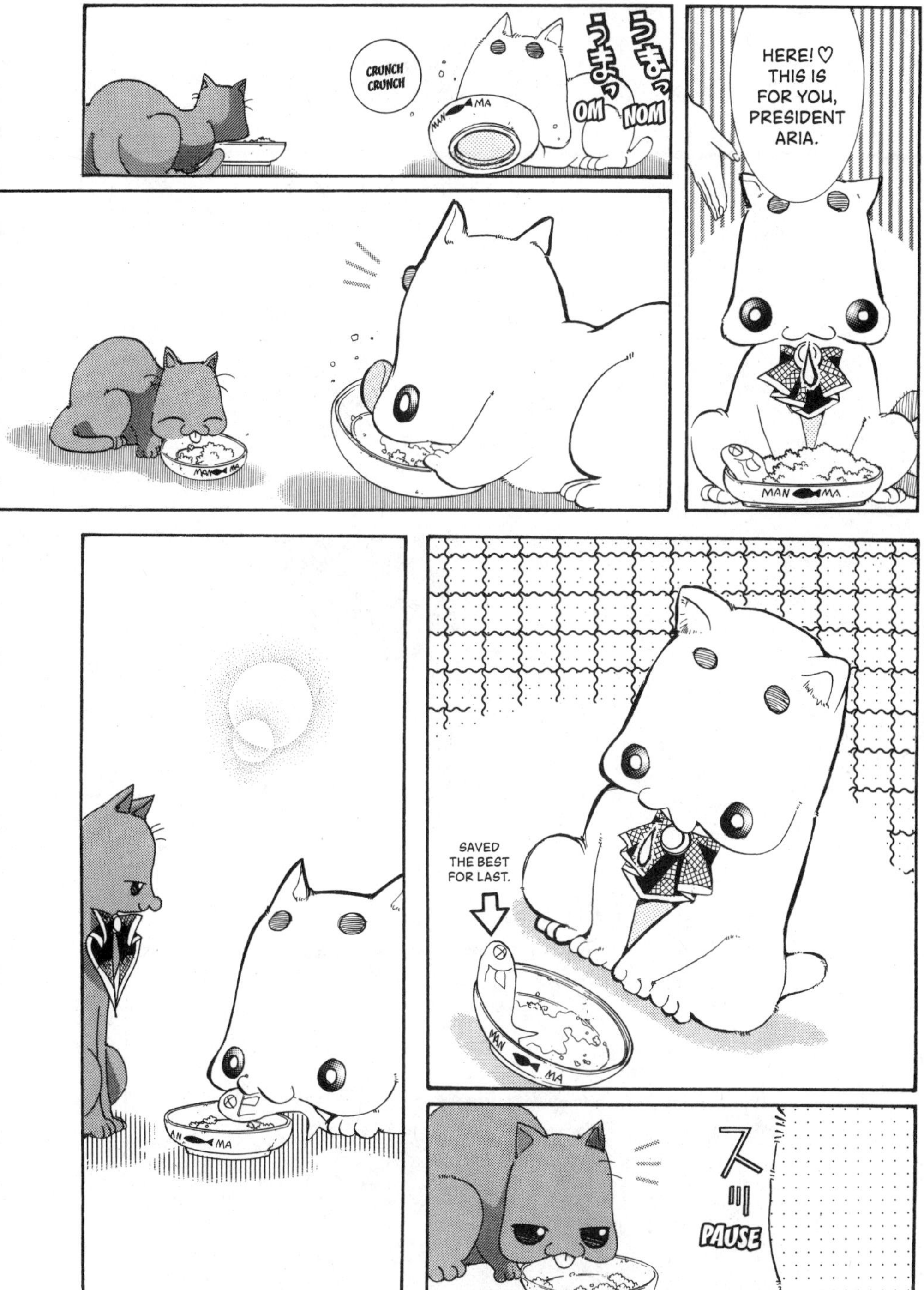
HERE! ♡ THIS IS FOR YOU, PRESIDENT ARIA.
うまっ うまっ
NOM OM
CRUNCH CRUNCH
MAN MA
SAVED THE BEST FOR LAST.
スッ
PAUSE

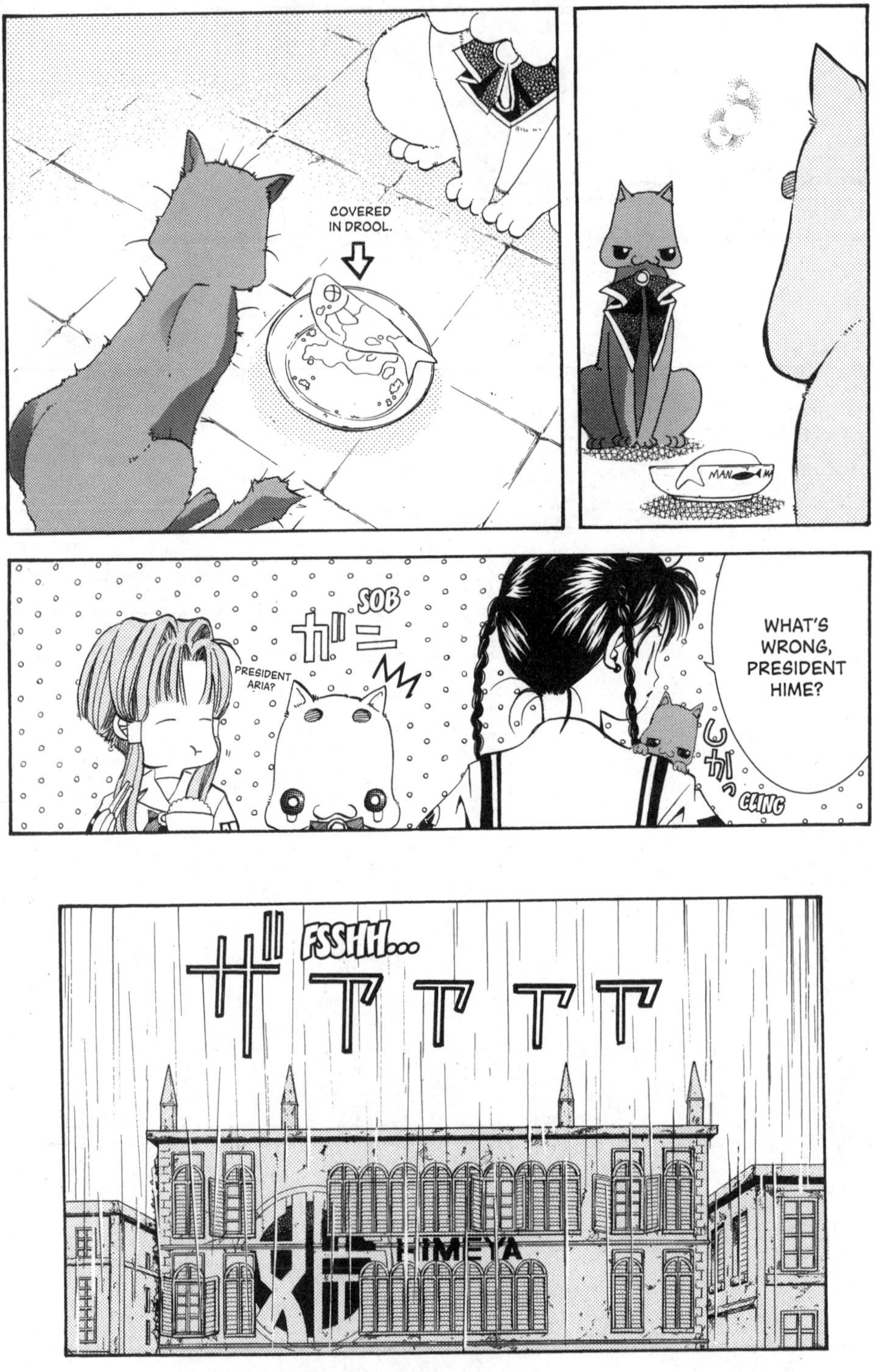
COVERED IN DROOL.
WHAT'S WRONG, PRESIDENT HIME?
CLING
SOB
PRESIDENT ARIA?
FSSHH...
ザァァァァ
HIMEYA

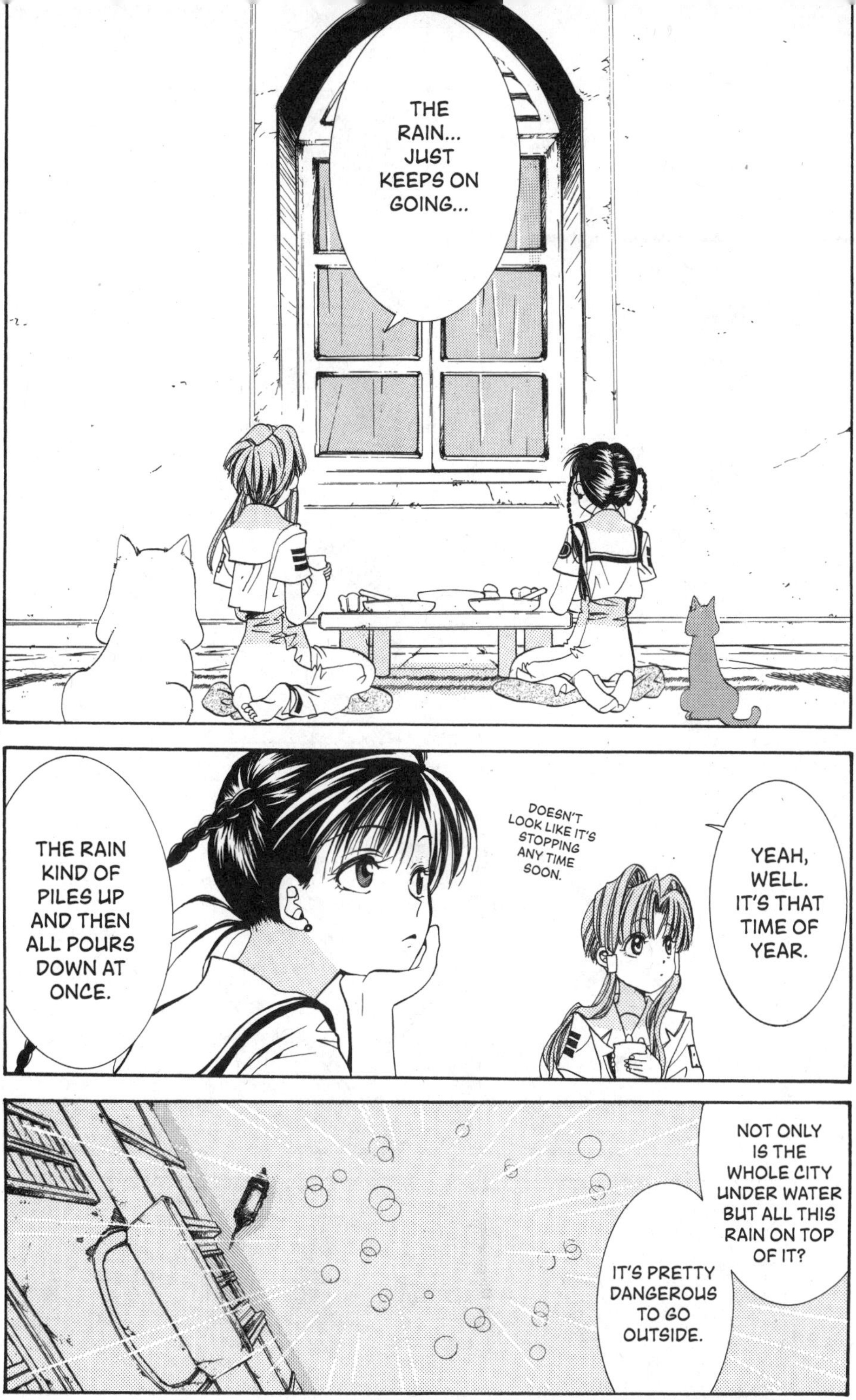
THE RAIN... JUST KEEPS ON GOING...
YEAH, WELL. IT'S THAT TIME OF YEAR.
DOESN'T LOOK LIKE IT'S STOPPING ANY TIME SOON.
THE RAIN KIND OF PILES UP AND THEN ALL POURS DOWN AT ONCE.
NOT ONLY IS THE WHOLE CITY UNDER WATER BUT ALL THIS RAIN ON TOP OF IT?
IT'S PRETTY DANGEROUS TO GO OUTSIDE.

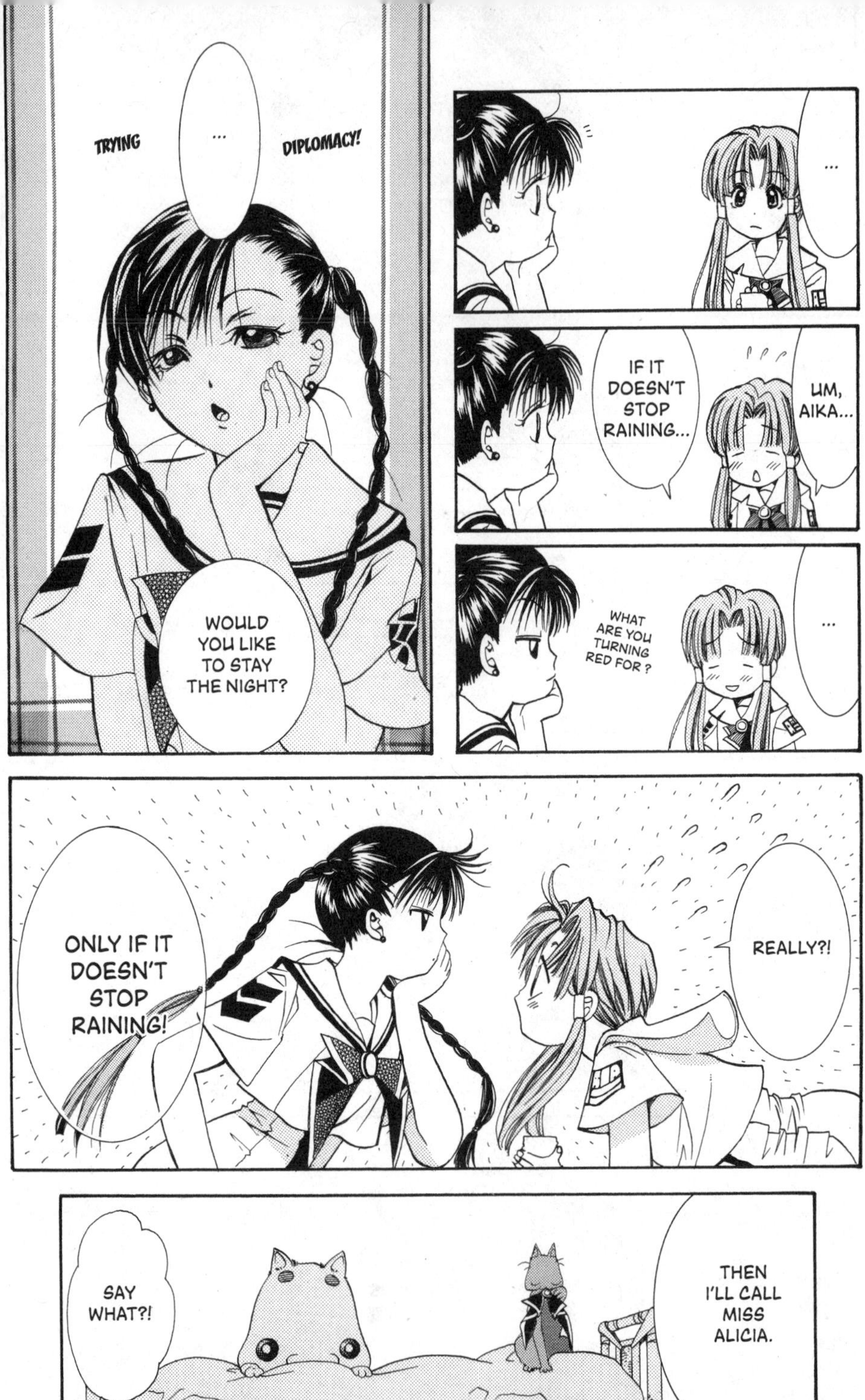
...
UM, AIKA...
IF IT DOESN'T STOP RAINING...
...
WHAT ARE YOU TURNING RED FOR ?
...
TRYING DIPLOMACY!
WOULD YOU LIKE TO STAY THE NIGHT?
REALLY?!
ONLY IF IT DOESN'T STOP RAINING!
THEN I'LL CALL MISS ALICIA.
SAY WHAT?!

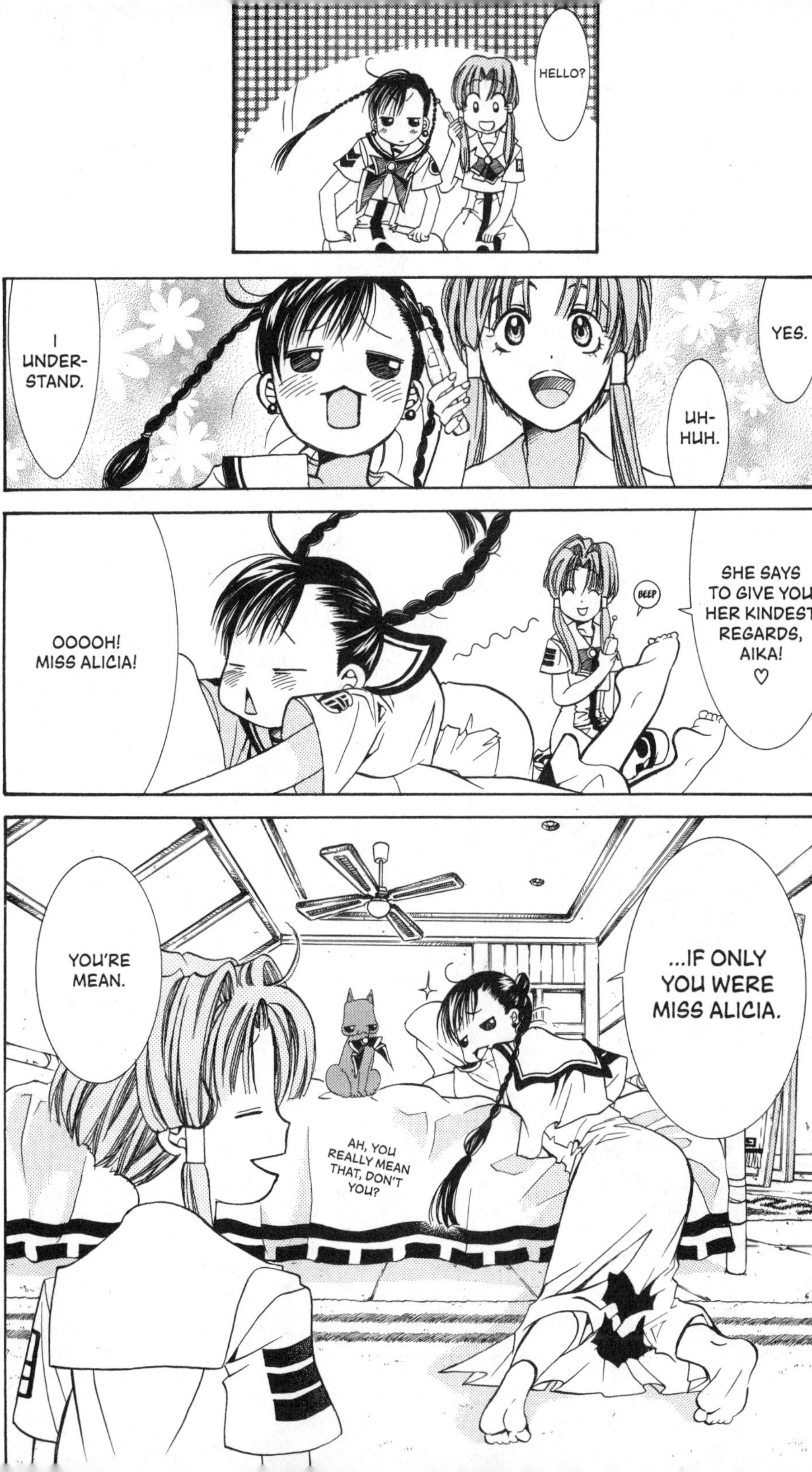
HELLO?
YES.
UH-HUH.
I UNDER-STAND.
SHE SAYS TO GIVE YOU HER KINDEST REGARDS, AIKA! ♡
BEEP
OOOOH! MISS ALICIA!
...IF ONLY YOU WERE MISS ALICIA.
AH, YOU REALLY MEAN THAT, DON'T YOU?
YOU'RE MEAN.

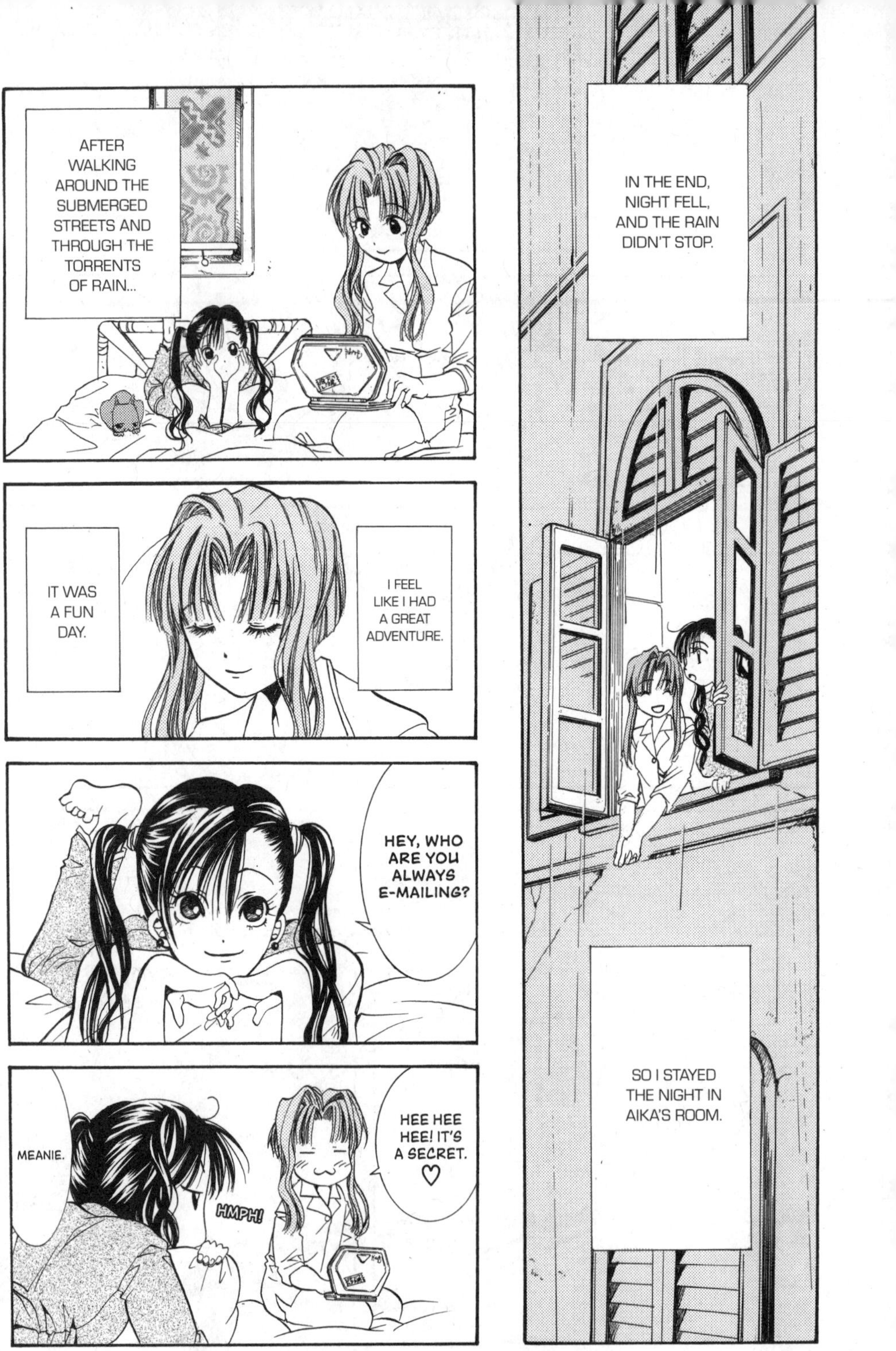
IN THE END, NIGHT FELL, AND THE RAIN DIDN'T STOP.
SO I STAYED THE NIGHT IN AIKA'S ROOM.
AFTER WALKING AROUND THE SUBMERGED STREETS AND THROUGH THE TORRENTS OF RAIN...
I FEEL LIKE I HAD A GREAT ADVENTURE.
IT WAS A FUN DAY.
HEY, WHO ARE YOU ALWAYS E-MAILING?
HEE HEE HEE! IT'S A SECRET. ♡
HMPH!
MEANIE.

FFSSHH

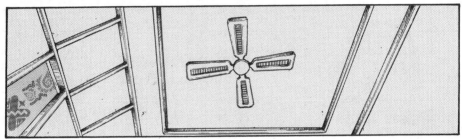

IT'S EXCITING TO SLEEP UNDER AN UNFAMILIAR CEILING.

GOOD NIGHT.

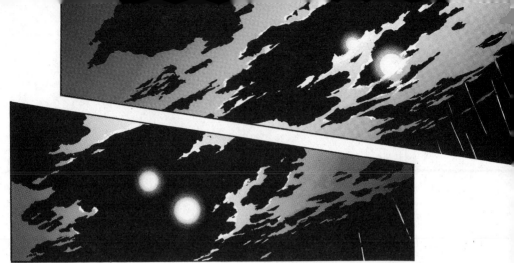

む
く
FWIP

...HUH?

HUH?

THERE'S NO
SOUND OF
RAINDROPS?

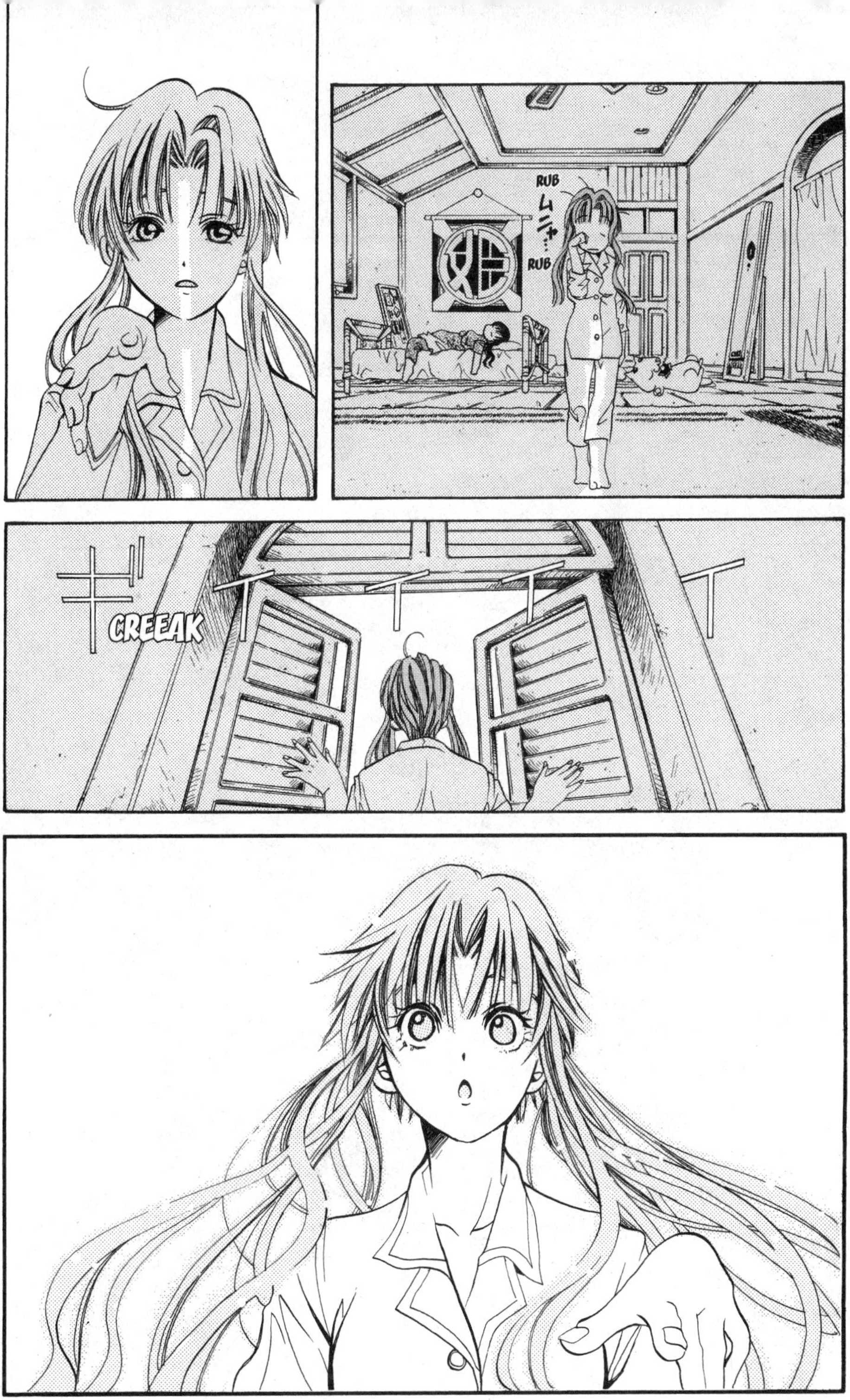
RUB
ムニャ…
RUB
CREEAK

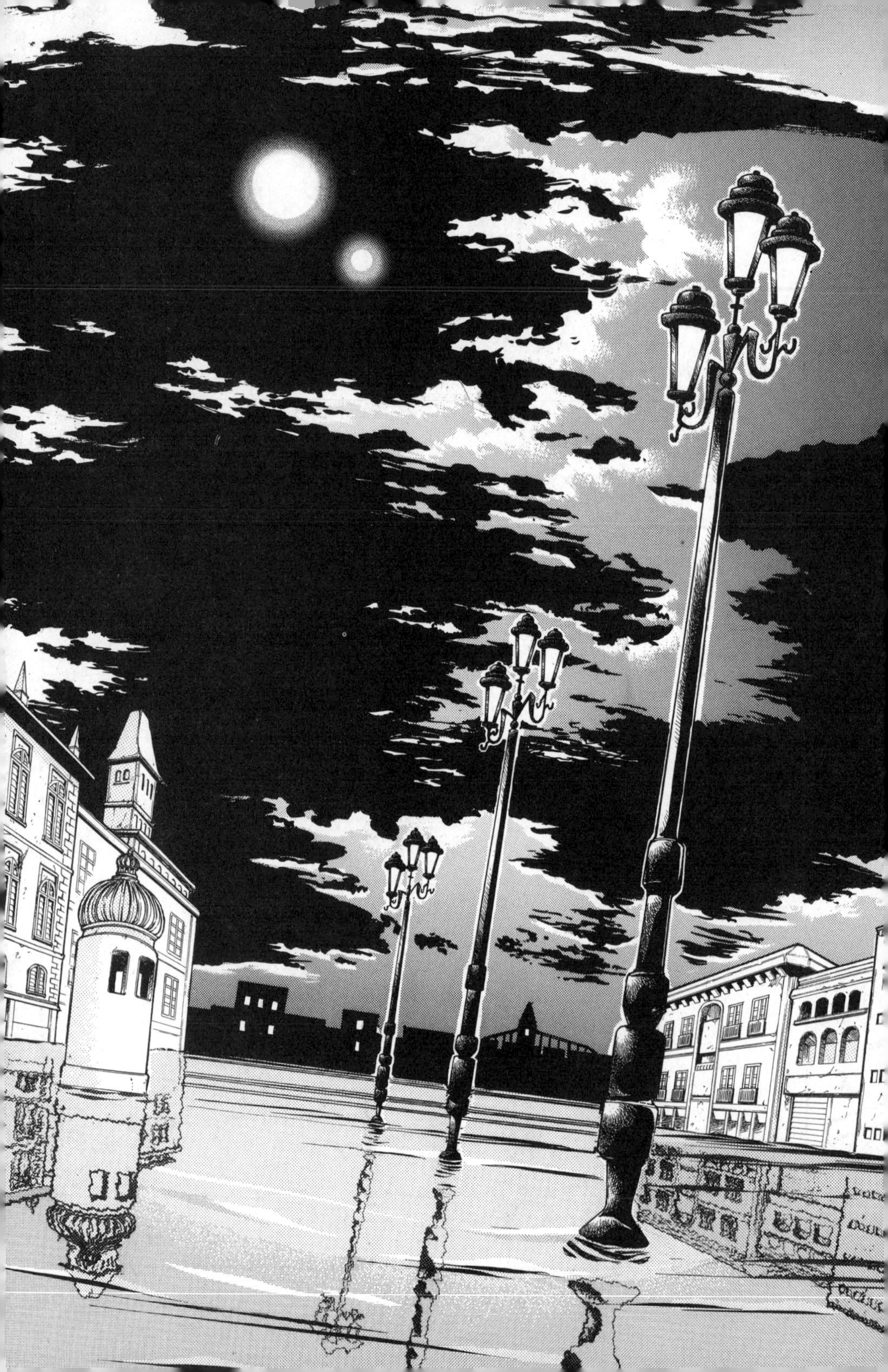

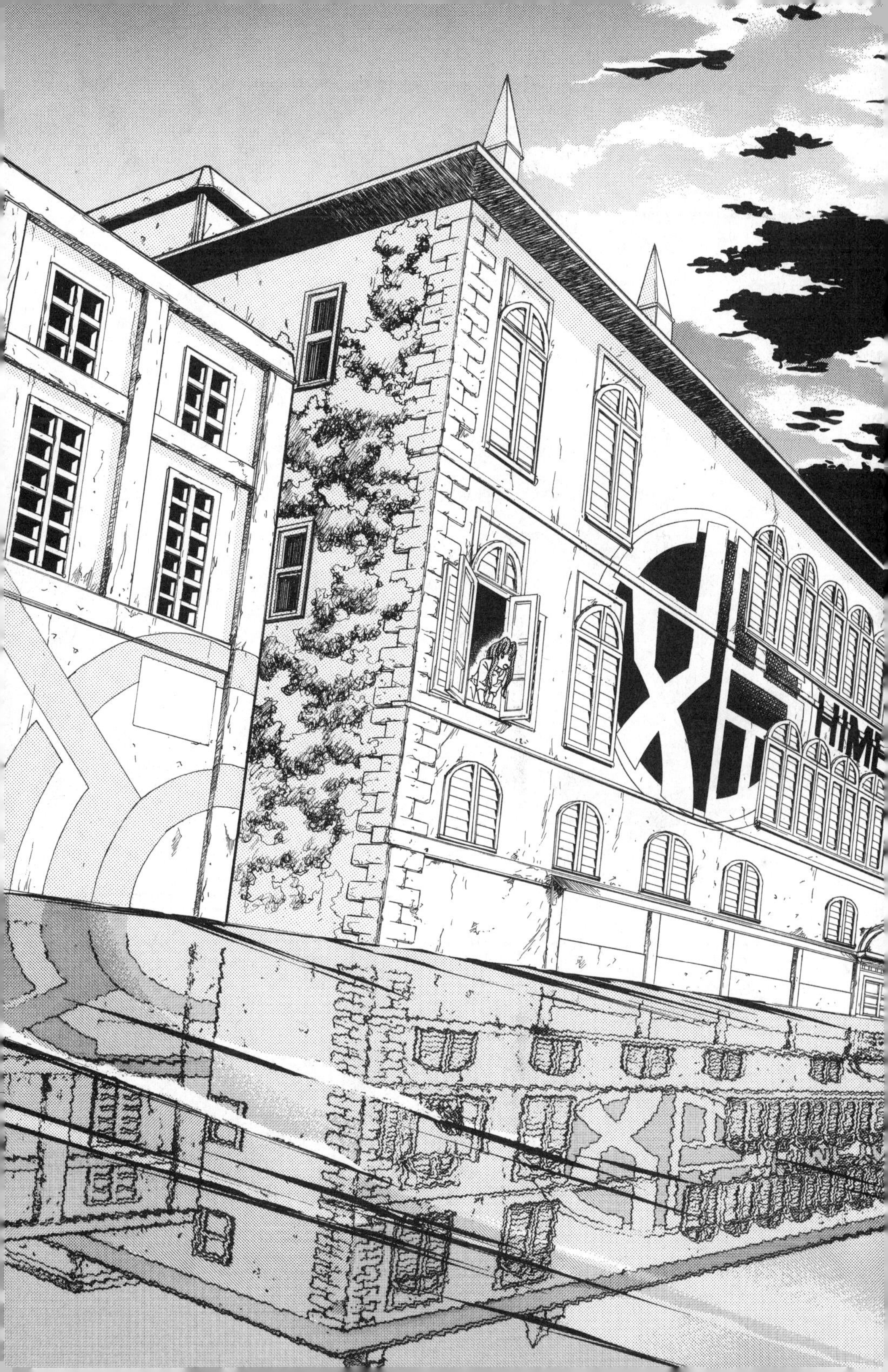
HIME

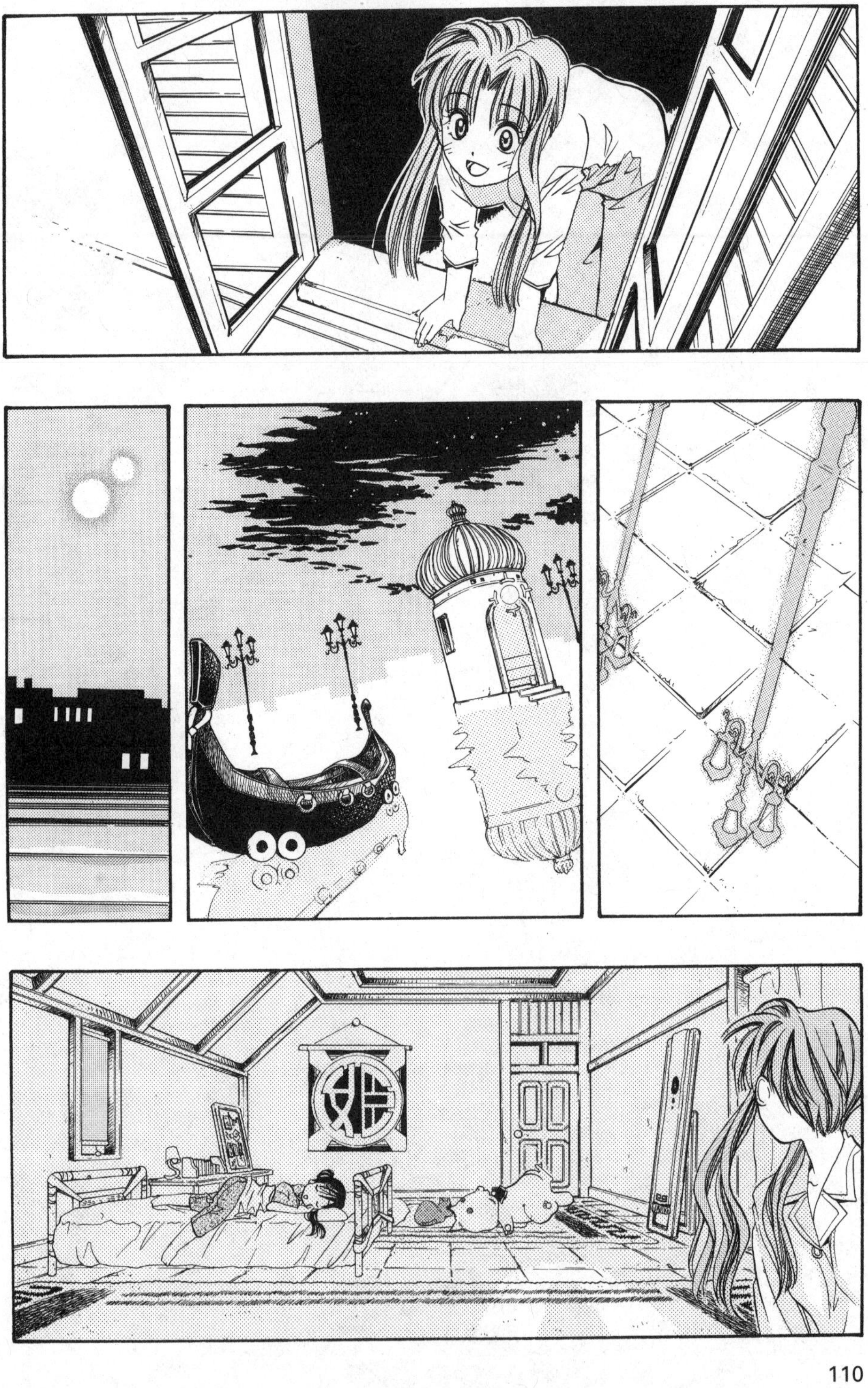

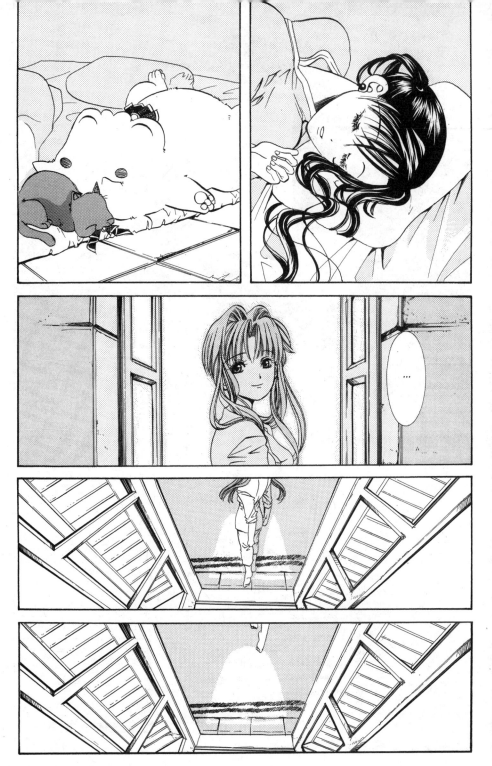

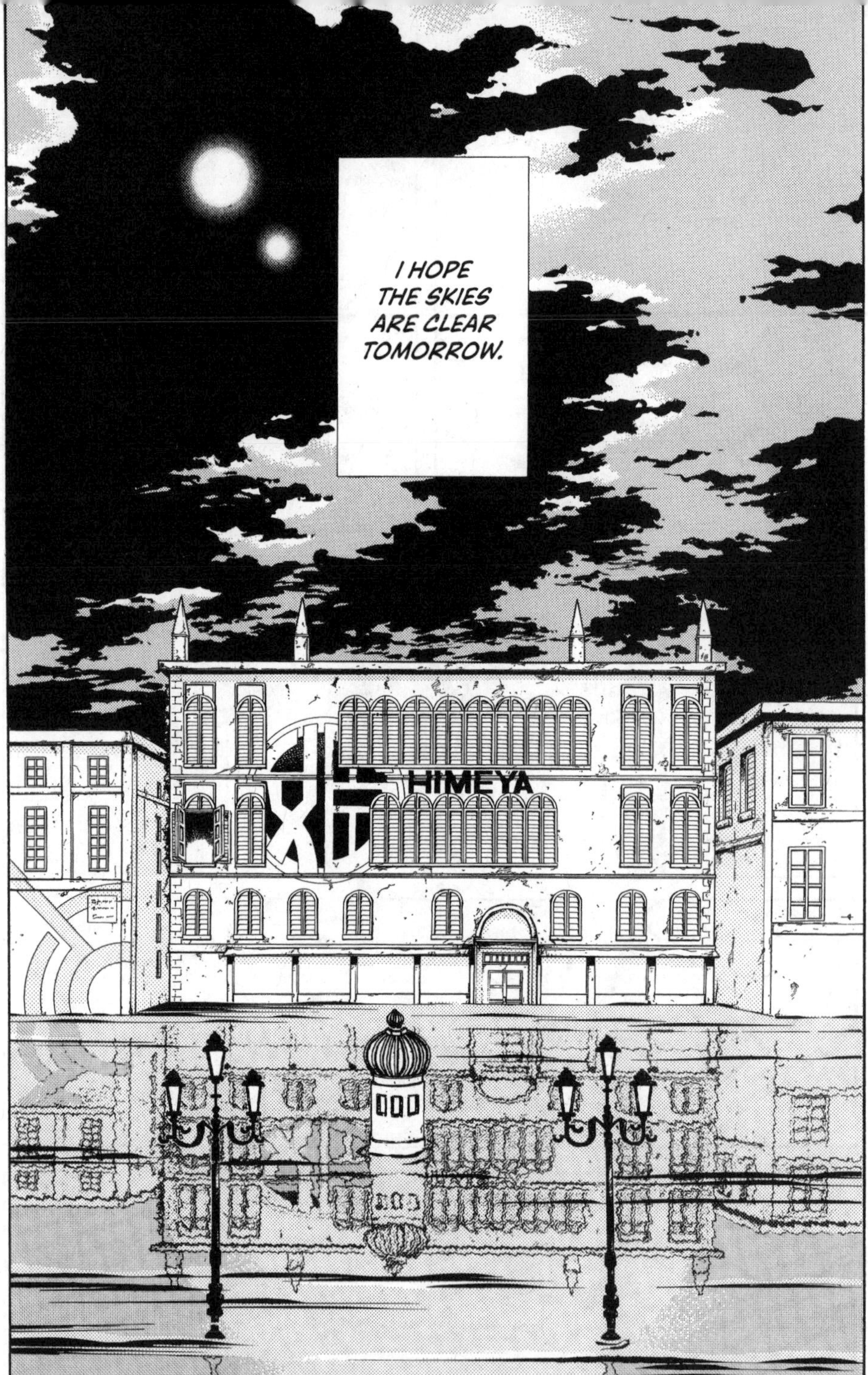
I HOPE THE SKIES ARE CLEAR TOMORROW.
HIMEYA

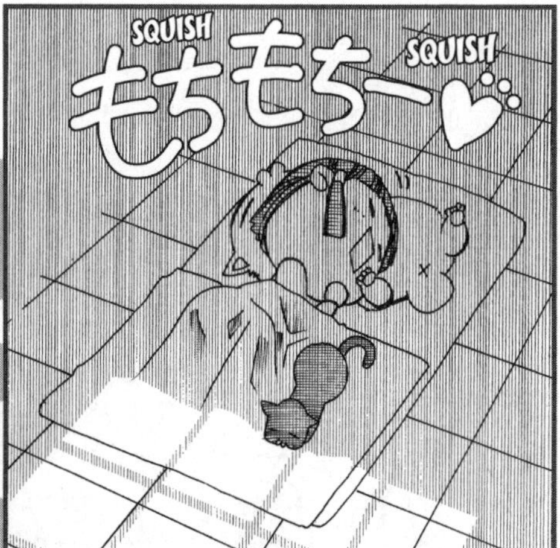
SQUISH
もちもちー
SQUISH

ARIA
The MASTERPIECE

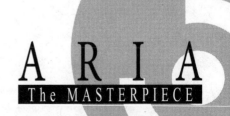

Navigation 04
The Kingdom of Cats

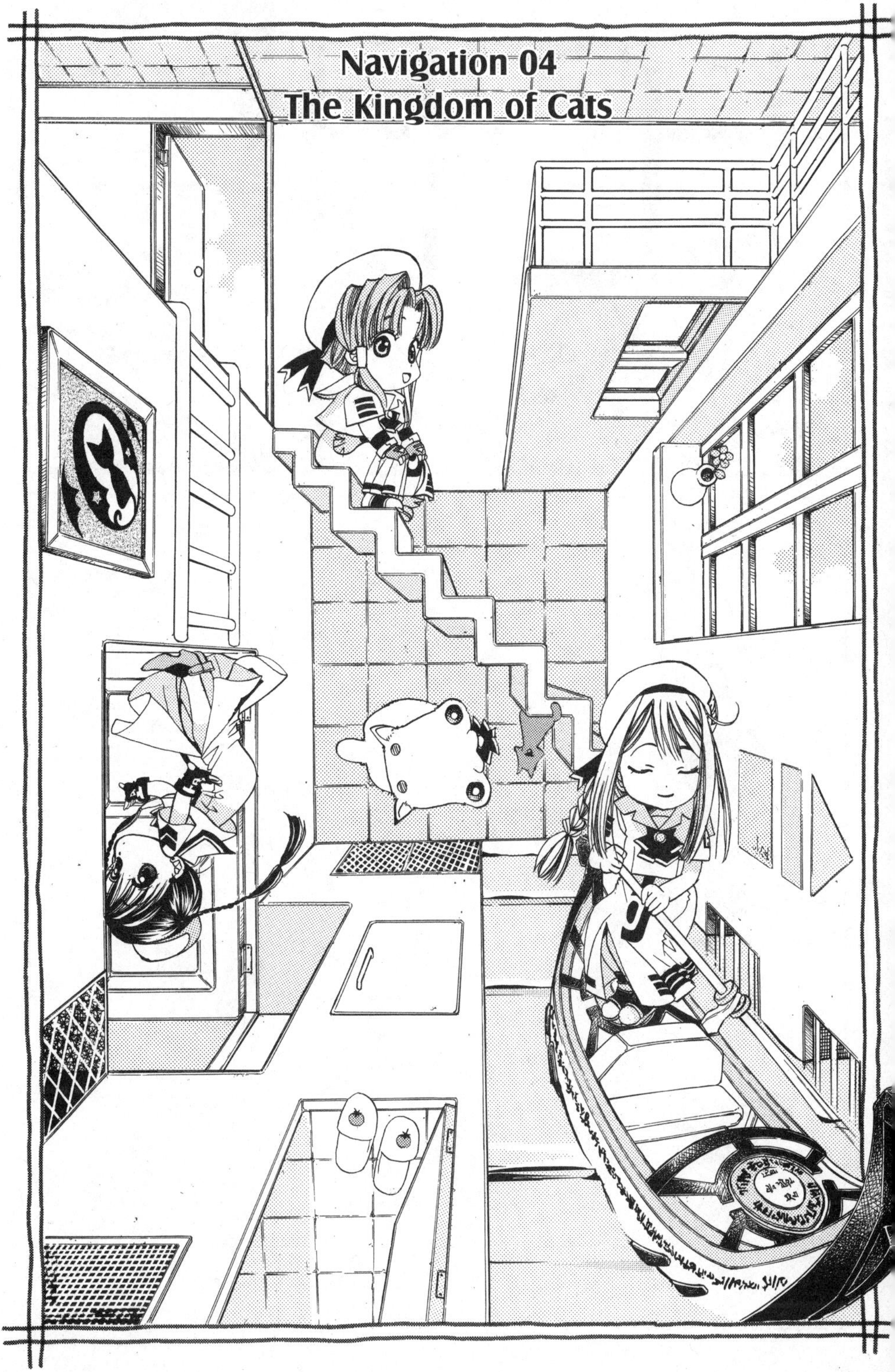

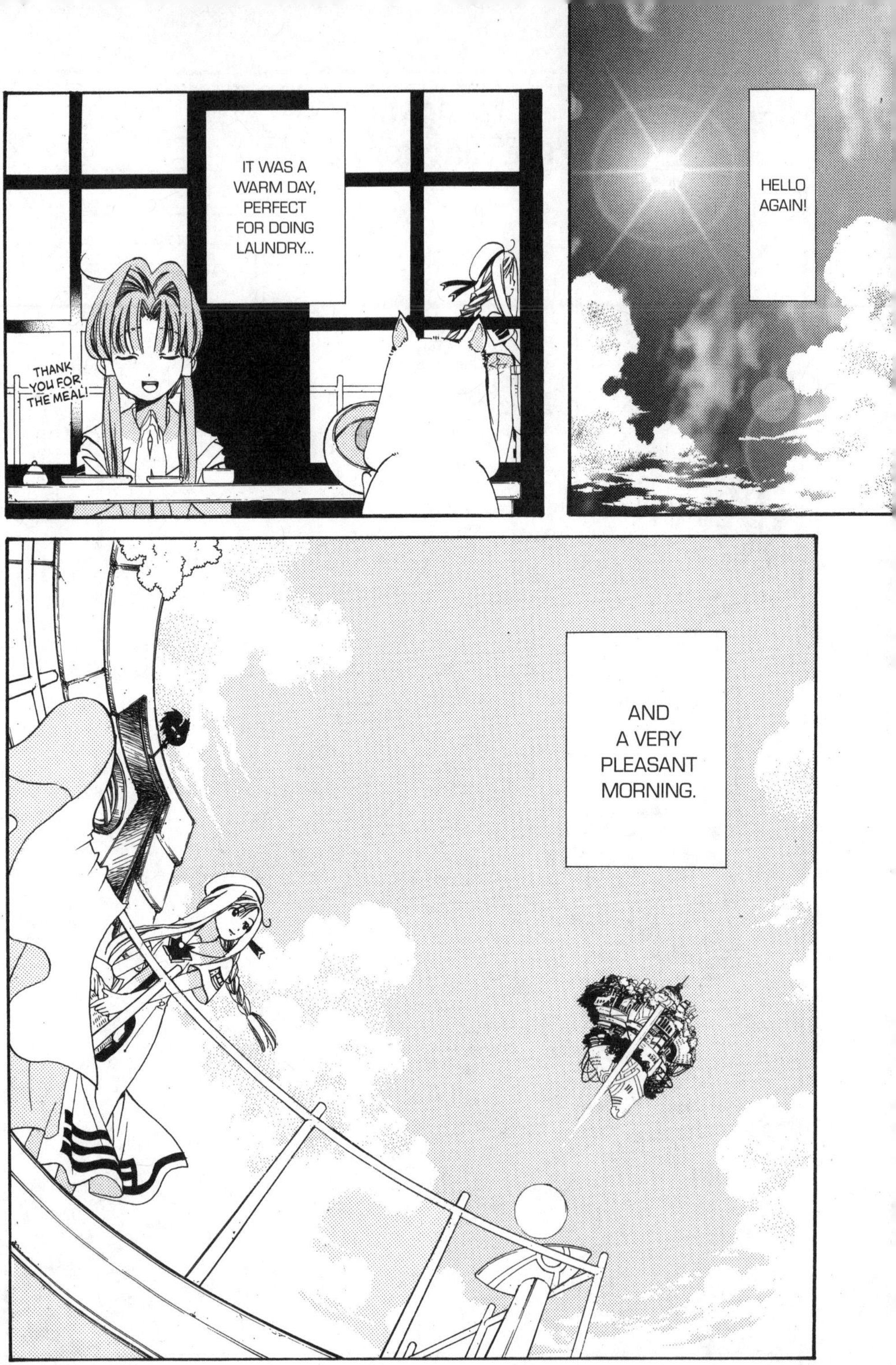
HELLO AGAIN!
IT WAS A WARM DAY, PERFECT FOR DOING LAUNDRY...
THANK YOU FOR THE MEAL!
AND A VERY PLEASANT MORNING.

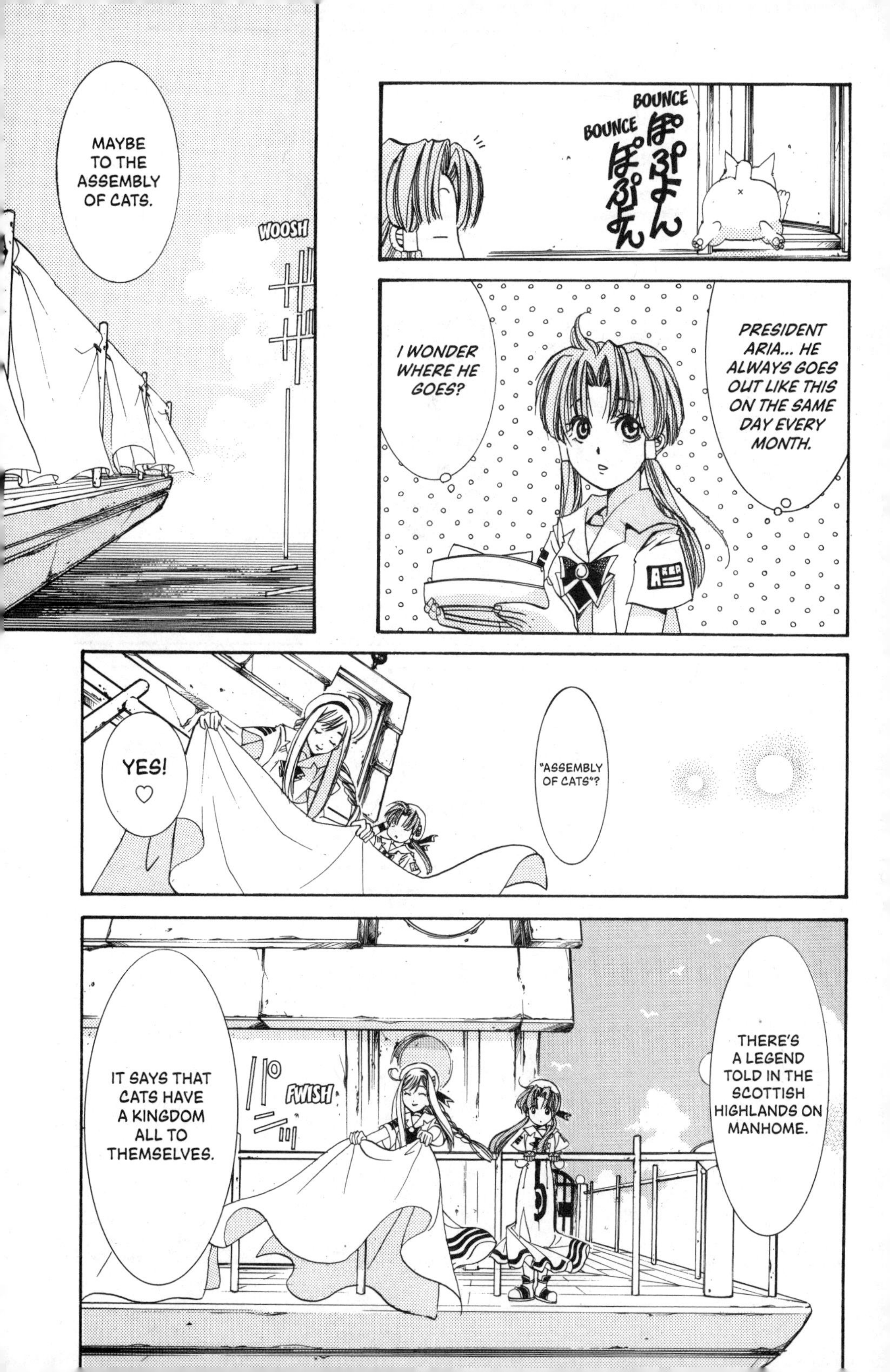
BOUNCE
ぽぷよん
BOUNCE
ぽぷよん
PRESIDENT ARIA... HE ALWAYS GOES OUT LIKE THIS ON THE SAME DAY EVERY MONTH.
I WONDER WHERE HE GOES?
WOOSH
MAYBE TO THE ASSEMBLY OF CATS.
"ASSEMBLY OF CATS"?
YES! ♡
THERE'S A LEGEND TOLD IN THE SCOTTISH HIGHLANDS ON MANHOME.
FWISH
IT SAYS THAT CATS HAVE A KINGDOM ALL TO THEMSELVES.

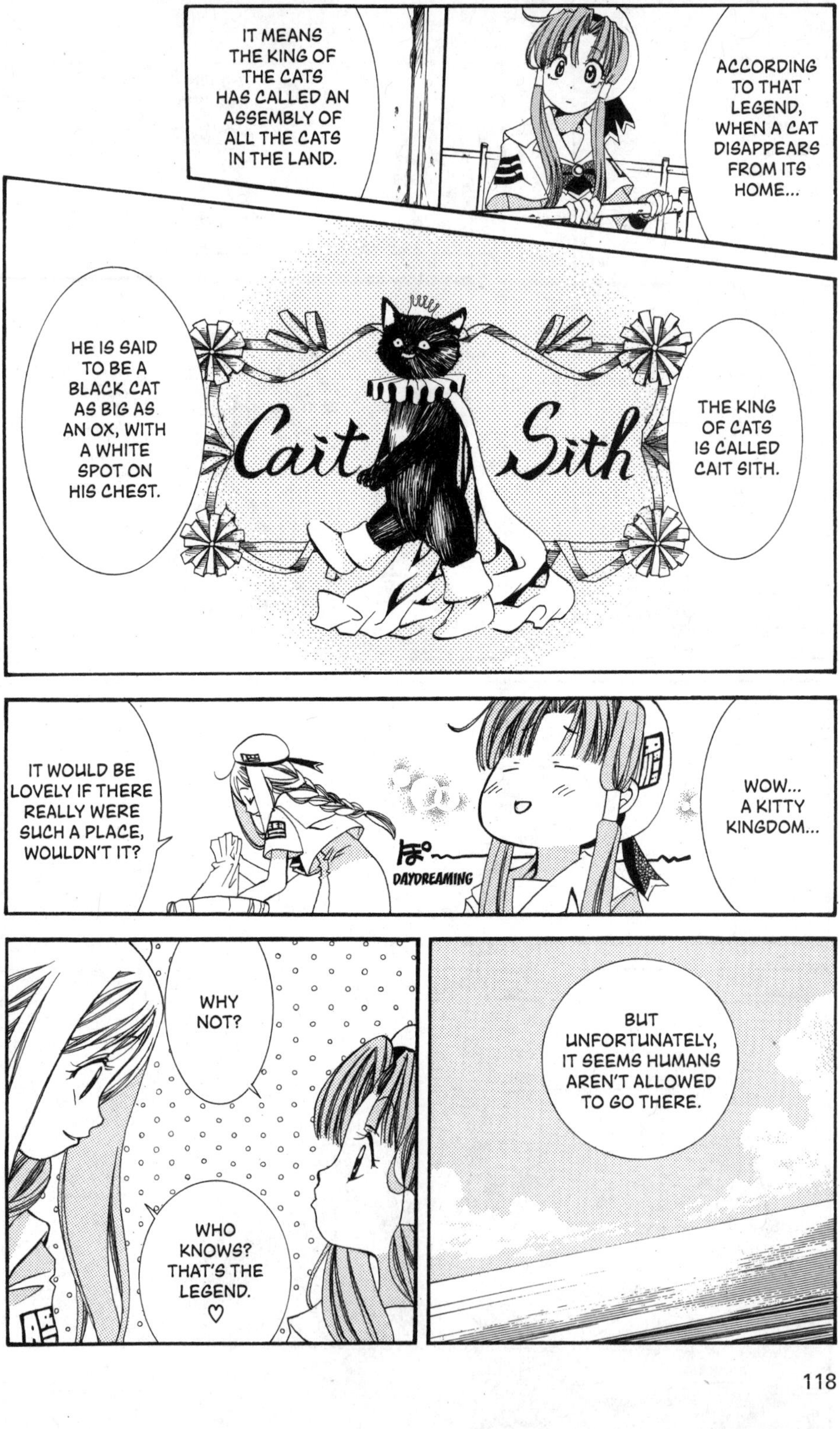
ACCORDING TO THAT LEGEND, WHEN A CAT DISAPPEARS FROM ITS HOME...
IT MEANS THE KING OF THE CATS HAS CALLED AN ASSEMBLY OF ALL THE CATS IN THE LAND.
THE KING OF CATS IS CALLED CAIT SITH.
Cait Sith
HE IS SAID TO BE A BLACK CAT AS BIG AS AN OX, WITH A WHITE SPOT ON HIS CHEST.
WOW... A KITTY KINGDOM...
DAYDREAMING
IT WOULD BE LOVELY IF THERE REALLY WERE SUCH A PLACE, WOULDN'T IT?
BUT UNFORTUNATELY, IT SEEMS HUMANS AREN'T ALLOWED TO GO THERE.
WHY NOT?
WHO KNOWS? THAT'S THE LEGEND. ♡

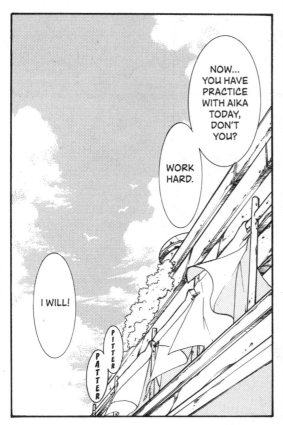

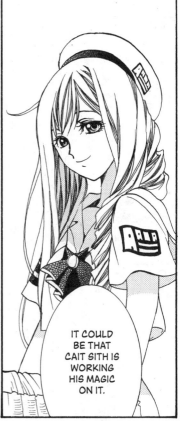

IT COULD BE THAT CAIT SITH IS WORKING HIS MAGIC ON IT.
NOW... YOU HAVE PRACTICE WITH AIKA TODAY, DON'T YOU?
WORK HARD.
I WILL!
PITTER
PATTER
...SO?
SO LET'S FOLLOW PRESIDENT ARIA!
OH, YOU DON'T NEED TO PRACTICE?

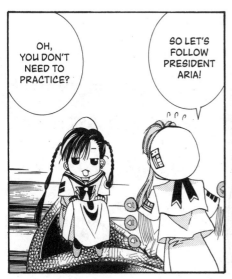

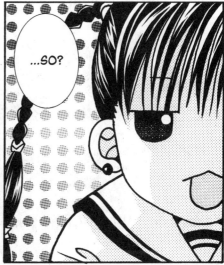

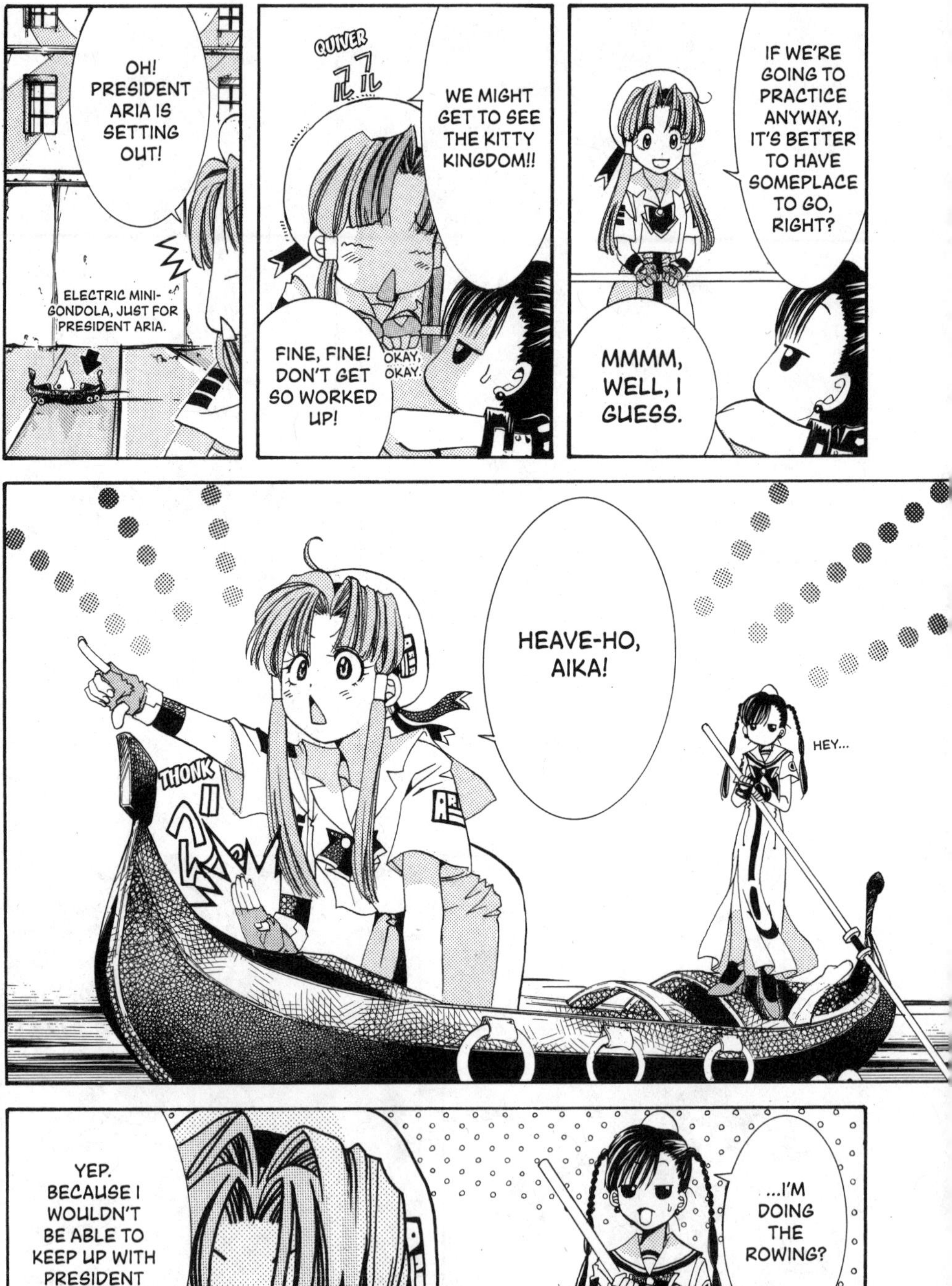
IF WE'RE GOING TO PRACTICE ANYWAY, IT'S BETTER TO HAVE SOMEPLACE TO GO, RIGHT?
MMMM, WELL, I GUESS.
QUIVER
WE MIGHT GET TO SEE THE KITTY KINGDOM!!
OKAY, OKAY.
FINE, FINE! DON'T GET SO WORKED UP!
OH! PRESIDENT ARIA IS SETTING OUT!
ELECTRIC MINI-GONDOLA, JUST FOR PRESIDENT ARIA.
HEAVE-HO, AIKA!
HEY...
THONK
...I'M DOING THE ROWING?
YEP. BECAUSE I WOULDN'T BE ABLE TO KEEP UP WITH PRESIDENT ARIA.

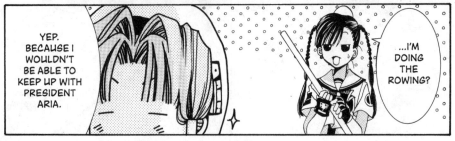

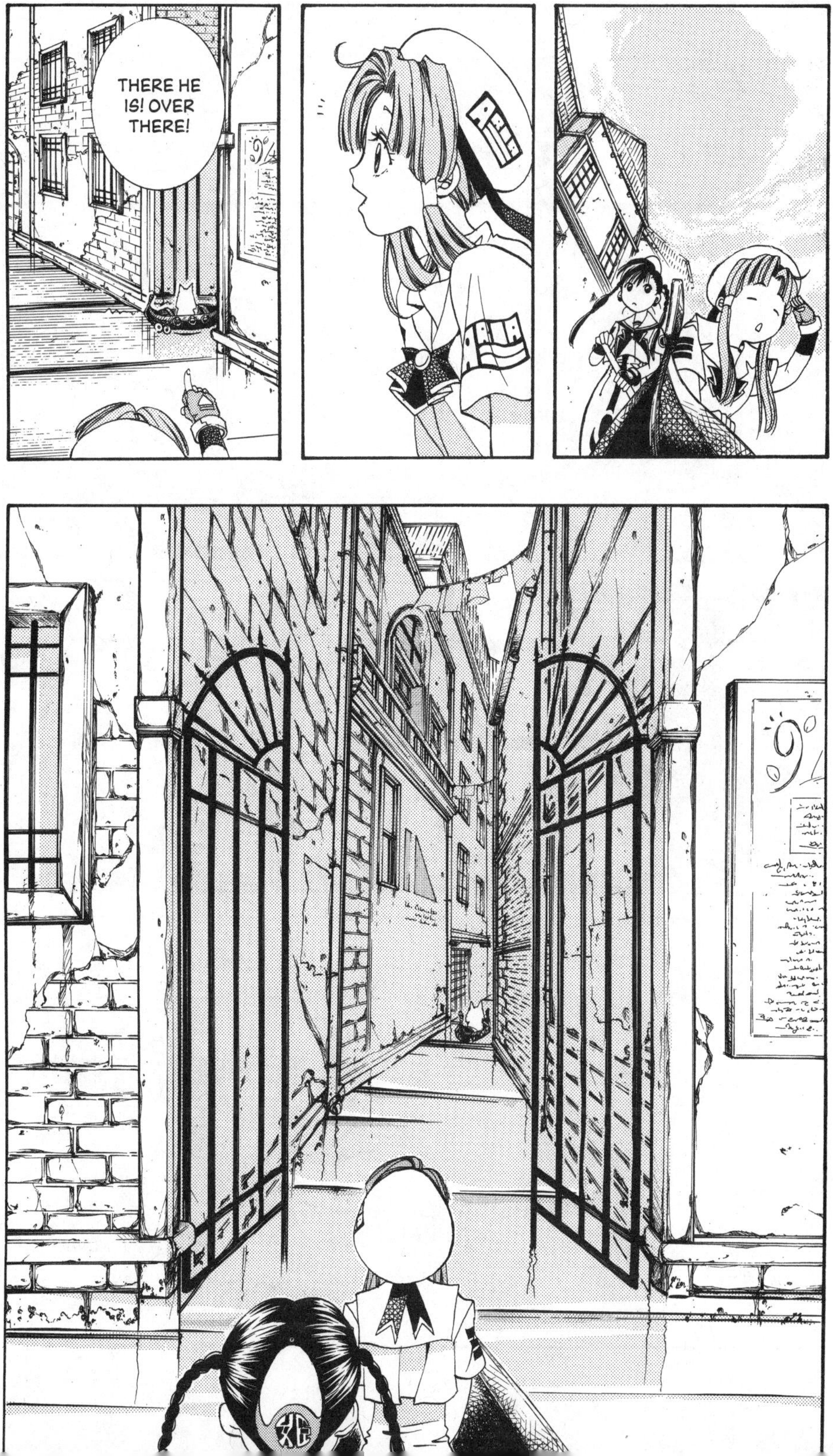
THERE HE IS! OVER THERE!

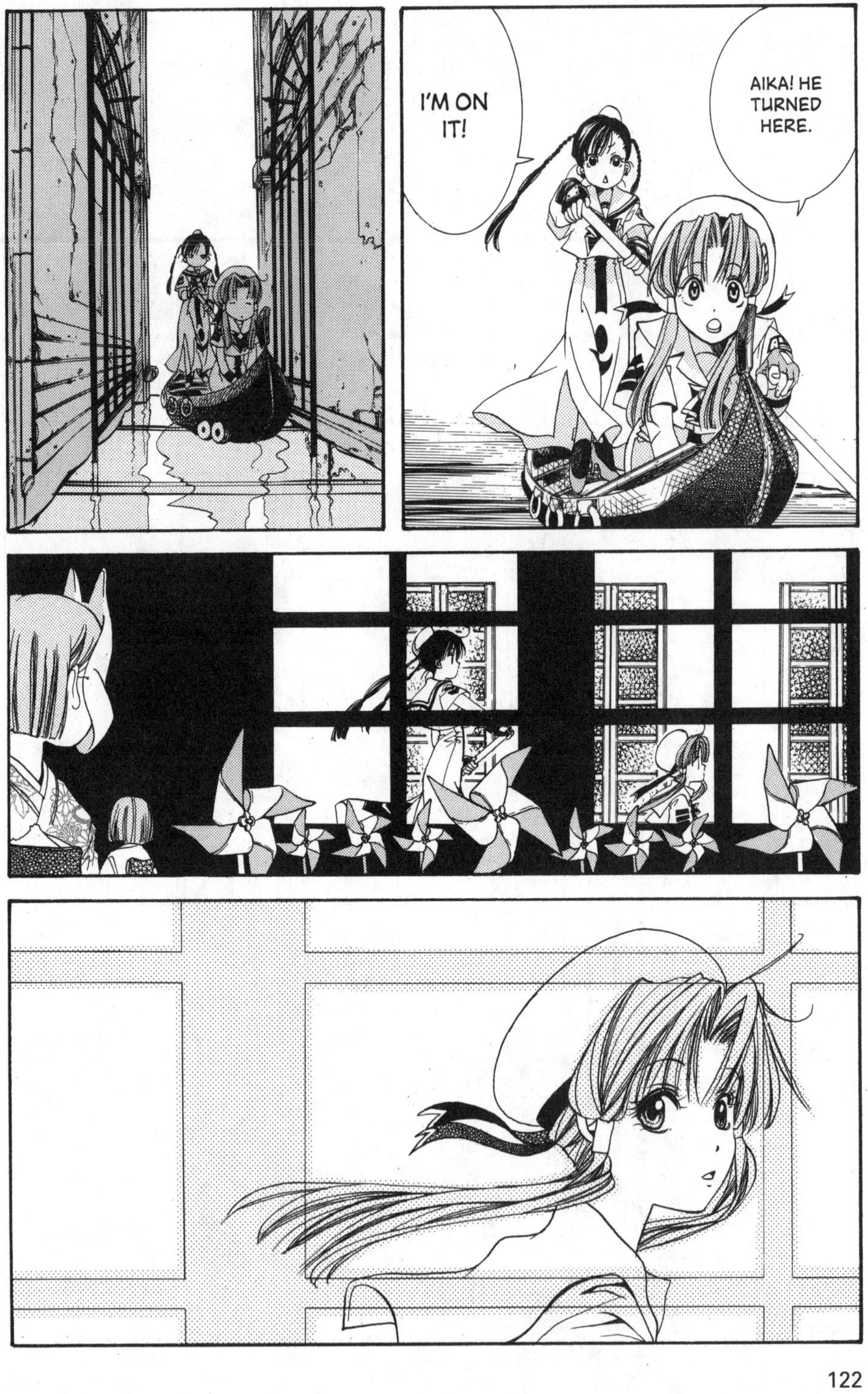
AIKA! HE TURNED HERE.
I'M ON IT!

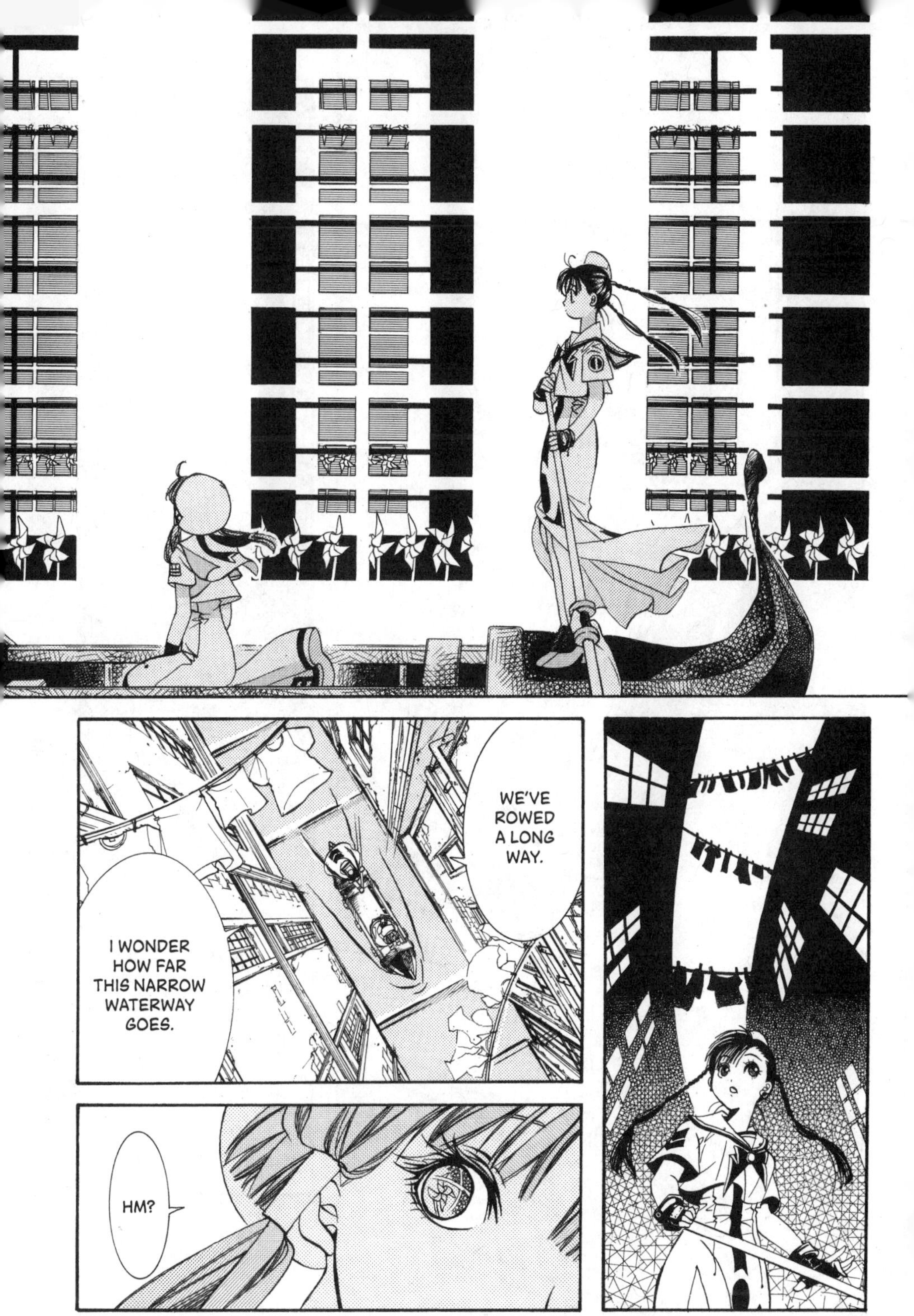
WE'VE ROWED A LONG WAY.
I WONDER HOW FAR THIS NARROW WATERWAY GOES.
HM?

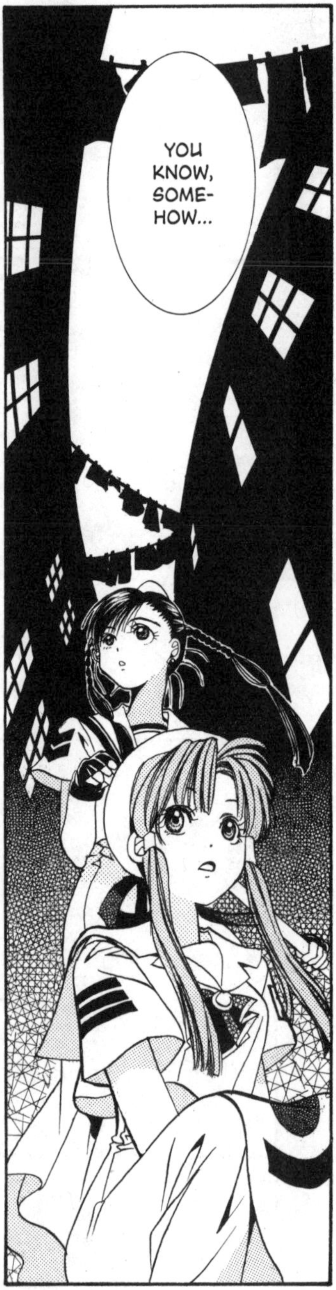
YOU KNOW, SOME-HOW...

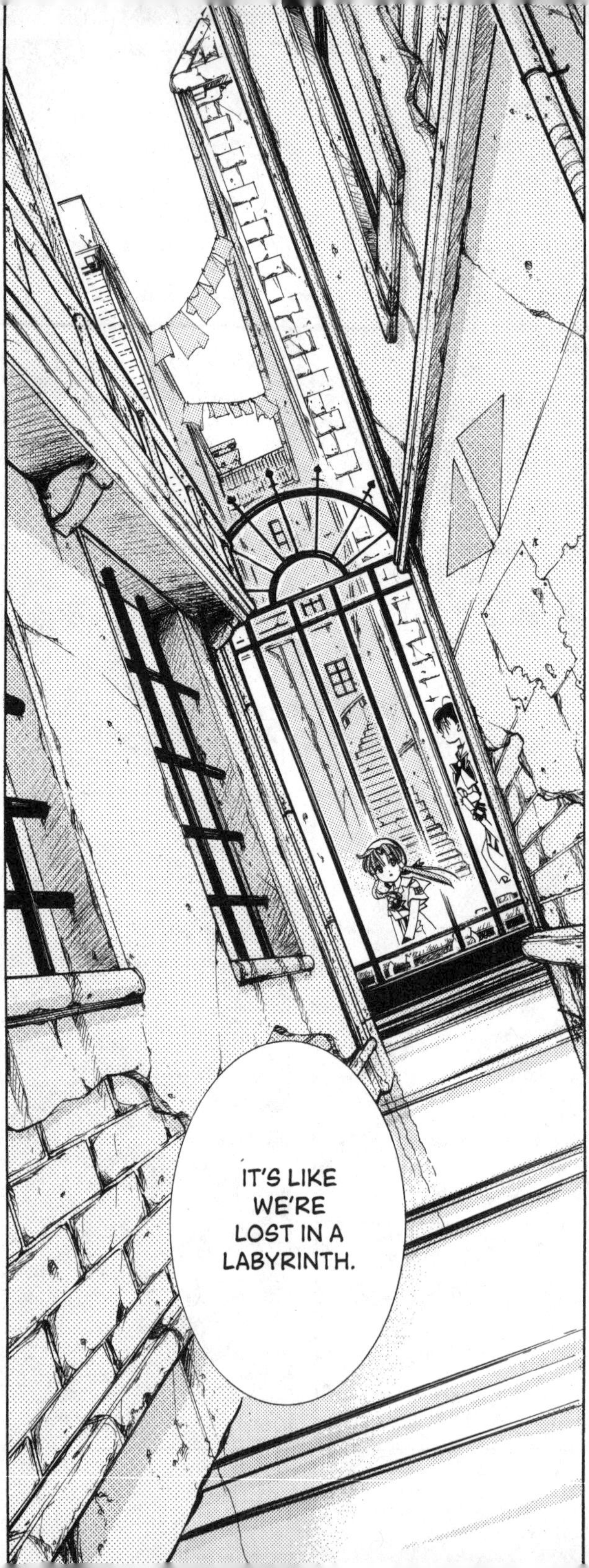
IT'S LIKE WE'RE LOST IN A LABYRINTH.

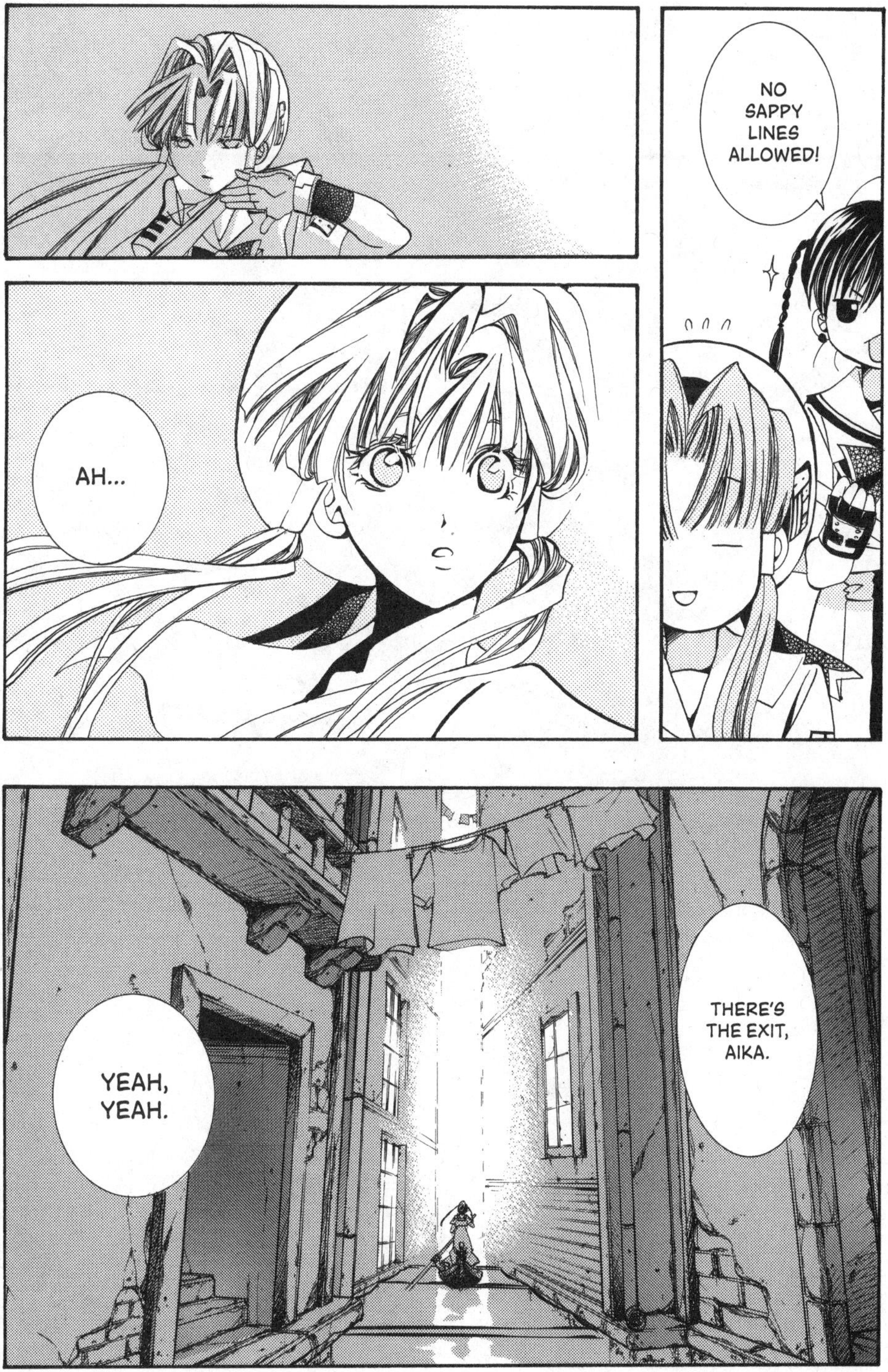
NO SAPPY LINES ALLOWED!
AH...
THERE'S THE EXIT, AIKA.
YEAH, YEAH.

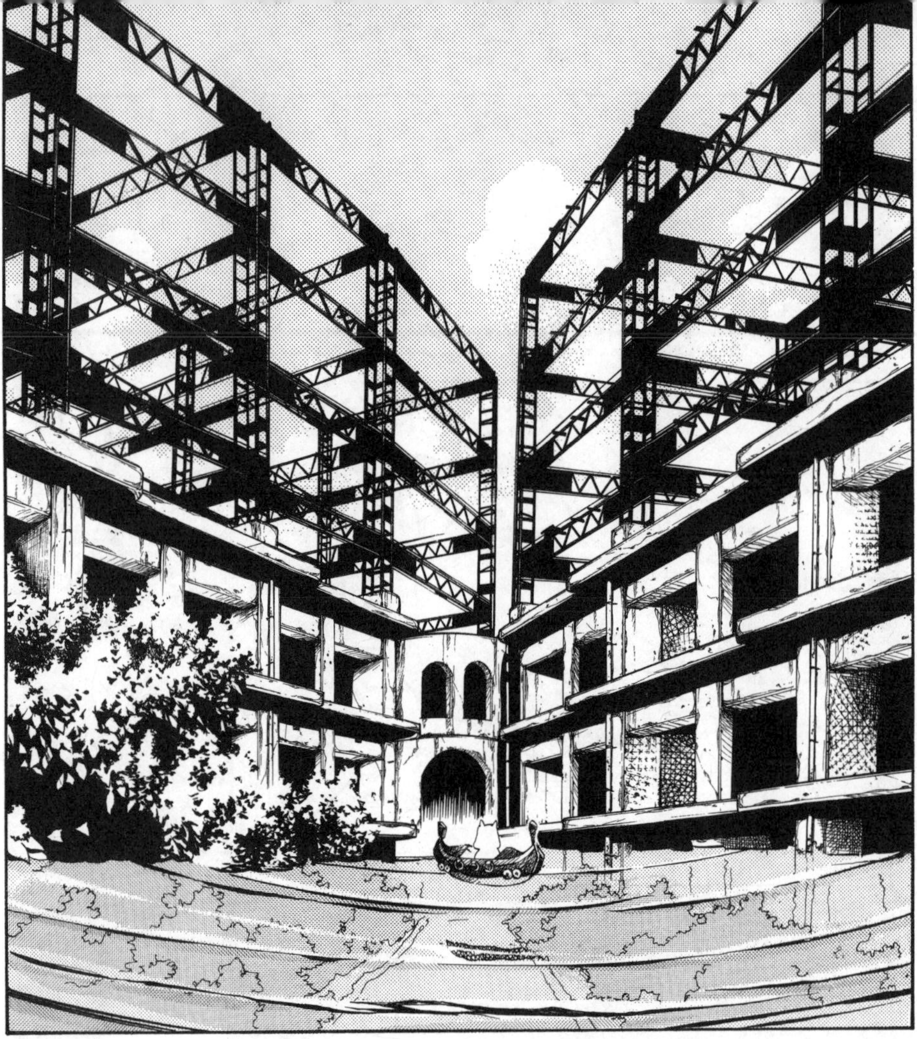

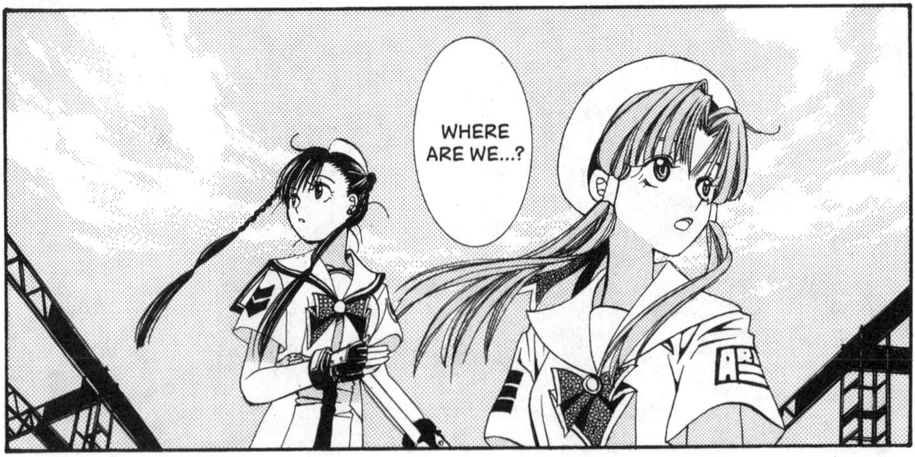
WHERE ARE WE...?

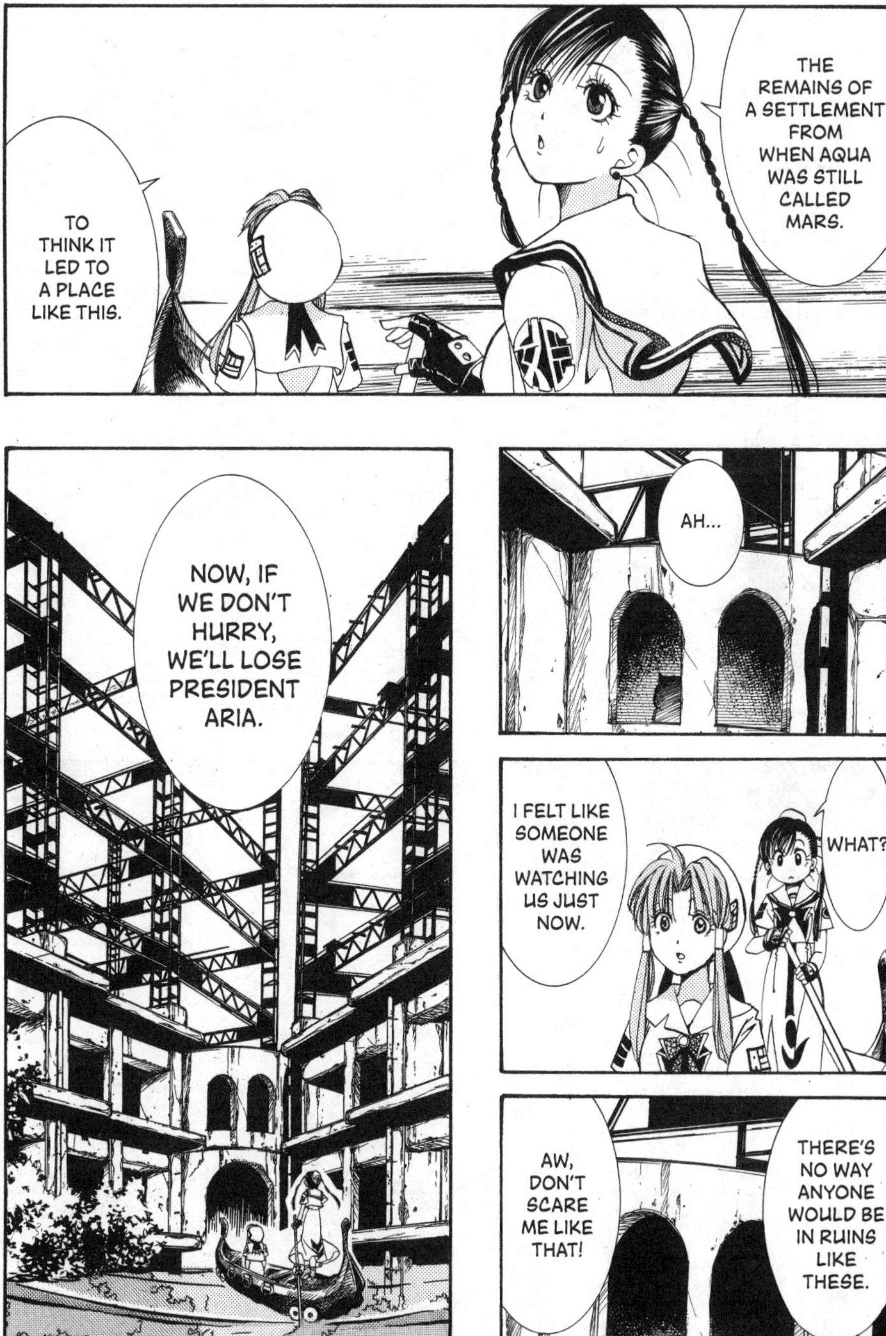
THE REMAINS OF A SETTLEMENT FROM WHEN AQUA WAS STILL CALLED MARS.
TO THINK IT LED TO A PLACE LIKE THIS.
AH...
WHAT?
I FELT LIKE SOMEONE WAS WATCHING US JUST NOW.
THERE'S NO WAY ANYONE WOULD BE IN RUINS LIKE THESE.
AW, DON'T SCARE ME LIKE THAT!
NOW, IF WE DON'T HURRY, WE'LL LOSE PRESIDENT ARIA.

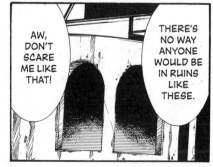

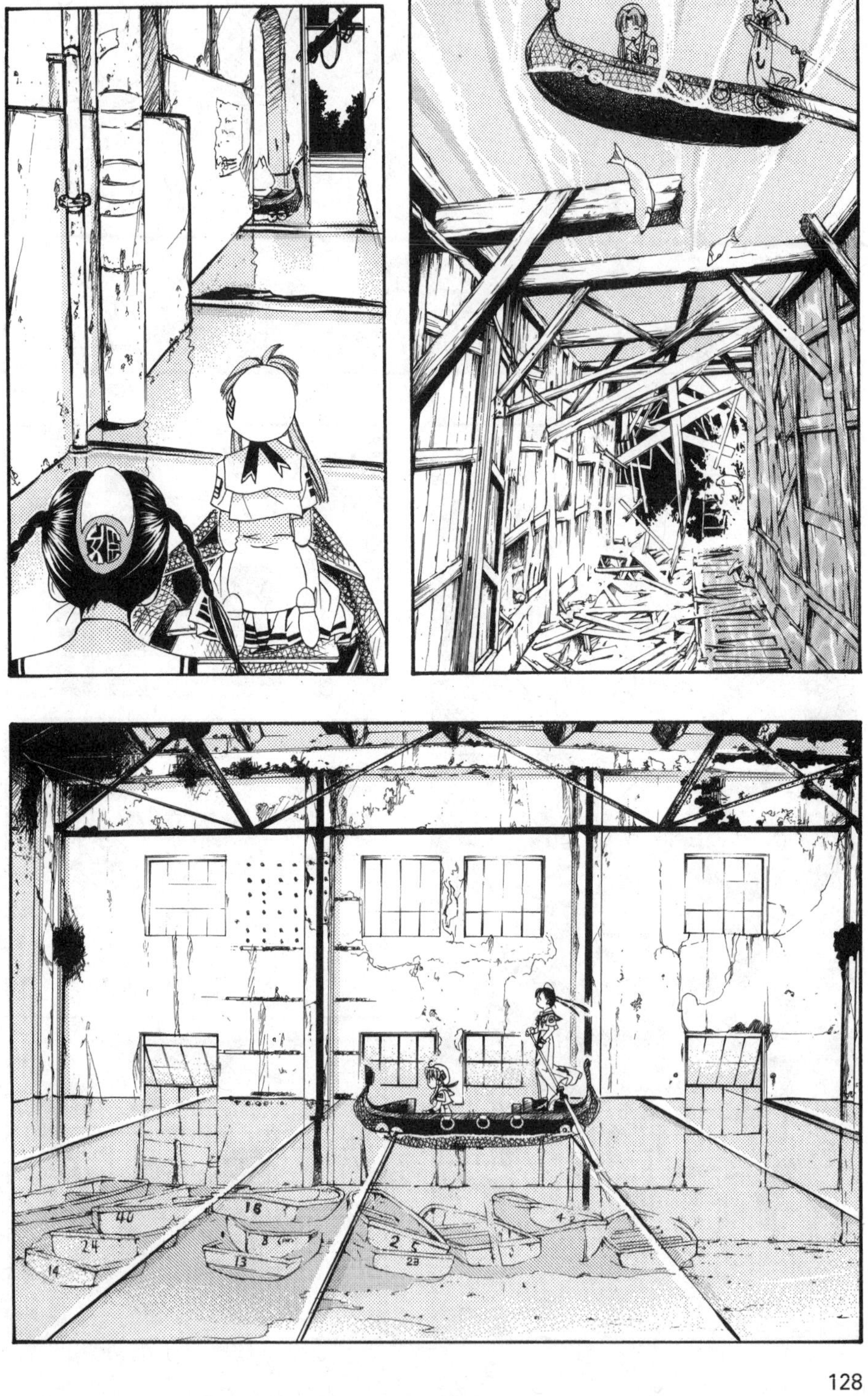

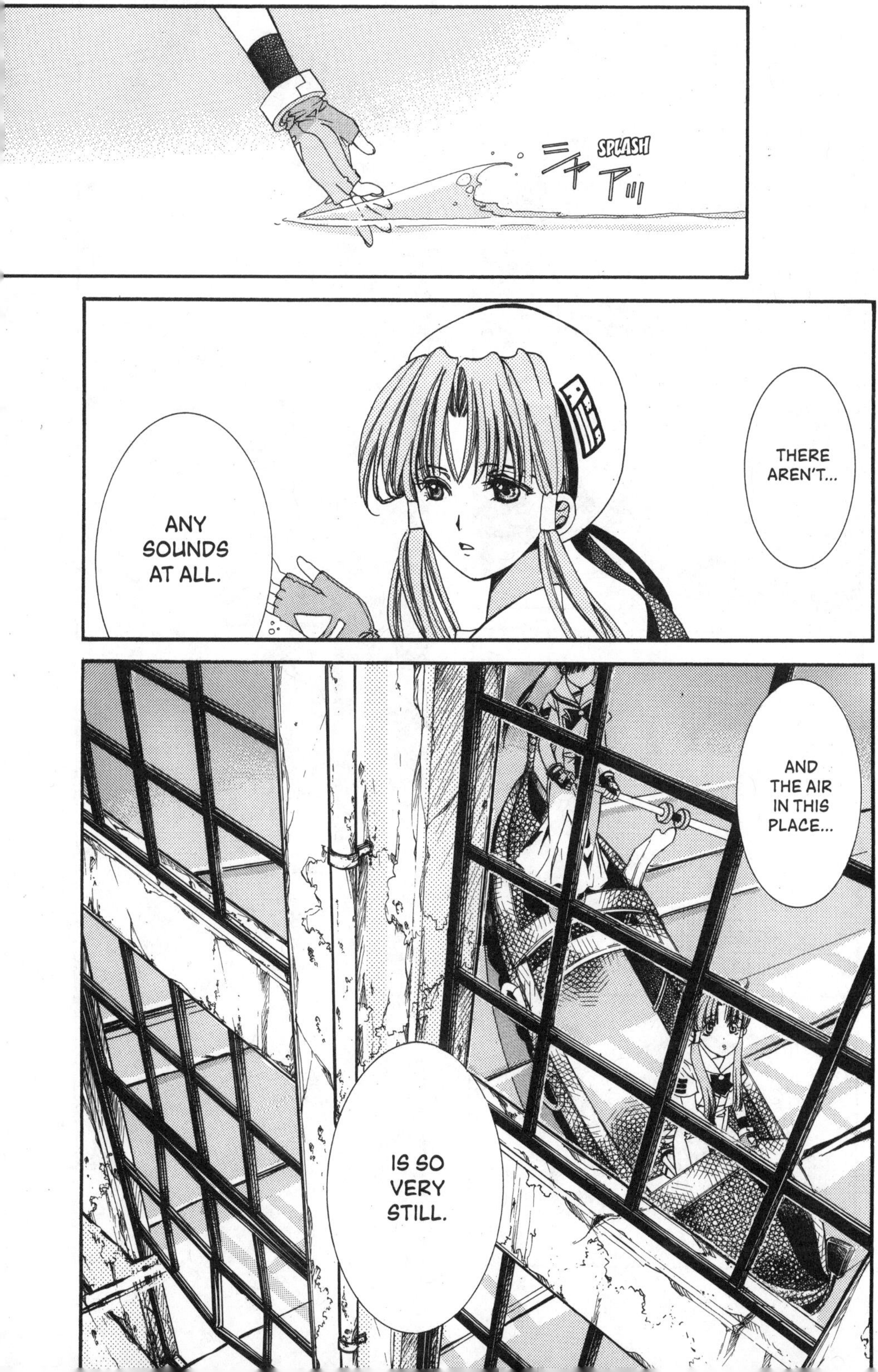
シャアッ
SPLASH
THERE AREN'T...
ANY SOUNDS AT ALL.
AND THE AIR IN THIS PLACE...
IS SO VERY STILL.

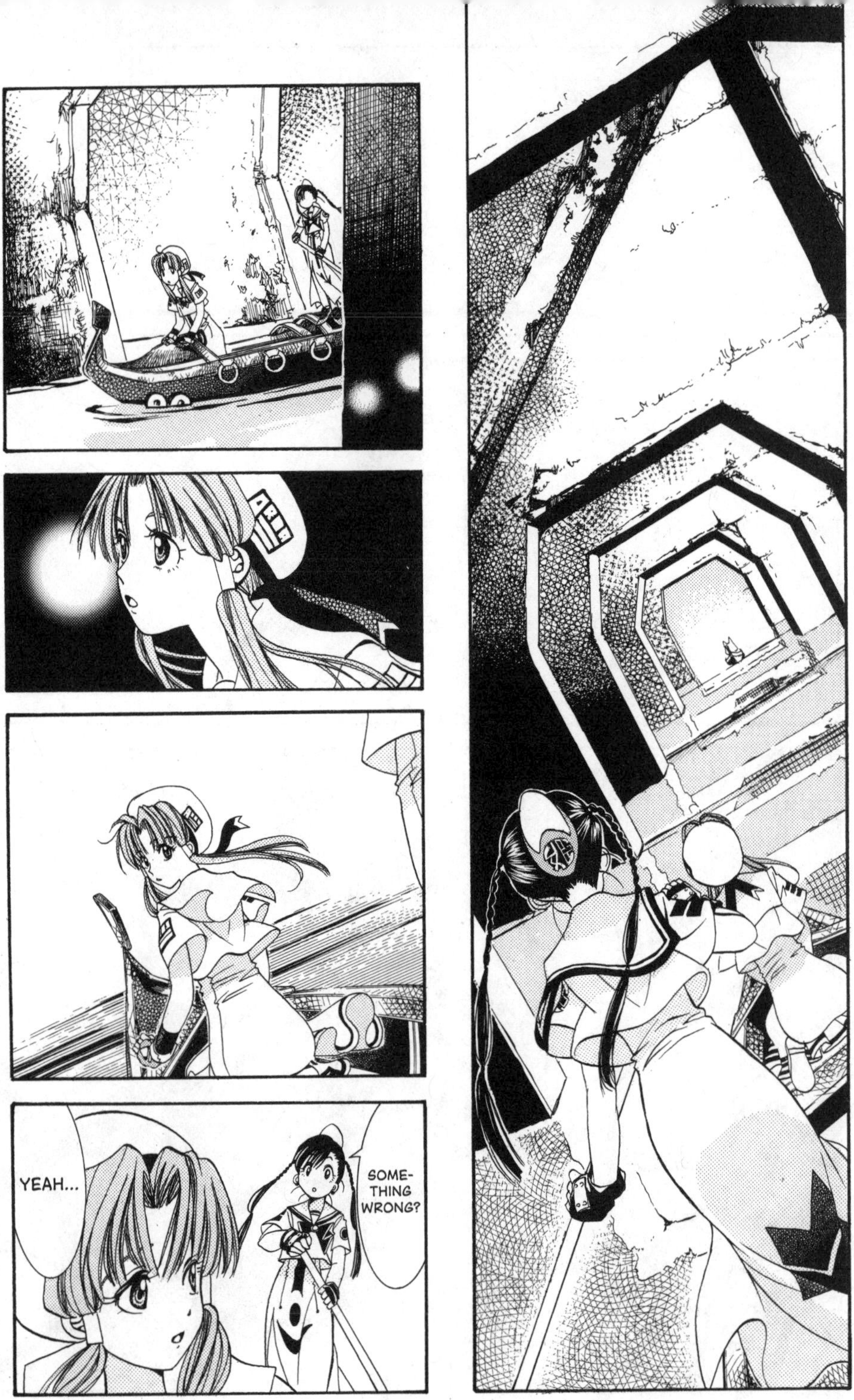
SOME-THING WRONG?
YEAH...

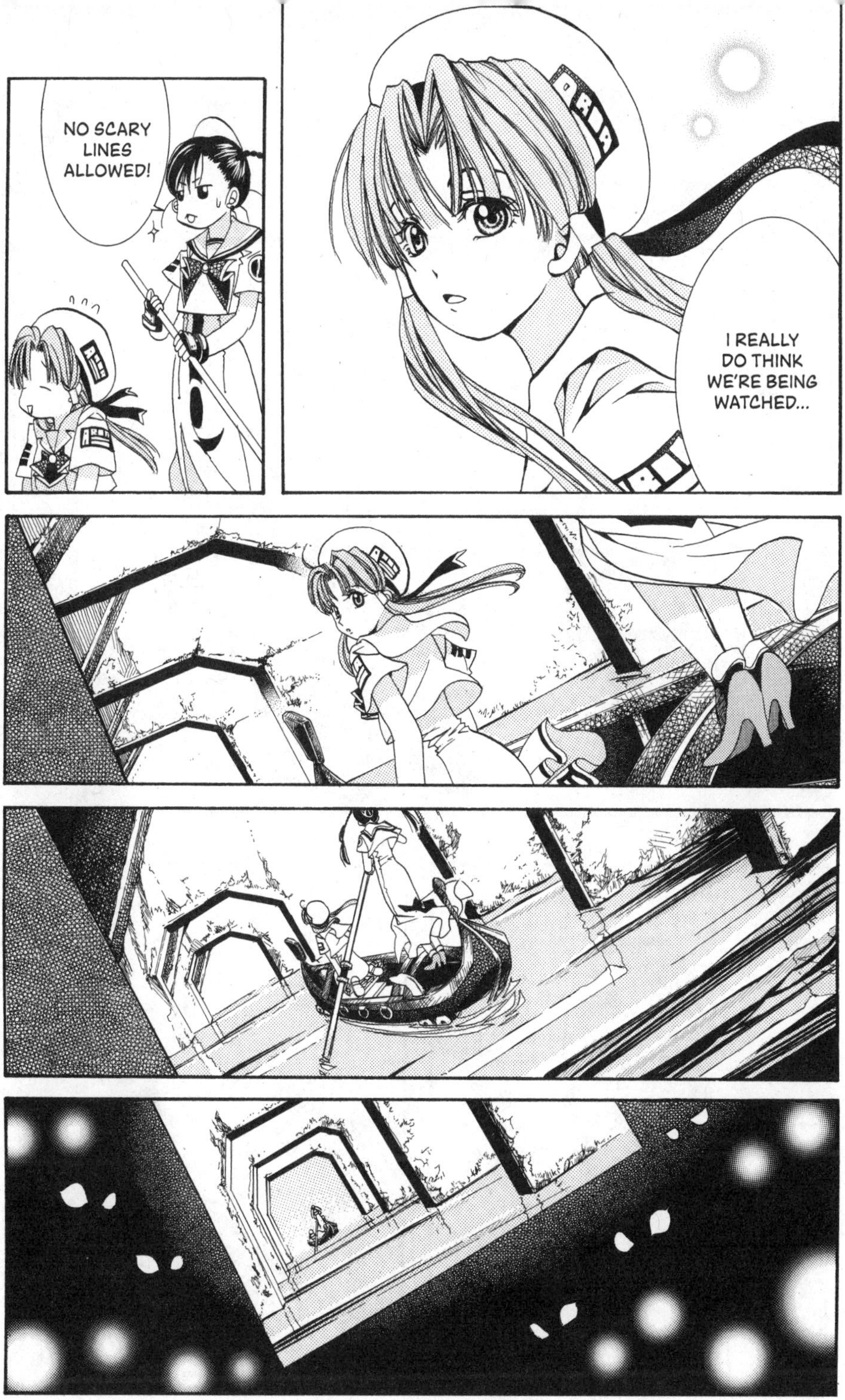
I REALLY DO THINK WE'RE BEING WATCHED...
NO SCARY LINES ALLOWED!

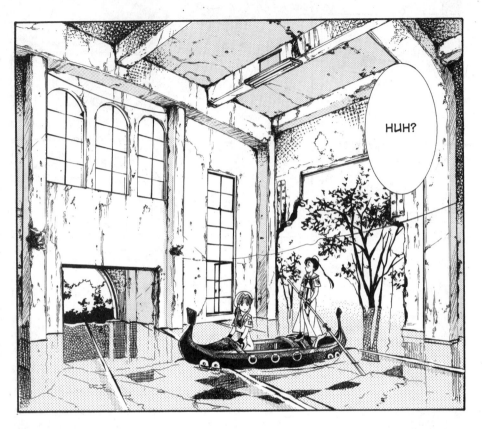

HUH?
I LOST PRESIDENT ARIA.
WAIT, WHAT?!
IT'S OKAY. THIS DREARY PLACE ONLY HAS ONE WAY OUT ANYWAY.
WE WON'T GET LOST.

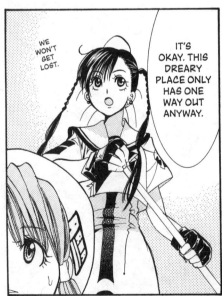

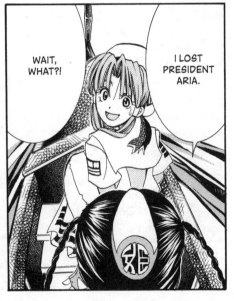

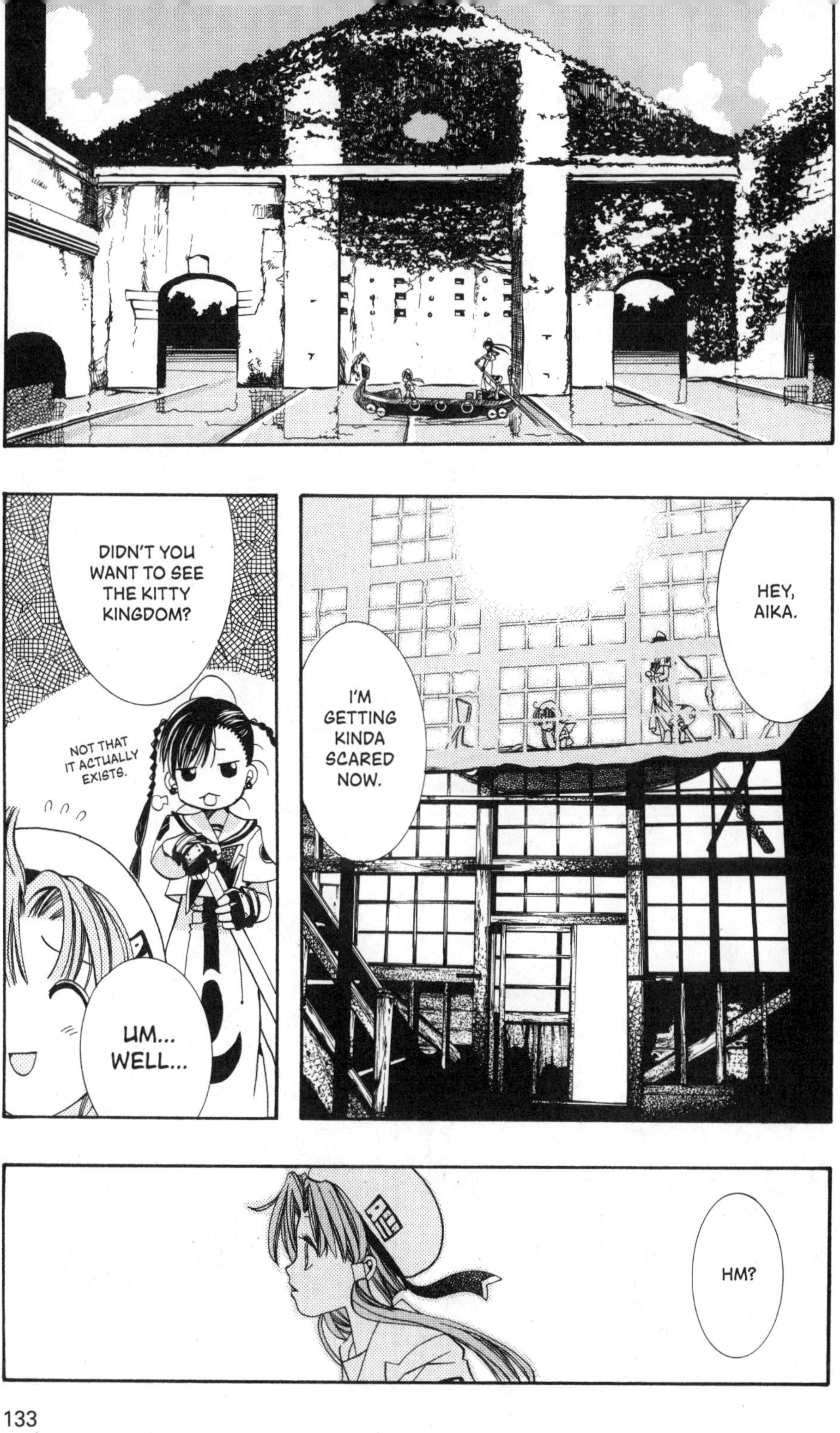
HEY, AIKA.
I'M GETTING KINDA SCARED NOW.
DIDN'T YOU WANT TO SEE THE KITTY KINGDOM?
NOT THAT IT ACTUALLY EXISTS.
UM... WELL...
HM?

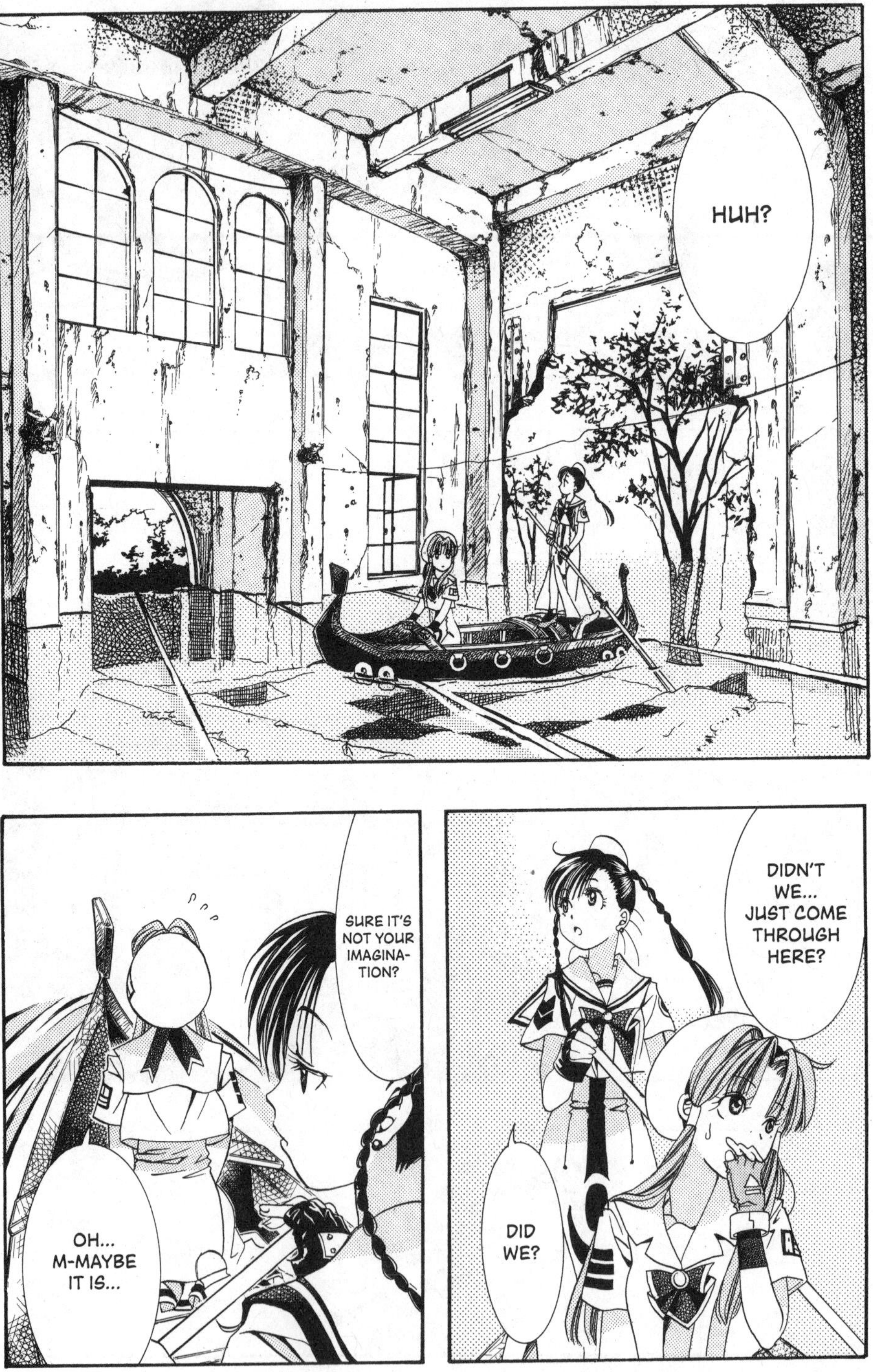
HUH?
DIDN'T WE... JUST COME THROUGH HERE?
DID WE?
SURE IT'S NOT YOUR IMAGINATION?
OH... M-MAYBE IT IS...

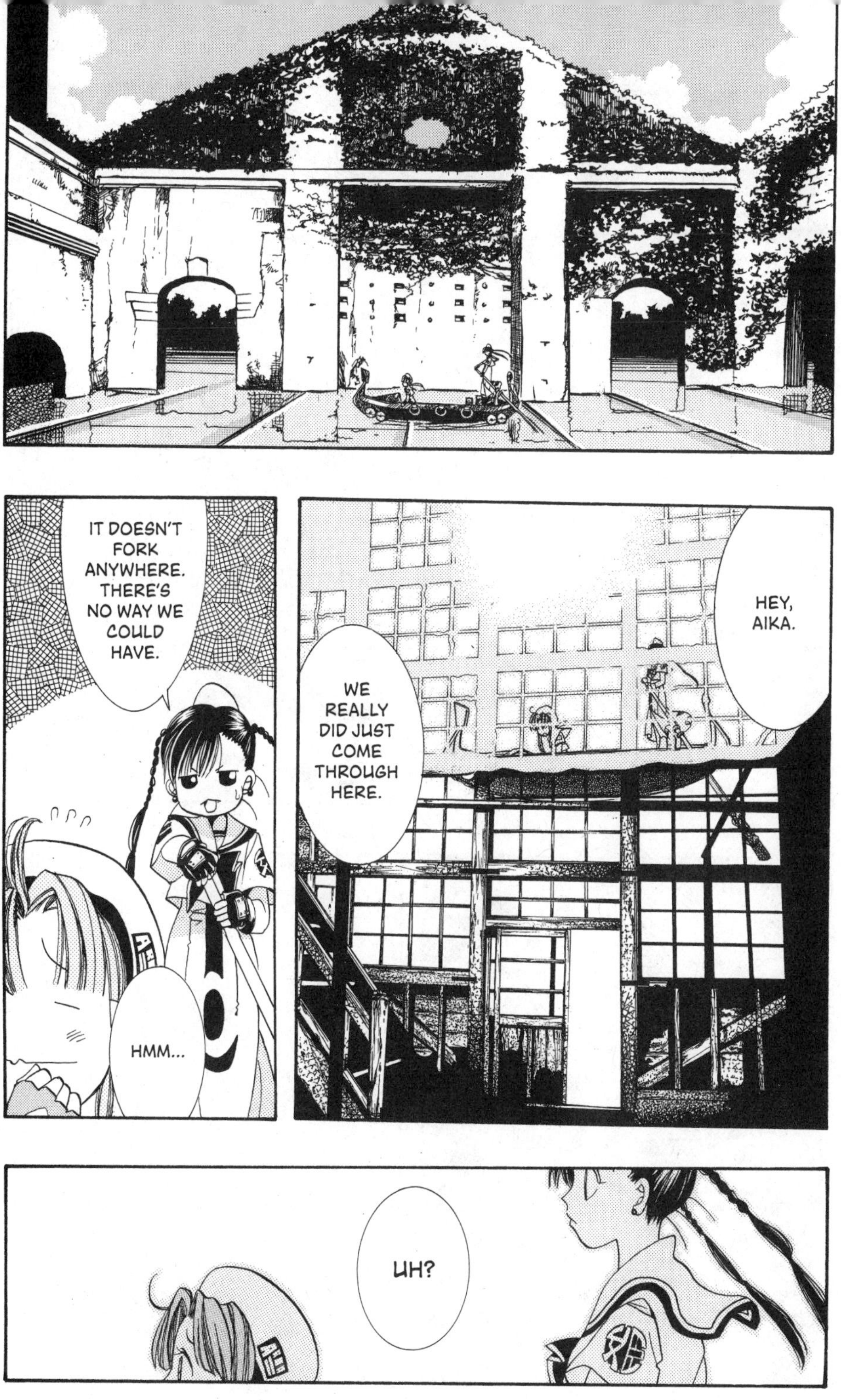
HEY, AIKA.
WE REALLY DID JUST COME THROUGH HERE.
IT DOESN'T FORK ANYWHERE. THERE'S NO WAY WE COULD HAVE.
HMM...
UH?

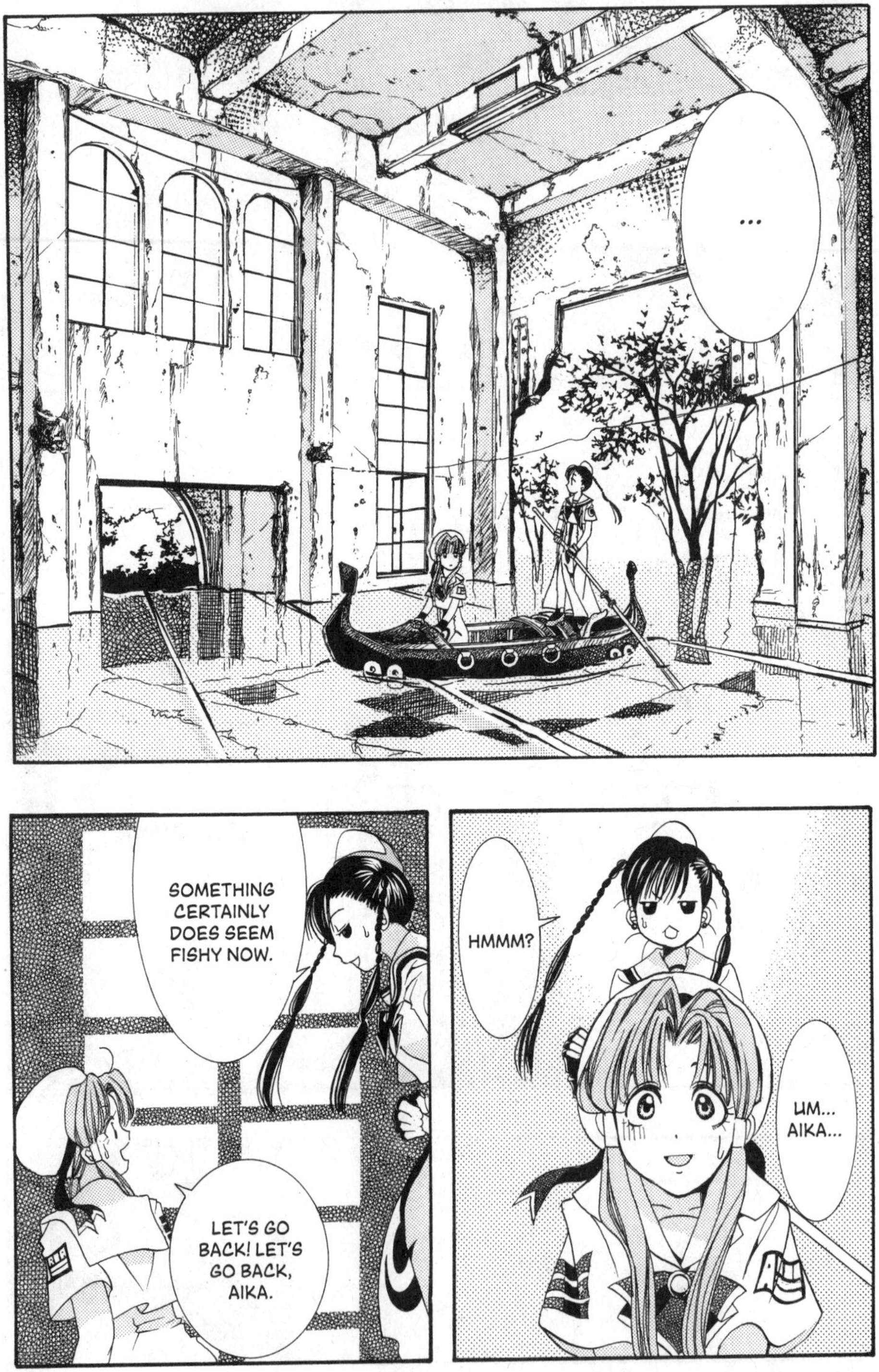
...
HMMM?
UM... AIKA...
SOMETHING CERTAINLY DOES SEEM FISHY NOW.
LET'S GO BACK! LET'S GO BACK, AIKA.

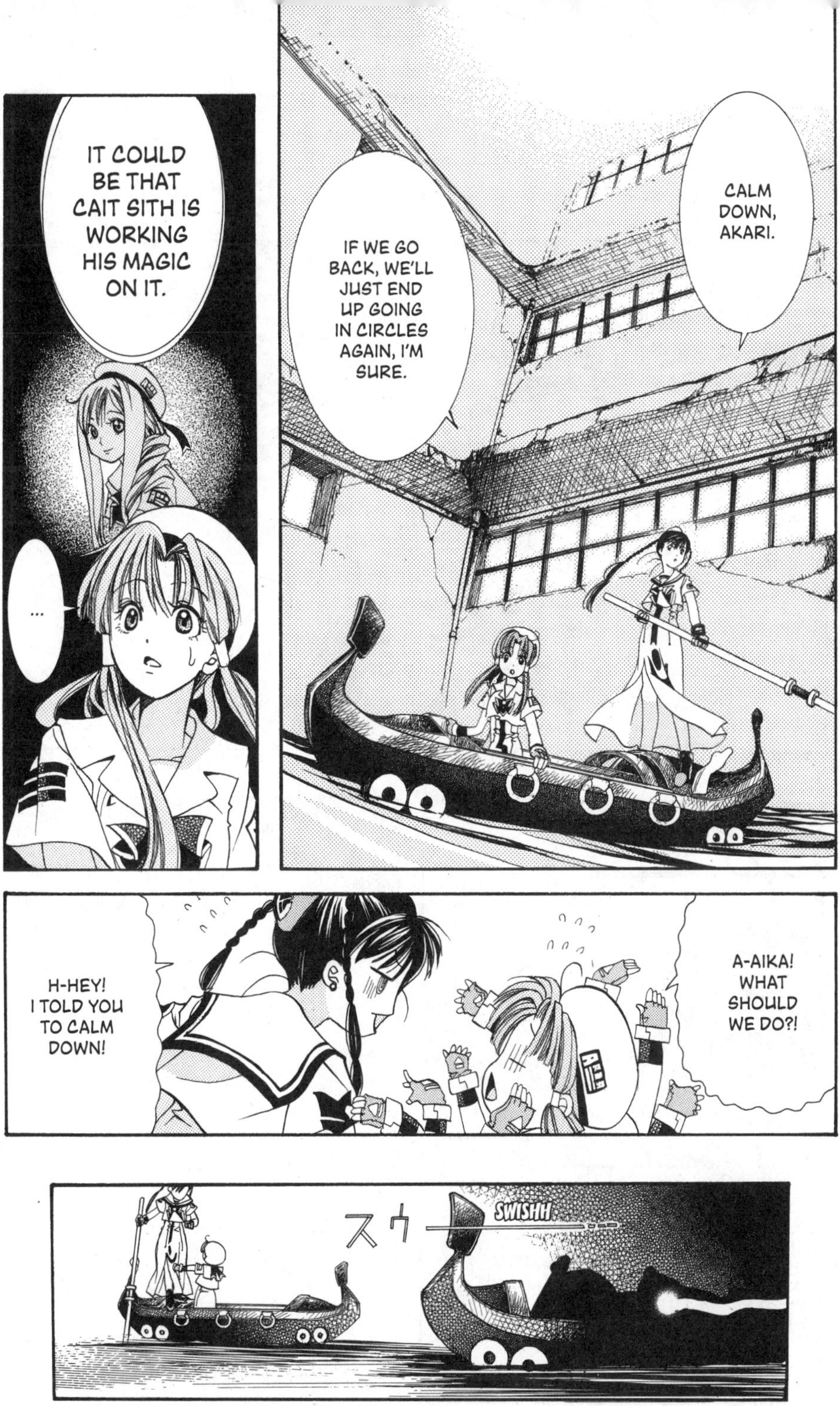
CALM DOWN, AKARI.
IF WE GO BACK, WE'LL JUST END UP GOING IN CIRCLES AGAIN, I'M SURE.
IT COULD BE THAT CAIT SITH IS WORKING HIS MAGIC ON IT.
...
A-AIKA! WHAT SHOULD WE DO?!
H-HEY! I TOLD YOU TO CALM DOWN!
スウー
SWISHH

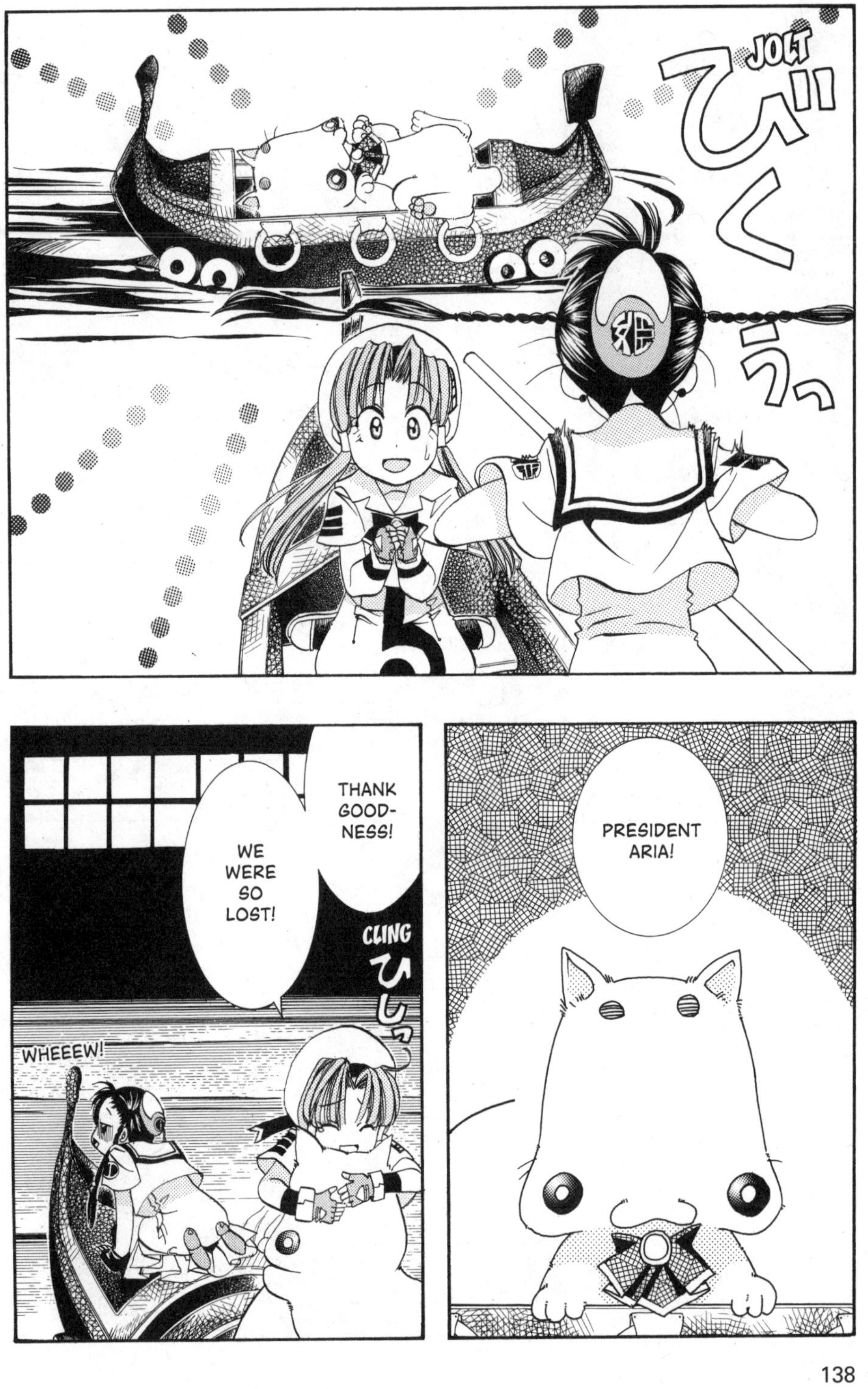
JOLT
びくうっ
PRESIDENT ARIA!
THANK GOODNESS!
WE WERE SO LOST!
CLING
ひしっ
WHEEEW!

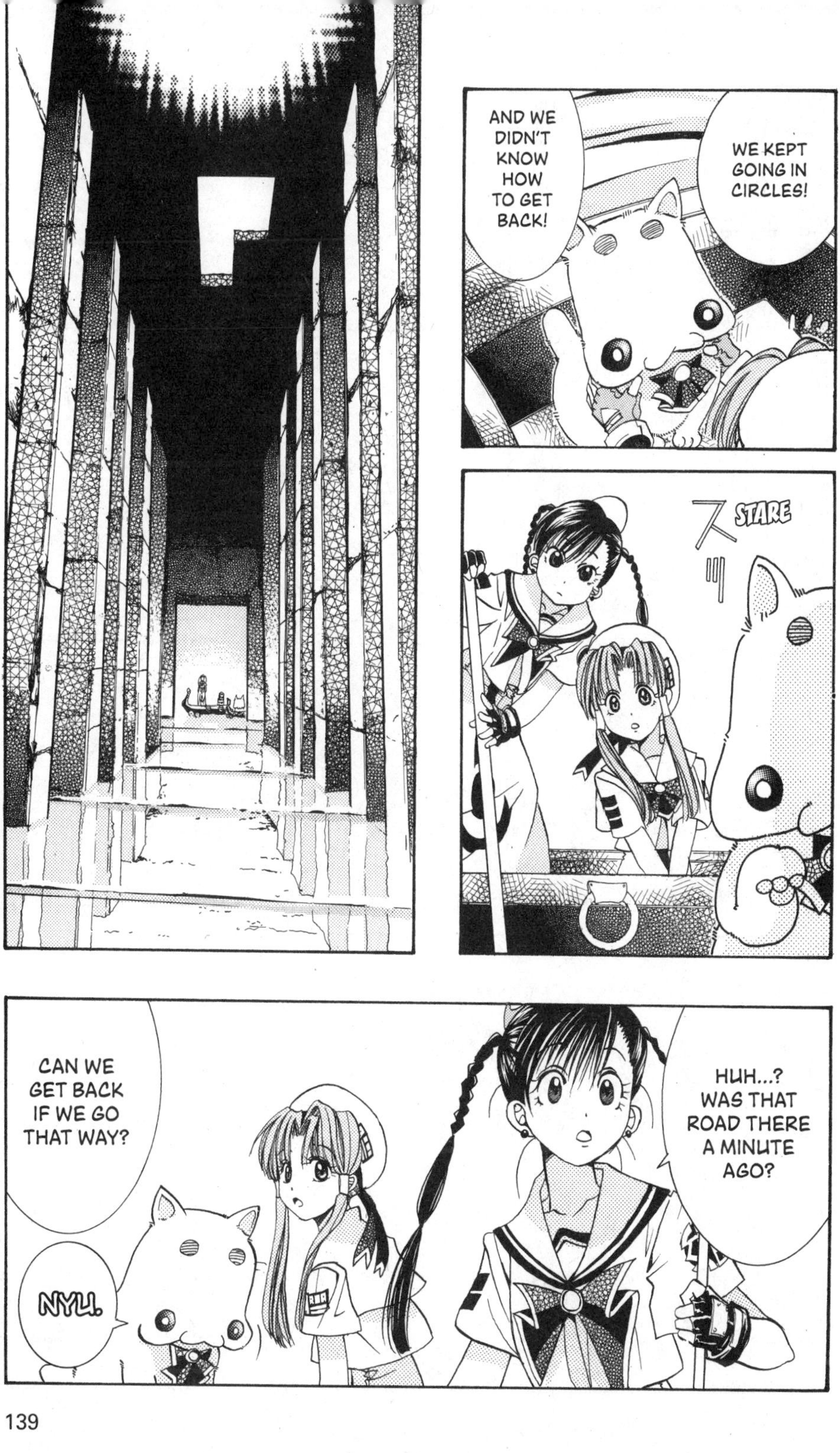
WE KEPT GOING IN CIRCLES!
AND WE DIDN'T KNOW HOW TO GET BACK!
スッ
STARE
HUH...? WAS THAT ROAD THERE A MINUTE AGO?
CAN WE GET BACK IF WE GO THAT WAY?
NYU.

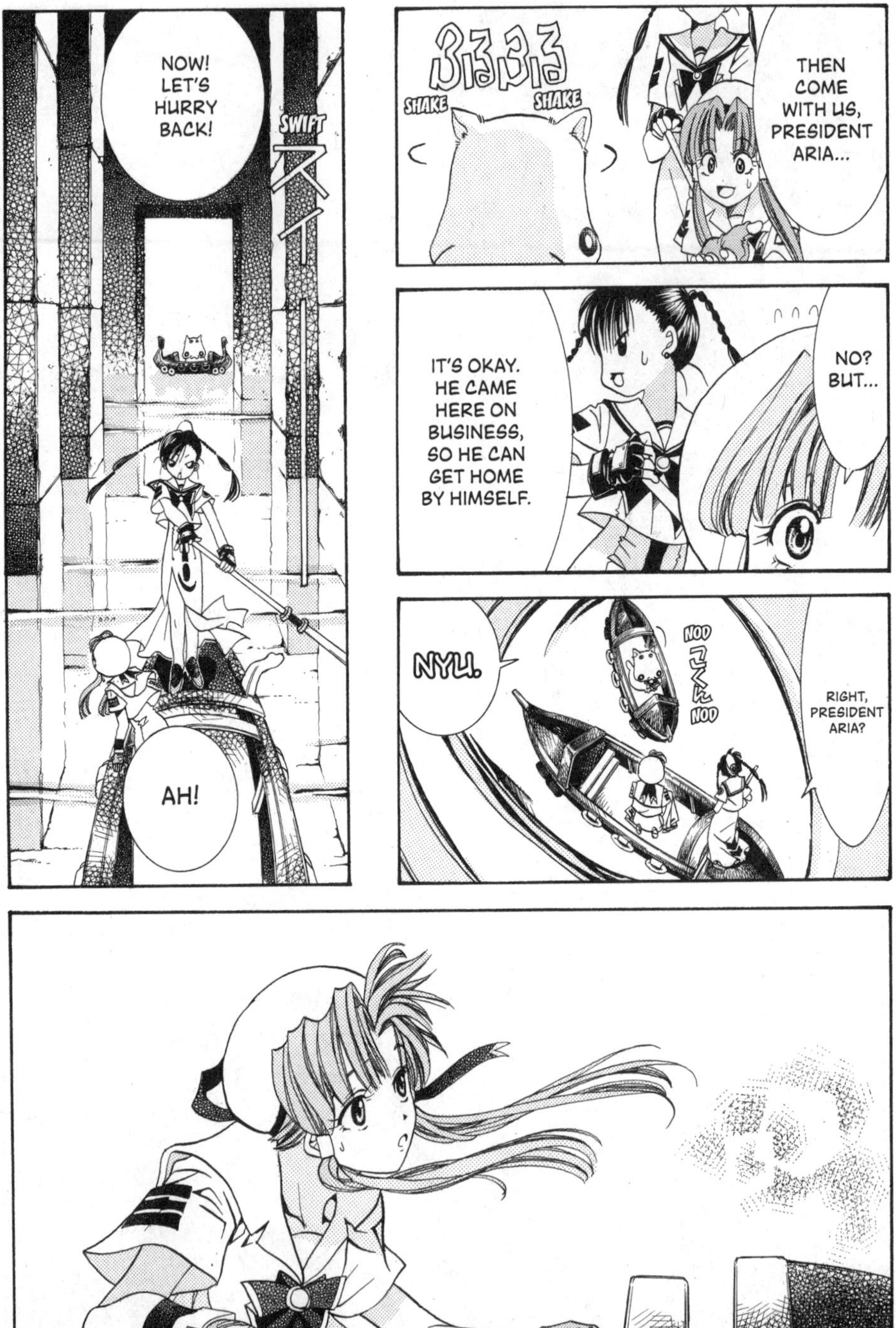
THEN COME WITH US, PRESIDENT ARIA...
ふるふる
SHAKE
SHAKE
NO? BUT...
IT'S OKAY. HE CAME HERE ON BUSINESS, SO HE CAN GET HOME BY HIMSELF.
RIGHT, PRESIDENT ARIA?
NOD
こくん
NOD
NYU.
NOW! LET'S HURRY BACK!
SWIFT
スイー
AH!

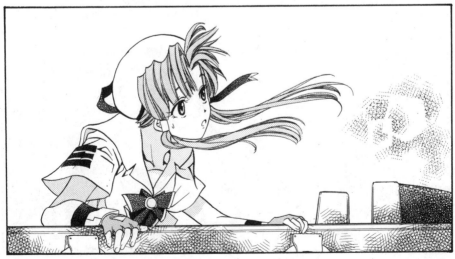

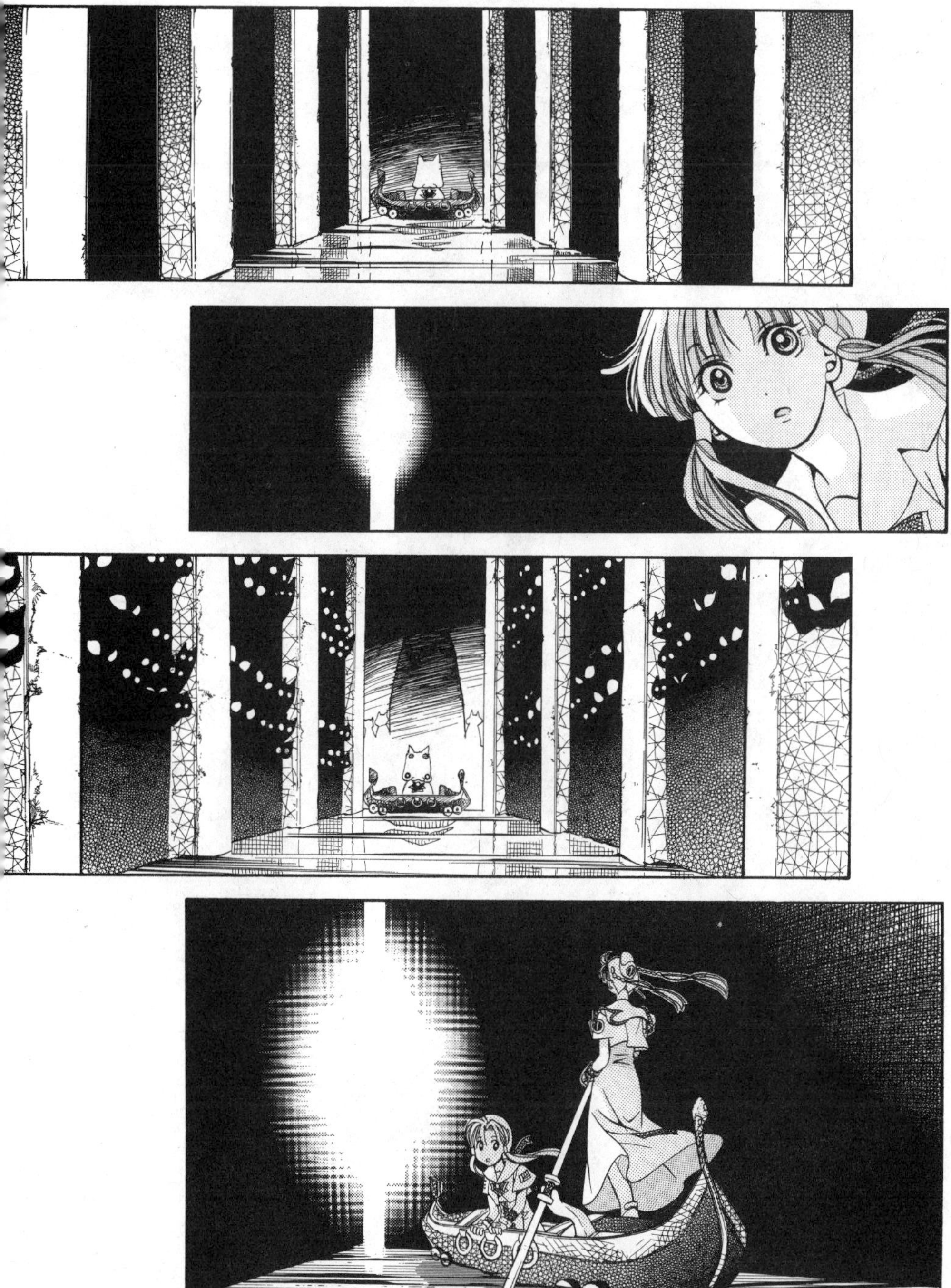

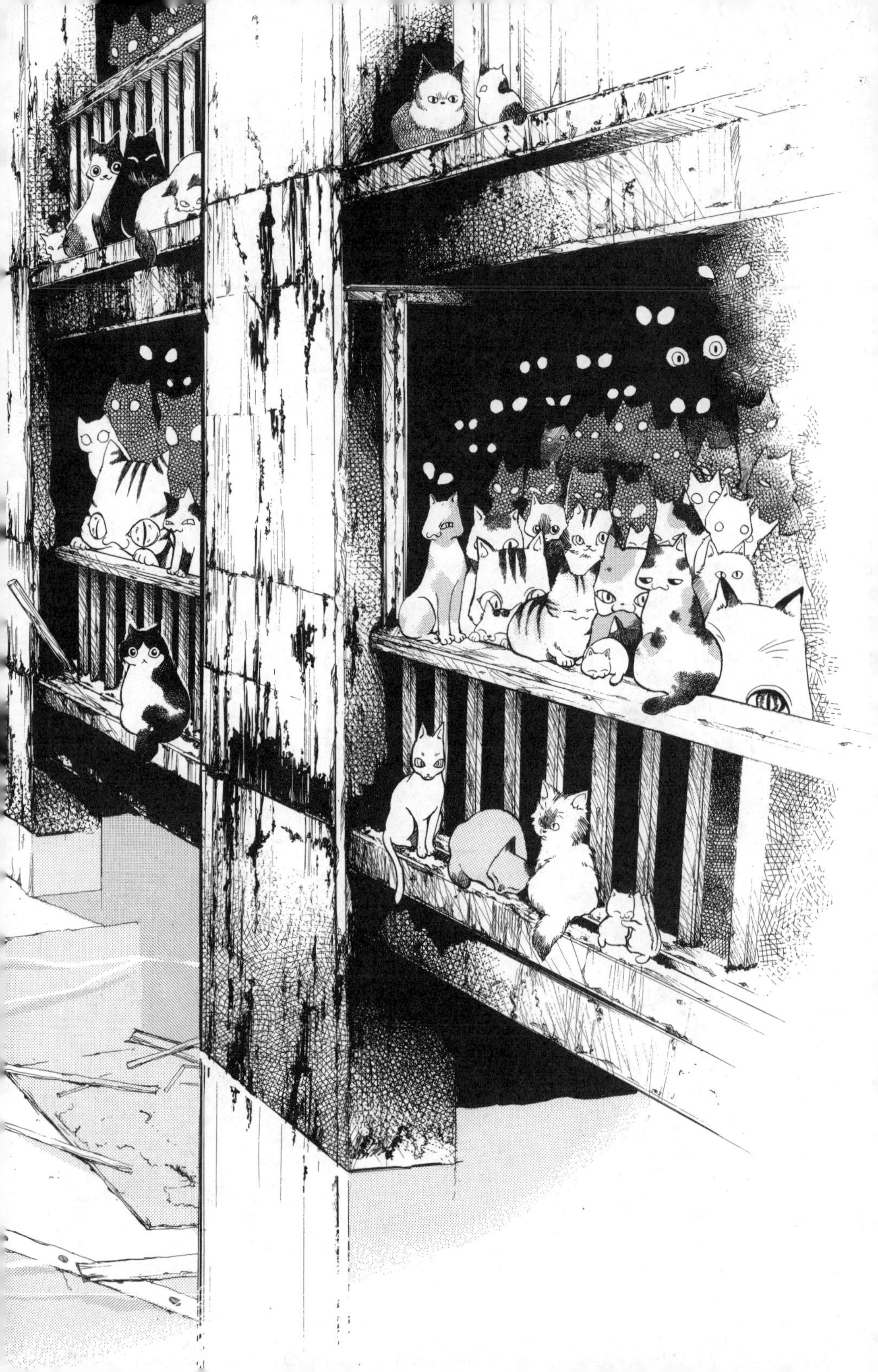

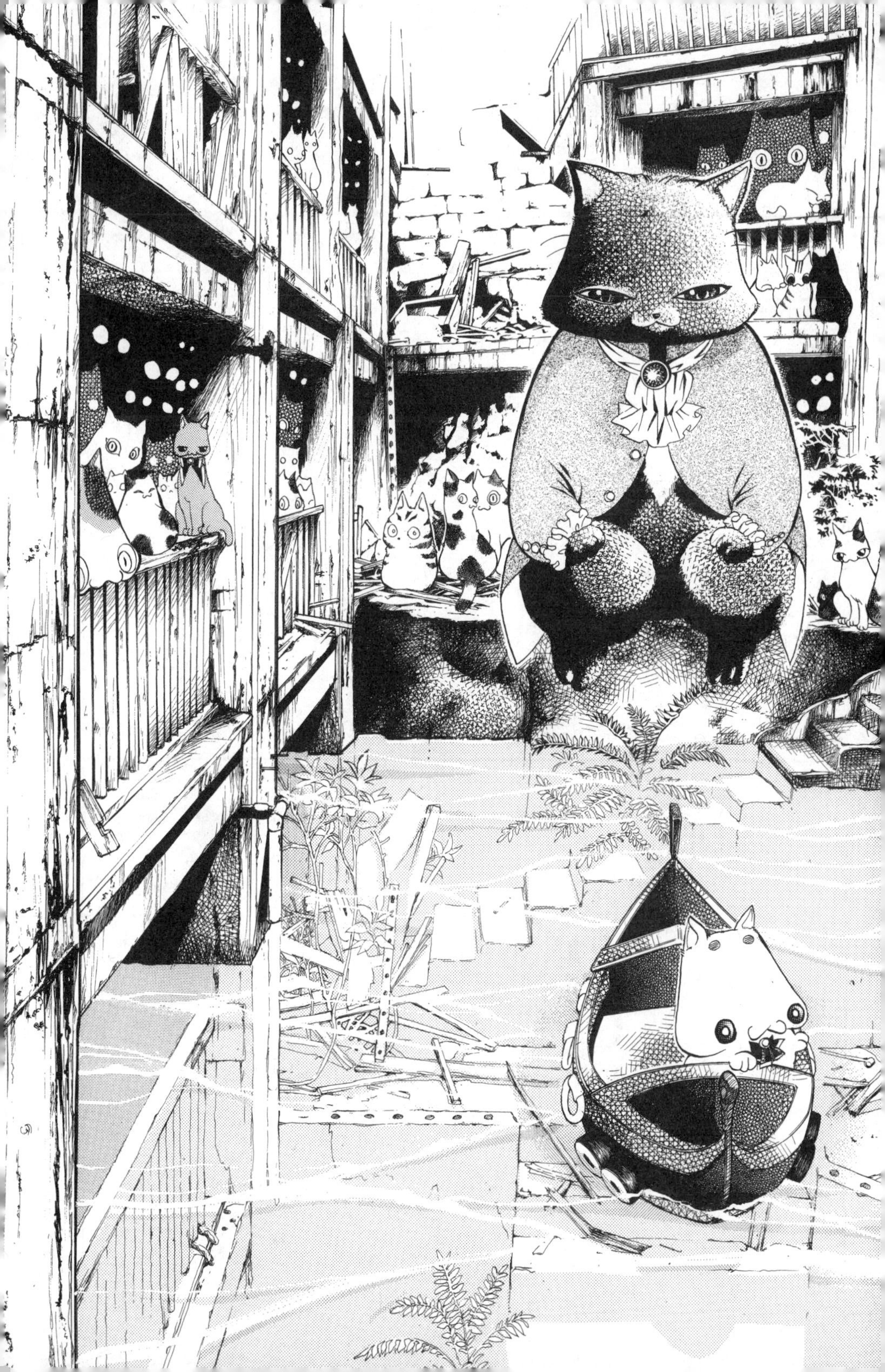

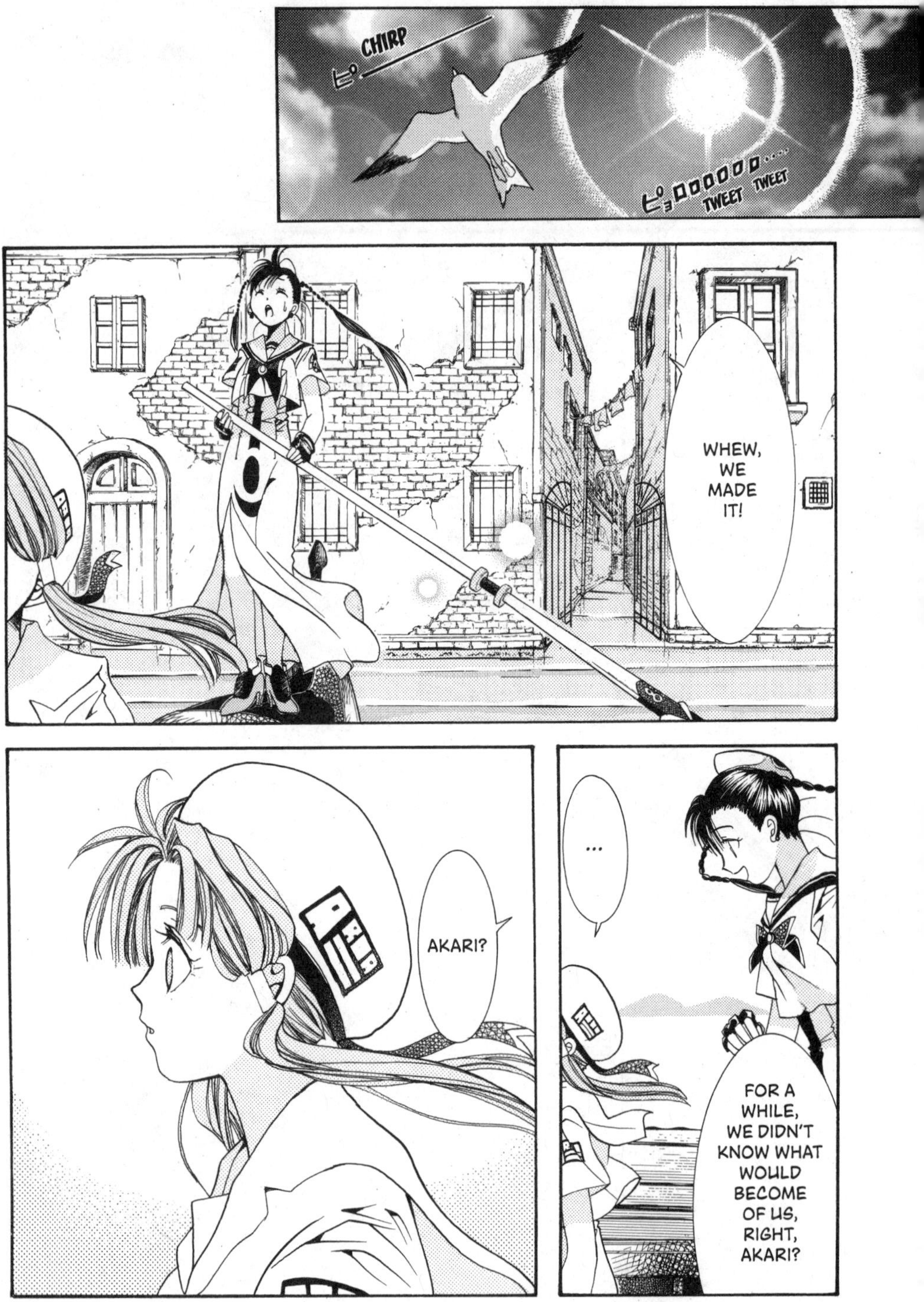
ピ CHIRP
ピョロロロロロロ.... TWEET TWEET
WHEW, WE MADE IT!
...
FOR A WHILE, WE DIDN'T KNOW WHAT WOULD BECOME OF US, RIGHT, AKARI?
AKARI?

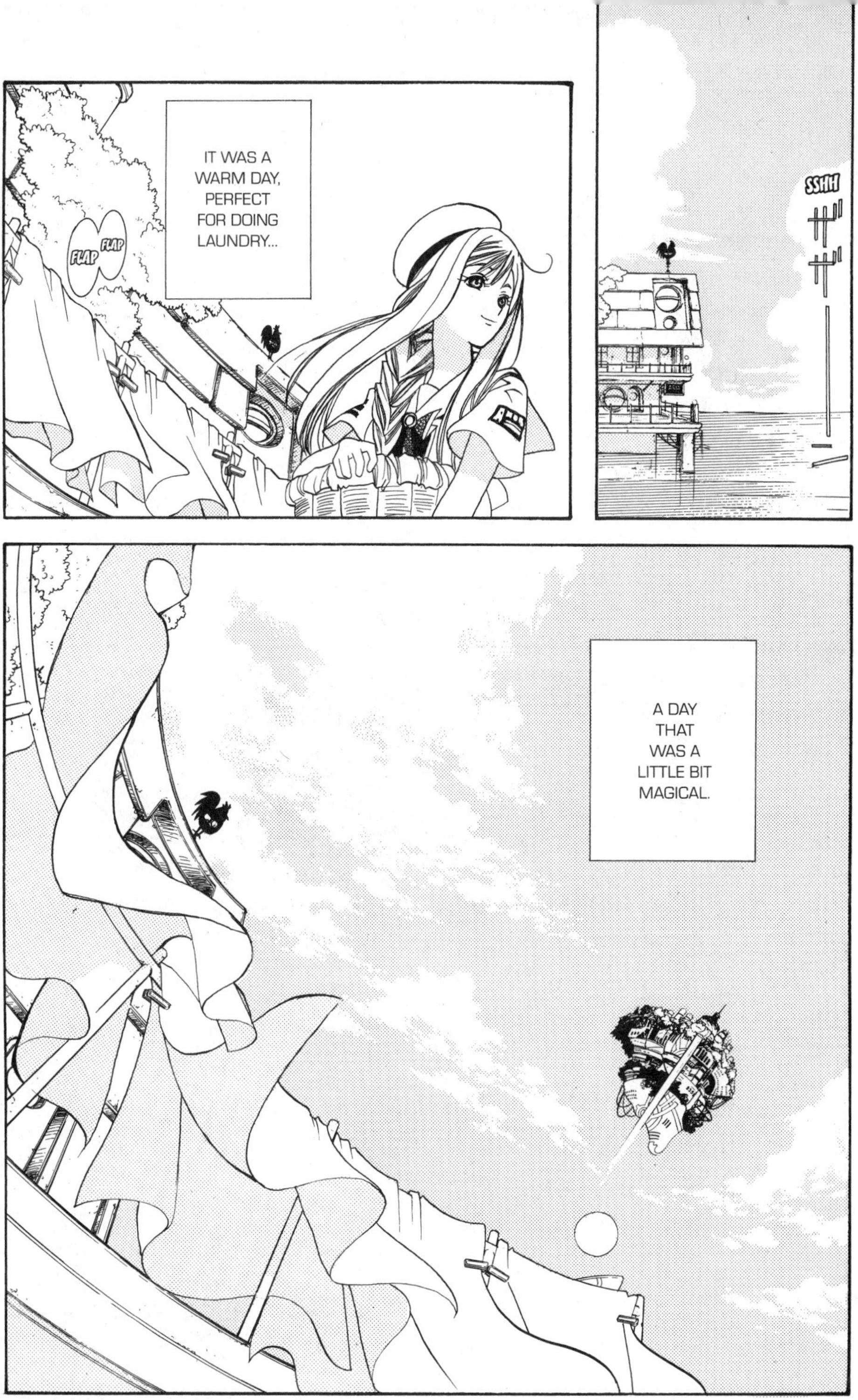
SSHH
IT WAS A WARM DAY, PERFECT FOR DOING LAUNDRY...
FLAP FLAP
A DAY THAT WAS A LITTLE BIT MAGICAL.

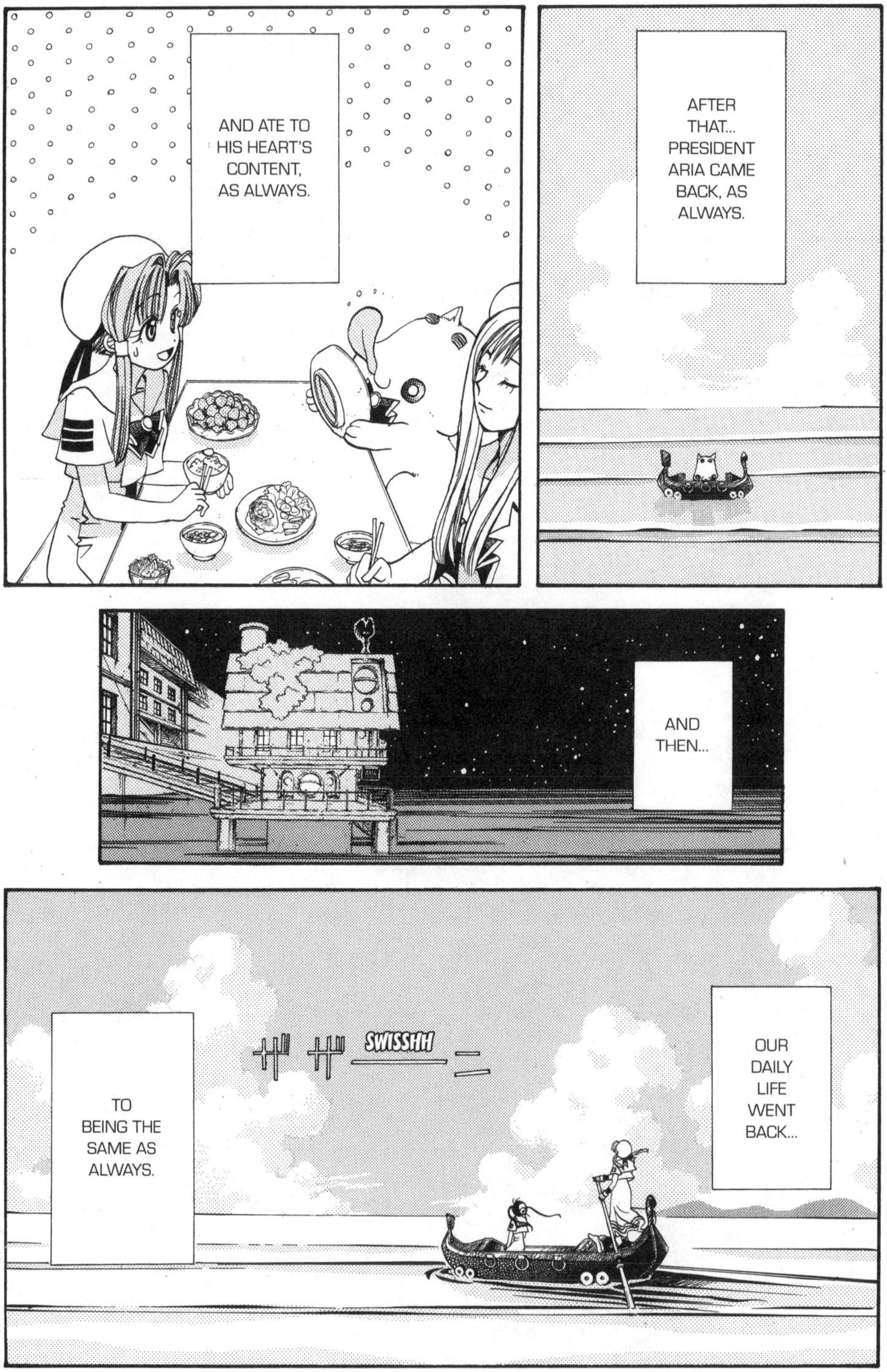
AFTER THAT... PRESIDENT ARIA CAME BACK, AS ALWAYS.
AND ATE TO HIS HEART'S CONTENT, AS ALWAYS.
AND THEN...
OUR DAILY LIFE WENT BACK...
SWISSHH
TO BEING THE SAME AS ALWAYS.

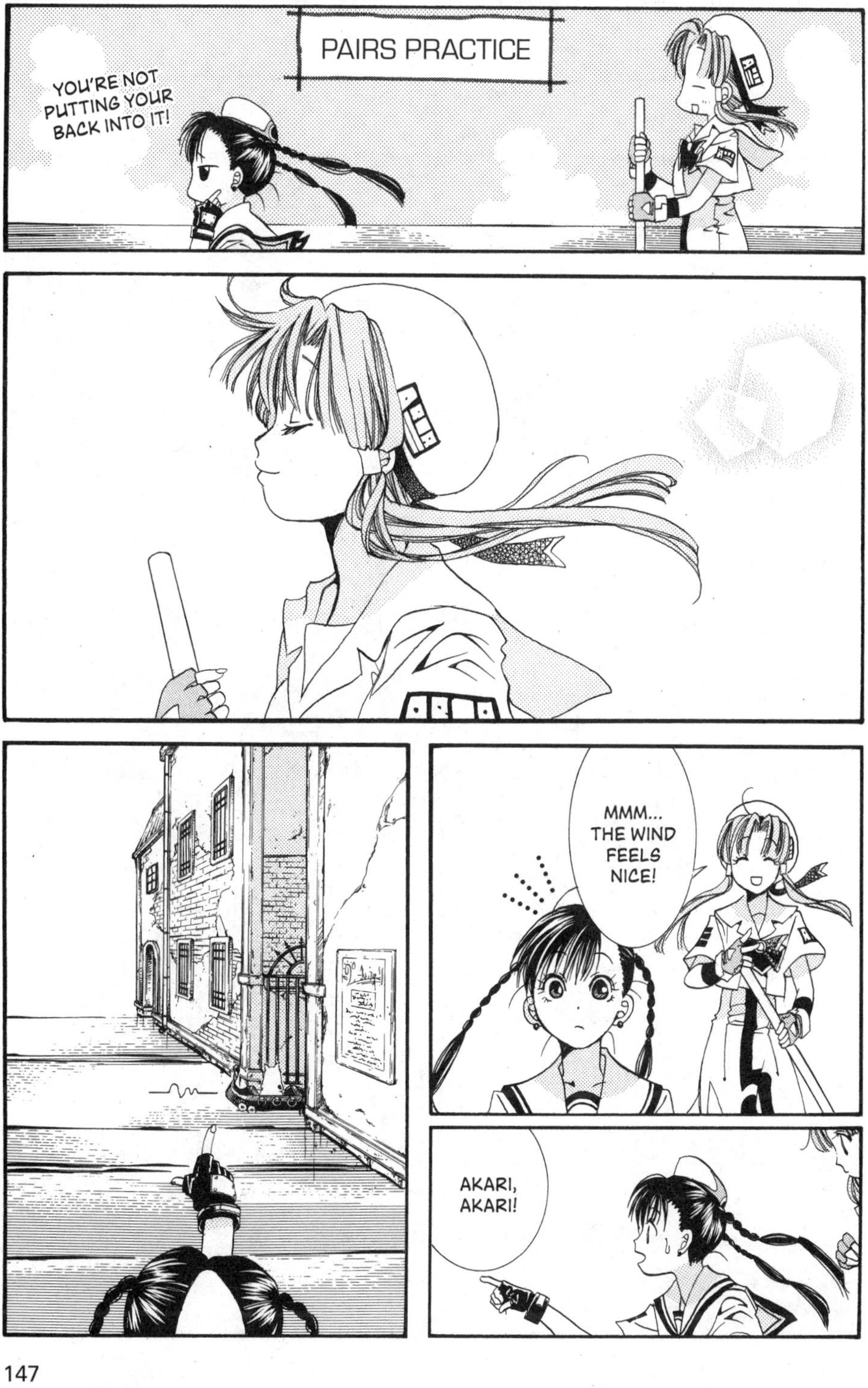
PAIRS PRACTICE
YOU'RE NOT PUTTING YOUR BACK INTO IT!
MMM... THE WIND FEELS NICE!
AKARI, AKARI!

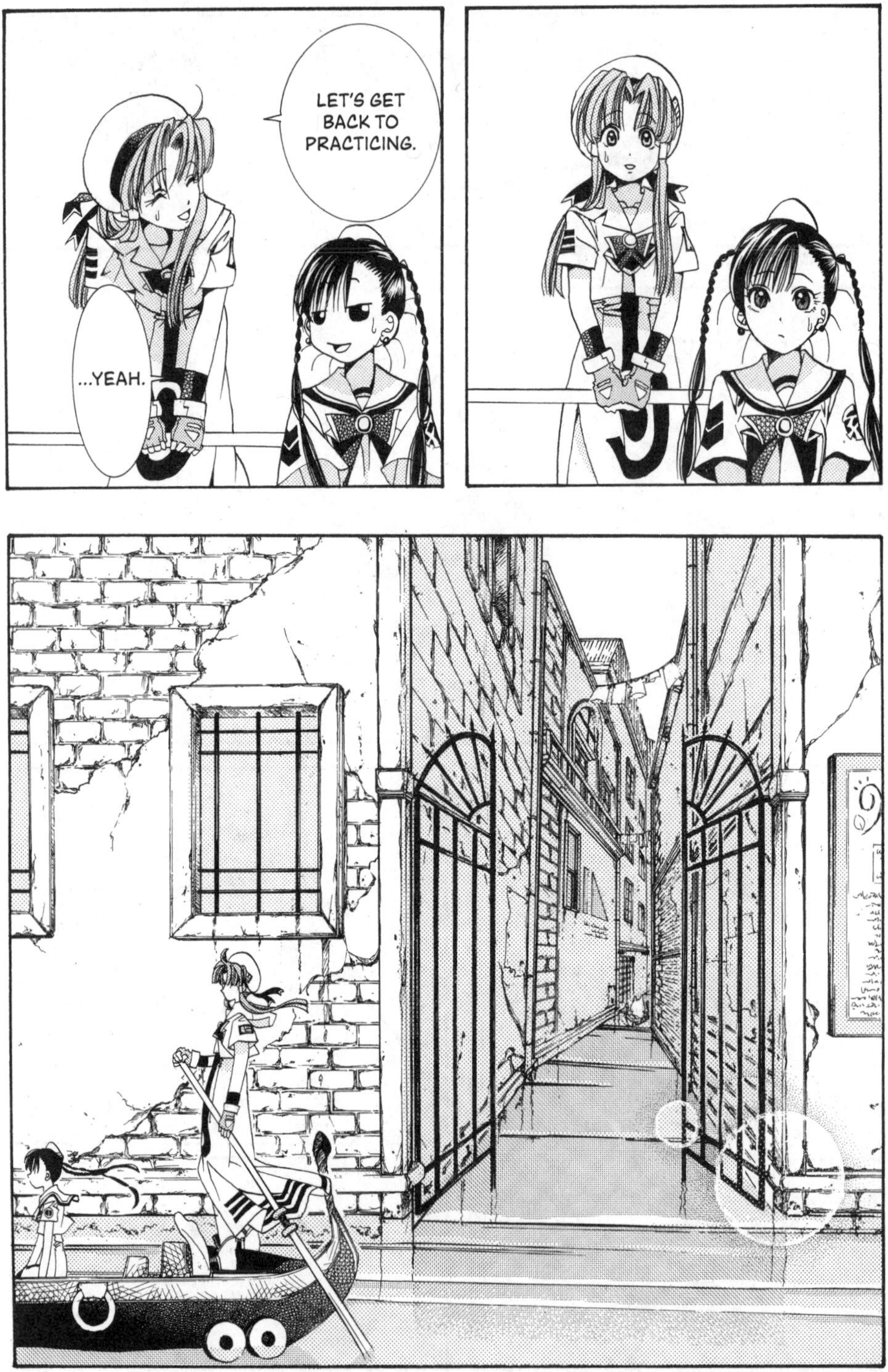
LET'S GET BACK TO PRACTICING.
...YEAH.

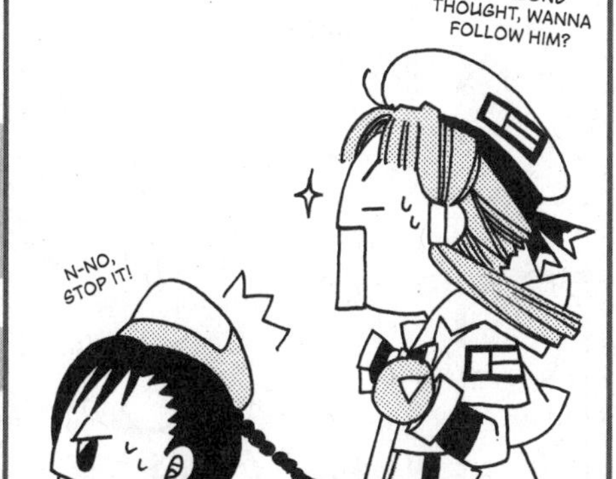
ON SECOND THOUGHT, WANNA FOLLOW HIM?
N-NO, STOP IT!

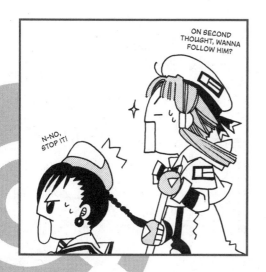

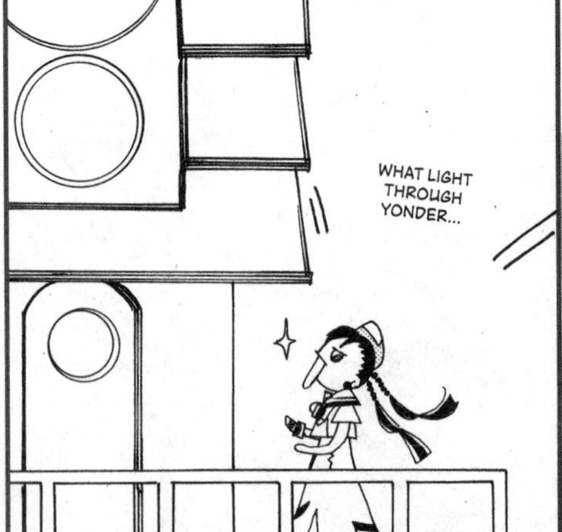
WHAT LIGHT THROUGH YONDER...

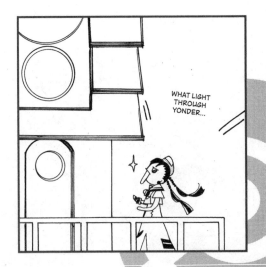

Navigation 05
The Hill of Hope

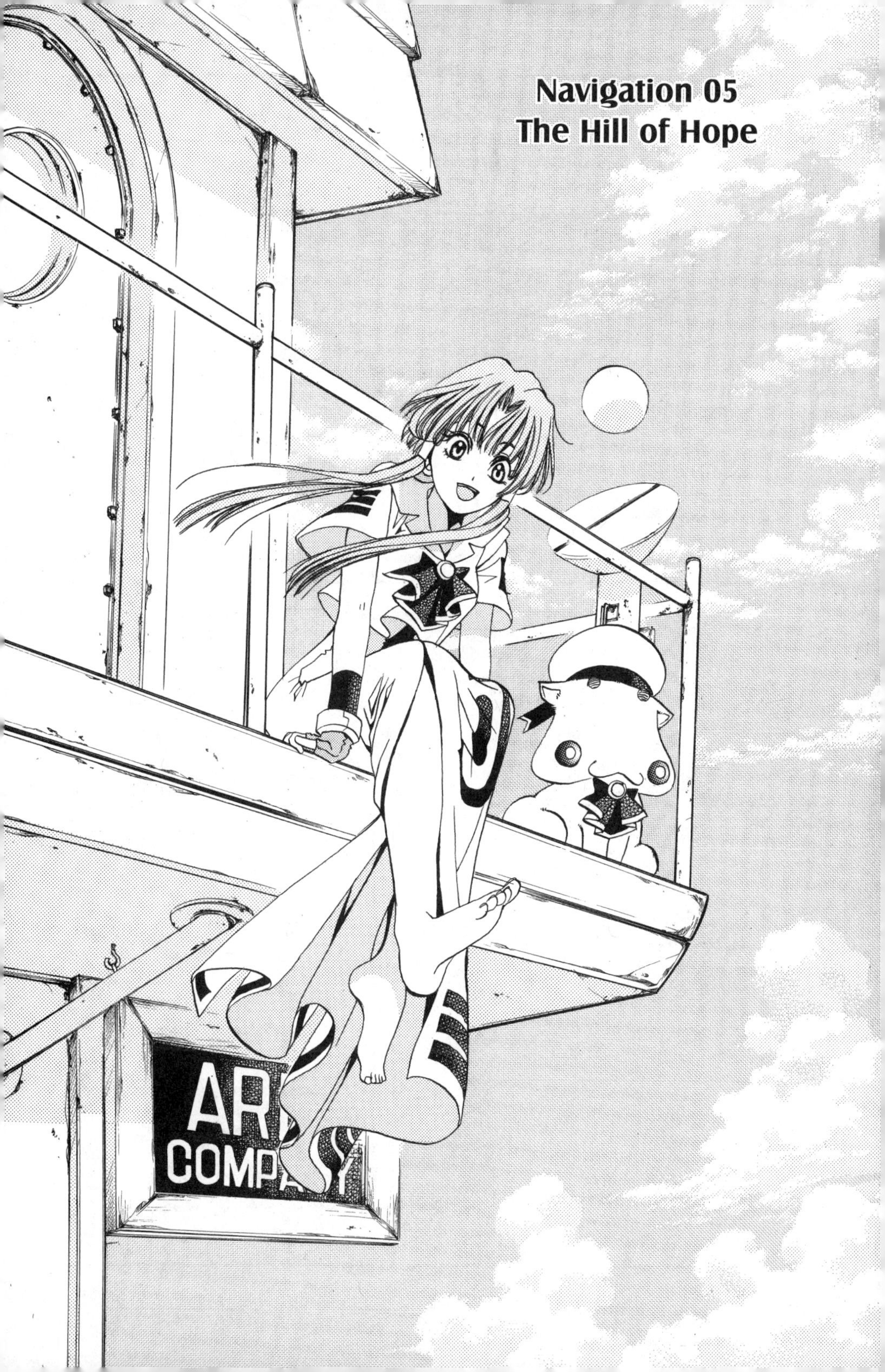
AR
COMPA

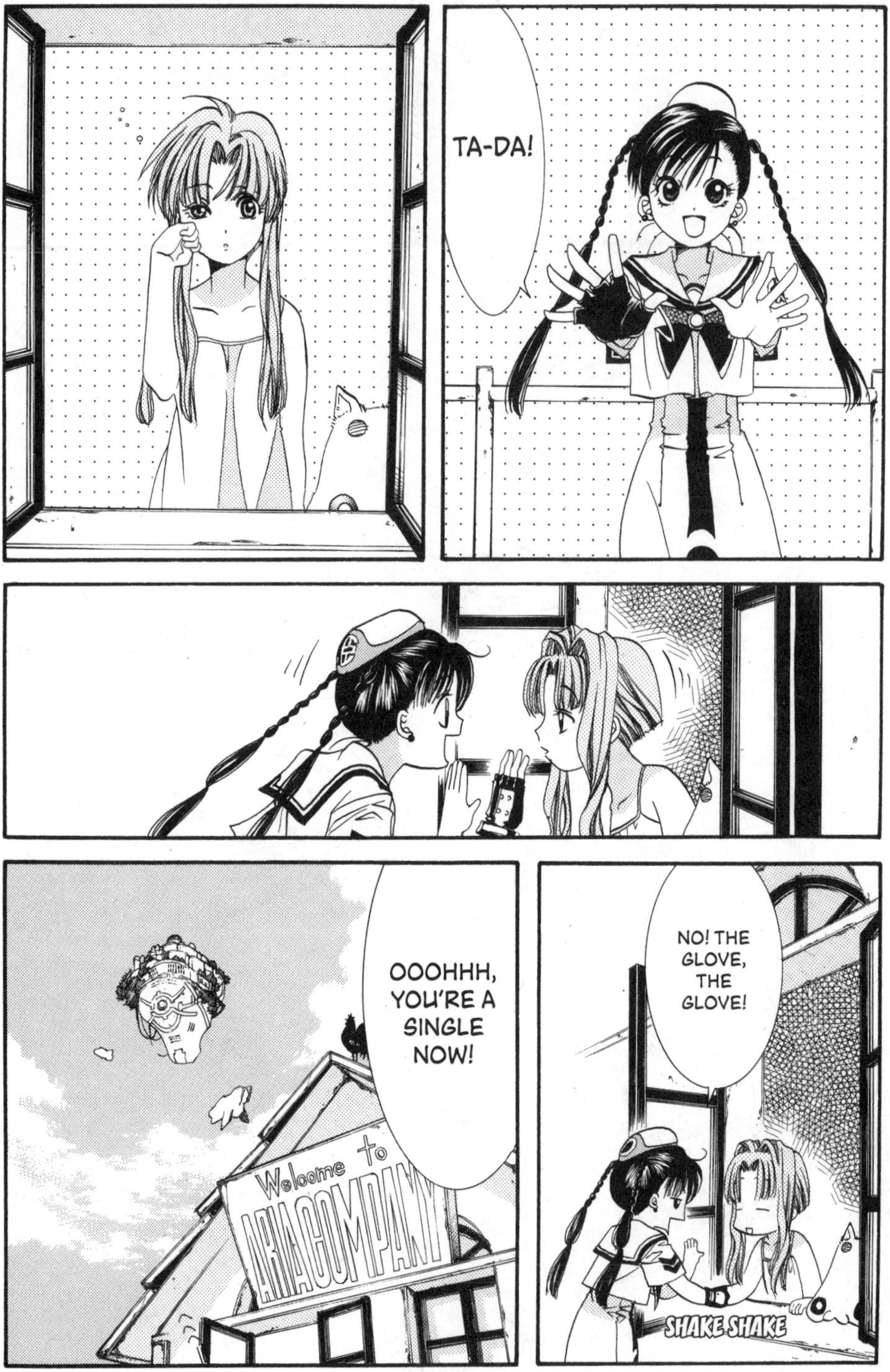
TA-DA!
NO! THE GLOVE, THE GLOVE!
SHAKE SHAKE
OOOHHH, YOU'RE A SINGLE NOW!
Welcome to
ARIA COMPANY

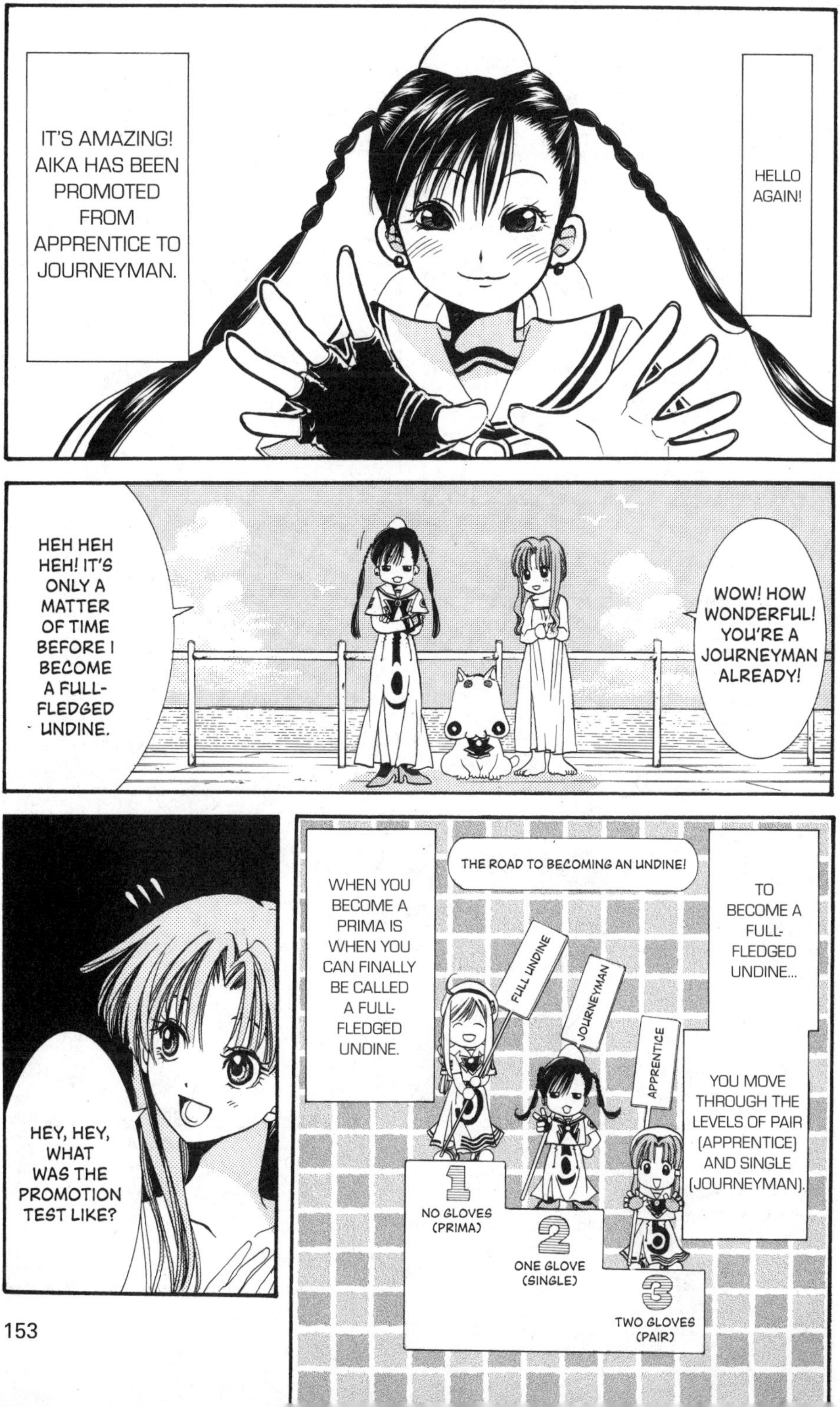
HELLO AGAIN!
IT'S AMAZING! AIKA HAS BEEN PROMOTED FROM APPRENTICE TO JOURNEYMAN.
WOW! HOW WONDERFUL! YOU'RE A JOURNEYMAN ALREADY!
HEH HEH HEH! IT'S ONLY A MATTER OF TIME BEFORE I BECOME A FULL-FLEDGED UNDINE.
THE ROAD TO BECOMING AN UNDINE!
TO BECOME A FULL-FLEDGED UNDINE...
YOU MOVE THROUGH THE LEVELS OF PAIR (APPRENTICE) AND SINGLE (JOURNEYMAN).
WHEN YOU BECOME A PRIMA IS WHEN YOU CAN FINALLY BE CALLED A FULL-FLEDGED UNDINE.
APPRENTICE
JOURNEYMAN
FULL UNDINE
3
TWO GLOVES (PAIR)
2
ONE GLOVE (SINGLE)
1
NO GLOVES (PRIMA)
HEY, HEY, WHAT WAS THE PROMOTION TEST LIKE?

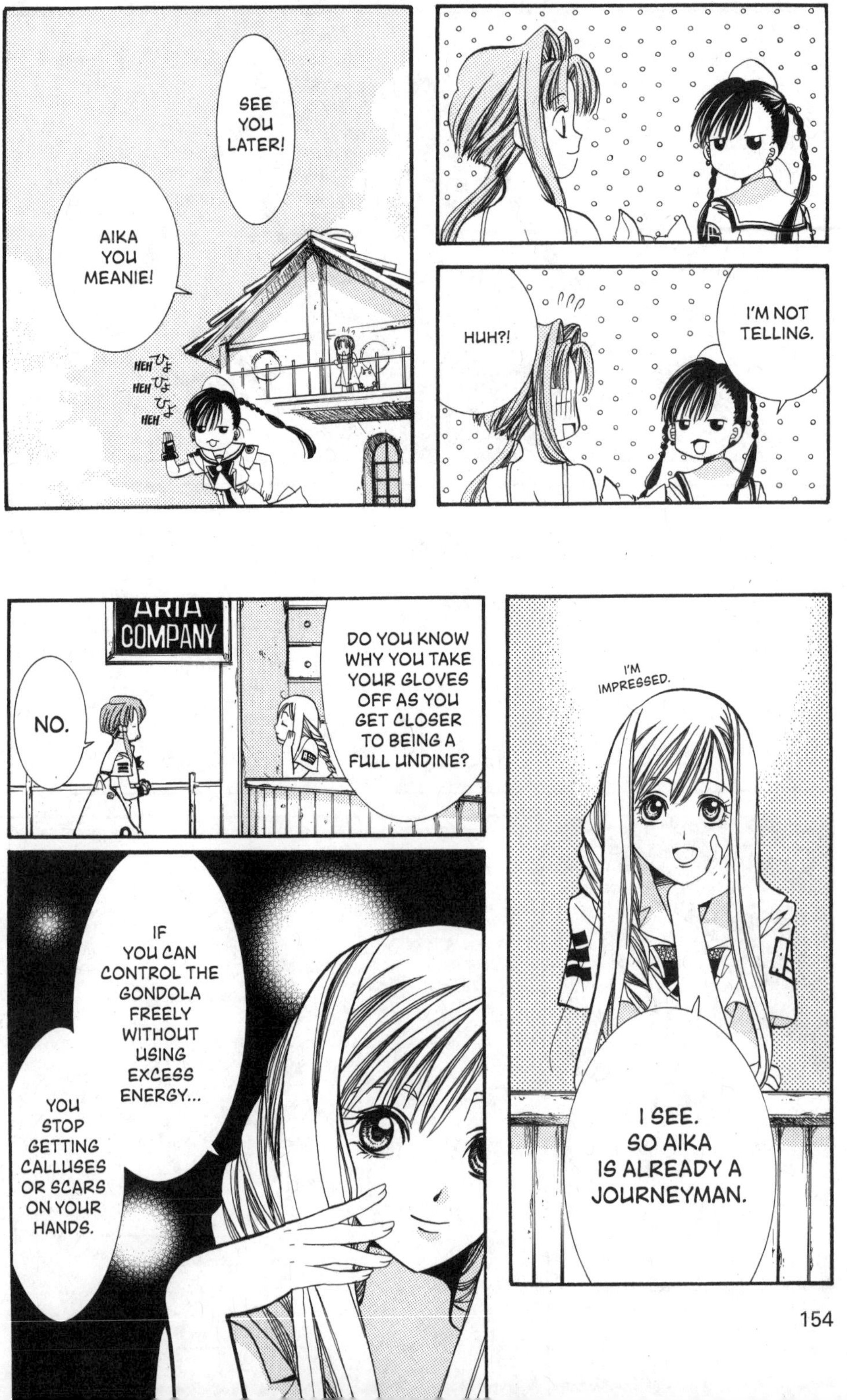

I'M NOT TELLING.
HUH?!
SEE YOU LATER!
AIKA YOU MEANIE!
HEH ひよ HEH ひよ ひよ HEH
I'M IMPRESSED.
I SEE. SO AIKA IS ALREADY A JOURNEYMAN.
ARIA COMPANY
DO YOU KNOW WHY YOU TAKE YOUR GLOVES OFF AS YOU GET CLOSER TO BEING A FULL UNDINE?
NO.
IF YOU CAN CONTROL THE GONDOLA FREELY WITHOUT USING EXCESS ENERGY...
YOU STOP GETTING CALLUSES OR SCARS ON YOUR HANDS.

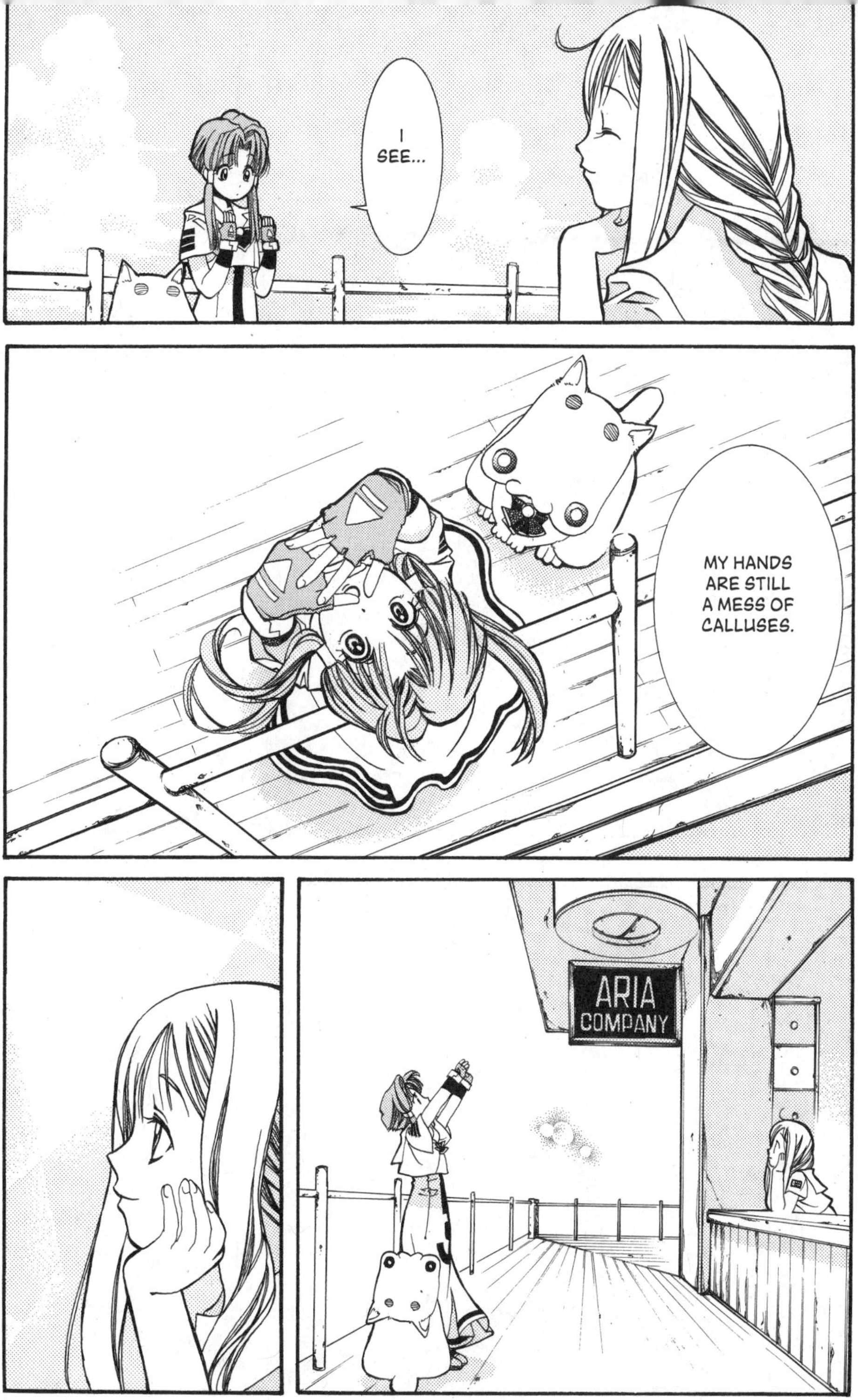
I SEE...
MY HANDS ARE STILL A MESS OF CALLUSES.
ARIA COMPANY

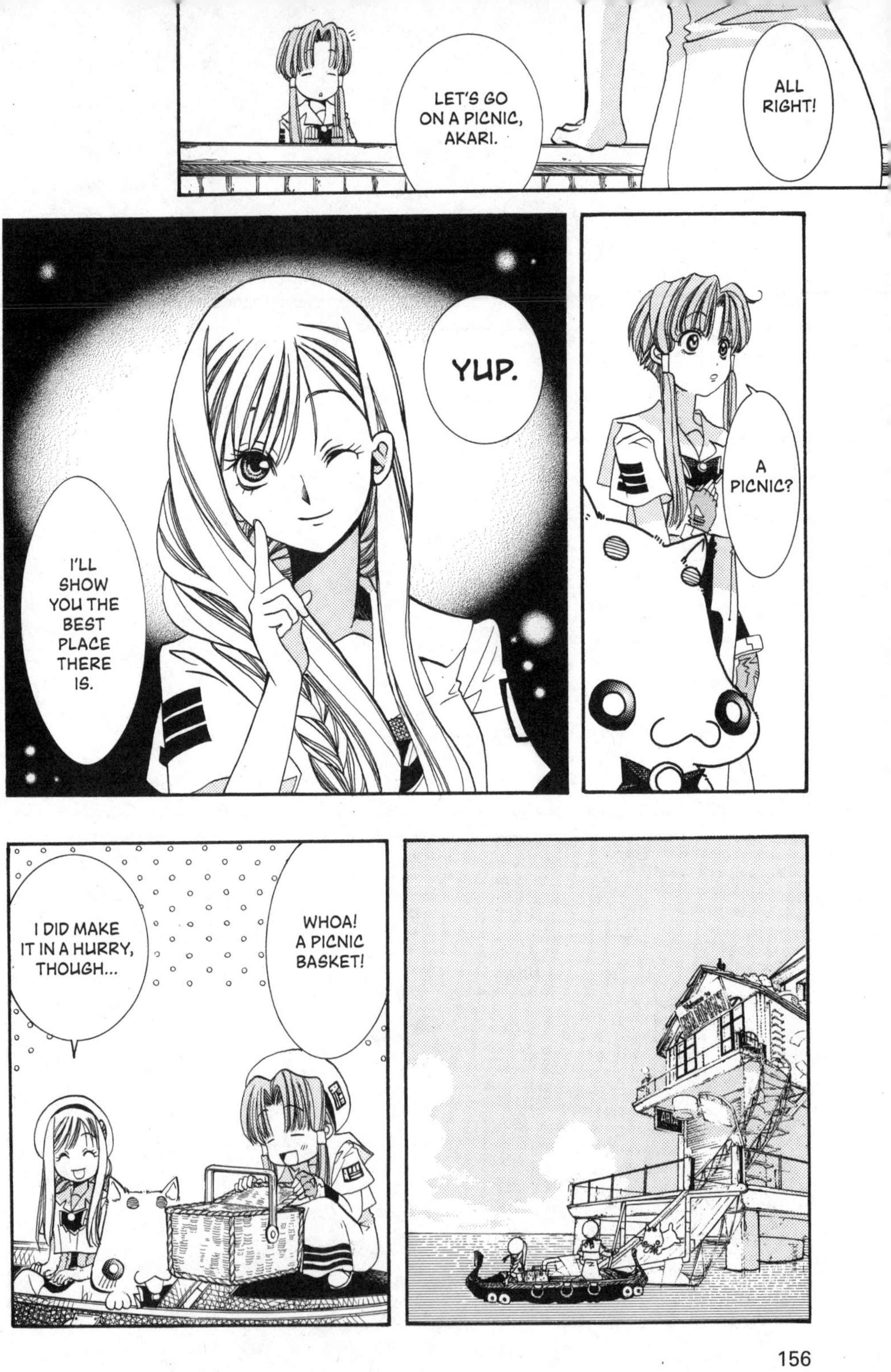
ALL RIGHT!
LET'S GO ON A PICNIC, AKARI.
A PICNIC?
YUP.
I'LL SHOW YOU THE BEST PLACE THERE IS.
WHOA! A PICNIC BASKET!
I DID MAKE IT IN A HURRY, THOUGH...

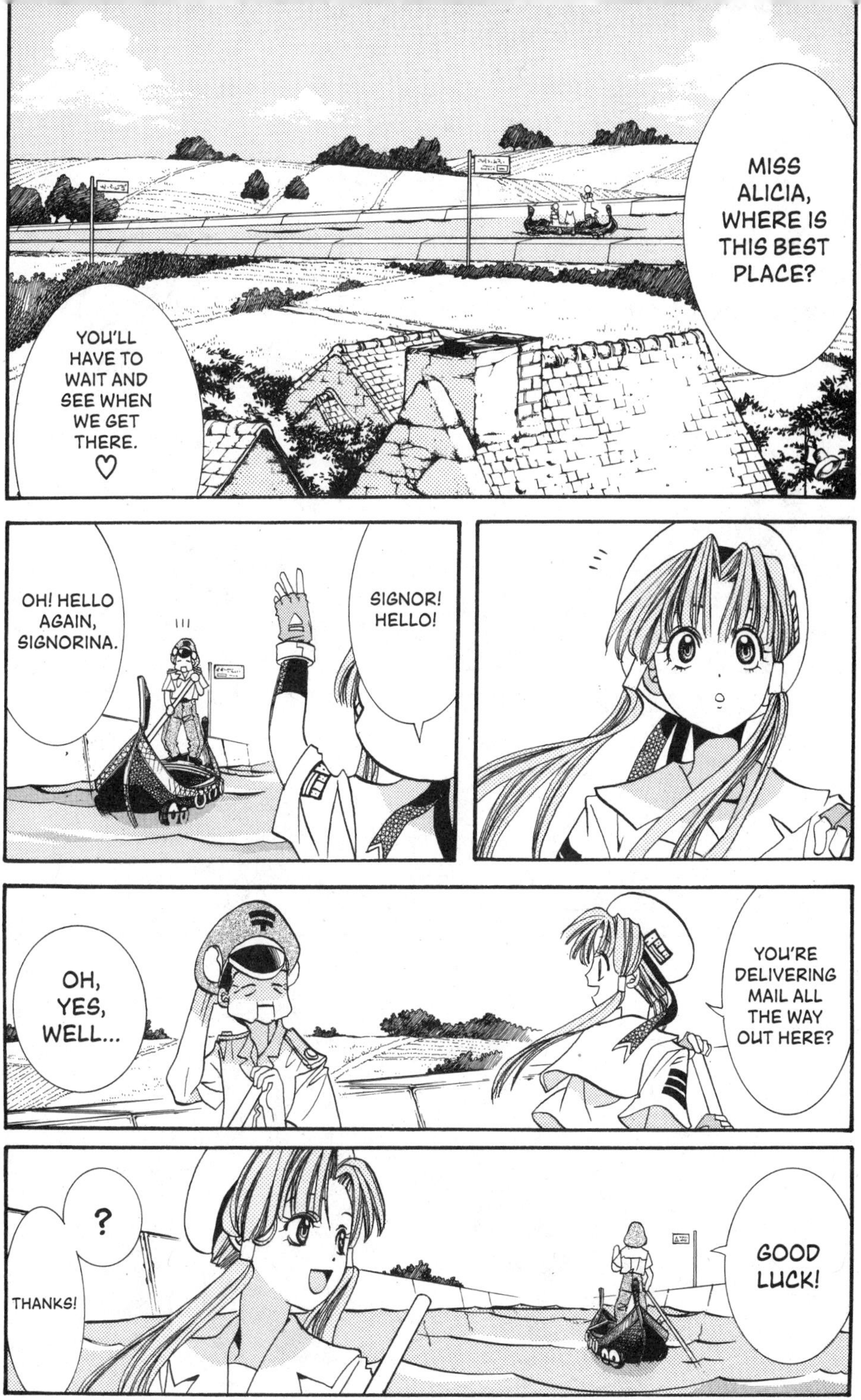
MISS ALICIA, WHERE IS THIS BEST PLACE?
YOU'LL HAVE TO WAIT AND SEE WHEN WE GET THERE. ♡
SIGNOR! HELLO!
OH! HELLO AGAIN, SIGNORINA.
YOU'RE DELIVERING MAIL ALL THE WAY OUT HERE?
OH, YES, WELL...
GOOD LUCK!
?
THANKS!

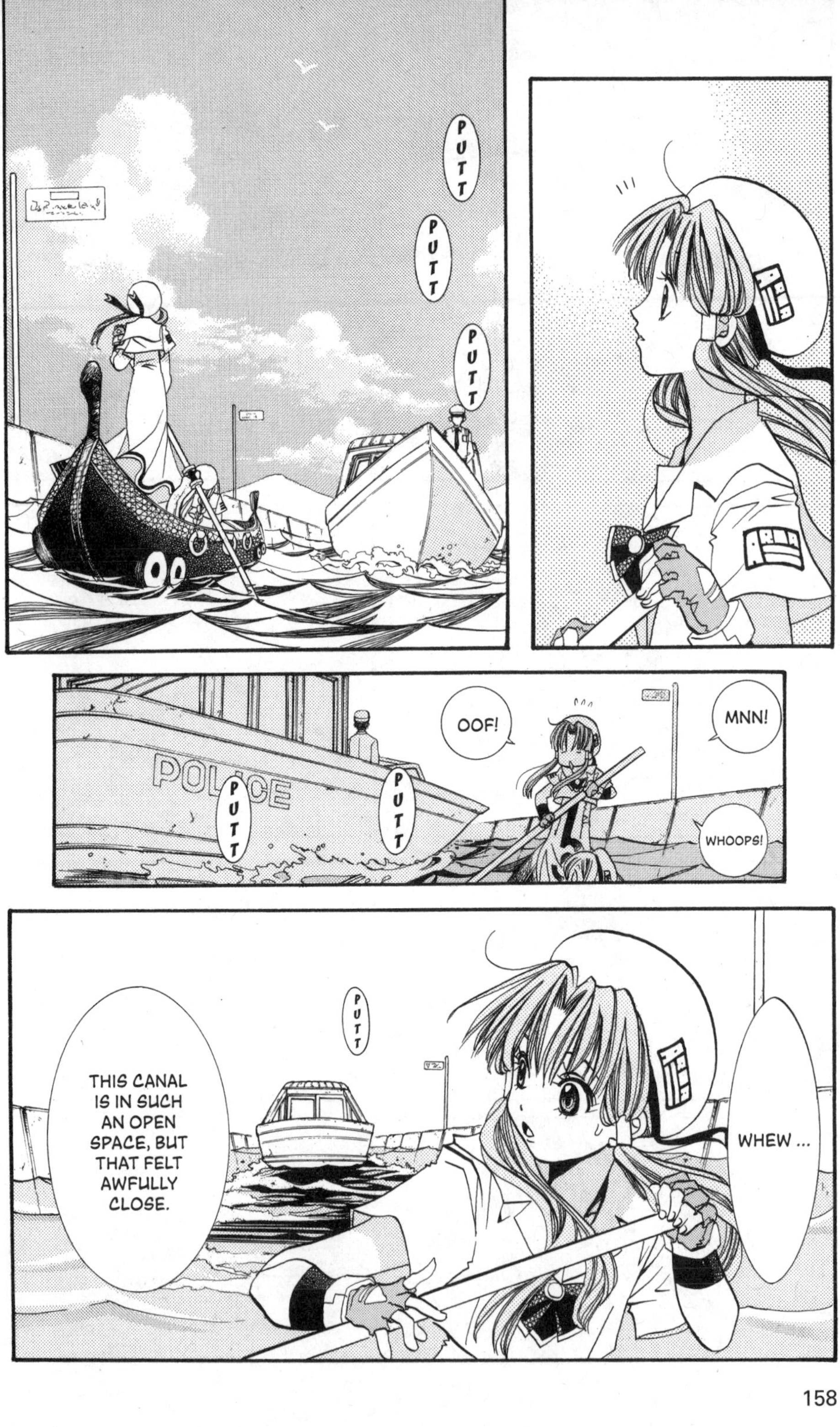
PUTT
PUTT
PUTT
MNN!
OOF!
WHOOPS!
PUTT
PUTT
WHEW ...
PUTT
THIS CANAL IS IN SUCH AN OPEN SPACE, BUT THAT FELT AWFULLY CLOSE.

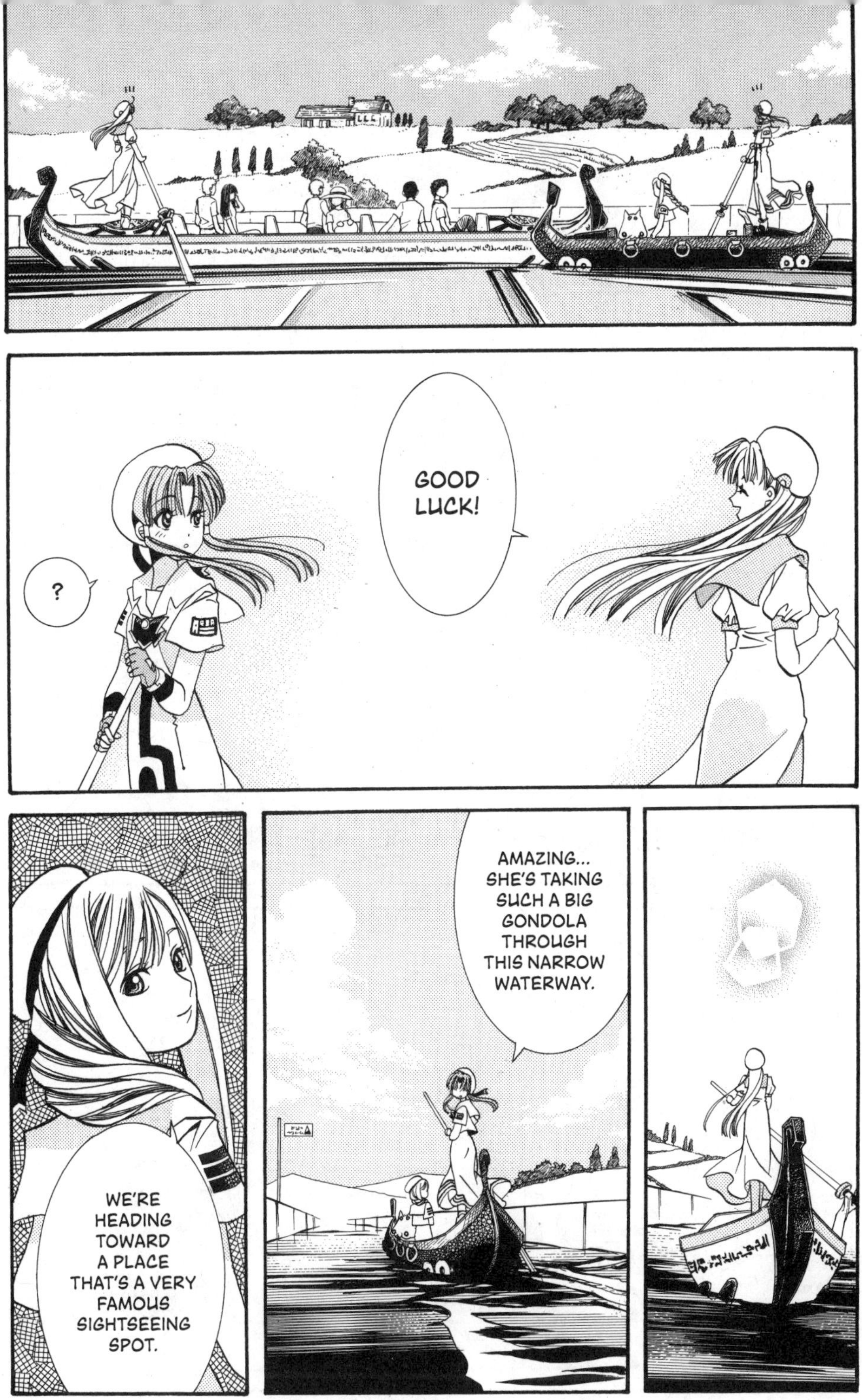
GOOD LUCK!
?
AMAZING... SHE'S TAKING SUCH A BIG GONDOLA THROUGH THIS NARROW WATERWAY.
WE'RE HEADING TOWARD A PLACE THAT'S A VERY FAMOUS SIGHTSEEING SPOT.

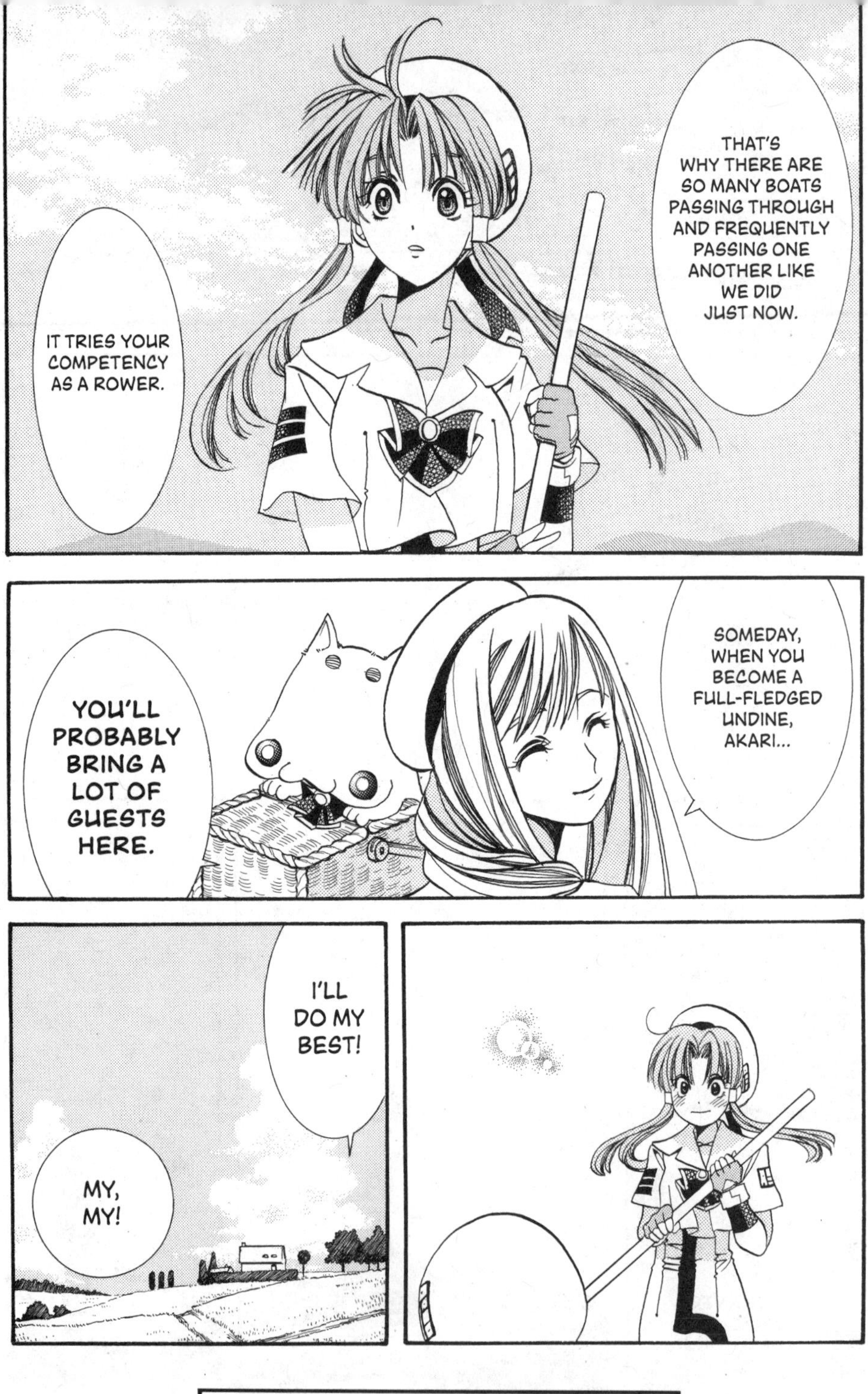
THAT'S WHY THERE ARE SO MANY BOATS PASSING THROUGH AND FREQUENTLY PASSING ONE ANOTHER LIKE WE DID JUST NOW.
IT TRIES YOUR COMPETENCY AS A ROWER.
SOMEDAY, WHEN YOU BECOME A FULL-FLEDGED UNDINE, AKARI...
YOU'LL PROBABLY BRING A LOT OF GUESTS HERE.
I'LL DO MY BEST!
MY, MY!

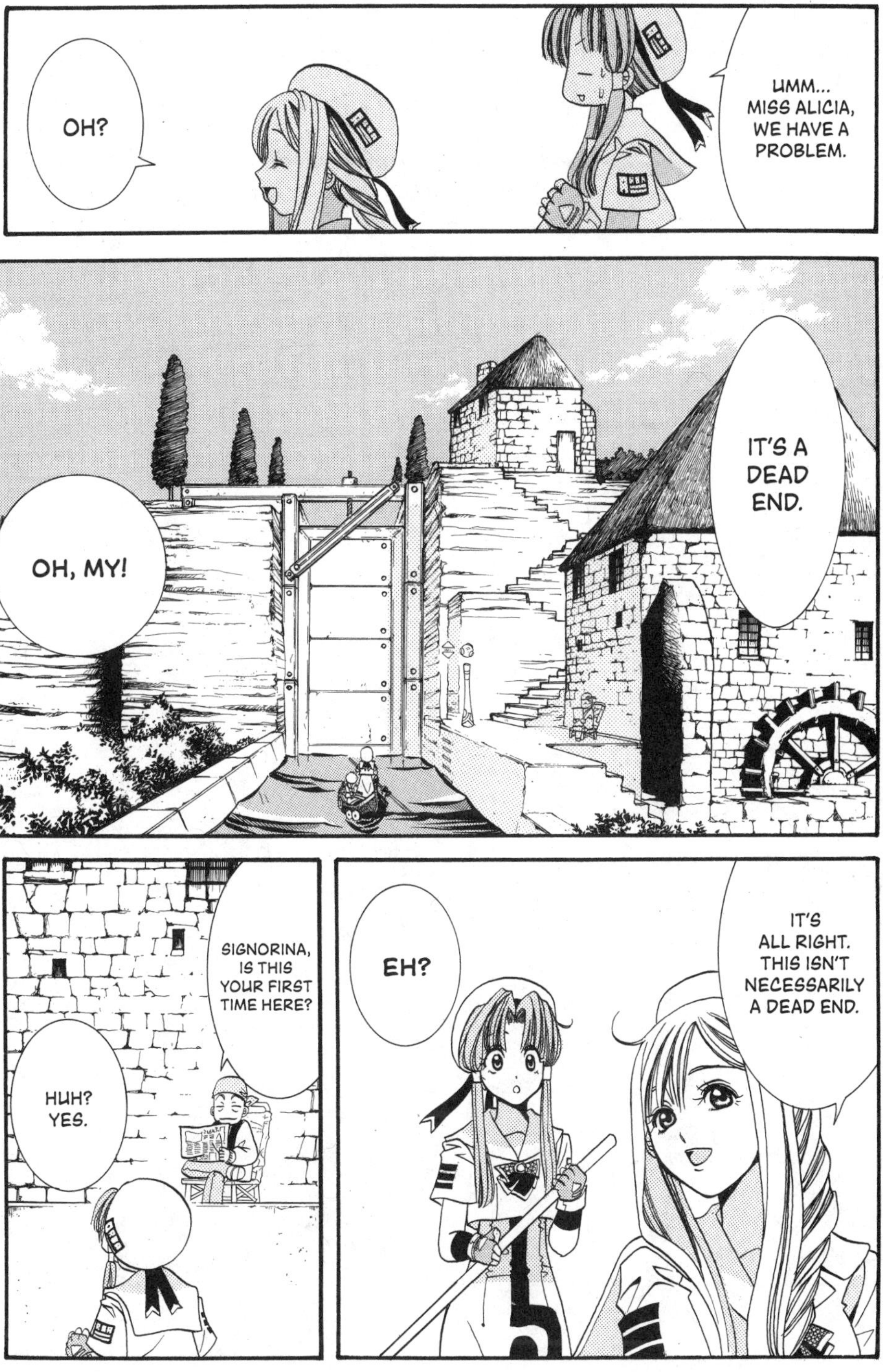
UMM... MISS ALICIA, WE HAVE A PROBLEM.
OH?
IT'S A DEAD END.
OH, MY!
IT'S ALL RIGHT. THIS ISN'T NECESSARILY A DEAD END.
EH?
SIGNORINA, IS THIS YOUR FIRST TIME HERE?
HUH? YES.

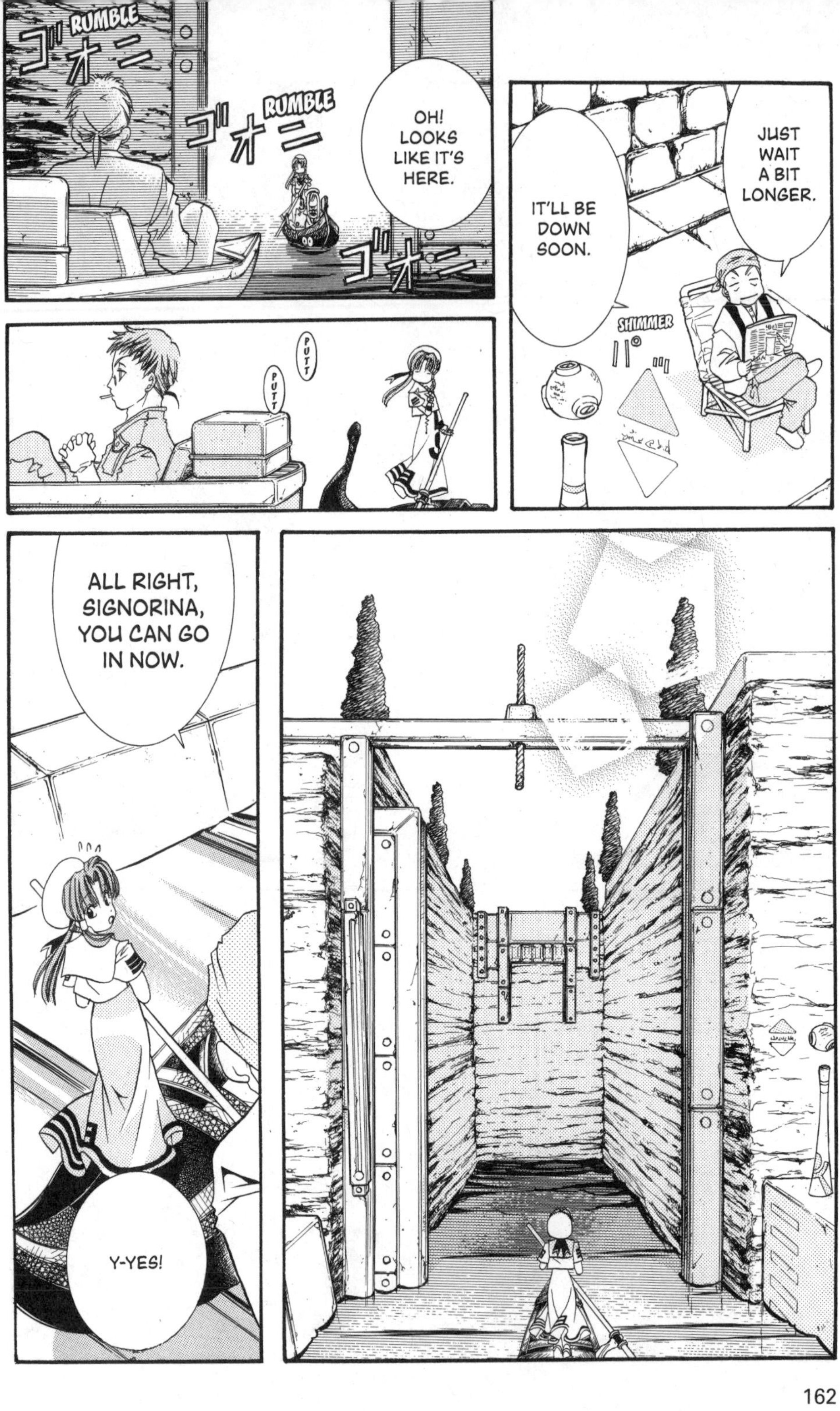
JUST WAIT A BIT LONGER.
IT'LL BE DOWN SOON.
SHIMMER
RUMBLE
RUMBLE
OH! LOOKS LIKE IT'S HERE.
PUTT
PUTT
ALL RIGHT, SIGNORINA, YOU CAN GO IN NOW.
Y-YES!

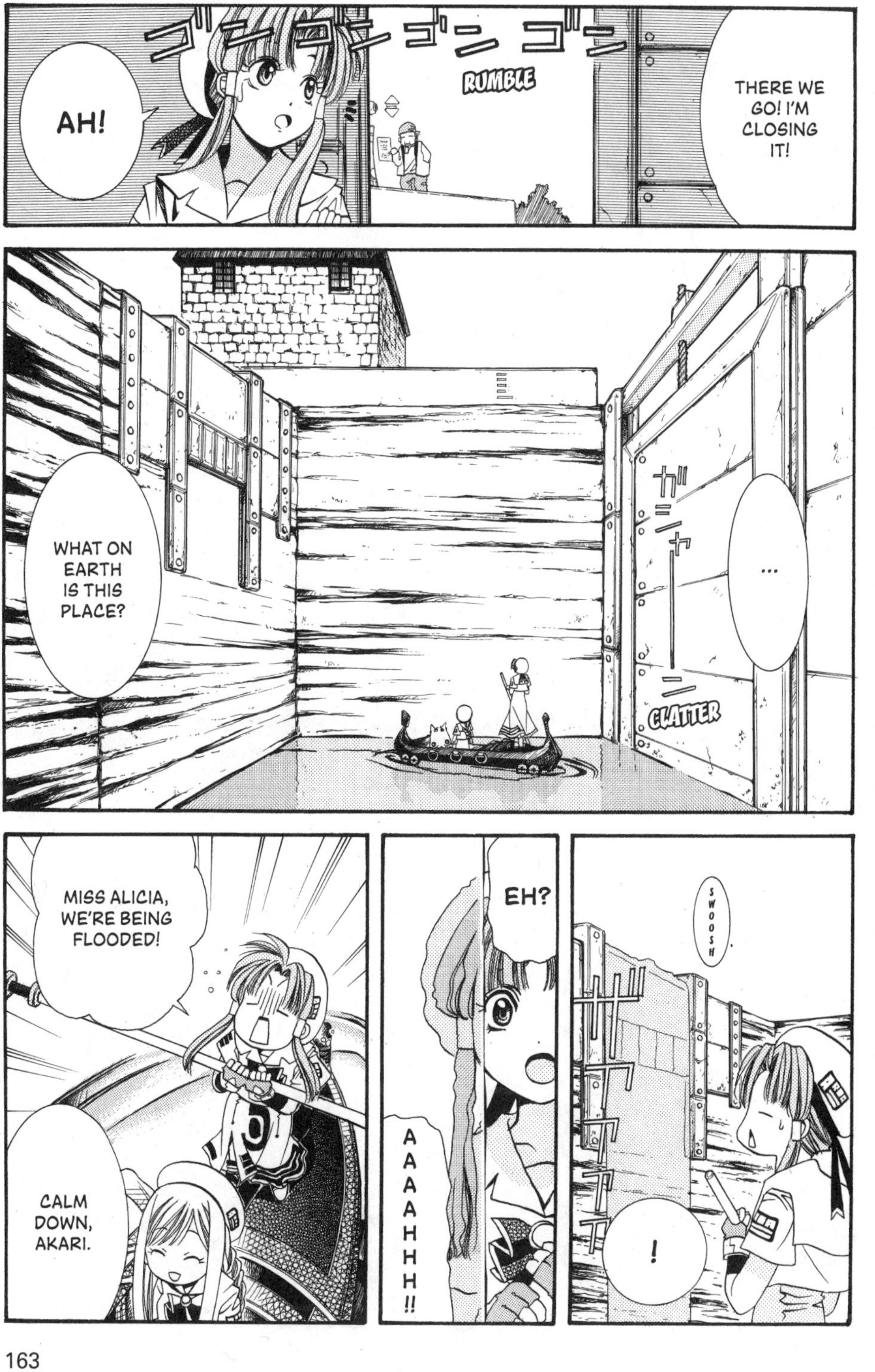
THERE WE GO! I'M CLOSING IT!
RUMBLE
AH!
...
CLATTER
WHAT ON EARTH IS THIS PLACE?
SWOOSH
!
EH?
AAAAAHHH!!
MISS ALICIA, WE'RE BEING FLOODED!
CALM DOWN, AKARI.

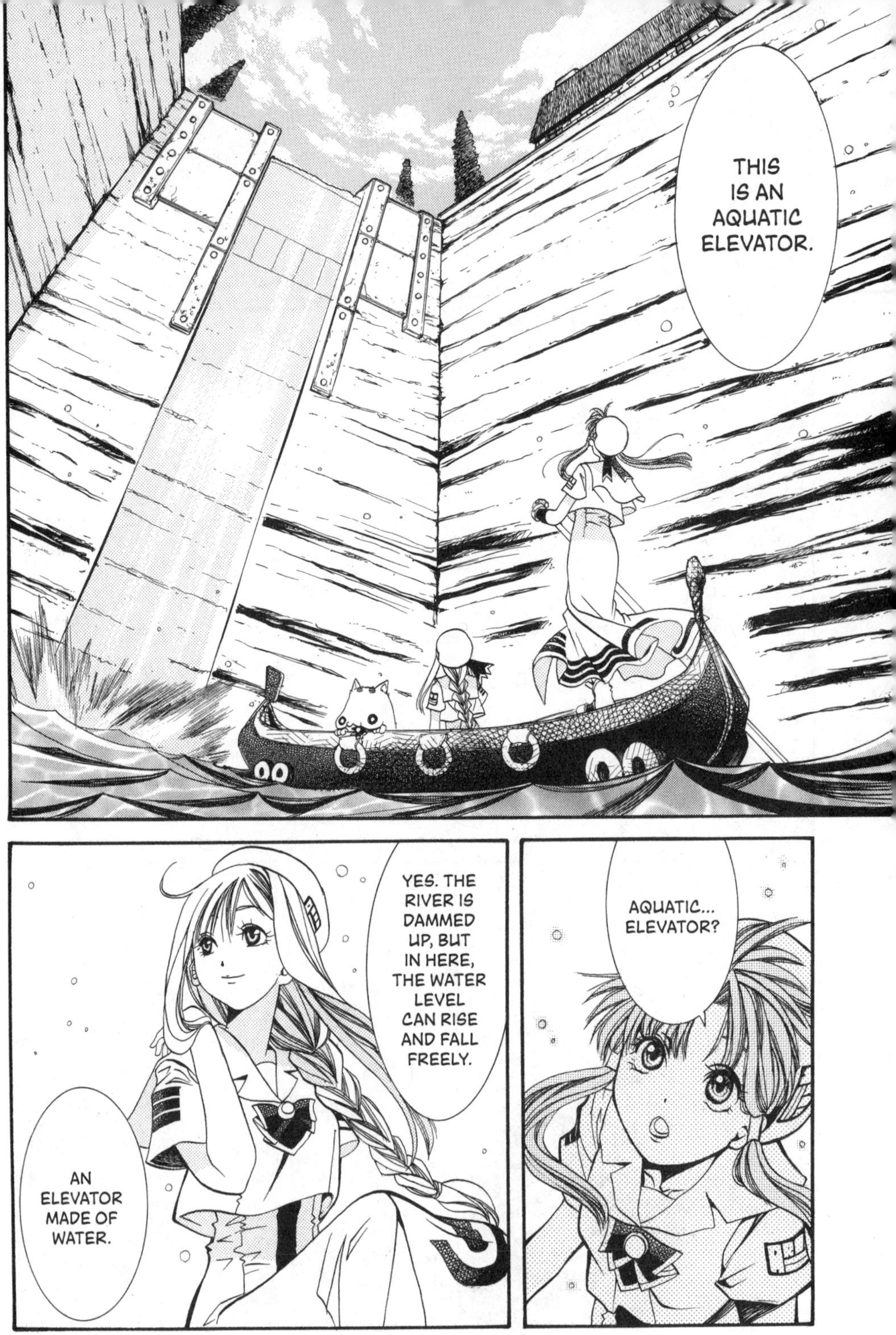
THIS IS AN AQUATIC ELEVATOR.
AQUATIC... ELEVATOR?
YES. THE RIVER IS DAMMED UP, BUT IN HERE, THE WATER LEVEL CAN RISE AND FALL FREELY.
AN ELEVATOR MADE OF WATER.

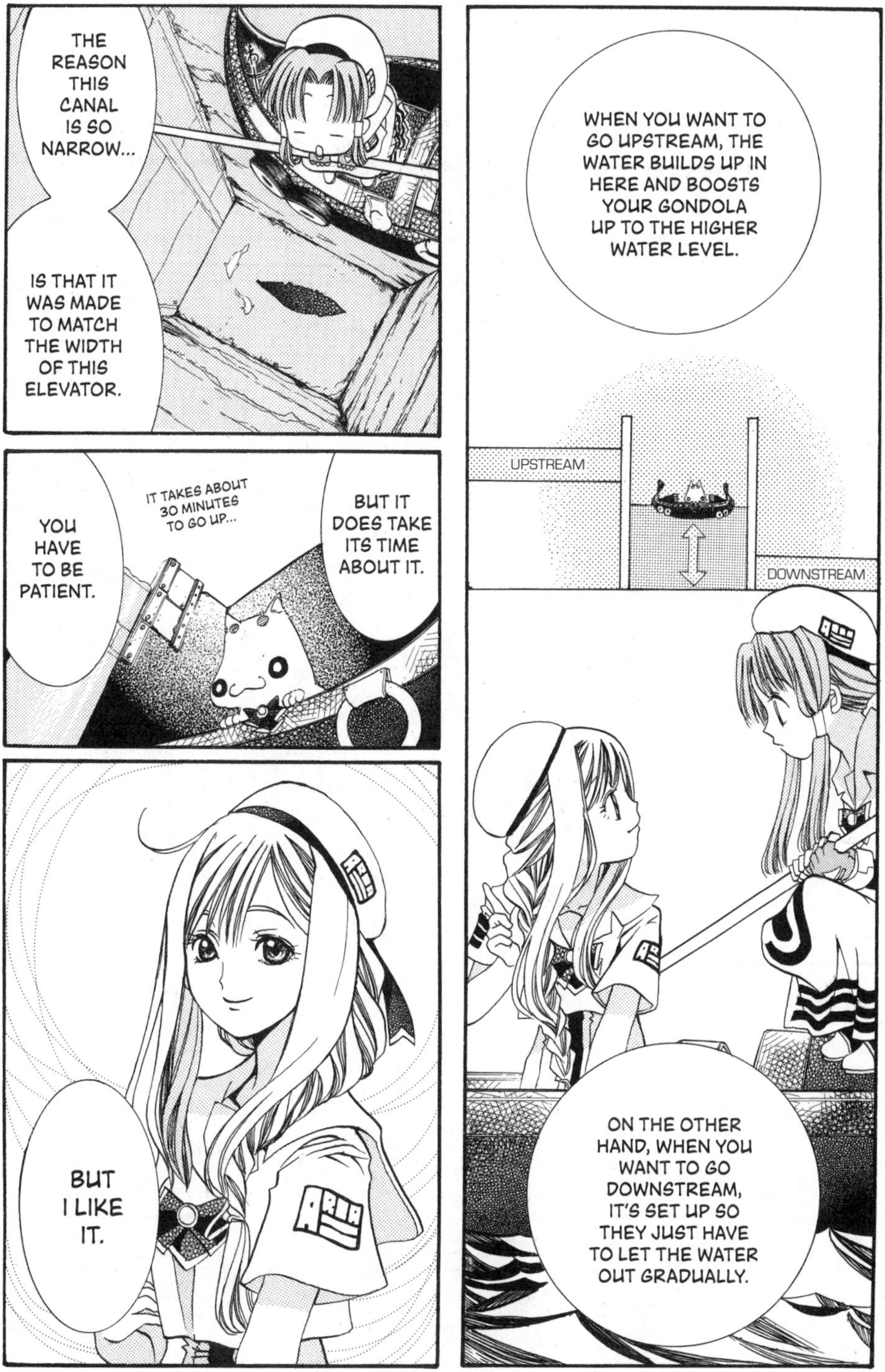
THE REASON THIS CANAL IS SO NARROW...
IS THAT IT WAS MADE TO MATCH THE WIDTH OF THIS ELEVATOR.
WHEN YOU WANT TO GO UPSTREAM, THE WATER BUILDS UP IN HERE AND BOOSTS YOUR GONDOLA UP TO THE HIGHER WATER LEVEL.
UPSTREAM
DOWNSTREAM
ON THE OTHER HAND, WHEN YOU WANT TO GO DOWNSTREAM, IT'S SET UP SO THEY JUST HAVE TO LET THE WATER OUT GRADUALLY.
BUT IT DOES TAKE ITS TIME ABOUT IT.
IT TAKES ABOUT 30 MINUTES TO GO UP...
YOU HAVE TO BE PATIENT.
BUT I LIKE IT.

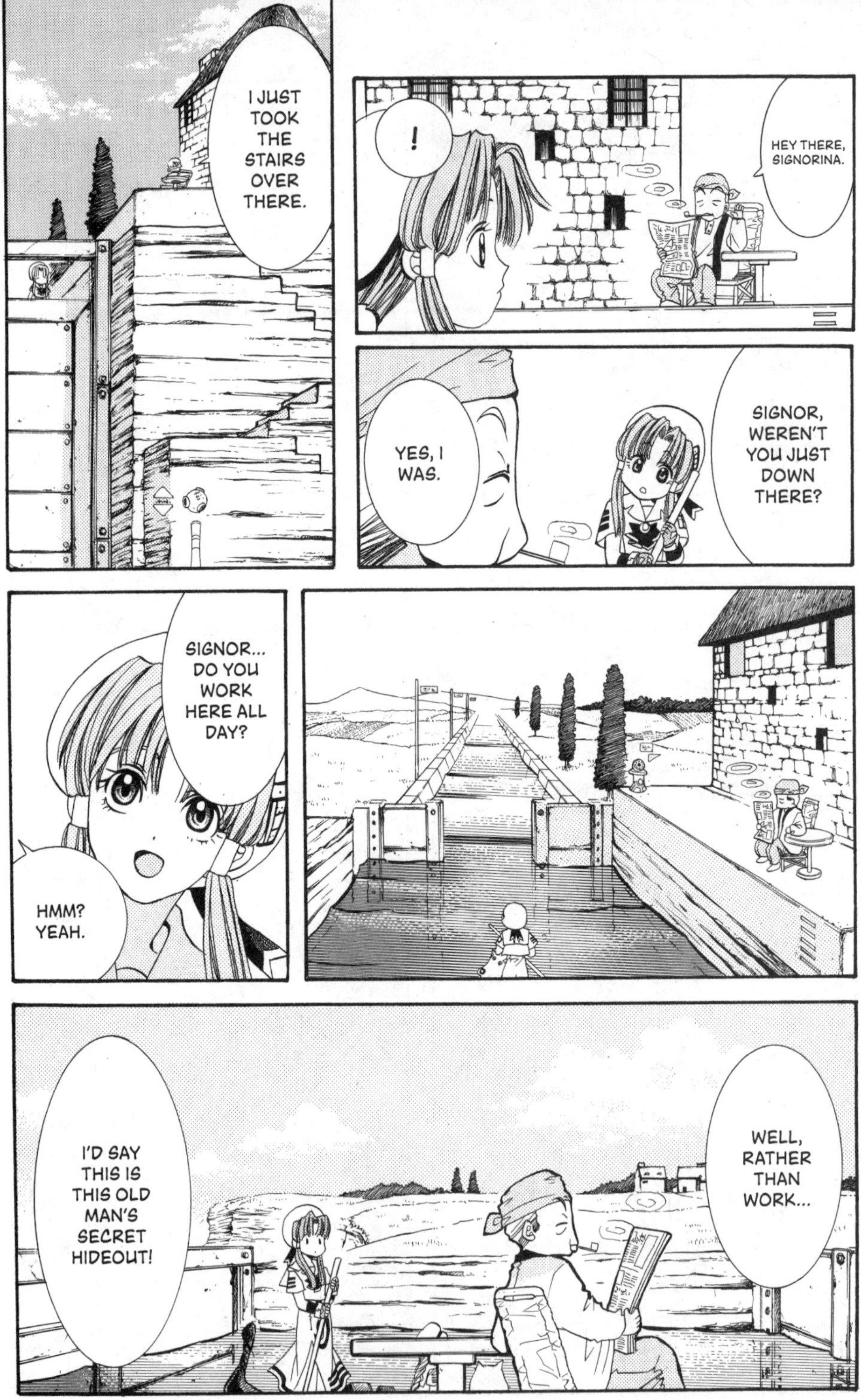
HEY THERE, SIGNORINA.
!
SIGNOR, WEREN'T YOU JUST DOWN THERE?
YES, I WAS.
I JUST TOOK THE STAIRS OVER THERE.
SIGNOR... DO YOU WORK HERE ALL DAY?
HMM? YEAH.
WELL, RATHER THAN WORK...
I'D SAY THIS IS THIS OLD MAN'S SECRET HIDEOUT!

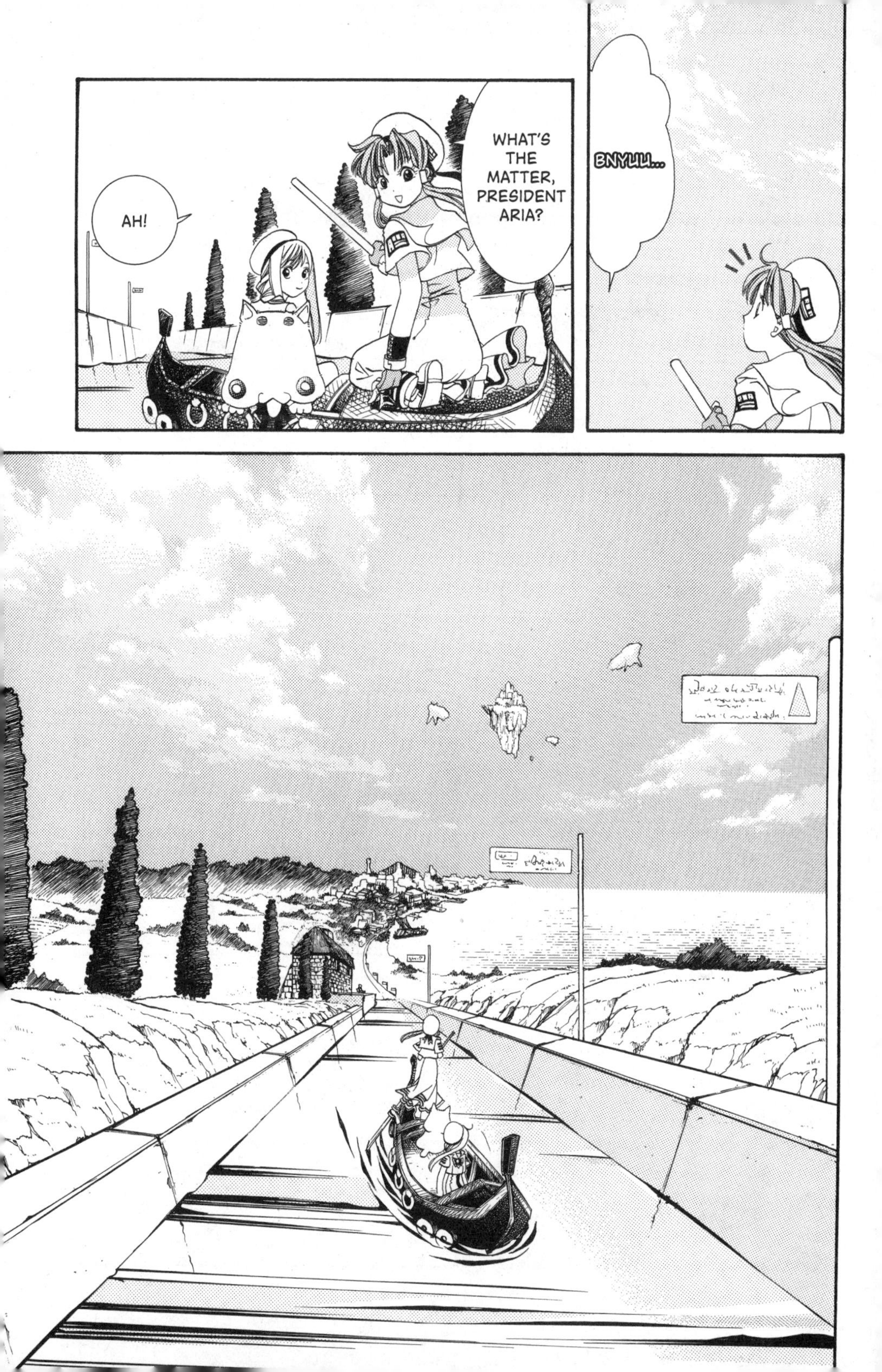
BNYUU...
WHAT'S THE MATTER, PRESIDENT ARIA?
AH!

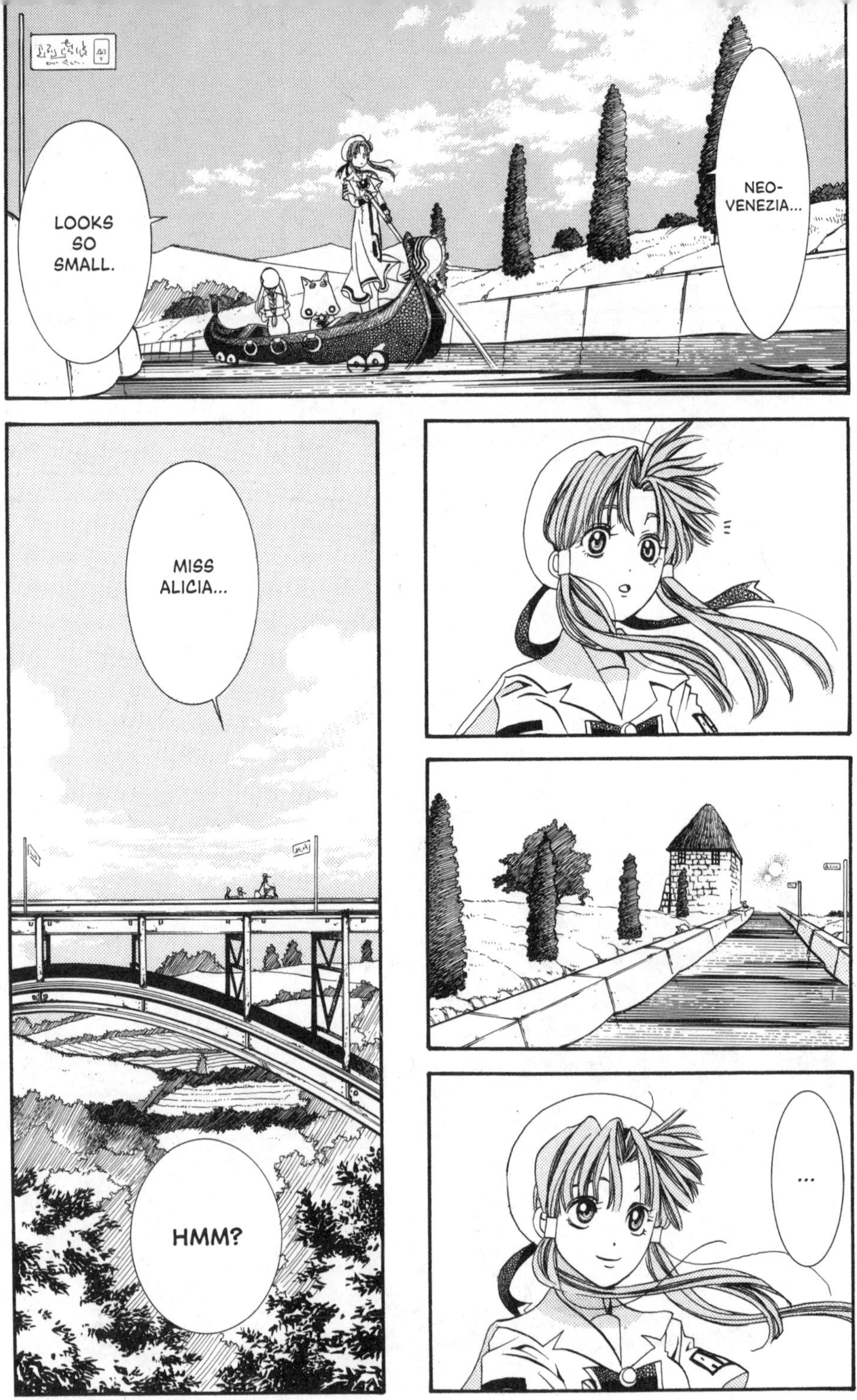
NEO-VENEZIA...
LOOKS SO SMALL.
...
MISS ALICIA...
HMM?

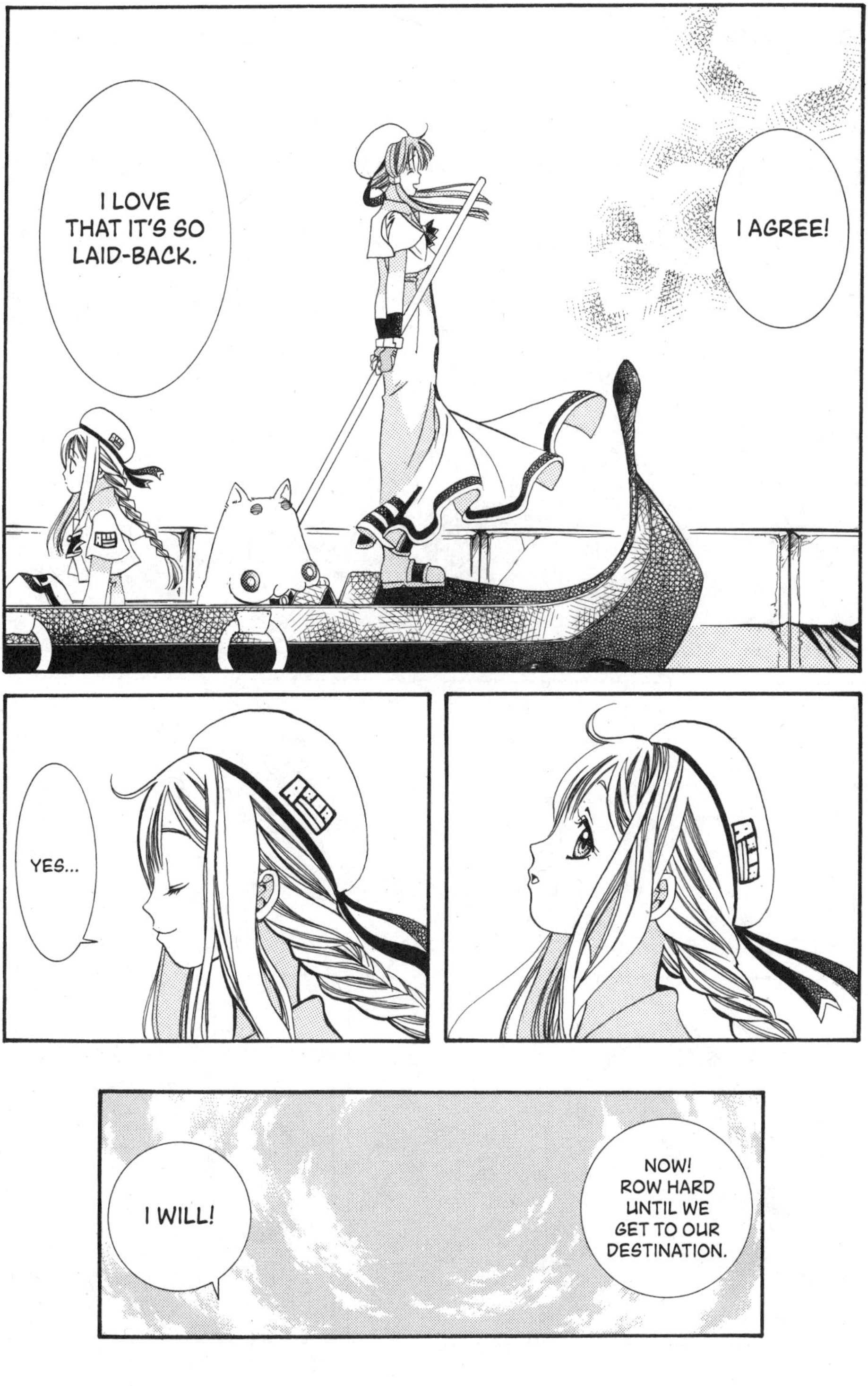
I AGREE!
I LOVE THAT IT'S SO LAID-BACK.
YES...
NOW! ROW HARD UNTIL WE GET TO OUR DESTINATION.
I WILL!

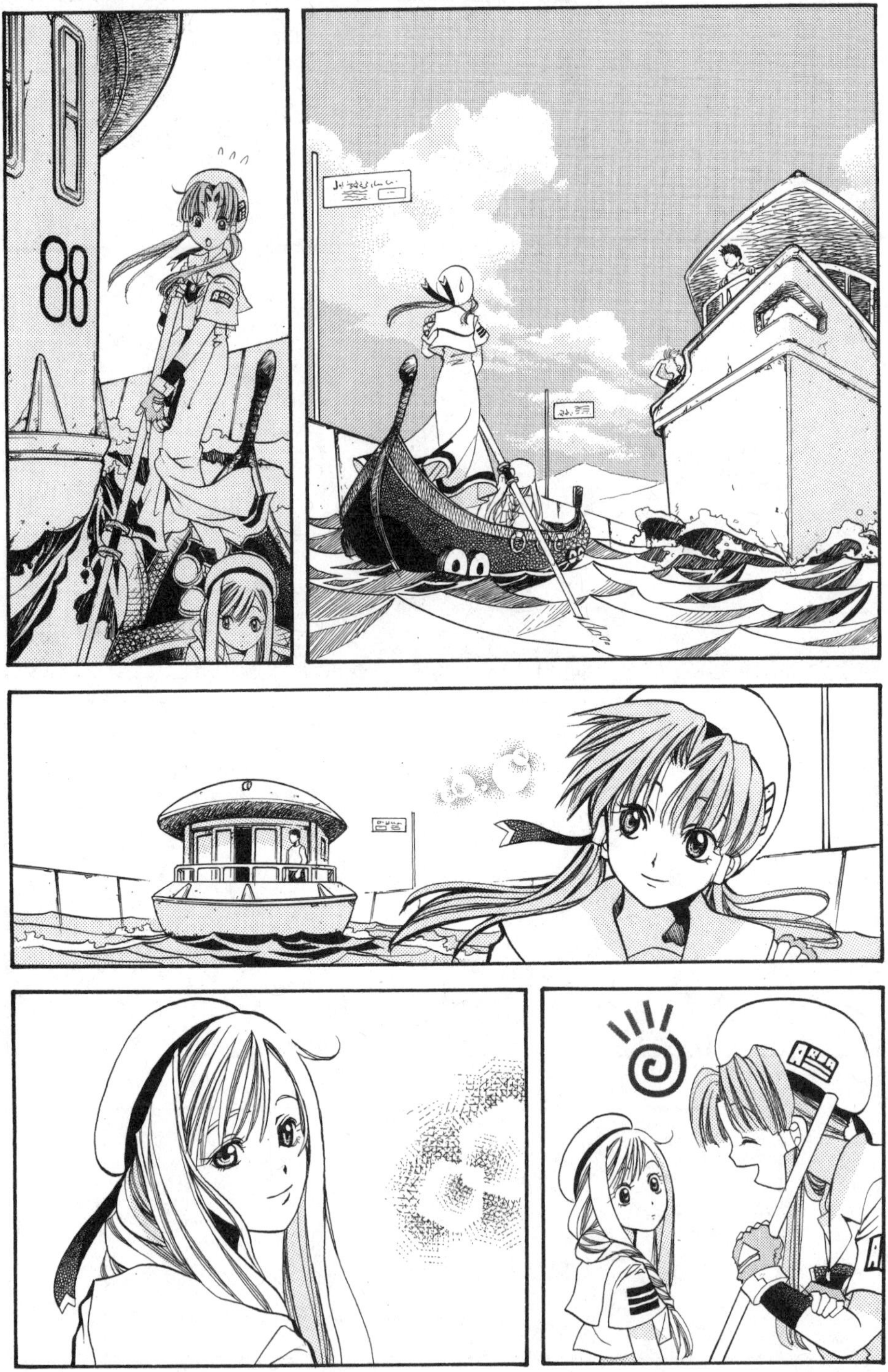
88

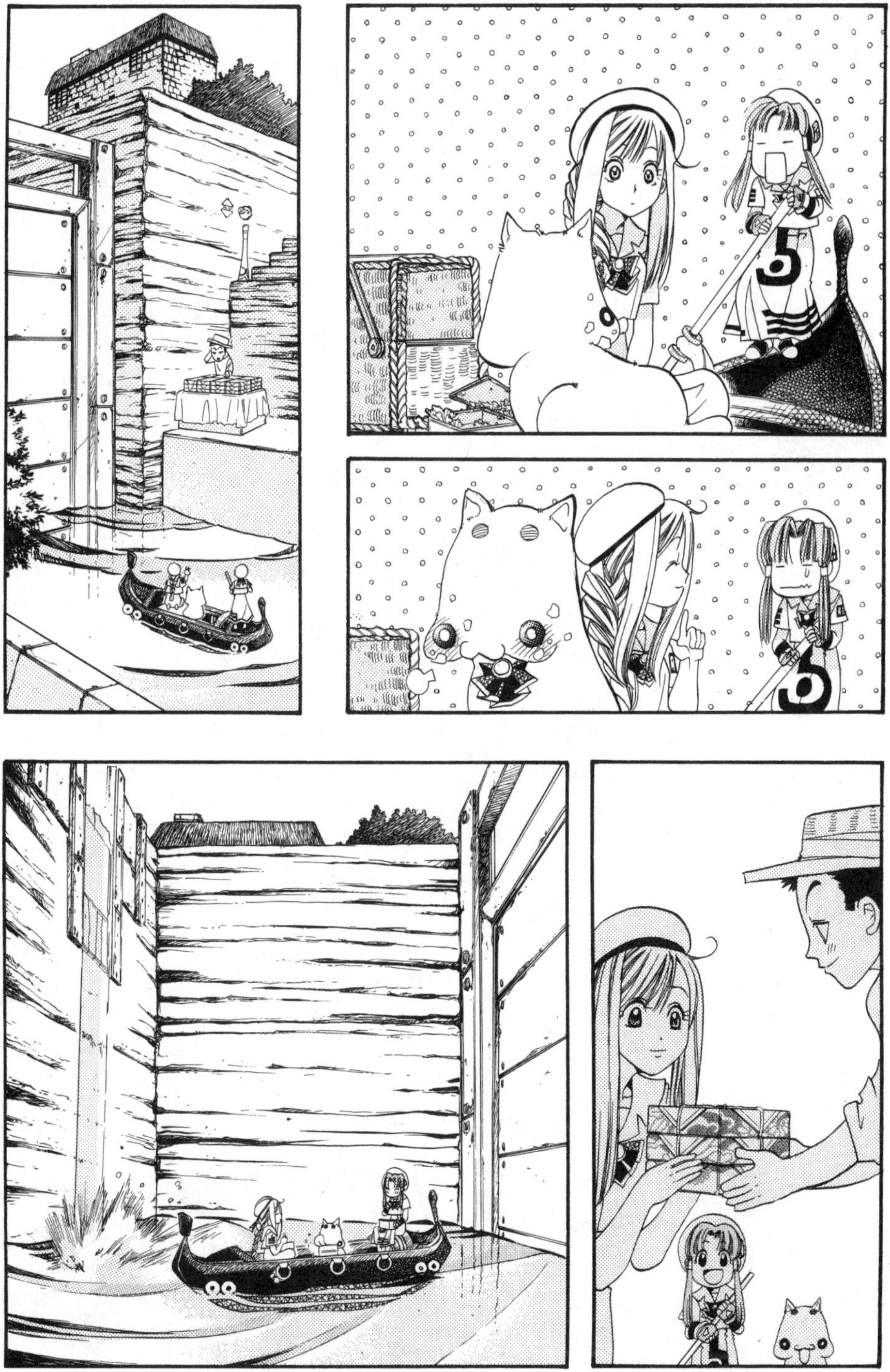

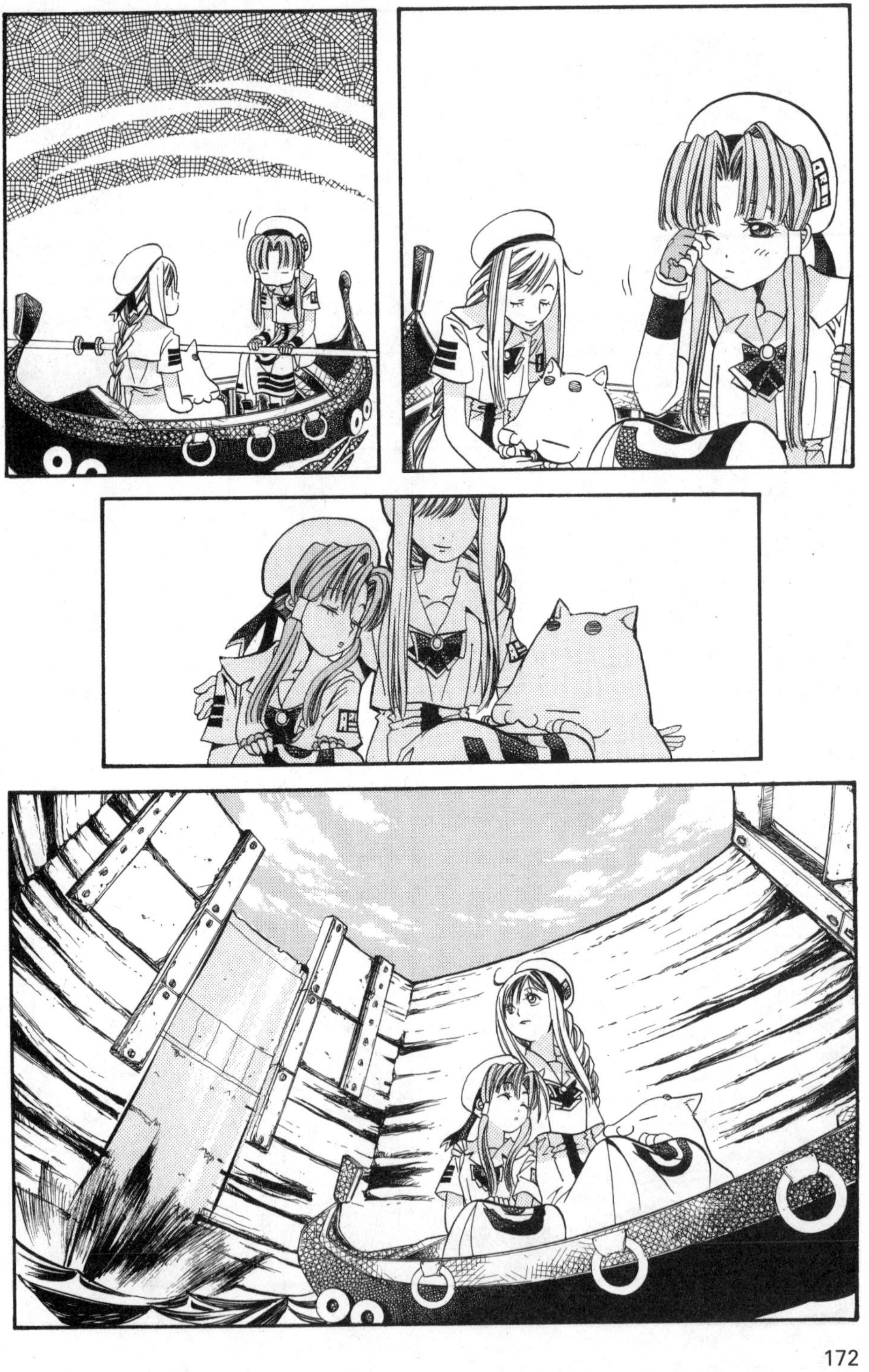

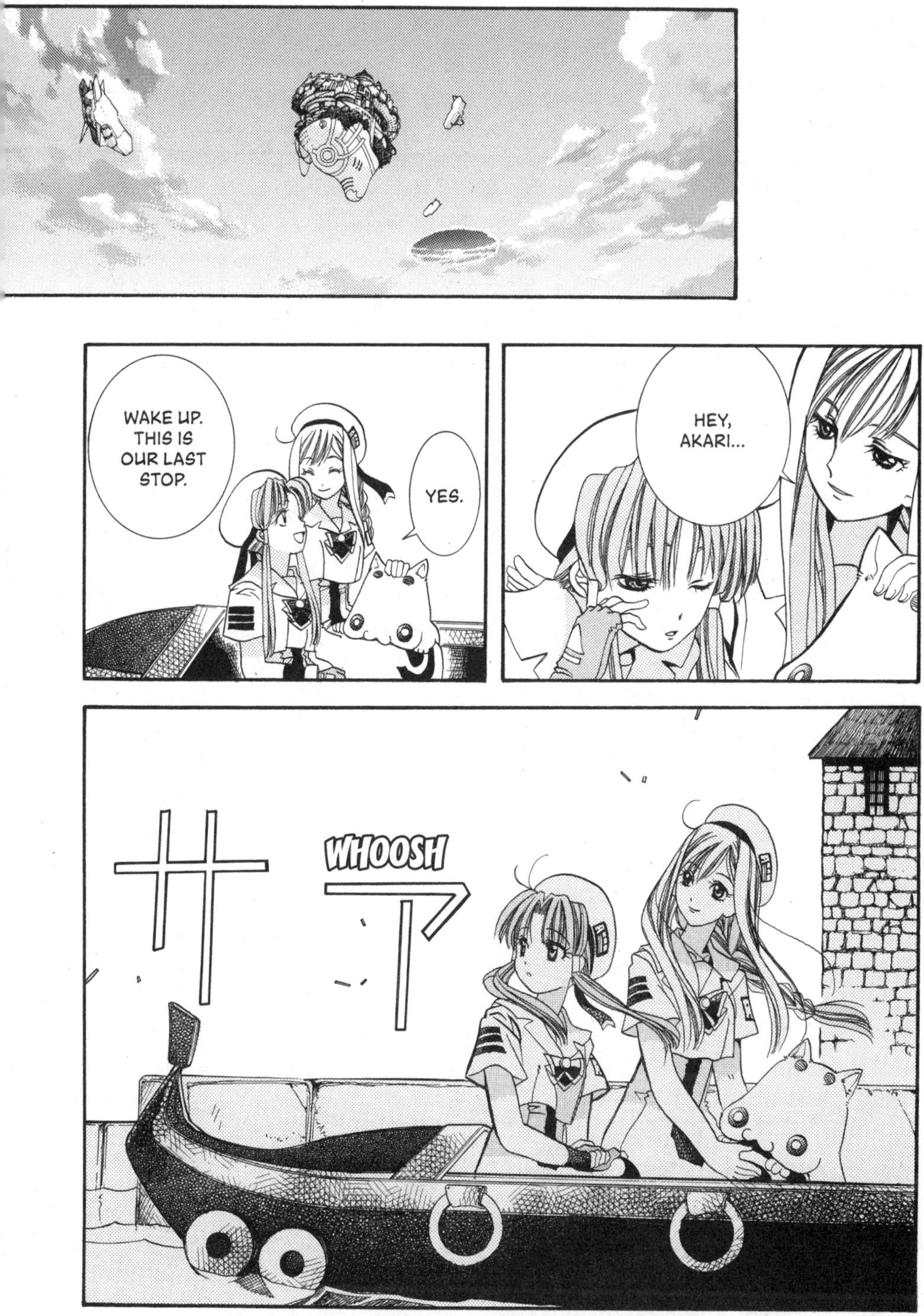
HEY, AKARI...
WAKE UP. THIS IS OUR LAST STOP.
YES.
サア
WHOOSH

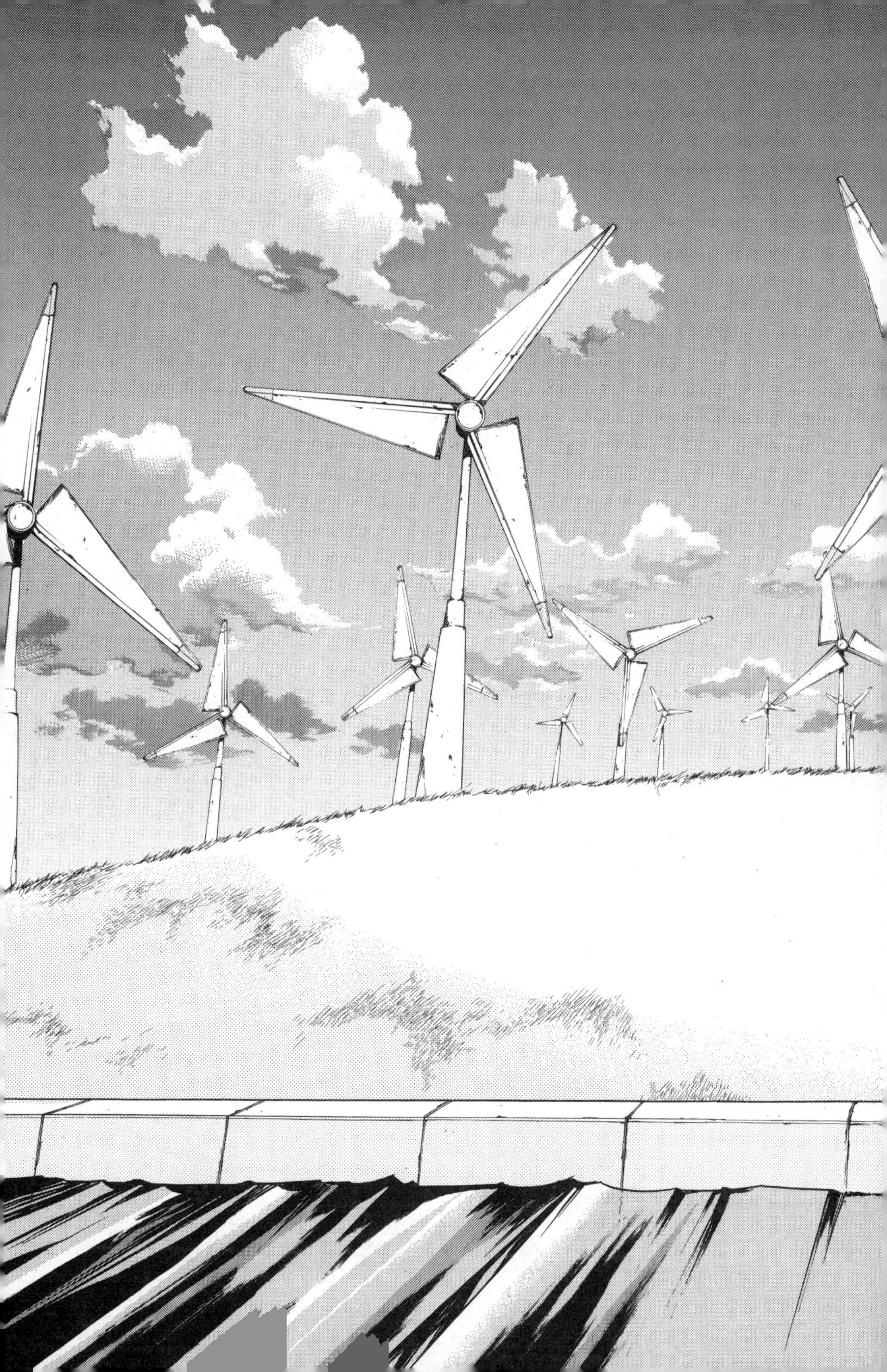

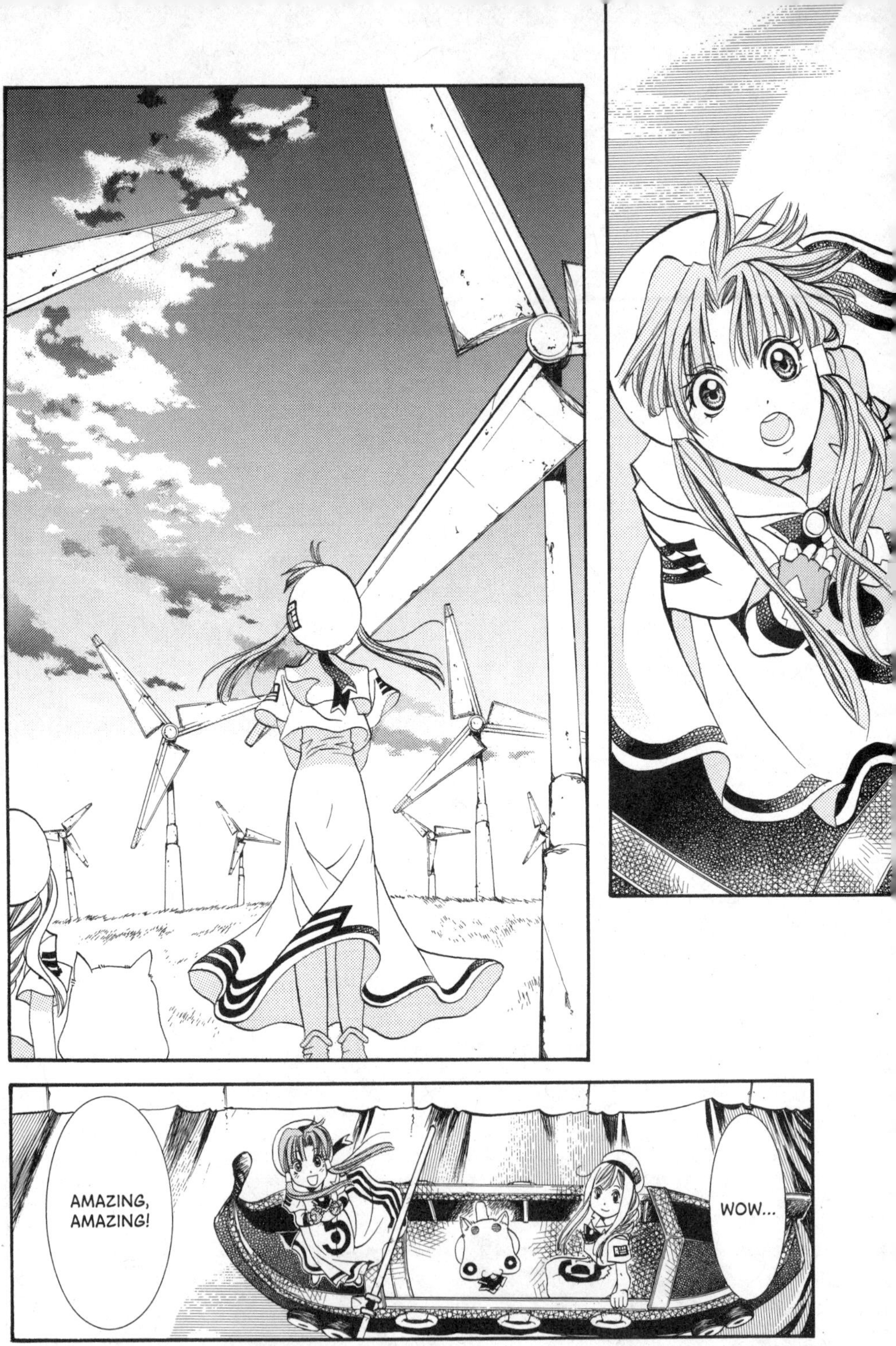
WOW...
AMAZING, AMAZING!

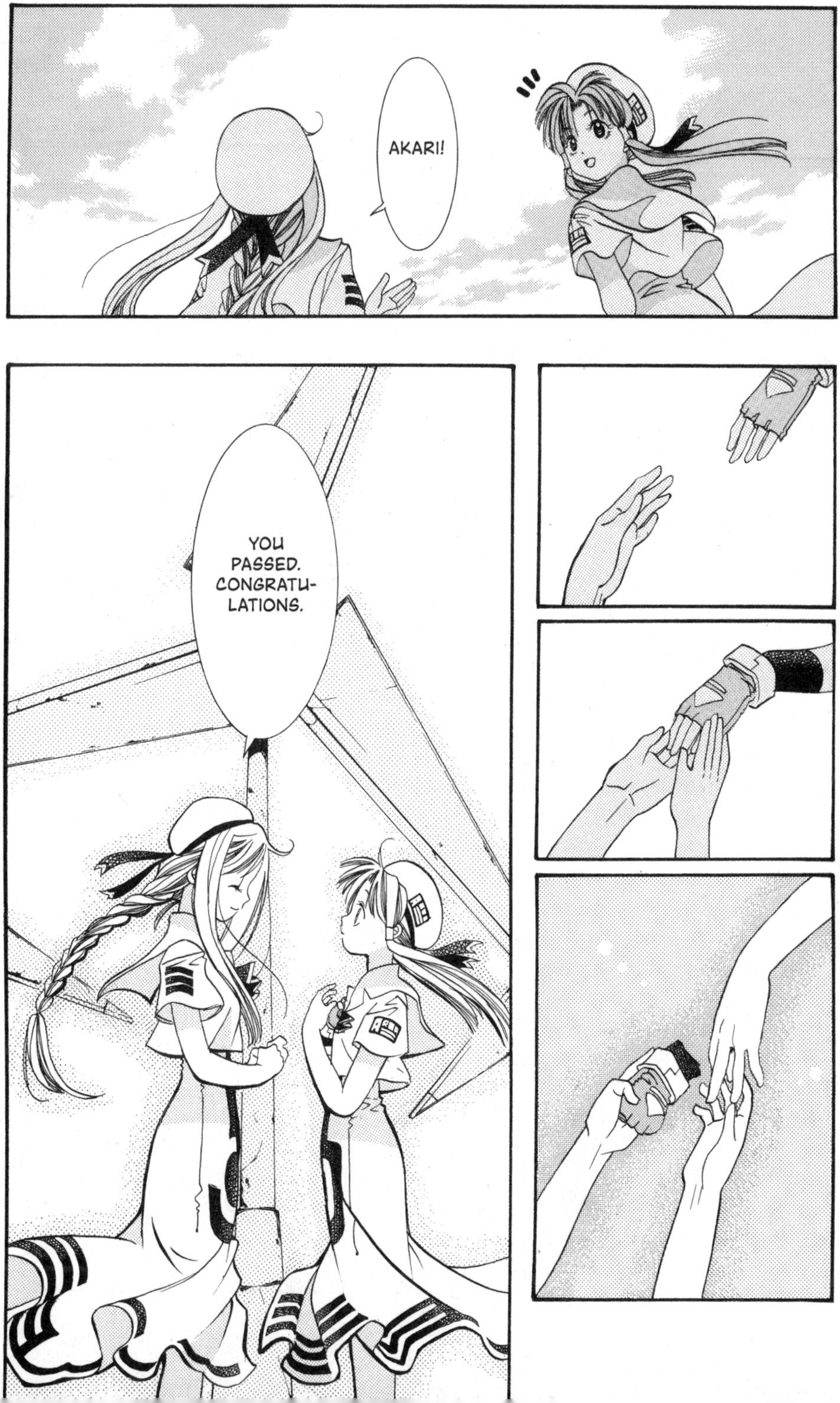
AKARI!
YOU PASSED. CONGRATU- LATIONS.

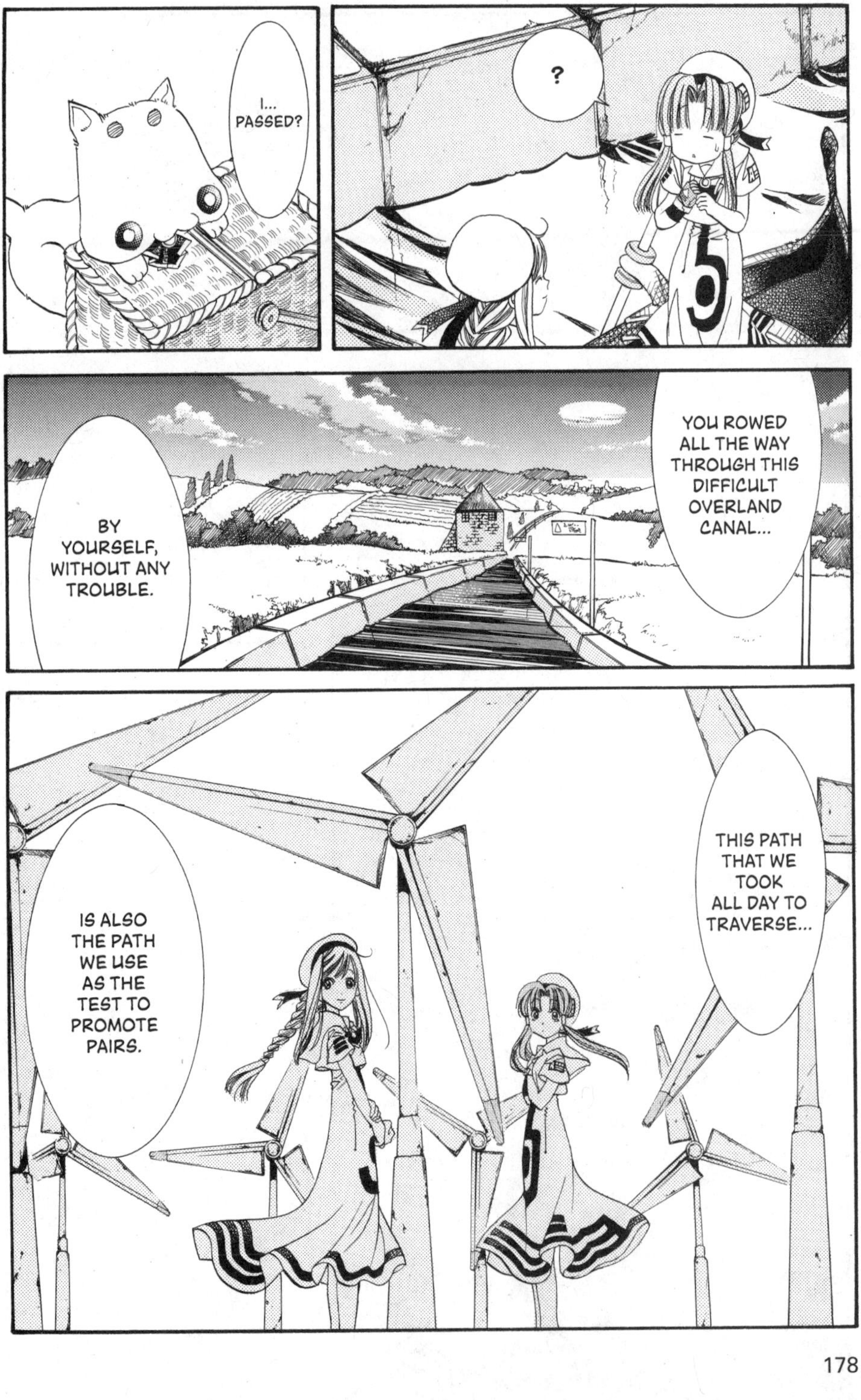
?
I... PASSED?
YOU ROWED ALL THE WAY THROUGH THIS DIFFICULT OVERLAND CANAL...
BY YOURSELF, WITHOUT ANY TROUBLE.
THIS PATH THAT WE TOOK ALL DAY TO TRAVERSE...
IS ALSO THE PATH WE USE AS THE TEST TO PROMOTE PAIRS.

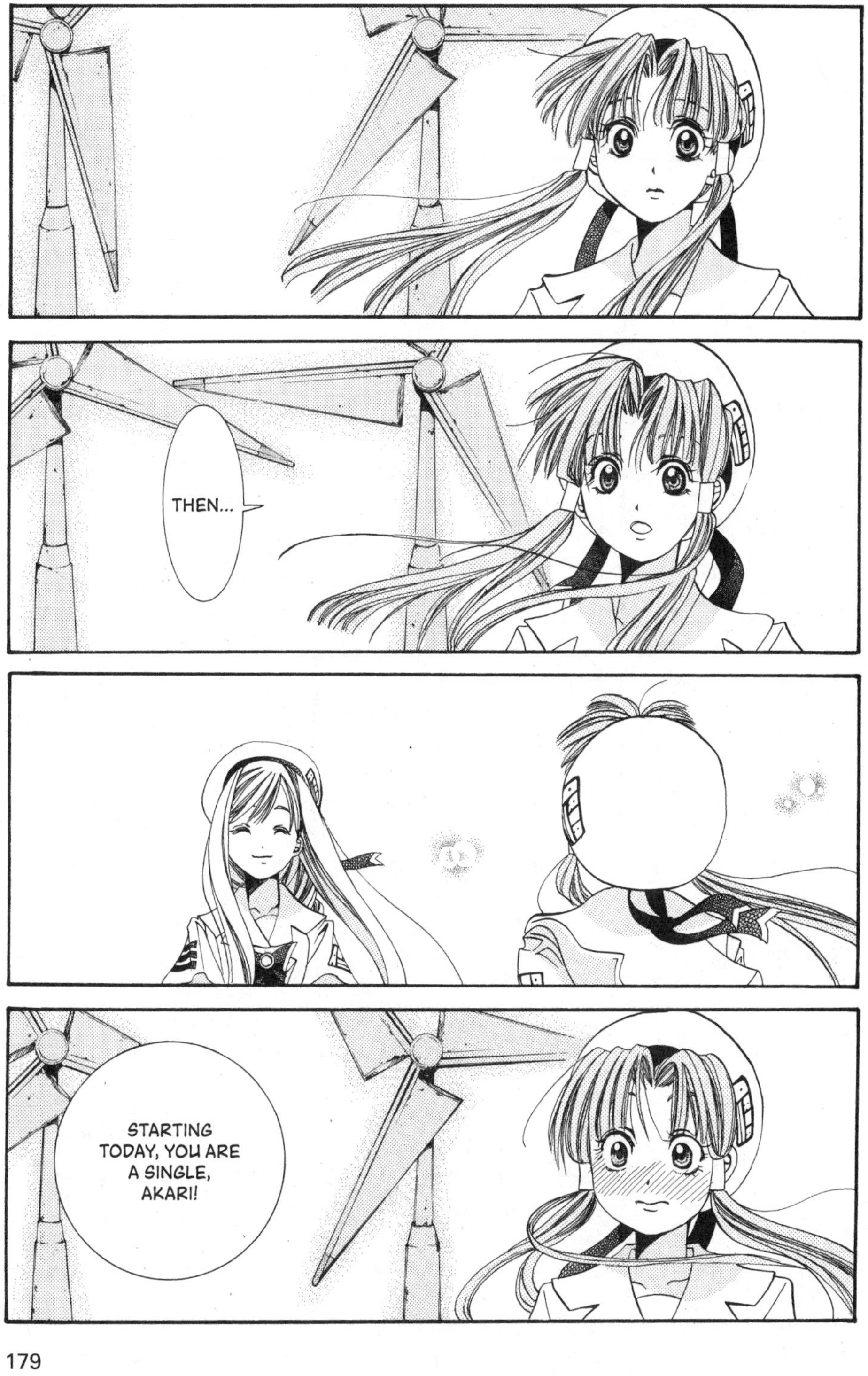
THEN...
STARTING TODAY, YOU ARE A SINGLE, AKARI!

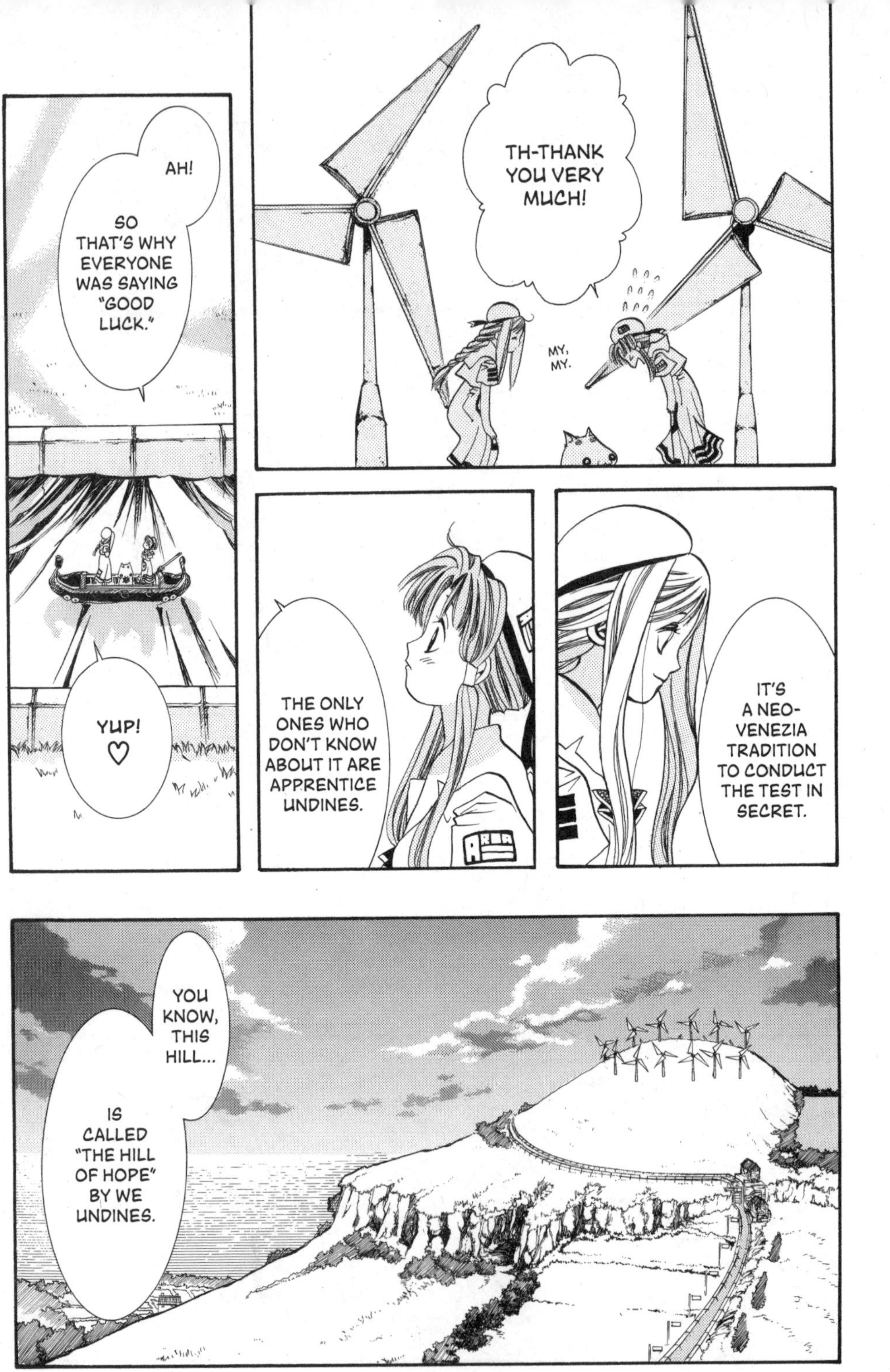
TH-THANK YOU VERY MUCH!
MY, MY.
IT'S A NEO-VENEZIA TRADITION TO CONDUCT THE TEST IN SECRET.
THE ONLY ONES WHO DON'T KNOW ABOUT IT ARE APPRENTICE UNDINES.
AH!
SO THAT'S WHY EVERYONE WAS SAYING "GOOD LUCK."
YUP! ♡
YOU KNOW, THIS HILL...
IS CALLED "THE HILL OF HOPE" BY WE UNDINES.

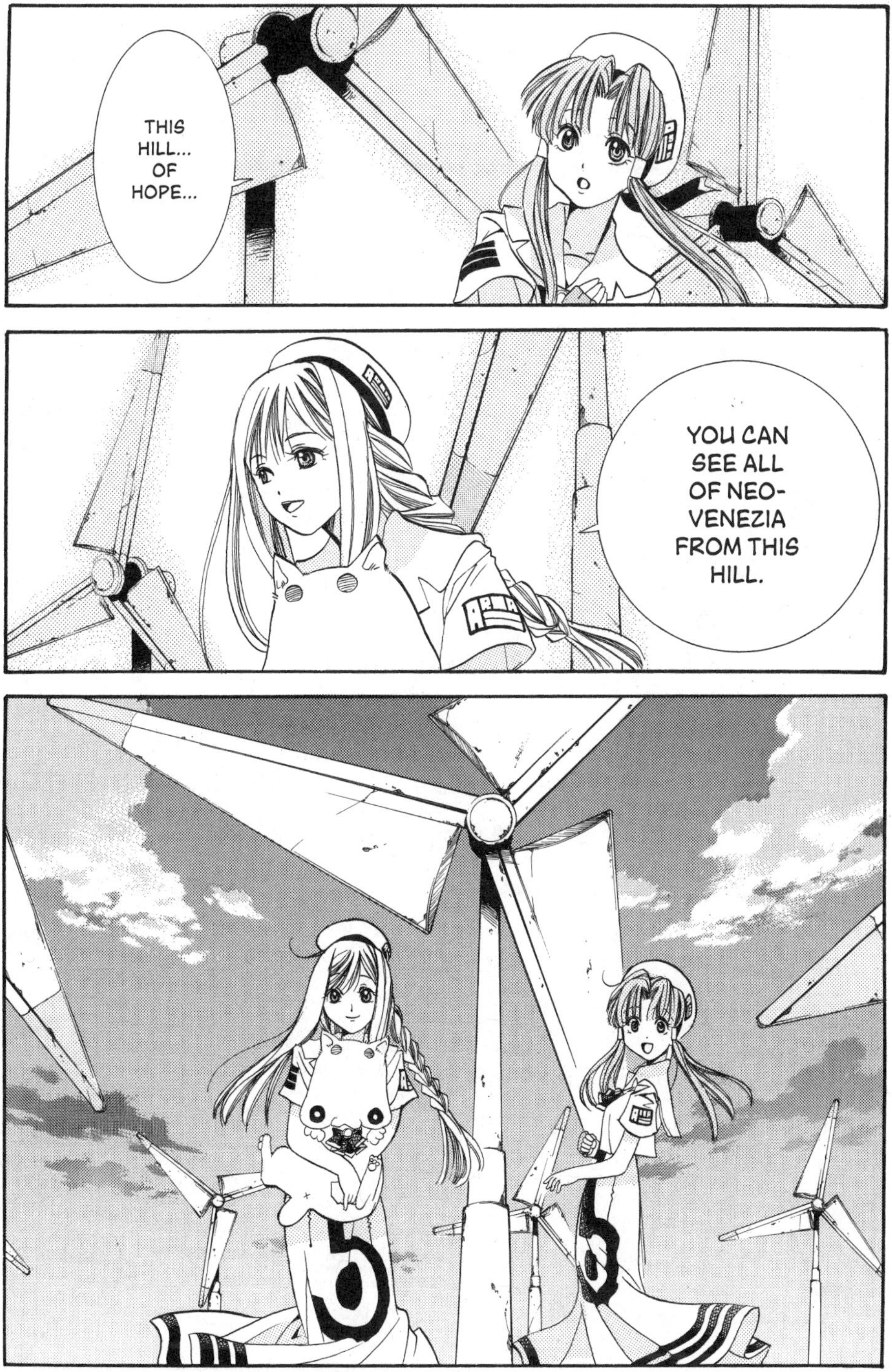
THIS HILL... OF HOPE...
YOU CAN SEE ALL OF NEO-VENEZIA FROM THIS HILL.

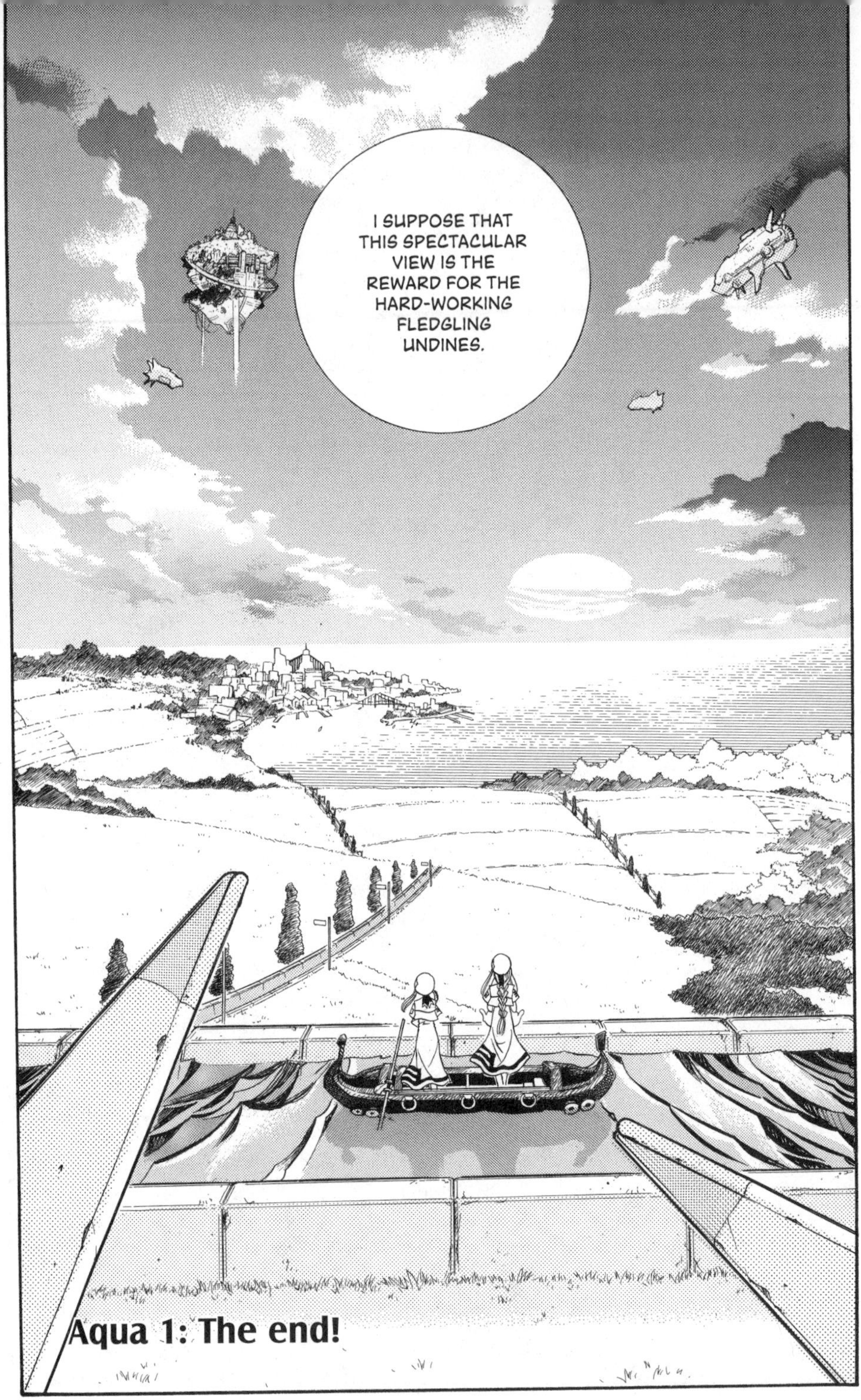
I SUPPOSE THAT THIS SPECTACULAR VIEW IS THE REWARD FOR THE HARD-WORKING FLEDGLING UNDINES.
Aqua 1: The end!

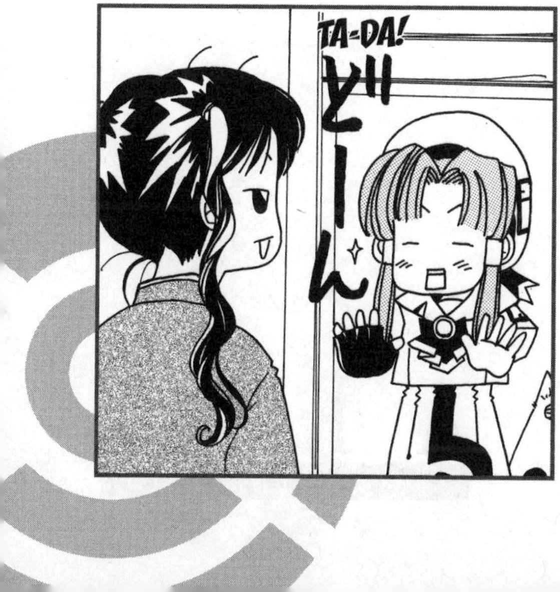
TA-DA!
どーん

ARIA
The MASTERPIECE

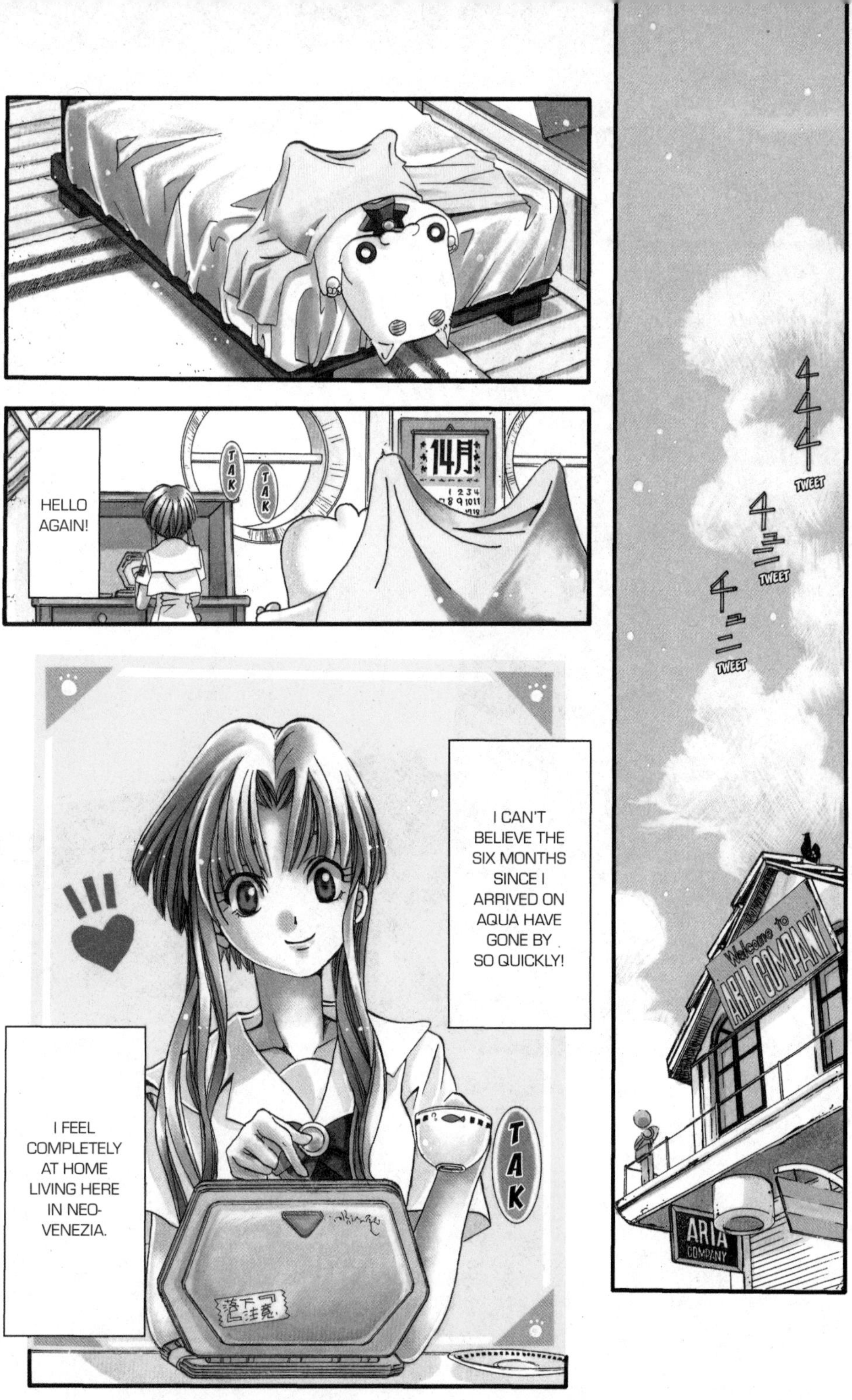
TWEET
TWEET
TWEET
Welcome to
ARIA COMPANY
ARIA
COMPANY
HELLO AGAIN!
TAK
TAK
14月
I CAN'T BELIEVE THE SIX MONTHS SINCE I ARRIVED ON AQUA HAVE GONE BY SO QUICKLY!
TAK
I FEEL COMPLETELY AT HOME LIVING HERE IN NEO-VENEZIA.

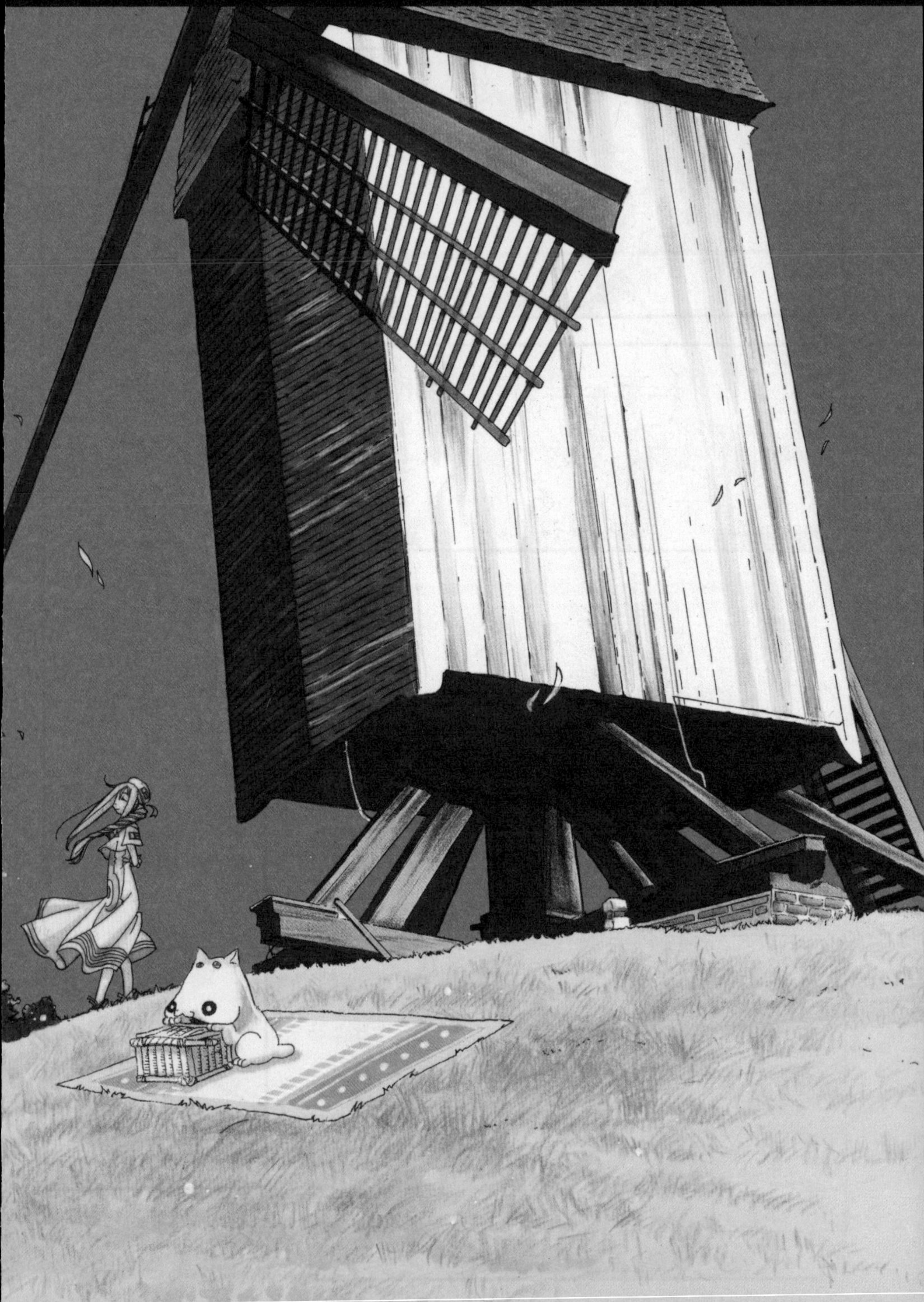

Navigation 06
My First Guest

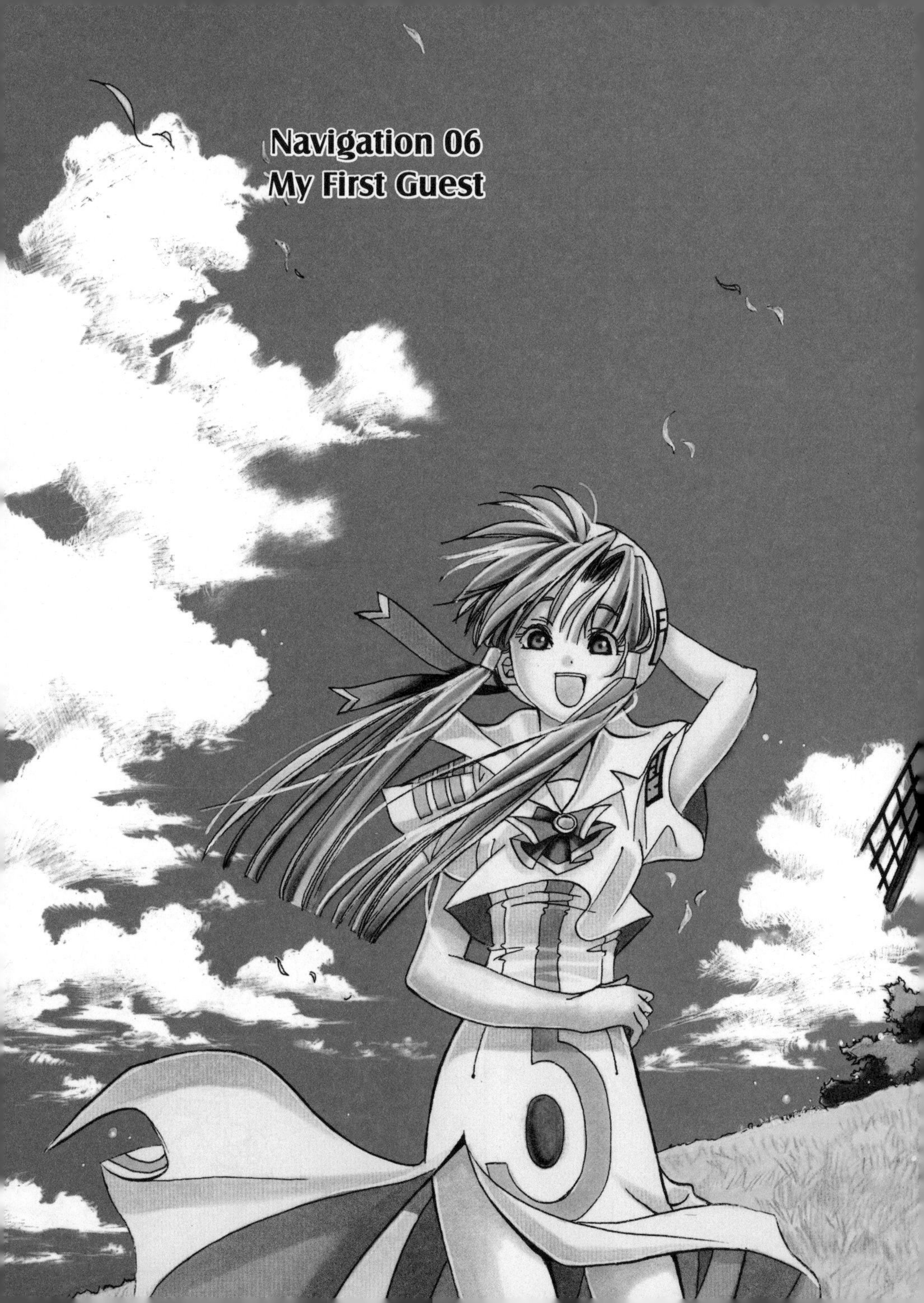

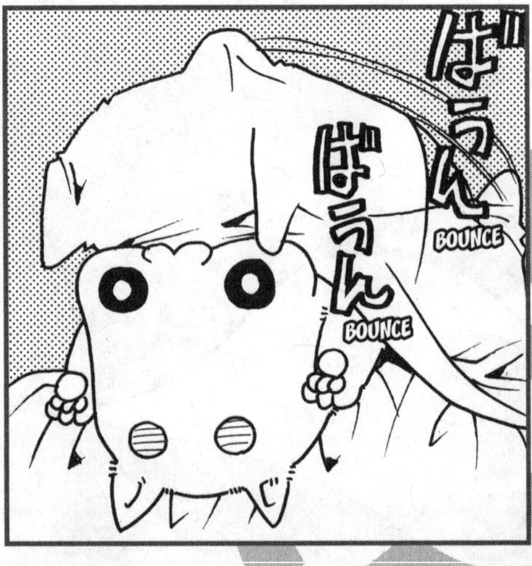
ぼうん
BOUNCE
ぼうん
BOUNCE

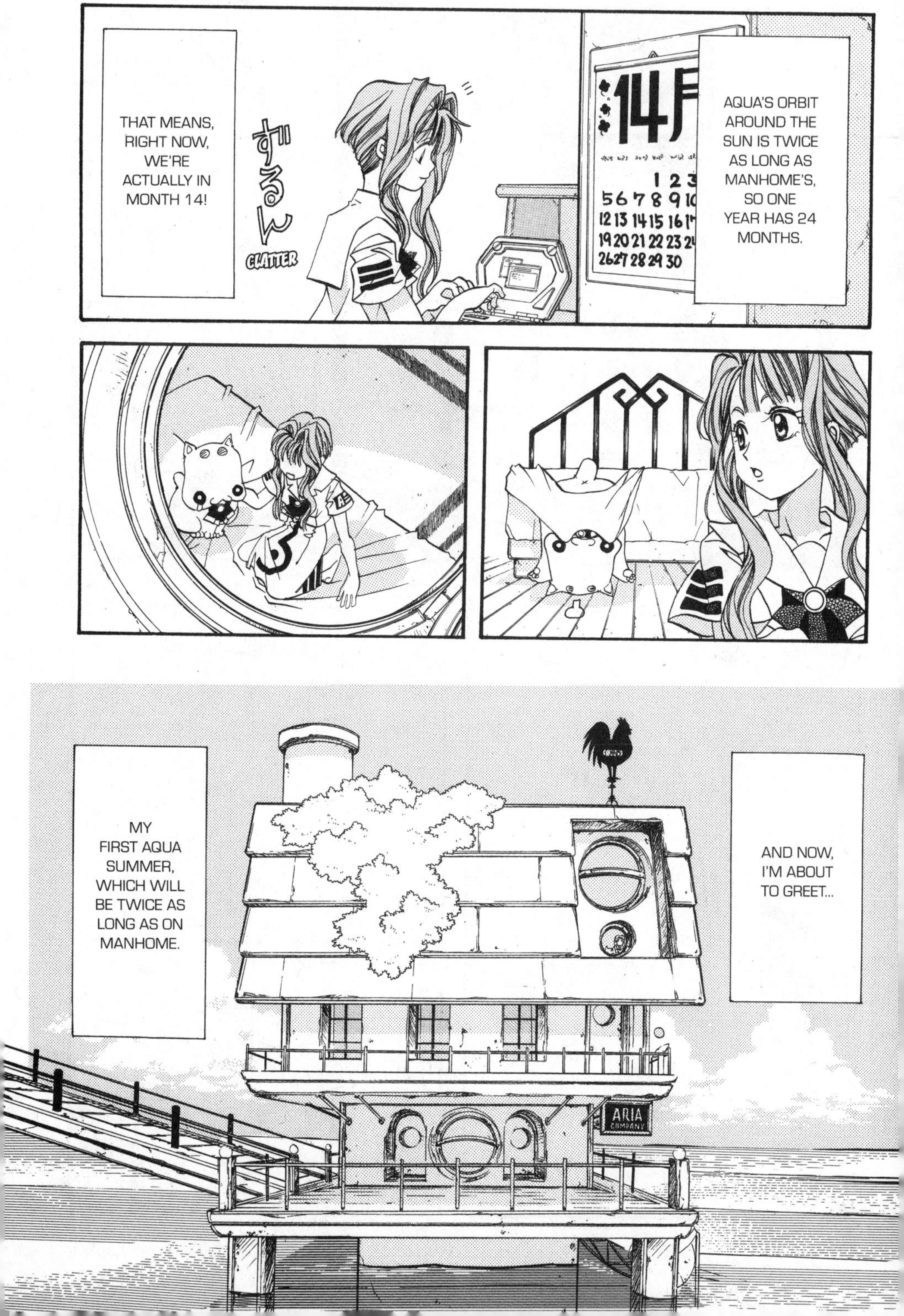
AQUA'S ORBIT AROUND THE SUN IS TWICE AS LONG AS MANHOME'S, SO ONE YEAR HAS 24 MONTHS.
14月
THAT MEANS, RIGHT NOW, WE'RE ACTUALLY IN MONTH 14!
ずるん
CLATTER
AND NOW, I'M ABOUT TO GREET...
MY FIRST AQUA SUMMER, WHICH WILL BE TWICE AS LONG AS ON MANHOME.
ARIA COMPANY

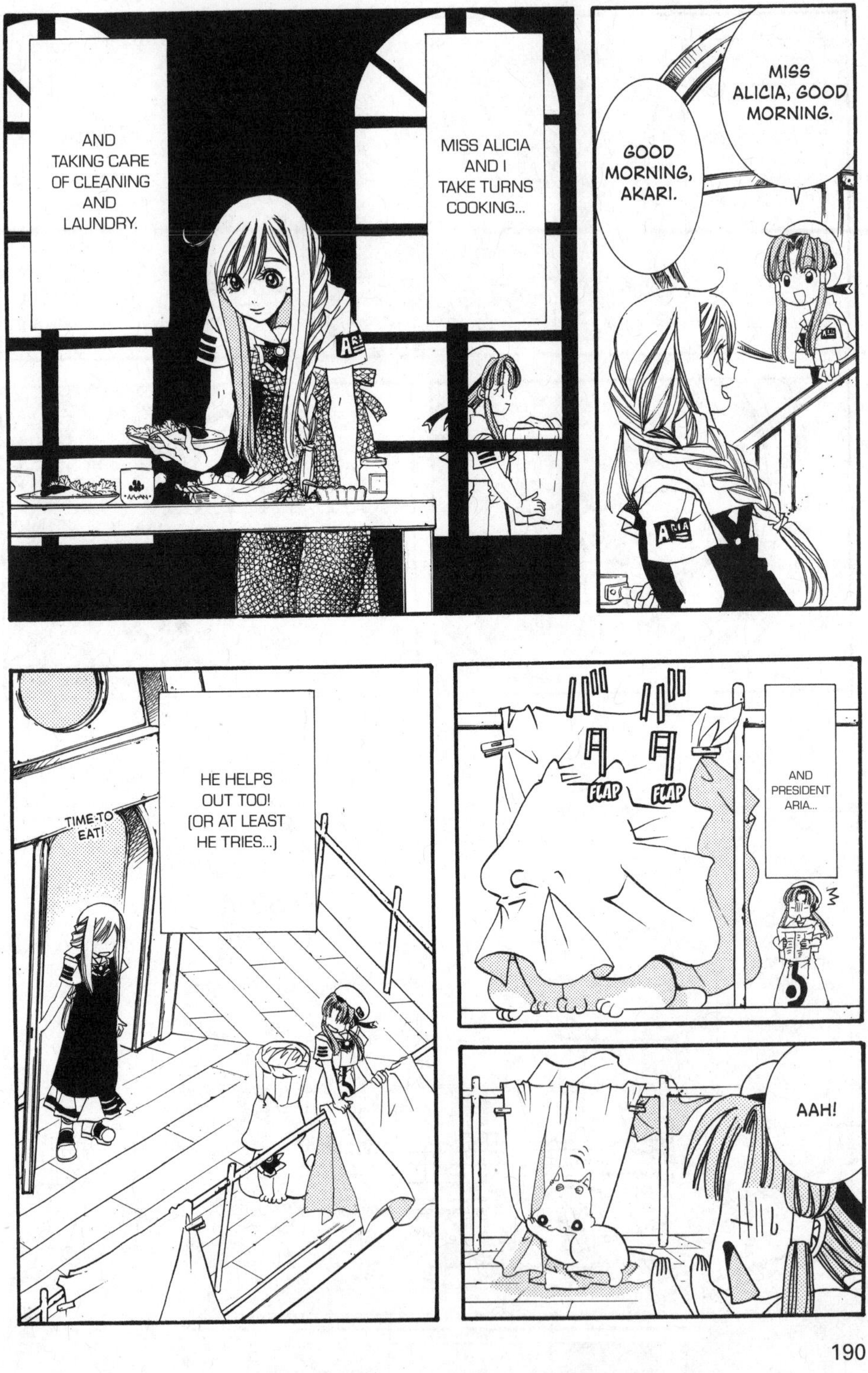
MISS ALICIA, GOOD MORNING.
GOOD MORNING, AKARI.
MISS ALICIA AND I TAKE TURNS COOKING...
AND TAKING CARE OF CLEANING AND LAUNDRY.
AND PRESIDENT ARIA...
FLAP
FLAP
AAH!
HE HELPS OUT TOO! (OR AT LEAST HE TRIES...)
TIME TO EAT!

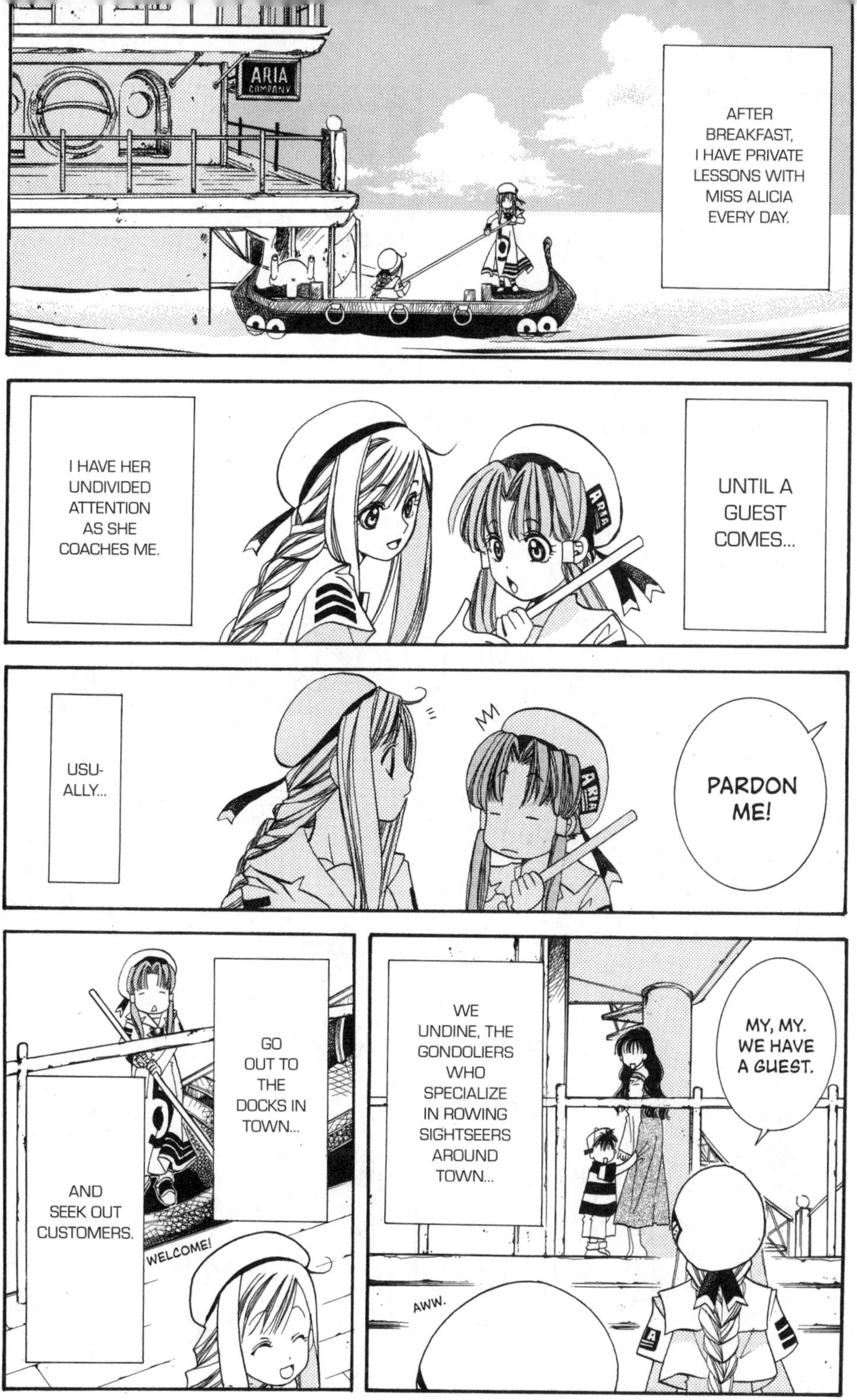
ARIA COMPANY
AFTER BREAKFAST, I HAVE PRIVATE LESSONS WITH MISS ALICIA EVERY DAY.
I HAVE HER UNDIVIDED ATTENTION AS SHE COACHES ME.
UNTIL A GUEST COMES...
ARIA
PARDON ME!
USU-ALLY...
MY, MY. WE HAVE A GUEST.
WE UNDINE, THE GONDOLIERS WHO SPECIALIZE IN ROWING SIGHTSEERS AROUND TOWN...
AWW.
GO OUT TO THE DOCKS IN TOWN...
AND SEEK OUT CUSTOMERS.
WELCOME!

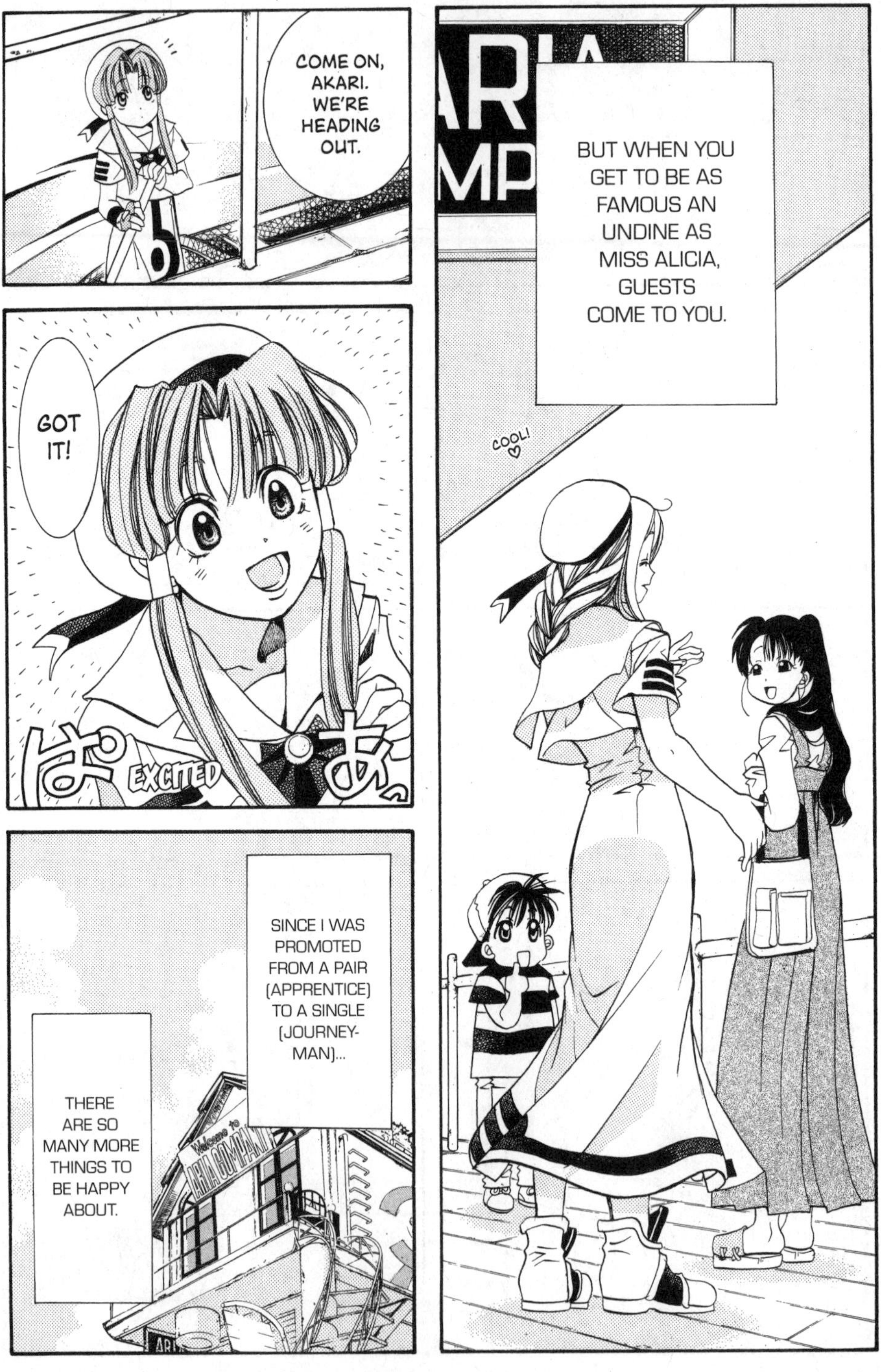
BUT WHEN YOU GET TO BE AS FAMOUS AN UNDINE AS MISS ALICIA, GUESTS COME TO YOU.
COOL! ♡
COME ON, AKARI. WE'RE HEADING OUT.
GOT IT!
ぱあっ
EXCITED
SINCE I WAS PROMOTED FROM A PAIR (APPRENTICE) TO A SINGLE (JOURNEY-MAN)...
THERE ARE SO MANY MORE THINGS TO BE HAPPY ABOUT.
Welcome to ARIA COMPANY

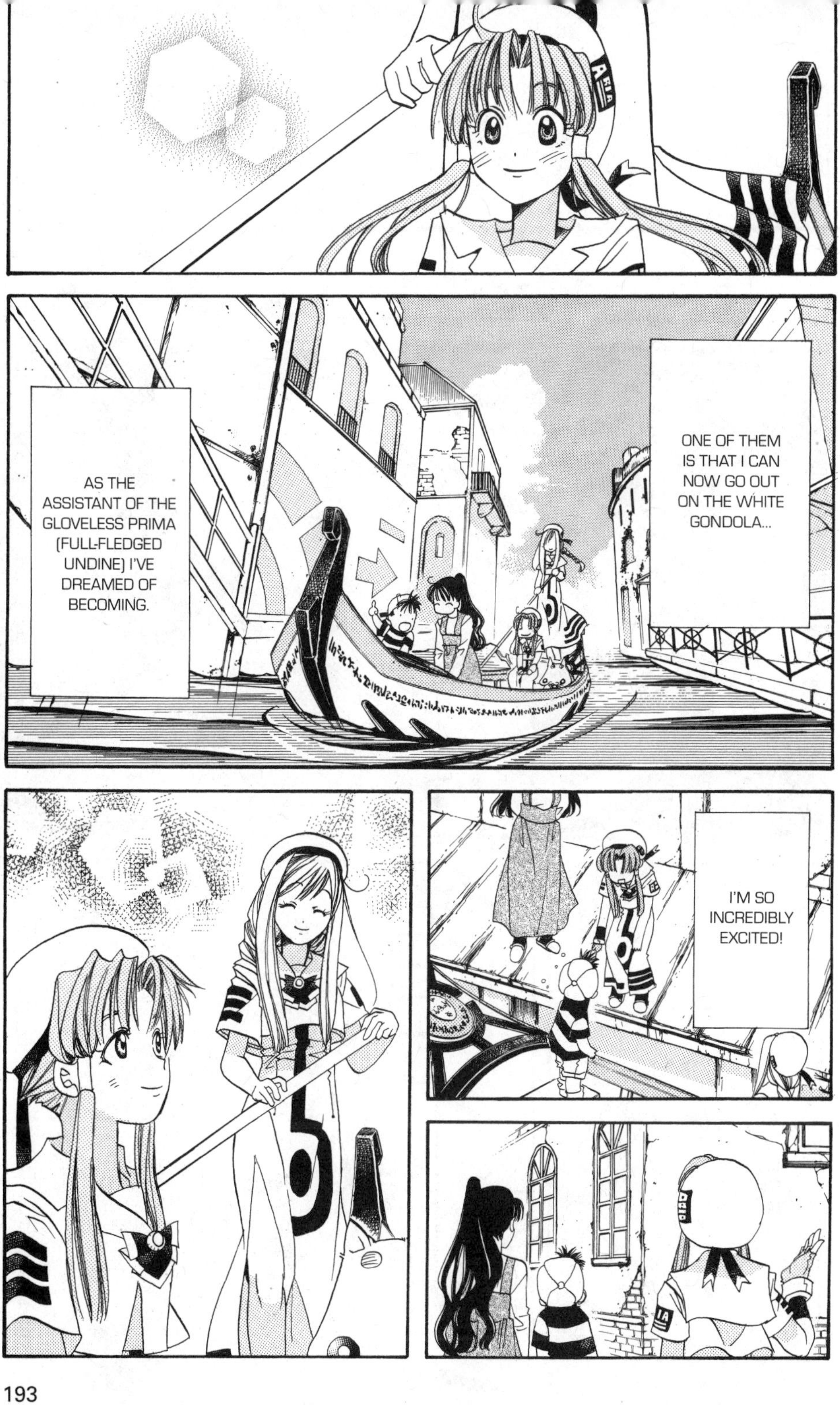
ONE OF THEM IS THAT I CAN NOW GO OUT ON THE WHITE GONDOLA...
AS THE ASSISTANT OF THE GLOVELESS PRIMA (FULL-FLEDGED UNDINE) I'VE DREAMED OF BECOMING.
I'M SO INCREDIBLY EXCITED!

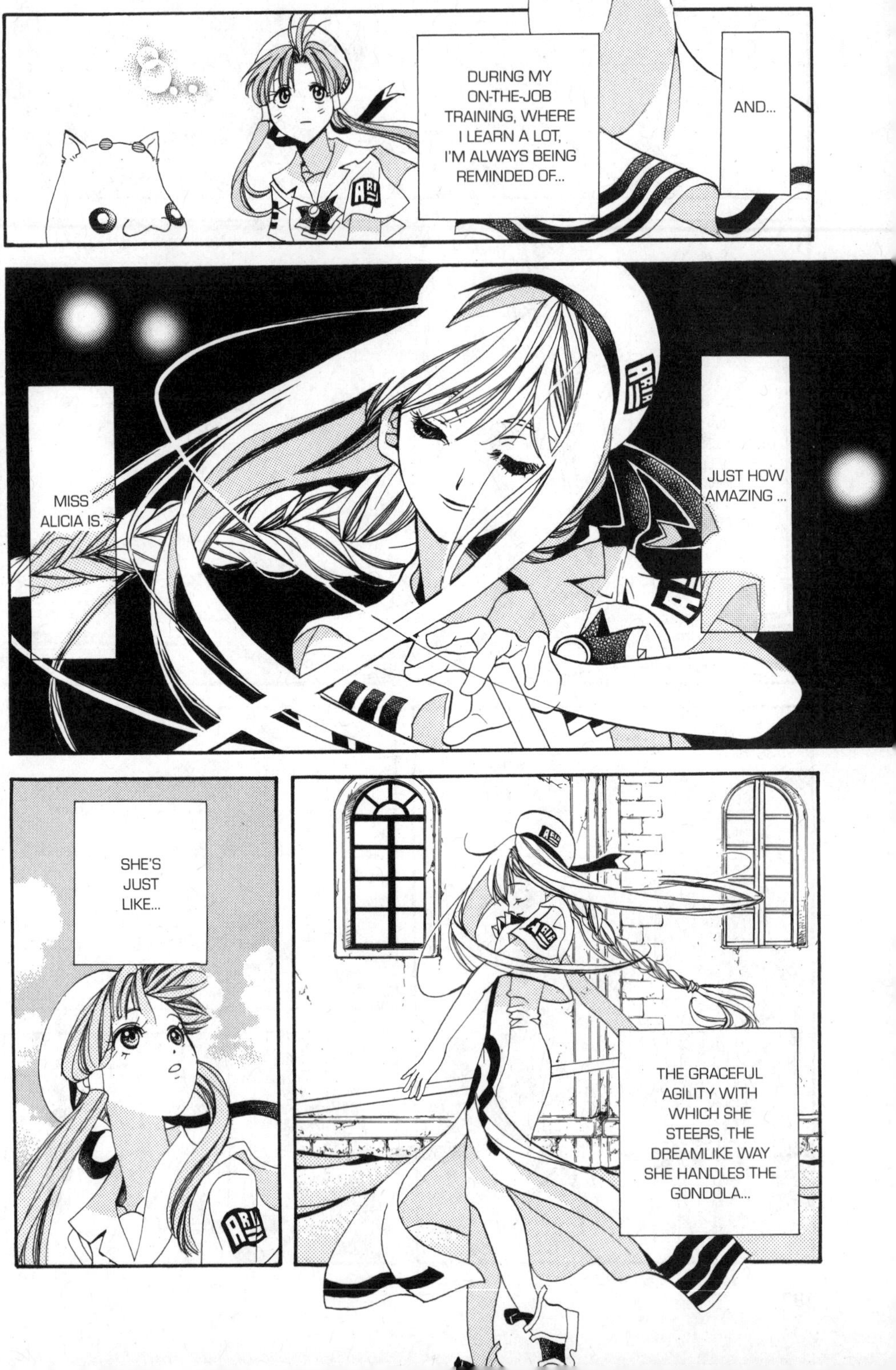
AND...
DURING MY ON-THE-JOB TRAINING, WHERE I LEARN A LOT, I'M ALWAYS BEING REMINDED OF...
JUST HOW AMAZING ...
MISS ALICIA IS.
THE GRACEFUL AGILITY WITH WHICH SHE STEERS, THE DREAMLIKE WAY SHE HANDLES THE GONDOLA...
SHE'S JUST LIKE...

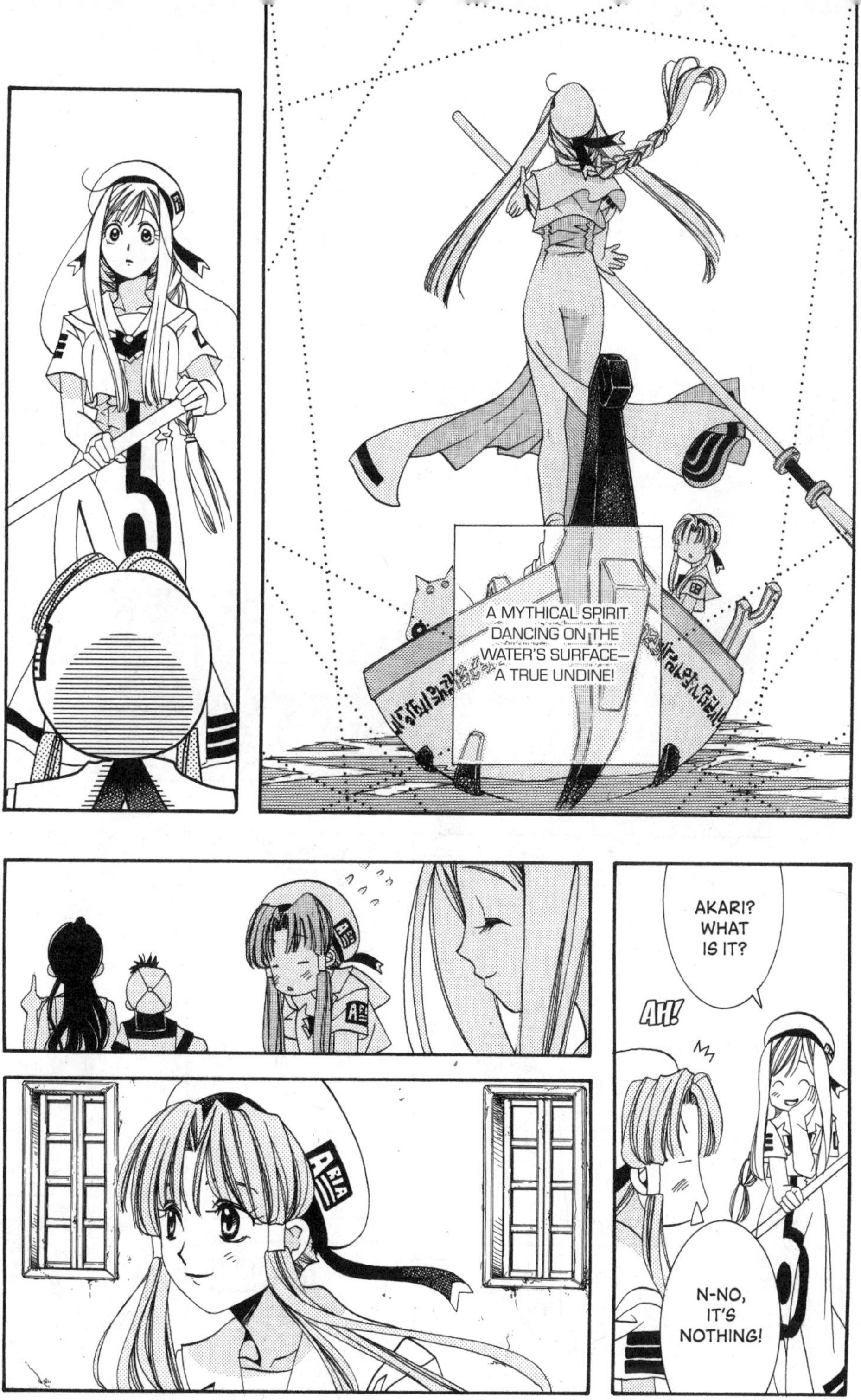
A MYTHICAL SPIRIT DANCING ON THE WATER'S SURFACE— A TRUE UNDINE!
AKARI? WHAT IS IT?
AH!
N-NO, IT'S NOTHING!

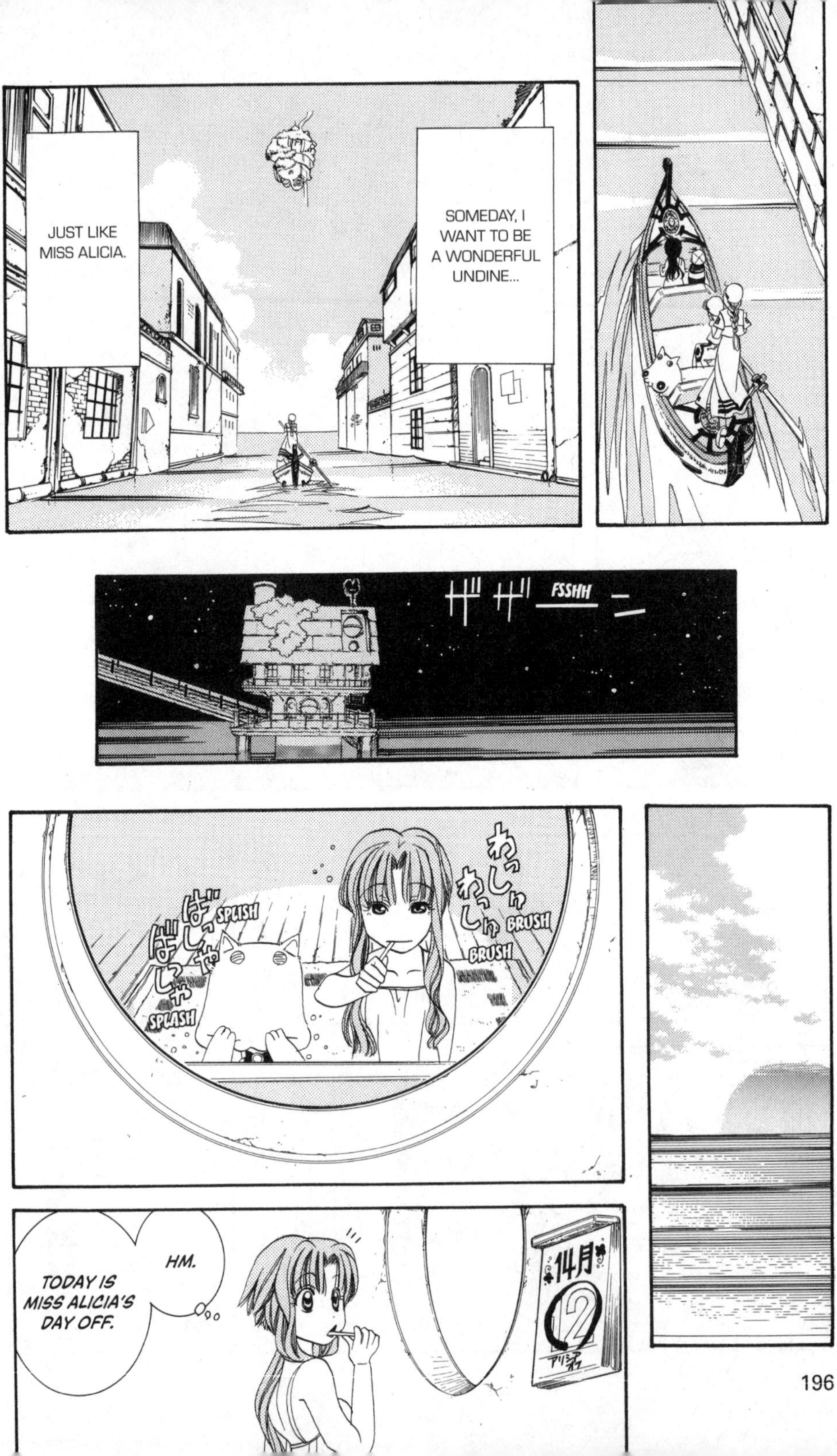
SOMEDAY, I WANT TO BE A WONDERFUL UNDINE...
JUST LIKE MISS ALICIA.
ザザ ーー
FSSHH
わっしゅ わっしゅ
BRUSH
BRUSH
ぱしゃ ぱしゃ
SPLISH
SPLASH
14月
12
アリシア オフ
HM.
TODAY IS MISS ALICIA'S DAY OFF.

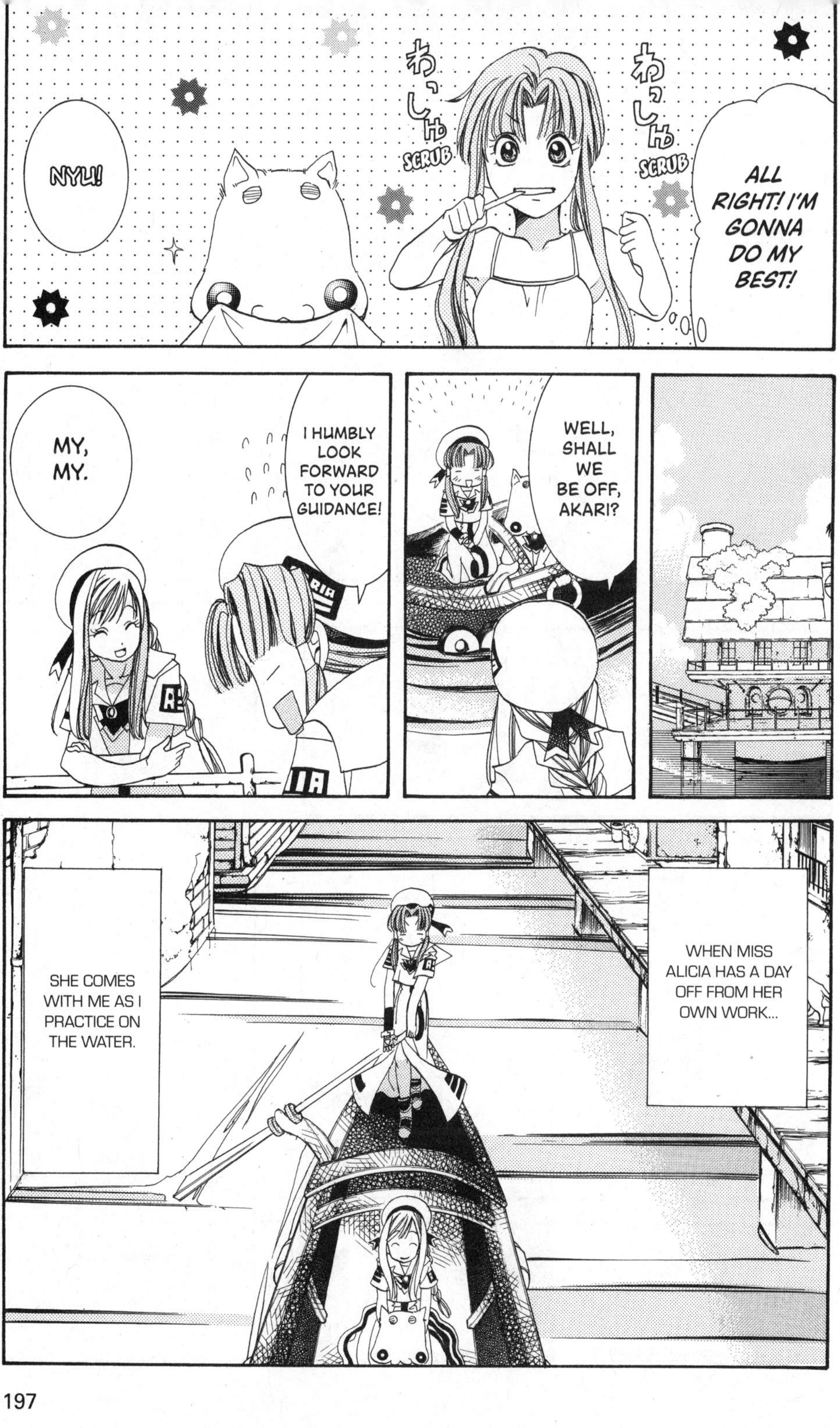
わっしゅ
SCRUB
ALL RIGHT! I'M GONNA DO MY BEST!
わっしゅ
SCRUB
NYU!
WELL, SHALL WE BE OFF, AKARI?
I HUMBLY LOOK FORWARD TO YOUR GUIDANCE!
MY, MY.
WHEN MISS ALICIA HAS A DAY OFF FROM HER OWN WORK...
SHE COMES WITH ME AS I PRACTICE ON THE WATER.

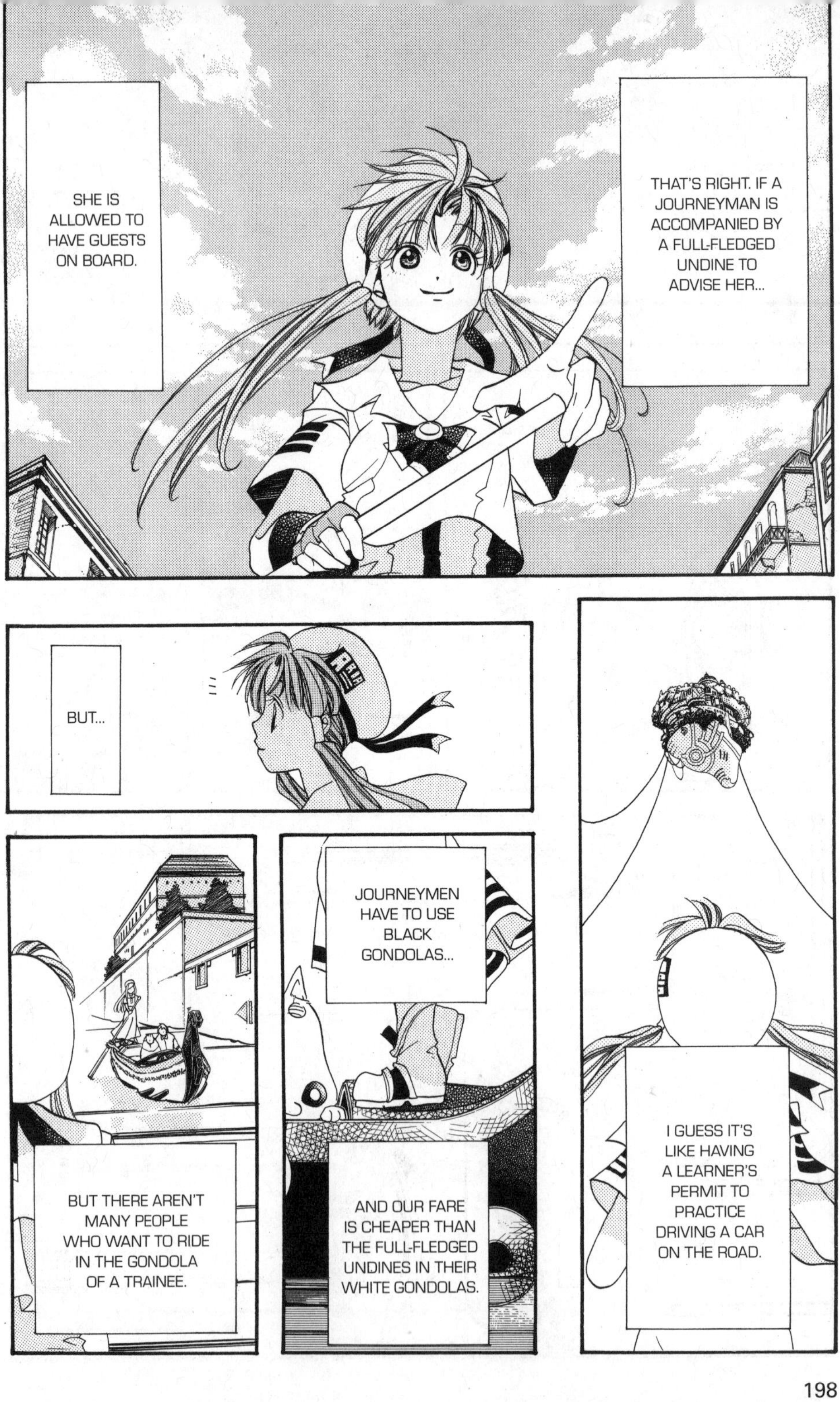
THAT'S RIGHT. IF A JOURNEYMAN IS ACCOMPANIED BY A FULL-FLEDGED UNDINE TO ADVISE HER...
SHE IS ALLOWED TO HAVE GUESTS ON BOARD.
I GUESS IT'S LIKE HAVING A LEARNER'S PERMIT TO PRACTICE DRIVING A CAR ON THE ROAD.
BUT...
JOURNEYMEN HAVE TO USE BLACK GONDOLAS...
AND OUR FARE IS CHEAPER THAN THE FULL-FLEDGED UNDINES IN THEIR WHITE GONDOLAS.
BUT THERE AREN'T MANY PEOPLE WHO WANT TO RIDE IN THE GONDOLA OF A TRAINEE.

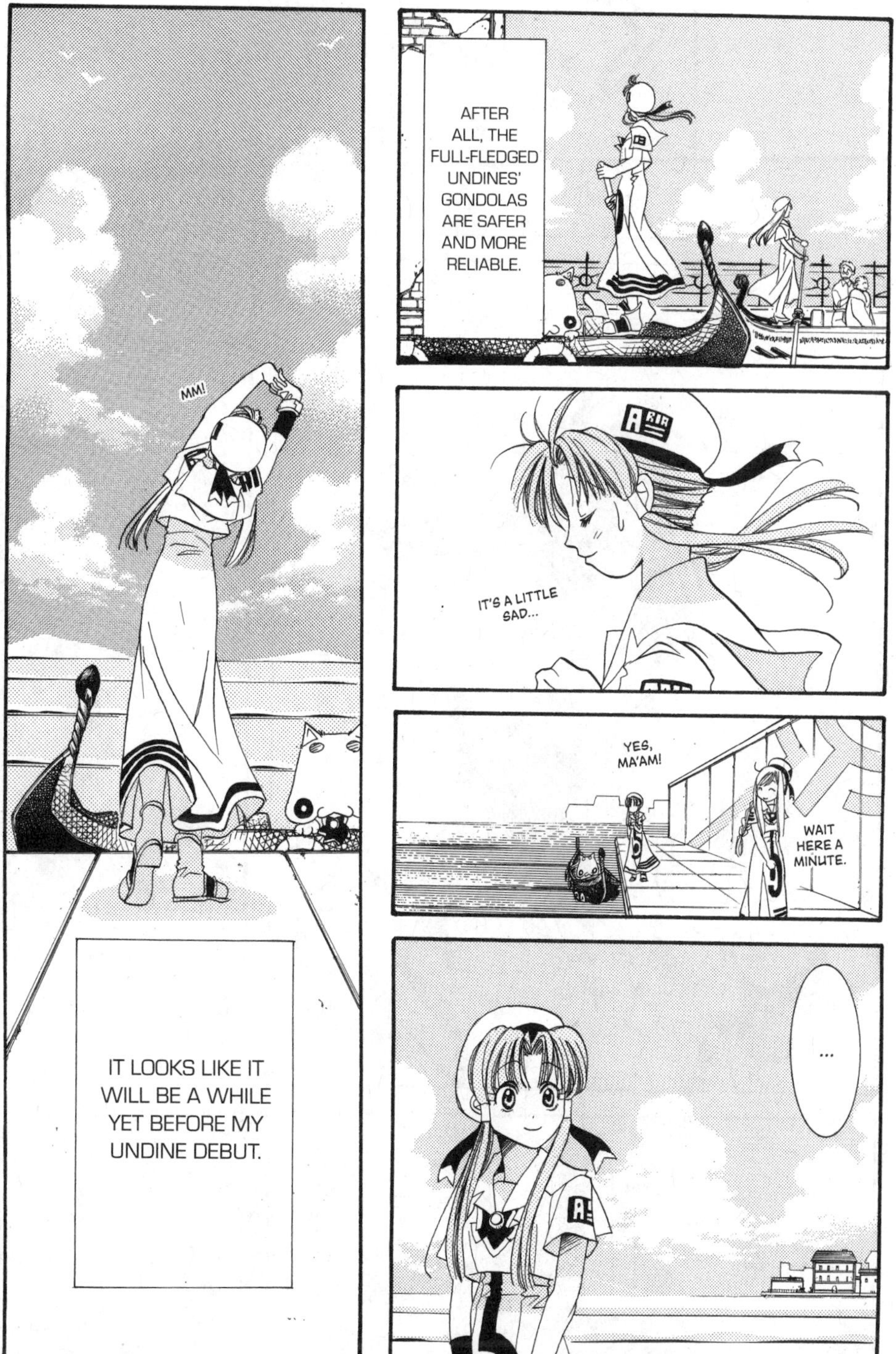
AFTER ALL, THE FULL-FLEDGED UNDINES' GONDOLAS ARE SAFER AND MORE RELIABLE.
IT'S A LITTLE SAD...
WAIT HERE A MINUTE.
YES, MA'AM!
...
MM!
IT LOOKS LIKE IT WILL BE A WHILE YET BEFORE MY UNDINE DEBUT.

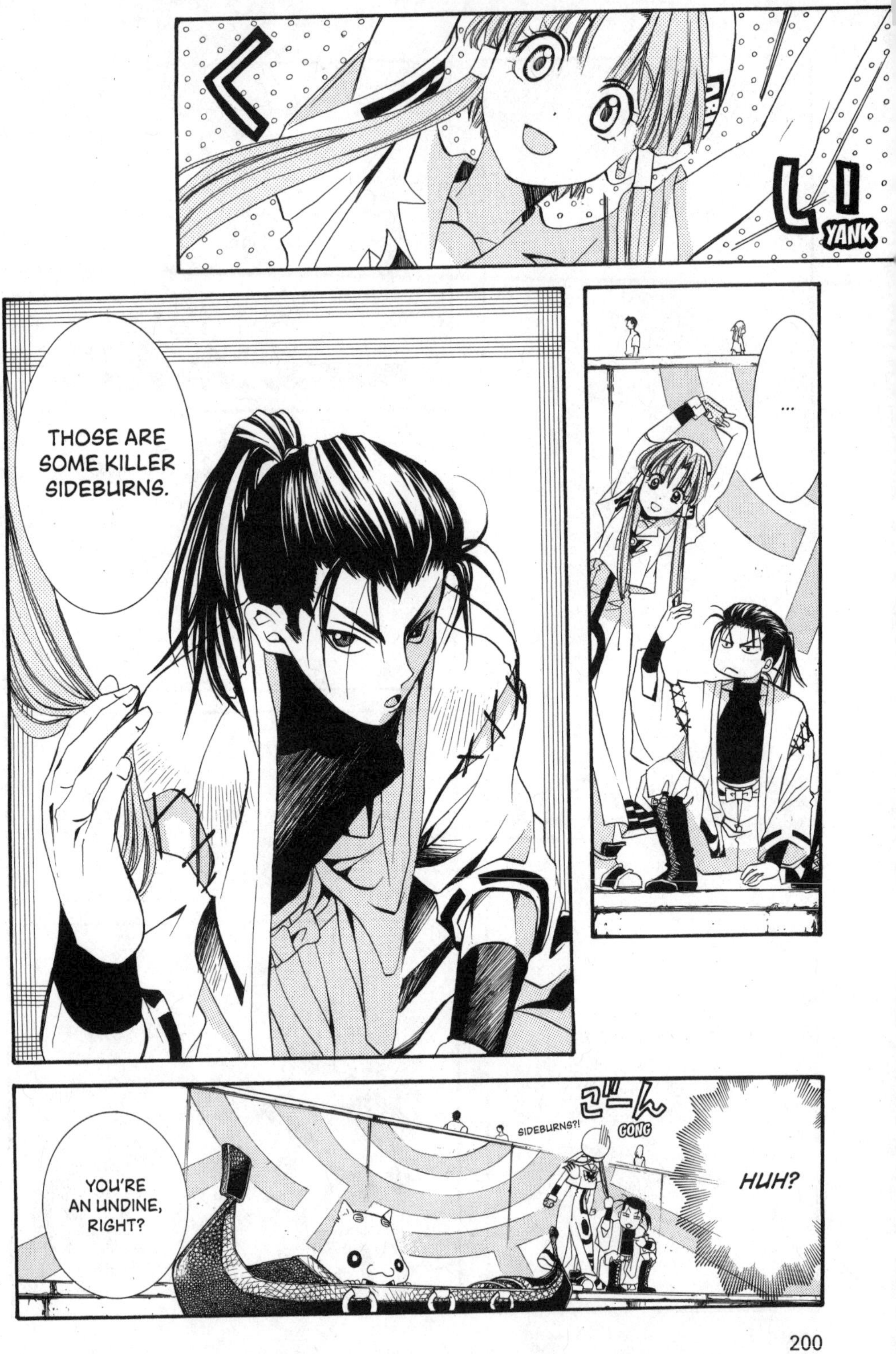
YANK
...
THOSE ARE SOME KILLER SIDEBURNS.
ごーん
GONG
SIDEBURNS?!
HUH?
YOU'RE AN UNDINE, RIGHT?

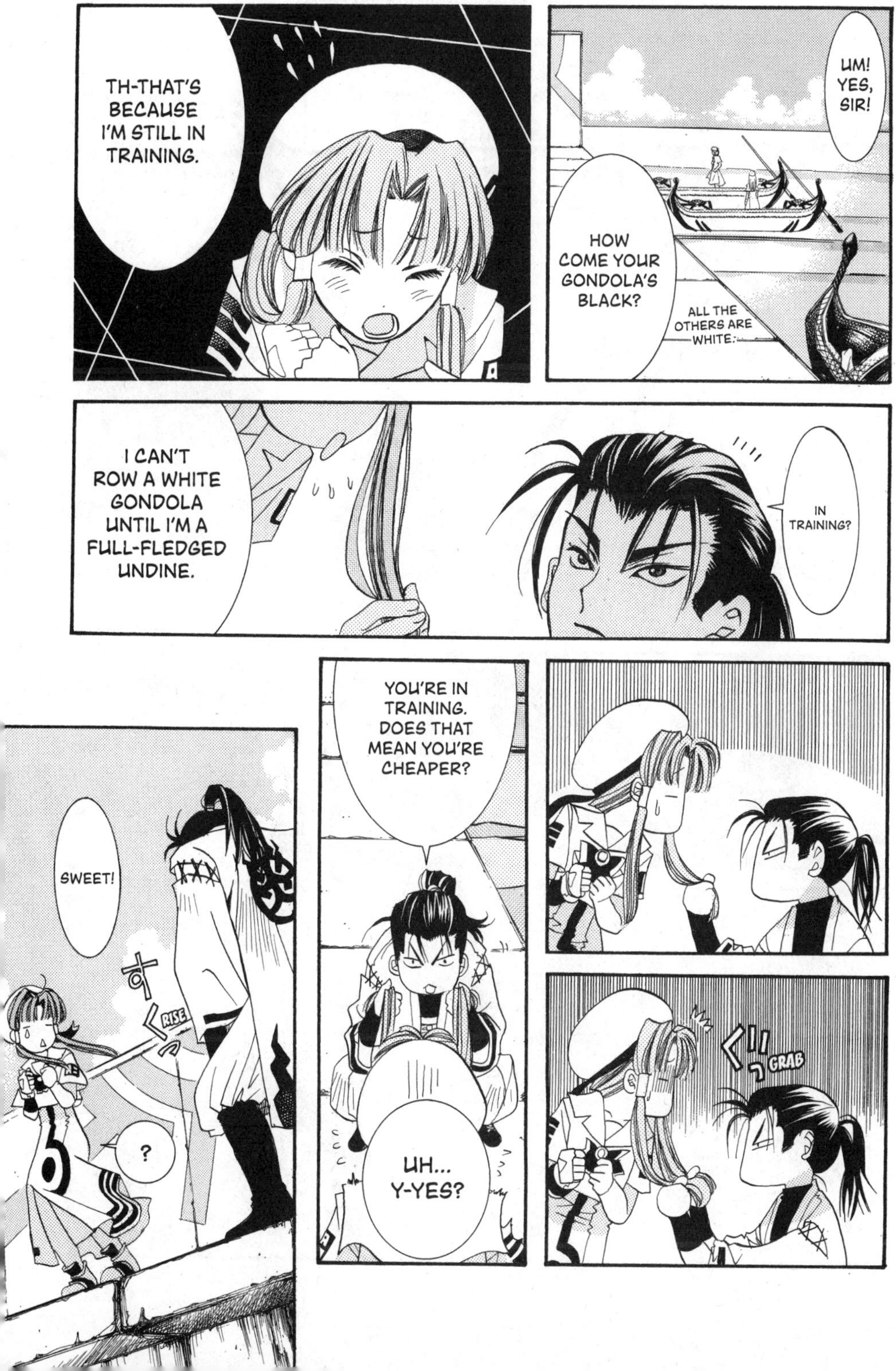

UM! YES, SIR!
HOW COME YOUR GONDOLA'S BLACK?
ALL THE OTHERS ARE WHITE.
TH-THAT'S BECAUSE I'M STILL IN TRAINING.
IN TRAINING?
I CAN'T ROW A WHITE GONDOLA UNTIL I'M A FULL-FLEDGED UNDINE.
GRAB
YOU'RE IN TRAINING. DOES THAT MEAN YOU'RE CHEAPER?
UH... Y-YES?
SWEET!
すくっ
RISE
?

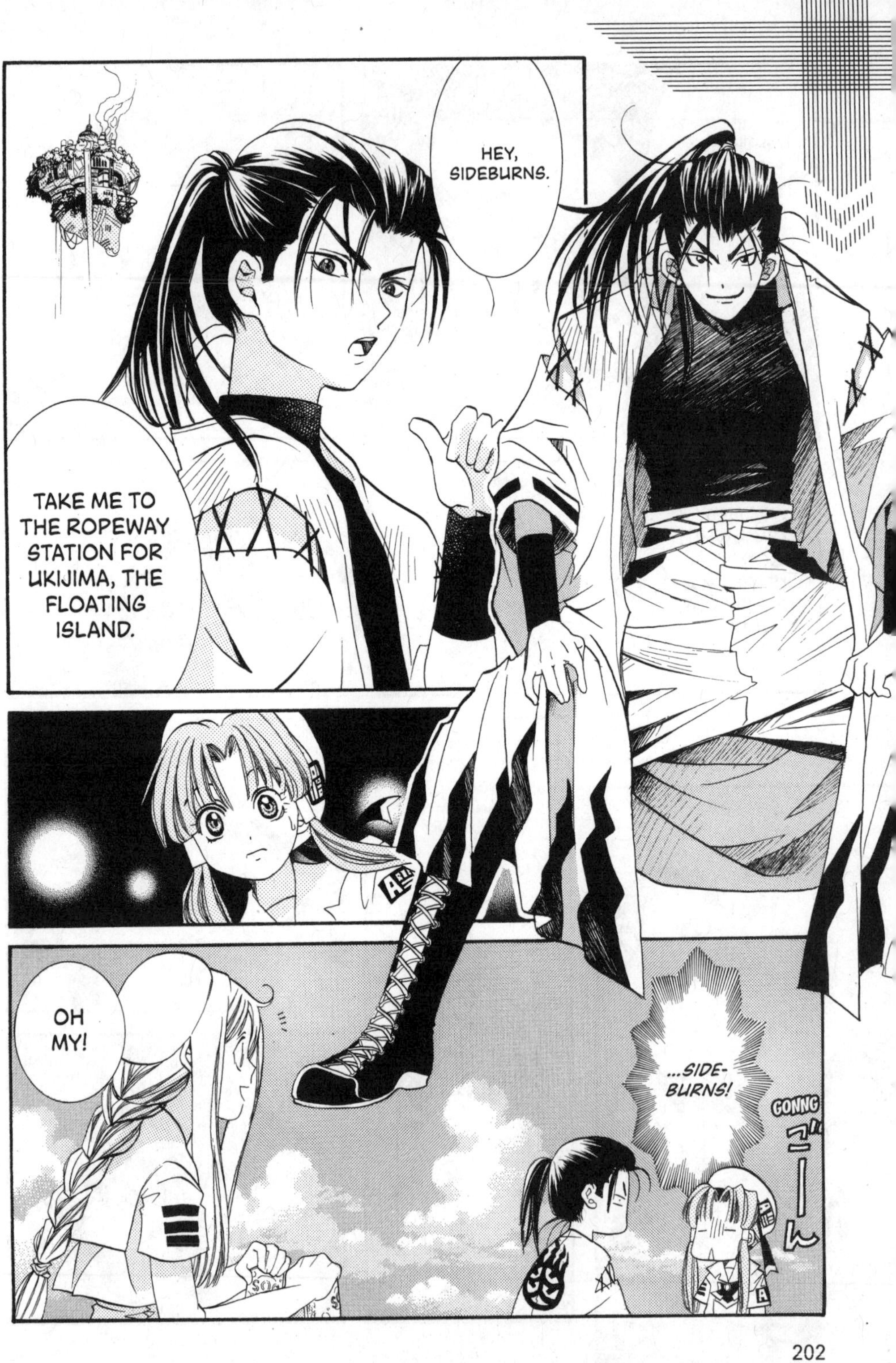
HEY, SIDEBURNS.
TAKE ME TO THE ROPEWAY STATION FOR UKIJIMA, THE FLOATING ISLAND.
...SIDE-BURNS!
GONNG
ごーん
OH MY!

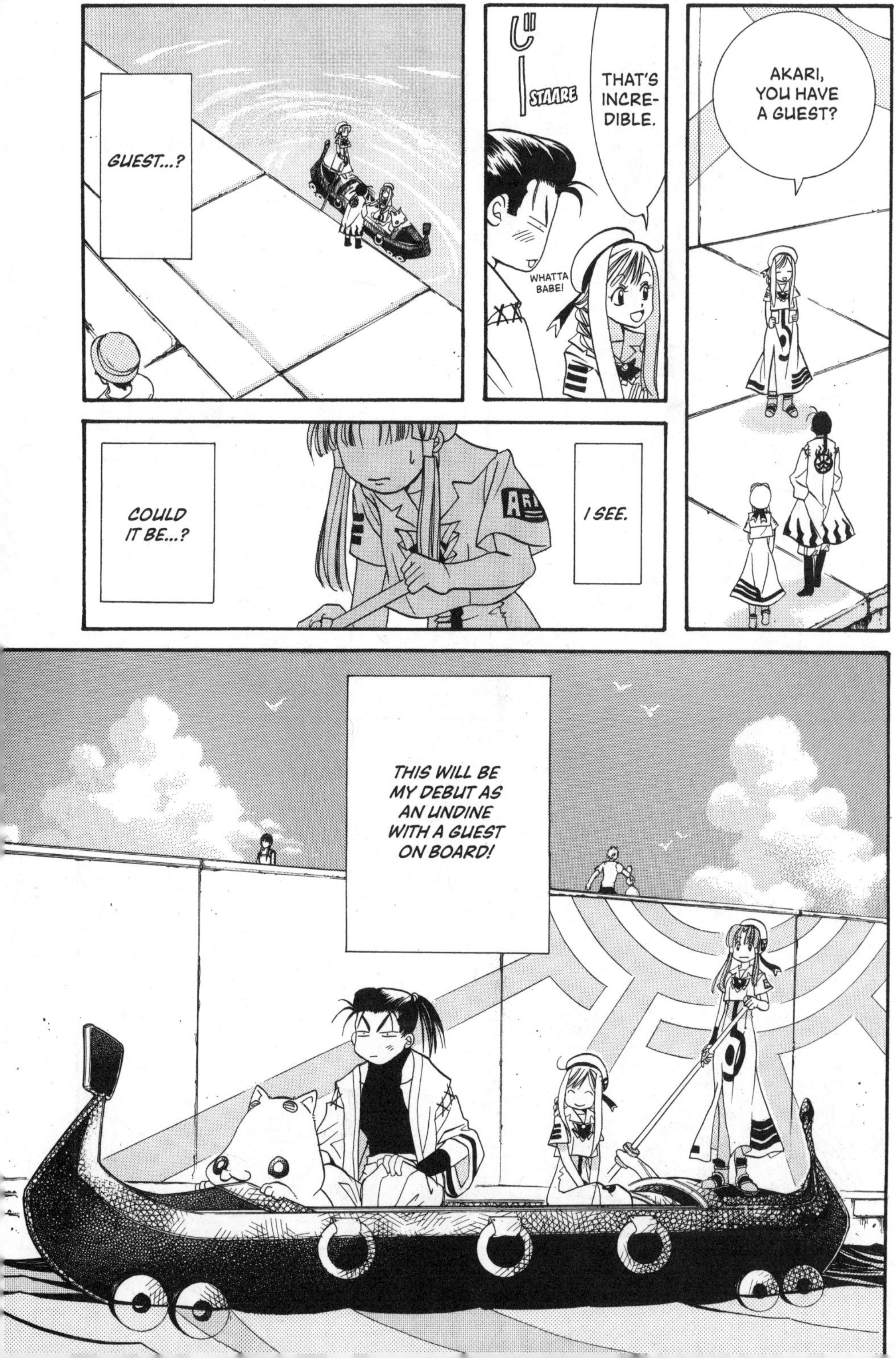
AKARI, YOU HAVE A GUEST?
STAARE
THAT'S INCREDIBLE.
WHATTA BABE!
GUEST...?
I SEE.
COULD IT BE...?
THIS WILL BE MY DEBUT AS AN UNDINE WITH A GUEST ON BOARD!

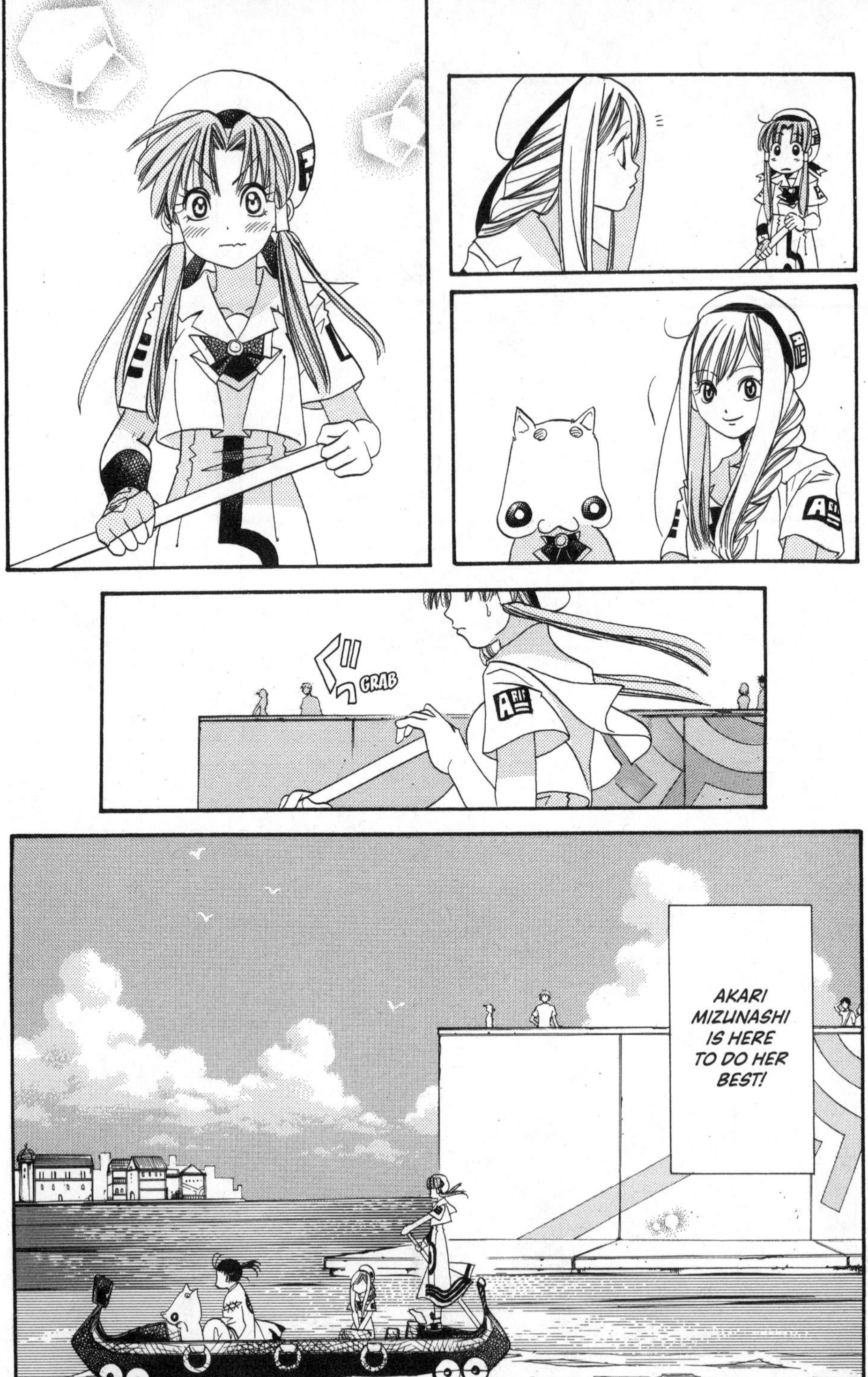

ぐいっ
GRAB
AKARI MIZUNASHI IS HERE TO DO HER BEST!

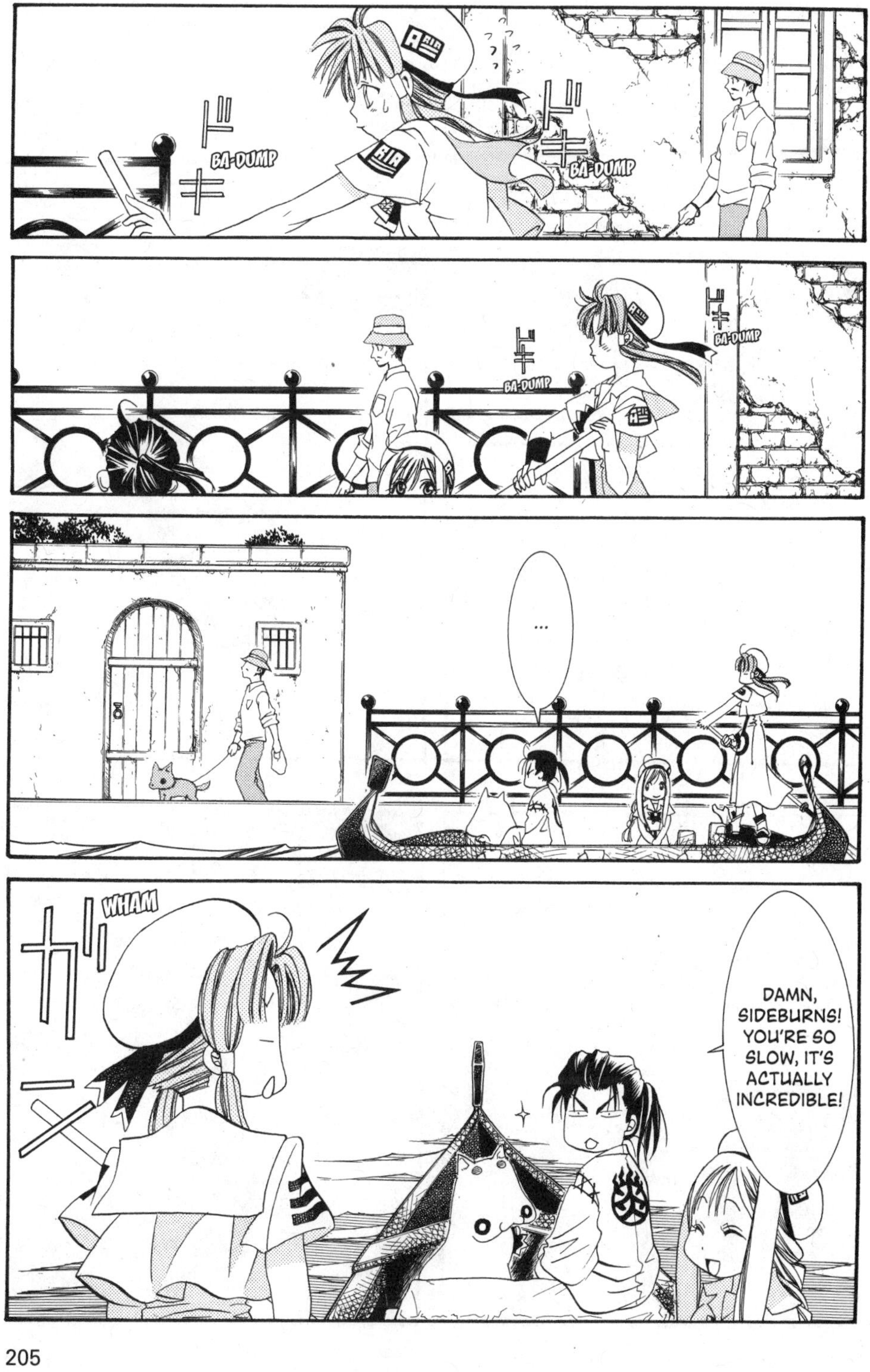
ドキ
BA-DUMP
ドキ
BA-DUMP
ドキ
BA-DUMP
ドキ
BA-DUMP
...
DAMN, SIDEBURNS! YOU'RE SO SLOW, IT'S ACTUALLY INCREDIBLE!
WHAM

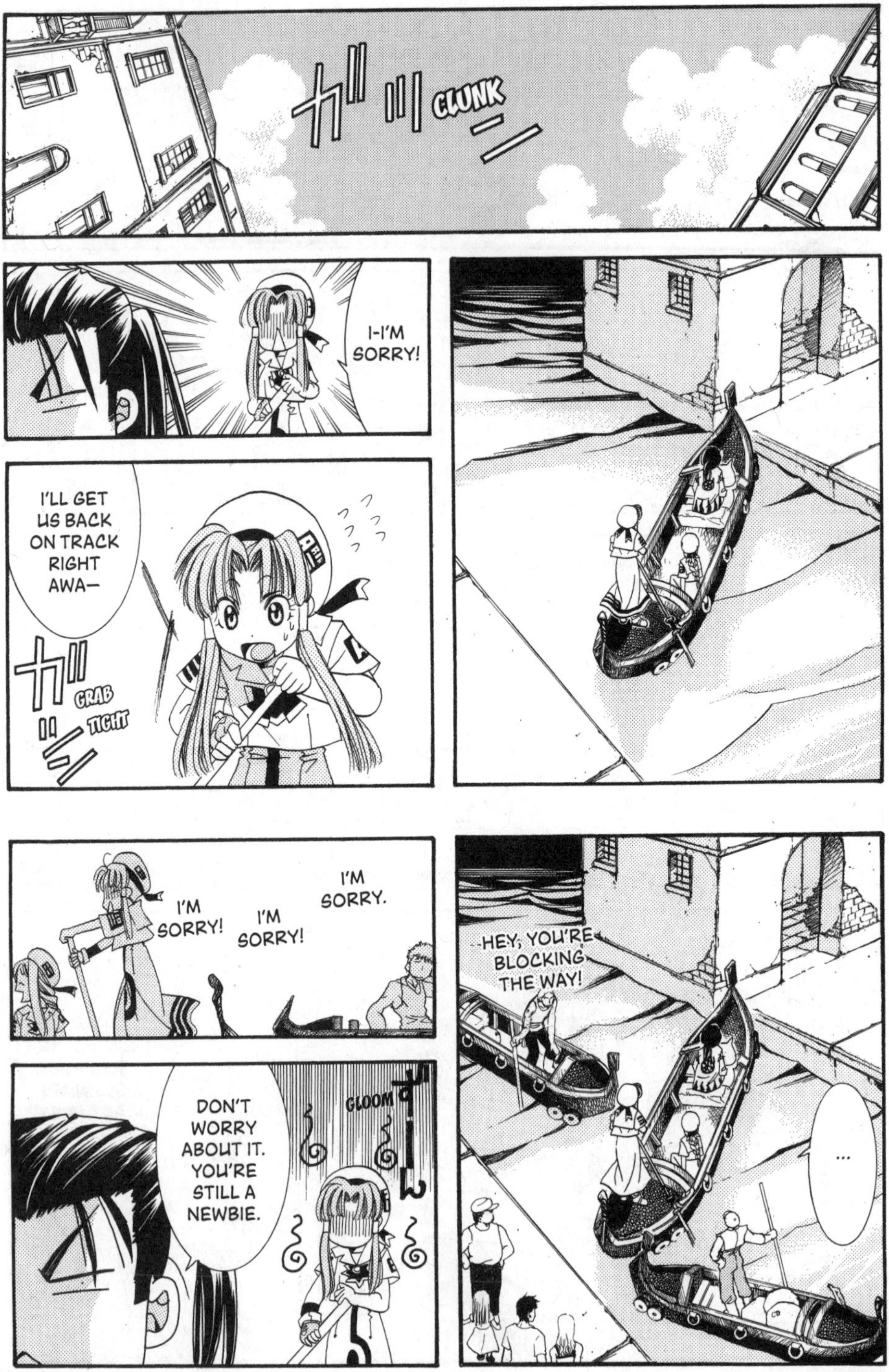
CLUNK
I-I'M SORRY!
I'LL GET US BACK ON TRACK RIGHT AWA—
GRAB TIGHT
HEY, YOU'RE BLOCKING THE WAY!
...
I'M SORRY.
I'M SORRY!
I'M SORRY!
DON'T WORRY ABOUT IT. YOU'RE STILL A NEWBIE.
GLOOM

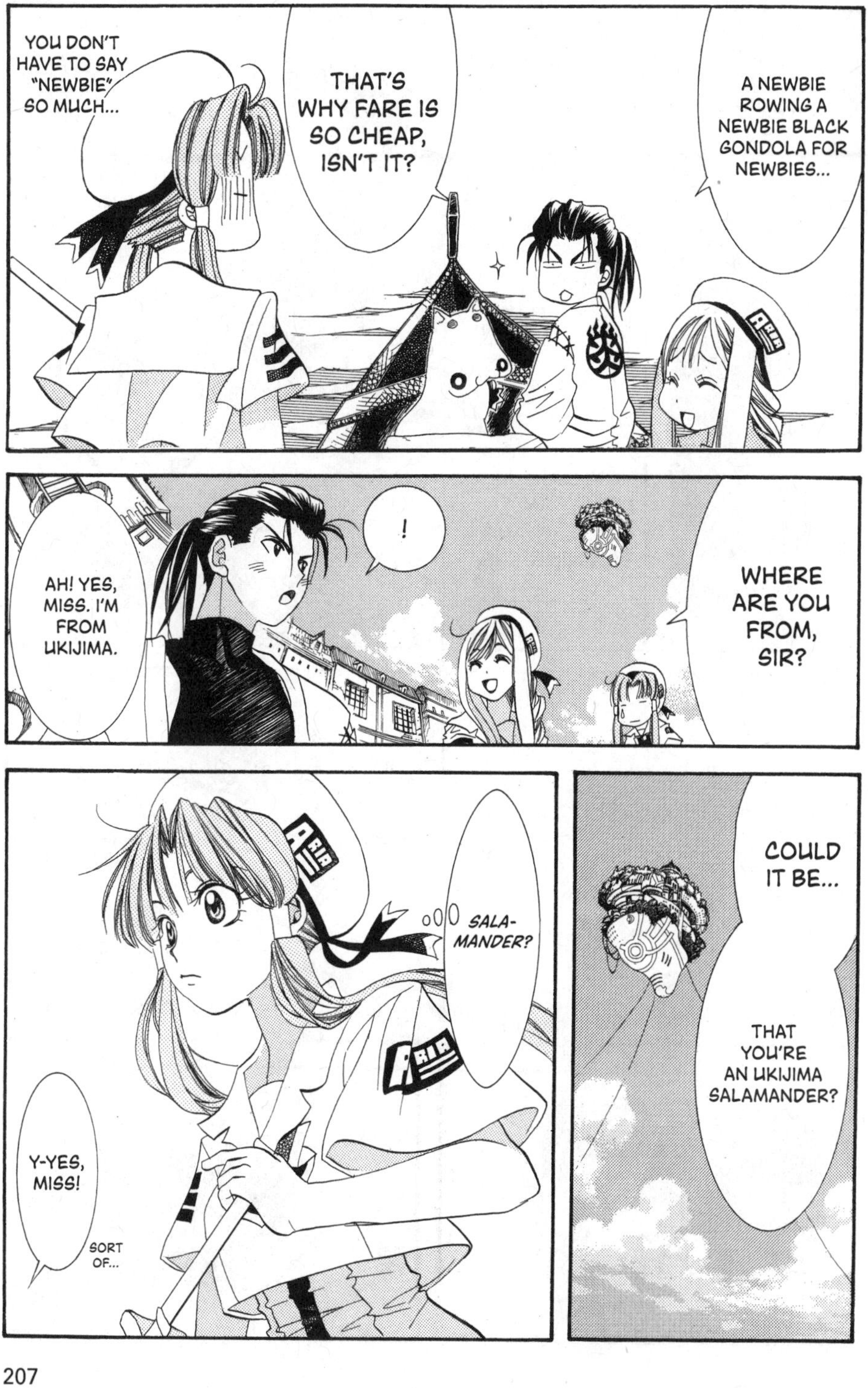
A NEWBIE ROWING A NEWBIE BLACK GONDOLA FOR NEWBIES...
THAT'S WHY FARE IS SO CHEAP, ISN'T IT?
YOU DON'T HAVE TO SAY "NEWBIE" SO MUCH...
WHERE ARE YOU FROM, SIR?
!
AH! YES, MISS. I'M FROM UKIJIMA.
COULD IT BE...
THAT YOU'RE AN UKIJIMA SALAMANDER?
SALAMANDER?
Y-YES, MISS!
SORT OF...

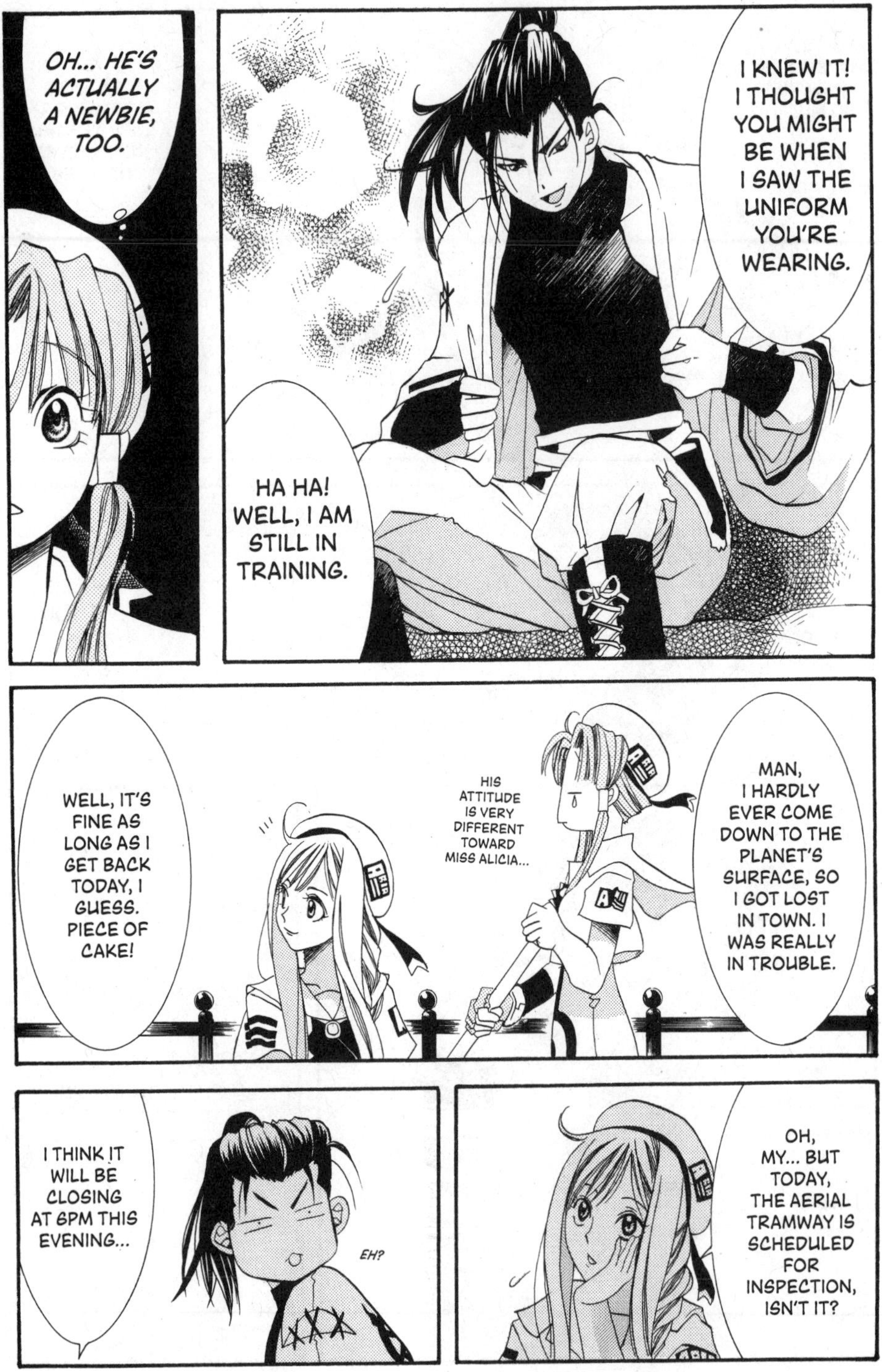
I KNEW IT! I THOUGHT YOU MIGHT BE WHEN I SAW THE UNIFORM YOU'RE WEARING.
HA HA! WELL, I AM STILL IN TRAINING.
OH... HE'S ACTUALLY A NEWBIE, TOO.
MAN, I HARDLY EVER COME DOWN TO THE PLANET'S SURFACE, SO I GOT LOST IN TOWN. I WAS REALLY IN TROUBLE.
HIS ATTITUDE IS VERY DIFFERENT TOWARD MISS ALICIA...
WELL, IT'S FINE AS LONG AS I GET BACK TODAY, I GUESS. PIECE OF CAKE!
OH, MY... BUT TODAY, THE AERIAL TRAMWAY IS SCHEDULED FOR INSPECTION, ISN'T IT?
EH?
I THINK IT WILL BE CLOSING AT 6PM THIS EVENING...

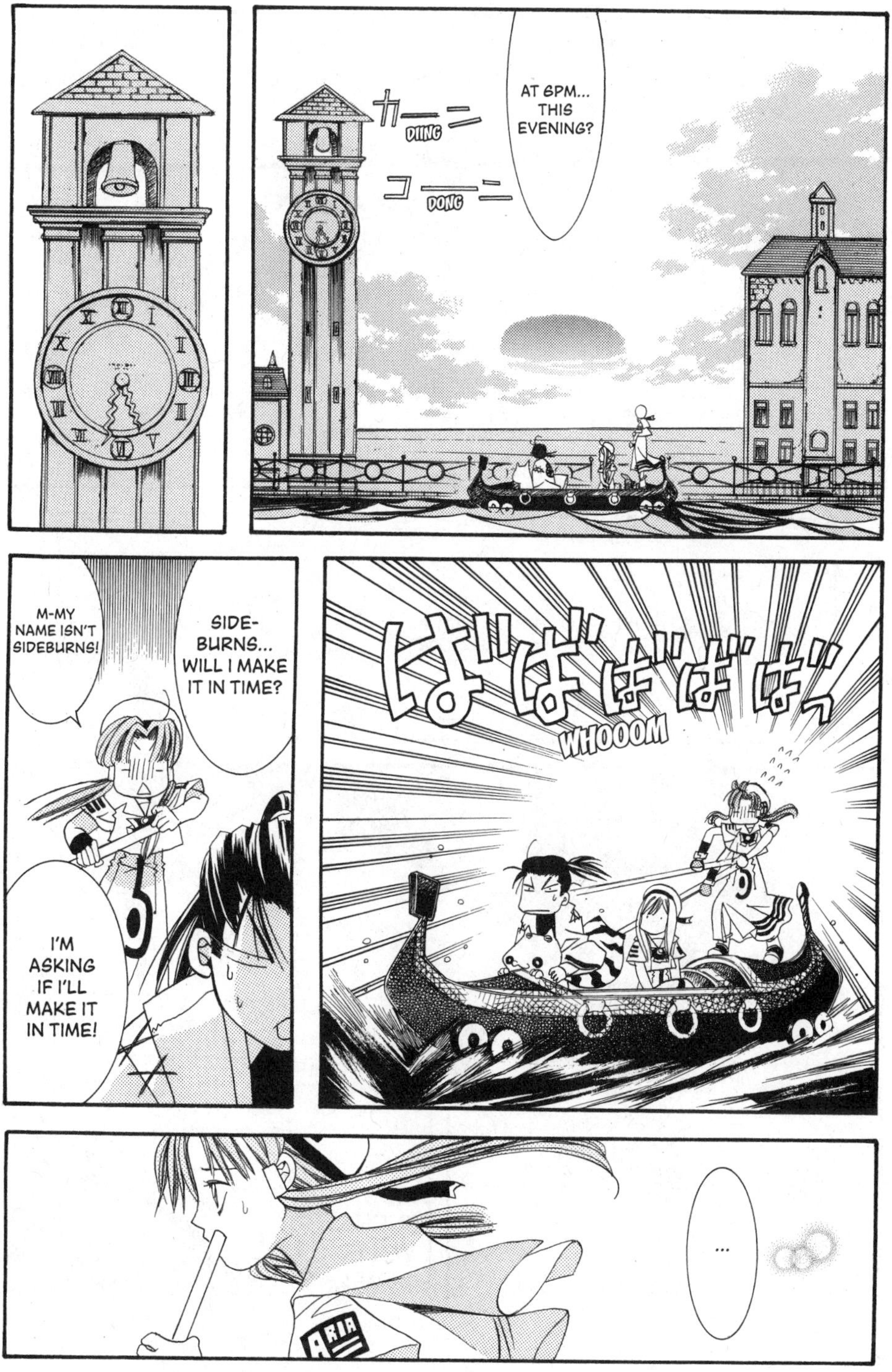
カーン
DIING
コーン
DONG
AT 6PM... THIS EVENING?
ばばばばばっ
WHOOOM
SIDE-BURNS... WILL I MAKE IT IN TIME?
M-MY NAME ISN'T SIDEBURNS!
I'M ASKING IF I'LL MAKE IT IN TIME!
...

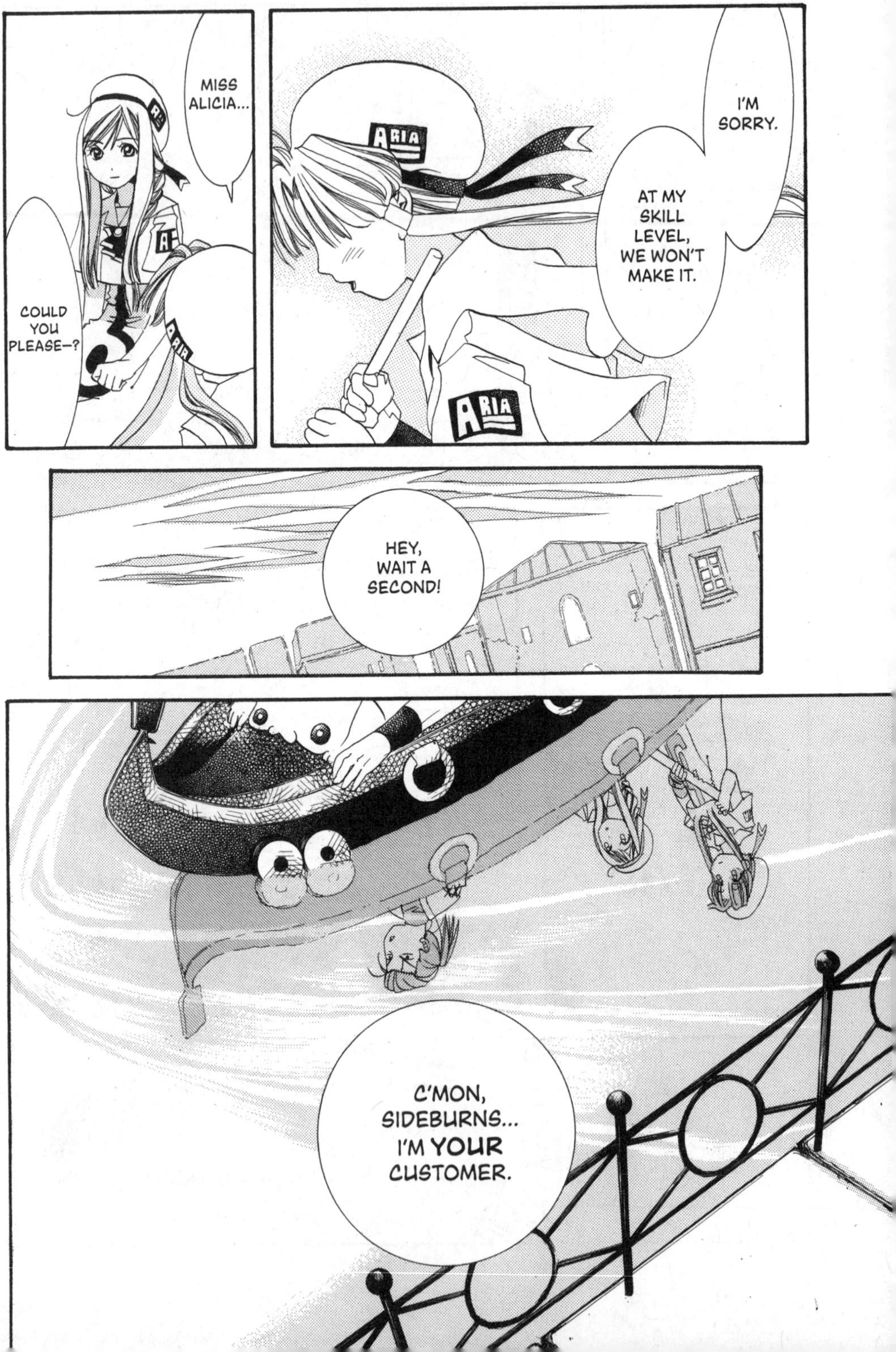
I'M SORRY.
AT MY SKILL LEVEL, WE WON'T MAKE IT.
MISS ALICIA...
COULD YOU PLEASE—?
HEY, WAIT A SECOND!
C'MON, SIDEBURNS... I'M **YOUR** CUSTOMER.

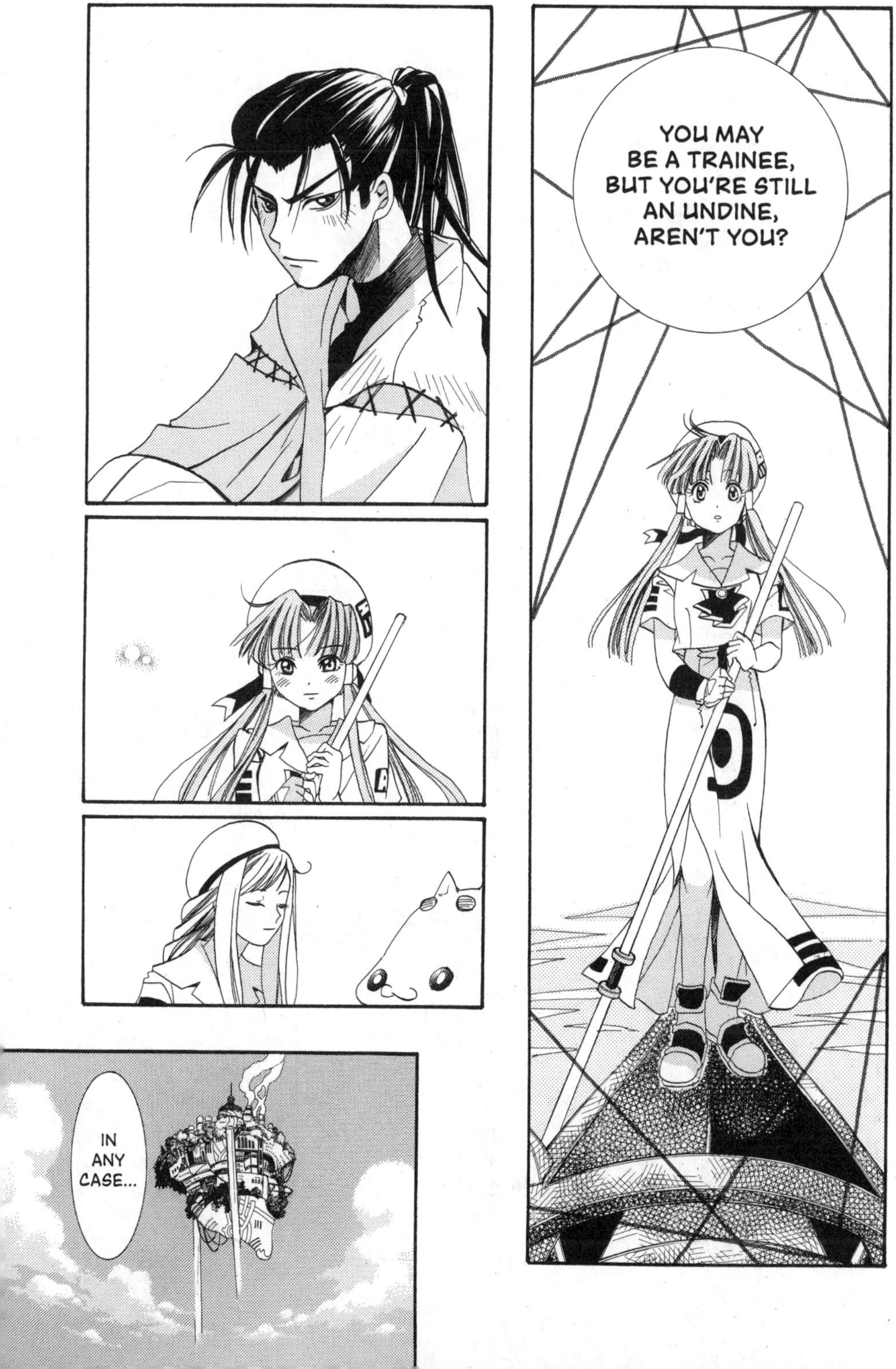
YOU MAY BE A TRAINEE, BUT YOU'RE STILL AN UNDINE, AREN'T YOU?
IN ANY CASE...

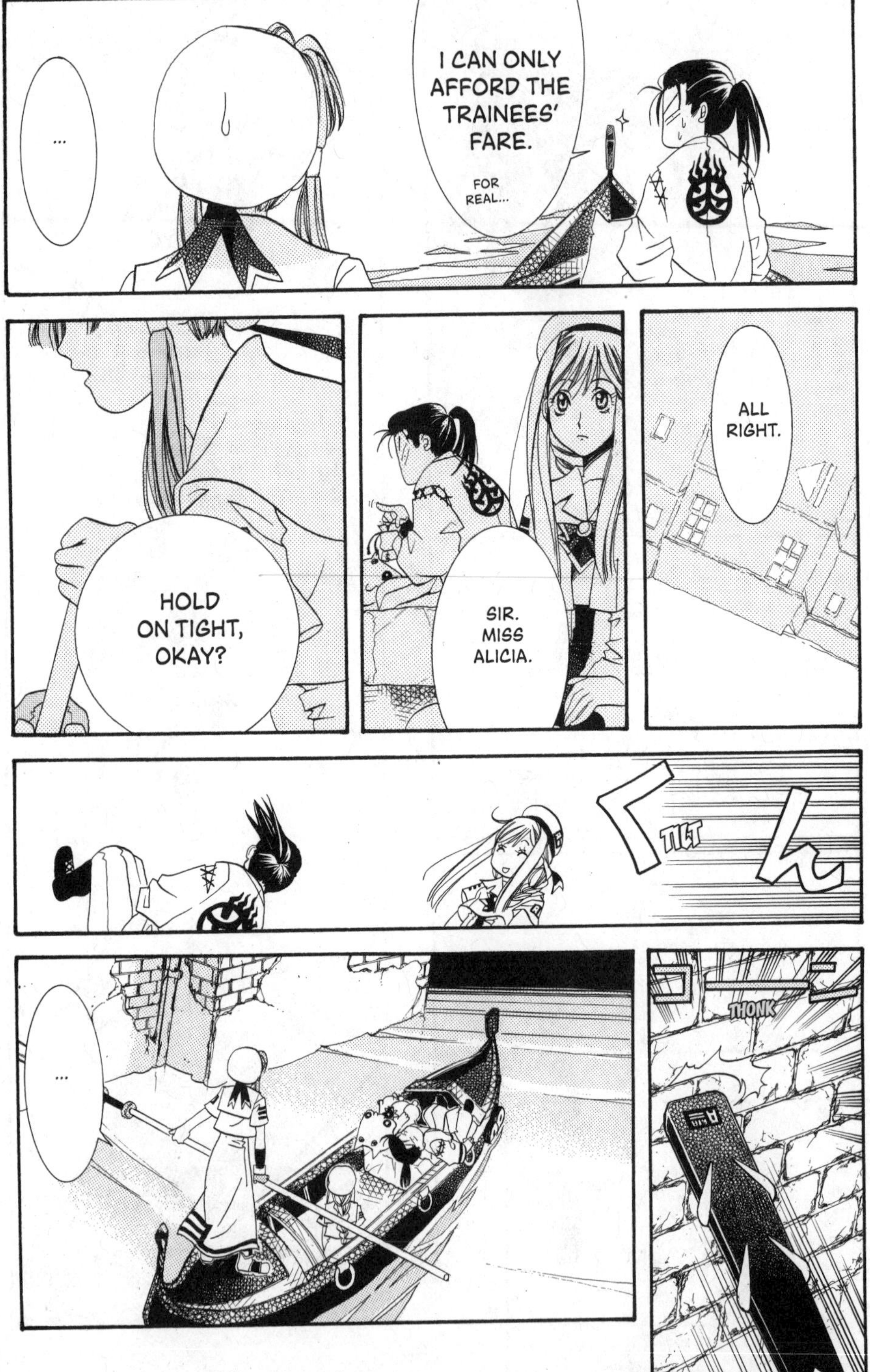
I CAN ONLY AFFORD THE TRAINEES' FARE.
FOR REAL...
...
ALL RIGHT.
SIR. MISS ALICIA.
HOLD ON TIGHT, OKAY?
TILT
THONK
...

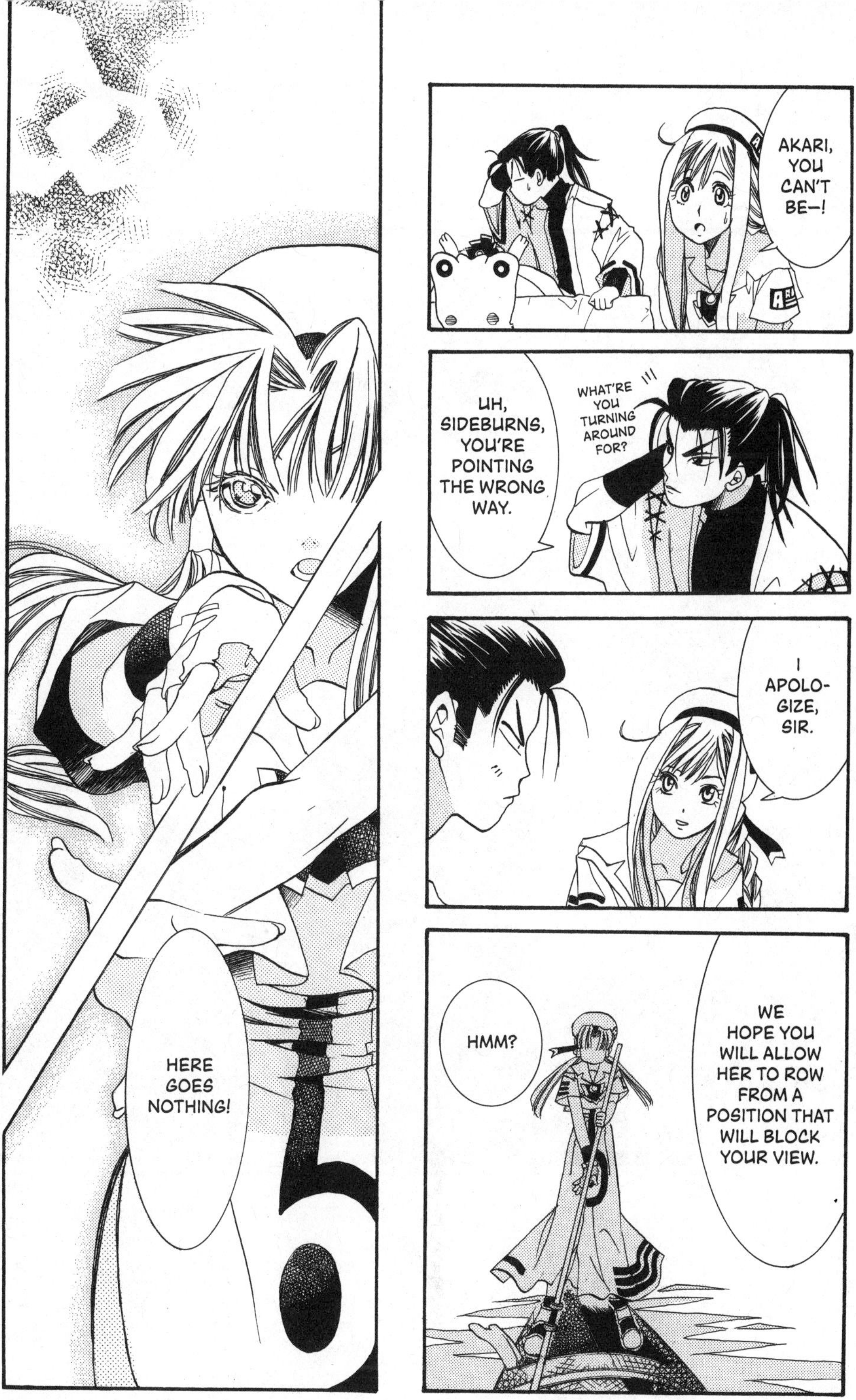
AKARI, YOU CAN'T BE—!
WHAT'RE YOU TURNING AROUND FOR?
UH, SIDEBURNS, YOU'RE POINTING THE WRONG WAY.
I APOLO-GIZE, SIR.
WE HOPE YOU WILL ALLOW HER TO ROW FROM A POSITION THAT WILL BLOCK YOUR VIEW.
HMM?
HERE GOES NOTHING!

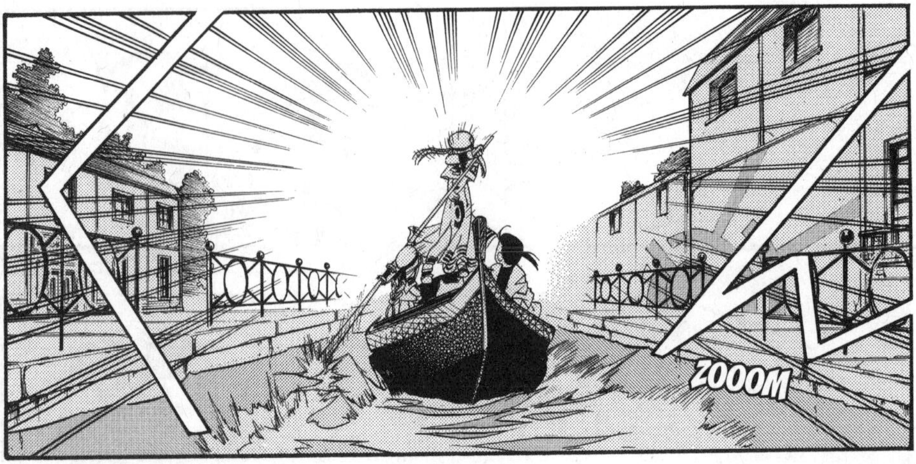
ZOOOM

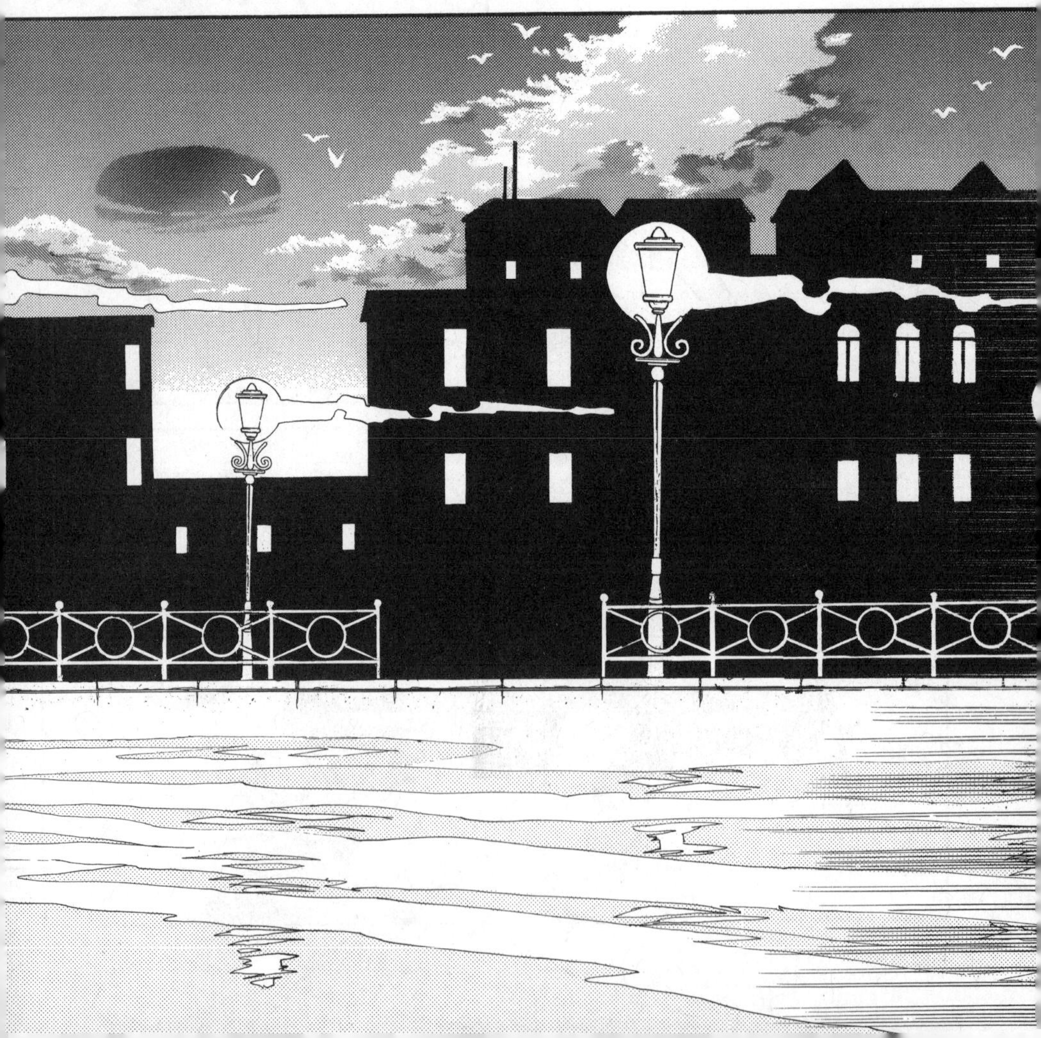

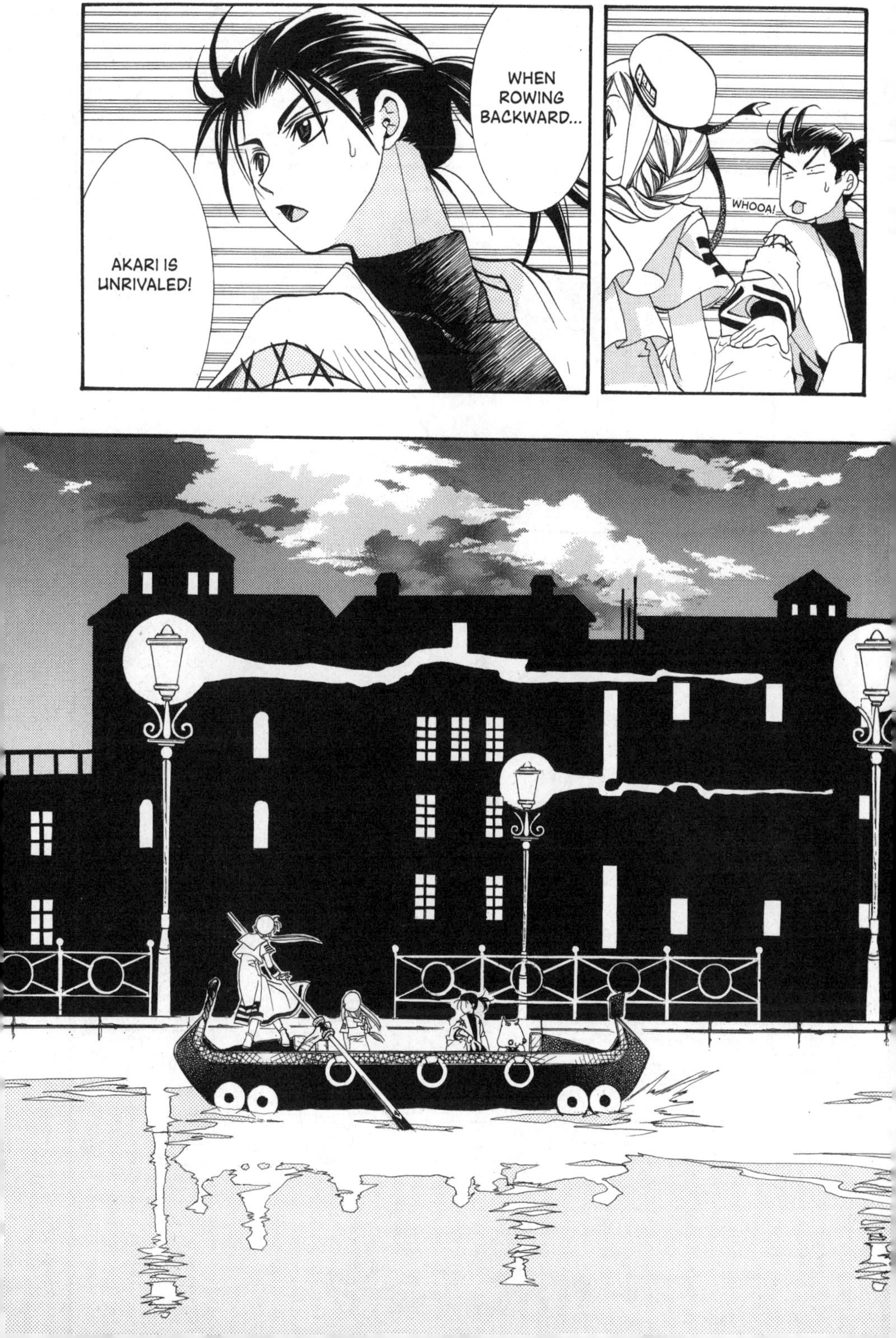
WHOOA!
WHEN ROWING BACKWARD...
AKARI IS UNRIVALED!

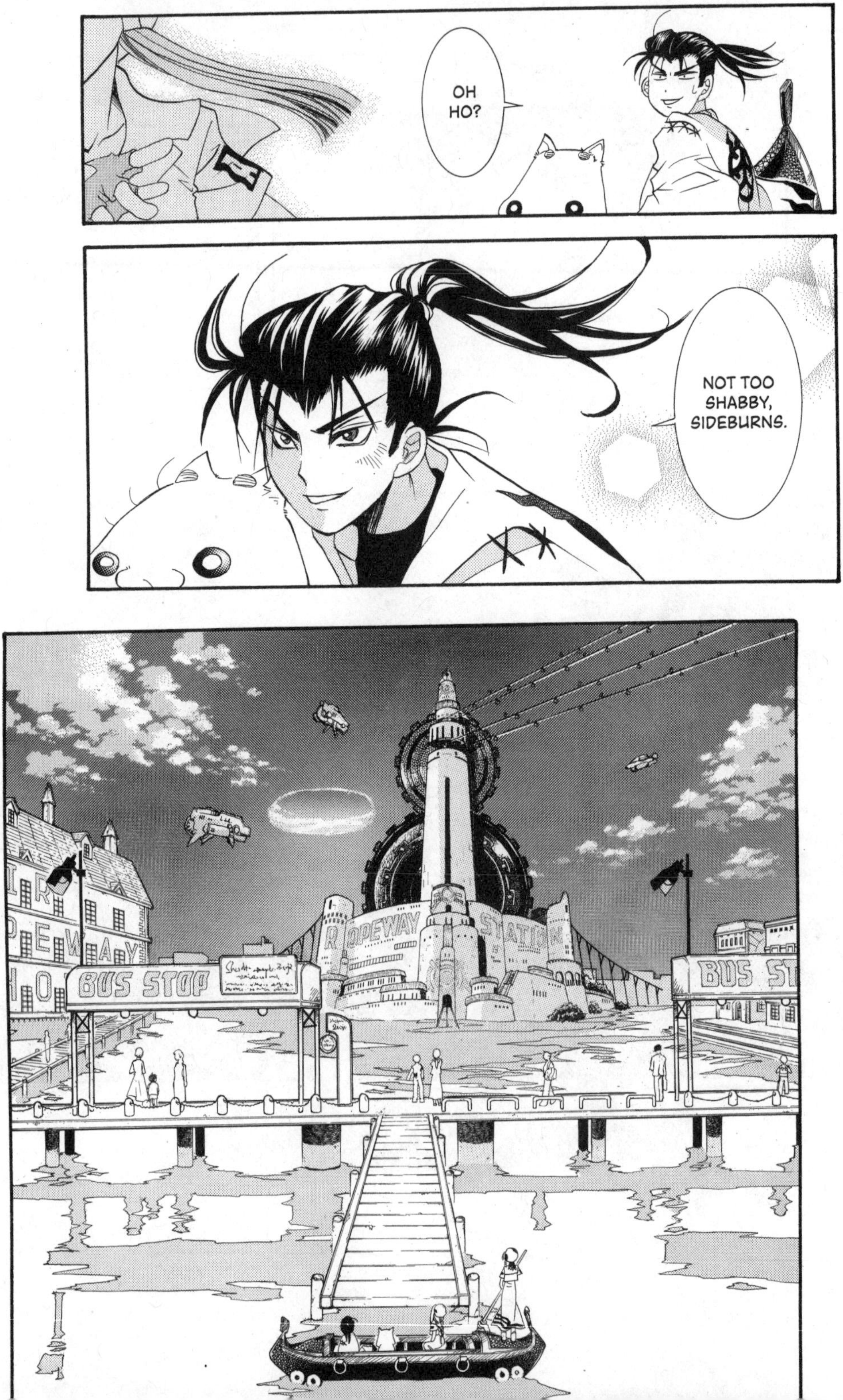
OH HO?
NOT TOO SHABBY, SIDEBURNS.
ROPEWAY STATION
BUS STOP

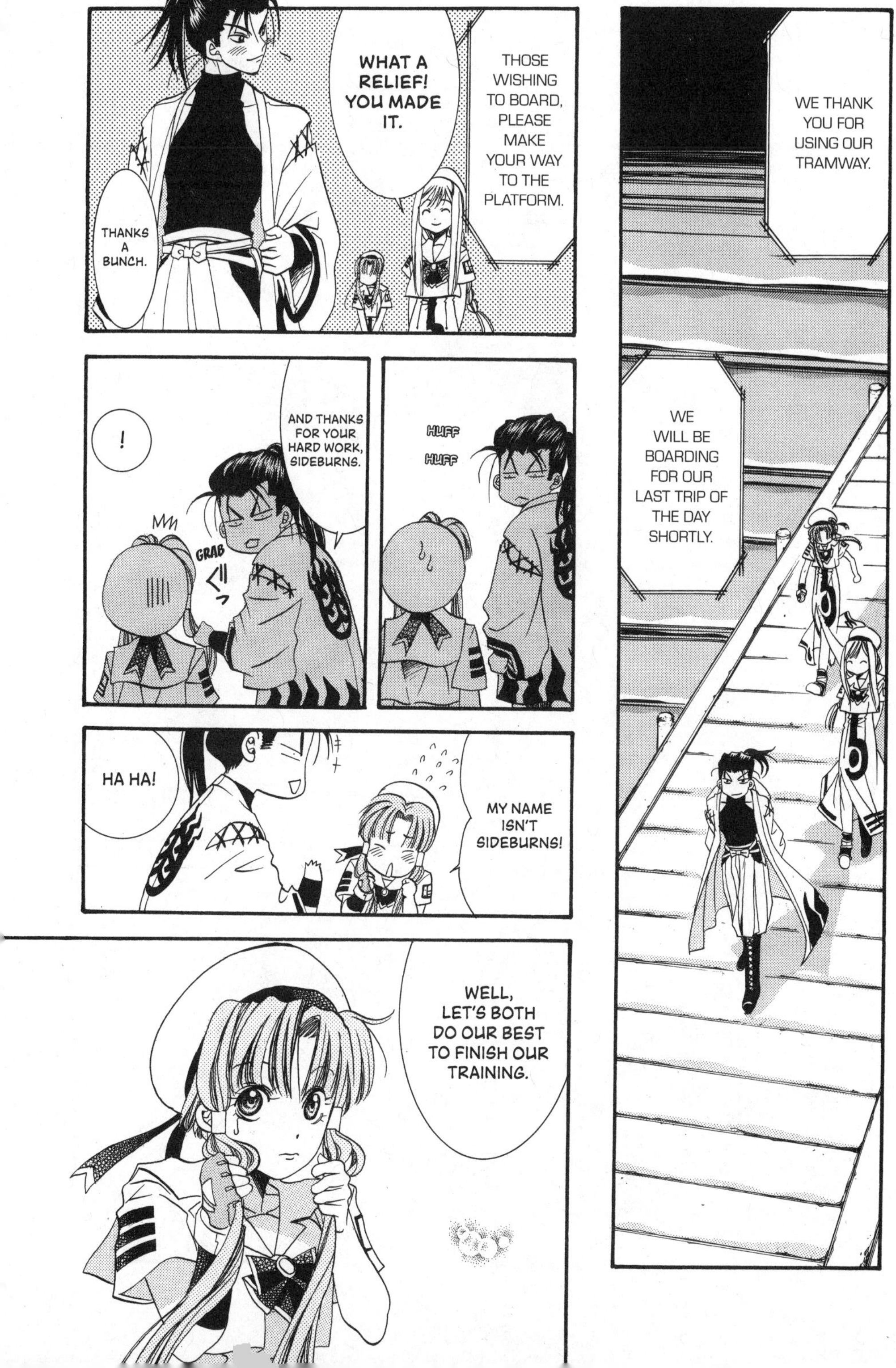
WE THANK YOU FOR USING OUR TRAMWAY.
WE WILL BE BOARDING FOR OUR LAST TRIP OF THE DAY SHORTLY.
THOSE WISHING TO BOARD, PLEASE MAKE YOUR WAY TO THE PLATFORM.
WHAT A RELIEF! YOU MADE IT.
THANKS A BUNCH.
HUFF
HUFF
AND THANKS FOR YOUR HARD WORK, SIDEBURNS.
!
GRAB
MY NAME ISN'T SIDEBURNS!
HA HA!
WELL, LET'S BOTH DO OUR BEST TO FINISH OUR TRAINING.

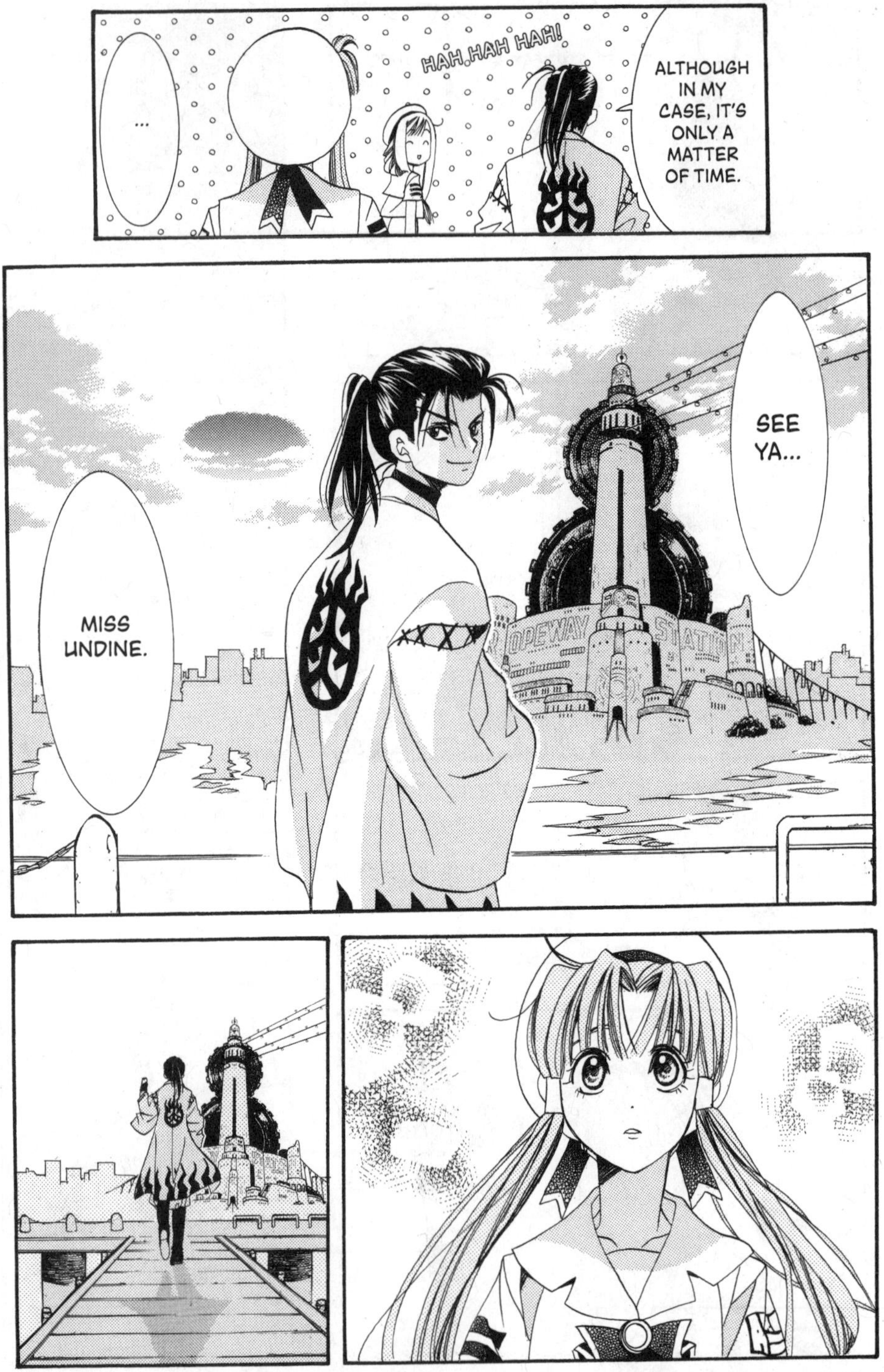
ALTHOUGH IN MY CASE, IT'S ONLY A MATTER OF TIME.
HAH HAH HAH!
...
SEE YA...
MISS UNDINE.

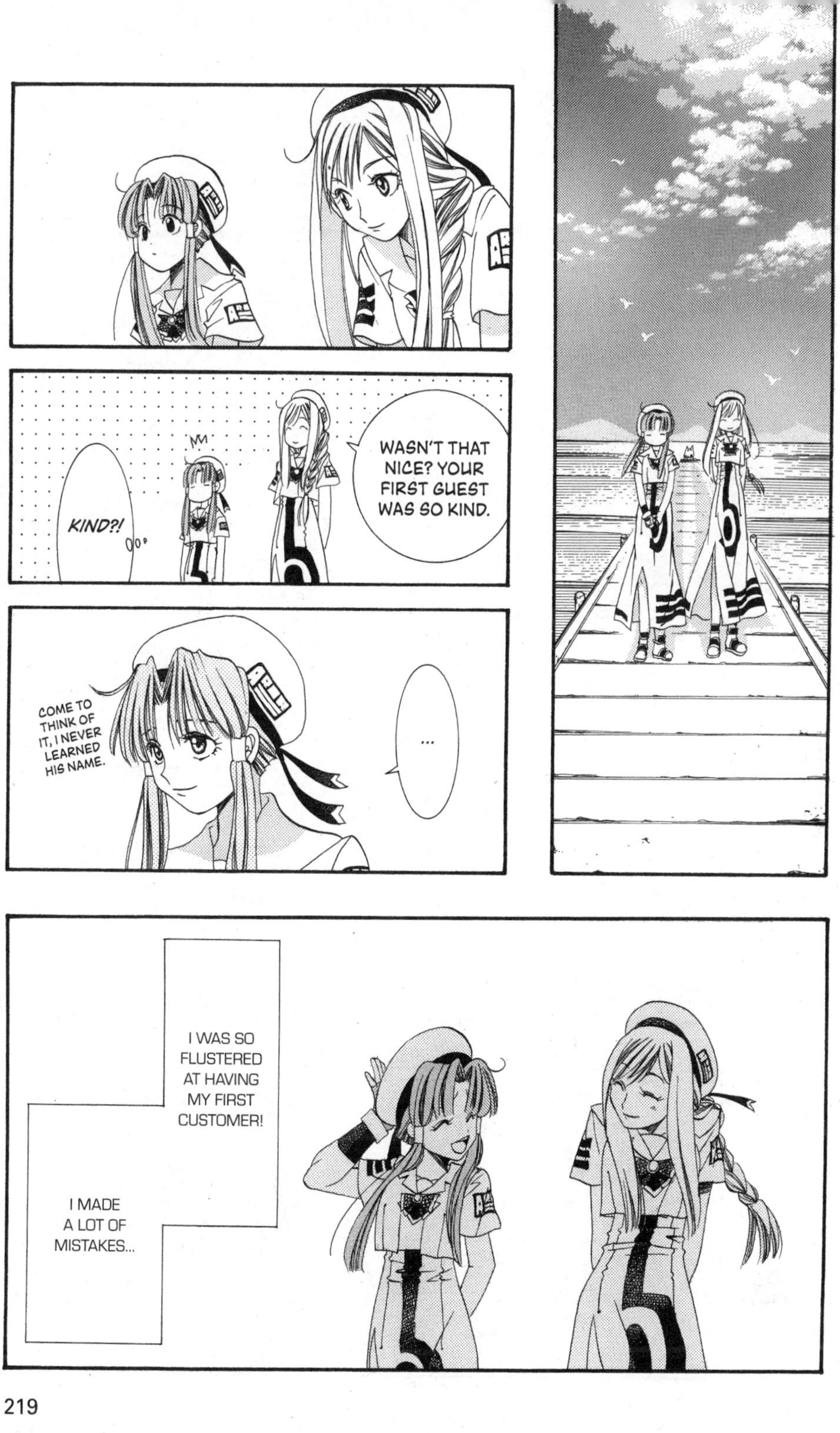
WASN'T THAT NICE? YOUR FIRST GUEST WAS SO KIND.
KIND?!
...
COME TO THINK OF IT, I NEVER LEARNED HIS NAME.
I WAS SO FLUSTERED AT HAVING MY FIRST CUSTOMER!
I MADE A LOT OF MISTAKES...

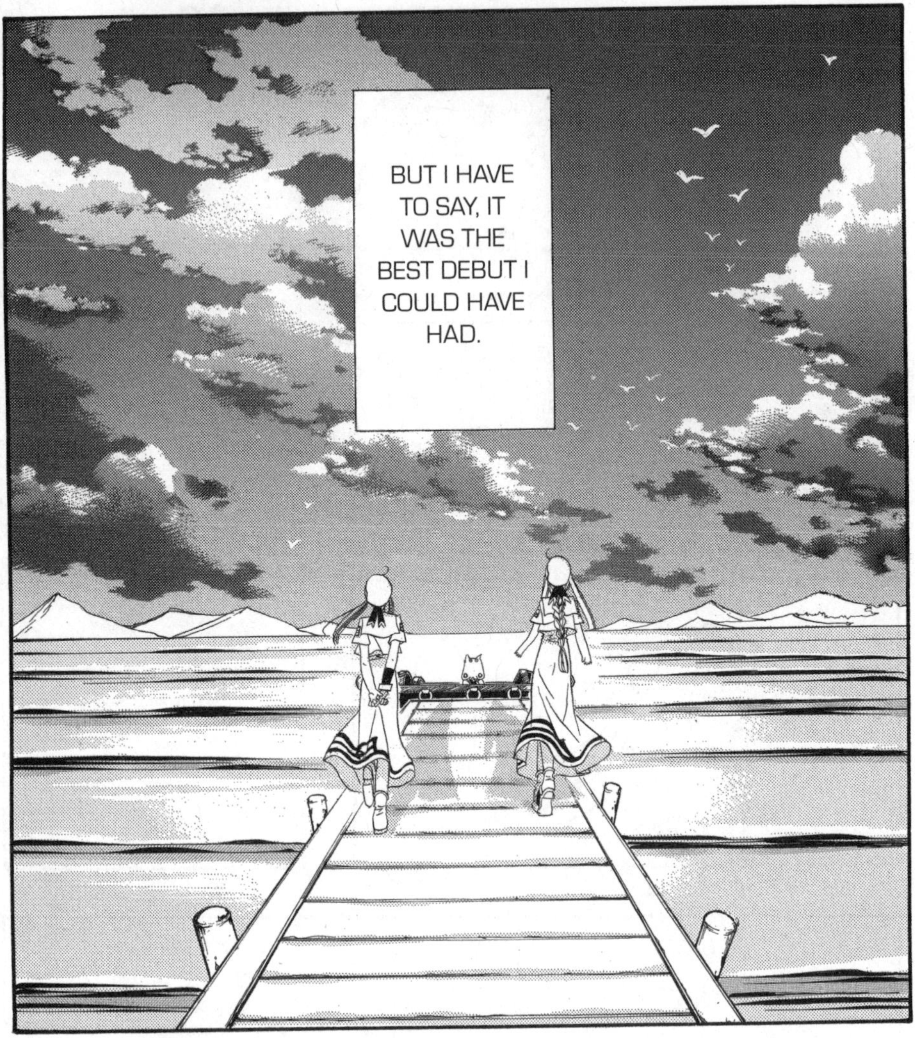
BUT I HAVE TO SAY, IT WAS THE BEST DEBUT I COULD HAVE HAD.
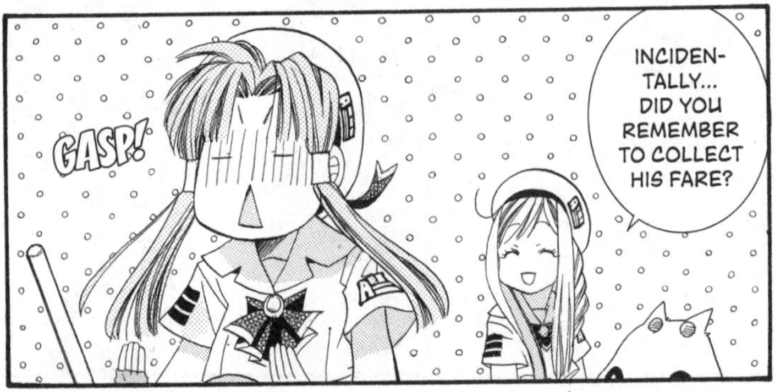
INCIDEN-TALLY... DID YOU REMEMBER TO COLLECT HIS FARE?
GASP!

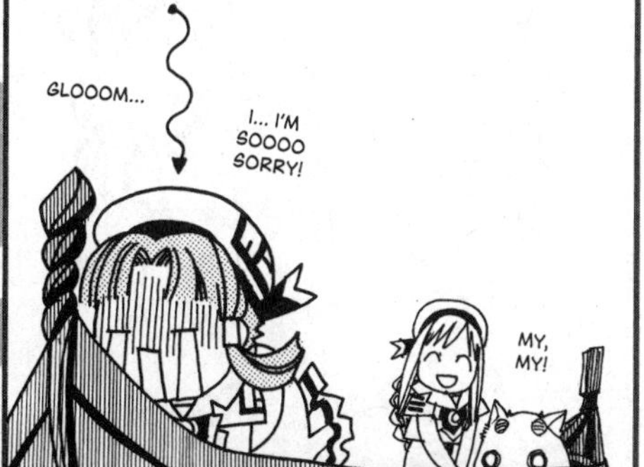
GLOOOM...
I... I'M SOOOO SORRY!
MY, MY!

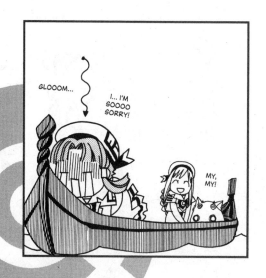

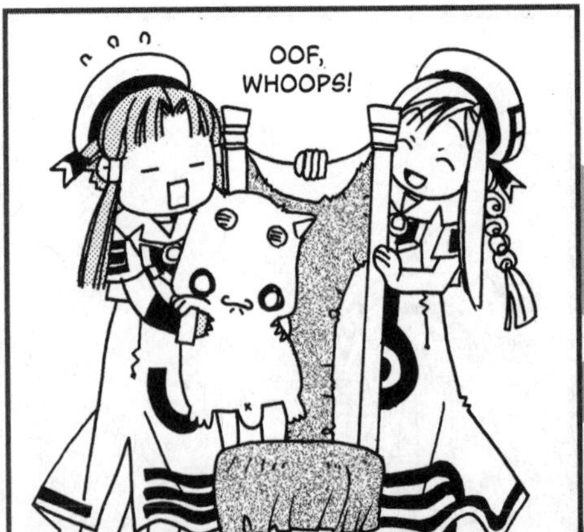
OOF,
WHOOPS!

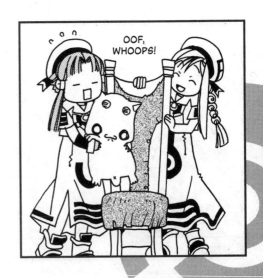

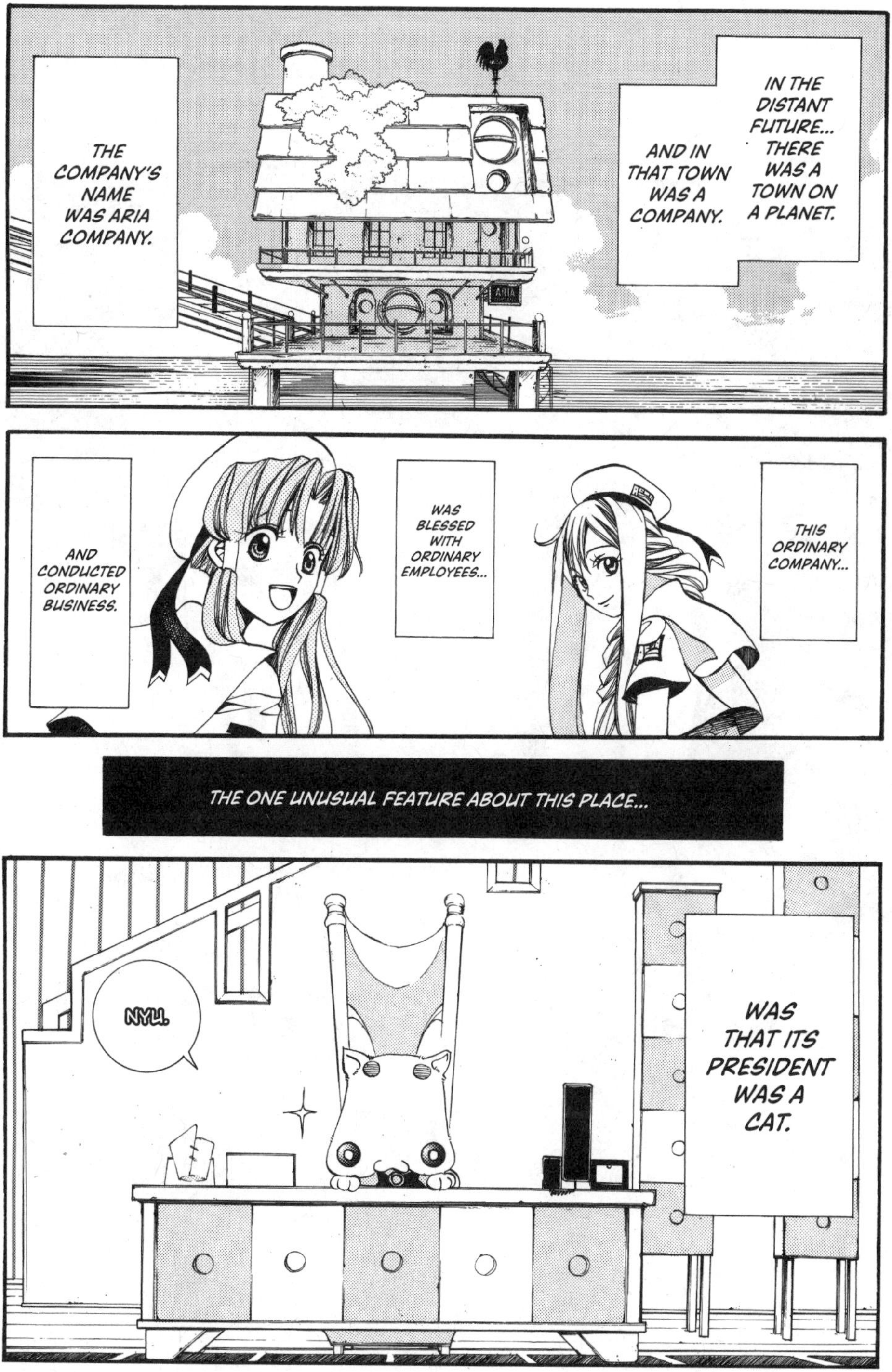
IN THE DISTANT FUTURE... THERE WAS A TOWN ON A PLANET.
AND IN THAT TOWN WAS A COMPANY.
THE COMPANY'S NAME WAS ARIA COMPANY.
THIS ORDINARY COMPANY...
WAS BLESSED WITH ORDINARY EMPLOYEES...
AND CONDUCTED ORDINARY BUSINESS.
THE ONE UNUSUAL FEATURE ABOUT THIS PLACE...
WAS THAT ITS PRESIDENT WAS A CAT.
NYU.

Navigation 07
It's Hard Being President

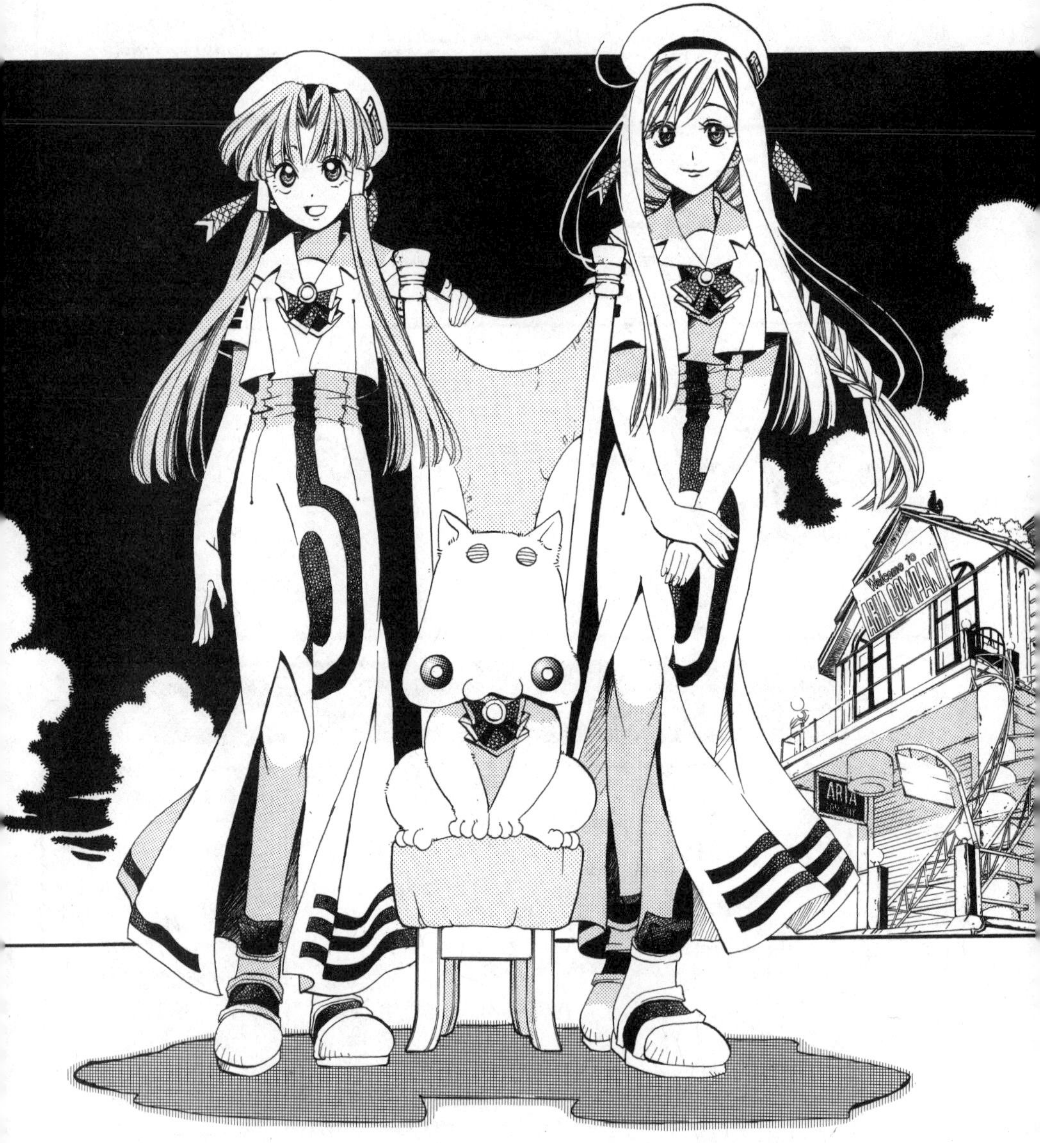
Welcome to
ARIA COMPANY
ARIA

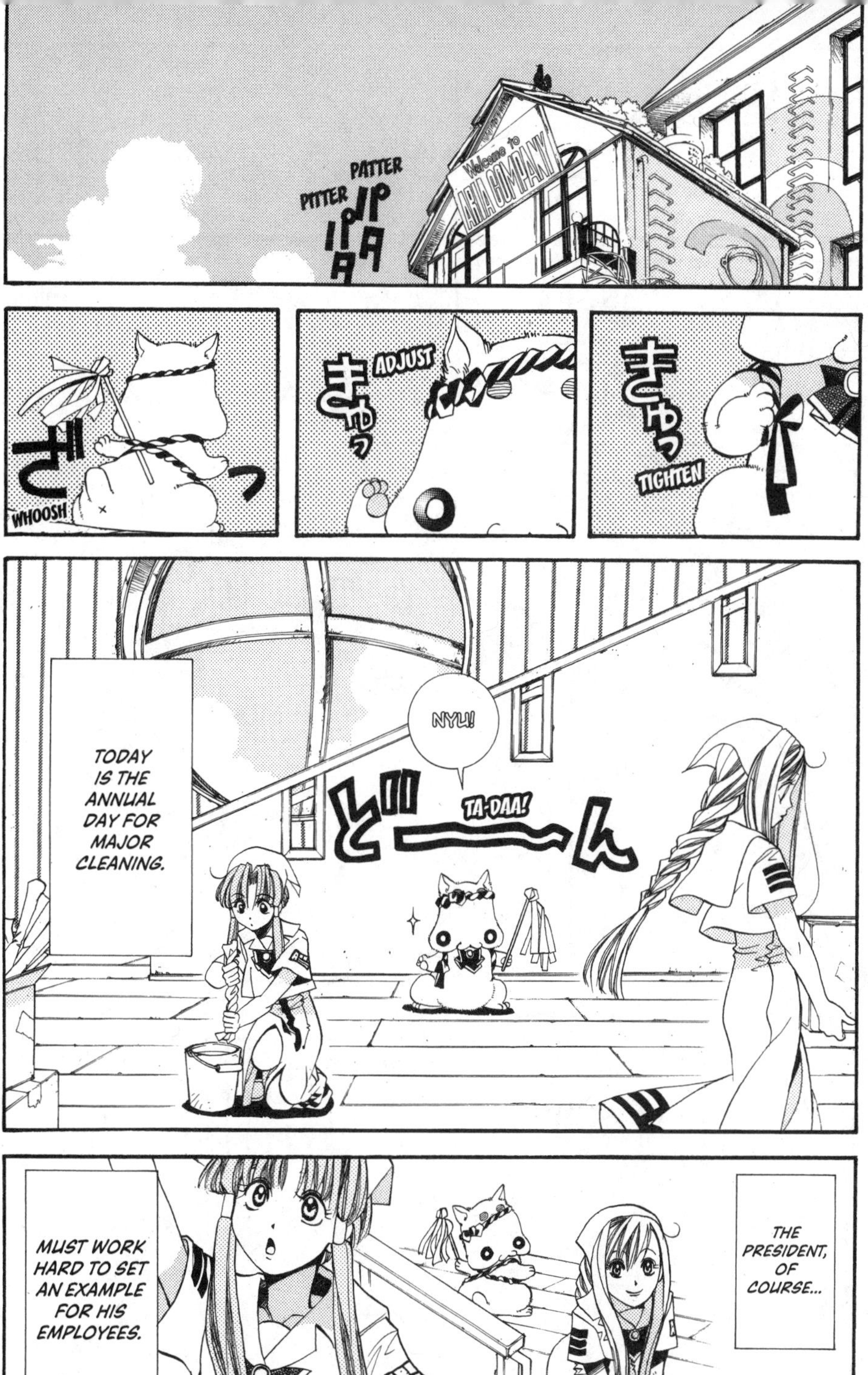
Welcome to
ARIA COMPANY
PITTER
PATTER
TIGHTEN
ADJUST
WHOOSH
TODAY IS THE ANNUAL DAY FOR MAJOR CLEANING.
NYU!
TA-DAA!
THE PRESIDENT, OF COURSE...
MUST WORK HARD TO SET AN EXAMPLE FOR HIS EMPLOYEES.

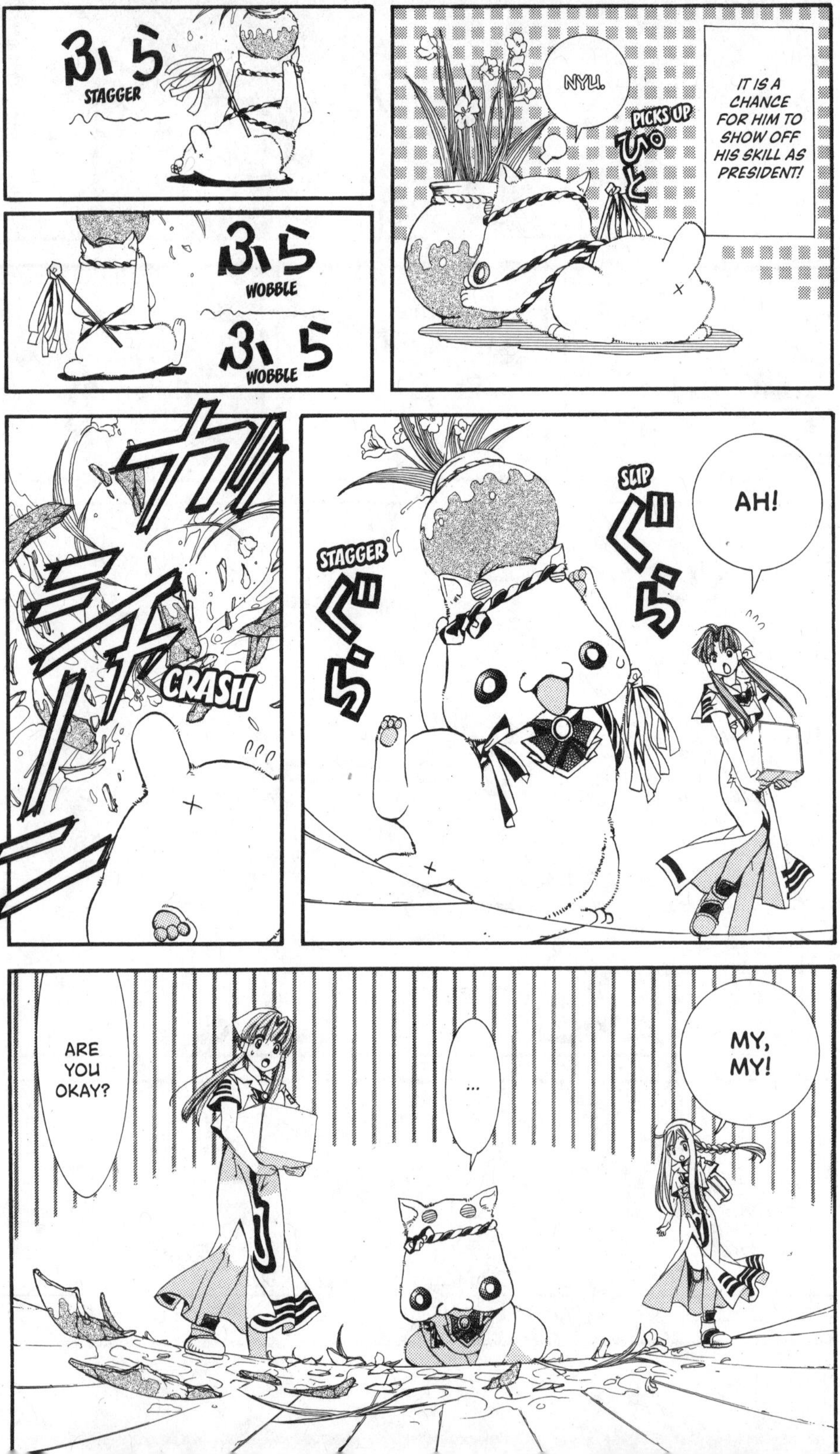

IT IS A CHANCE FOR HIM TO SHOW OFF HIS SKILL AS PRESIDENT!
NYU.
PICKS UP
ふら
STAGGER
ふら
WOBBLE
ふら
WOBBLE
AH!
SLIP
ぐら
STAGGER
ぐら
CRASH
MY, MY!
...
ARE YOU OKAY?

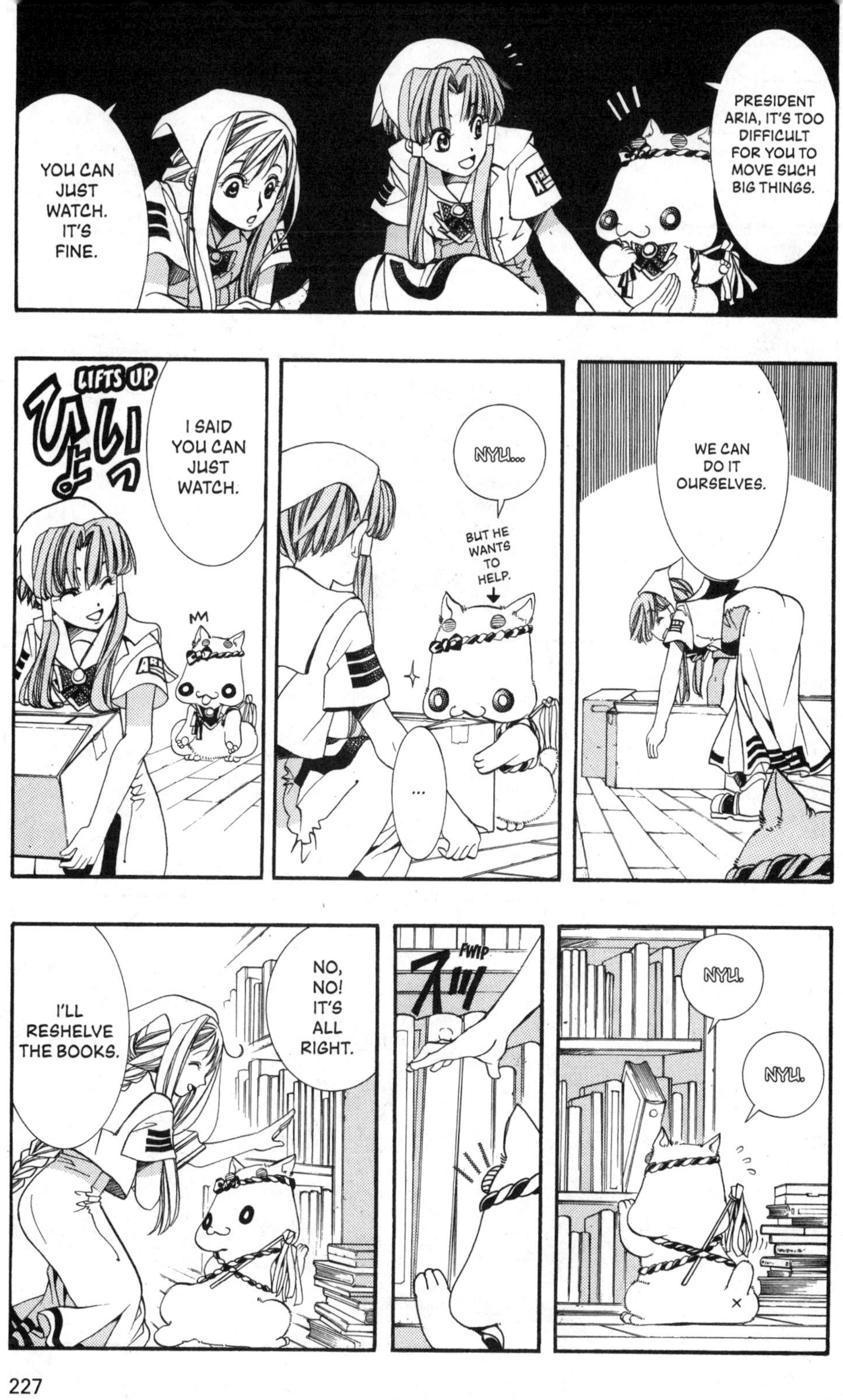
PRESIDENT ARIA, IT'S TOO DIFFICULT FOR YOU TO MOVE SUCH BIG THINGS.
YOU CAN JUST WATCH. IT'S FINE.
WE CAN DO IT OURSELVES.
NYU...
BUT HE WANTS TO HELP.
...
LIFTS UP
ひょいっ
I SAID YOU CAN JUST WATCH.
NYU.
NYU.
FWIP
スッ
NO, NO! IT'S ALL RIGHT.
I'LL RESHELVE THE BOOKS.

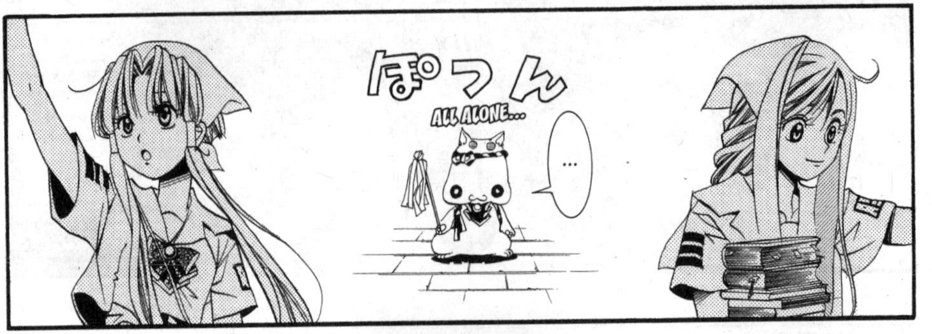
ぽつん
ALL ALONE...
...

PRESIDENT ARIA WAS DEPRESSED.

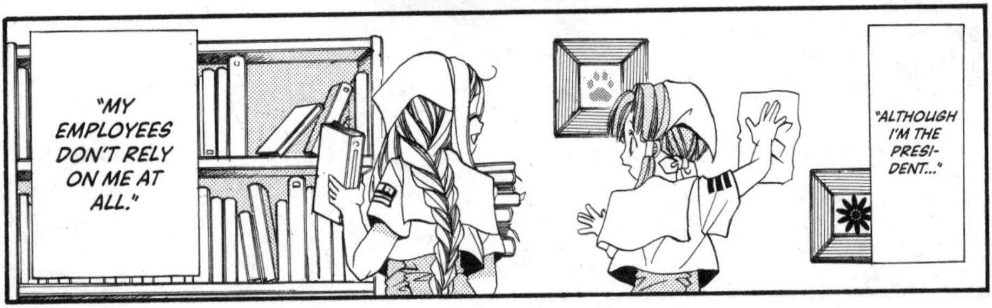
"ALTHOUGH I'M THE PRESIDENT..."
"MY EMPLOYEES DON'T RELY ON ME AT ALL."

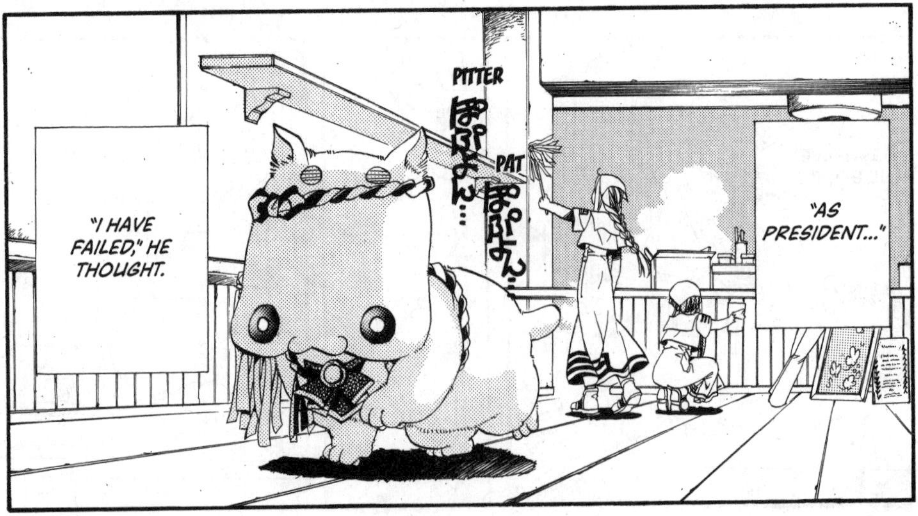
"AS PRESIDENT..."
PITTER
ぽふぽふ…
PAT
ぽふぽふ…
"I HAVE FAILED," HE THOUGHT.

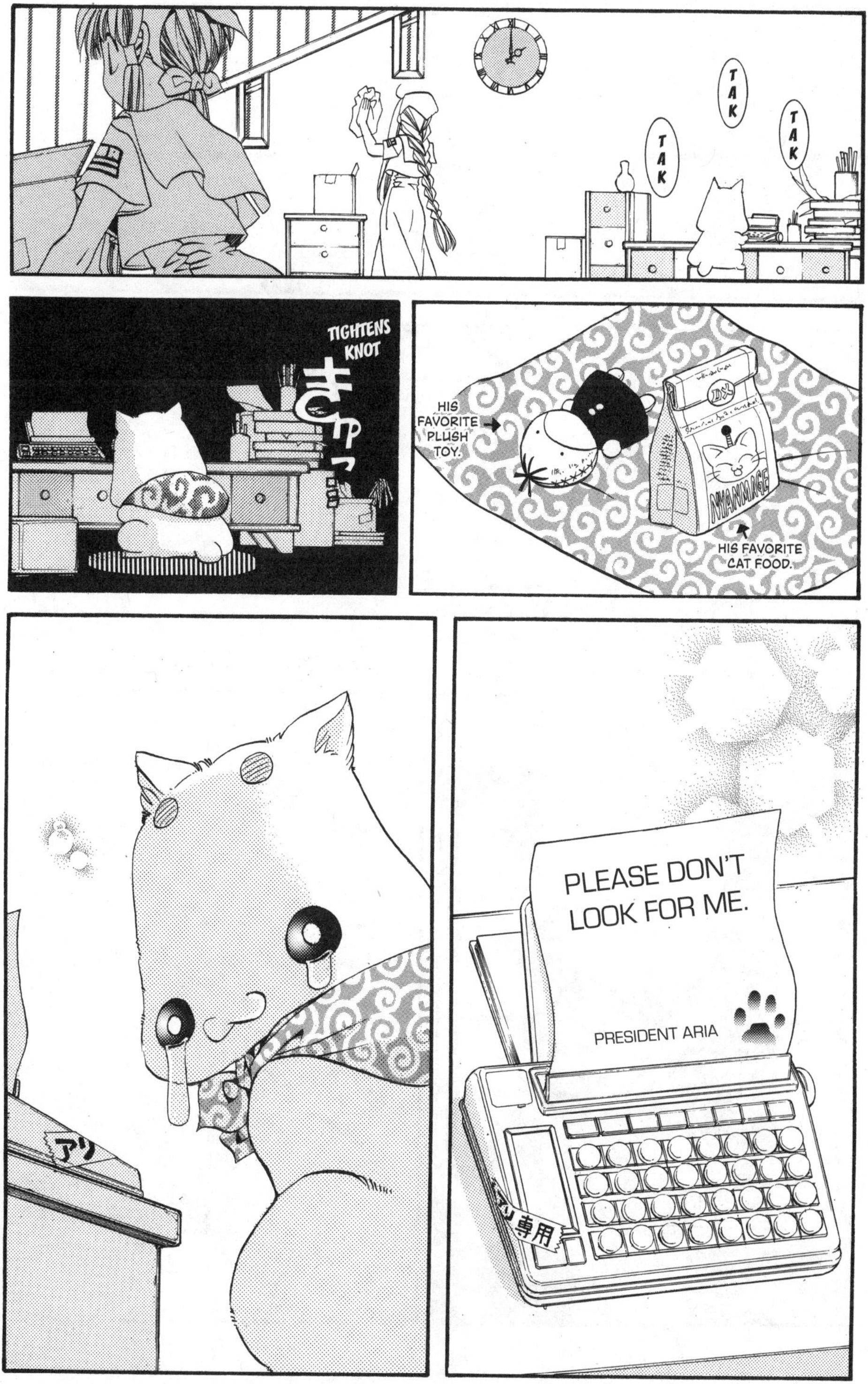
TAK
TAK
TAK
HIS FAVORITE PLUSH TOY.
DX
NYANMAGE
HIS FAVORITE CAT FOOD.
TIGHTENS KNOT
きゅっ
PLEASE DON'T LOOK FOR ME.
PRESIDENT ARIA
アリ専用
アリ

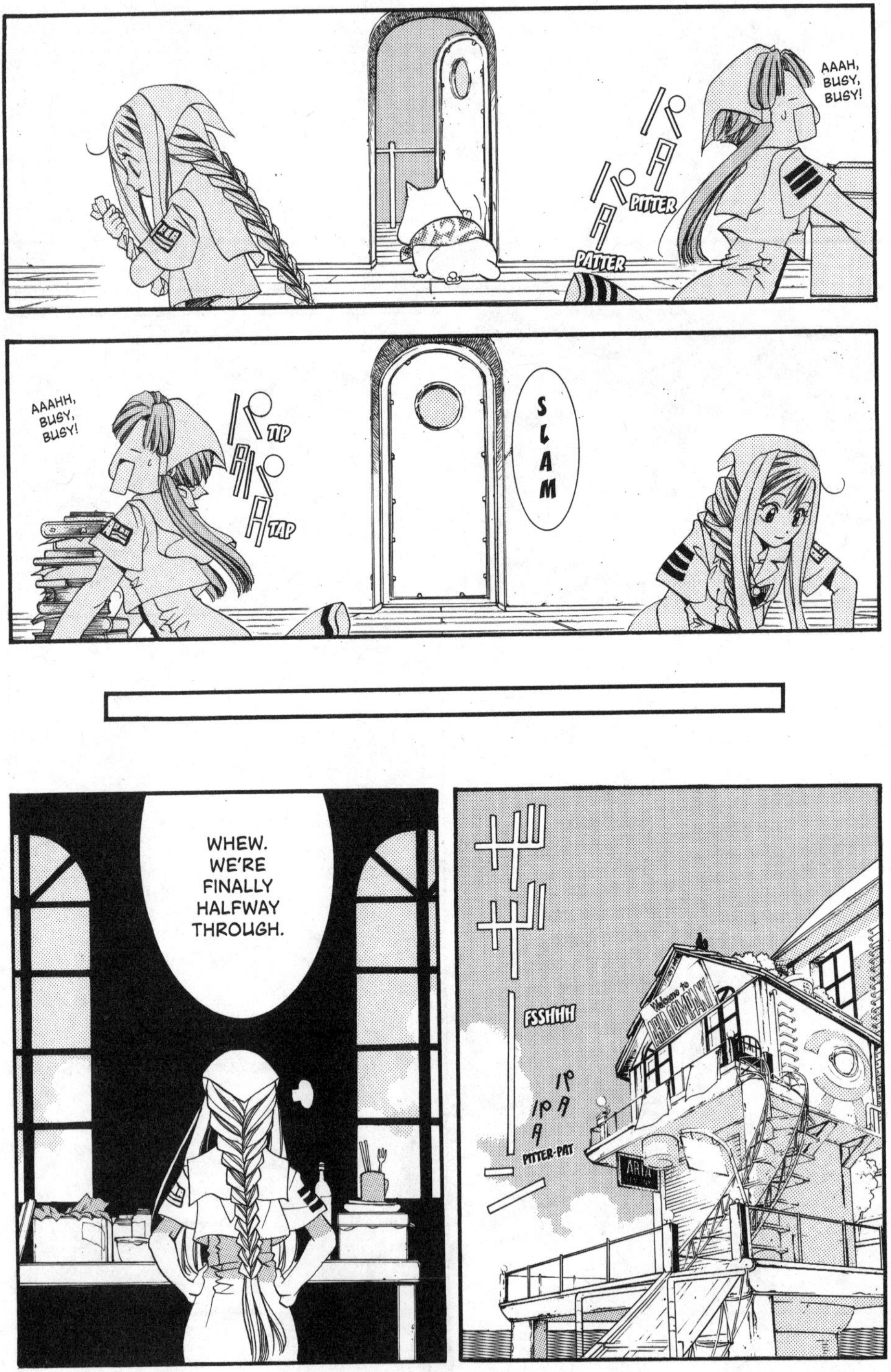
AAAH, BUSY, BUSY!
PITTER
PATTER
SLAM
AAAHH, BUSY, BUSY!
TIP
TAP
FSSHHH
PITTER-PAT
Welcome to ARIA COMPANY
ARIA
WHEW. WE'RE FINALLY HALFWAY THROUGH.

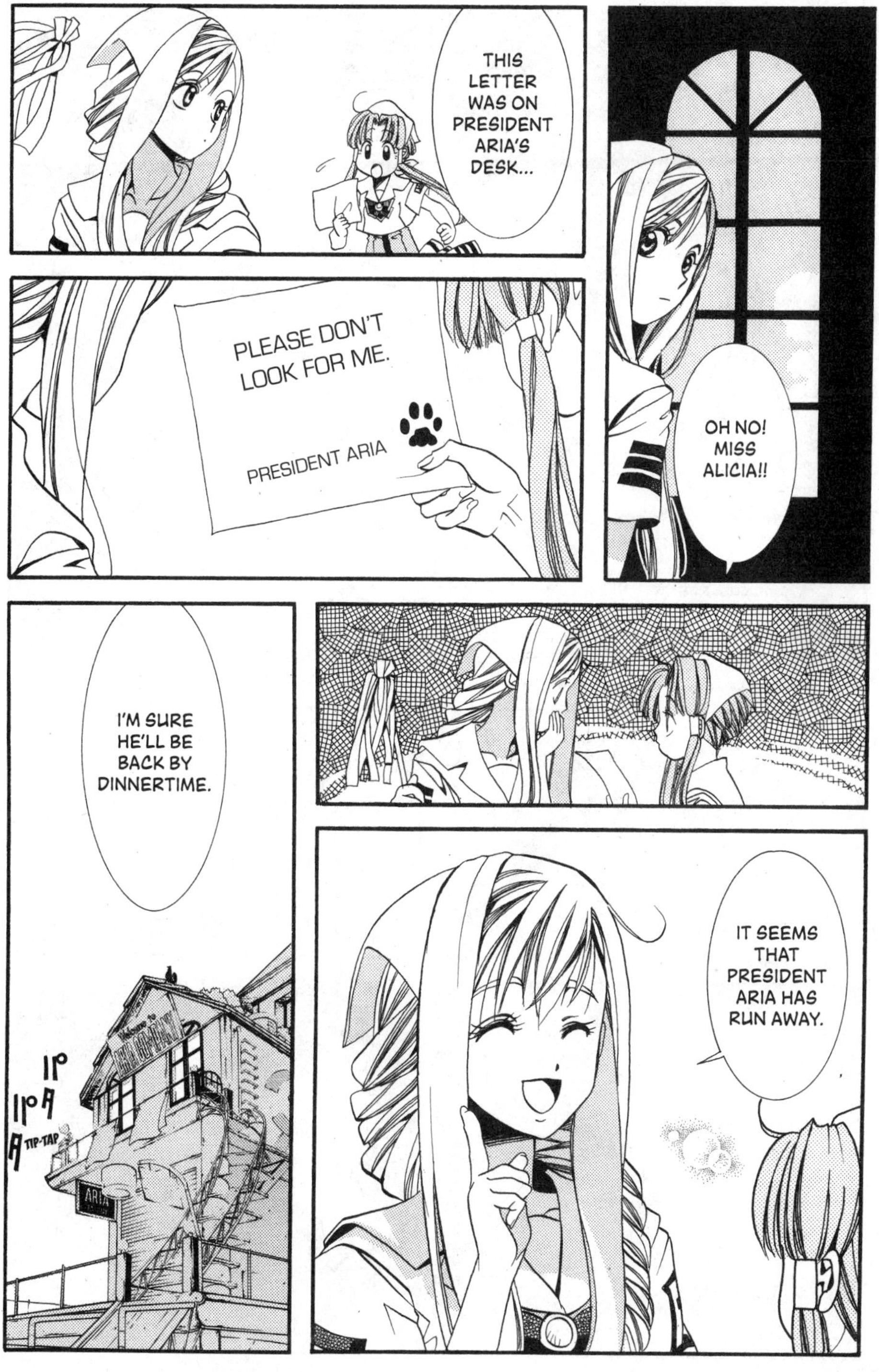
OH NO! MISS ALICIA!!
THIS LETTER WAS ON PRESIDENT ARIA'S DESK...
PLEASE DON'T LOOK FOR ME.
PRESIDENT ARIA
IT SEEMS THAT PRESIDENT ARIA HAS RUN AWAY.
I'M SURE HE'LL BE BACK BY DINNERTIME.
TIP-TAP
ARIA

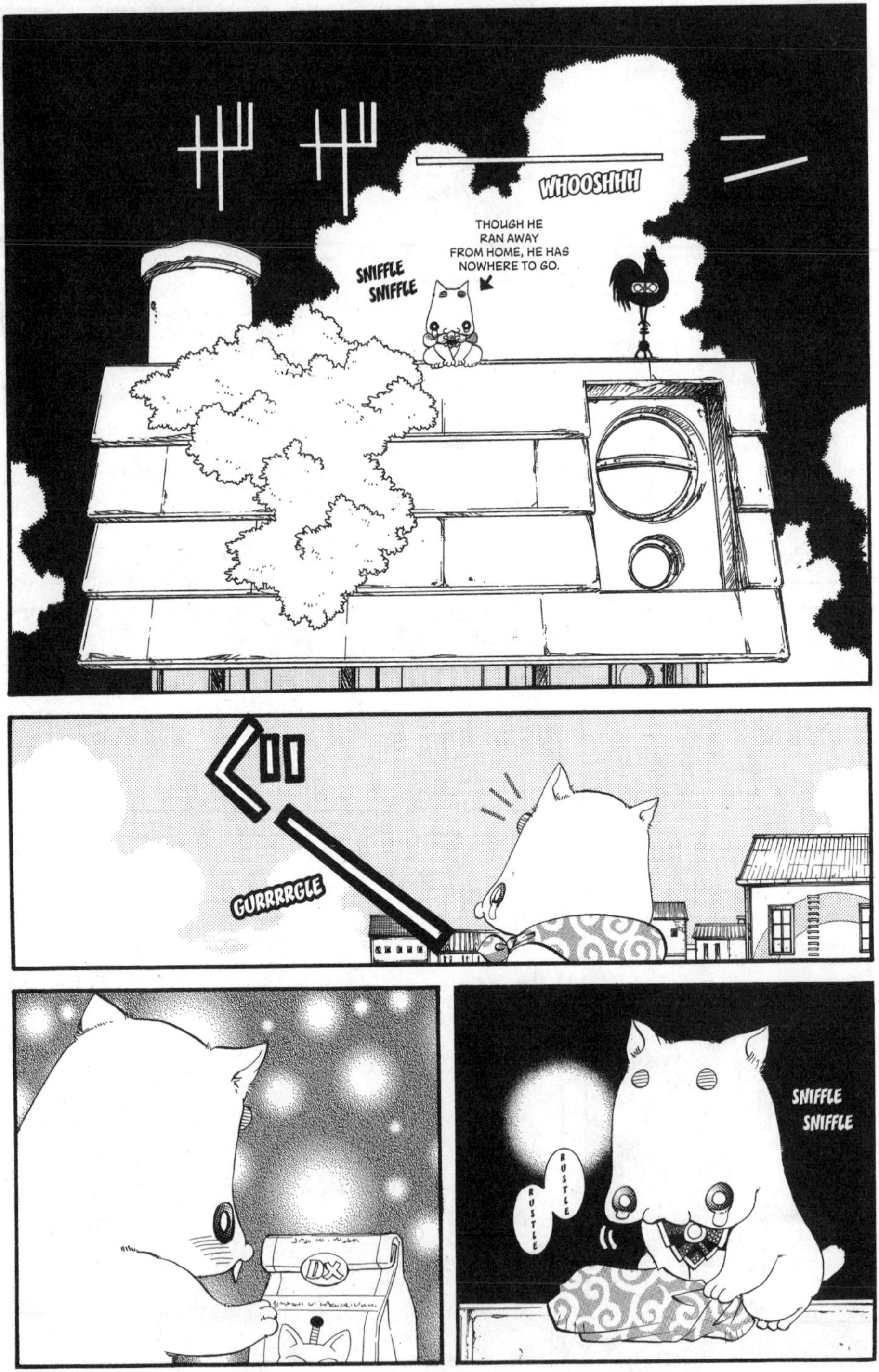
WHOOSHHH
THOUGH HE RAN AWAY FROM HOME, HE HAS NOWHERE TO GO.
SNIFFLE SNIFFLE
GURRRRGLE
SNIFFLE SNIFFLE
RUSTLE RUSTLE
DX

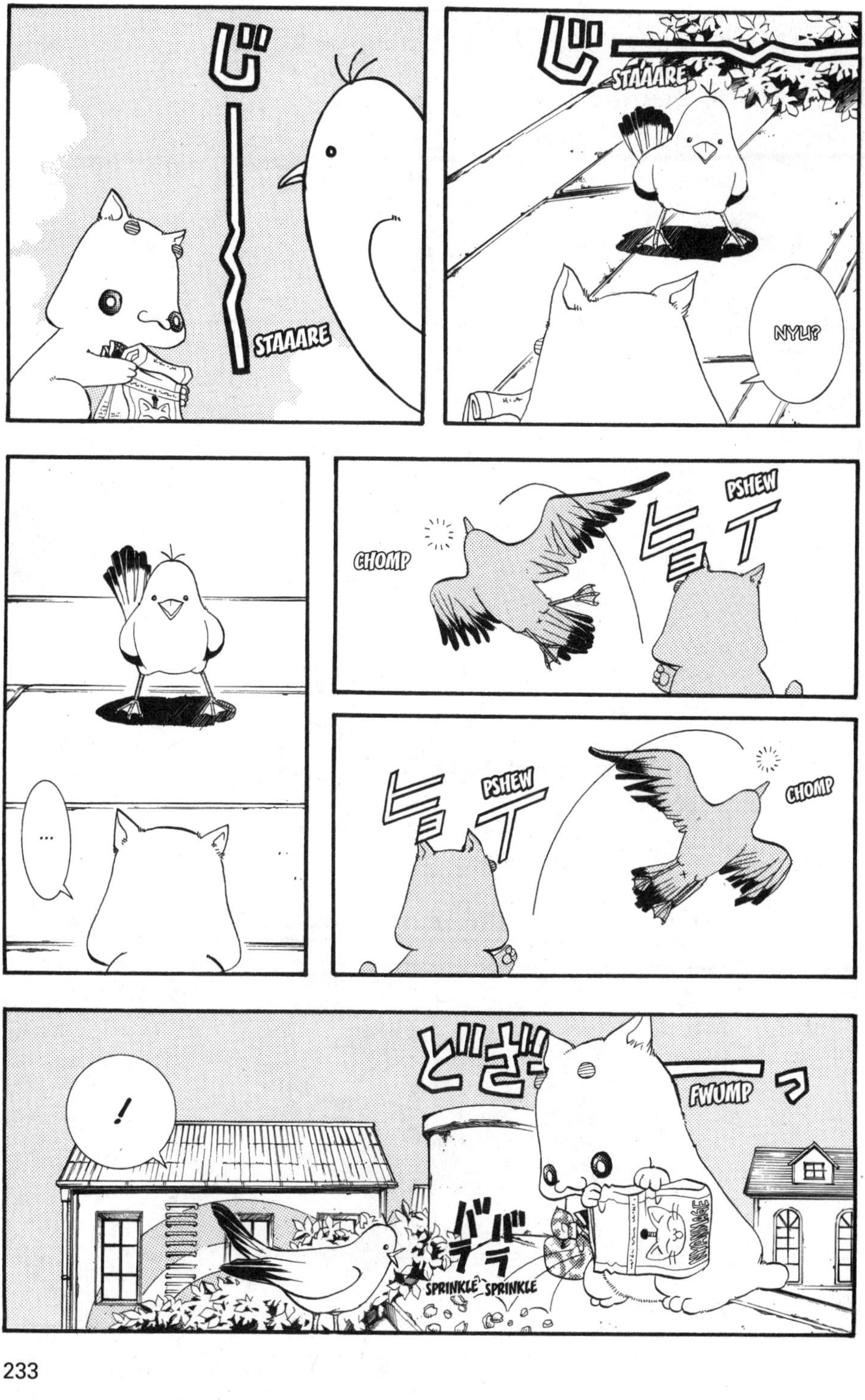

じーー
STAAARE
NYU?
じーー
STAAARE
ヒョイ
PSHEW
CHOMP
ヒョイ
PSHEW
CHOMP
...
どさーっ
FWUMP
!
バラバラ
SPRINKLE SPRINKLE

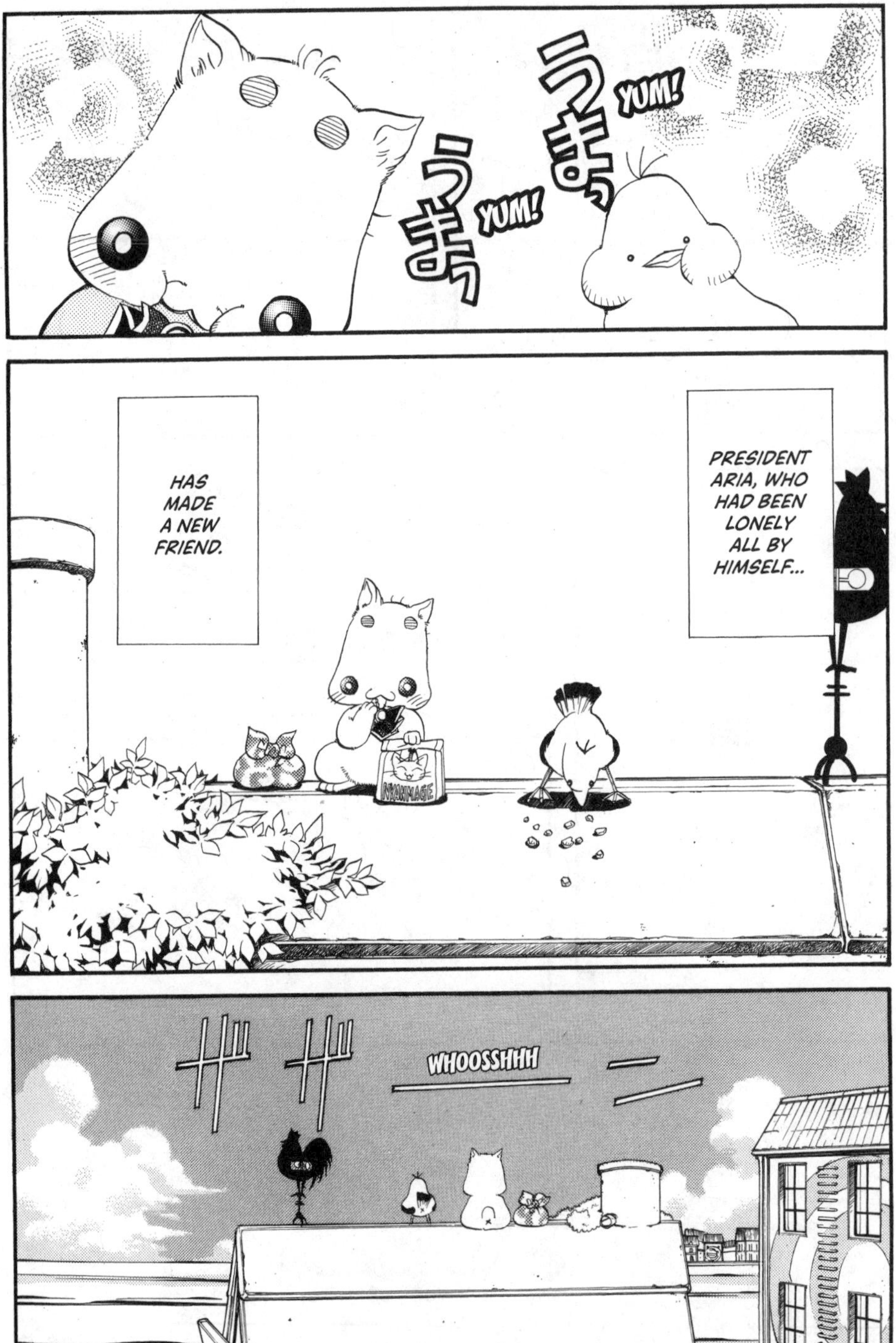
うまっ
YUM!
うまっ
YUM!
PRESIDENT ARIA, WHO HAD BEEN LONELY ALL BY HIMSELF...
HAS MADE A NEW FRIEND.
NYANMAGE
WHOOSSHHH

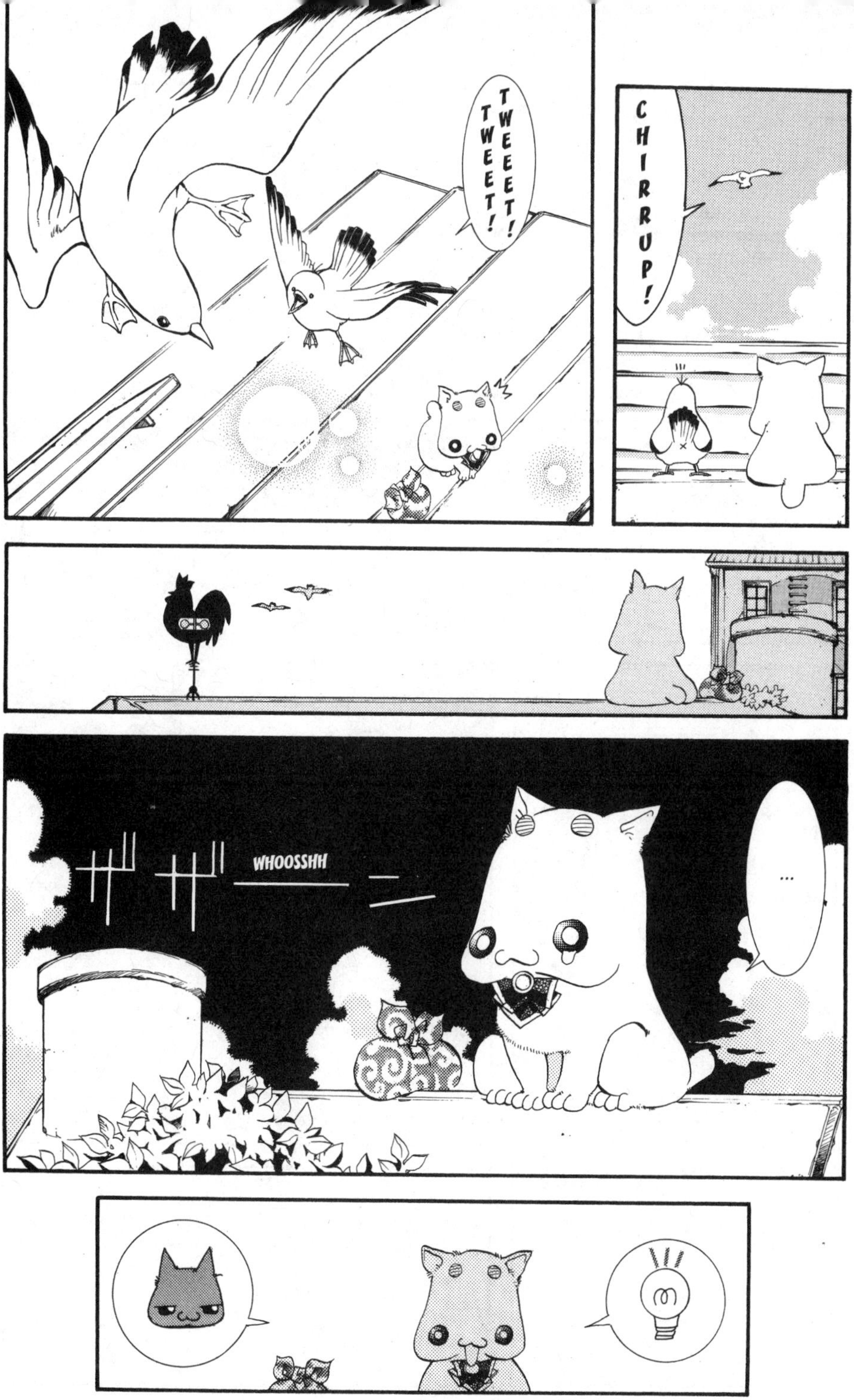
CHIRRUP!
TWEEET! TWEEET!
WHOOSSHH
...

LET'S GO VISIT PRESIDENT HIME.

THAT'S RIGHT.

SURELY PRESIDENT HIME WILL UNDERSTAND HOW HE FEELS.

PRESIDENT HIME IS IN THE SAME LINE OF WORK.

PRESIDENT ARIA RAN WITH ALL HIS MIGHT.

BOUNCE

BOUNCE

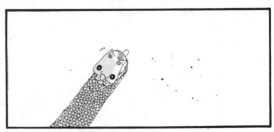

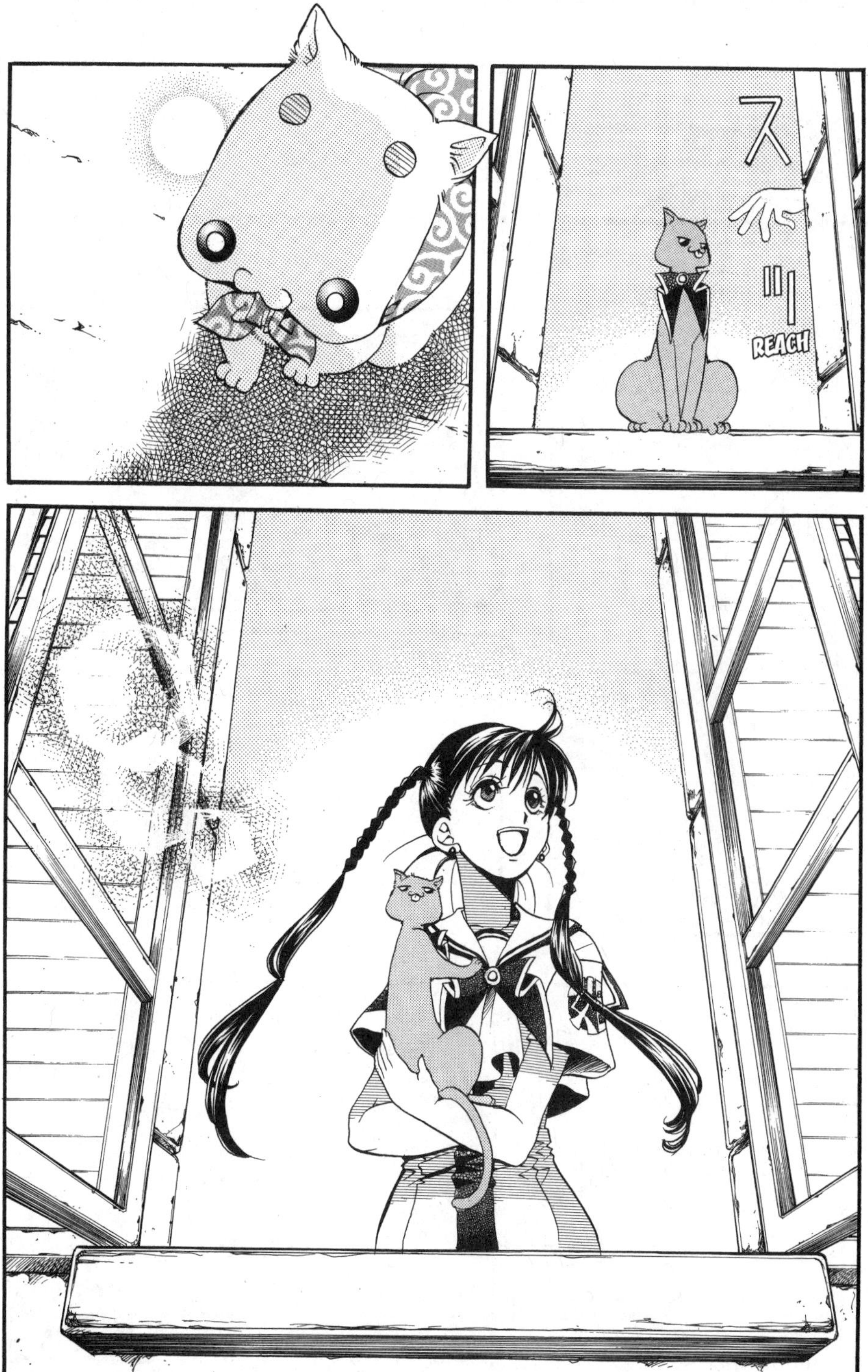
スッ
REACH

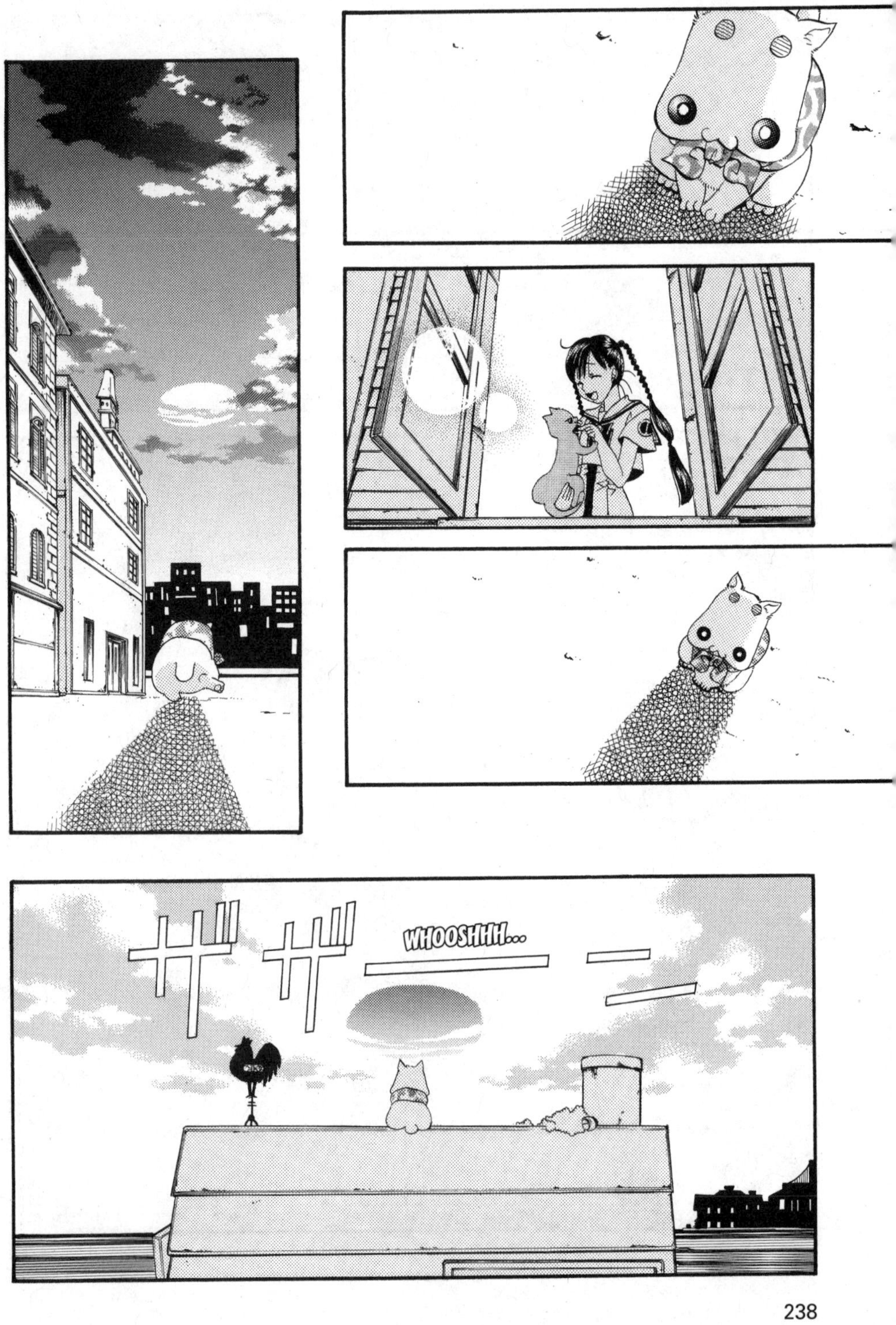
ザザーー
WHOOSHHH...

HAVING NOWHERE TO GO...

PRESIDENT ARIA ENDED UP BACK AT HIS COMPANY AFTER ALL.

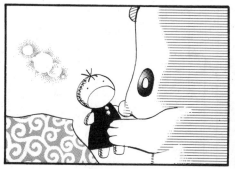

RUMMAGE

RUMMAGE

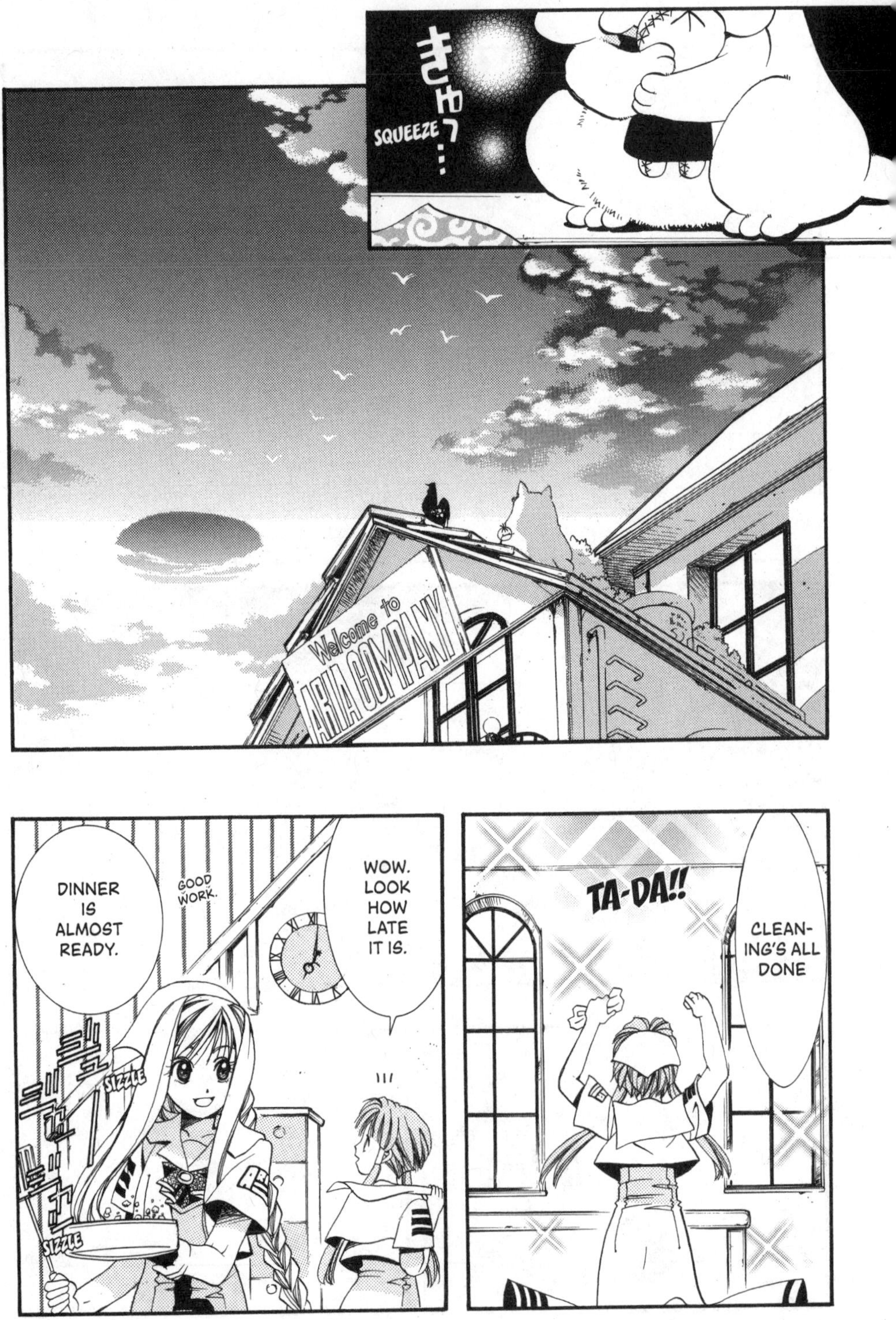

きゅっ
SQUEEZE
Welcome to
ARIA COMPANY
TA-DA!!
CLEANING'S ALL DONE
WOW. LOOK HOW LATE IT IS.
GOOD WORK.
DINNER IS ALMOST READY.
SIZZLE
SIZZLE

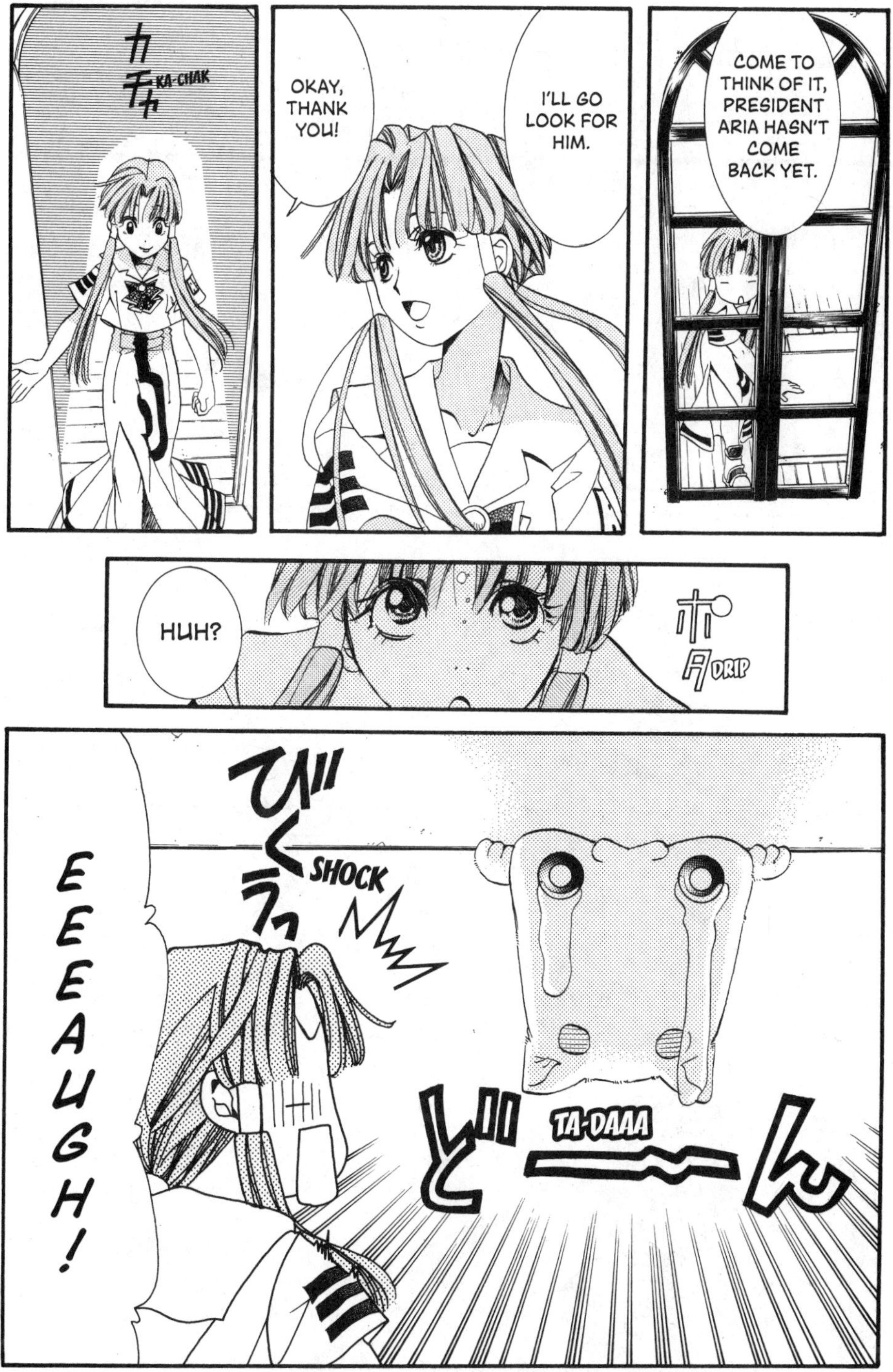
COME TO THINK OF IT, PRESIDENT ARIA HASN'T COME BACK YET.
I'LL GO LOOK FOR HIM.
OKAY, THANK YOU!
カチャ
KA-CHAK
HUH?
ポタ
DRIP
びくっ
SHOCK
どーん
TA-DAAA
EEEAUGH!

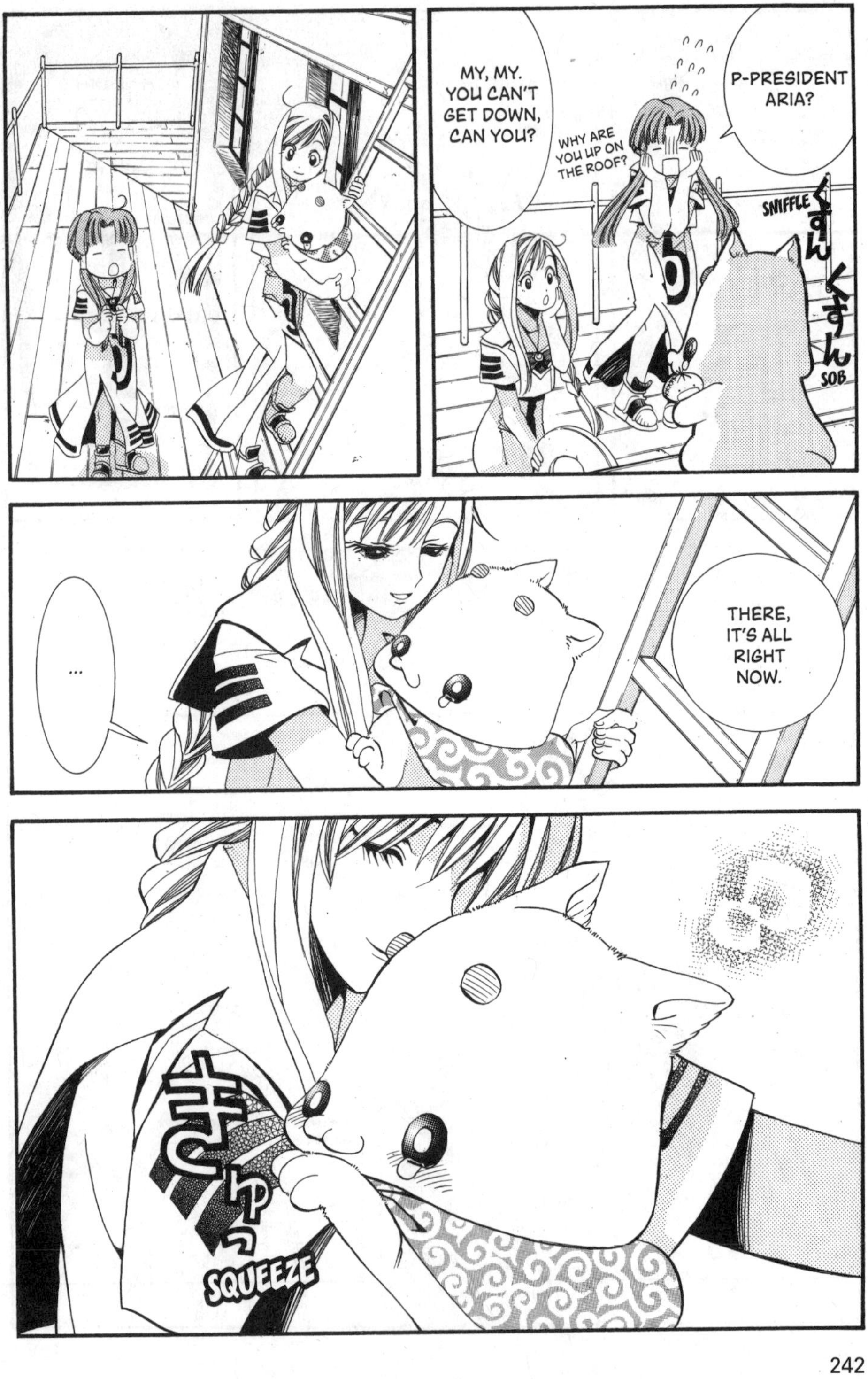
P-PRESIDENT ARIA?
SNIFFLE くすん
くすん SOB
WHY ARE YOU UP ON THE ROOF?
MY, MY. YOU CAN'T GET DOWN, CAN YOU?
THERE, IT'S ALL RIGHT NOW.
...
きゅっ
SQUEEZE

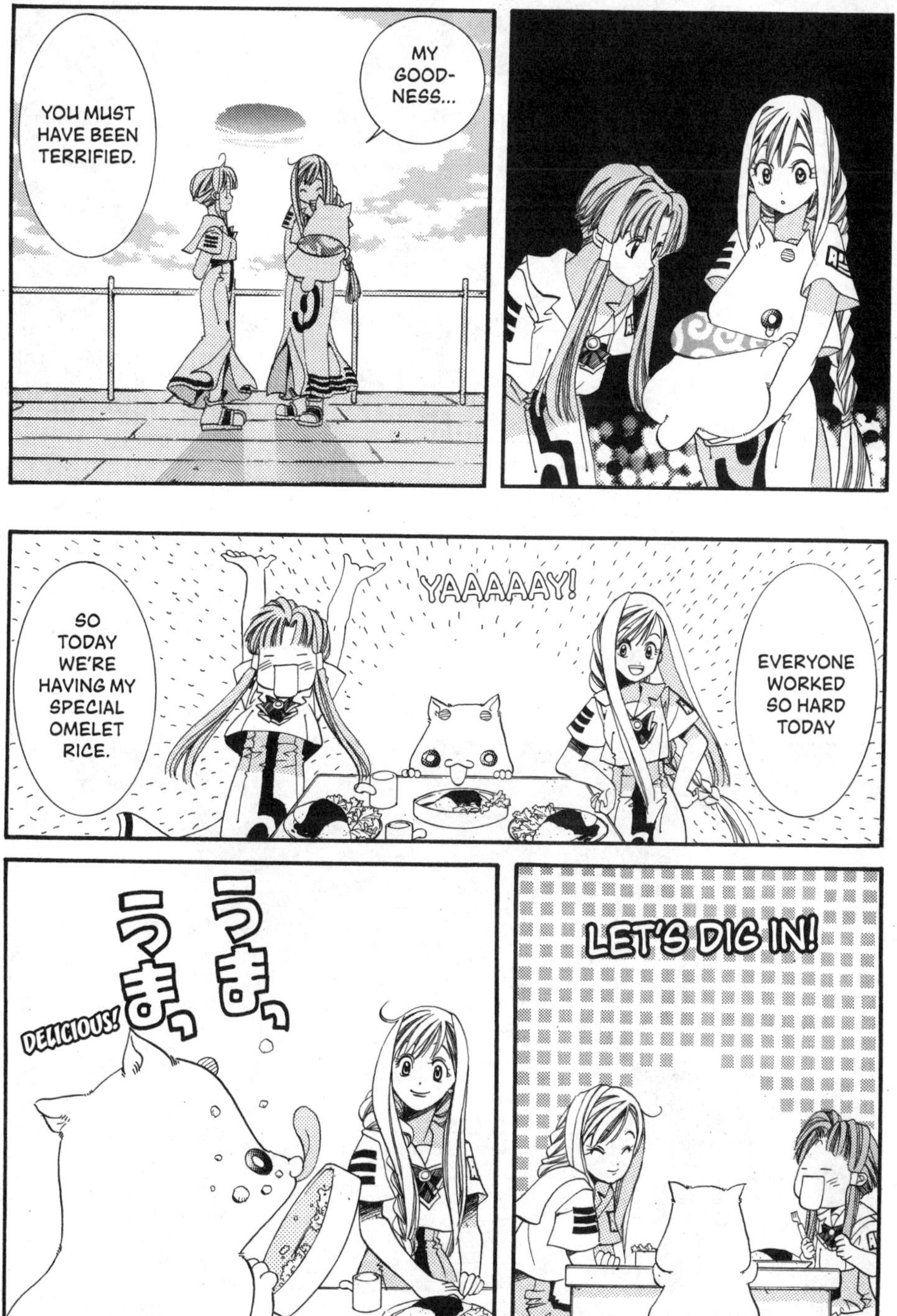
MY GOODNESS...
YOU MUST HAVE BEEN TERRIFIED.
EVERYONE WORKED SO HARD TODAY
SO TODAY WE'RE HAVING MY SPECIAL OMELET RICE.
YAAAAAY!
LET'S DIG IN!
うまっ うまっ
DELICIOUS!

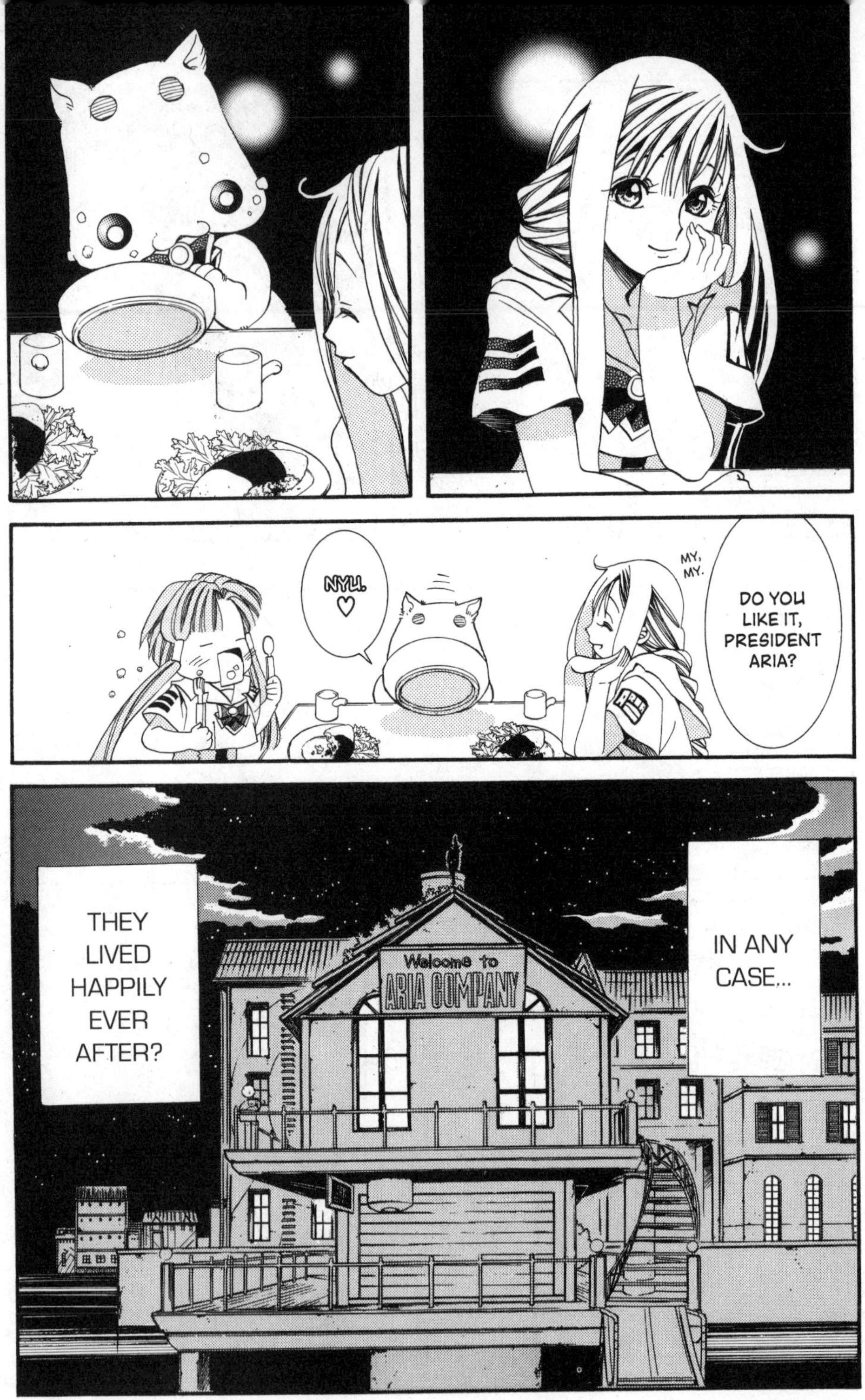
MY, MY.
DO YOU LIKE IT, PRESIDENT ARIA?
NYU. ♥
IN ANY CASE...
Welcome to ARIA COMPANY
THEY LIVED HAPPILY EVER AFTER?

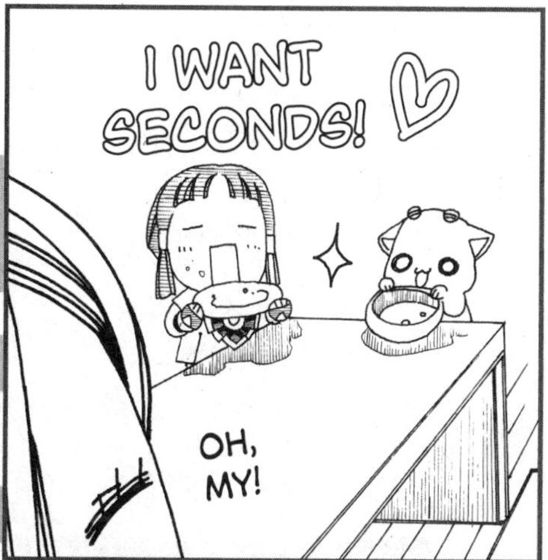
I WANT SECONDS!
OH, MY!

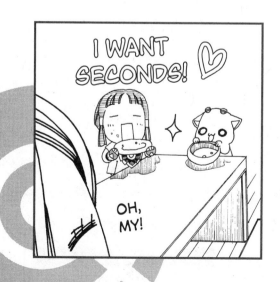

ARIA
The MASTERPIECE

Navigation 08
Night-light Bells

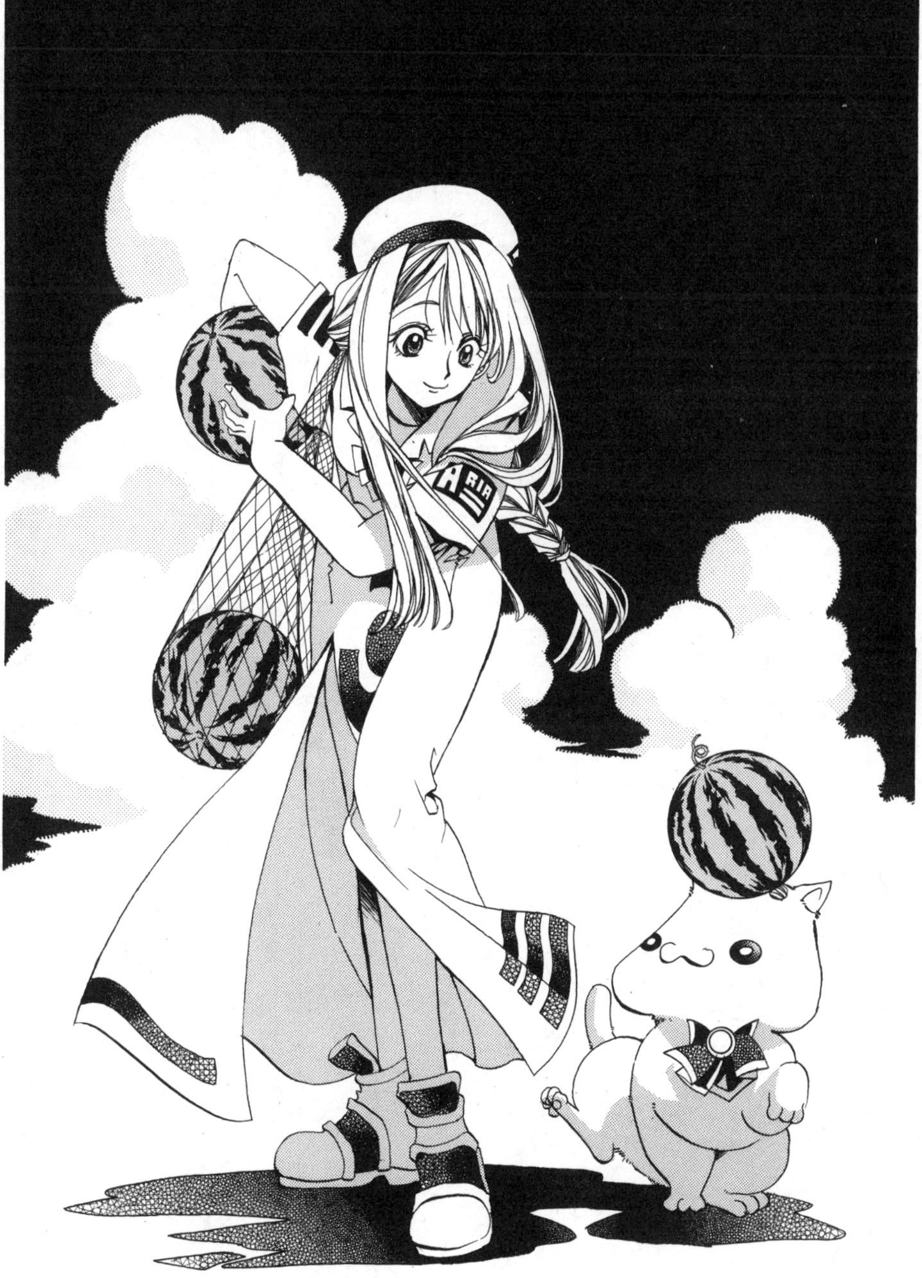

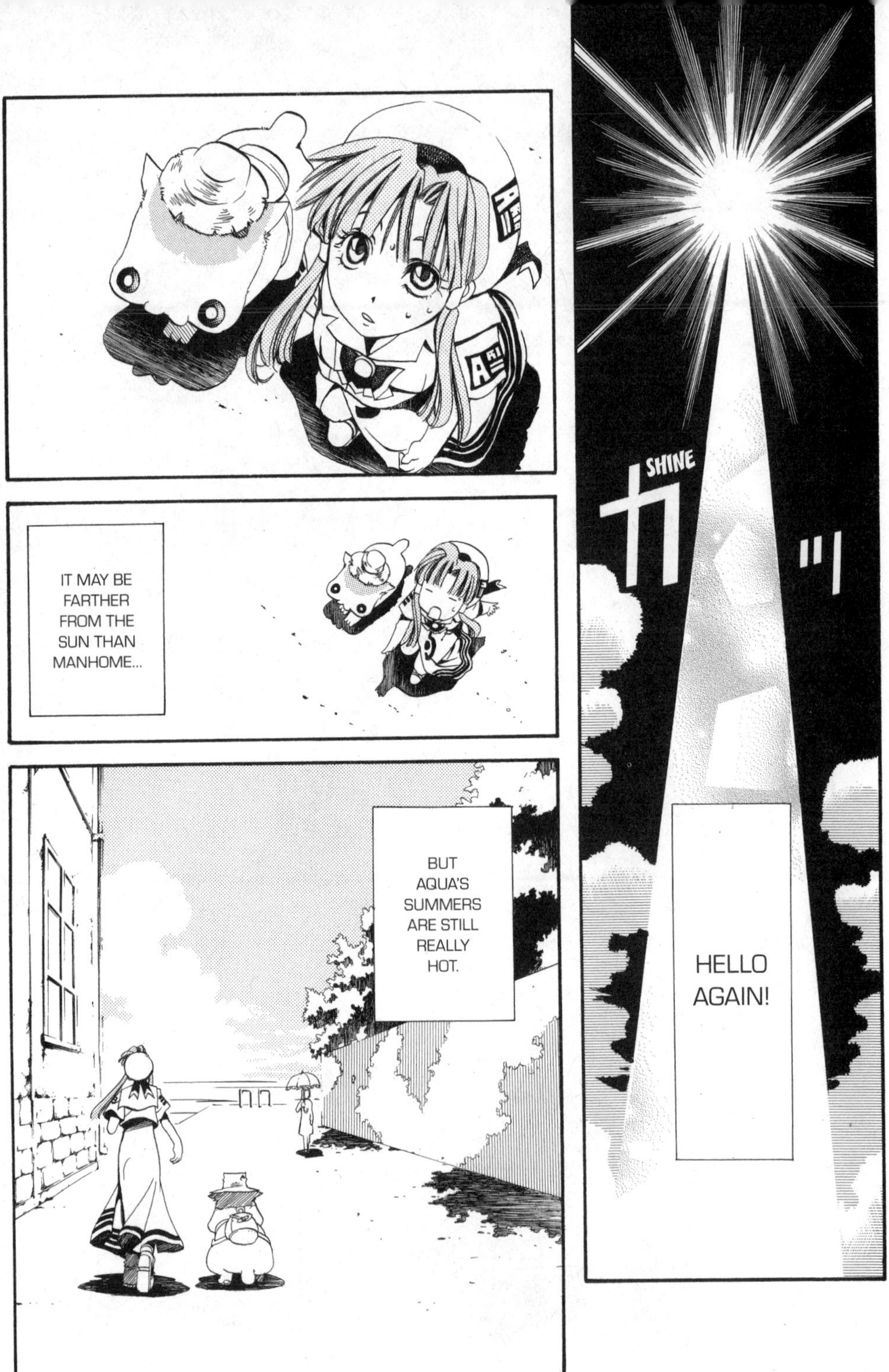
SHINE
カッ
HELLO AGAIN!
IT MAY BE FARTHER FROM THE SUN THAN MANHOME...
BUT AQUA'S SUMMERS ARE STILL REALLY HOT.

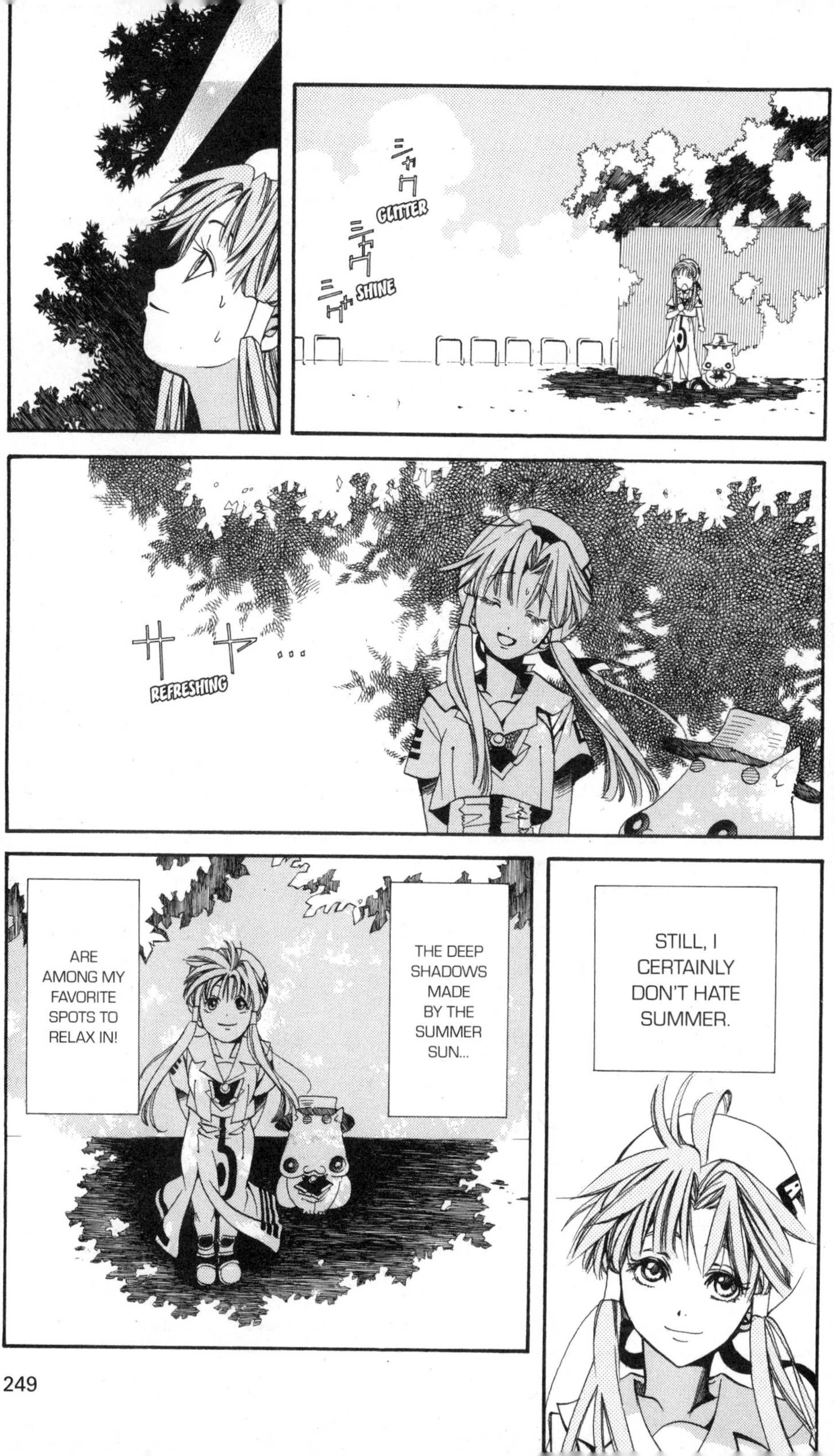
GLITTER
SHINE
サヤ...
REFRESHING
STILL, I CERTAINLY DON'T HATE SUMMER.
THE DEEP SHADOWS MADE BY THE SUMMER SUN...
ARE AMONG MY FAVORITE SPOTS TO RELAX IN!

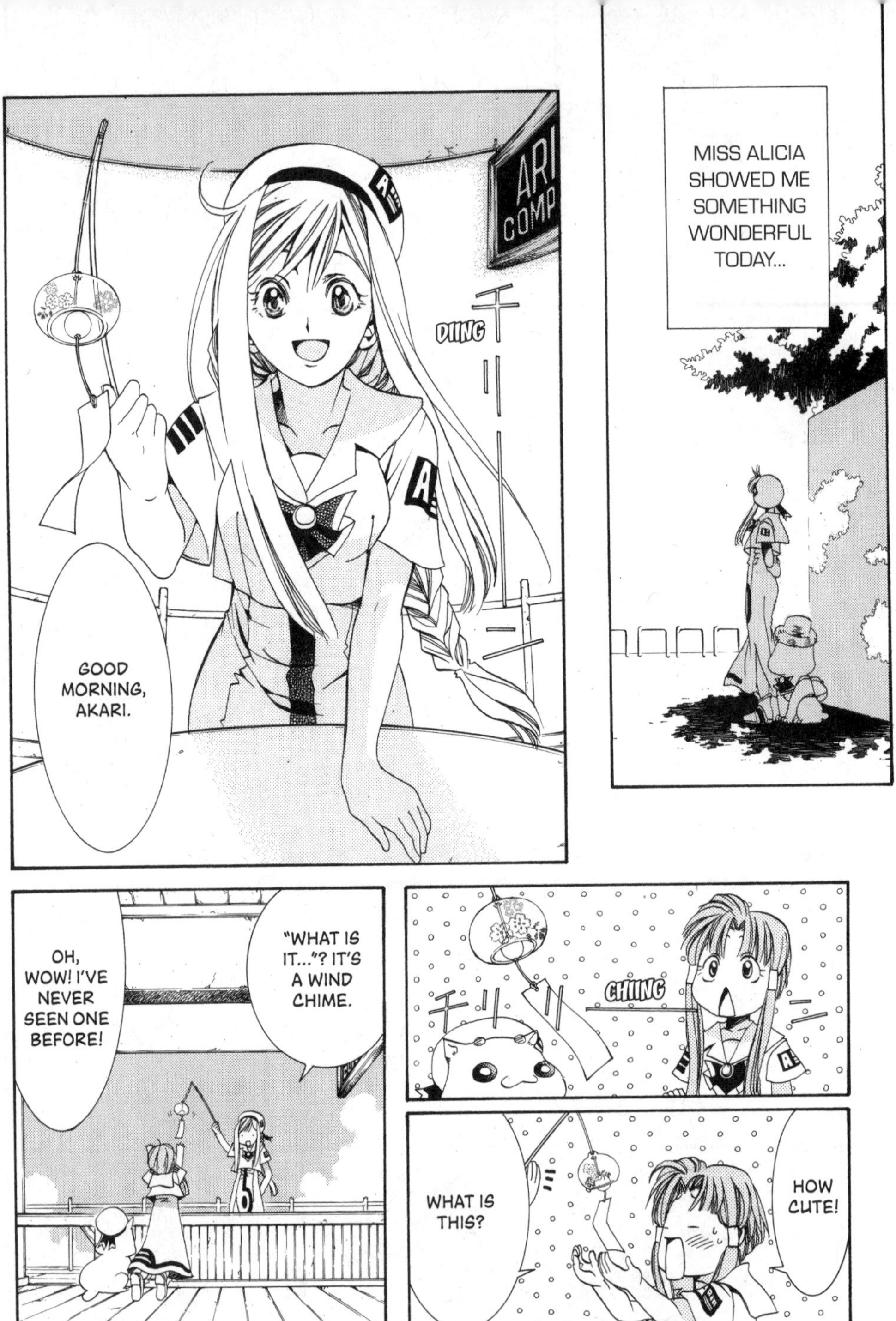
MISS ALICIA SHOWED ME SOMETHING WONDERFUL TODAY...
DIING
GOOD MORNING, AKARI.
CHIING
HOW CUTE!
WHAT IS THIS?
"WHAT IS IT..."? IT'S A WIND CHIME.
OH, WOW! I'VE NEVER SEEN ONE BEFORE!

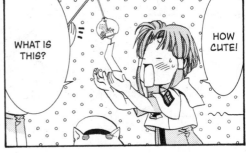

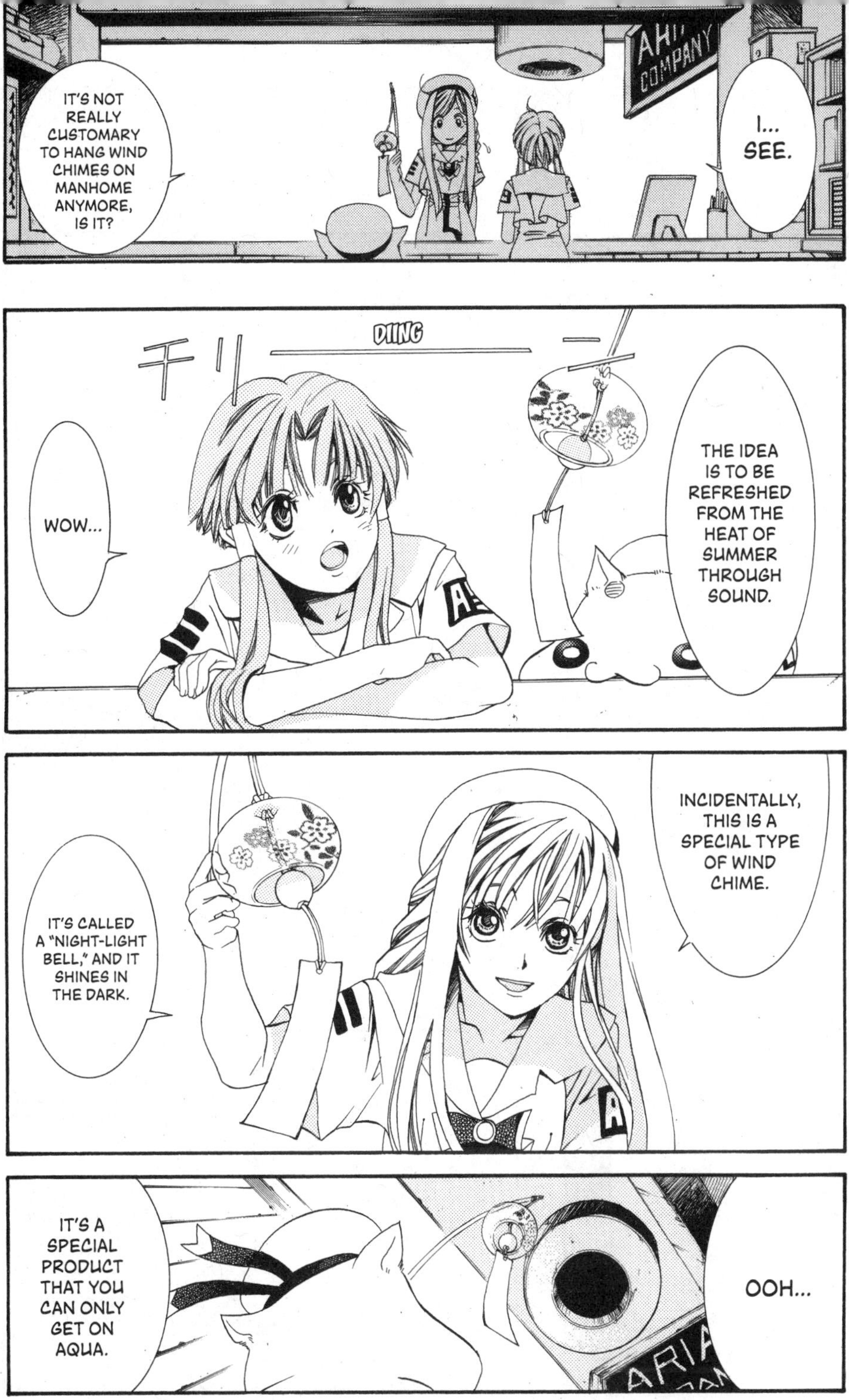
I... SEE.
IT'S NOT REALLY CUSTOMARY TO HANG WIND CHIMES ON MANHOME ANYMORE, IS IT?
DIING
チリ
THE IDEA IS TO BE REFRESHED FROM THE HEAT OF SUMMER THROUGH SOUND.
WOW...
INCIDENTALLY, THIS IS A SPECIAL TYPE OF WIND CHIME.
IT'S CALLED A "NIGHT-LIGHT BELL," AND IT SHINES IN THE DARK.
OOH...
IT'S A SPECIAL PRODUCT THAT YOU CAN ONLY GET ON AQUA.
ARIA

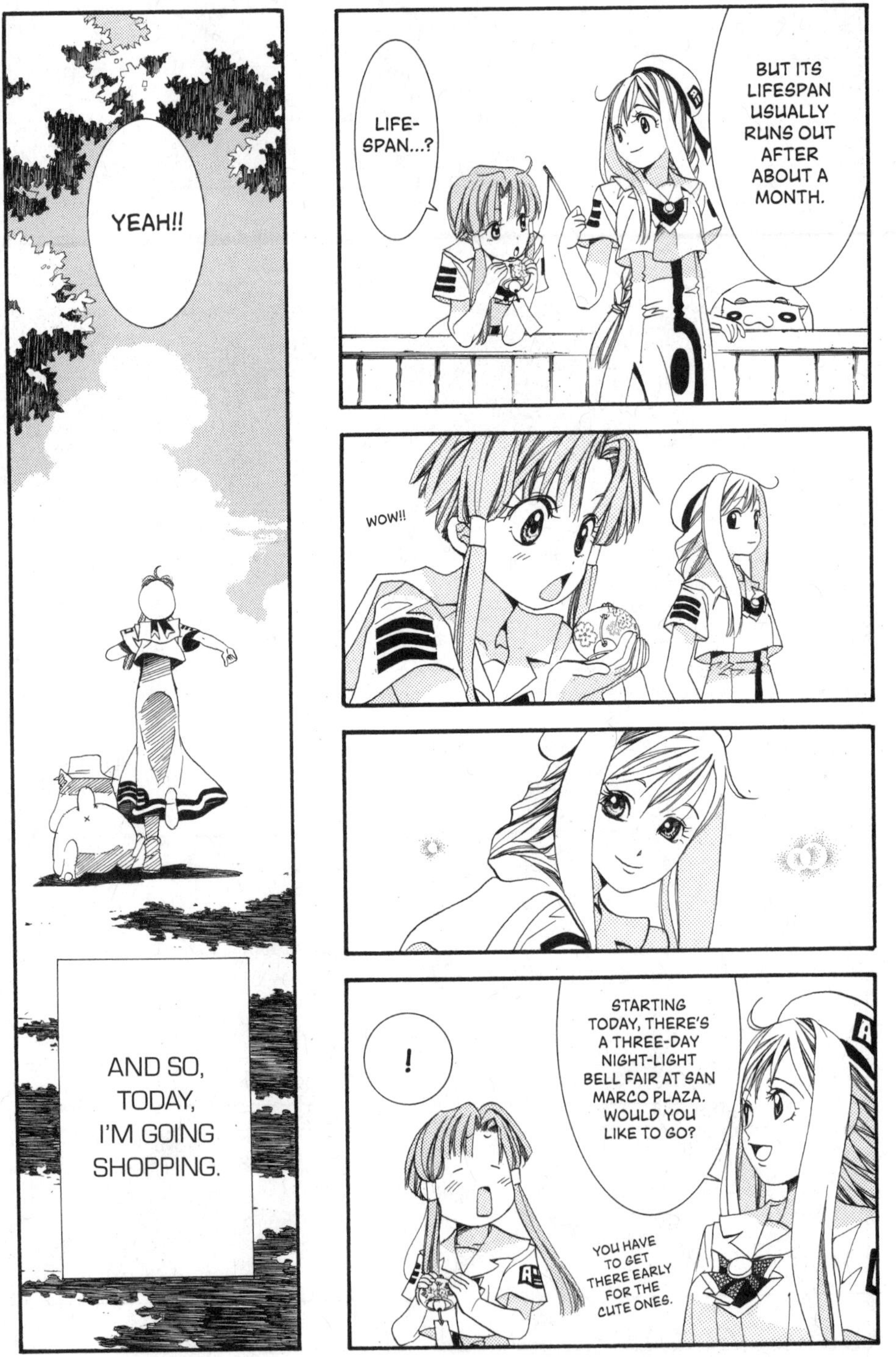
BUT ITS LIFESPAN USUALLY RUNS OUT AFTER ABOUT A MONTH.
LIFE-SPAN...?
WOW!!
STARTING TODAY, THERE'S A THREE-DAY NIGHT-LIGHT BELL FAIR AT SAN MARCO PLAZA. WOULD YOU LIKE TO GO?
YOU HAVE TO GET THERE EARLY FOR THE CUTE ONES.
!
YEAH!!
AND SO, TODAY, I'M GOING SHOPPING.

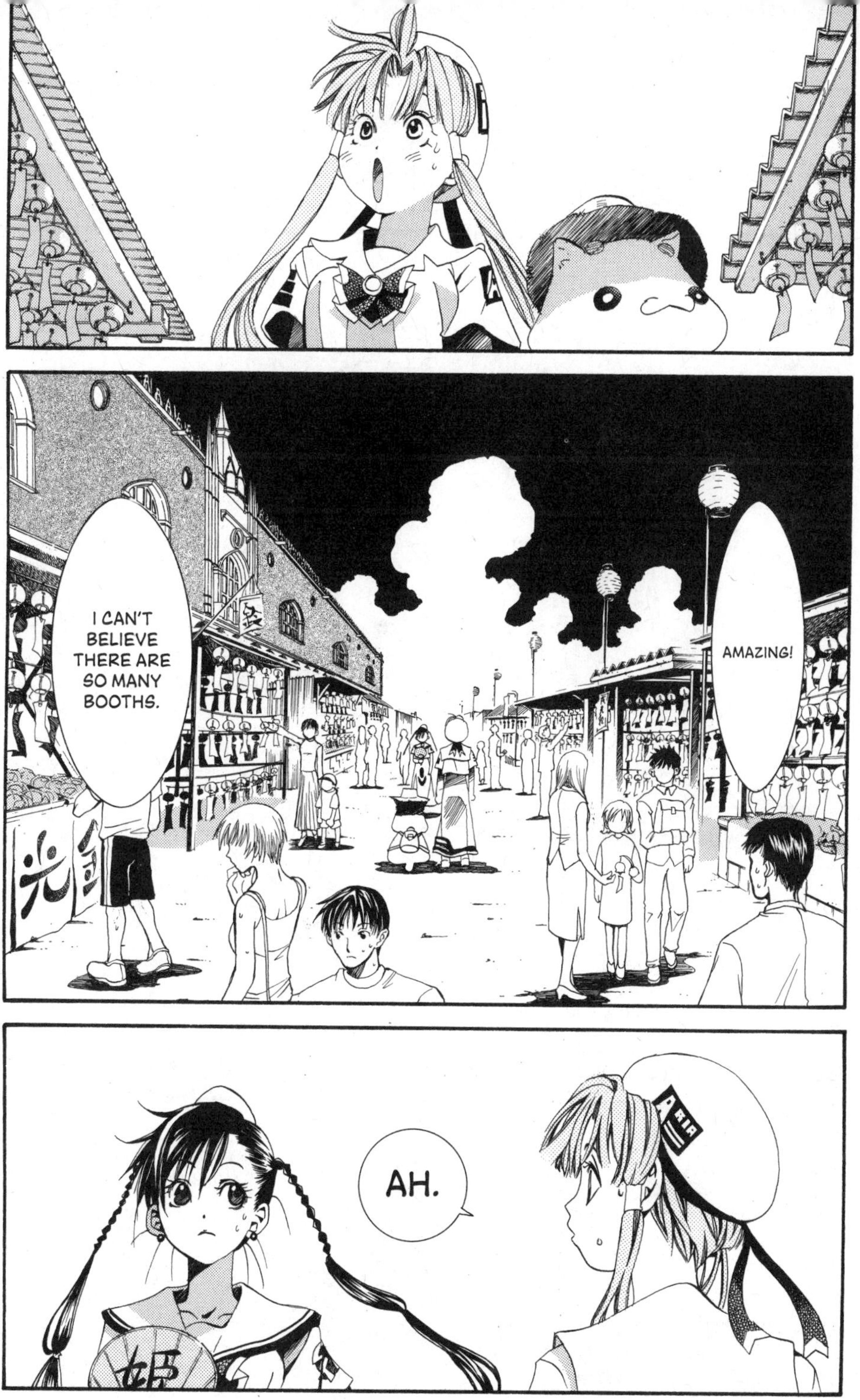
AMAZING!
I CAN'T BELIEVE THERE ARE SO MANY BOOTHS.
AH.

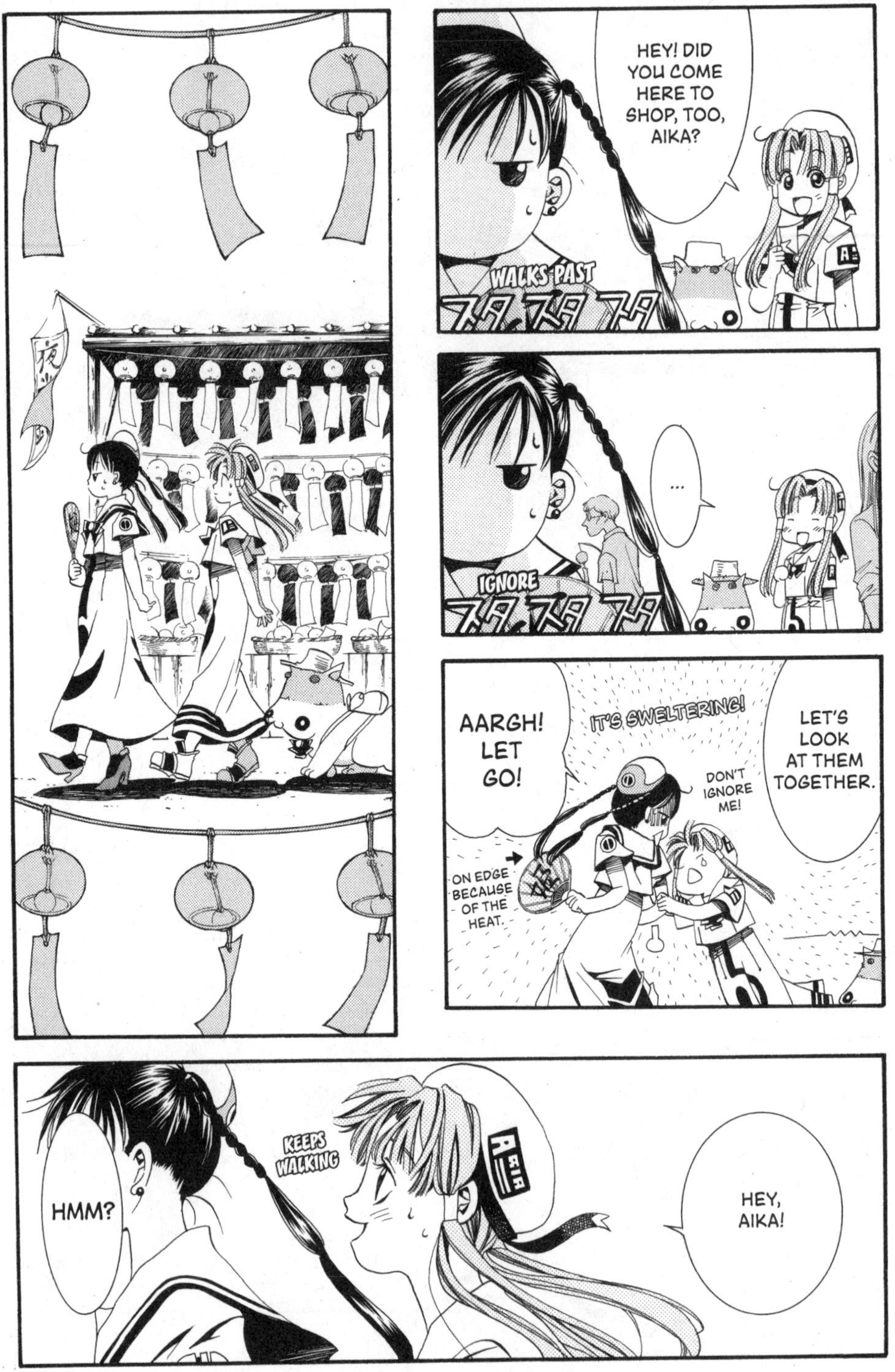

HEY! DID YOU COME HERE TO SHOP, TOO, AIKA?
WALKS PAST
スタ スタ スタ
...
IGNORE
スタ スタ スタ
LET'S LOOK AT THEM TOGETHER.
IT'S SWELTERING!
DON'T IGNORE ME!
AARGH! LET GO!
ON EDGE BECAUSE OF THE HEAT.
HEY, AIKA!
KEEPS WALKING
HMM?

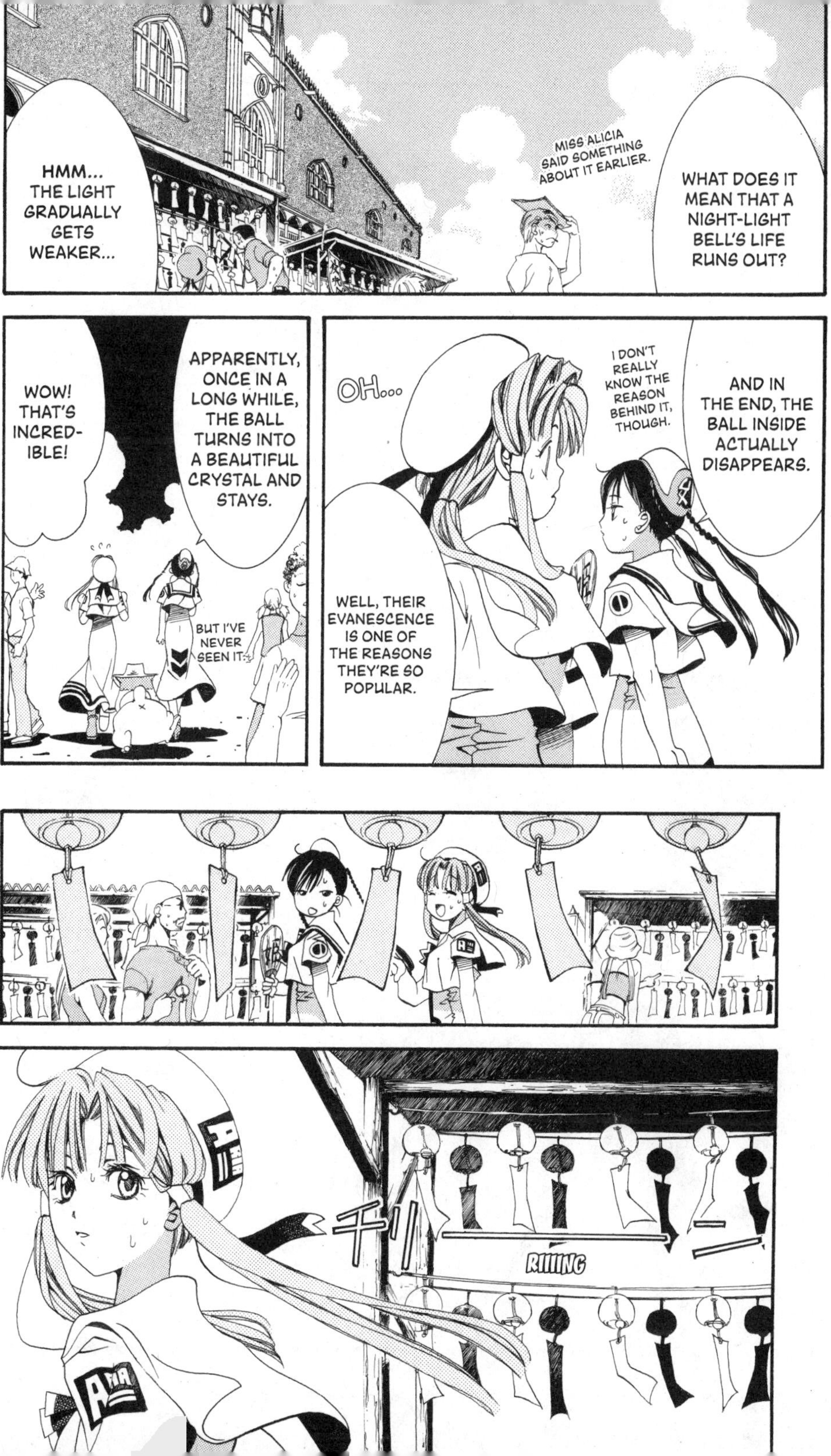
WHAT DOES IT MEAN THAT A NIGHT-LIGHT BELL'S LIFE RUNS OUT?
MISS ALICIA SAID SOMETHING ABOUT IT EARLIER.
HMM... THE LIGHT GRADUALLY GETS WEAKER...
AND IN THE END, THE BALL INSIDE ACTUALLY DISAPPEARS.
I DON'T REALLY KNOW THE REASON BEHIND IT, THOUGH.
OH...
WELL, THEIR EVANESCENCE IS ONE OF THE REASONS THEY'RE SO POPULAR.
APPARENTLY, ONCE IN A LONG WHILE, THE BALL TURNS INTO A BEAUTIFUL CRYSTAL AND STAYS.
BUT I'VE NEVER SEEN IT.
WOW! THAT'S INCRED-IBLE!
チリーーン
RIIIING

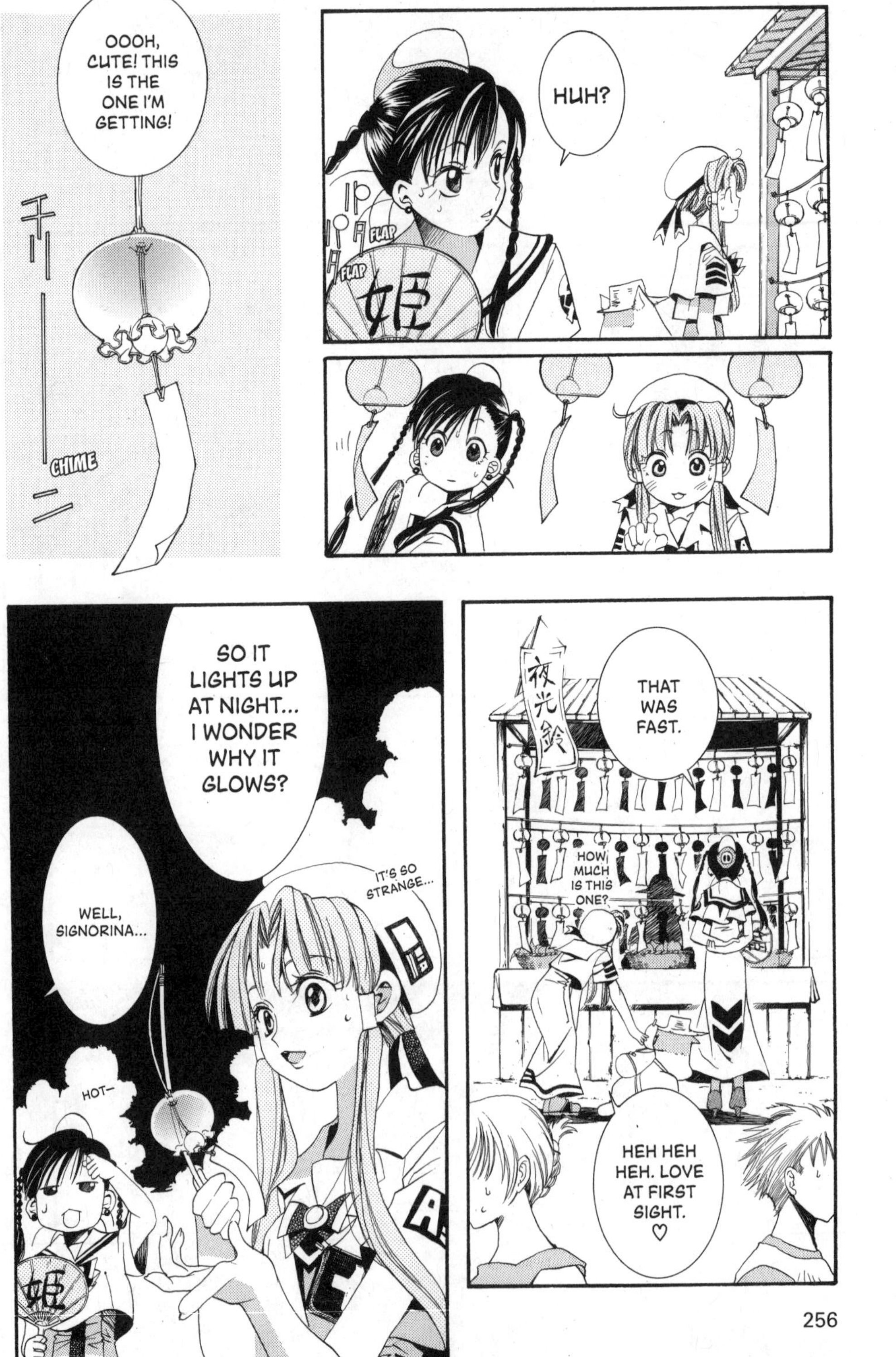
HUH?
FLAP
FLAP
姫
OOOH, CUTE! THIS IS THE ONE I'M GETTING!
CHIME
THAT WAS FAST.
夜光鈴
HOW MUCH IS THIS ONE?
HEH HEH HEH. LOVE AT FIRST SIGHT. ♡
SO IT LIGHTS UP AT NIGHT... I WONDER WHY IT GLOWS?
IT'S SO STRANGE...
WELL, SIGNORINA...
HOT—
姫

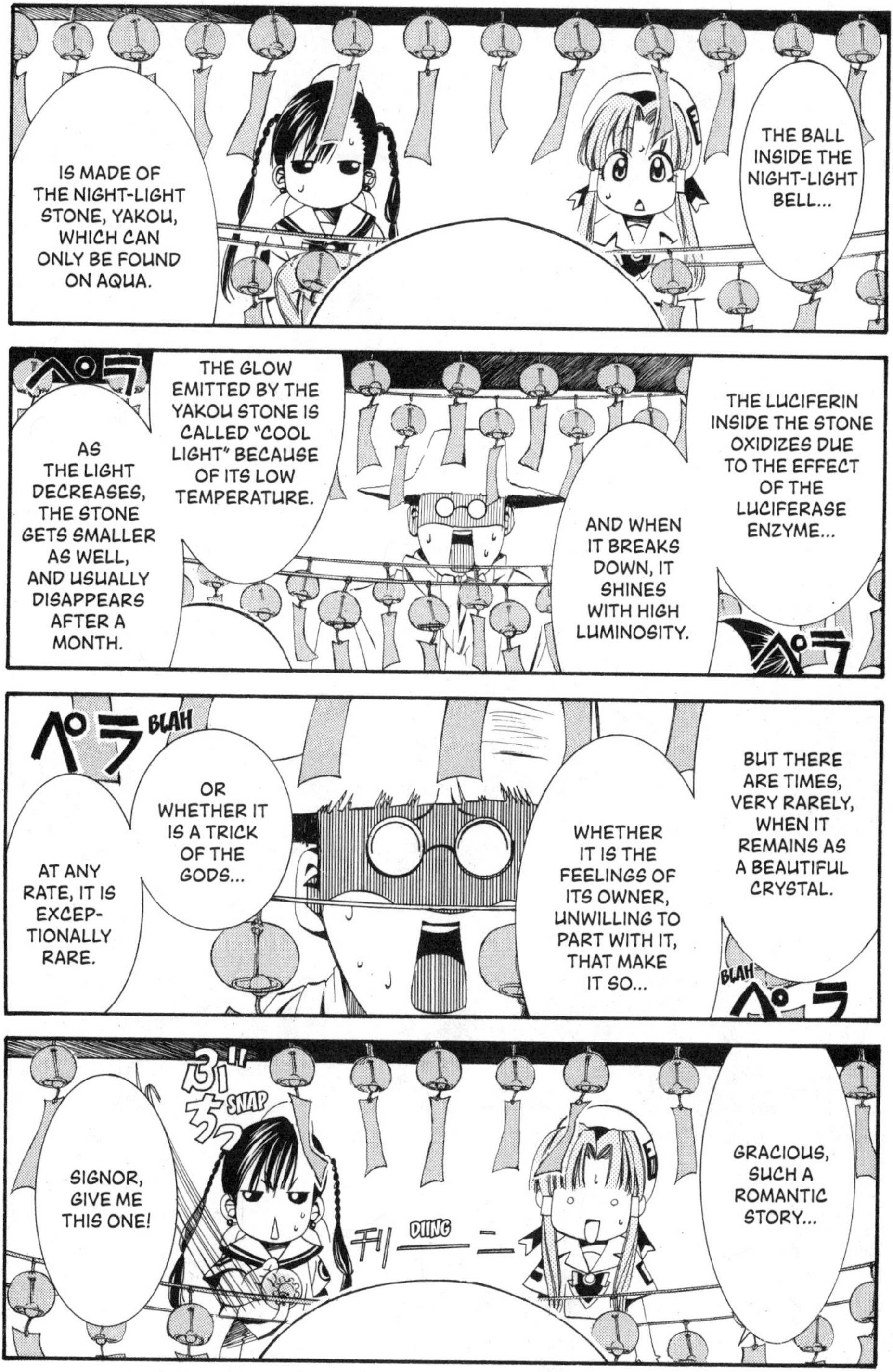
THE BALL INSIDE THE NIGHT-LIGHT BELL...
IS MADE OF THE NIGHT-LIGHT STONE, YAKOU, WHICH CAN ONLY BE FOUND ON AQUA.
THE LUCIFERIN INSIDE THE STONE OXIDIZES DUE TO THE EFFECT OF THE LUCIFERASE ENZYME...
AND WHEN IT BREAKS DOWN, IT SHINES WITH HIGH LUMINOSITY.
ペラ
THE GLOW EMITTED BY THE YAKOU STONE IS CALLED "COOL LIGHT" BECAUSE OF ITS LOW TEMPERATURE.
AS THE LIGHT DECREASES, THE STONE GETS SMALLER AS WELL, AND USUALLY DISAPPEARS AFTER A MONTH.
ペラ
BUT THERE ARE TIMES, VERY RARELY, WHEN IT REMAINS AS A BEAUTIFUL CRYSTAL.
WHETHER IT IS THE FEELINGS OF ITS OWNER, UNWILLING TO PART WITH IT, THAT MAKE IT SO...
ペラ BLAH
OR WHETHER IT IS A TRICK OF THE GODS...
AT ANY RATE, IT IS EXCEP-TIONALLY RARE.
ペラ BLAH
GRACIOUS, SUCH A ROMANTIC STORY...
DIING
SIGNOR, GIVE ME THIS ONE!
ぶちっ SNAP

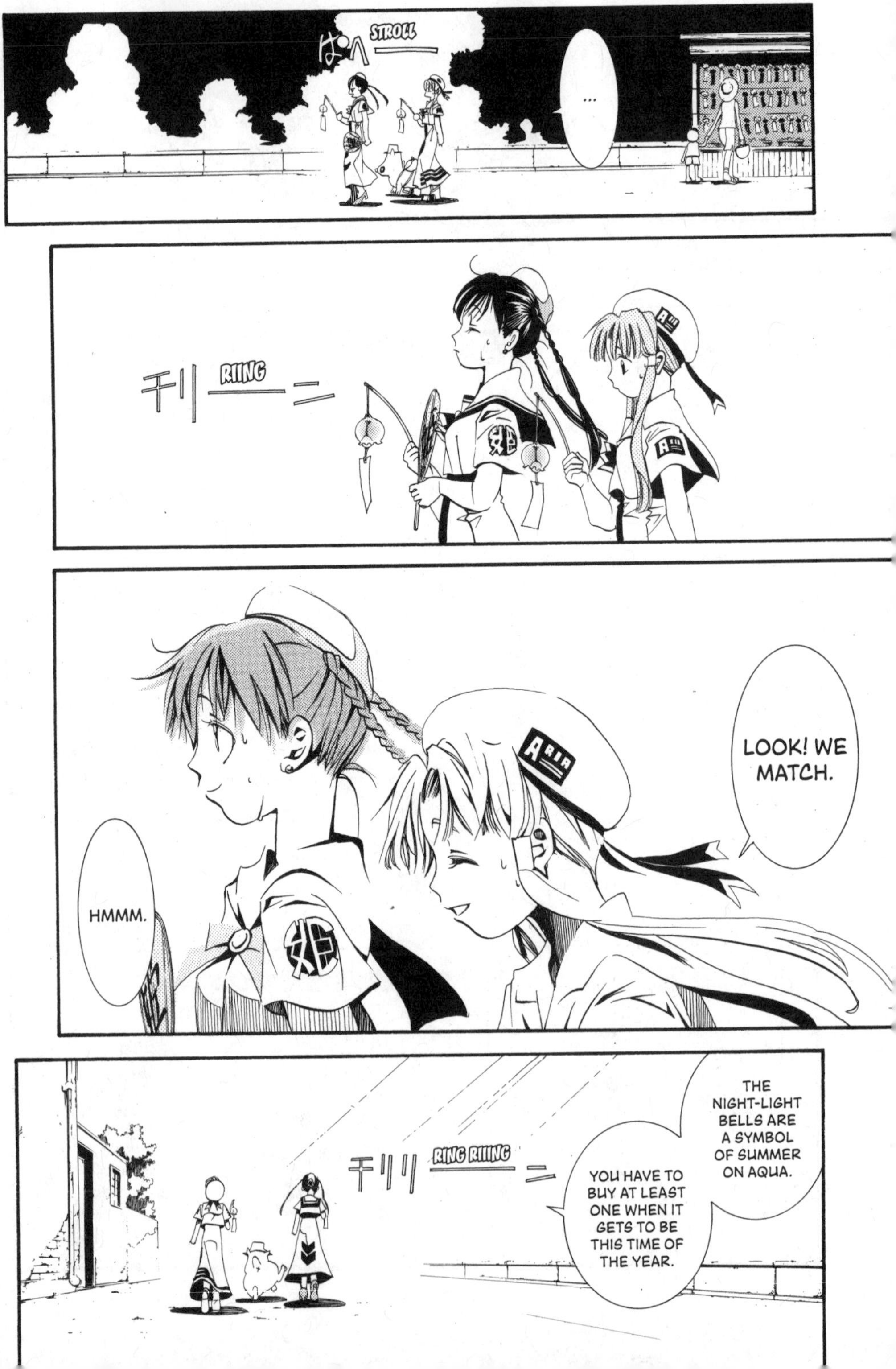
...
はへー
STROLL
チリーン
RIING
LOOK! WE MATCH.
HMMM.
THE NIGHT-LIGHT BELLS ARE A SYMBOL OF SUMMER ON AQUA.
YOU HAVE TO BUY AT LEAST ONE WHEN IT GETS TO BE THIS TIME OF THE YEAR.
チリリーン
RING RIIING

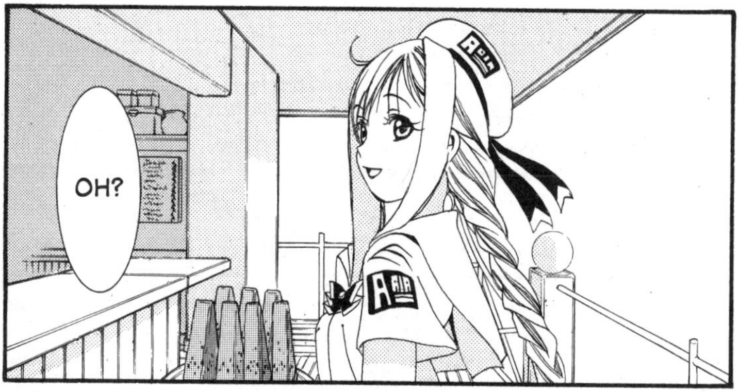
OH?

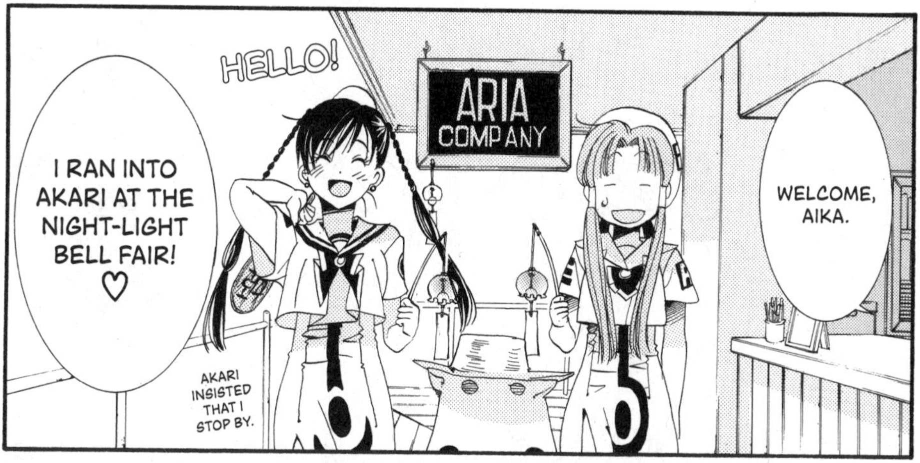
WELCOME, AIKA.
HELLO!
I RAN INTO AKARI AT THE NIGHT-LIGHT BELL FAIR! ♡
AKARI INSISTED THAT I STOP BY.
ARIA COMPANY

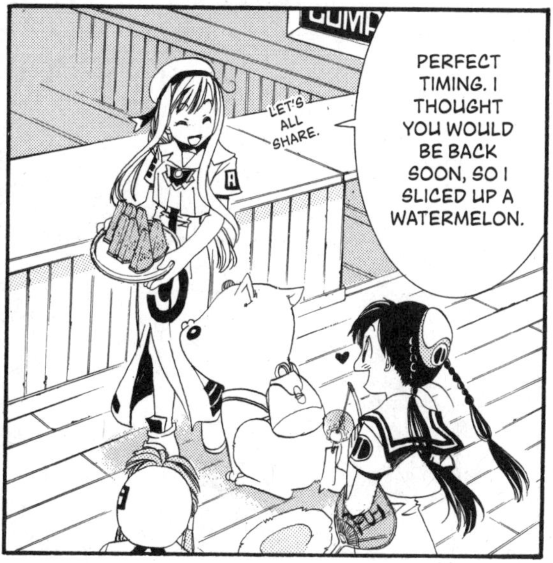
PERFECT TIMING. I THOUGHT YOU WOULD BE BACK SOON, SO I SLICED UP A WATERMELON.
LET'S ALL SHARE.

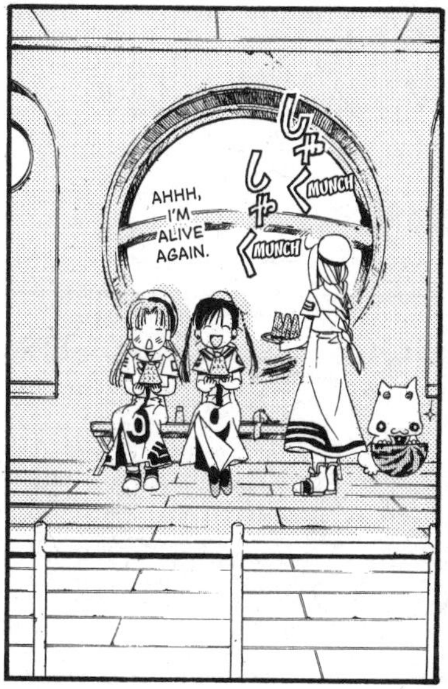
しゃく MUNCH
しゃく MUNCH
AHHH, I'M ALIVE AGAIN.

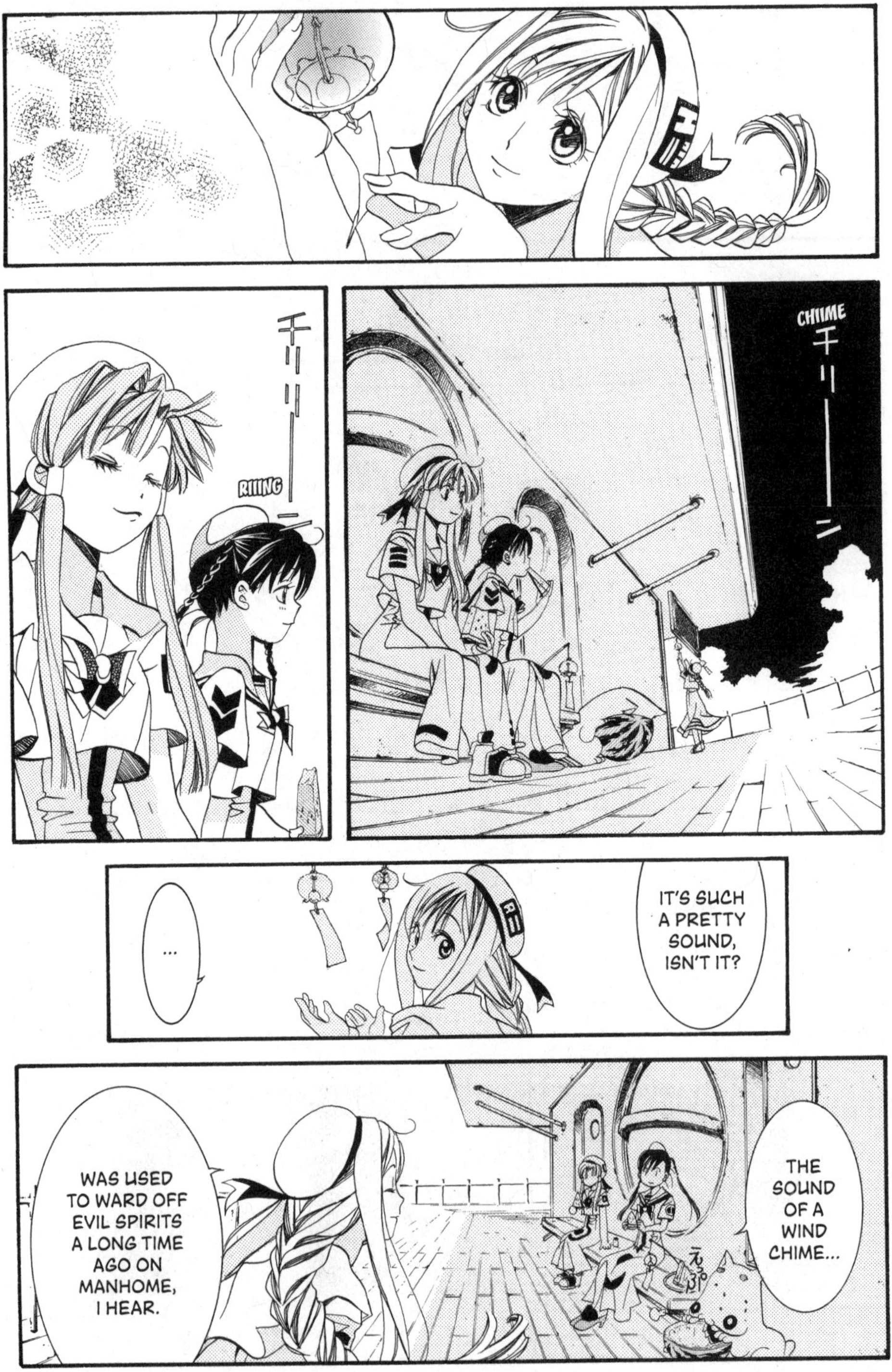
CHIIME
RIIING
IT'S SUCH A PRETTY SOUND, ISN'T IT?
...
THE SOUND OF A WIND CHIME...
WAS USED TO WARD OFF EVIL SPIRITS A LONG TIME AGO ON MANHOME, I HEAR.

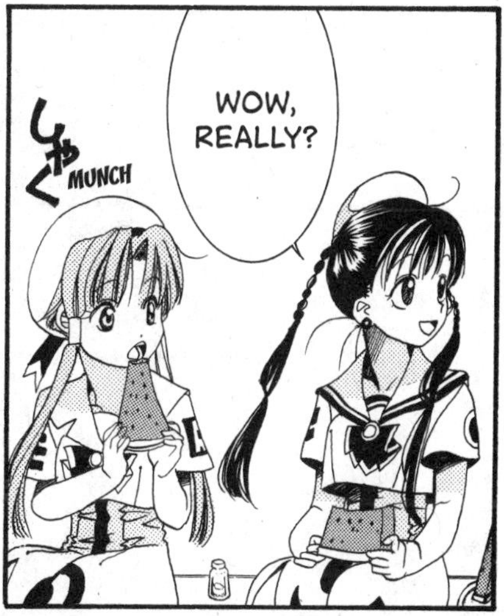
WOW, REALLY?
しゃく
MUNCH

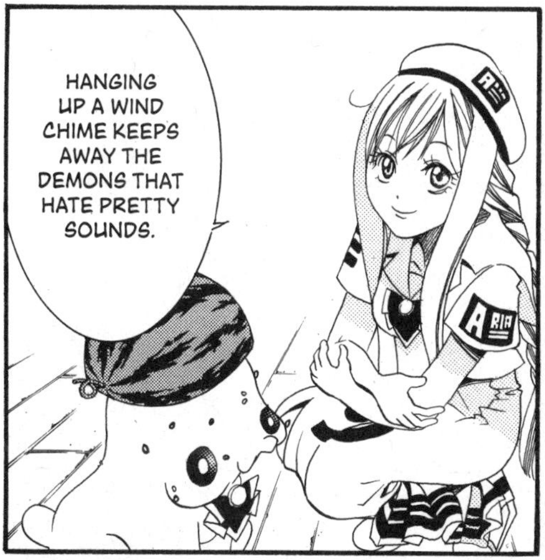
HANGING UP A WIND CHIME KEEPS AWAY THE DEMONS THAT HATE PRETTY SOUNDS.

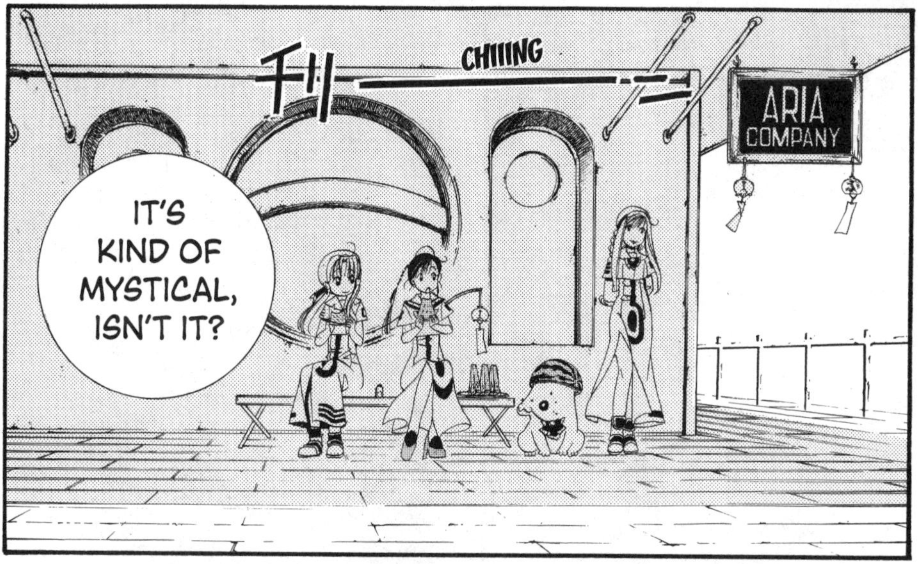
ARIA COMPANY
チリ
CHIIING
IT'S KIND OF MYSTICAL, ISN'T IT?

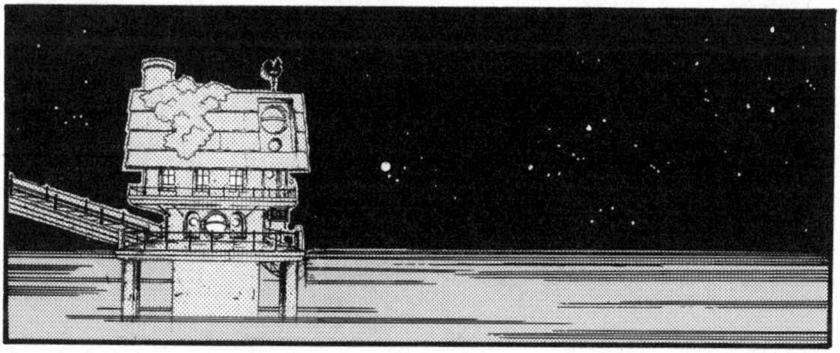

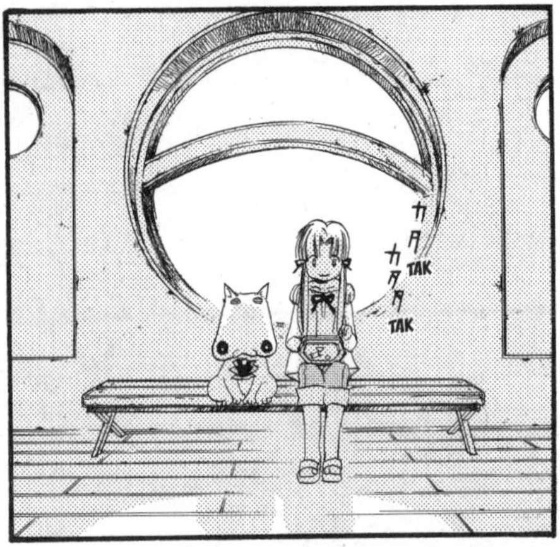
カタ
TAK
カタタ
TAK

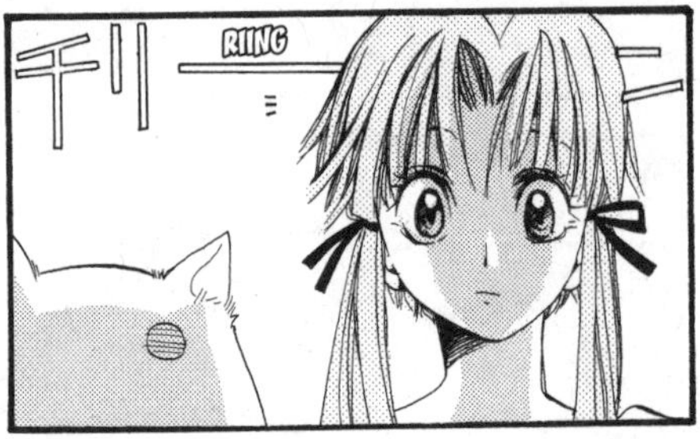
チリー
RIING

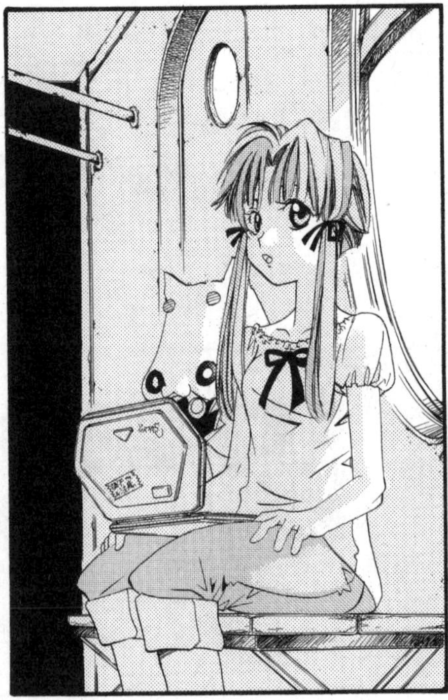

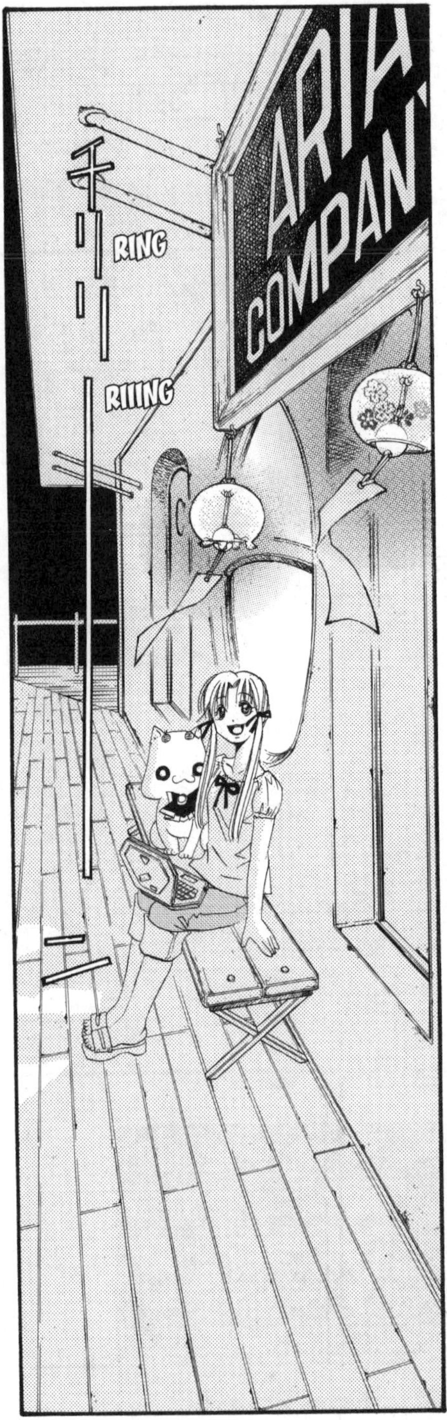
ARIA COMPAN
チリー
RING
RIIING

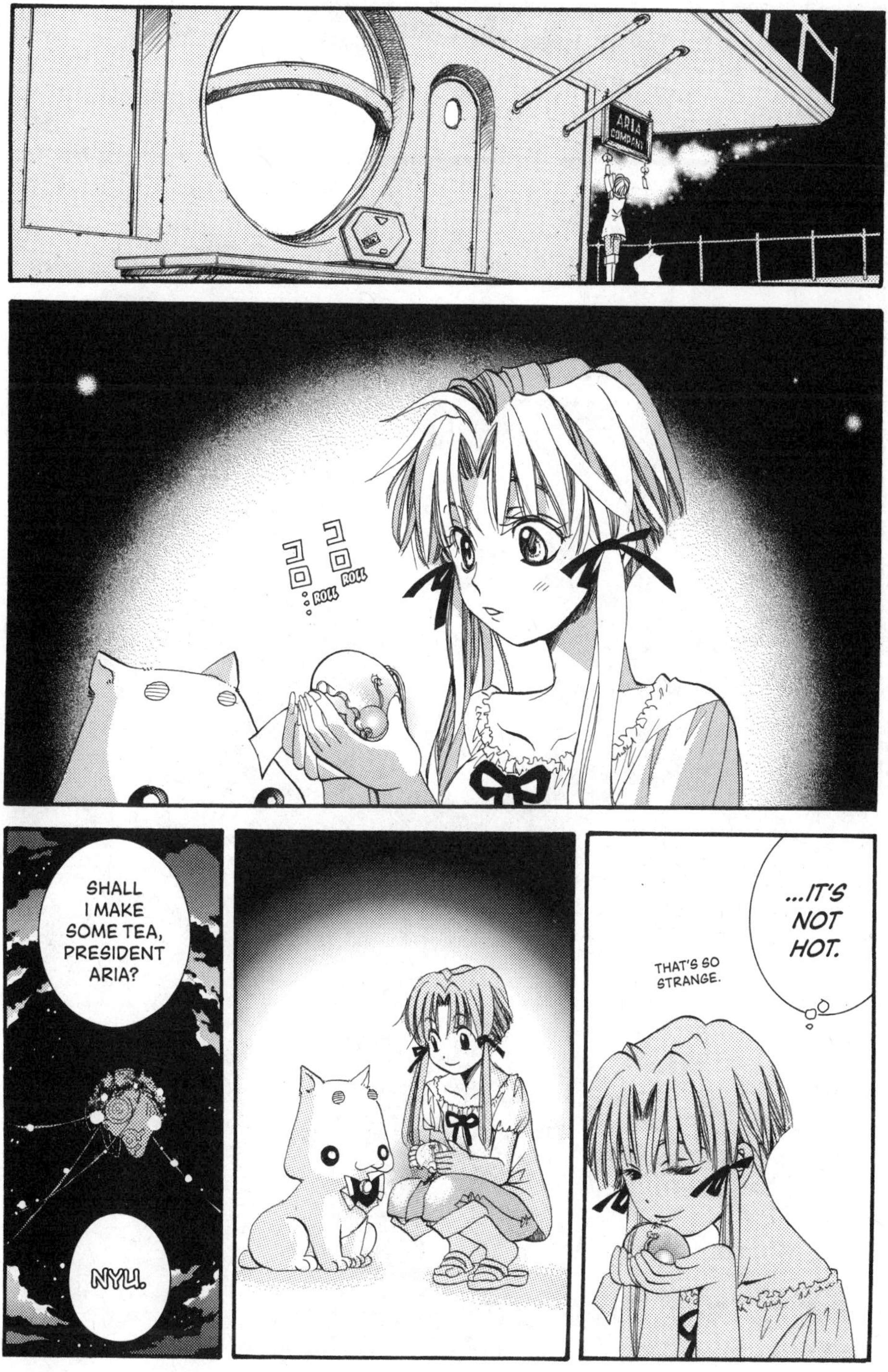
ARIA COMPANY
コロ ROLL
コロ ROLL
...IT'S NOT HOT.
THAT'S SO STRANGE.
SHALL I MAKE SOME TEA, PRESIDENT ARIA?
NYU.

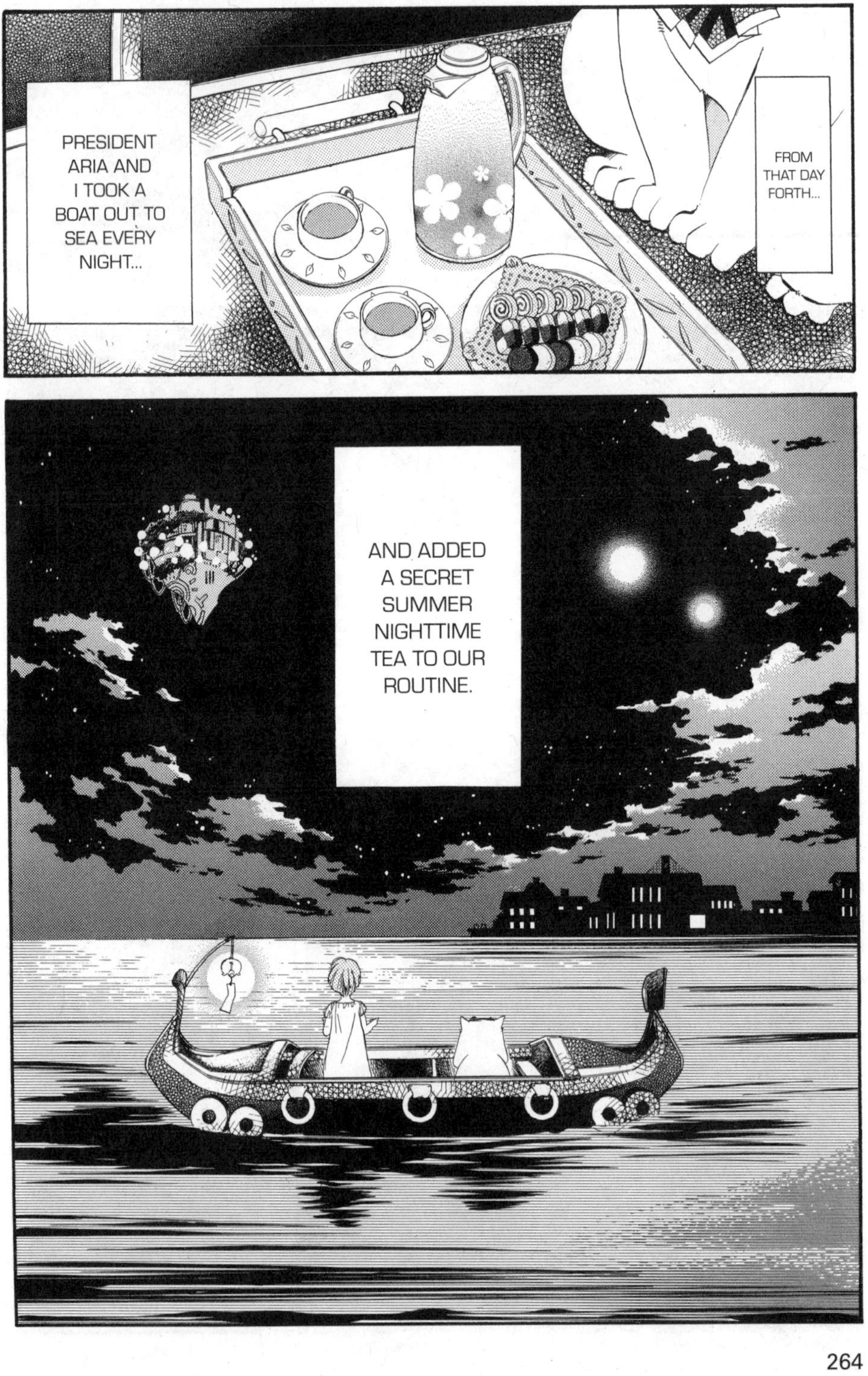
FROM THAT DAY FORTH...
PRESIDENT ARIA AND I TOOK A BOAT OUT TO SEA EVERY NIGHT...
AND ADDED A SECRET SUMMER NIGHTTIME TEA TO OUR ROUTINE.

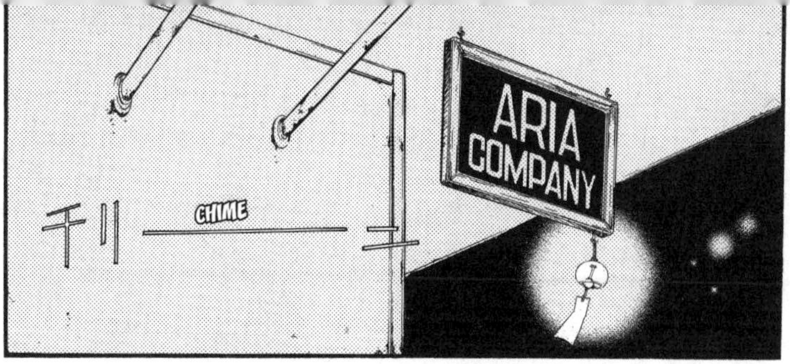
CHIME
ARIA COMPANY

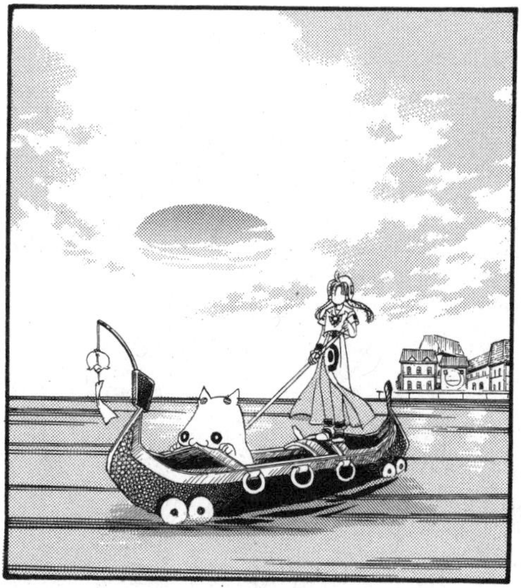

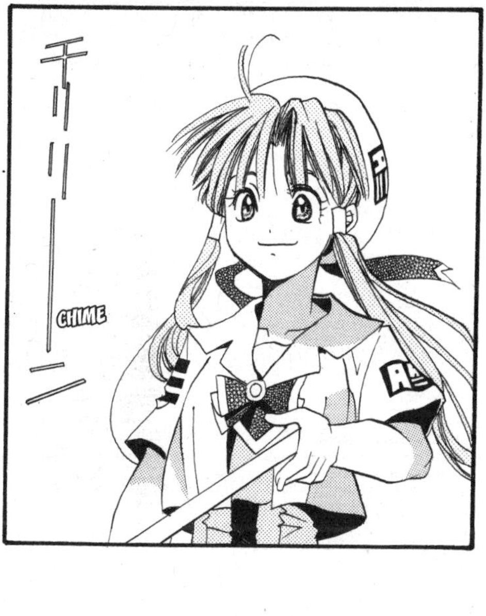
CHIME

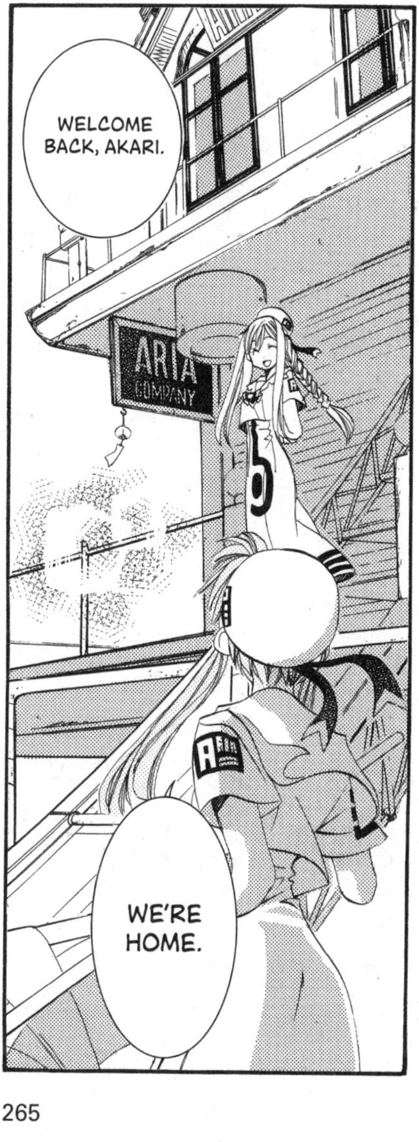
WELCOME BACK, AKARI.
ARIA COMPANY
WE'RE HOME.

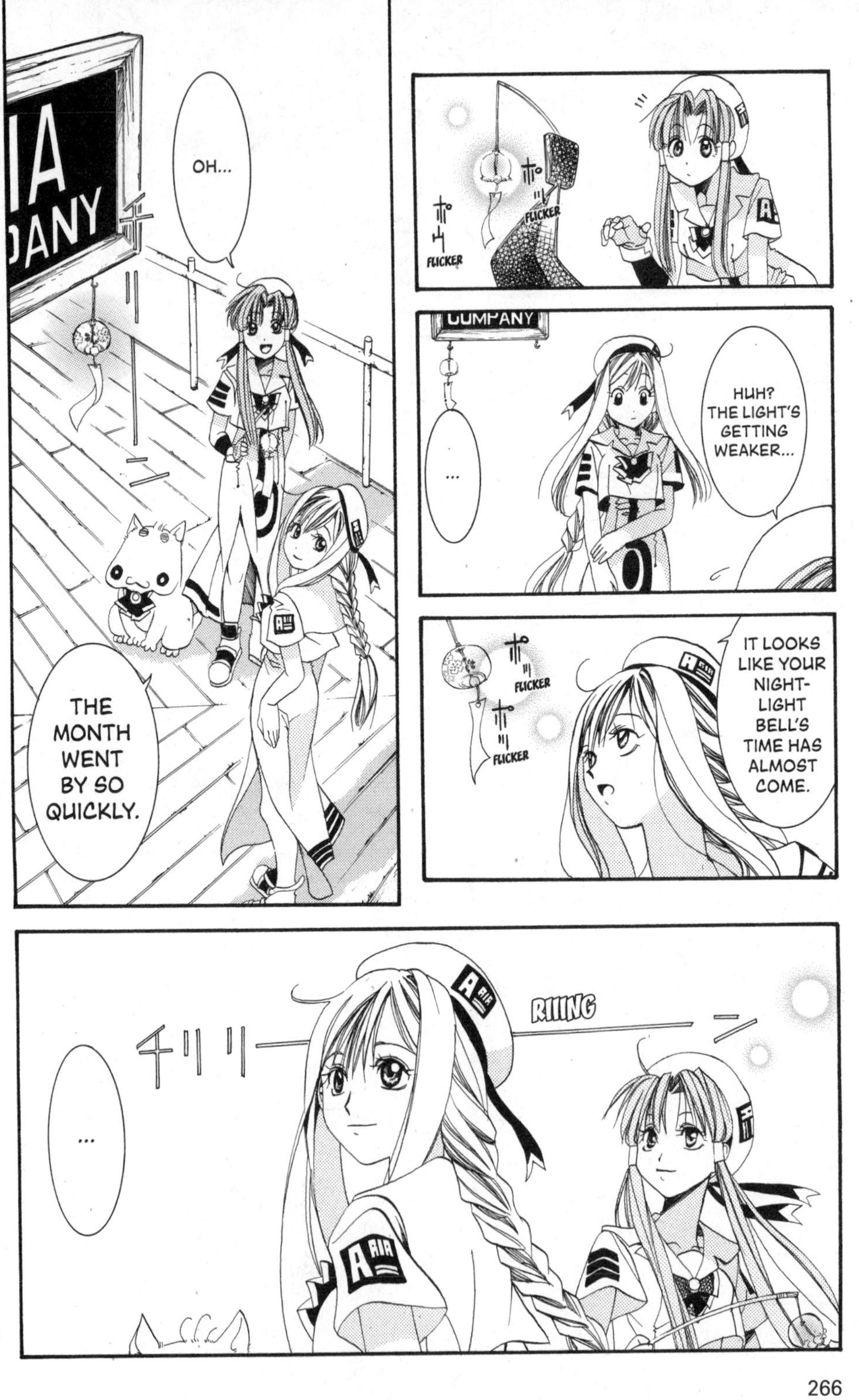
FLICKER
FLICKER
HUH? THE LIGHT'S GETTING WEAKER...
...
IT LOOKS LIKE YOUR NIGHT-LIGHT BELL'S TIME HAS ALMOST COME.
FLICKER
FLICKER
OH...
THE MONTH WENT BY SO QUICKLY.
RIIING
チリリー
...

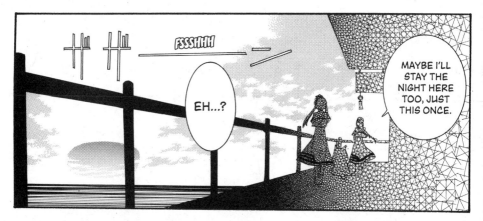

MAYBE I'LL STAY THE NIGHT HERE TOO, JUST THIS ONCE.

EH...?

FSSSHHH

THANK YOU.

FOR YOU, MISS ALICIA.

YES!

I SEE. SO YOU'VE BEEN HAVING TEATIME WITH PRESIDENT ARIA EVERY NIGHT.

EH? WHY IS THAT?

THEN I'M SURE YOU'LL BE SURPRISED TONIGHT.

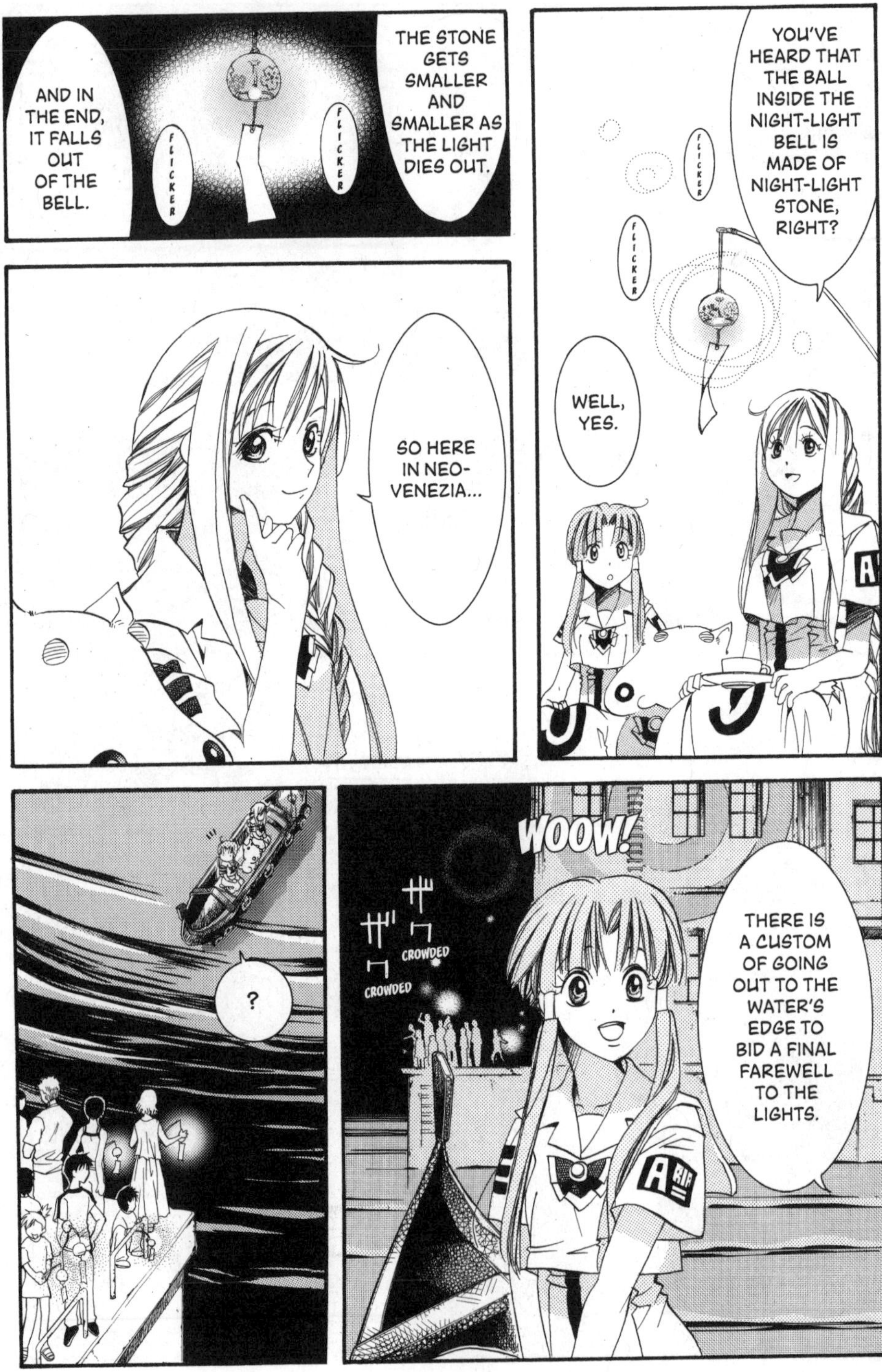
YOU'VE HEARD THAT THE BALL INSIDE THE NIGHT-LIGHT BELL IS MADE OF NIGHT-LIGHT STONE, RIGHT?
FLICKER
FLICKER
WELL, YES.
THE STONE GETS SMALLER AND SMALLER AS THE LIGHT DIES OUT.
FLICKER
FLICKER
AND IN THE END, IT FALLS OUT OF THE BELL.
SO HERE IN NEO-VENEZIA...
WOOW!
THERE IS A CUSTOM OF GOING OUT TO THE WATER'S EDGE TO BID A FINAL FAREWELL TO THE LIGHTS.
ザワ CROWDED
ザワ CROWDED
?

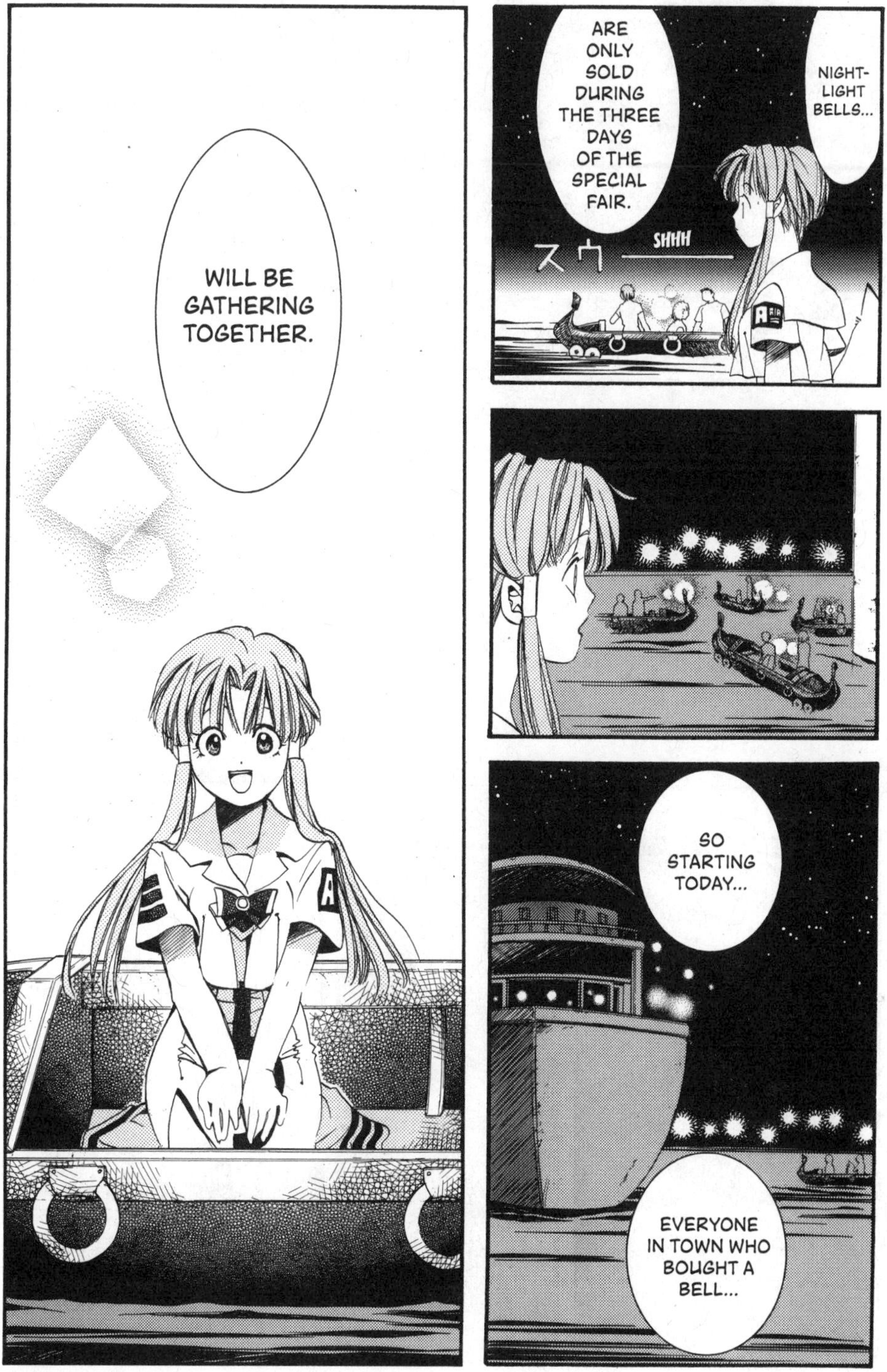
NIGHT-LIGHT BELLS...
ARE ONLY SOLD DURING THE THREE DAYS OF THE SPECIAL FAIR.
スウー
SHHH
SO STARTING TODAY...
EVERYONE IN TOWN WHO BOUGHT A BELL...
WILL BE GATHERING TOGETHER.

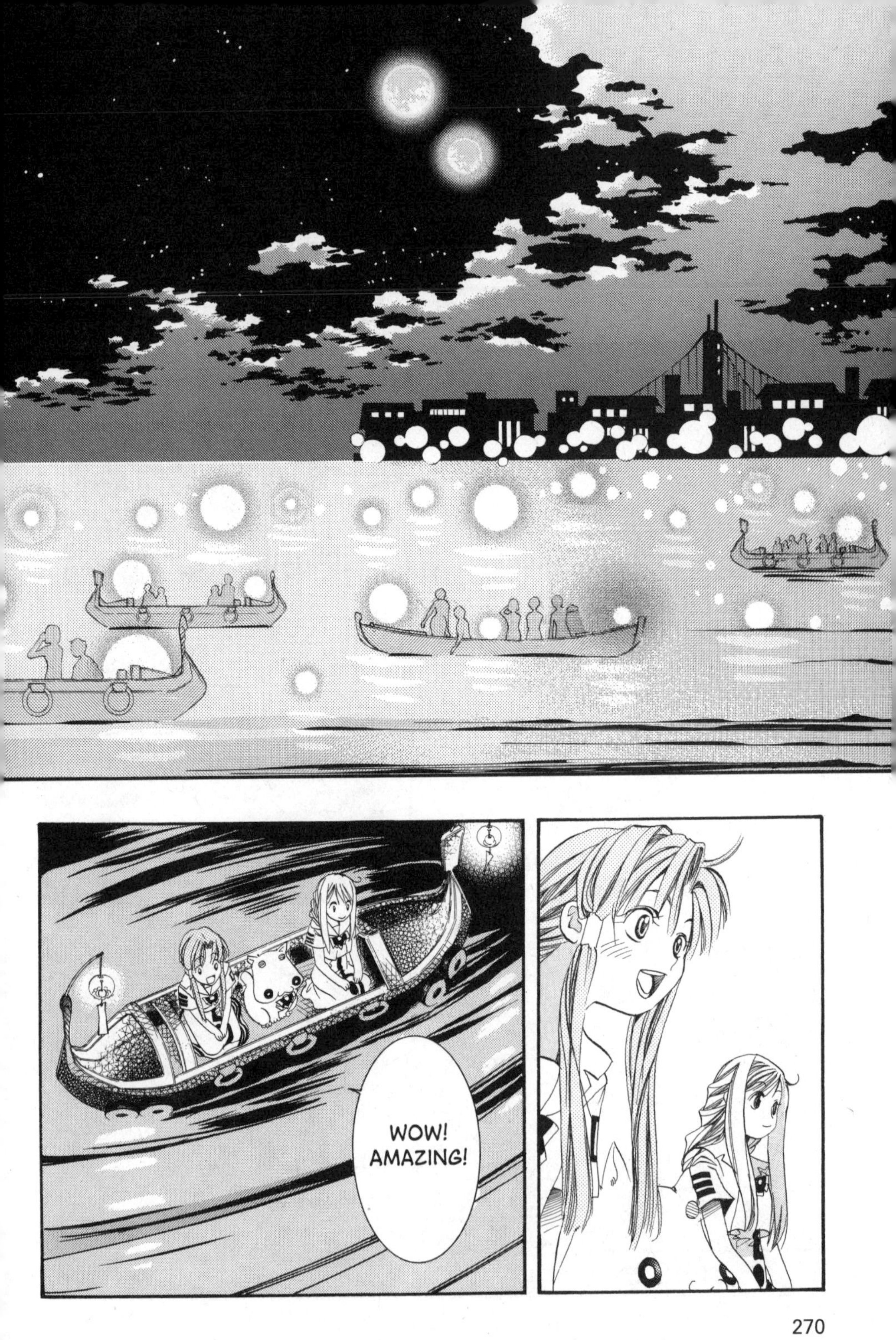
WOW! AMAZING!

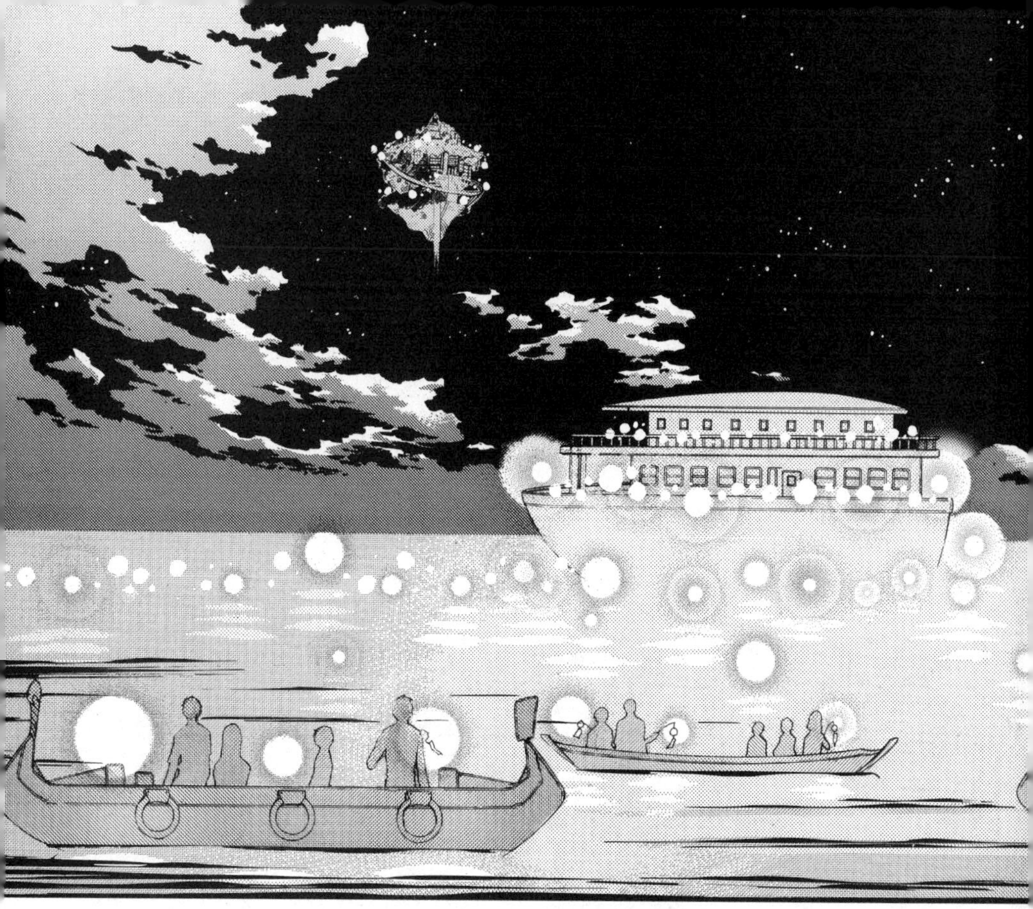

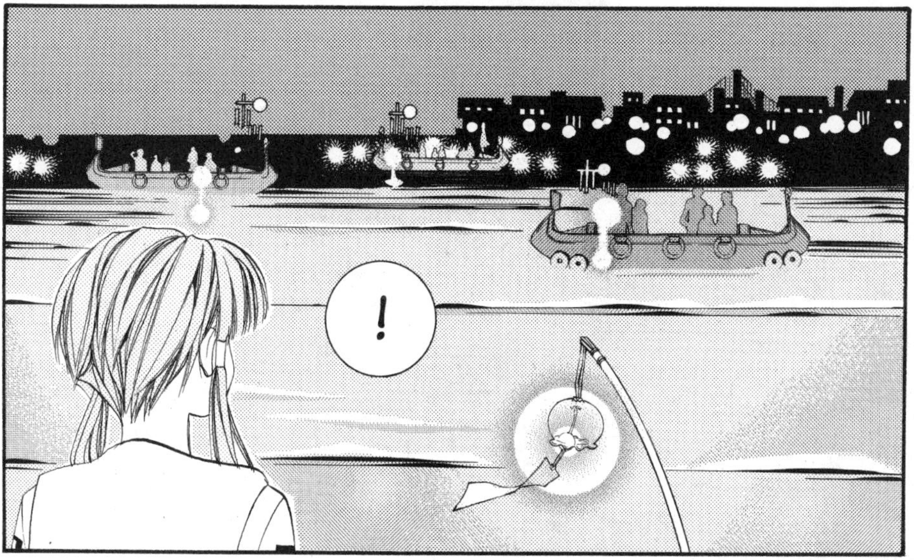
!

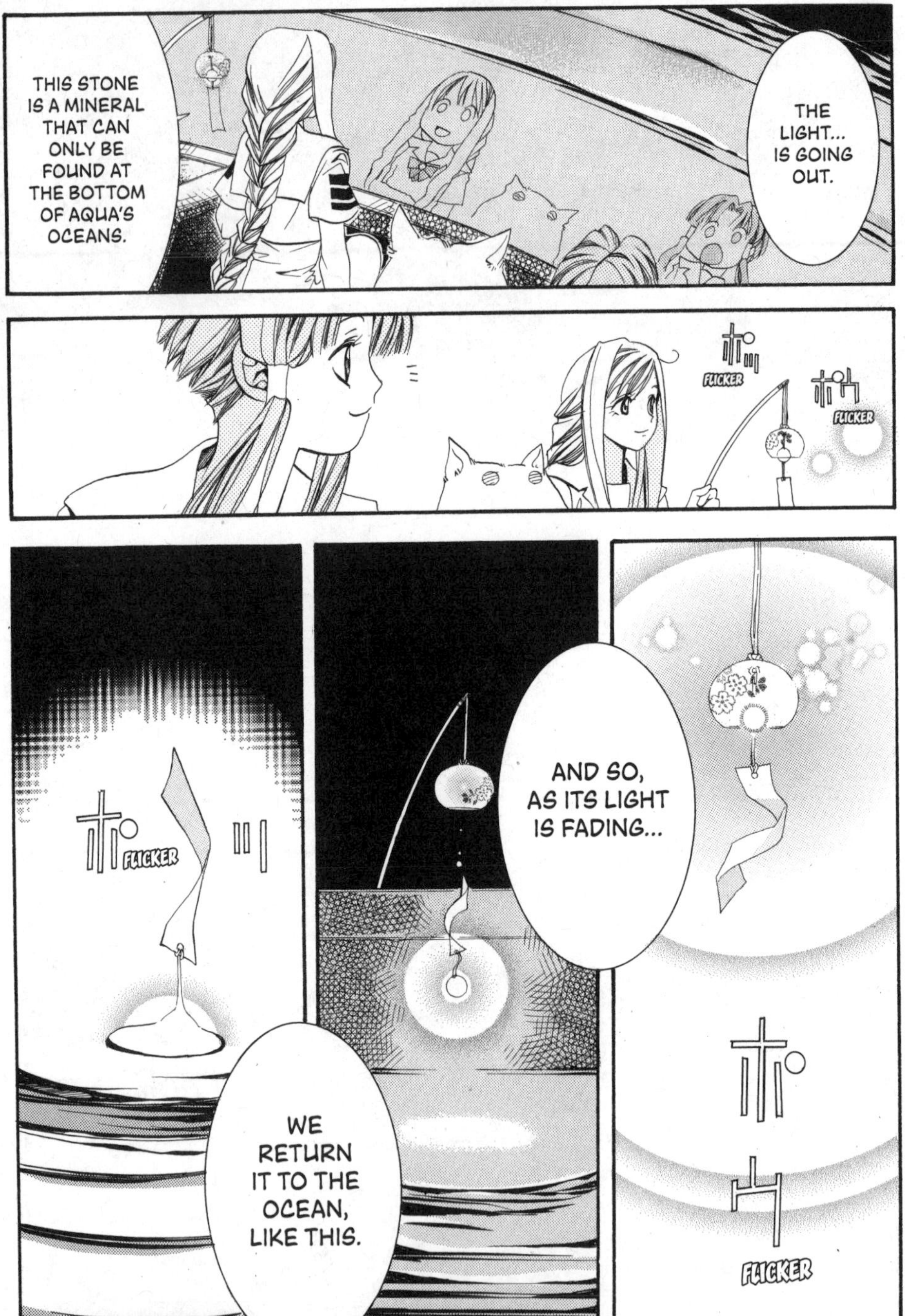
THE LIGHT... IS GOING OUT.
THIS STONE IS A MINERAL THAT CAN ONLY BE FOUND AT THE BOTTOM OF AQUA'S OCEANS.
FLICKER
FLICKER
FLICKER
AND SO, AS ITS LIGHT IS FADING...
WE RETURN IT TO THE OCEAN, LIKE THIS.
FLICKER

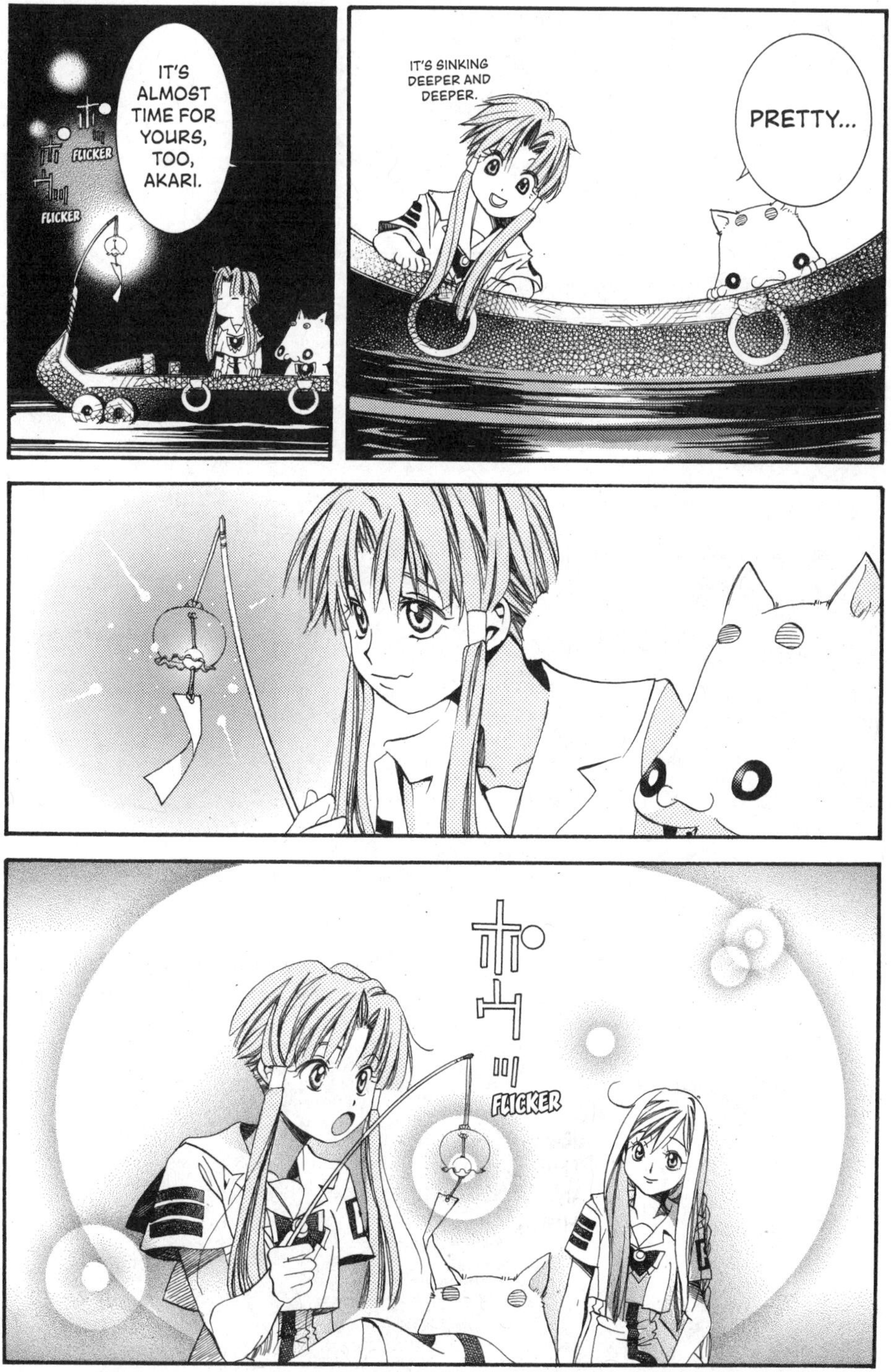
PRETTY...
IT'S SINKING DEEPER AND DEEPER.
IT'S ALMOST TIME FOR YOURS, TOO, AKARI.
FLICKER
FLICKER
ポウッ
FLICKER

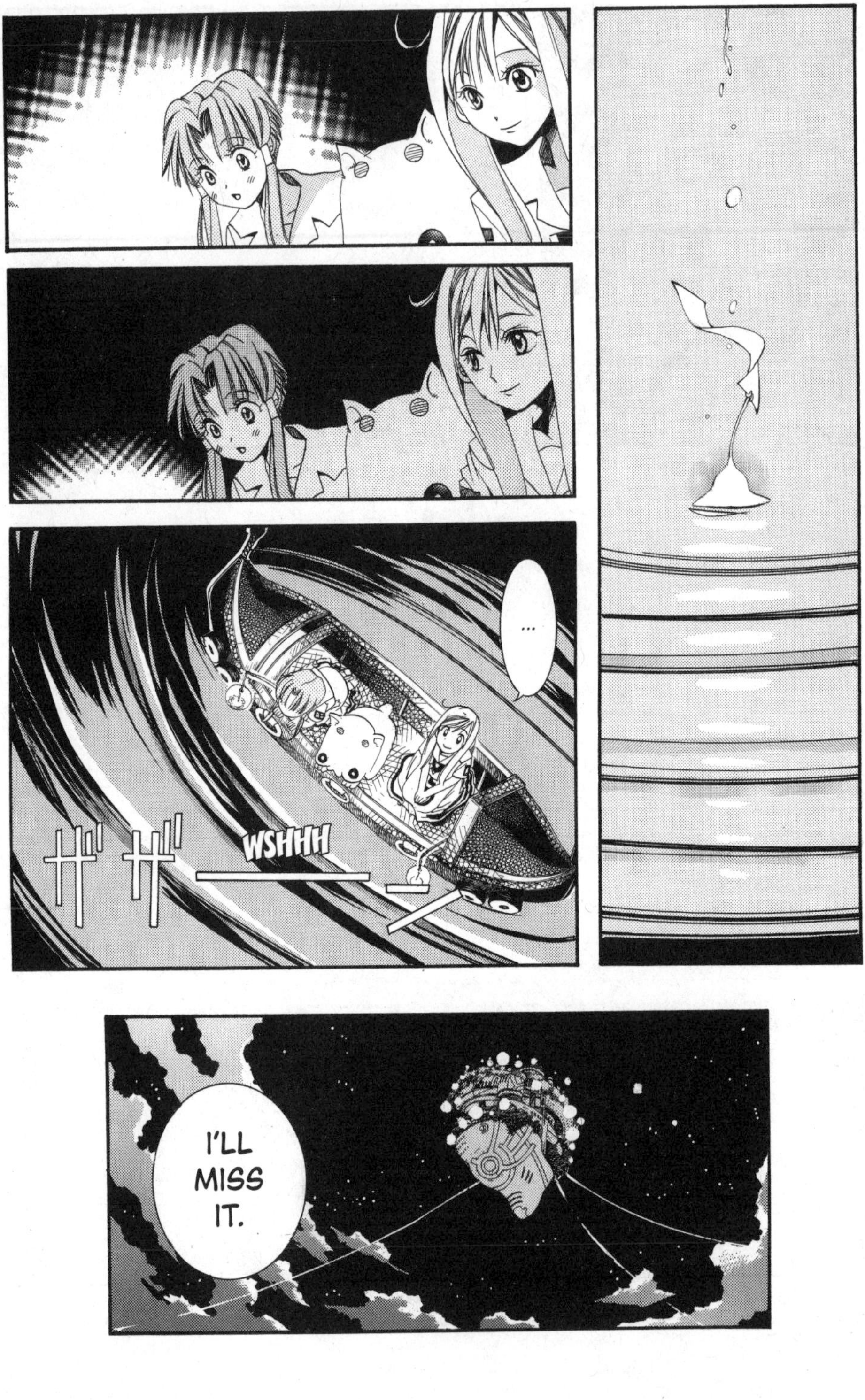
...
WSHHH
ザザ
I'LL MISS IT.

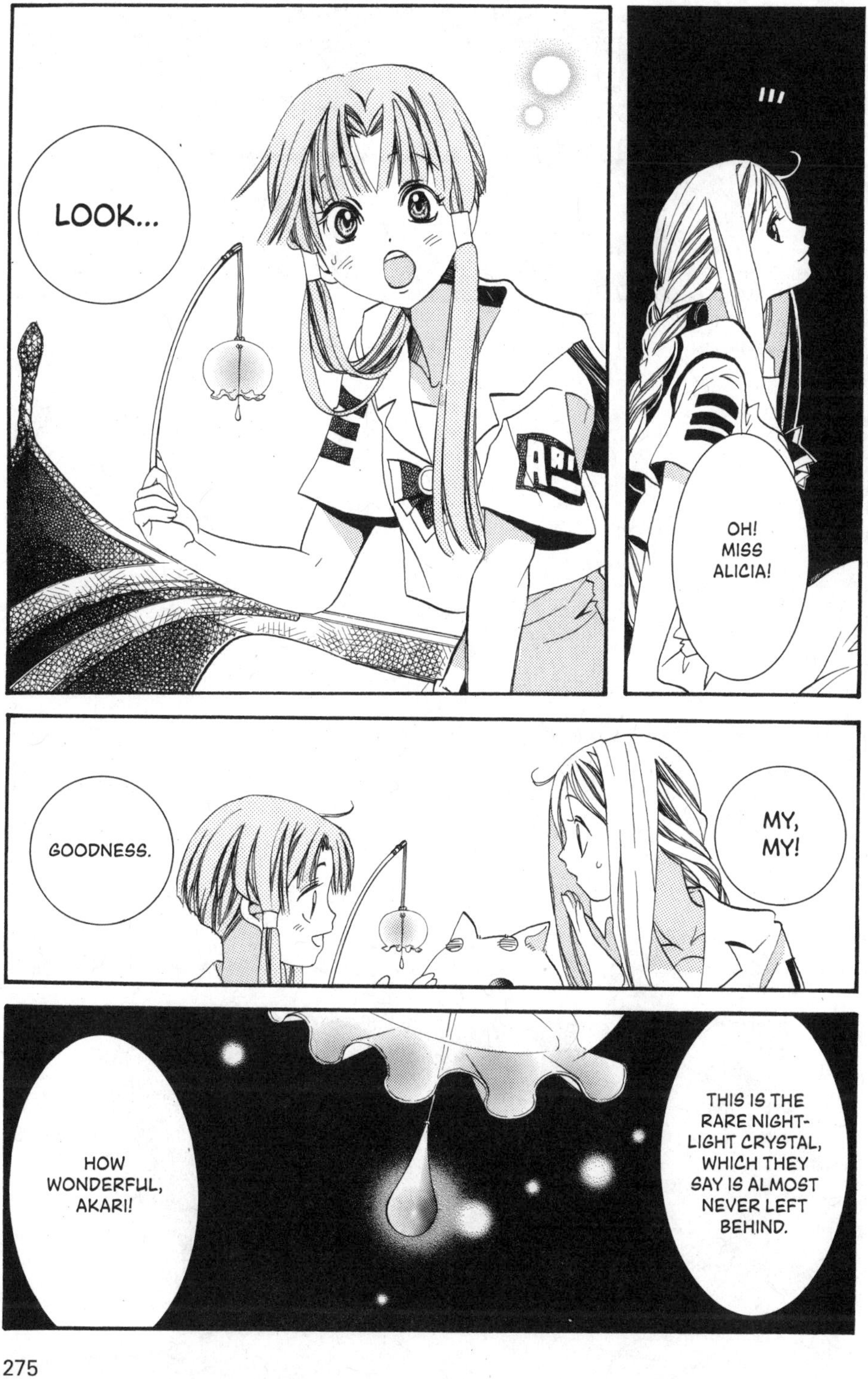
OH! MISS ALICIA!
LOOK...
MY, MY!
GOODNESS.
THIS IS THE RARE NIGHT-LIGHT CRYSTAL, WHICH THEY SAY IS ALMOST NEVER LEFT BEHIND.
HOW WONDERFUL, AKARI!

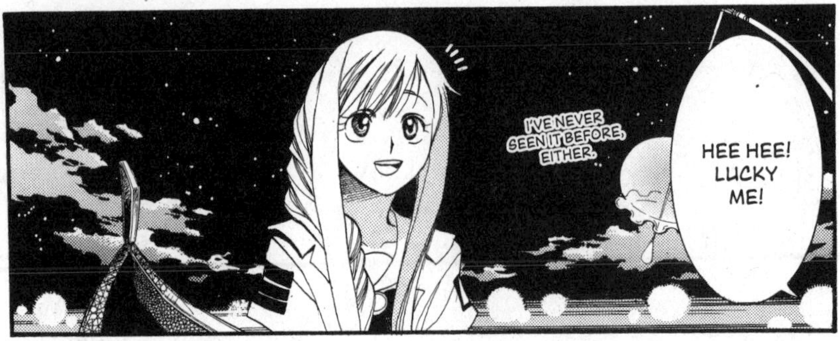
HEE HEE! LUCKY ME!
I'VE NEVER SEEN IT BEFORE, EITHER.

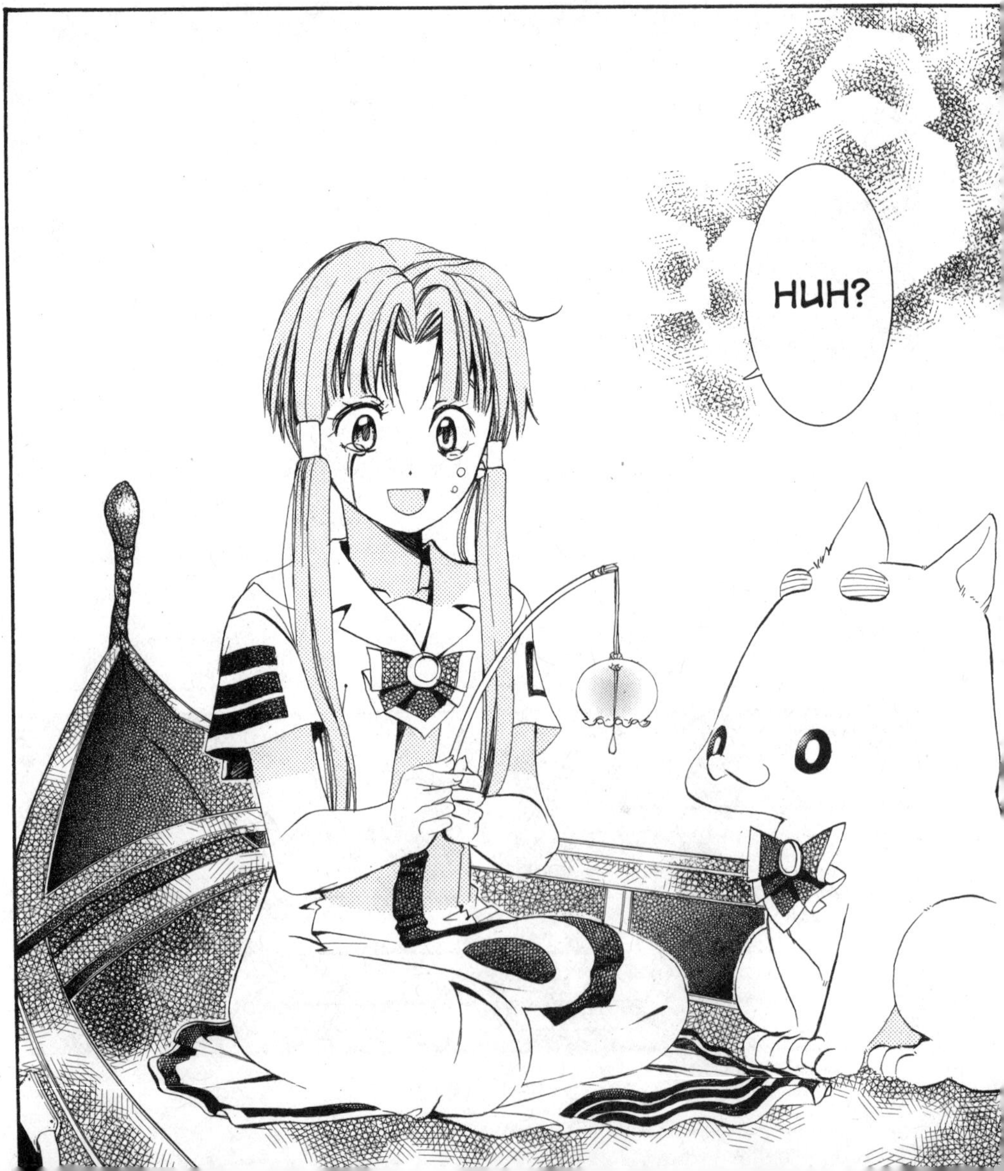
HUH?

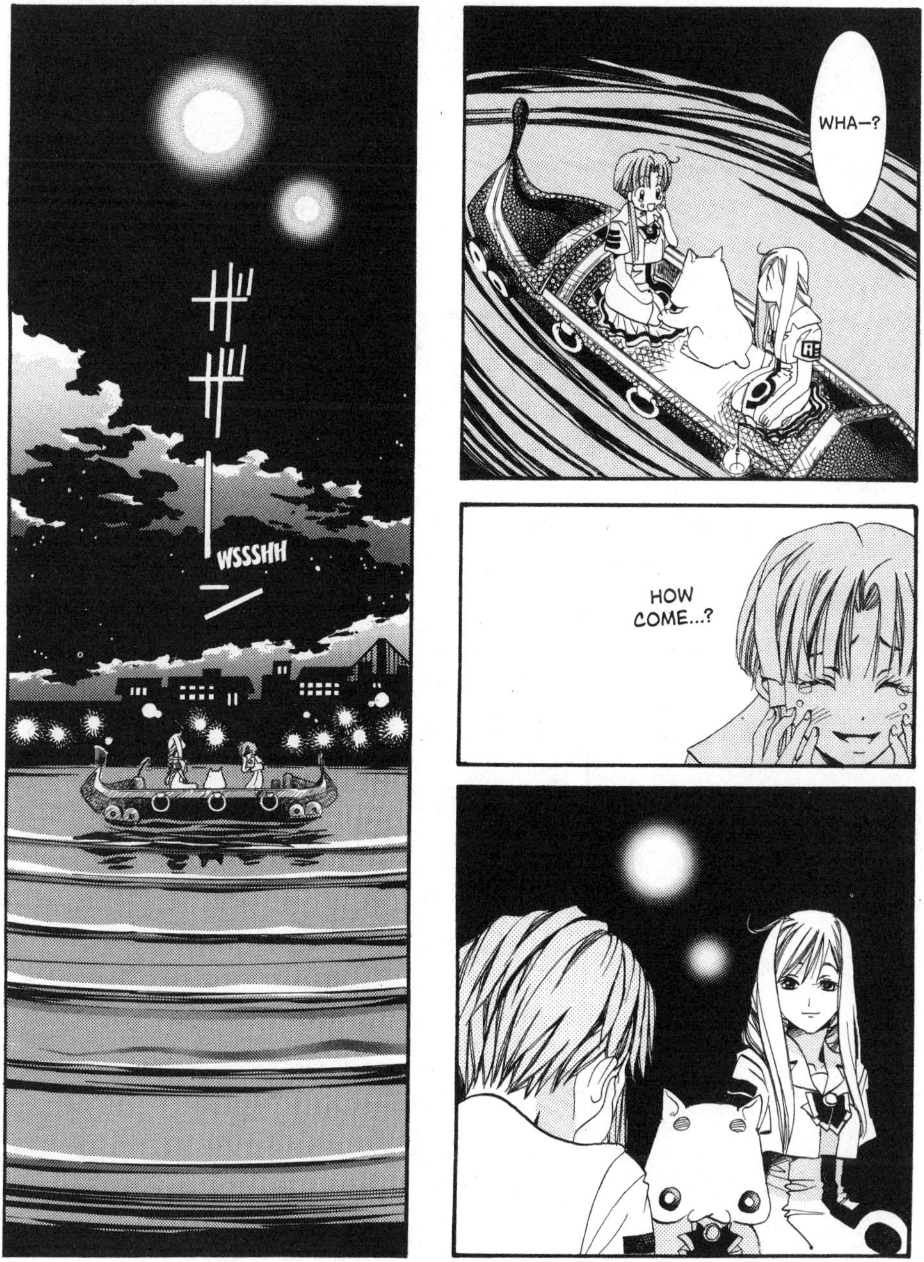
WHA–?
HOW COME...?
WSSSHH

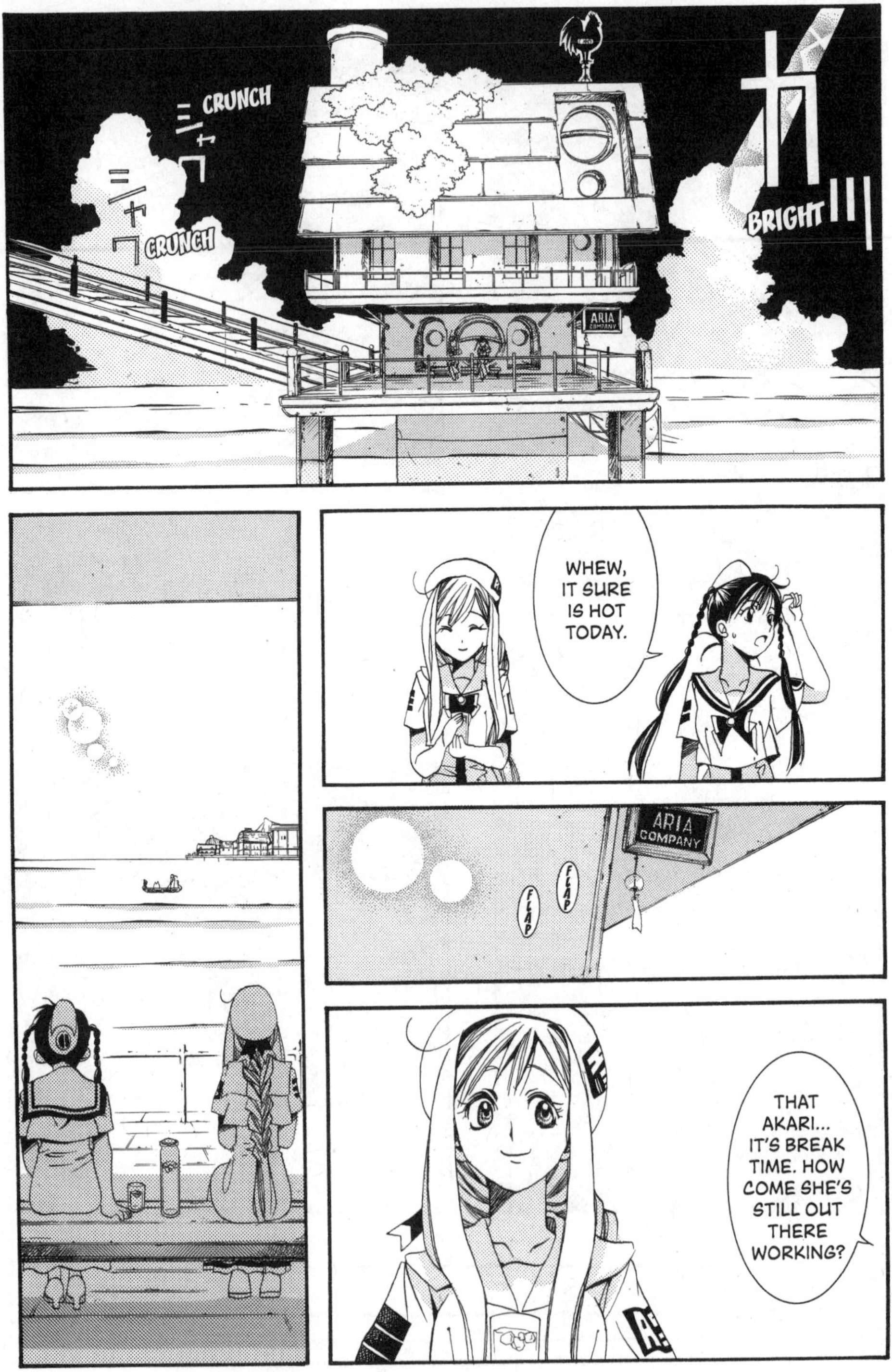

BRIGHT
シャク CRUNCH
シャク CRUNCH
WHEW, IT SURE IS HOT TODAY.
ARIA COMPANY
FLAP
FLAP
THAT AKARI... IT'S BREAK TIME. HOW COME SHE'S STILL OUT THERE WORKING?

DON'T FULLY
KNOW WHY
I WAS CRYING
THEN.

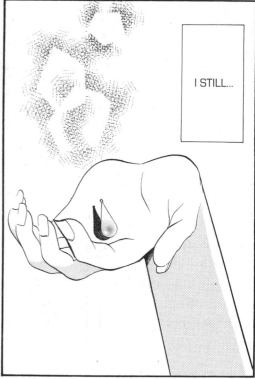

I STILL...

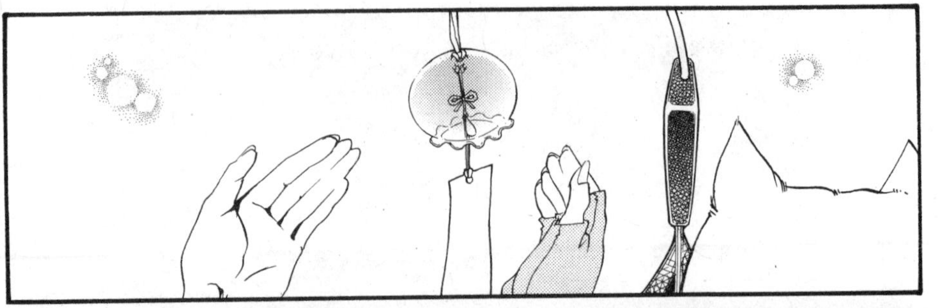

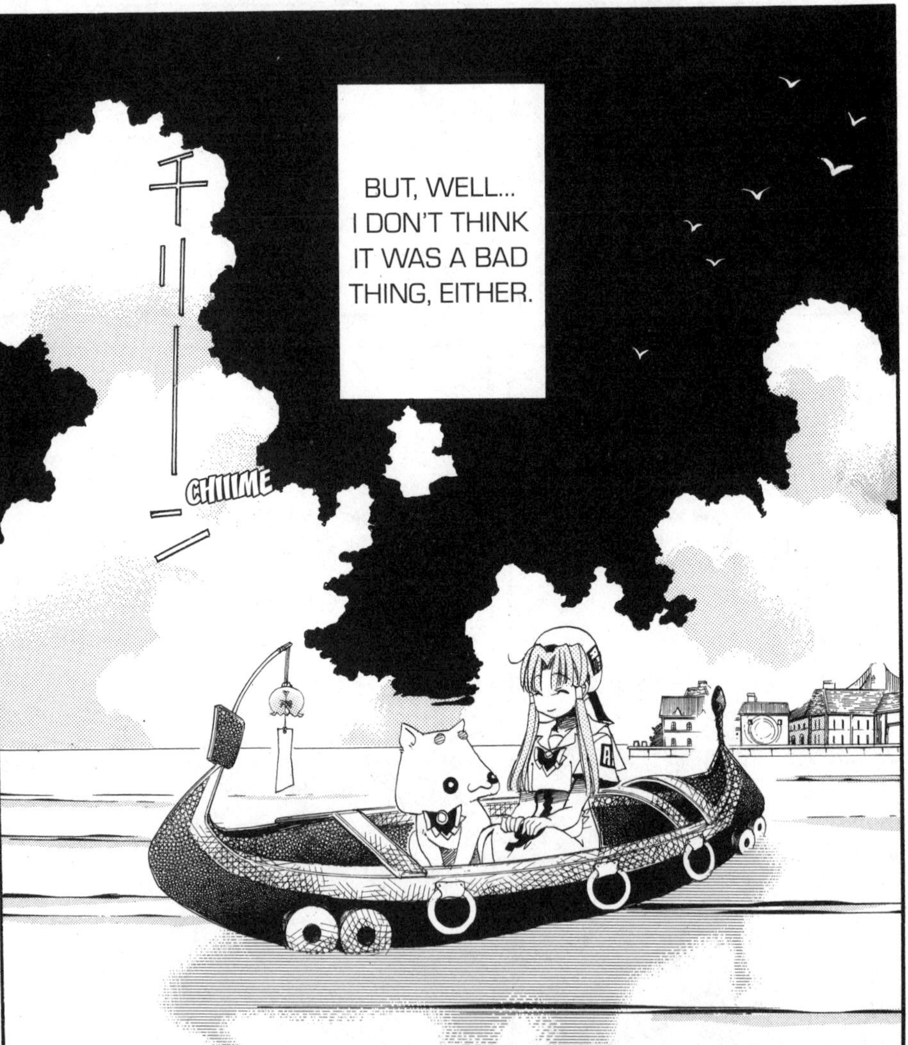
BUT, WELL... I DON'T THINK IT WAS A BAD THING, EITHER.
チリーン
CHIIIME

ARIA
The MASTERPIECE

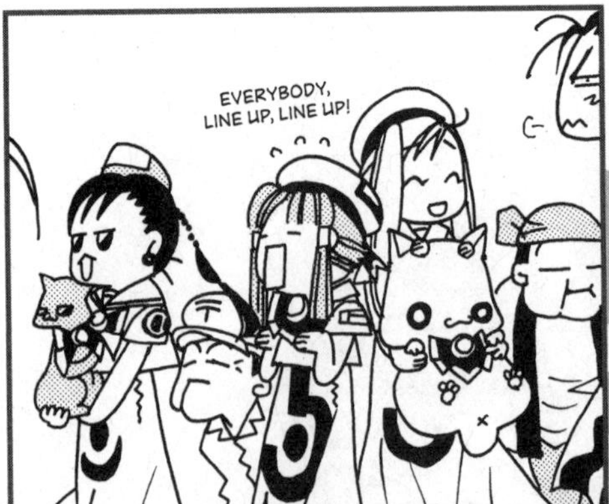
EVERYBODY,
LINE UP, LINE UP!

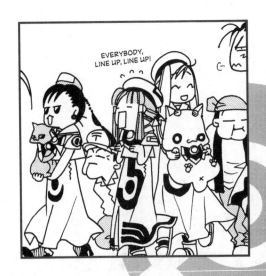

Navigation 09
Fireworks

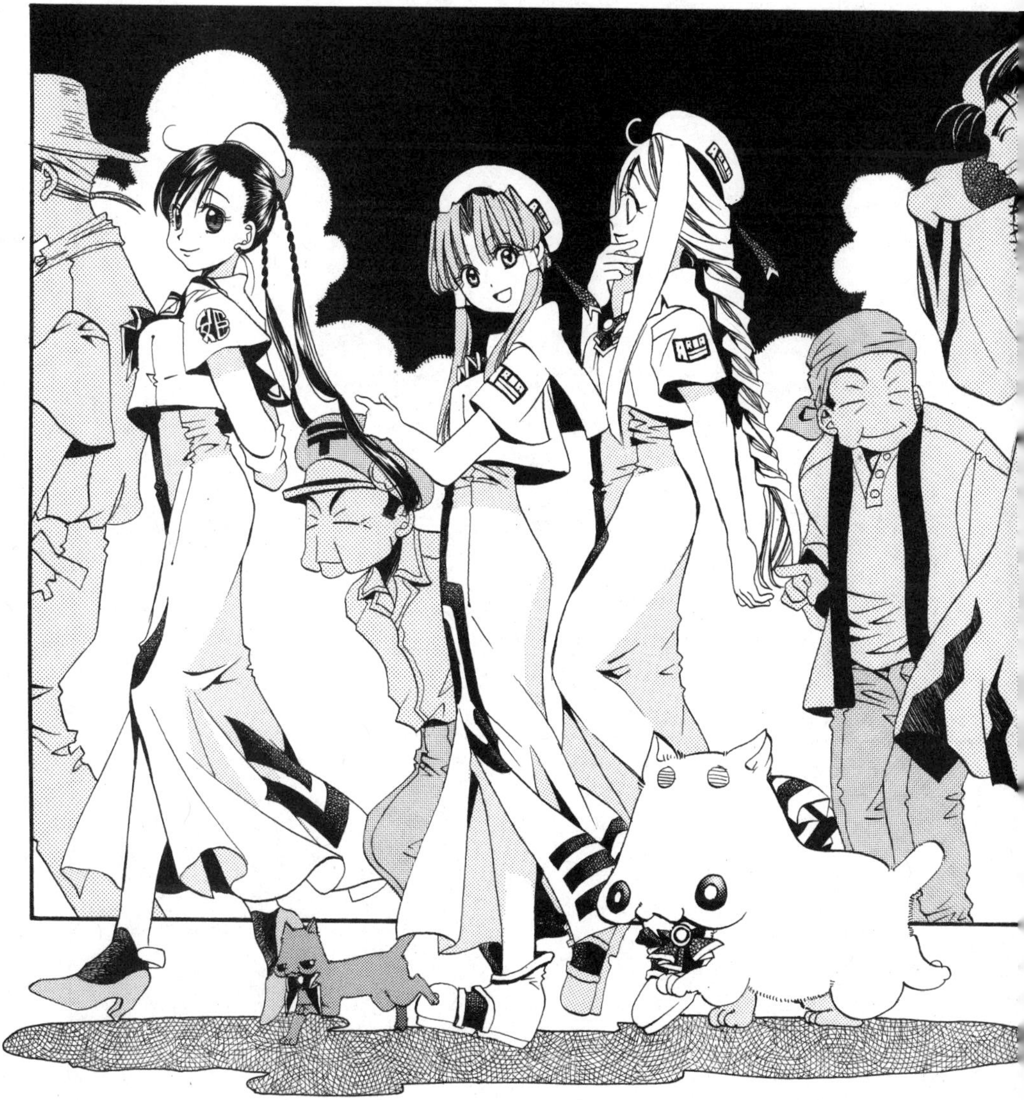

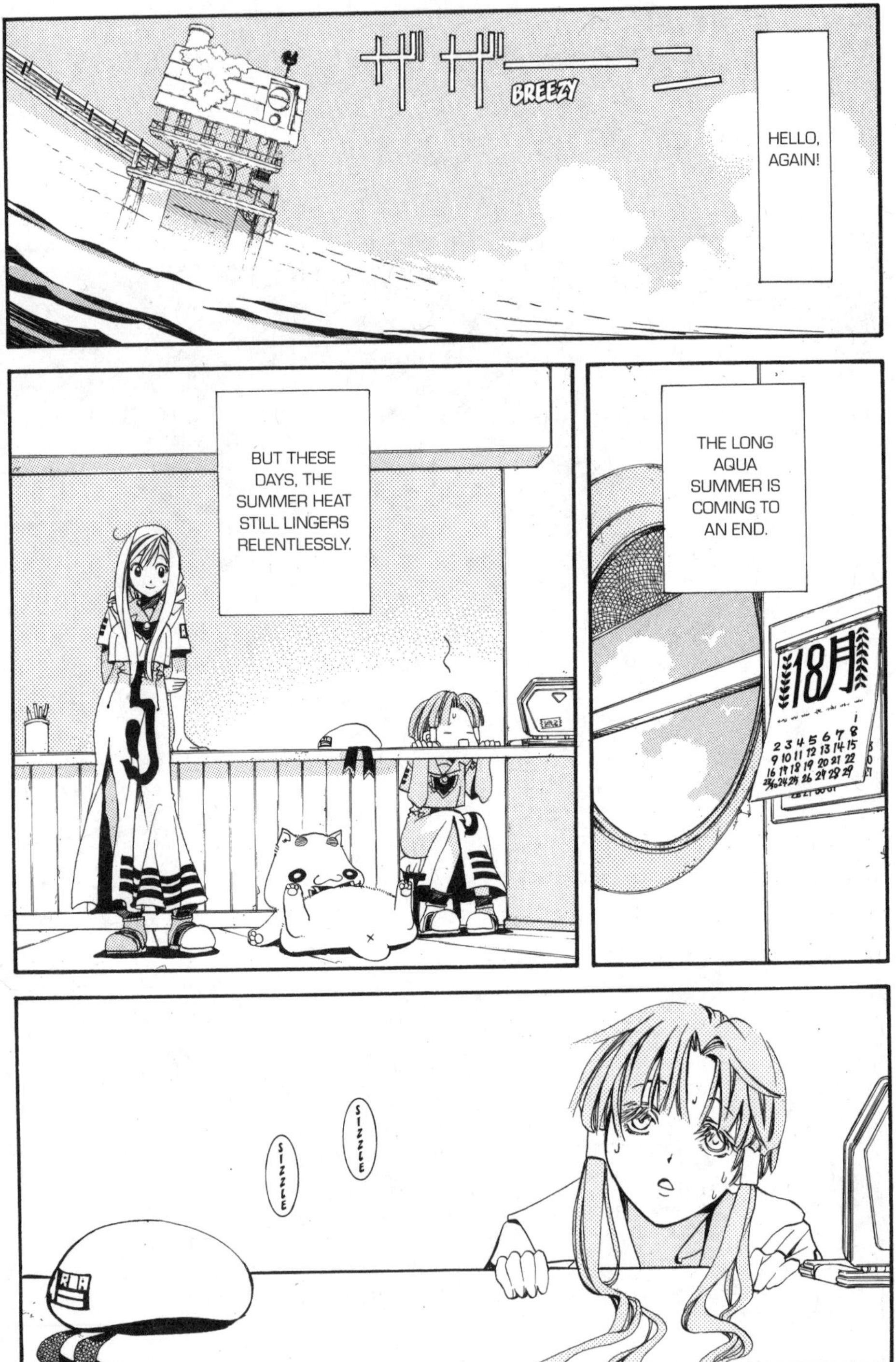
HELLO, AGAIN!
ザザー
BREEZY
THE LONG AQUA SUMMER IS COMING TO AN END.
18月
BUT THESE DAYS, THE SUMMER HEAT STILL LINGERS RELENTLESSLY.
SIZZLE
SIZZLE

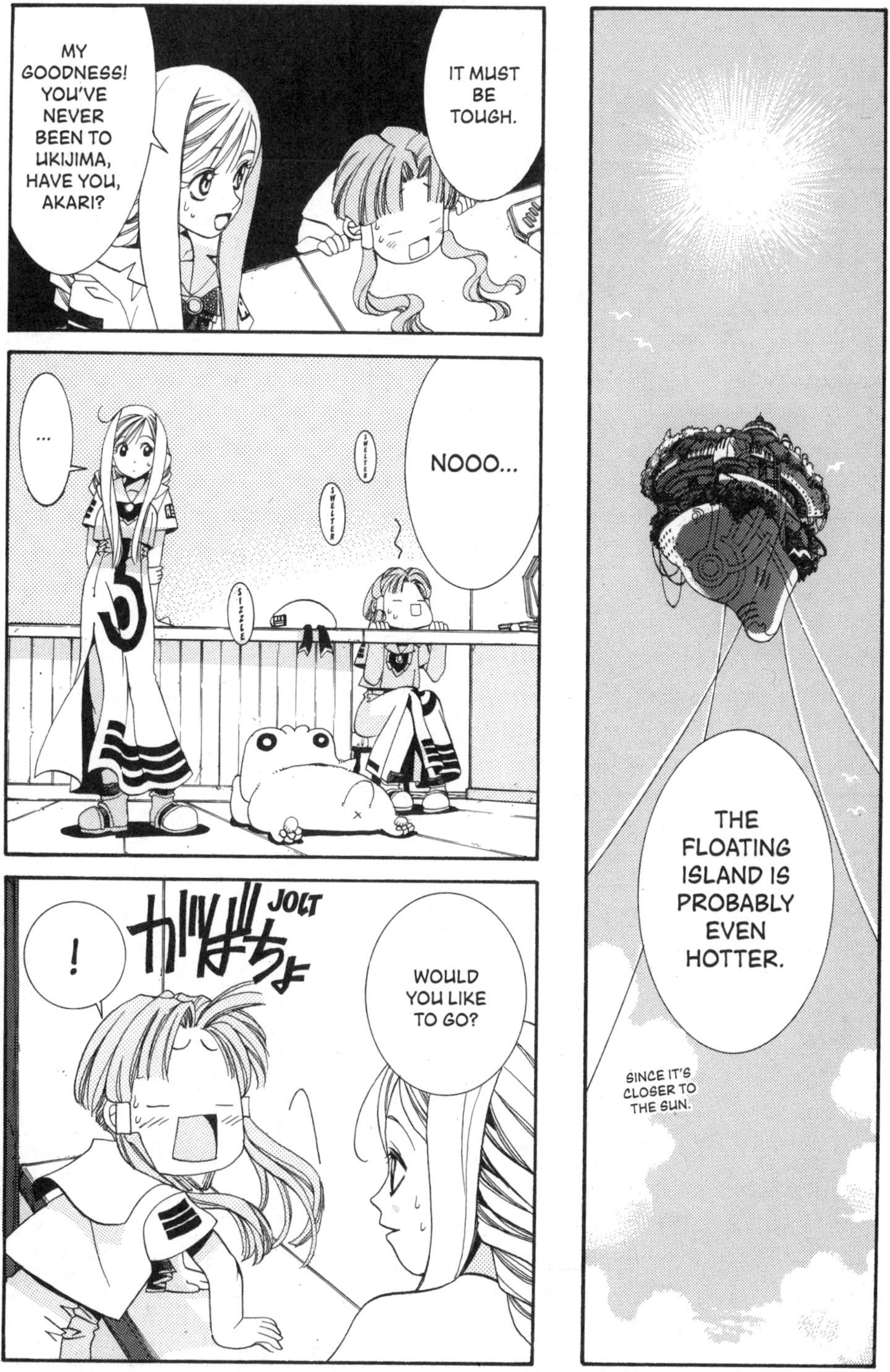
THE FLOATING ISLAND IS PROBABLY EVEN HOTTER.
SINCE IT'S CLOSER TO THE SUN.
IT MUST BE TOUGH.
MY GOODNESS! YOU'VE NEVER BEEN TO UKIJIMA, HAVE YOU, AKARI?
NOOO...
SWELTER
SWELTER
SIZZLE
...
WOULD YOU LIKE TO GO?
JOLT
!

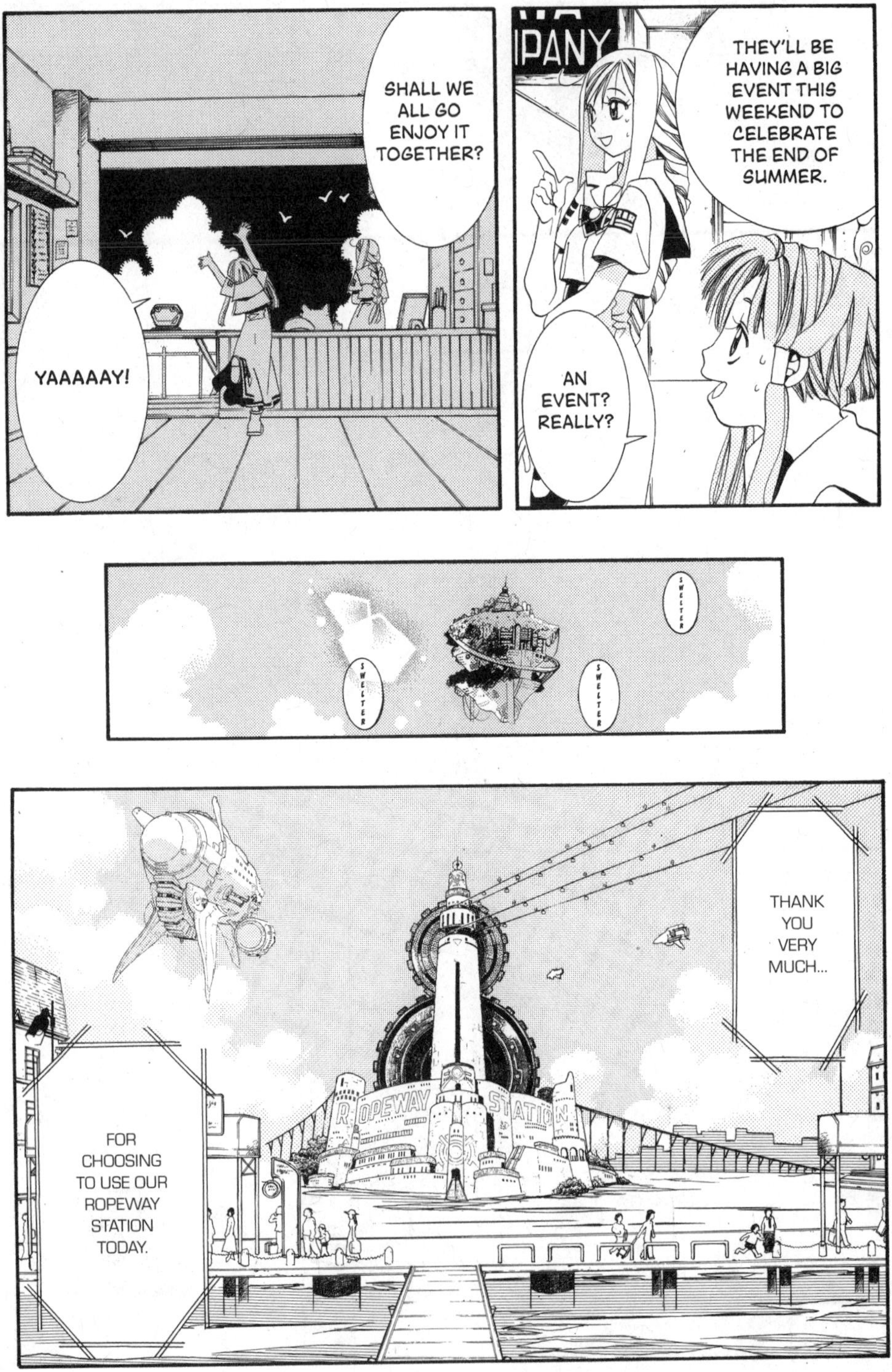
IPANY
THEY'LL BE HAVING A BIG EVENT THIS WEEKEND TO CELEBRATE THE END OF SUMMER.
AN EVENT? REALLY?
SHALL WE ALL GO ENJOY IT TOGETHER?
YAAAAAY!
SWELTER
SWELTER
SWELTER
THANK YOU VERY MUCH...
ROPEWAY STATION
FOR CHOOSING TO USE OUR ROPEWAY STATION TODAY.

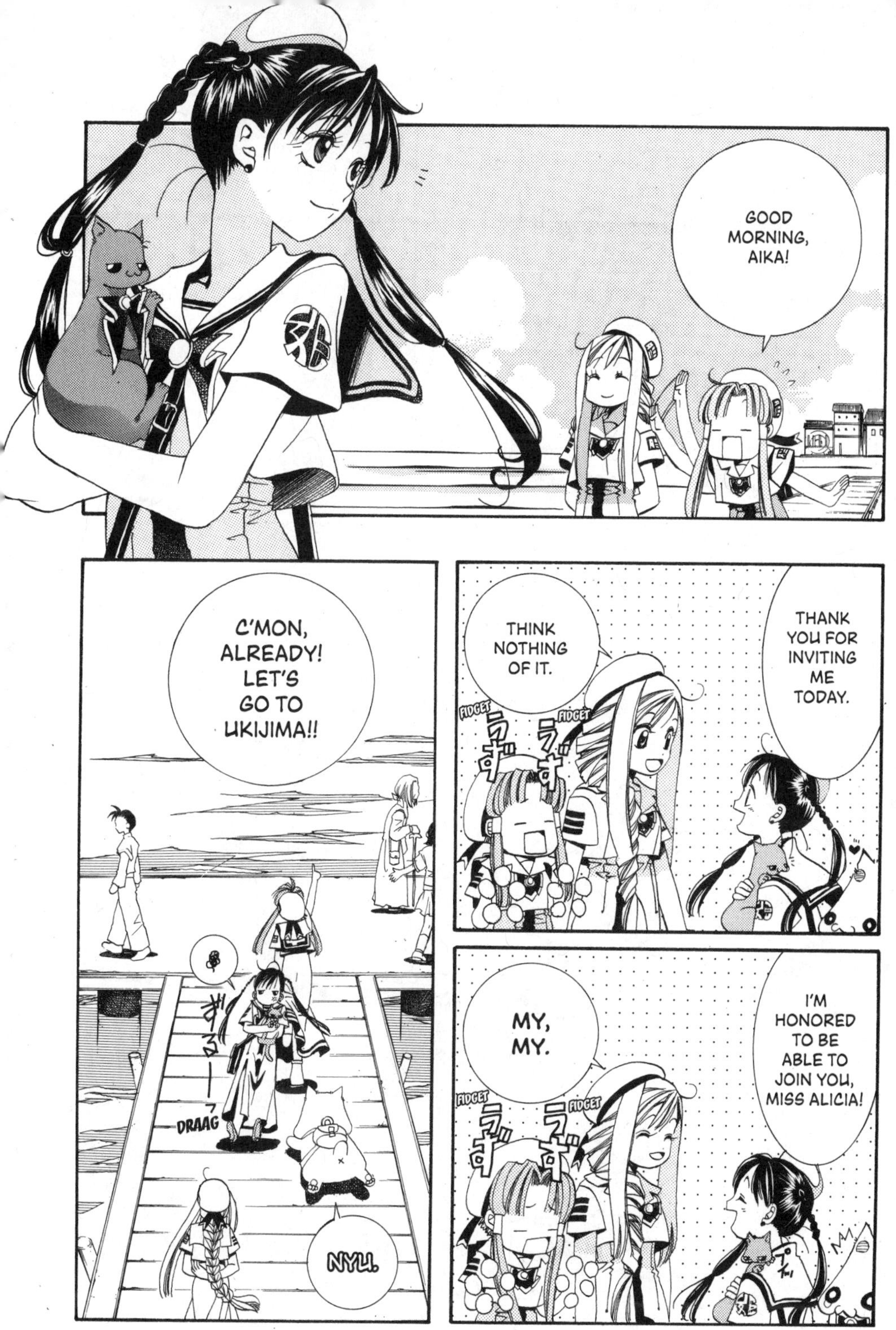
GOOD MORNING, AIKA!
THANK YOU FOR INVITING ME TODAY.
THINK NOTHING OF IT.
FIDGET
FIDGET
I'M HONORED TO BE ABLE TO JOIN YOU, MISS ALICIA!
MY, MY.
FIDGET
FIDGET
C'MON, ALREADY! LET'S GO TO UKIJIMA!!
DRAAG
NYU.

I CAN'T WAIT! I CAN'T WAIT!

RESTLESS そわ

EAGER そわ

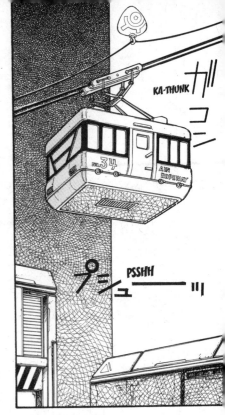

KA-THUNK カコン

AH...

ぺちっ？

SMACK

JEEZ! SIT STILL, WOULDJA?!

PSSHH プシュ————ﾘﾘ

WILTING... しゅーん

MY, MY.

HMM?

OH YES, AKARI.

YOU KNOW, UKIJIMA ISN'T JUST UP THERE TO LOOK PRETTY.

KA-THUNK ゴトン

KA-THUNK ゴトン

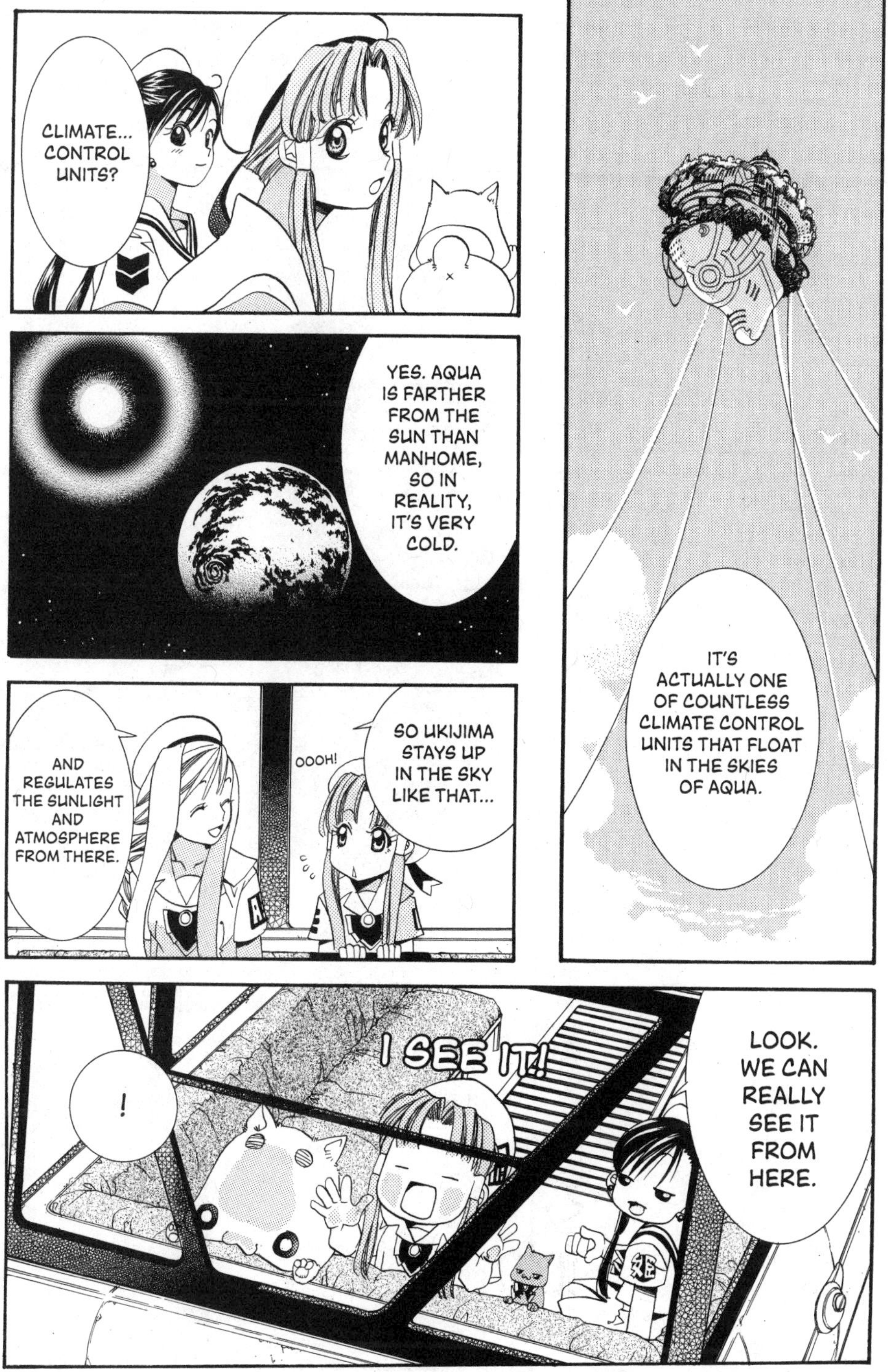
IT'S ACTUALLY ONE OF COUNTLESS CLIMATE CONTROL UNITS THAT FLOAT IN THE SKIES OF AQUA.
CLIMATE... CONTROL UNITS?
YES. AQUA IS FARTHER FROM THE SUN THAN MANHOME, SO IN REALITY, IT'S VERY COLD.
SO UKIJIMA STAYS UP IN THE SKY LIKE THAT...
OOOH!
AND REGULATES THE SUNLIGHT AND ATMOSPHERE FROM THERE.
LOOK. WE CAN REALLY SEE IT FROM HERE.
I SEE IT!
!

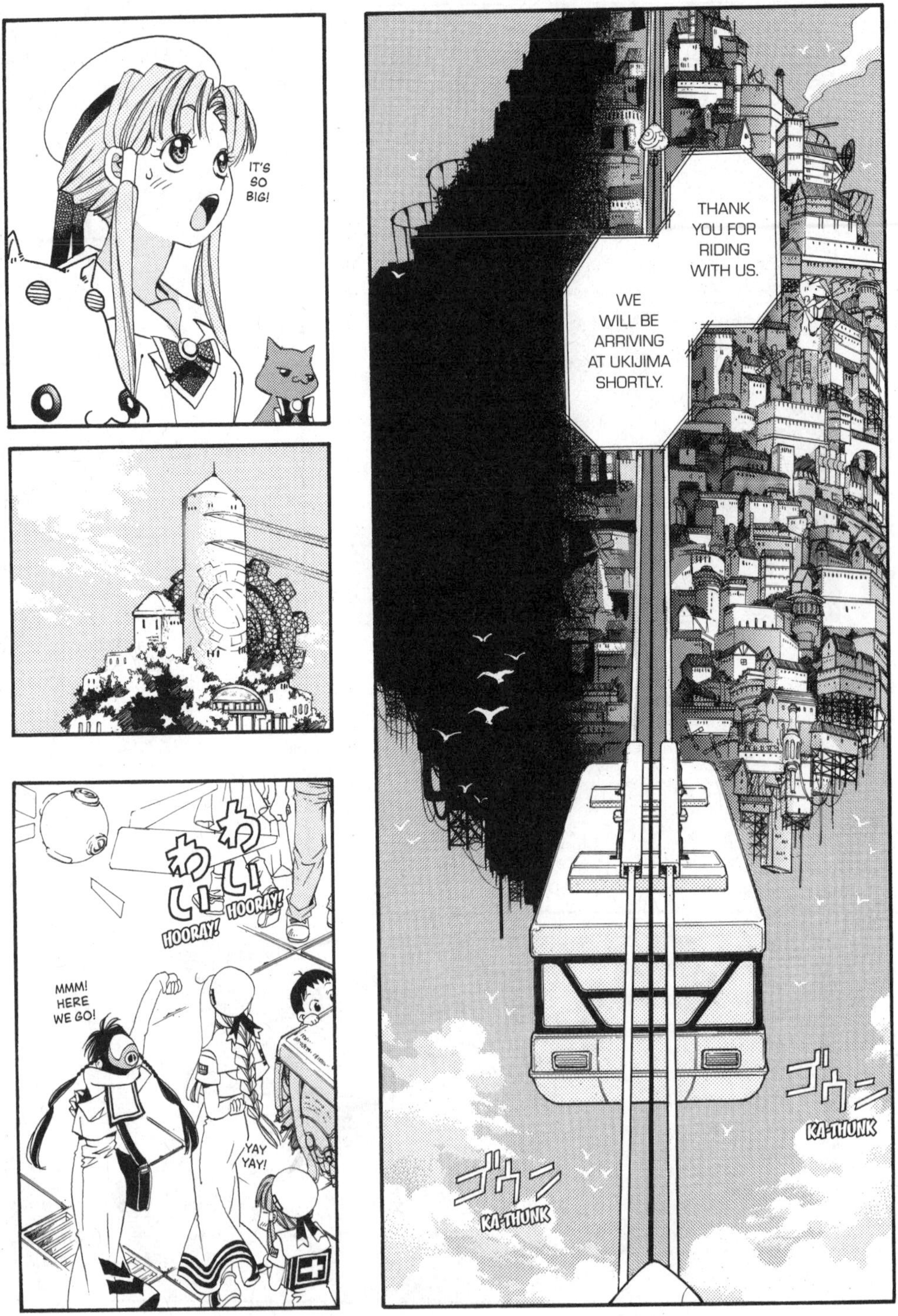
THANK YOU FOR RIDING WITH US.
WE WILL BE ARRIVING AT UKIJIMA SHORTLY.
ゴウン
KA-THUNK
ゴウン
KA-THUNK
IT'S SO BIG!
わいわい
HOORAY!
HOORAY!
MMM! HERE WE GO!
YAY YAY!

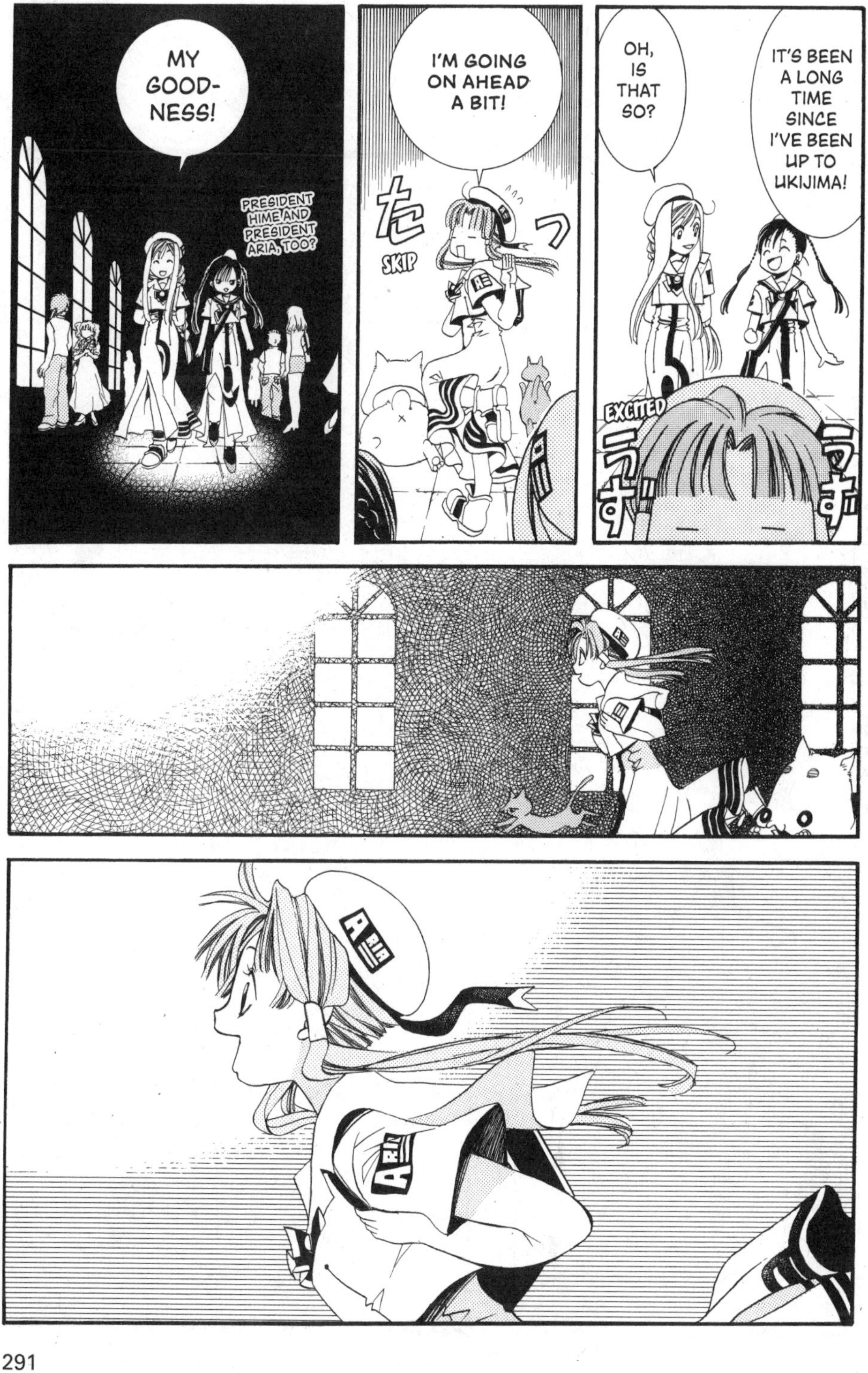
IT'S BEEN A LONG TIME SINCE I'VE BEEN UP TO UKIJIMA!
OH, IS THAT SO?
EXCITED
I'M GOING ON AHEAD A BIT!
SKIP
MY GOOD-NESS!
PRESIDENT HIME AND PRESIDENT ARIA, TOO?

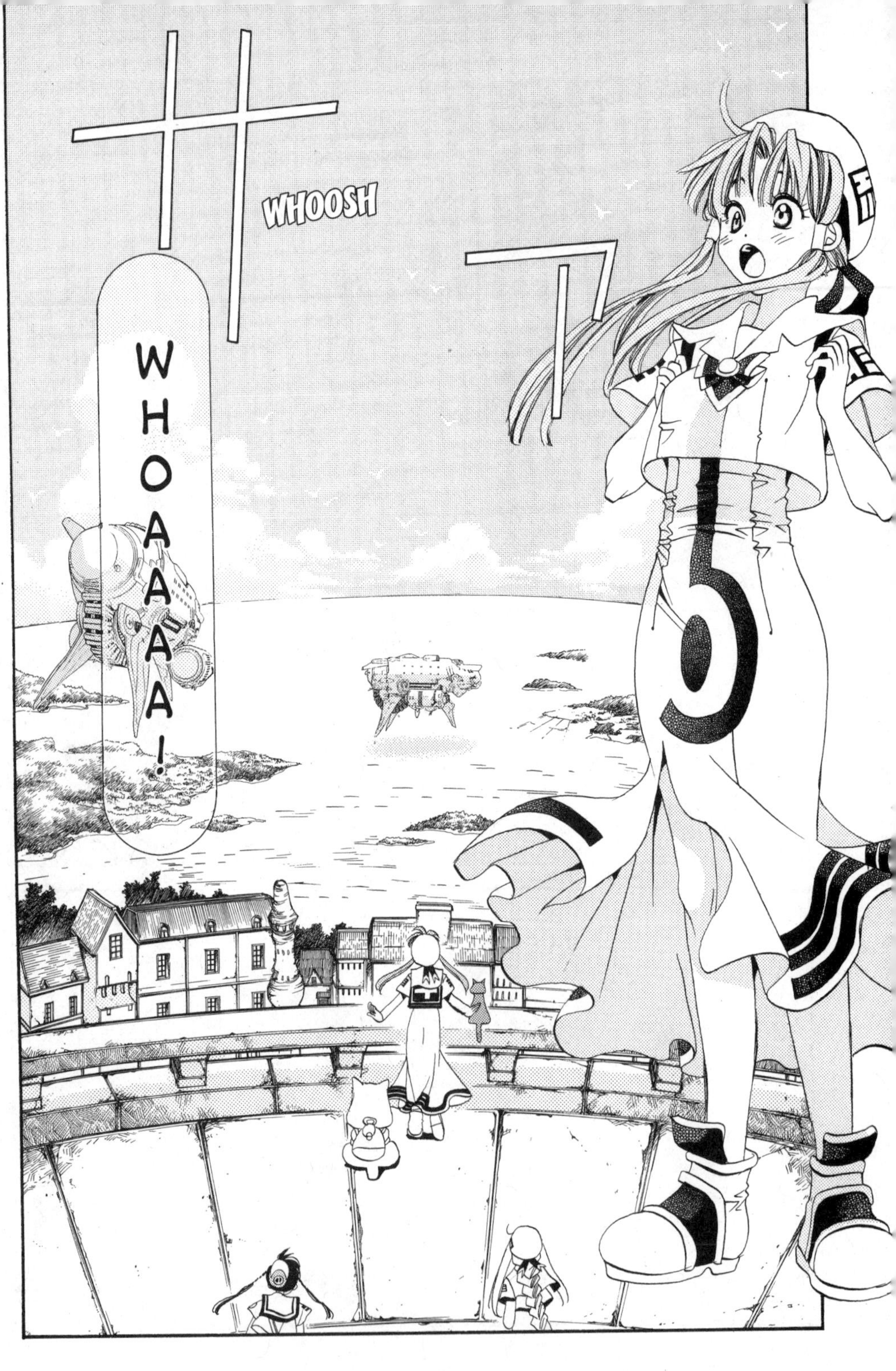
WHOOSH
WHOAAAAA!

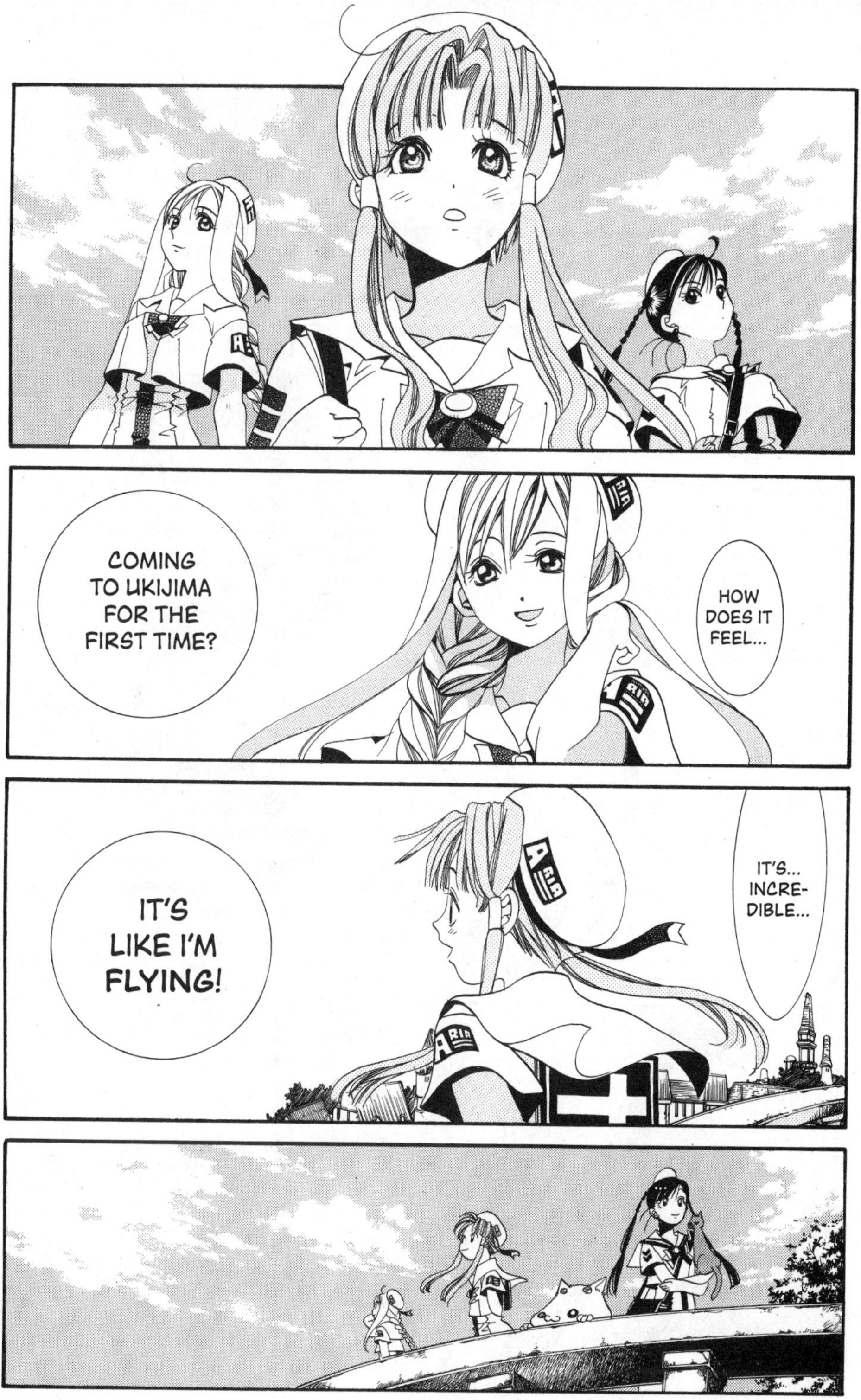
HOW DOES IT FEEL...
COMING TO UKIJIMA FOR THE FIRST TIME?
IT'S... INCREDIBLE...
IT'S LIKE I'M FLYING!

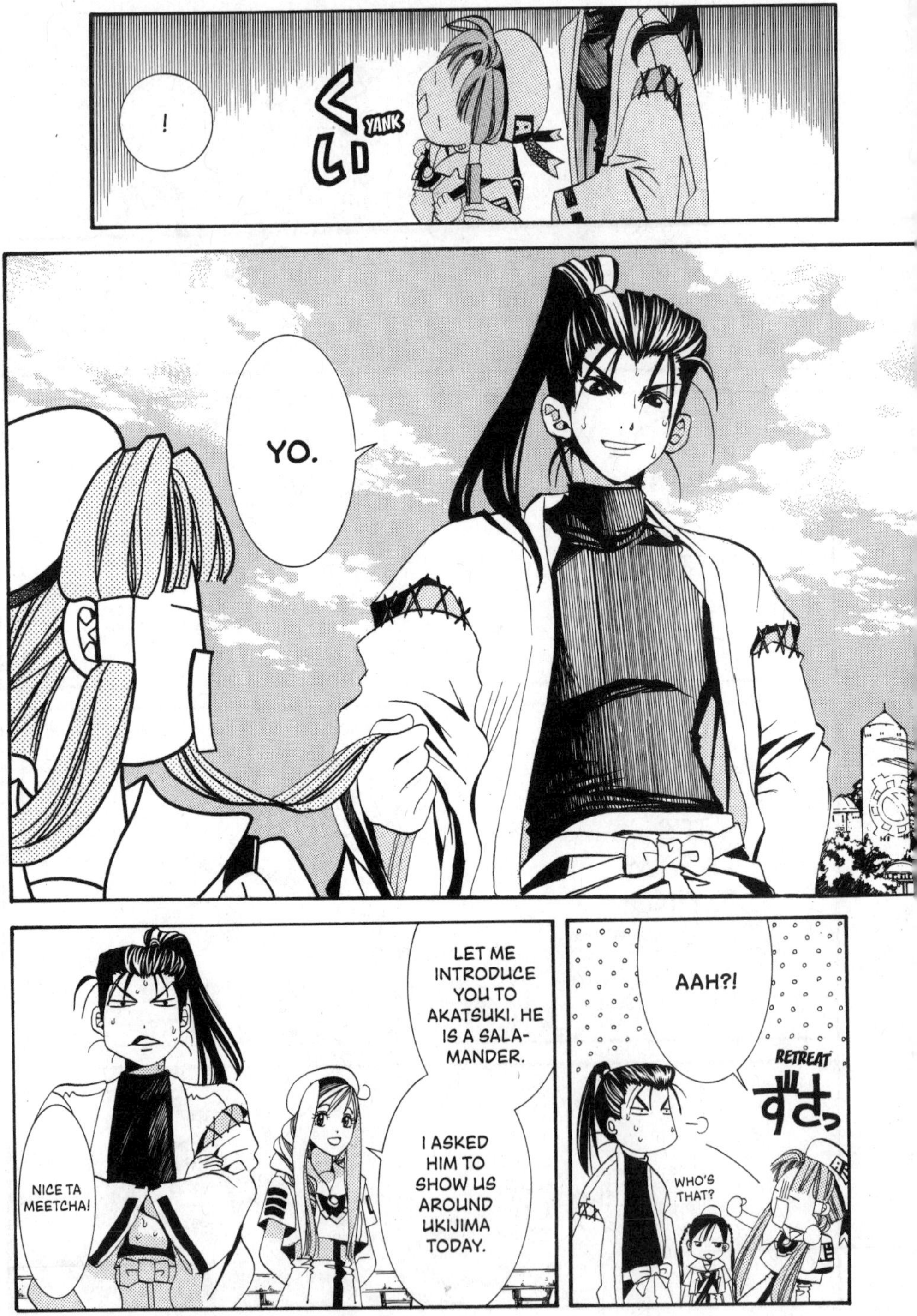
YANK
くい
!
YO.
AAH?!
RETREAT
ずさっ
WHO'S THAT?
LET ME INTRODUCE YOU TO AKATSUKI. HE IS A SALAMANDER.
I ASKED HIM TO SHOW US AROUND UKIJIMA TODAY.
NICE TA MEETCHA!

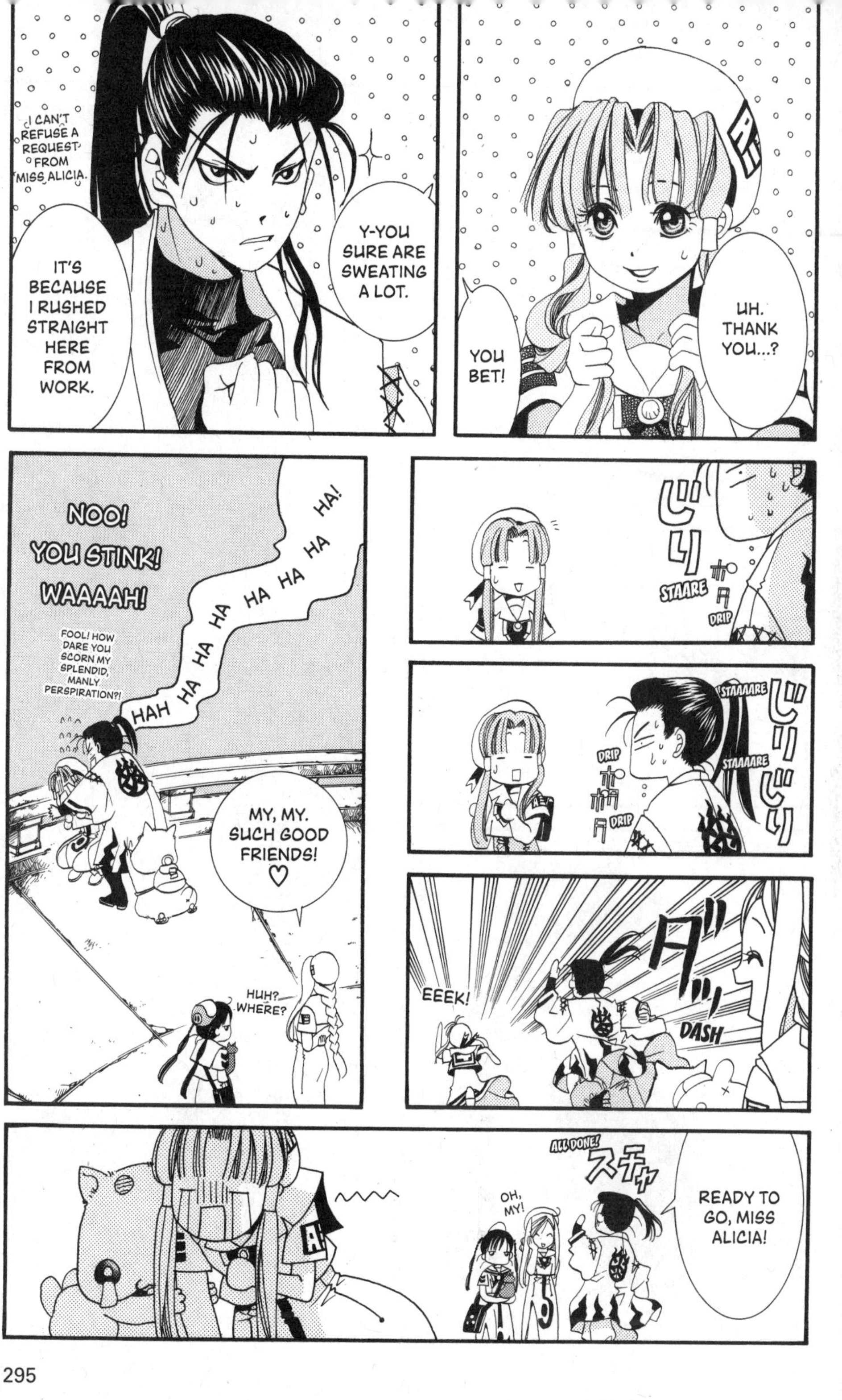
UH. THANK YOU...?
YOU BET!
Y-YOU SURE ARE SWEATING A LOT.
I CAN'T REFUSE A REQUEST FROM MISS ALICIA.
IT'S BECAUSE I RUSHED STRAIGHT HERE FROM WORK.
じり
STAARE
DRIP
STAAAARE
STAAAARE
DRIP
DRIP
ダッ
DASH
EEEK!
HAH HA HA HA HA HA HA HA!
NOO! YOU STINK! WAAAAH!
FOOL! HOW DARE YOU SCORN MY SPLENDID, MANLY PERSPIRATION?!
MY, MY. SUCH GOOD FRIENDS! ♡
HUH? WHERE?
READY TO GO, MISS ALICIA!
ALL DONE!
スチャ
OH, MY!

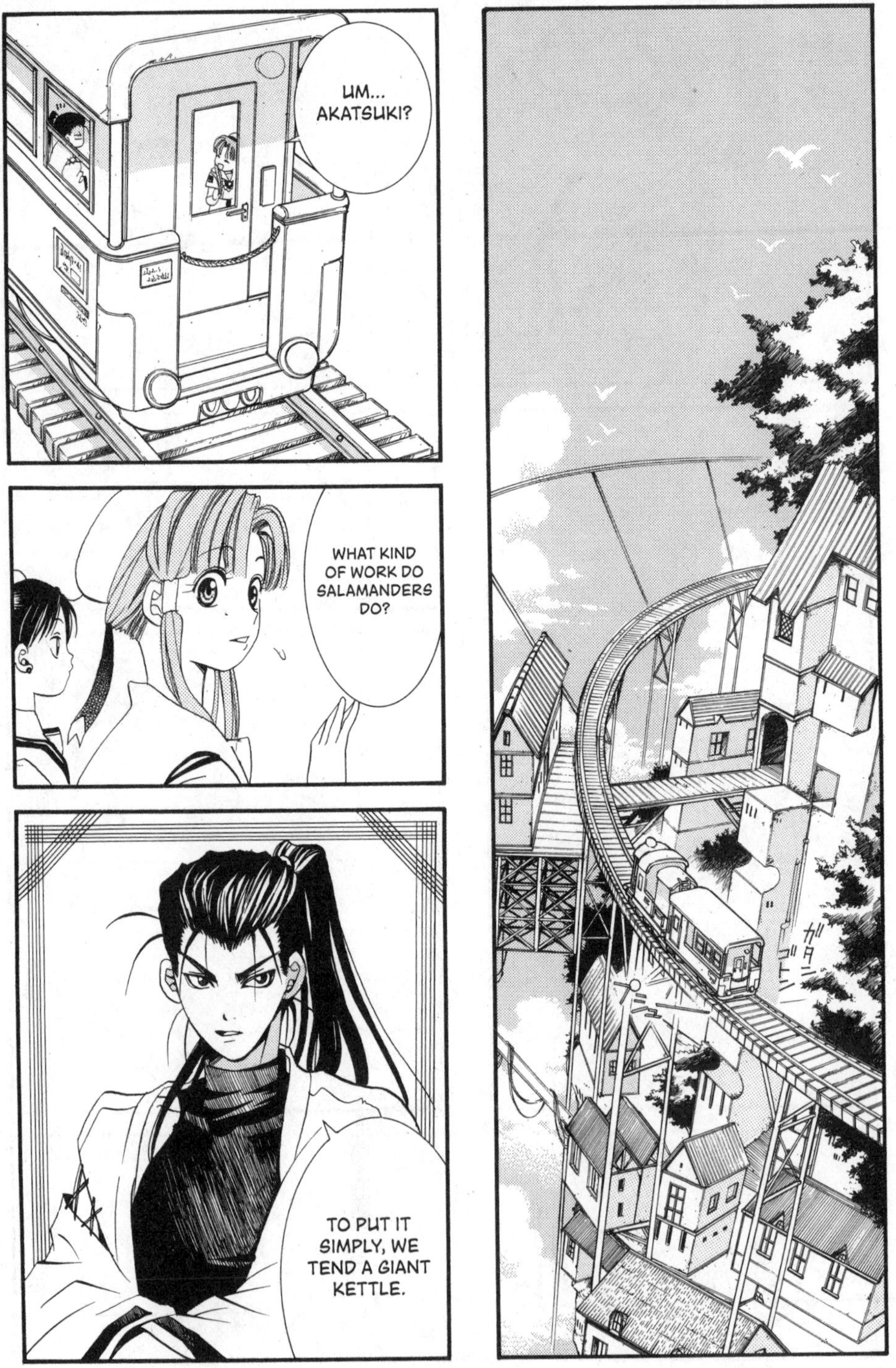
ガタン ゴトン
UM... AKATSUKI?
WHAT KIND OF WORK DO SALAMANDERS DO?
TO PUT IT SIMPLY, WE TEND A GIANT KETTLE.

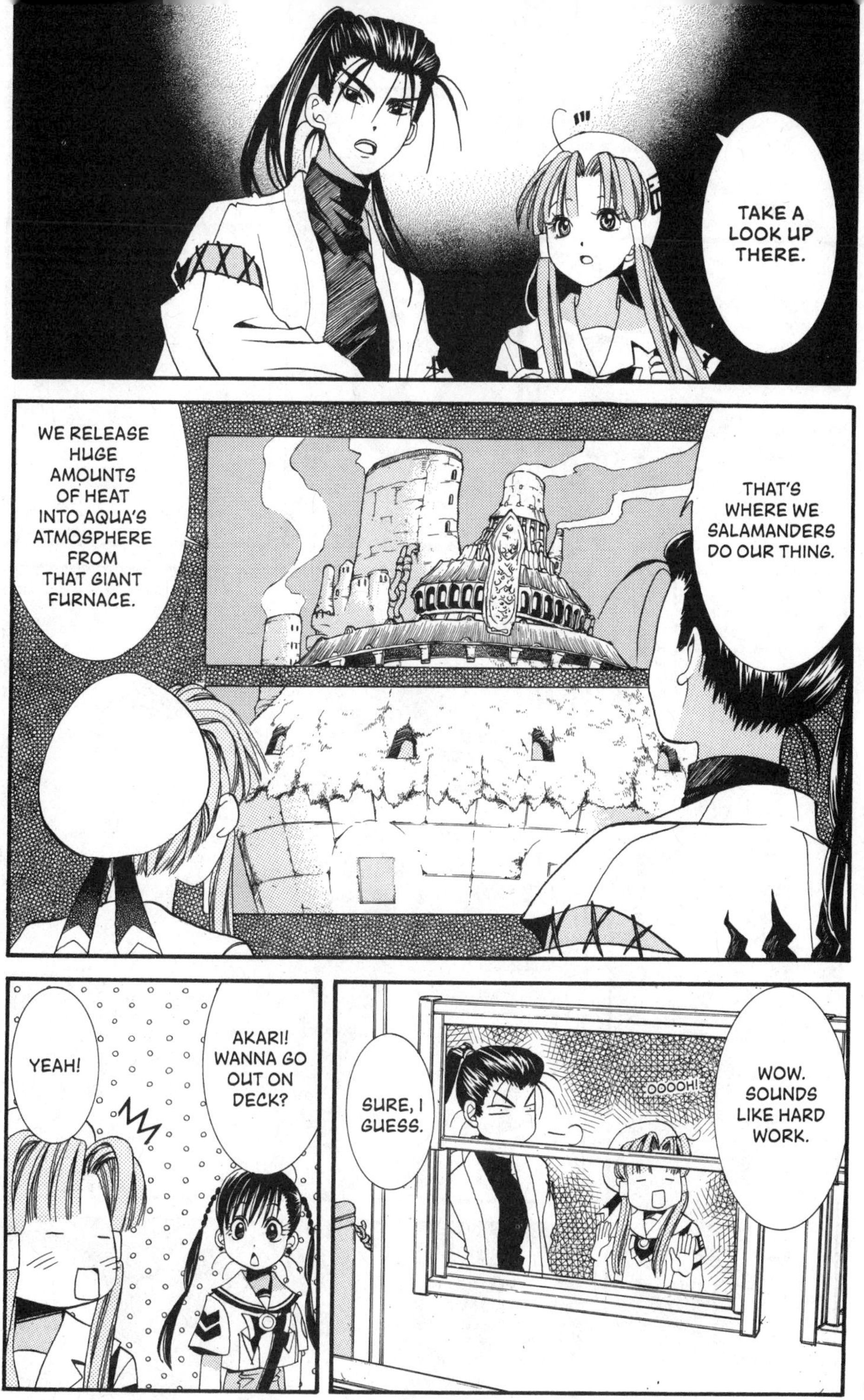
TAKE A LOOK UP THERE.
THAT'S WHERE WE SALAMANDERS DO OUR THING.
WE RELEASE HUGE AMOUNTS OF HEAT INTO AQUA'S ATMOSPHERE FROM THAT GIANT FURNACE.
WOW. SOUNDS LIKE HARD WORK.
OOOOH!
SURE, I GUESS.
AKARI! WANNA GO OUT ON DECK?
YEAH!

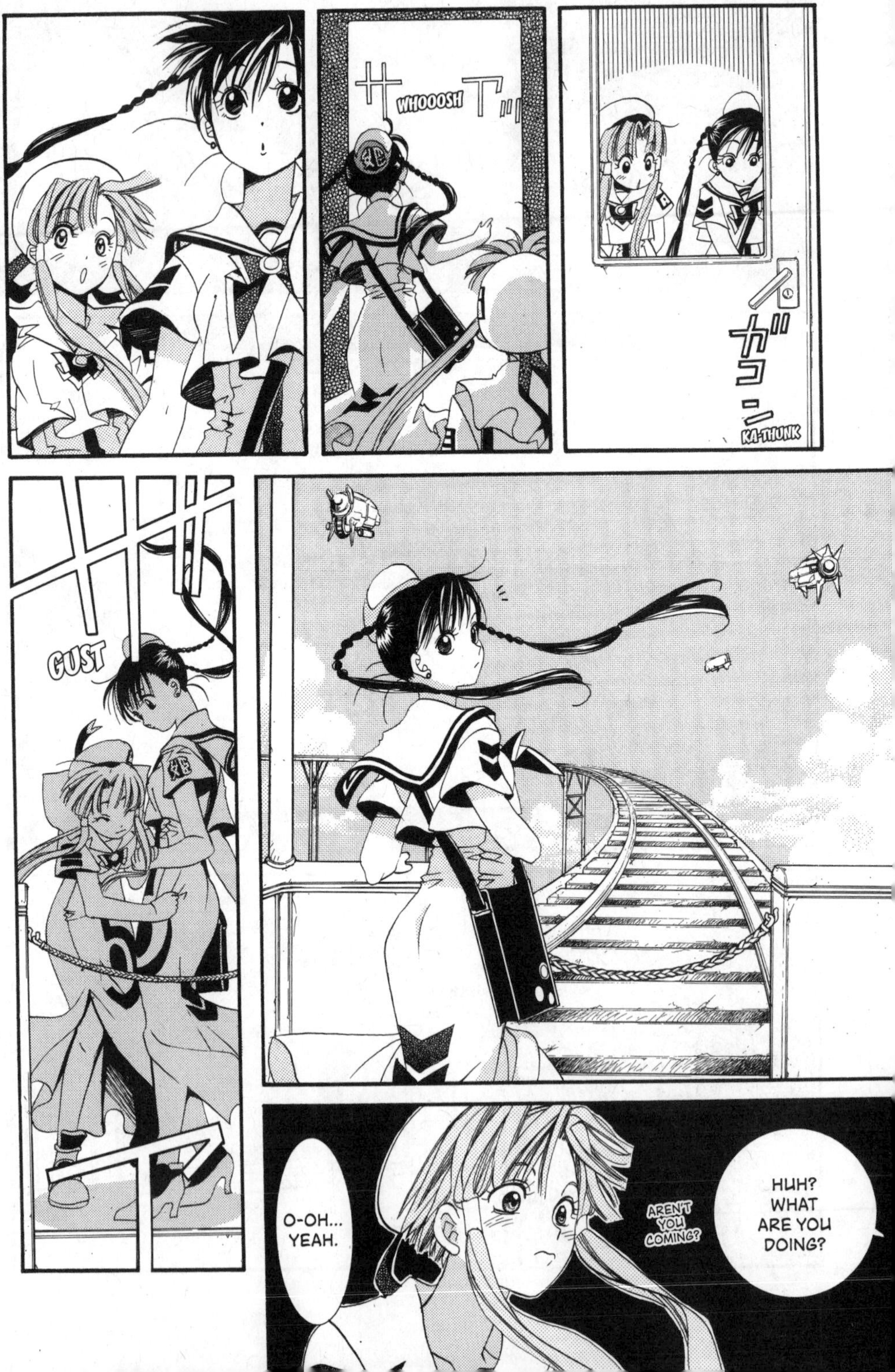
KA-THUNK
WHOOOSH
GUST
HUH? WHAT ARE YOU DOING?
AREN'T YOU COMING?
O-OH... YEAH.

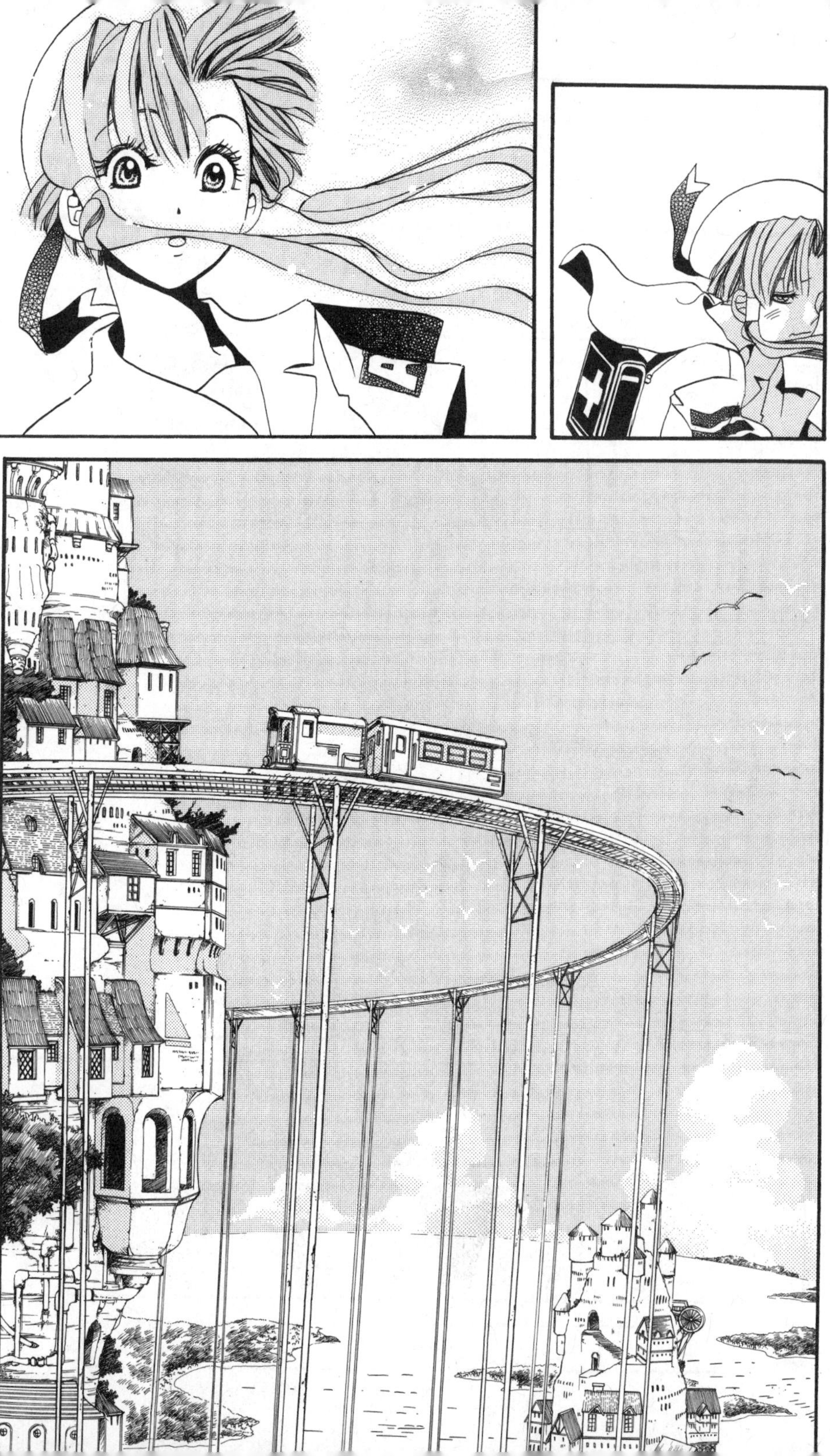

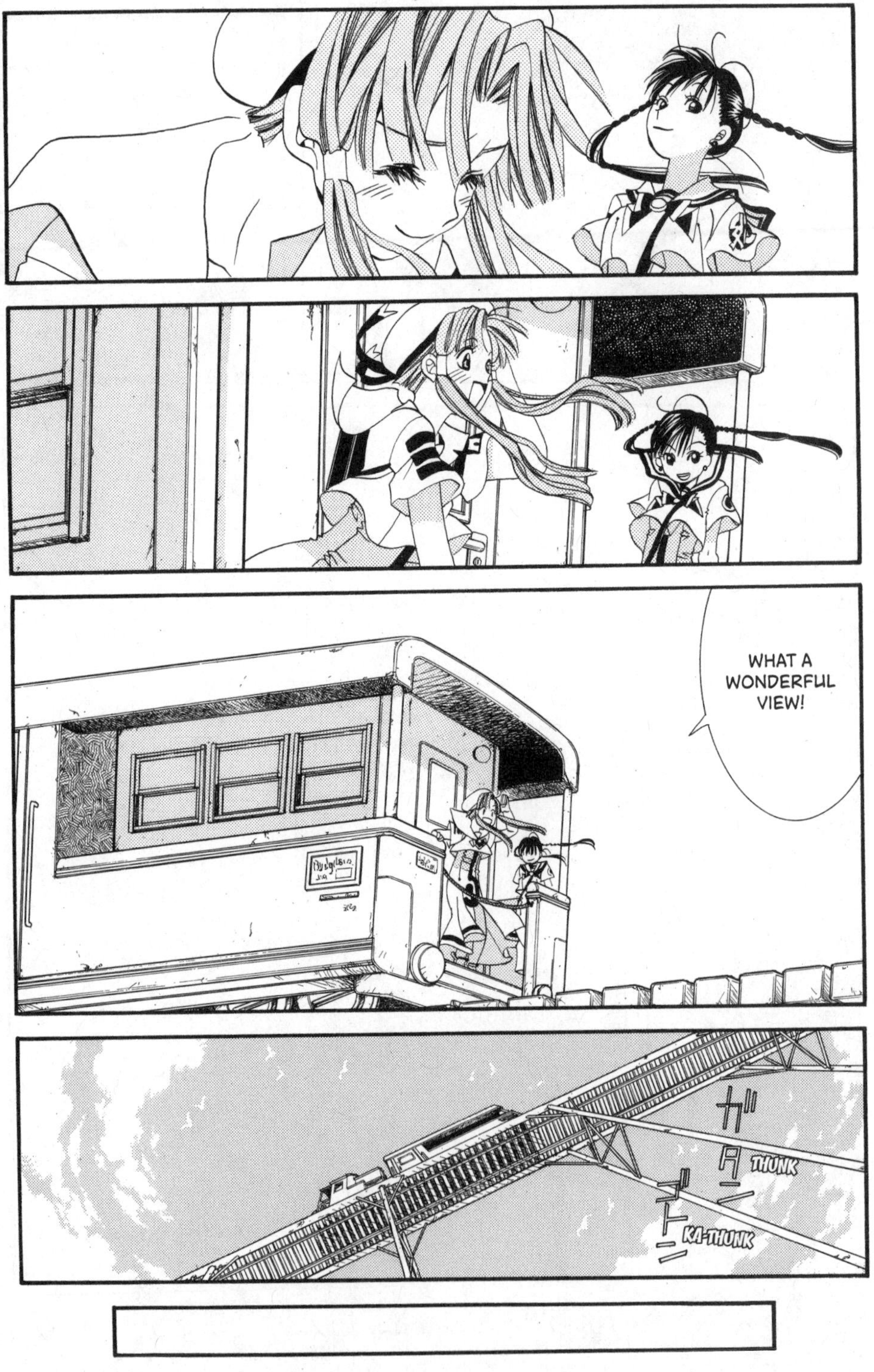
WHAT A WONDERFUL VIEW!
THUNK
KA-THUNK

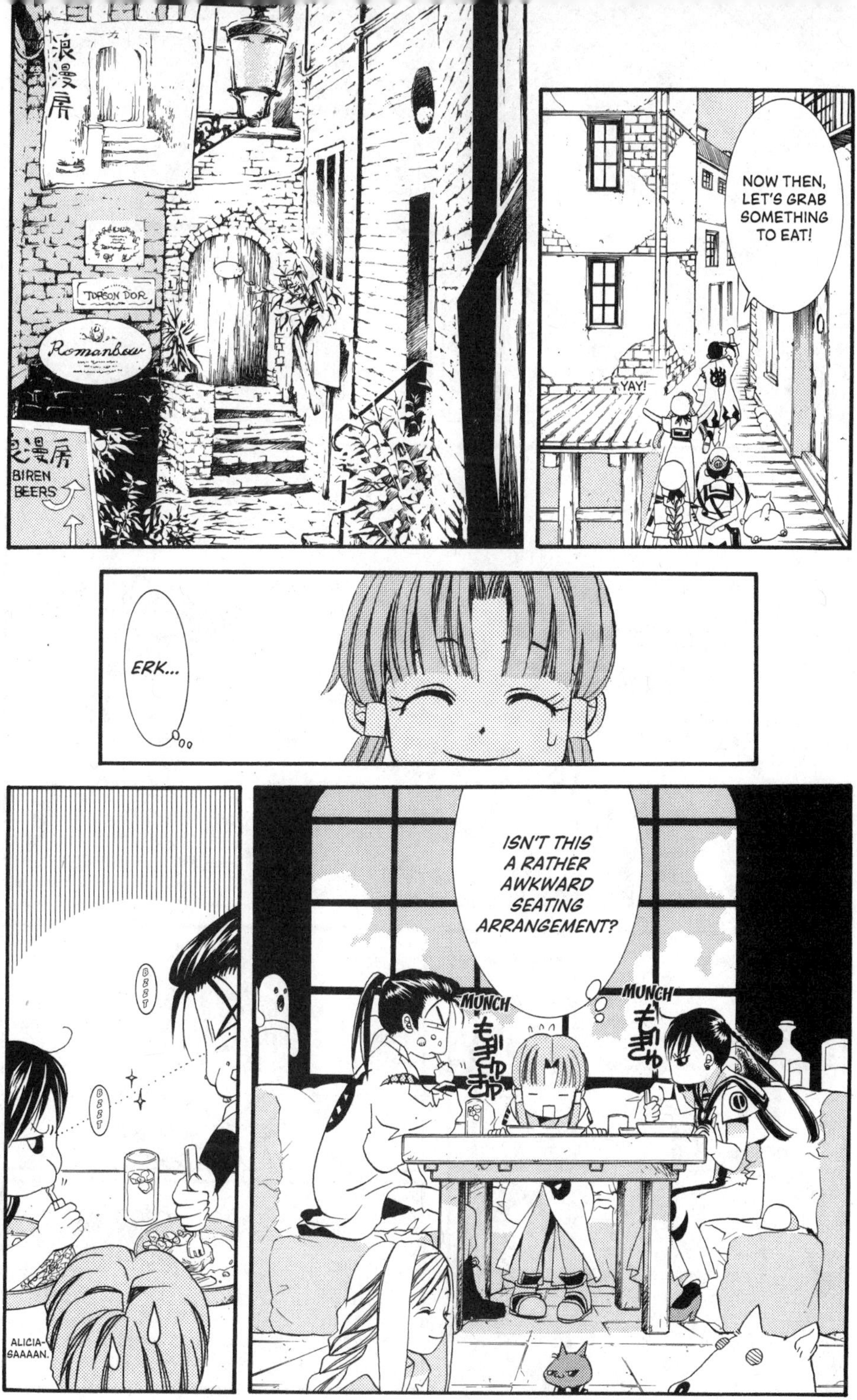
NOW THEN, LET'S GRAB SOMETHING TO EAT!
YAY!
浪漫房
TOISON DOR
Romanbow
浪漫房
BIREN BEERS
ERK...
ISN'T THIS A RATHER AWKWARD SEATING ARRANGEMENT?
MUNCH
もぎゅ
MUNCH
もぎゅもぎゅ
BZZT
BZZT
ALICIA-SAAAAN.

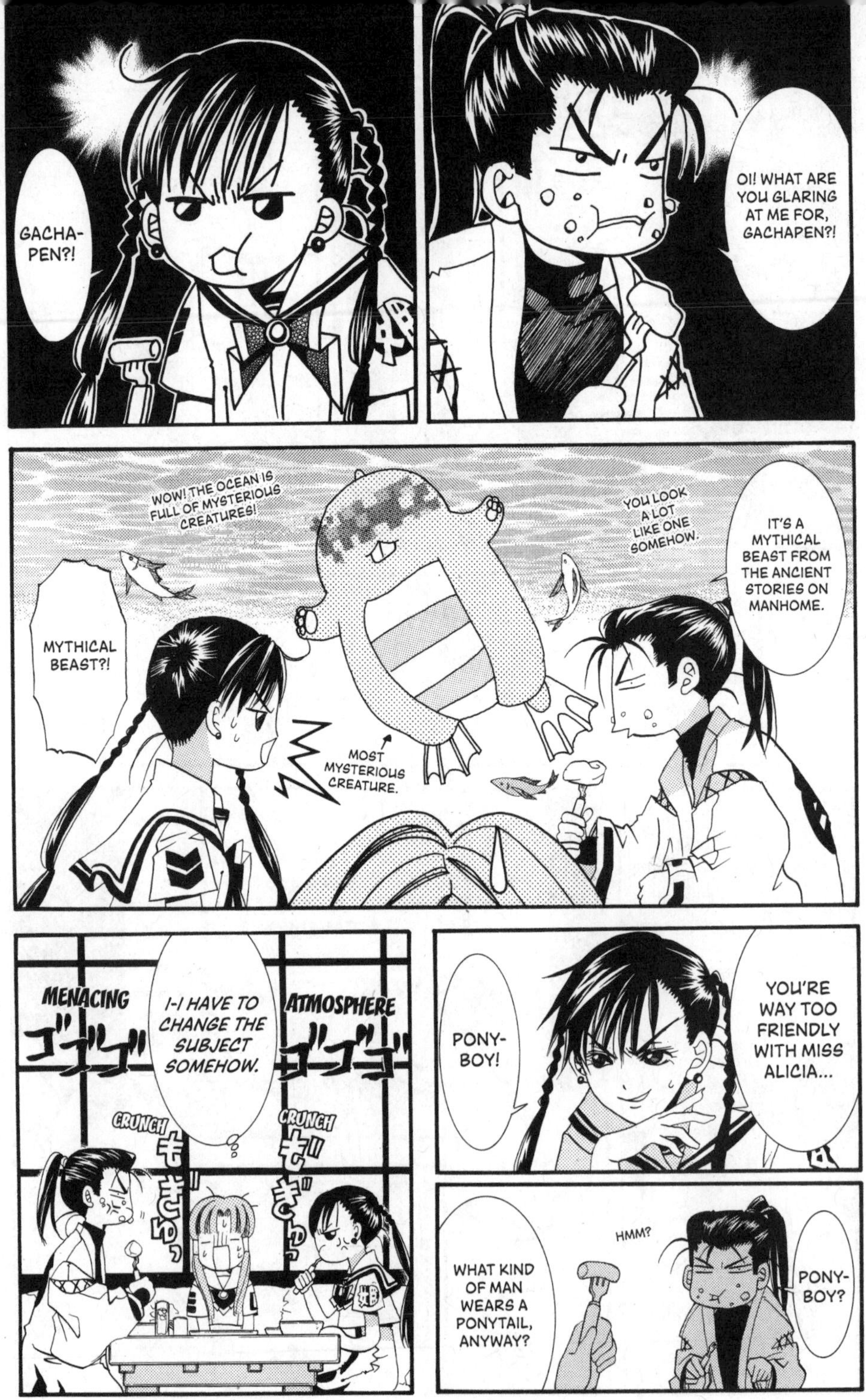
OI! WHAT ARE YOU GLARING AT ME FOR, GACHAPEN?!
GACHA-PEN?!
IT'S A MYTHICAL BEAST FROM THE ANCIENT STORIES ON MANHOME.
YOU LOOK A LOT LIKE ONE SOMEHOW.
WOW! THE OCEAN IS FULL OF MYSTERIOUS CREATURES!
MYTHICAL BEAST?!
MOST MYSTERIOUS CREATURE.
YOU'RE WAY TOO FRIENDLY WITH MISS ALICIA...
PONY-BOY!
PONY-BOY?
HMM?
WHAT KIND OF MAN WEARS A PONYTAIL, ANYWAY?
ATMOSPHERE
ゴゴゴ
I-I HAVE TO CHANGE THE SUBJECT SOMEHOW.
MENACING
ゴゴゴ
CRUNCH
もぎゅっ
CRUNCH
もぎゅっ

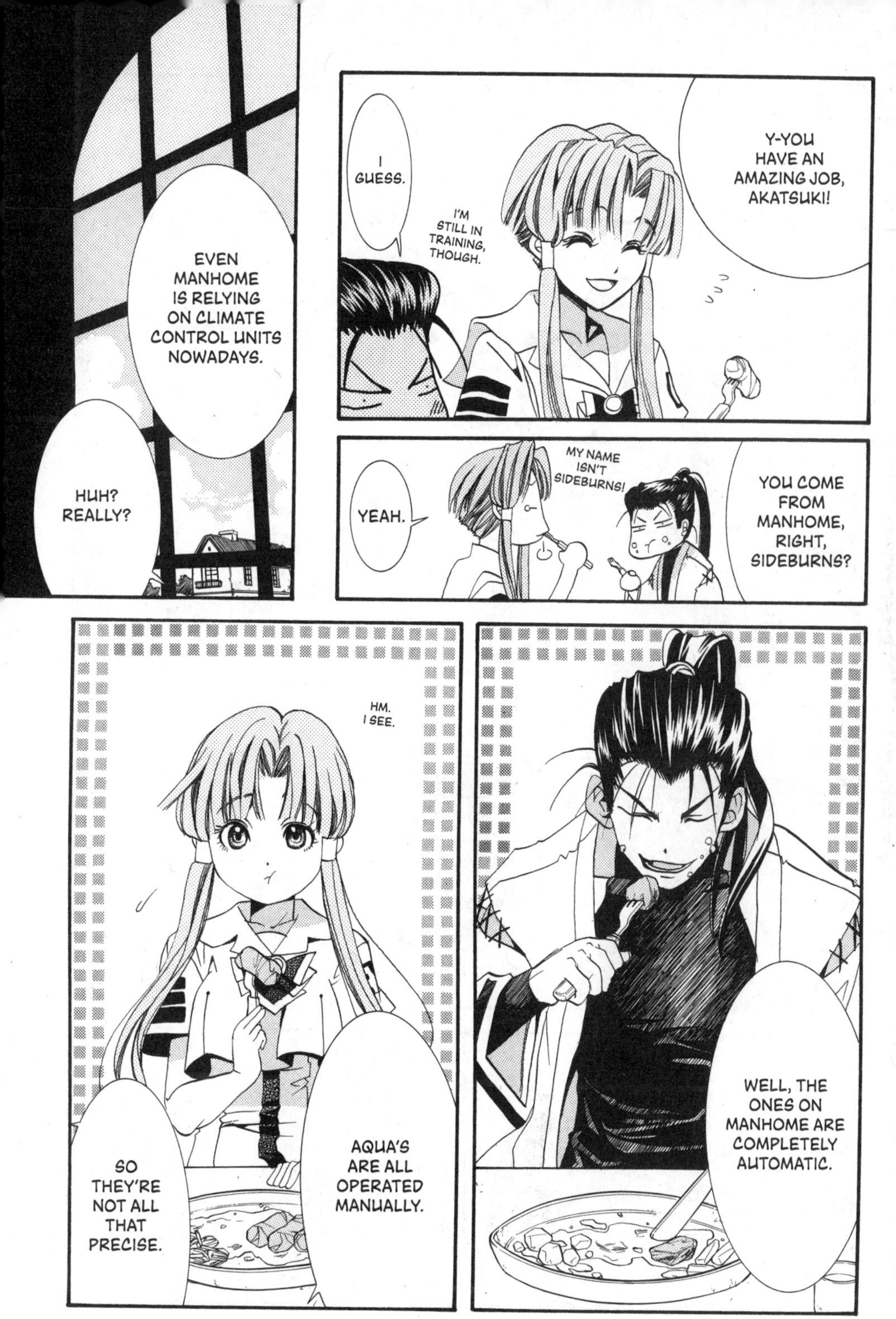
Y-YOU HAVE AN AMAZING JOB, AKATSUKI!
I GUESS.
I'M STILL IN TRAINING, THOUGH.
YOU COME FROM MANHOME, RIGHT, SIDEBURNS?
MY NAME ISN'T SIDEBURNS!
YEAH.
EVEN MANHOME IS RELYING ON CLIMATE CONTROL UNITS NOWADAYS.
HUH? REALLY?
WELL, THE ONES ON MANHOME ARE COMPLETELY AUTOMATIC.
HM. I SEE.
AQUA'S ARE ALL OPERATED MANUALLY.
SO THEY'RE NOT ALL THAT PRECISE.

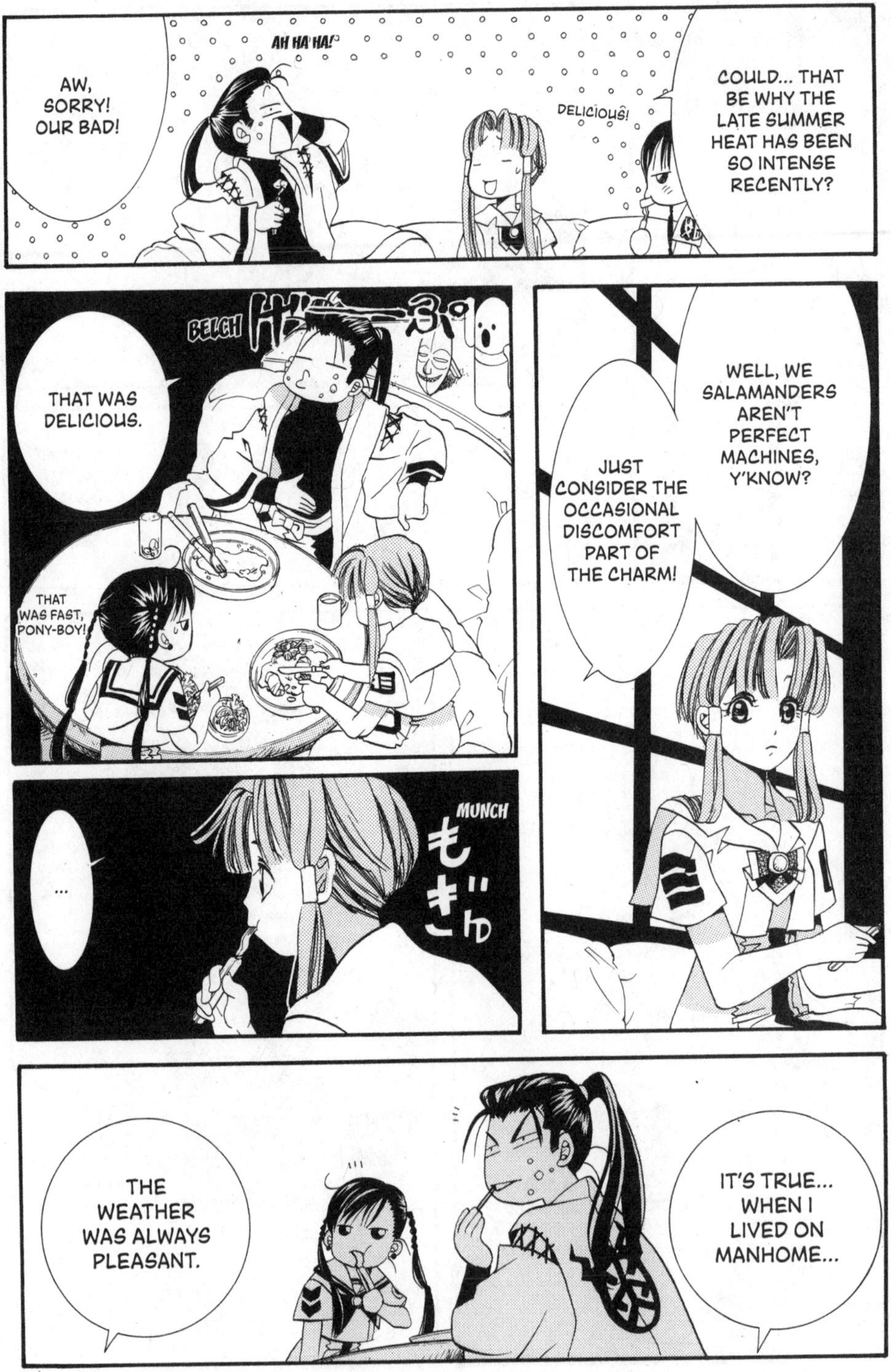
COULD... THAT BE WHY THE LATE SUMMER HEAT HAS BEEN SO INTENSE RECENTLY?
DELICIOUS!
AH HA HA!
AW, SORRY! OUR BAD!
WELL, WE SALAMANDERS AREN'T PERFECT MACHINES, Y'KNOW?
JUST CONSIDER THE OCCASIONAL DISCOMFORT PART OF THE CHARM!
BELCH
THAT WAS DELICIOUS.
THAT WAS FAST, PONY-BOY!
MUNCH
もぎゅ
...
IT'S TRUE... WHEN I LIVED ON MANHOME...
THE WEATHER WAS ALWAYS PLEASANT.

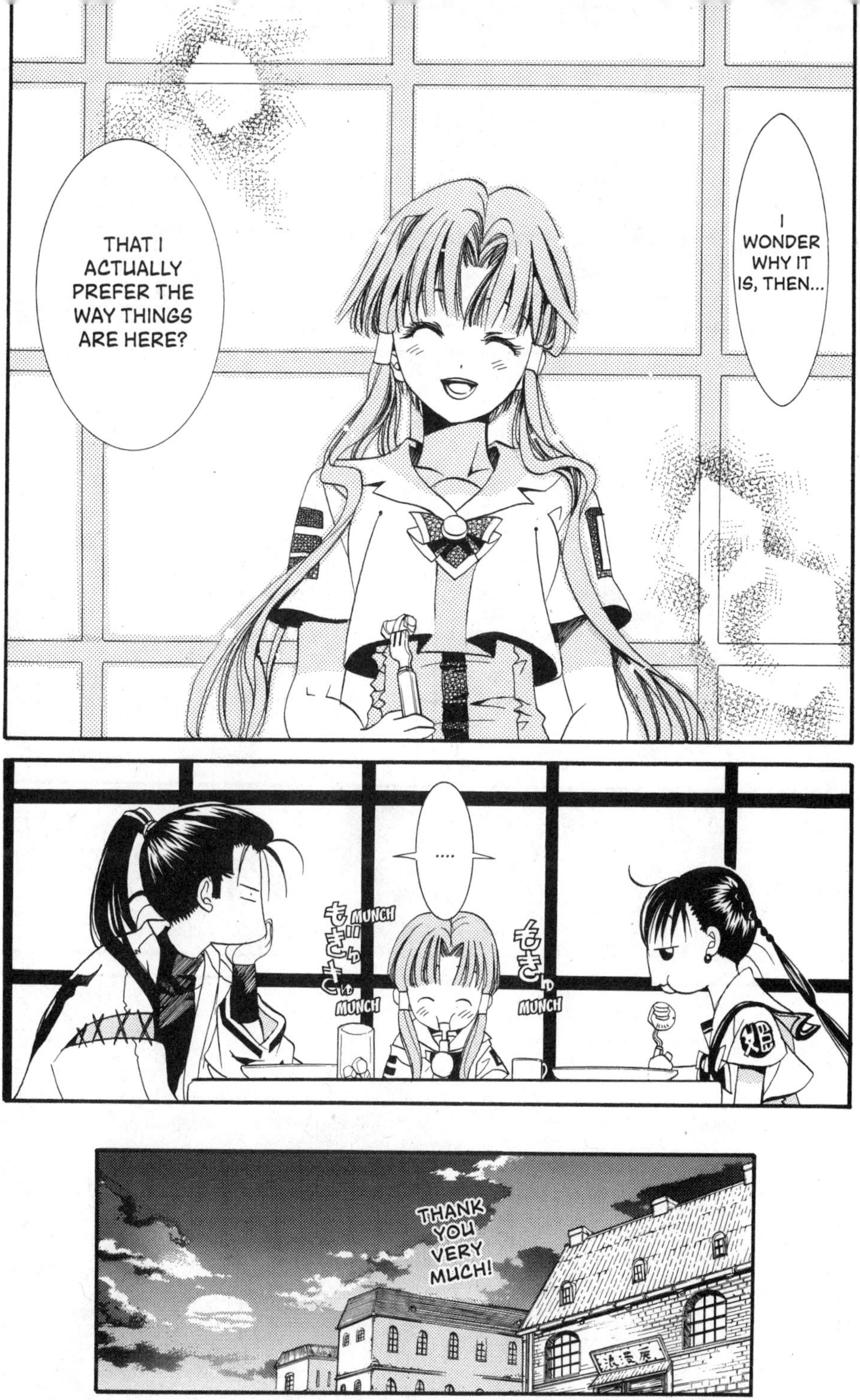
I WONDER WHY IT IS, THEN...
THAT I ACTUALLY PREFER THE WAY THINGS ARE HERE?
....
MUNCH
MUNCH
MUNCH
THANK YOU VERY MUCH!

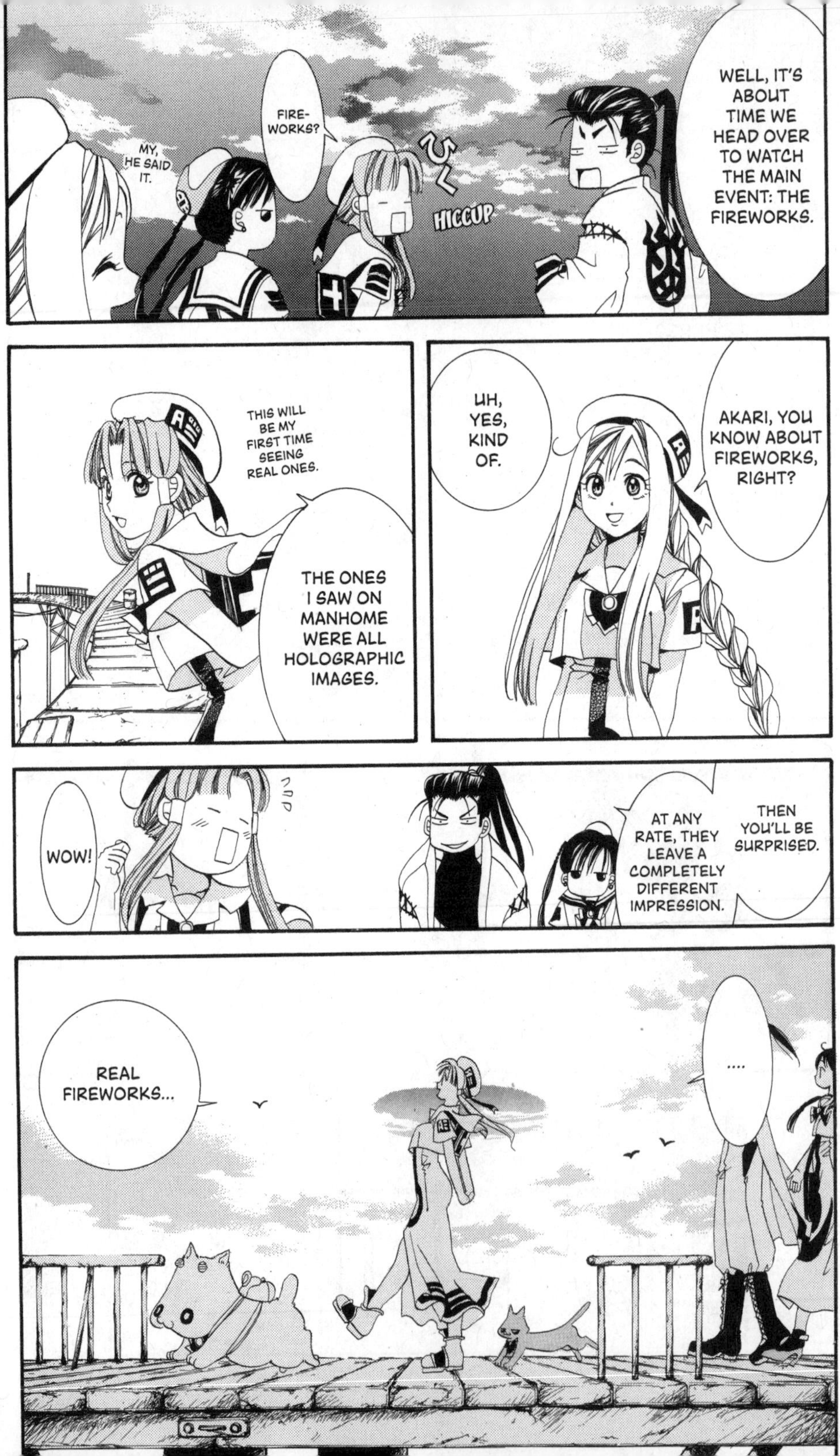
WELL, IT'S ABOUT TIME WE HEAD OVER TO WATCH THE MAIN EVENT: THE FIREWORKS.
FIRE-WORKS?
HICCUP
MY, HE SAID IT.
AKARI, YOU KNOW ABOUT FIREWORKS, RIGHT?
UH, YES, KIND OF.
THIS WILL BE MY FIRST TIME SEEING REAL ONES.
THE ONES I SAW ON MANHOME WERE ALL HOLOGRAPHIC IMAGES.
THEN YOU'LL BE SURPRISED.
AT ANY RATE, THEY LEAVE A COMPLETELY DIFFERENT IMPRESSION.
WOW!
....
REAL FIREWORKS...

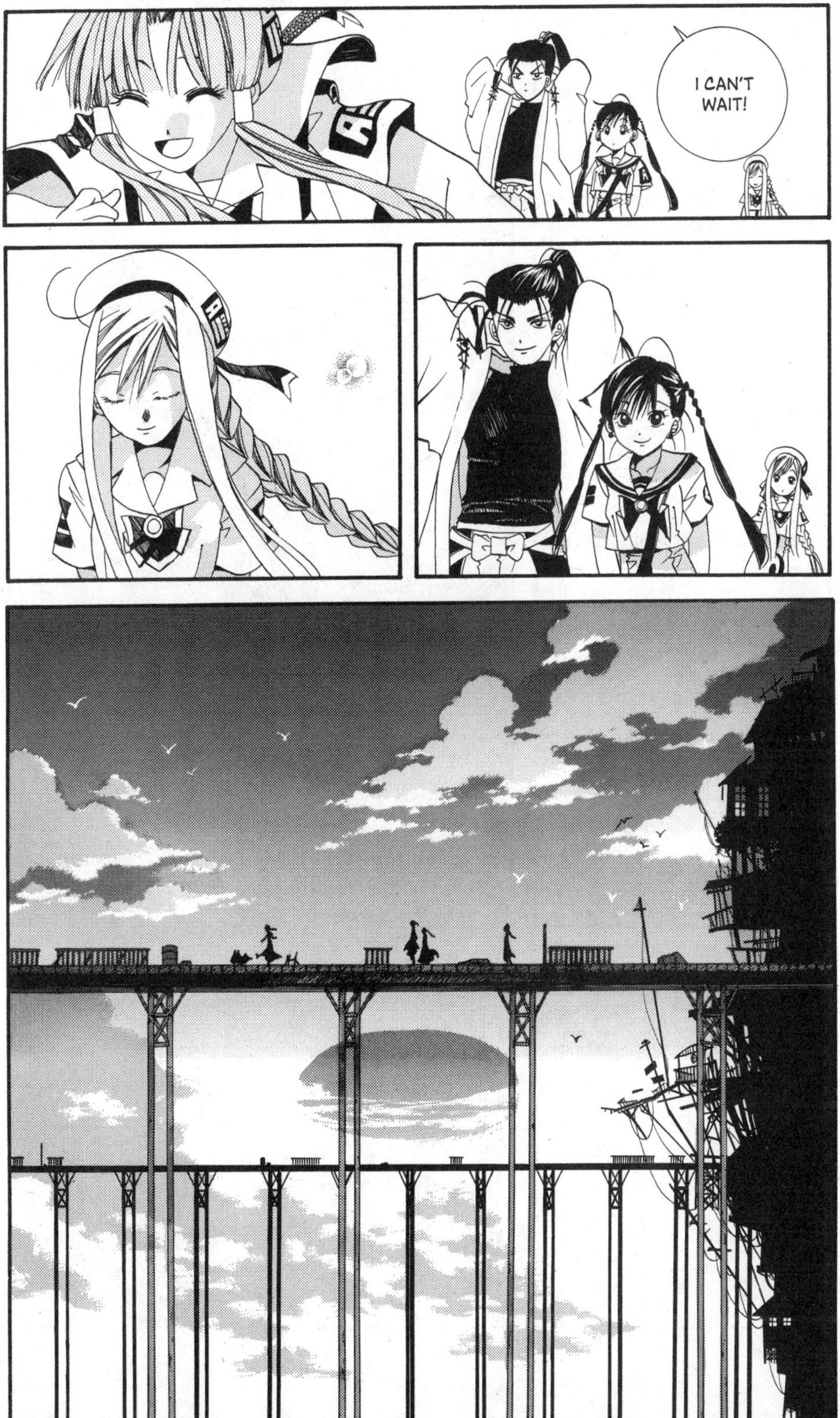
I CAN'T
WAIT!

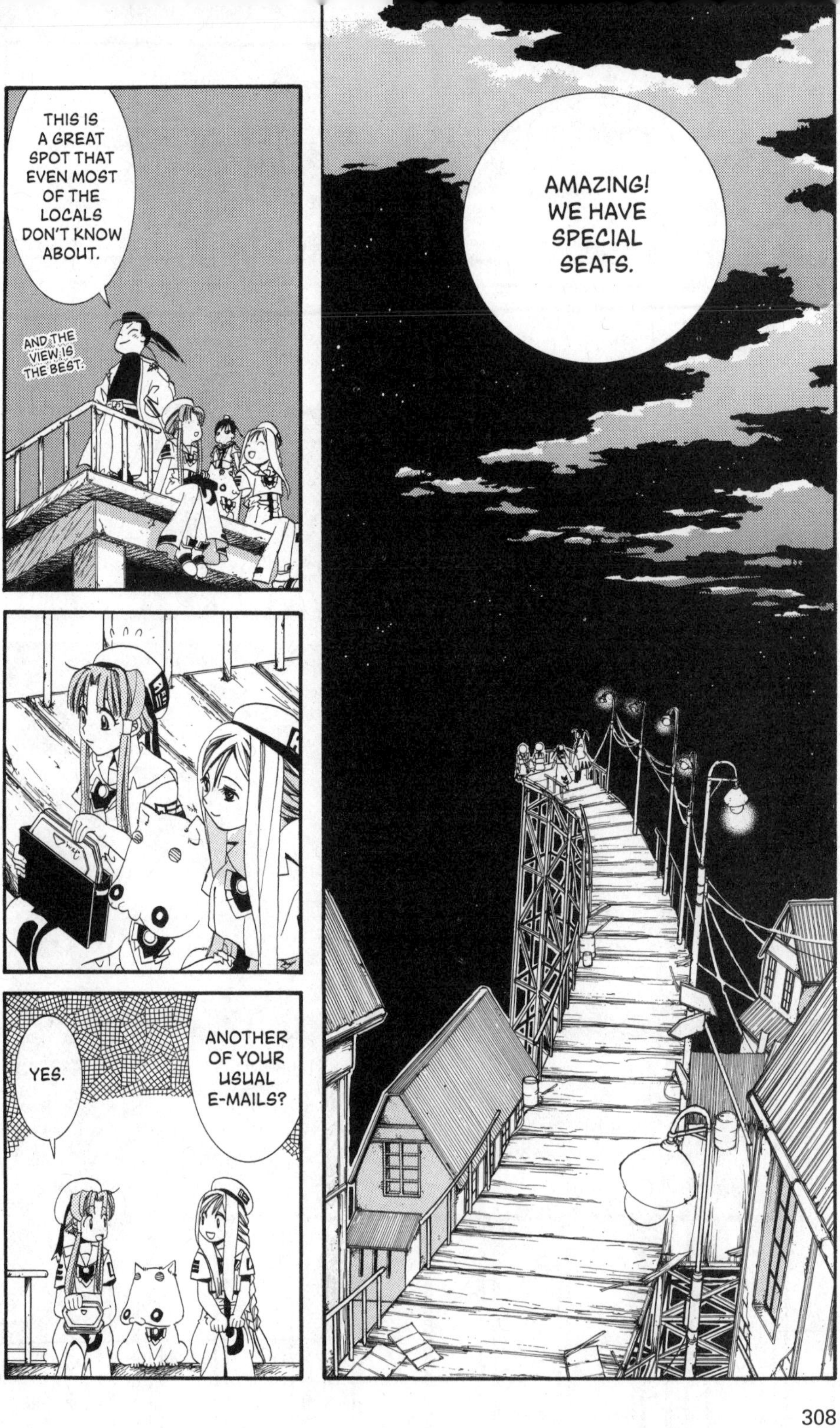
AMAZING! WE HAVE SPECIAL SEATS.
THIS IS A GREAT SPOT THAT EVEN MOST OF THE LOCALS DON'T KNOW ABOUT.
AND THE VIEW IS THE BEST.
ANOTHER OF YOUR USUAL E-MAILS?
YES.

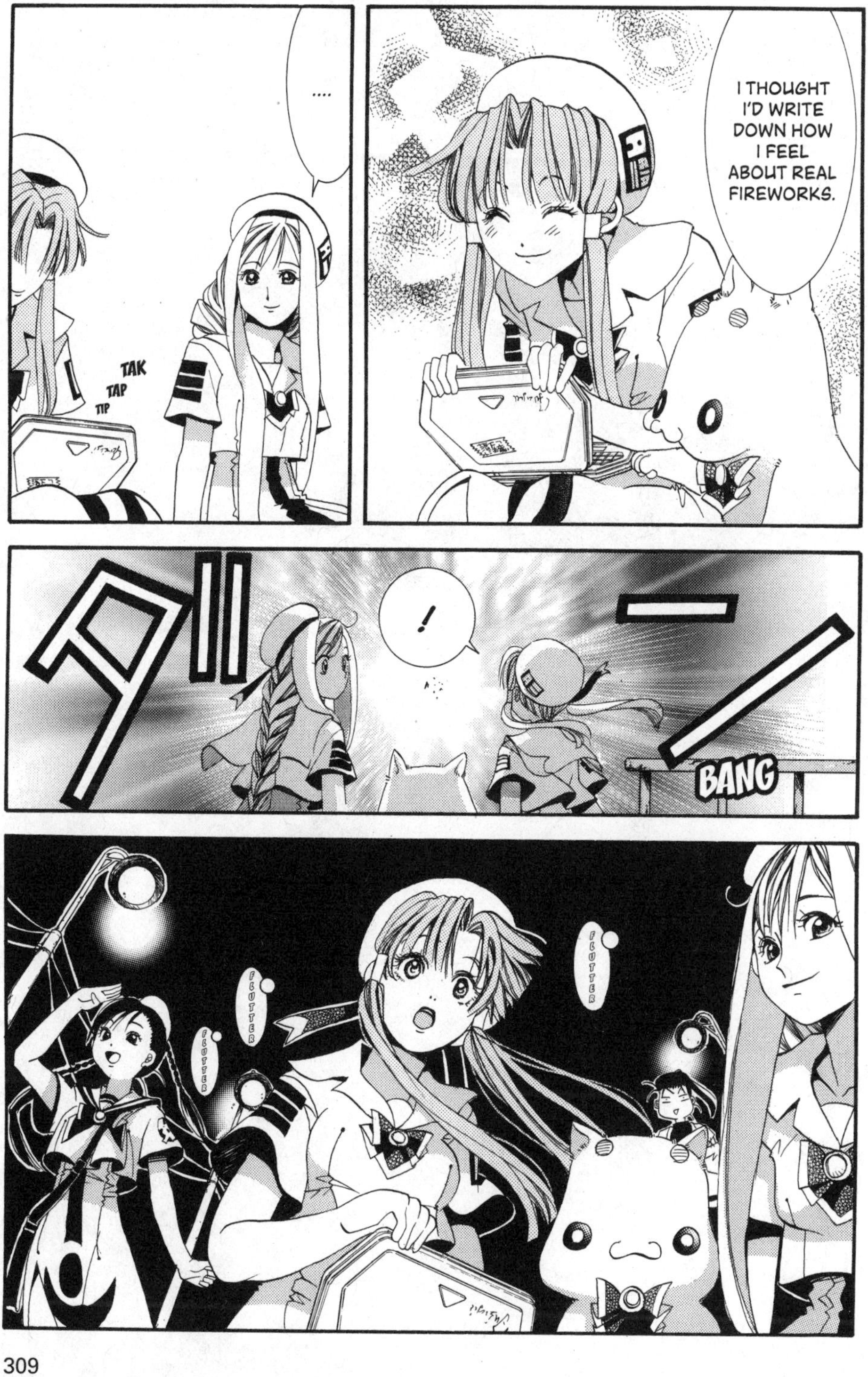
I THOUGHT I'D WRITE DOWN HOW I FEEL ABOUT REAL FIREWORKS.
....
TAK
TAP
TIP
!
BANG
FLUTTER
FLUTTER
FLUTTER

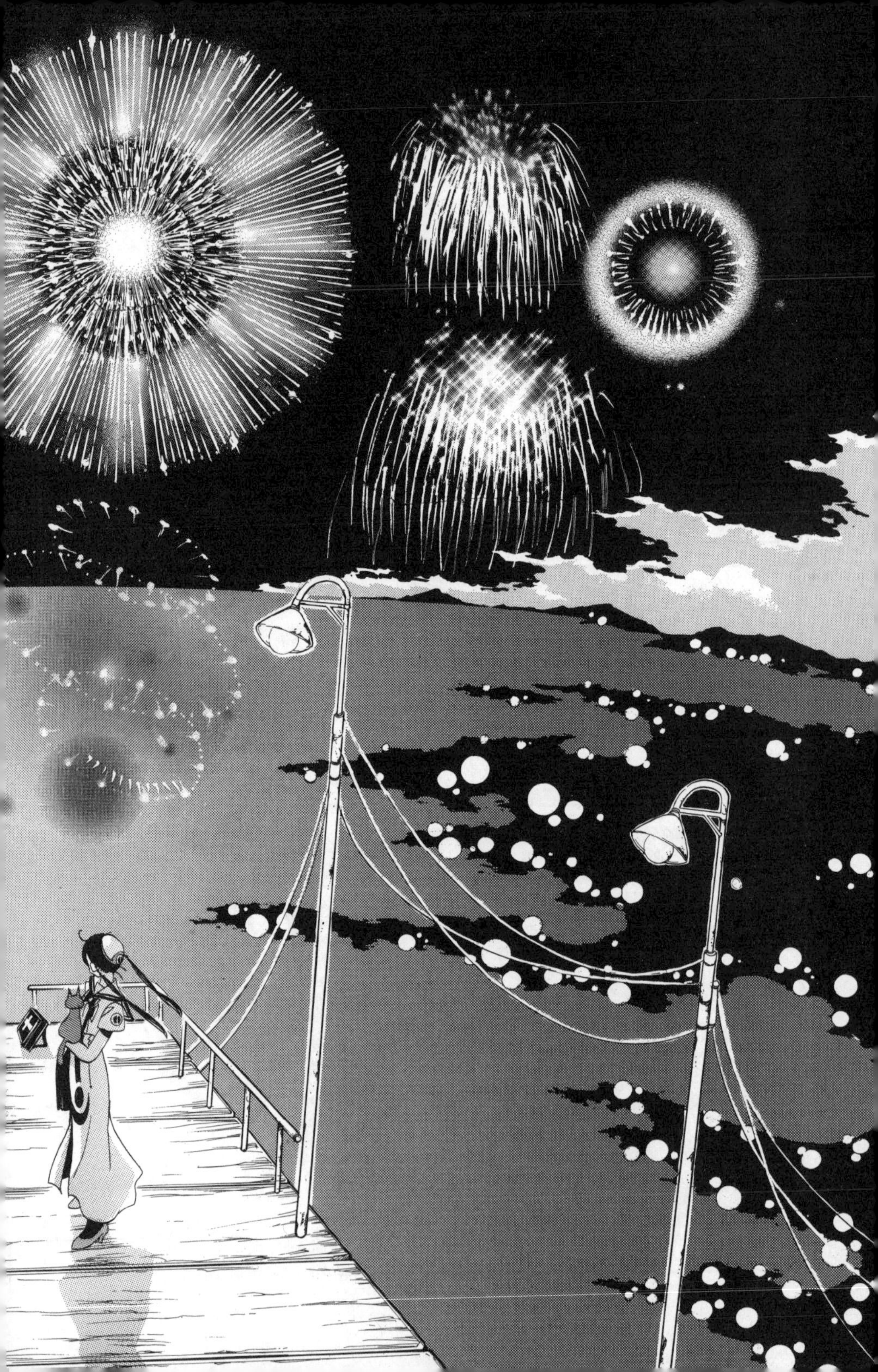

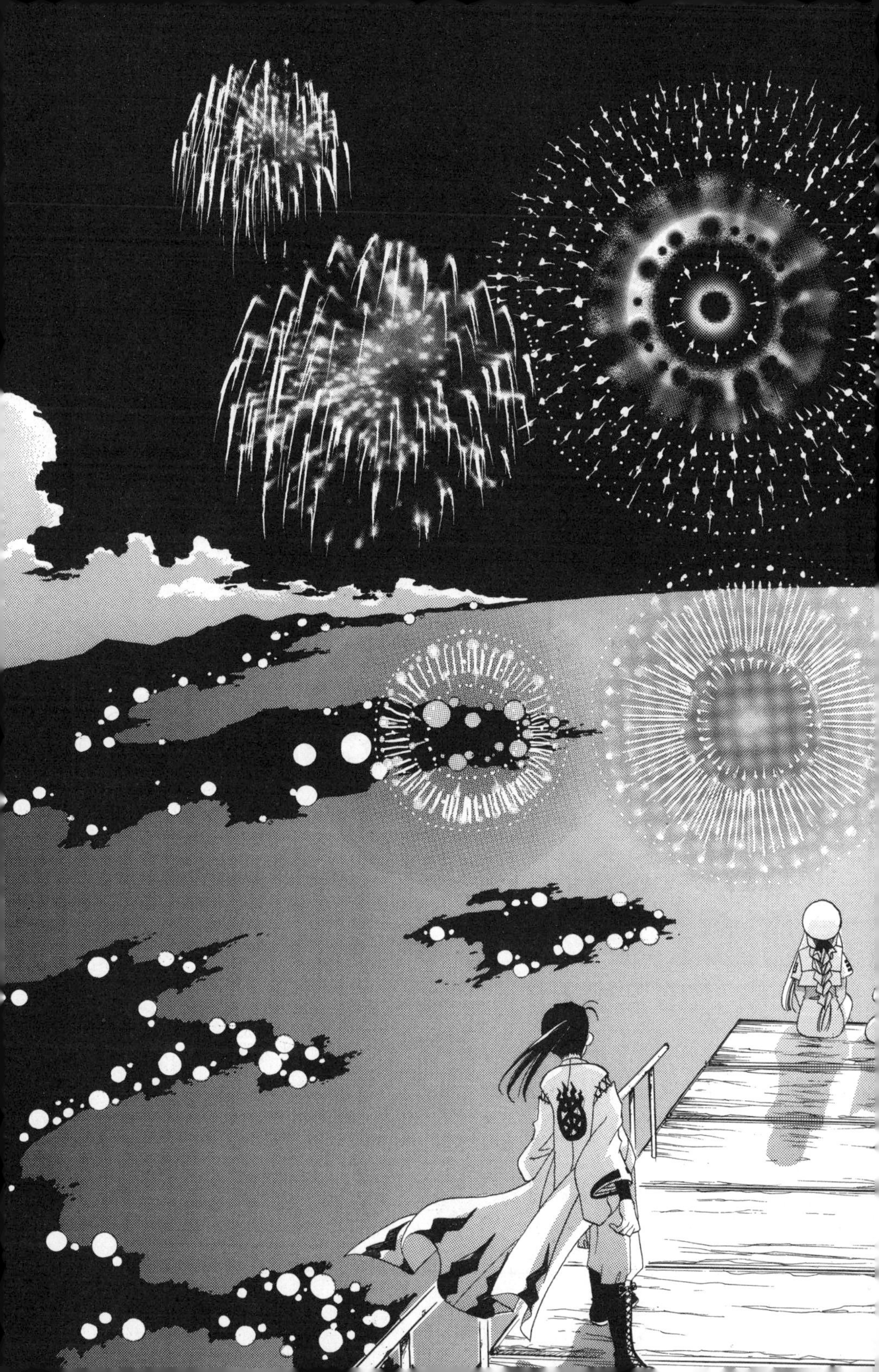

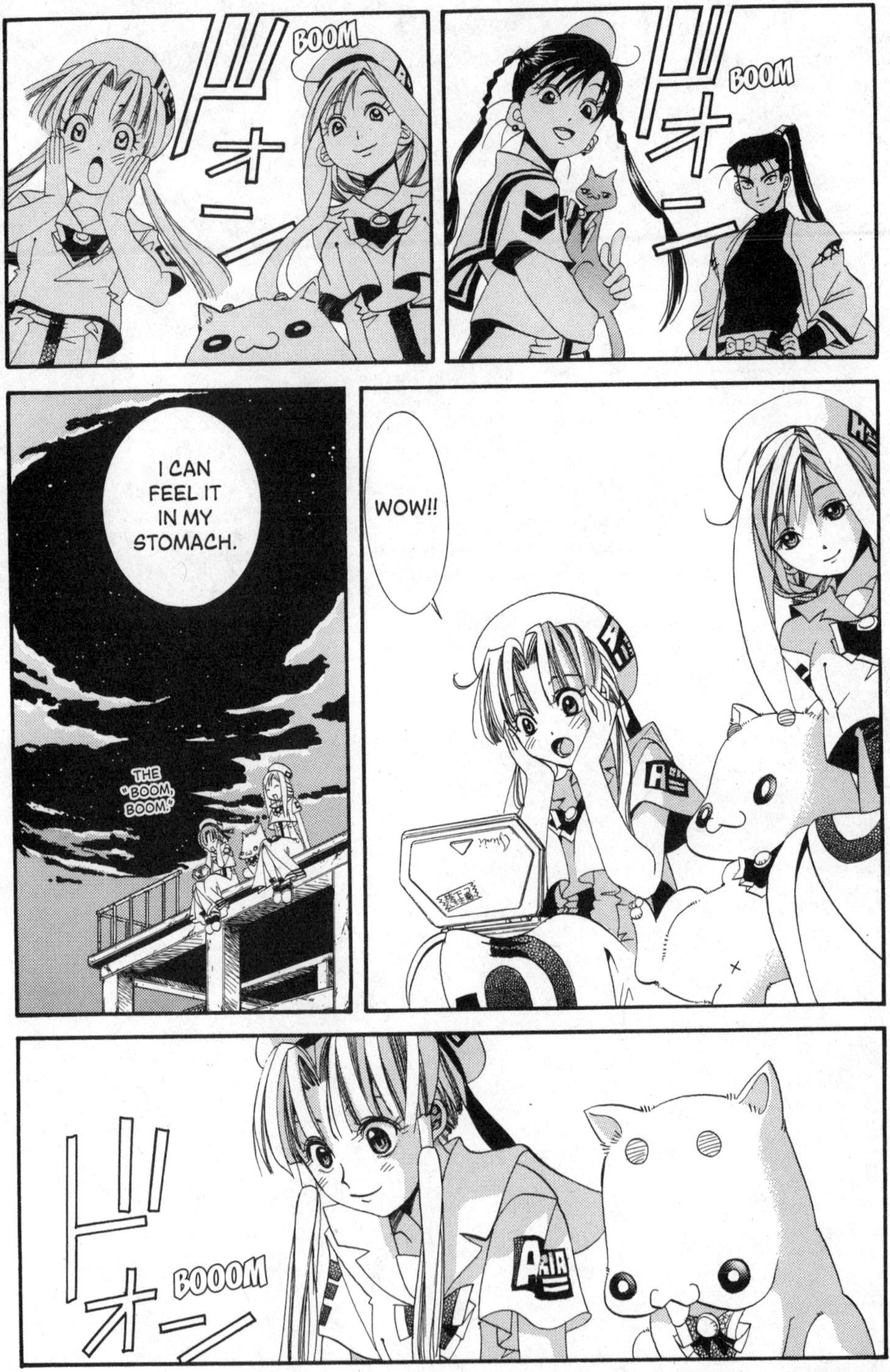
BOOM
BOOM
WOW!!
I CAN FEEL IT IN MY STOMACH.
THE "BOOM, BOOM."
BOOOM

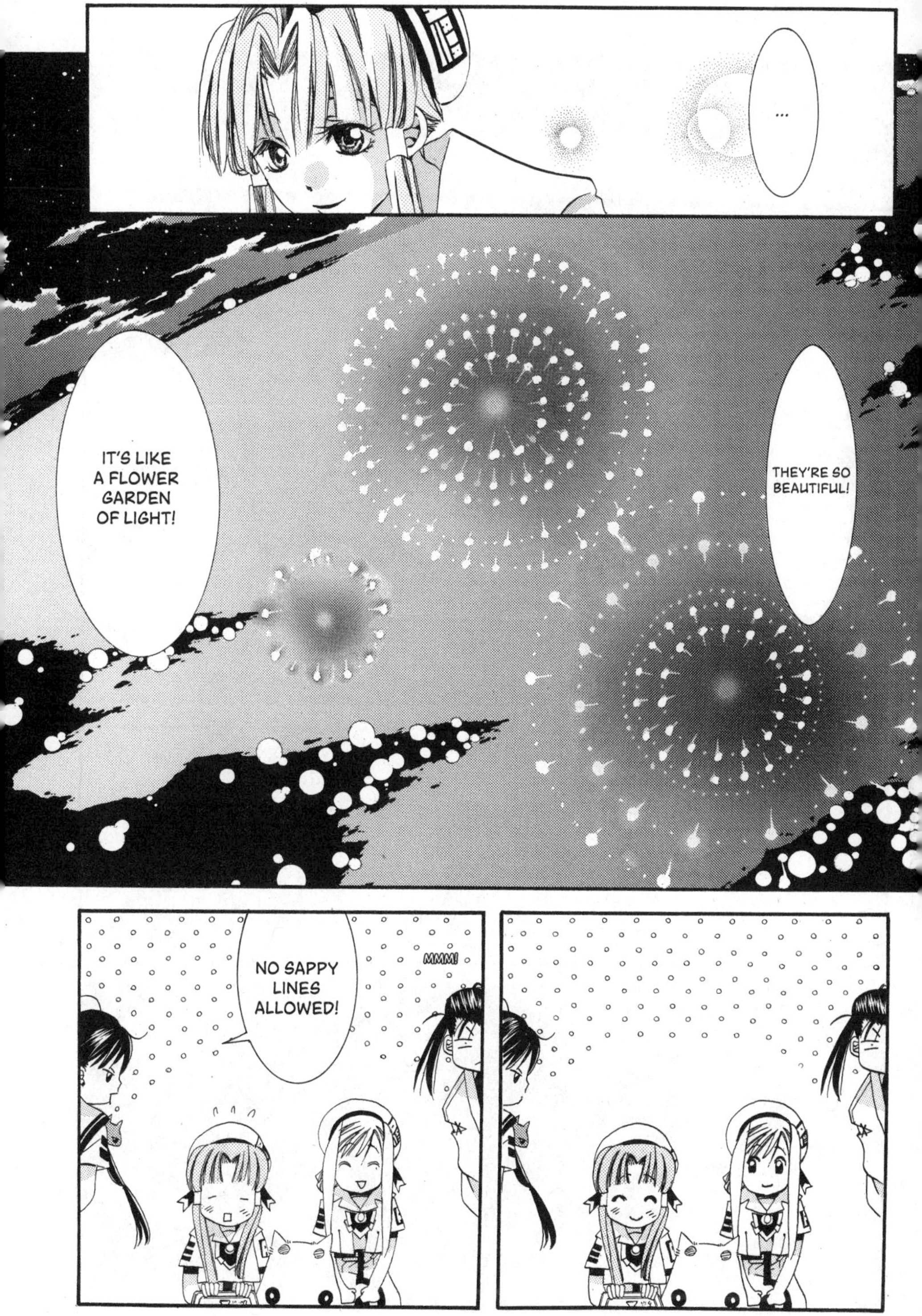
...
THEY'RE SO BEAUTIFUL!
IT'S LIKE A FLOWER GARDEN OF LIGHT!
MMM!
NO SAPPY LINES ALLOWED!

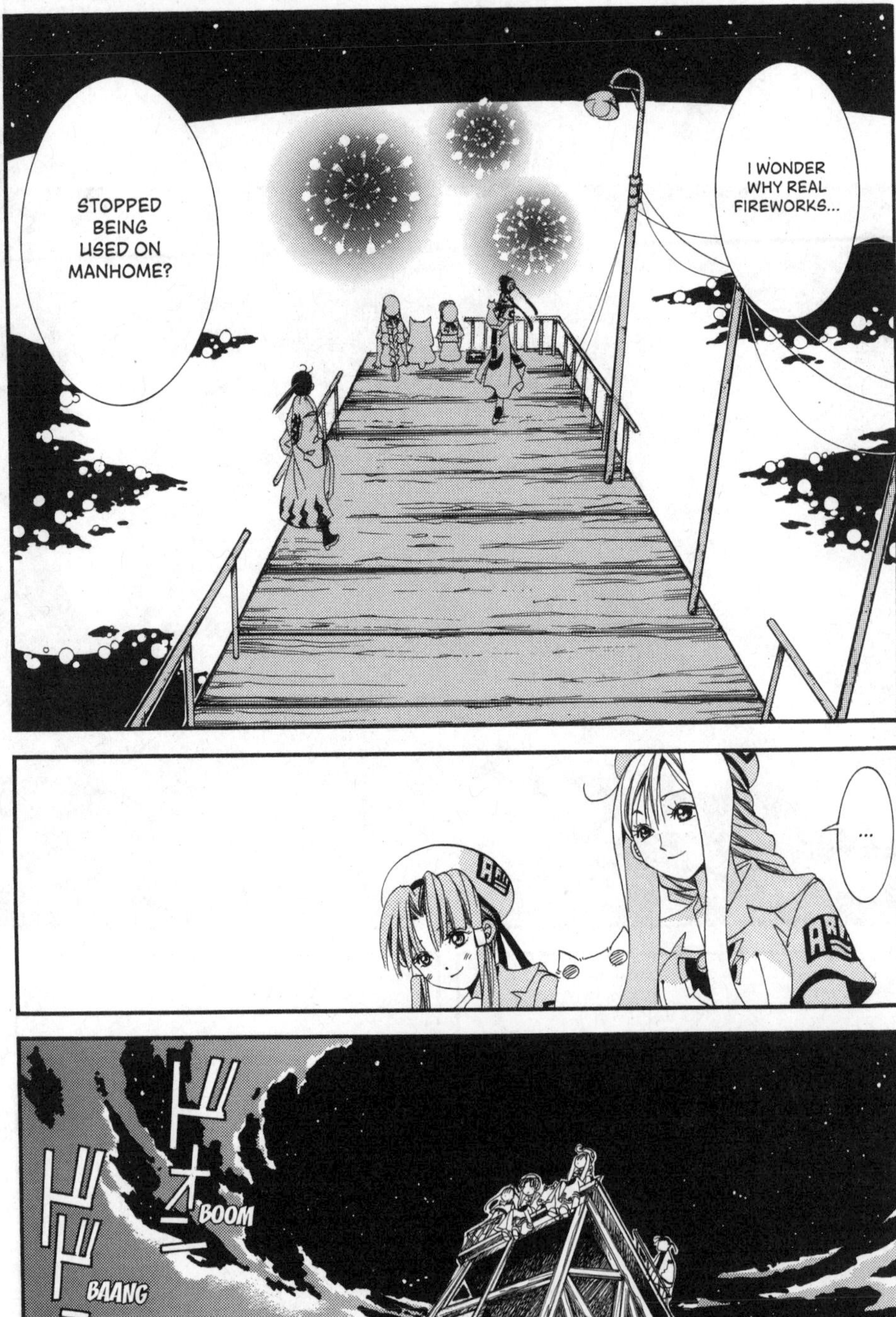
I WONDER WHY REAL FIREWORKS...
STOPPED BEING USED ON MANHOME?
...
BOOM
BAANG

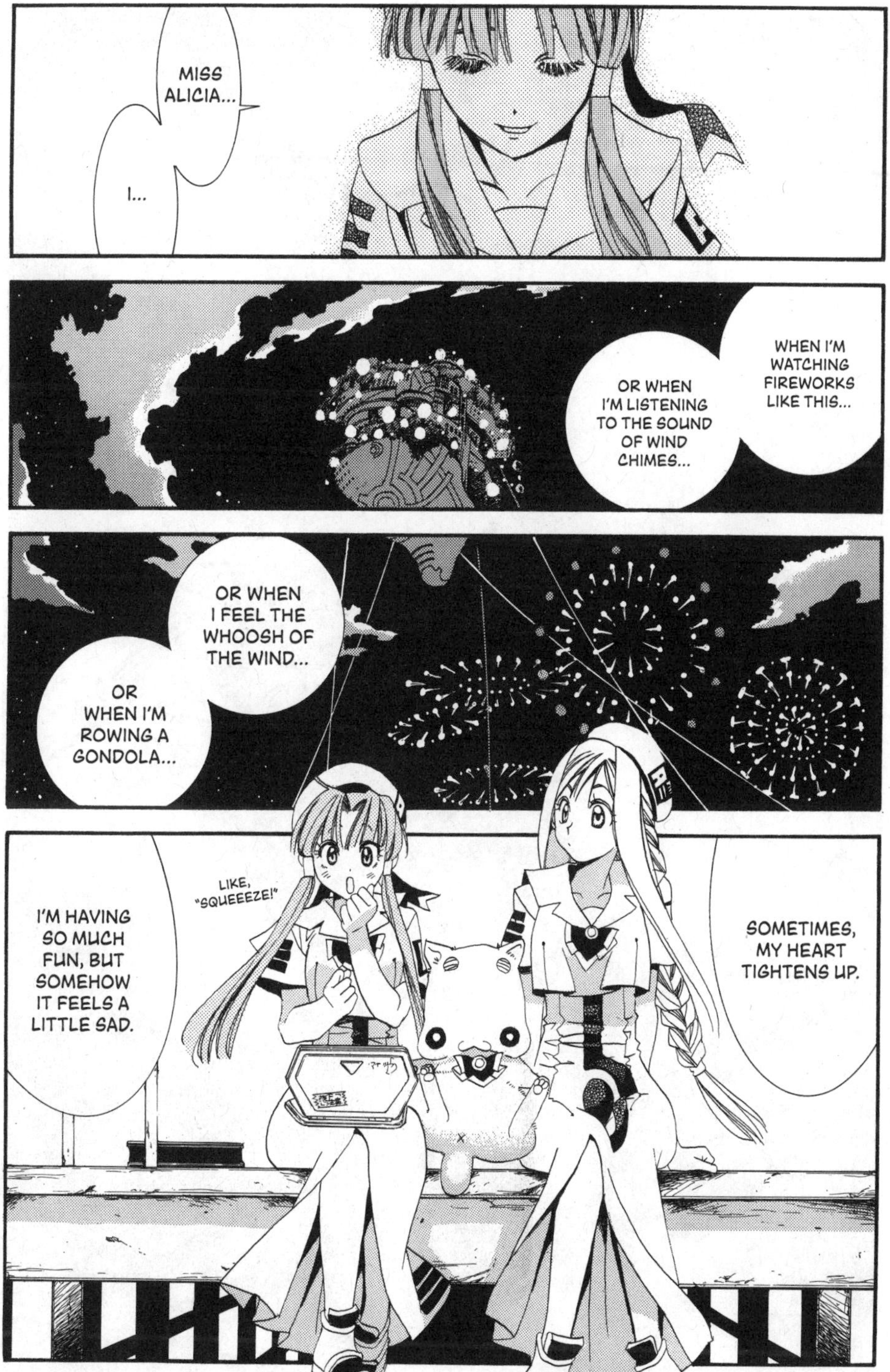
MISS ALICIA...
I...
WHEN I'M WATCHING FIREWORKS LIKE THIS...
OR WHEN I'M LISTENING TO THE SOUND OF WIND CHIMES...
OR WHEN I FEEL THE WHOOSH OF THE WIND...
OR WHEN I'M ROWING A GONDOLA...
SOMETIMES, MY HEART TIGHTENS UP.
LIKE, "SQUEEEZE!"
I'M HAVING SO MUCH FUN, BUT SOMEHOW IT FEELS A LITTLE SAD.

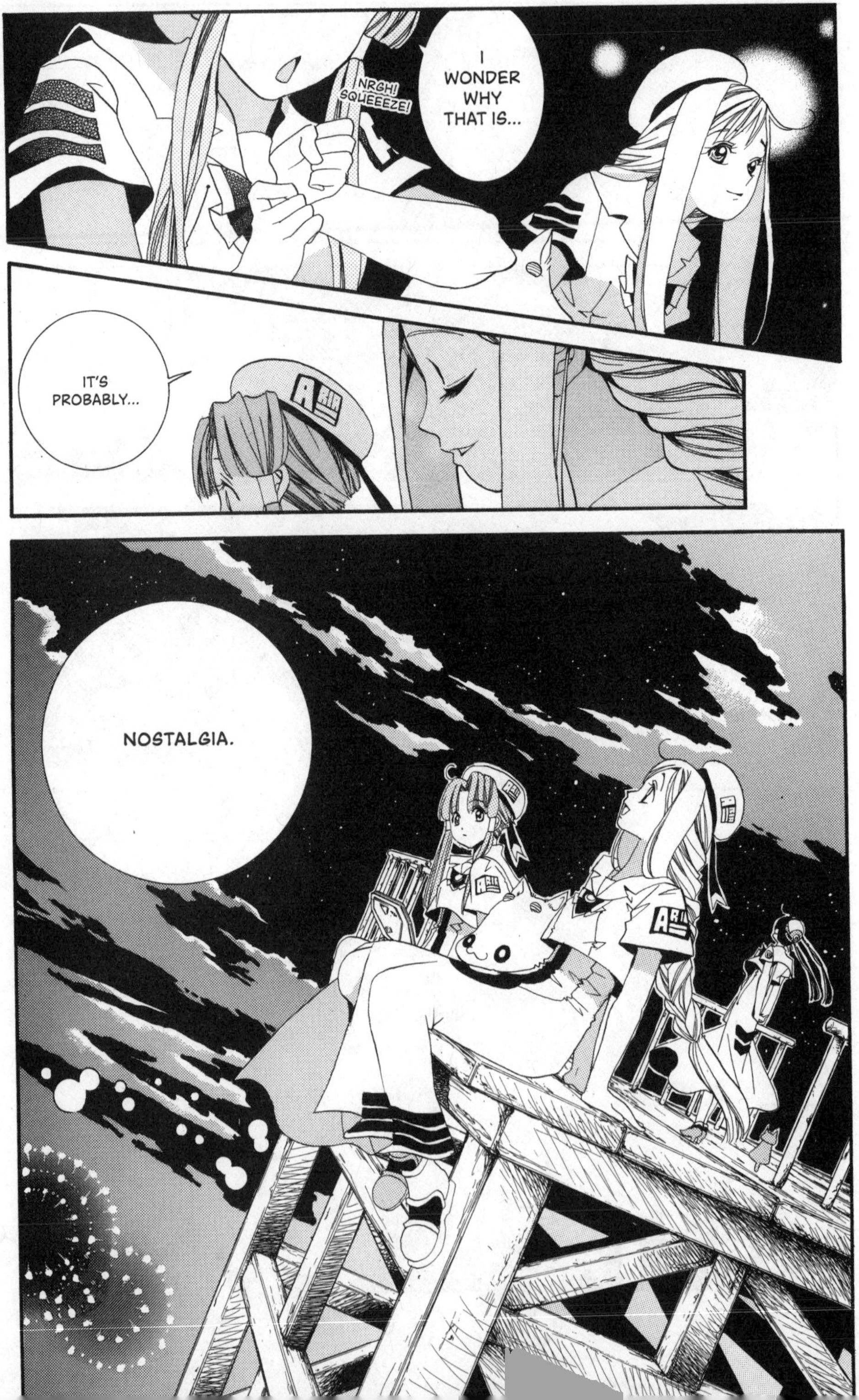
I WONDER WHY THAT IS...
NRGH! SQUEEEZE!
IT'S PROBABLY...
NOSTALGIA.

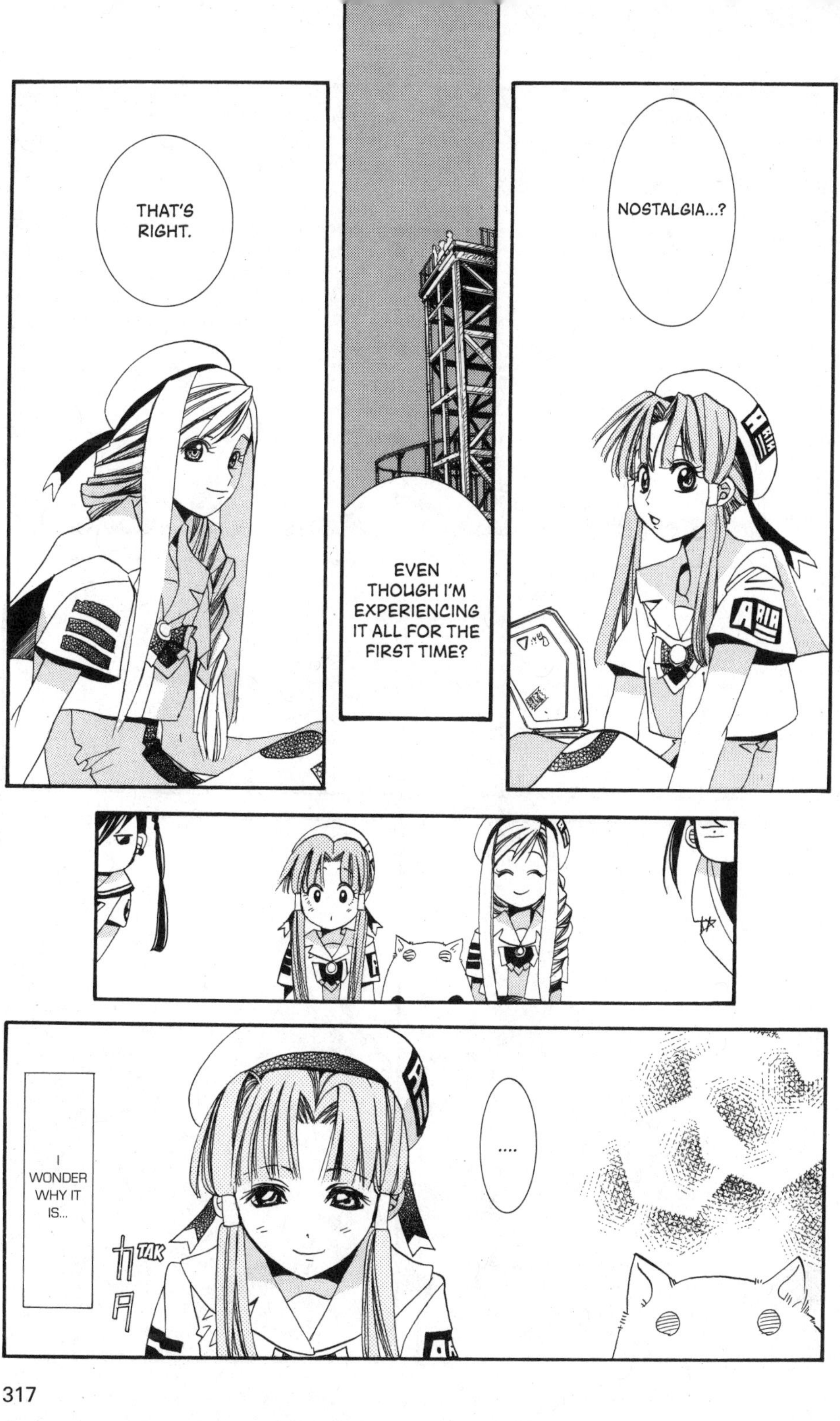
NOSTALGIA...?
EVEN THOUGH I'M EXPERIENCING IT ALL FOR THE FIRST TIME?
THAT'S RIGHT.
....
I WONDER WHY IT IS...
TAK

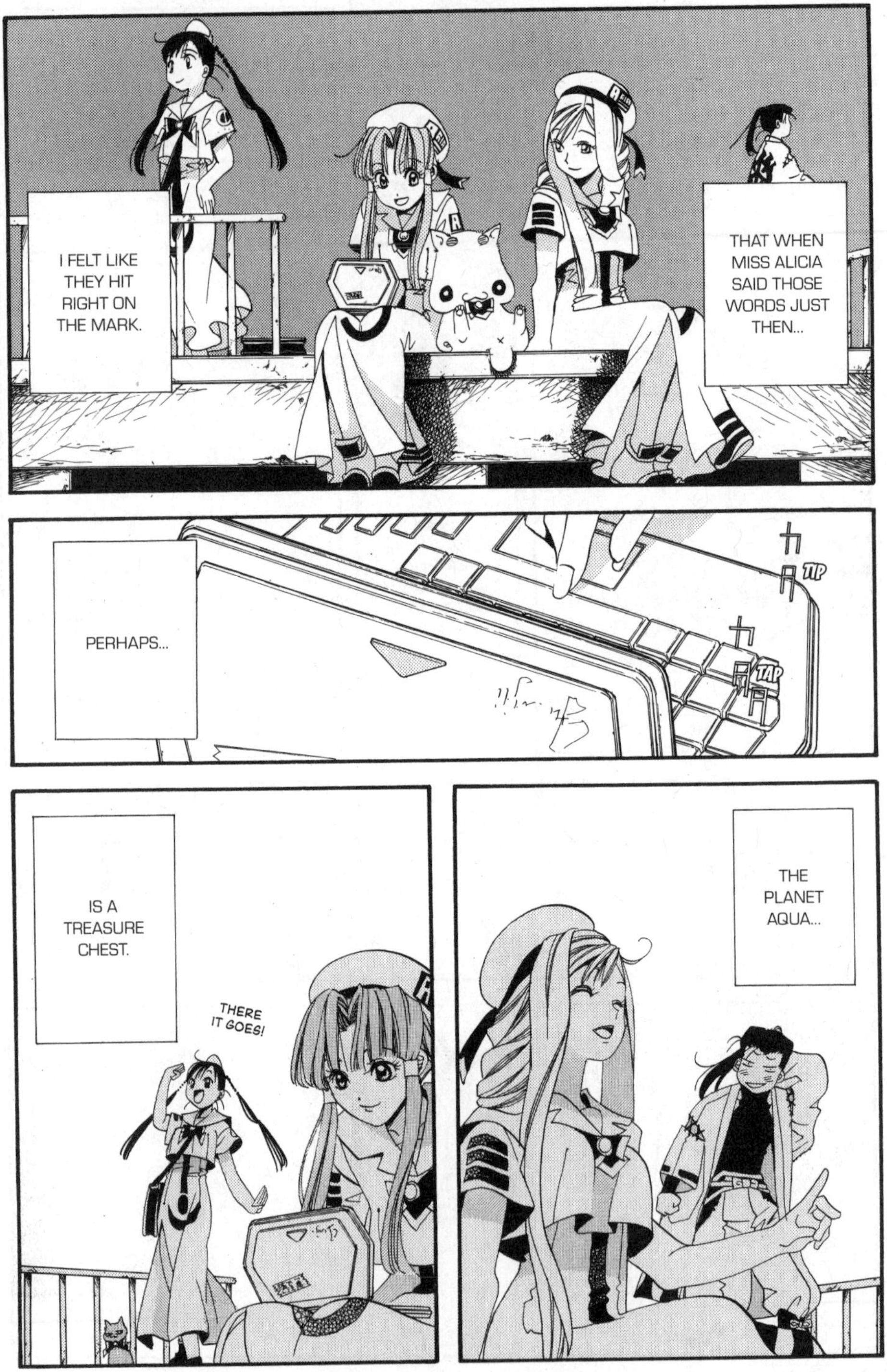
THAT WHEN MISS ALICIA SAID THOSE WORDS JUST THEN...
I FELT LIKE THEY HIT RIGHT ON THE MARK.
TIP
TAP
PERHAPS...
THE PLANET AQUA...
IS A TREASURE CHEST.
THERE IT GOES!

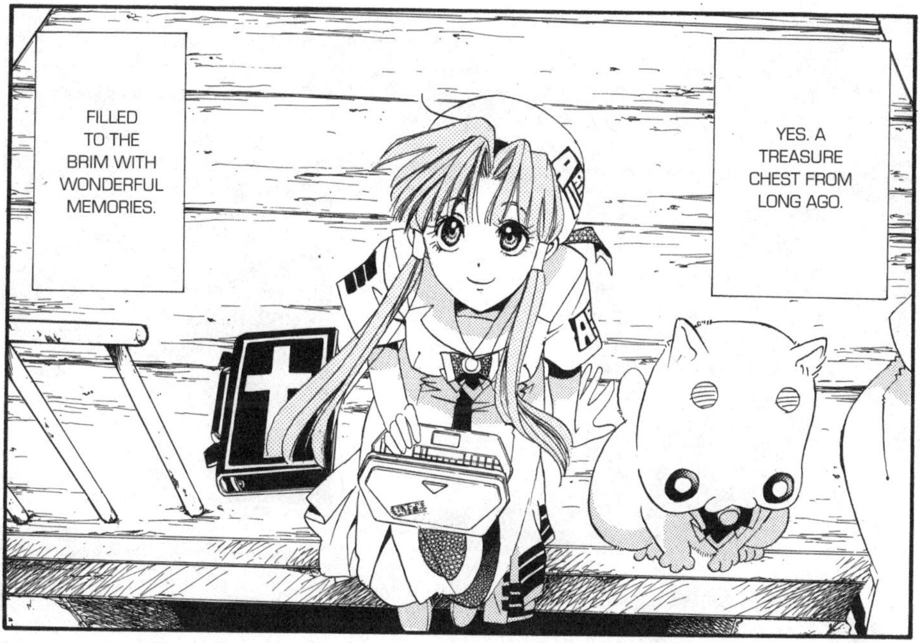
YES. A TREASURE CHEST FROM LONG AGO.
FILLED TO THE BRIM WITH WONDERFUL MEMORIES.

THAT'S WHY IT FEELS SO NOSTALGIC.

THAT'S WHY IT'S SO DEAR TO ME.

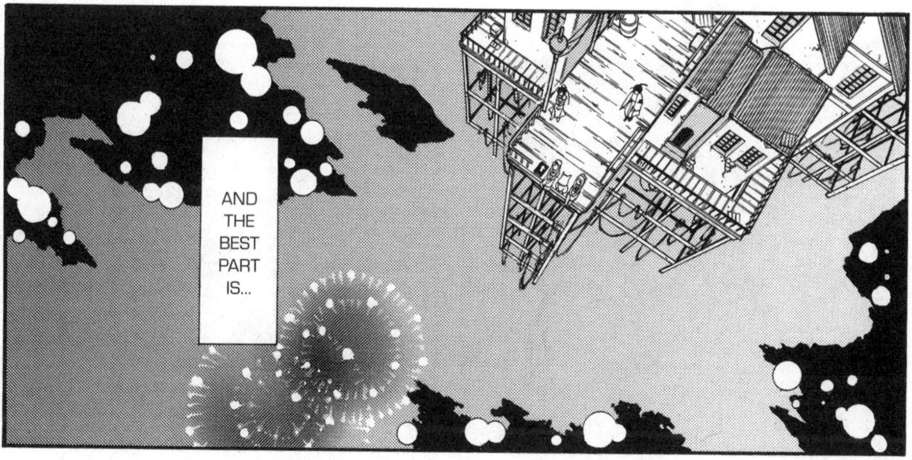
AND THE BEST PART IS...

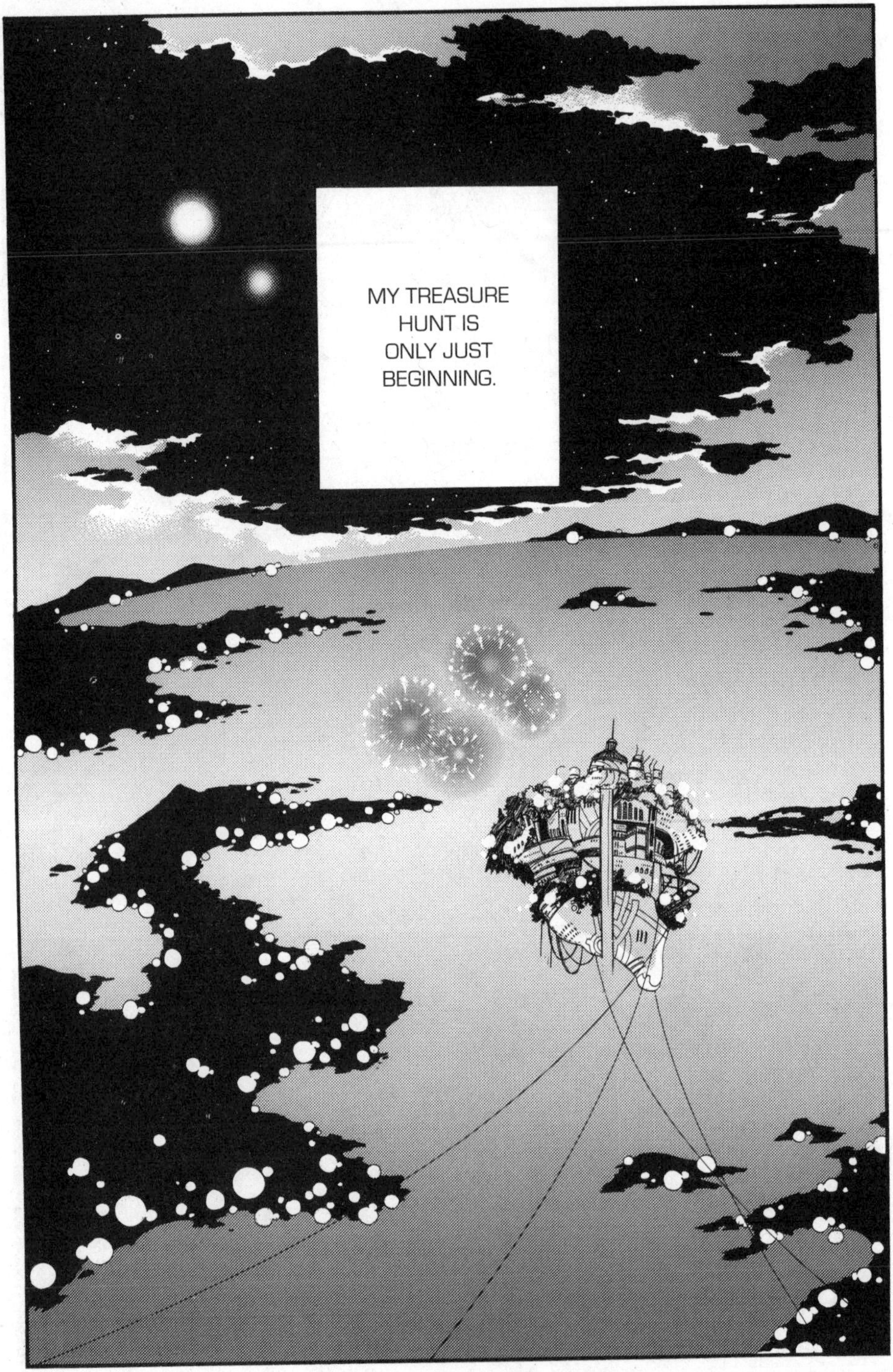
MY TREASURE
HUNT IS
ONLY JUST
BEGINNING.

ARIA The MASTERPIECE
VOYAGE.1 FINE

Aria The Masterpiece Volume 1
Manga by Kozue Amano

Editor - Lena Atanassova
Marketing Associate - Kae Winters
Technology and Digital Media Assistant - Phillip Hong
Graphic Design - Phillip Hong
Original Translation - Alethea & Athena Nibley
Retouching and Lettering - Vibrraant Publishing Studio
Editor-in-Chief & Publisher - Stu Levy

A  Manga

TOKYOPOP and 👁 are trademarks or registered trademarks of TOKYOPOP Inc.

TOKYOPOP inc.
5200 W Century Blvd
Suite 705
Los Angeles, CA 90045 USA

E-mail: info@TOKYOPOP.com
Come visit us online at www.TOKYOPOP.com

f www.facebook.com/TOKYOPOP
🐦 www.twitter.com/TOKYOPOP
📌 www.pinterest.com/TOKYOPOP
📷 www.instagram.com/TOKYOPOP

ISBN: 978-1-4278-6000-2
First TOKYOPOP Printing: February 2019
10 9 8 7 6 5 4 3 2 1
Printed in CANADA

STOP

THIS IS THE BACK OF THE BOOK!

How do you read manga-style? It's simple! Let's practice -- just start in the top right panel and follow the numbers below!

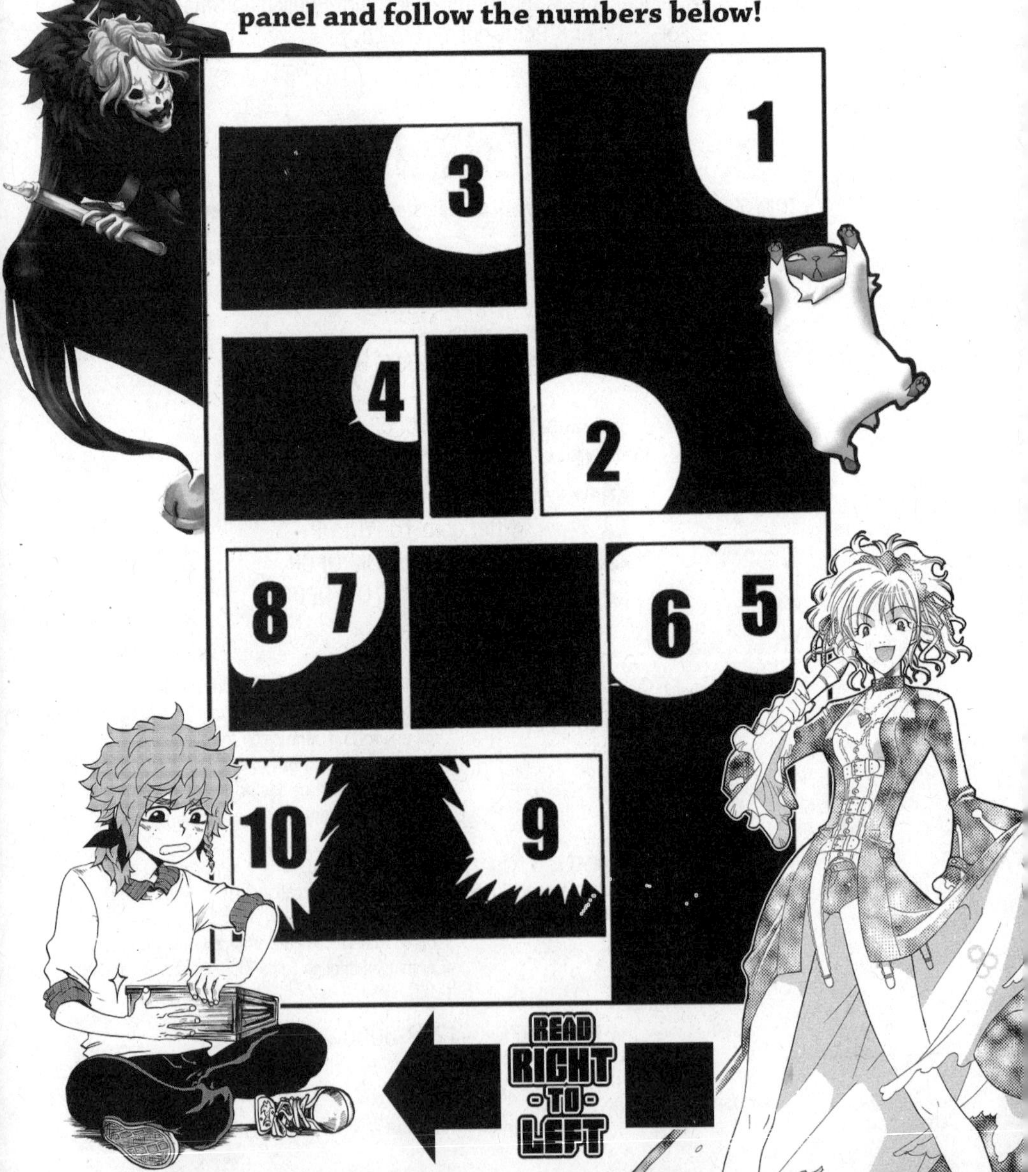
1
2
3
4
5
6
7
8
9
10
READ RIGHT -TO- LEFT

Crimson from ***Kamo*** / Fairy Cat from ***Grimms Manga Tales***
Morrey from ***Goldfisch*** / Princess Ai from ***Princess Ai***